THE LABORATORY METHOD OF CHANGING AND LEARNING

THEORY AND APPLICATION

Edited by

KENNETH D. BENNE

LELAND P. BRADFORD

JACK R. GIBB

RONALD O. LIPPITT

Science and Behavior Books, Inc.
Palo Alto, California 94306

Library of Congress Card Number 74-32598
ISBN 0-8314-0042-X

Typography by Penguin ≈ Santa Clara, California

TABLE OF CONTENTS

PREFACE

Ten years ago three of us — Leland P. Bradford, Jack Gibb and Kenneth D. Benne — edited a book called *T GROUP THEORY AND LABORATORY METHOD.* That book explored some aspects of laboratory method as a way of stimulating, supporting, and guiding processes of change in human systems. But its major emphasis was upon the T Group or training group, one of the principal formats in which laboratory method had been originally applied and developed. The book has reached a large and receptive audience of readers in the United States and in other countries as well. It has been published in Japanese and German translations.

Two years ago, Ronald Lippitt, one of the originators of laboratory method, joined our editorial group. Our early intention was to revise the T Group book. But as we examined what had happened to laboratory method during the past decade, a new focus emerged. The theoretical and research base of laboratory method has been significantly elaborated and refined between 1964 and 1974. The technologies supporting the applications of laboratory method have been greatly diversified and differentiated. The original focus of laboratory method on the face-to-face group has continued. Significant variations in group training have been invented and tested. And new foci of application have emerged. Laboratory method has been successfully applied in changing and renewing larger human systems — organizations, institutions, and communities of various magnitudes. It has also been focused effectively on stimulating and supporting processes of individual and personal growth. The professionalization of laboratory practice has been notably advanced during the past ten years.

PREFACE

We decided, therefore, to focus this book upon a sampling of the entire range of current applications of laboratory method in group training and education, in personal growth laboratories, in organizational and community development. In the book, we have tried both to explicate the conceptual and moral foundations and to describe and explain a wide range of applications of laboratory method. It is thus a contribution to both theory and practice. We have also surveyed recent developments in the professionalization of laboratory practice.

We have been fortunate in convincing distinguished colleagues to contribute chapters on aspects of laboratory method in which they are particularly well versed. These contributions have supplemented significantly our own interpretive efforts.

This book should be of interest to all those who found the T Group book helpful. In general, these were applied social scientists and professionals interested in the educative and reeducative uses of small group processes. This volume should also be of interest both to psychotherapists and to social scientists and professionals concerned with problems and processes of change in larger social systems.

We recognize and appreciate the early support given to our writing project by Learning Resources Corporation.

We are grateful to the critics and colleagues, beyond the circle of authors, who furnished indispensable materials in the preparation of Chapters 4 and 11.

We are grateful also to Martha Bradford, Emilie Cherry, Mary Paine, and Judith Raymond, who helped to put the manuscript into publishable shape.

Kenneth D. Benne
Leland P. Bradford
Jack R. Gibb
Ronald O. Lippitt

PART I

LABORATORY METHOD:

DEFINITION

AND

REVIEW

PART I

INTRODUCTION

Because this book discusses a relatively recent innovation in education, it is appropriate for this introduction to begin with a brief account of its origins and development. More comprehensive accounts have been given elsewhere. [1/2/3/4]

HISTORY OF THE LABORATORY METHOD OF LEARNING AND CHANGING.

Origins of the Method. The beginnings of the laboratory method may properly be said to start during the summer of 1946 at a State Workshop on Inter-Group Relations at the State Teachers College in New Britain, Connecticut. It was there that the concept of the unstructured T Group was first discovered. Since then, of course, the concepts and methods have become diversified and have spread into many institutional settings and into many parts of the world.

While this method of education had its origins in 1946, there were, of course, antecedent concepts and events which contributed to the main discovery. The four major leaders at Connecticut, Kurt Lewin, Kenneth D. Benne, Leland P. Bradford, and Ronald Lippitt, each brought different knowledges and experiences which made the events at Connecticut feasible and possible. Kurt Lewin brought high competence in research concepts and methodologies, original theories of group dynamics and of the processes of social change, and an active interest in action-research as a tool for social improvement. Kenneth Benne brought knowledge of philosophy, particularly educational philosophy, as well as experiences in the use of workshop and discussion methods of learning and in intercultural education. Leland Bradford contributed knowledge and experience from the growing field of adult education as well as a background in educational psychology and knowledge of workshop methods and discussion experiments in adult education. Ronald Lippitt brought knowledge of social psychology, particularly of group behavior, through his work with Lewin, skills in research technologies, and a background in educational theory through his work with Piaget.

The event and discovery at Connecticut were serendipitously reached. Observations fed back to groups, group members, and leaders, about their individual and group behavior at the end of each day by trained research observers on the staff seemed to do more to stimulate interest in the behavior of those involved, more learning, and more change and insights than did the formal program itself. Furthermore, it seemed clear that the experience, plus feedback and analysis, induced more learning about personal and group behavior than did lectures or seminars on the subject.

It was on the basis of experience with a method of stimulating and supporting learning that seemed more effective than any other tried before, that "The National Training Laboratory in Group Development" (NTLGD) was organized by Benne, Bradford and Lippitt (Kurt Lewin died in early 1947) and held its first residential laboratory in the summer of 1947 at Gould Academy in Bethel, Maine. This laboratory was sponsored by the Research Center for Group Dynamics then at MIT; The National Education Association; Teachers College, Columbia University; Springfield College; U.C.L.A.; and Cornell University. A basic grant for research was made by the Office of Naval Research. The extensive research projects — there were six members on the training and more than thirty on the research staff of this first laboratory — were under the direction of John R. P. French, Jr., of the Research Center for Group Dynamics.[5]

Heterogeneous Laboratories at Bethel, Maine. In the beginning, the laboratory sessions at Bethel were heterogeneous as far as delegate composition was concerned. Such laboratories have continued through the years, although many other kinds of sessions with different and more homogeneous populations have been designed since. In preparation for the first three-week session in 1947, three staff papers were prepared as basic documents for NTLGD. They were an analysis of the Change-Agent Role, an analysis of the Phases of Group Growth and

Development, and a paper prepared by Kenneth Benne dealing with democratic ethics, scientific method, and social engineering.

The basic design of the three-week laboratory session, with its announced purposes of helping participants gain in self-understanding, in understanding and skill in group membership and leadership, and in understanding of the processes of encouraging social change, and the skills required in such efforts was to divide participants into Basic Skill Training Groups (later to become T Groups) for a large part of each day with a trainer and a training observer in each group. The observer fed back his observations during the last half-hour of each two-hour session and invited group discussion of his observations. Supplementing sessions of these face-to-face groups, there were theory lectures in the morning, dealing with individual and group behavior and change; skill-practice exercises and special interest groups in the afternoon, dealing with skills of encouraging change back home and problems of resistance to be faced. Skills of role-playing and action-research were also included in the afternoon program. Evenings generally were spent in general sessions focused on current social issues of the times, or on problems within the laboratory community.

The session in the summer of 1948 was largely a duplication of the 1947 session with a few exceptions. The observer became part of the trainer team in each group, and feedback was introduced immediately after each event rather than at the end of a session. Participants were trained to be observers as well as participants and were encouraged to feed back their feelings and observations where appropriate. In 1948 a psychiatrist was brought on the staff as a counselor to any individual who experienced undue stress. Thus the first two years formed a foundational block in the development of laboratory method.

The 1949 session saw the beginning of major changes in the heterogeneous laboratory programs. More clinically oriented staff members were added and greater attention was given to intrapersonal and interpersonal behavior, with less attention paid to group behavior and problems of social change. Naturally, there were disagreements between sociologists and social and clinical psychologists over the major emphasis to be given in the program. For a number of years this issue was compromised by devoting half the day, with one set of staff, to individual behavior and the other half of the day to role behavior and problems of organizational and societal change. As the years have gone by, the Basic Human Relations Laboratory (as it has come to be called) has turned its attention more to intrapersonal and interpersonal behavior, while other programs have become more concerned with problems and skills in the area of social change. In the middle and later fifties and in the sixties, nonverbal, body-awareness, and movement methods became prevalent and fitted into the Personal Growth Laboratories and programs labeled Therapy for Normals and Encounter Groups in many parts of the country. Their emphasis was emphatically on individual behavior.

Regional Developments. It was inevitable and wise that many regional counterparts to NTLGD (by the middle fifties it was renamed National Training Laboratories) should be established. In 1952, the Western Training Laboratory, sponsored by U.C.L.A., was organized. By 1954 a few more major laboratories, sponsored by various universities, had formed. By the sixties nearly a dozen such programs were in existence in the United States. Many of these later merged with NTL to widen the scope of the movement. Happily, the regional laboratories were divergent in the foci of their experimentation.

The Development of Occupational Laboratories. The founders of NTL at first had held to the idea that it would be unwise to hold laboratory programs for a single occupation because it was felt that such groups would tend to deal with only "there-and-then" work situations rather than "here-and-now" laboratory behavior. But we were urged to try and launched a number of occupational programs. In 1956, we started the first Management Work Conference for middle management people, largely from business and industry. This program still is going strong. The first Church Workers Laboratory was sponsored in conjunction with the National Council of Churches in the same year. In 1957, the first Key Executive Laboratory for top managers in industry and business was begun. In 1959, NTL sponsored the first Educators Laboratory. And in 1960 the first Community Workers Laboratory and the first Higher Education Laboratory, which eventually included teams of faculty members and administrators, along with students, were launched. In 1965, NTL held the first Presidents Conference, still being offered, for presidents of major industries and businesses, along with heads of other kinds of organizations.

Occupational laboratories have proved to be of great value to their participants. They have brought laboratory methods into organizations as part of internal processes of organizational change. They have, while maintaining some emphasis on training in intrapersonal and interpersonal behavior, given greater emphasis to skill practice relevant to the back-home situations participants face and have encouraged training in processes of social change. The Basic Human Relations programs and the occupational laboratories have, taken together, continued, though somewhat divergently, the purposes inherent in the origins of laboratory method.

Organizational Development. While the originators of NTL had done pioneer organizational development work before NTL was started, it was not until the late fifties and early sixties that organizational development work became an important part of NTL's activities. Since the formation of an organizational development network of leaders within various organizations concerned with continuing renewal of their organizations, many contracts for developmental work with institutions were carried out by NTL and by members of its network of trainers. Laboratory programs concerned with organizational development and skills of effective consulting were conducted by NTL and increasingly by other organizations, including universities and other centers and consulting firms. The range of organizations worked with has extended from industries to educational systems, to health agencies, to churches, and to a variety of other community organizations. Richard Beckhard in Chapter 18 gives an account of organizational development work in its current state of evolution.

Community Development. Although the first Community Workers Laboratory was held in 1960 and signaled NTL's entrance into this field, the founders of NTL had been concerned with training community leaders as far back as the Connecticut program of 1946 and had worked with various community groups and national organizations almost from the beginning. Sometimes with grants and sometimes with payments from local organizations, NTL has worked in community development programs from the beginning sixties through the present. Eva Schindler-Rainman in Chapter 19 gives a picture of some of the ways in which laboratory methods are currently being employed in programs of community development.

Movement into Other Countries. Although the first European team from Austria came to Bethel in 1954, and a group of twenty-seven Europeans came as teams from seven nations in 1955, the major growth of laboratory method in other countries really developed in the sixties. In Puerto Rico from 1956 until the middle sixties, NTL helped to conduct laboratories and trained trainers who worked not only in Puerto Rico, but from time to time in various countries of Central and South America. In 1964, the European Institute for Trans-national Studies in Group and Organization Development (EIT) was formed, with members from most West European countries. This organization is still viable. The Australian Institute of Human Relations began its work in 1968.

In 1960-1961, Donald Nylen, working with the Ford Foundation, experimented, first in Nigeria and then in other

African countries, in adapting laboratory methods for training leaders in those countries. India has developed programs of laboratory training and organizational development with centers in Calcutta, Bombay, New Delhi, and Udaipur. Laboratory training and consultation have developed in Canada, Japan, New Zealand, and in various other countries as well.

Career of the NTL Institute. As already mentioned, NTL started out in 1947 as the National Training Laboratory in Group Development. With the help of grants from the Carnegie Corporation in the late forties and early fifties, NTL developed a national headquarters and a year-round program as part of the Division of Adult Education of the National Education Association. In the middle fifties, its name was changed to the National Training Laboratories as more representative of its changing activities. In 1963, it was separated from the Adult Education Division and made a separate unit in the National Education Association. In 1967, the NTL Institute for Applied Behavioral Science was established as an institution separate from but affiliated with NEA. It is now known as the NTL Institute and has removed itself from connection with any other organization or institution. In 1967, when the NTL Institute for Applied Behavioral Science was formed, several program divisions were established within it: the Center for Community Affairs; the Center for Educational Programs; the Center for International Programs; the Center for Organizational Development; the Black Affairs Center, and the Center for Administration. In 1968-69, a Center for Voluntarism was added on a special basis. Some of these Centers still exist in the latest reorganization of NTL Institute. The four major Centers that now compose it are: Center for Development of Individual Potential; Center for Macro-System Change; Center for Professional Development; and Center for System Development. These four centers now conduct over a hundred laboratory programs each year and fulfill contracts with many organizations and institutions. The brief account of the changing organization of NTL gives an accurate, though sketchy, picture of the evolution of laboratory practice both in the varying demands of its changing clientele for services and the specializations that have emerged among laboratory practitioners. We have chosen to highlight the career of NTL because of its role in originating and spreading laboratory practices. We recognize that laboratory practices are now sponsored by many centers other than NTL.

Professional Training of Laboratory Practitioners. With the advent of the European teams in the middle fifties, the beginnings of formal programs for training trainers, change-agents, and consultants began. Up to that time most training of new trainers was accomplished through processes of apprenticeship. It was not until 1960 that such programs were given focal attention. During the sixties, four programs emerged. One was for behavioral scientists seeking professional training in laboratory method, most of whom had their homes in colleges and universities. A second dealt primarily with individuals doing laboratory training and consultation within organizations and who did not necessarily have advanced degrees in the social and behavioral sciences. The third endeavored to train consultants, trainers, and counselors for work in school systems. The fourth offered training for consultants, change-agents, and trainers who worked in community situations. Many of the trainers were indigenous leaders from poverty areas of cities. They included both blacks and whites. In 1970, the concept of the Learning Community was born as a format for professional development. In this format, after a core of basic training, simultaneous modules are scheduled. Each person may elect a module which fits his or her learning needs. Trainers, of course, have been developed in other NTL programs. And other organizations and institutions, including universities with degree programs, have joined the effort to professionalize training in laboratory methods. In the Netherlands, for example, a highly effective program, supported by governmental funding and with collaboration between professional and university resources, has been in existence for some time.

Thematic Programs. Beginning in the sixties a number of programs directed toward specific conceptual and skill areas have been planned and tested. Examples of these are laboratories and workshops in: Consultation Skills, Negotiation Skills, Power and System Change, Open Systems Planning, Conflict Management, and the Use of Media in Human Relations Education.

A FORWARD LOOK TO PART I

The purpose of Part I is essentially to introduce, describe, and define what the authors of this book mean by laboratory method as it has evolved in the twenty-five years of history sketched above. In Chapter 1, the editors seek to define laboratory method by giving snapshots of some of its applications. In Chapter 2, Kenneth Benne explores more deeply and tries to articulate the concepts and value orientations which undergird laboratory practice. In Chapter 3, Jack Gibb places laboratory method in the perspective of psychological and social research and provides an extensive bibliography of completed research connected with laboratory practice. In Chapter 4,

LABORATORY METHOD: DEFINITION AND REVIEW

Kenneth Benne has solicited comments and critiques of laboratory method from proponents of alternative modes of practice and of action and, in attempting to respond to these critics, has further clarified the ideology of laboratory practice.

FOOTNOTES AND REFERENCES

1. Ronald Lippitt, *Training in Community Relations,* Harper & Bros., New York, 1949.

2. Kenneth D. Benne, "History of the T-Group in the Laboratory Setting," a chapter in Bradford, L. P.; Gibb, J. R.; and Benne, K. D. (Eds.); *T-Group Theory and Laboratory Method,* John Wiley & Sons, Inc., New York, 1964.

3. L. P. Bradford, "Biography of an Institution," *Journal of Applied Behavioral Science, 2,* 3, 1967, pp. 127-143.

4. L. P. Bradford, *History of the National Training Laboratories, 1947-70.* (In preparation for publication.)

5. Emphasis on the original innovators of laboratory method in this account is, we hope, a pardonable exaggeration. It is not meant to obscure or to minimize the contributions which many others have made to the development of laboratory methods, through invention and testing of new designs and training technologies, through theorizing and research, and through the adaptive introduction of the method into various institutional and national environments. The number of such contributors now is numbered in the hundreds. We trust that the various chapters which follow will make this point abundantly clear.

CHAPTER 1

WHAT IS LABORATORY METHOD?

Kenneth D. Benne, Leland P. Bradford, Jack R. Gibb, and Ronald O. Lippitt

What is laboratory method? This entire book is a quest for justifiable answers to this question. The quest will lead readers through a variety of theoretical discussions and evaluations of the method as well as descriptions of its practical applications in various human and institutional settings.

Brief descriptions of cases representing some of the kinds of learning and change-oriented activities which laboratory method encompasses will be useful in launching our quest. This sampling of laboratory activities must of necessity be highly selective. Conservative estimates suggest that ten million people have experienced one or another application of laboratory method since its beginnings twenty-five years ago. Perhaps one million people now participate in one sort of laboratory activity or another each year. While the most extensive cultivation and use of the method have occurred in the United States, accelerating participation in laboratory activities is reported from Europe, Canada, Latin America, Japan, India, Australia, and from other countries as well.

SNAPSHOTS OF LABORATORY APPLICATIONS

Let us imagine that we are taking audiovisual snapshots of people engaged in laboratory activities from an imaginary helicopter flying over populated areas of the world. These will illustrate some of the kinds of activities in which a million people have been engaged during 1974.

Snapshot One

A hundred men and women have assembled in a place away from their homes and jobs to participate in a basic human relations laboratory. During their two weeks together, they will seek to build a learning community with the help of a staff of nine trainers or facilitators. They have come together as strangers. A cross-section of occupations, ages, races, and cultures or subcultures is present in the laboratory population. More than half of their time in the laboratory will be spent in one of several heterogeneous groups of about ten people each. These are known as training groups or T Groups. A staff trainer is assigned to work with each group.

The announcement of the laboratory promised an opportunity for participants to learn more about themselves as people and to learn better ways of communicating and working with other people.

Our imaginary camera focuses in on what is going on in one T Group which is in the midst of its fourth meeting. Joe has persisted in making subtle jokes about Bob. At first Bob laughed, but he has begun to feel hostile toward and uncomfortable with Joe. After a particularly cutting, jocular remark by Joe, a remark at which nearly all members of the group laughed, Betty stated that she didn't find the remark funny and was feeling sorry for Bob and angry with Joe. This led to a flurry of talk about the uses of wit and humor. Joe at first denied other than positive feeling toward Bob. The trainer invited members of the group, if they wished, to say what they were seeing and feeling about the relationship between Joe and Bob in the group. Most members reported that they saw Joe picking on Bob. Some tended, like Betty, to feel angry with Joe and sympathetic with Bob. Others saw Bob as setting himself up as a victim by being unduly apologetic and ingratiating when he spoke. These, like Joe, felt impatient with Bob for his avoidance of direct confrontations with others. As this discussion went on, Joe began to recognize his latent angry feeling toward Bob. He reported these feelings and said he now felt guilty about having such feelings. This guilt was probably behind his initial denial. He said he would explore his feelings further as the group continued to meet and he hoped Bob would help him do this. Bob also began to explore whether he normally expected hostile reactions from other men around him and showed his expectation through apology and ingratiation. These insights expressed by Joe and Bob led others to explore their reactions to other people and other episodes in the group's short history. The trainer supported this effort to learn from the here-and-now experiences of the people in the group and added a few observations and feelings of his own.[1]

Snapshot Two

Our imaginary camera now is focused on a meeting of forty people sitting around tables arranged in a large hollow square in the Junior High School Library of a city school. The name plates on the table in front of each participant show names like Pilecki, Hogan, Licardelli, Richards, and Applebaum. There are school administrators, teachers, counselors, and students in the group, along with parents and a few police officers, all from the same community. There are black people and white people in the group around the table. The school had experienced a disturbing clash between black students and white students two months before in which one teacher and three students were injured. The School Board called in consultants from a nearby university after this event. The Board had agreed to sponsor a program worked out jointly by Board members, school administrators, teachers and students, along with the consultants. The program is to include special continuing training for the student, faculty, parent, and other community leaders selected for leadership by their own constituent groups. The program also includes a series of less intensive two-day workshops which will eventually involve in participation 200 teachers from all levels of the school system and 500 students from the junior and senior high schools, along with 150 parent and other community leaders, black and white, Wasps, and ethnics. Our helicopter camera has focused in on one of these two-day workshops. A closer look shows two trainers, one white and one black, among the people around the hollow square.

The trainers began with an interview with each person in public session. The interviews had two purposes: to offer participants an opportunity to introduce themselves to the group and give some idea of their backgrounds, racial, religious, ethnic, occupational, and to start building an agenda for follow-up work by identifying issues and problems in the school and community that members consider important and in need of continuing joint work.

The interviews of individuals by the trainers, with others listening and gradually joining in, make it respectable to speak of ethnic, racial, occupational, and age differences and attitudes without the tensions and inhibitions felt in everyday social intercourse. They help individuals appreciate how influential religious, ethnic, and social class backgrounds have been in shaping their own and others' attitudes and actions — and how diverse these backgrounds are. They bring out information which helps to generate openness and trust among individuals from different groups and which define issues and problems that need to be worked on collaboratively. The trainers skillfully guide the interviewing, not judging what is said, encouraging open and risk-taking responses, often by modeling these qualities in their own behavior, while avoiding "psychotherapeutic" confessions and interventions and abrasive confrontations.

The next morning, "old friends" with a day's collaborative sharing behind them get down to work on immediate issues and problems already identified — sharpening them, adding others, picking out those they feel they might solve collaboratively, taking commitments to work on one or another of these in the future. The trainers guide the discussions which are now more open, more penetrating; anger and defiance still are there but are more openly and directly expressed and more listened to rather than reacted to by others, resistances to change melting around the edges. The process is not focused on exposing personal feelings and interpersonal relations as in a T Group, but rather on efforts to locate, clarify, and solve situational problems collaboratively across historically rooted and deeply defended barriers of race, ethnicity, social class, age, sex, professional, and volunteer status. The participants are learning hope for and commitment to resolving social conflicts by cooperative, problem-solving methods rather than by win-lose struggles and conflicts.[2]

Snapshot Three

Our imaginary camera now is focused on a meeting of the newly appointed president of a manufacturing company with his six vice-presidents. The new president is the fourth president this company has employed in the past eight years. He has asked two trainer-consultants, skilled in laboratory methods, to meet with him and the vice-presidents in a series of periodic three-day sessions away from their telephones and offices in plant headquarters in order to work on problems of building an administrative team in the company. They are in the second day of their first three-day laboratory. The consultants, as they have watched the group at work the first day, noted at the beginning of the second day's meeting that the vice-presidents talk publicly only of their successes, that they avoid identifying difficulties they are experiencing in their work and asking help in dealing with these, that they seem to support each other in avoiding open group discussion of problems within their departments or between departments. The president agrees with the consultants' observations and begins to scold the vice-presidents for not being more open. One consultant interrupts and asks the vice-presidents if the president's scolding has made them feel more free to expose their difficulties in open group discussion. After a long silence, one vice-president reports that the president's scolding has disappointed him. He had come to this meeting hoping that things would change in the company with a new president who seemed to want more teamwork, less competitive "individualism" among departments than preceding presidents had encouraged or allowed. He was afraid now that the new president would behave like the past presidents, talking teamwork and open sharing of difficulties, but not sharing his own difficulties, nor opening up himself to receive help from his colleagues. Two other vice-presidents came in to support the vice-president who spoke first.

One consultant asked the president if he wished to respond to what had been said. The president falteringly said that he saw now that his behavior had not squared with his professed commitment to sharing and teamwork. This discrepancy might be explained by (not excused by) the anxiety he felt about coming into a company that seems to eat up presidents. He really does need help, but he guesses he doesn't know how to ask for it. Will the vice-presidents be willing to help him learn to be a team member? He went on to say that he is bothered by a problem of fights between factions in the company's Board of Directors. The factions are so busy fighting each other that good decisions seldom get made. Will the vice-presidents give him suggestions about what he might do? A lively discussion developed in which some good ideas were generated and developed by the group. The president said he would think about the ideas and report back at a future meeting what ideas he had used and how they worked. The vice-president in charge of production then said that, if they were through with the president's difficulty for the time, he would like to get help on conflicts that continually break out between people in his department and people in the sales department. He asked Bob, vice-president of sales, if he too is concerned with these conflicts and if he wants to talk about them now publicly. After some hesitation, Bob expressed willingness to give it a try. One consultant then asked if Bob and Roy, the production chief, would work for awhile with the others in the group in finding out how they could best help Roy and Bob to understand and deal with their conflicts. The group discussed possible procedures for awhile and agreed upon a way of giving and receiving help which they were willing to try out and later evaluate.

After working awhile on the tensions between Bob's and Roy's departments in which all vice-presidents and the president took part, the consultants suggested that the group stop their substantive work for awhile and discuss and evaluate the way they had been working with each other. The discussion of their processes was animated — everybody did not agree but the differences did not block discussion. One vice-president said he was thinking about how he might help staff meetings in his department to become more open and cooperative. Another vice-president said, half-jokingly, to the president that maybe he should bring the consultants into his board meetings to do some teambuilding there.[3]

Snapshot Four

Our imaginary camera now focuses in on the lodge of Camp Woodland which is located ten miles from Lakeville, a medium-sized city. There are a number of school buses, a few charter buses and two dozen automobiles in the parking lot near the lodge. In the main hall of the lodge, a meeting is being called to order. There are 128 people in the meeting sitting at sixteen round tables each accommodating eight people. At the front of the room, the Executive Director of the city's United Fund is explaining how this Saturday Institute on "Working Together For Our City's Children and Youth" came into being. He said that he and the Superintendent of Schools had long been discouraged by the lack of common efforts on the part of the many agencies set up to serve the children and youth of Lakeville. They had called in a trainer-consultant to help them think about what, if anything, they might do about this condition. The consultant had urged them to convene a larger *ad hoc* planning group of fifteen, not to solve the problems but to think of ways of involving more of the people needed to invent effective approaches to problems of disunity in current programming for youth and children. The fifteen were "representative" of some of the major sectors of the city's organized life — education, religion, recreation, social welfare, industry, labor, local government, legal protection, and health, along with two young people. The *ad hoc* committee had identified and invited eighty-five key policy and program leaders in the city and sixty key young people who are influential in various sectors of the youth culture of the city to attend the Saturday Institute at Camp Woodland. The youth contingent includes young people who now are out of school, as well as others now attending high school and community college. The chairman said he was happy that 128 of the 140 invited were able to attend. He said they didn't expect the one-day meeting to solve all the problems but rather to locate priorities and make decisions about further needed work and planning, if any. He asked the trainer-consultant to explain the design of work for the day.

The trainer-consultant asked the groups at the tables, each of which included older and younger people from various segments of community life, to project images of potential for the year ahead — images of what would be good and achievable changes in the now inadequate lives of children and young people in Lakeville and images also of the collaborative activities which would be necessary to bring these improvements into being. The groups worked most of the morning on this task. The consultant asked the groups to hold "stop sessions" several times during the morning. In these sessions members assessed how well they were working together at their table — what factors were inhibiting and what were facilitating communication, how differences in priorities were being handled, how well "minority" views were being listened to and utilized.

By early afternoon, twelve priority images for improvement of the city's efforts in behalf of children and youth had been identified through the pooling of findings from all the table groups. Twelve temporary task forces were formed on a volunteer basis to work on strategies for moving ahead on the twelve priorities. These priorities included: "involving young people in decision-making;" "recruiting and training more volunteers;" "police-youth relations;" "coordinating job finding and apprenticeship opportunities;" and "improving use of community resources in educational programs."

By 4 P.M., task forces reported to a plenary session their preliminary diagnoses of action steps required for their special task, first steps to be taken, and ideas about involvement of specific agencies in support and funding of exchange efforts. By 5 P.M., every task force reported the selection of a convener, and the time, place, and agenda for the next meeting of the task force. A coordinating committee for the whole program was elected, representing all the task forces and including both adult and youth leaders. A tentative stock-taking meeting of all task forces at Camp Woodland in six months was voted unanimously. The trainer-consultant agreed to meet with the coordinating committee in a month's time to review progress and advise on process problems encountered by the task forces in their continuing work.[4]

Snapshot Five

The Ministries and Departments of Education from twelve nations are concerned with the lack of effective attention in their various countries to the development of international mindedness in young people through school and school-related programs. They are aware of numerous international conferences of educators which have met over the years to deal with this problem abstractly and cognitively. But they are also aware of the failure of these conferences to modify the nationalistic attitudes and behavior patterns which still dominate the thinking, valuations, and conduct of most of the educational leadership within each country.

An *ad hoc* committee of representatives of the Ministries of Education met in Copenhagen the previous year and retained a Danish consultant, skilled in laboratory method, to attend their meetings and to help them work through some of the relationship and attitudinal difficulties which they anticipated would impede their forward planning of action steps on the problem. He had helped them to identify blockages to open and trustful communication in their own meetings and to overcome some of these. The first action step they had agreed upon was to develop a team of professionals, influential citizens, and young people in each country. Their consultant had provided the names of skilled laboratory practitioners (applied social scientists) in each country. Each national group had employed the services of a practitioner from its own country. And each group had worked through a year's time in developing itself into a team. Their substantive focus had been on identifying the barriers and facilitators to developing school programs with a transnational focus in their own country.

The second step was to bring the twelve national teams together in a World Institute on "Educating for World-Mindedness." This institute also was to meet in Copenhagen for two weeks. The twelve consultants had come together in Copenhagen four days before the national teams assembled. During this time consultants had worked to develop themselves as a working team as they worked on a tentative design for the World Institute and solved technical problems of official languages and simultaneous translation.

Our imaginary camera now is focused on the meetings of the Institute. At first, each day is divided between meetings of national teams and meetings of cross-national groups of twelve with a representative from each national team. Their initial task is value exploration. The cross-national groups work on identifying value propositions about educational purpose and method on which they agree and others on which they differ. As they work on this task, they explore their own processes of value confrontation, of listening to each other, and of influencing each other with the help of a laboratory practitioner assigned to each group. The progress and difficulties of each cross-national group are shared and analyzed daily in meetings of national teams.

As value differences are clarified, the cross-national groups experience and analyze processes of creative compromise addressed to the handling of these differences. The management of work in a condition of value pluralism, handling power differentials, and reconciling minority with majority positions are skills which groups practiced as they encountered a need for these in their work. These skills are practiced and evaluated both in small groups and in plenary sessions of the Institute and the differences in small group and large group dynamics explored.

As the cross-national groups worked together, members developed loyalties to these groups which sometimes rivaled in intensity their loyalties to their own national teams. As conflicting loyalties surfaced, the consultants helped Institute members to understand and manage the dynamics of multiple loyalties, partly through sharing their own problems of competing loyalties as simultaneously nationals and members of an emerging world profession and through also sharing the ways in which they have tried to resolve these conflicts creatively. The relationship of multiple loyalty problems experienced and handled in the Institute to multiple loyalty problems which will occur in programs of international education were explored and learning experiences for school administrators, teachers, and students back home in the various nations in learning to handle multiple loyalties were imaged, evaluated and tentatively planned for.

During the second week of the Institute the teams worked on plans for continued cross-national work after the Institute is over, with national teams grouped on the basis of geographic regions. Part of the time each day was spent in regional task forces working on plans for follow-up work on world education in the nations of their region. All plans as they developed were checked back with national teams and criticisms from each nation considered in further regional planning and in simulated, anticipatory tryouts of aspects of the regional plans. The consultants worked for part of the time on designs for documentation and evaluation research for possible integration into action for programs in the nations and regions as these developed and on plans for sharing evaluation results among all national teams and programs on a continuing basis. Research ideas were considered by all national teams and regional task forces for inclusion in their plans, and problems of using action research as a tool of change back in the nations were explored and discussed.

DIFFERENCES AMONG LABORATORY APPLICATIONS

Several differences among activities in the five snapshots immediately are apparent.[5] The first of these is a difference in the targets of change for which various particular laboratory activities are designed. In the human relations laboratory, the changes sought were in the behavioral systems of the persons participating and in their understandings and skills of interpersonal and group relationships. In the intergroup workshop, meeting in the junior high school library, attention was on intergroup relations — on surfacing, accepting, and handling the deeply emotional difficulties which characterize relations among segregated groups and on experiencing and learning a problem-solving as over against a conflict approach to settling difficulties of differential yet common concern to many groups. Similar training has been conducted in military settings, industrial organizations, churches, and government agencies. In the team-building laboratory the focus was on improving working roles and role relationships within an established and functioning organization. While the organization in this case was an industrial organization, similar developmental work now is going on in hospitals, school systems, governmental agencies, as well as in other organizations in all parts of the world. In the Youth Institute, the emphasis was on imaging cooperative working relationships among non-communicating agencies with professed common purposes but with actively competitive and segregated programs and on planning step-wise work to bring these desired images into being. While the focus in the case was on problems of children in the urban community, similar approaches are being taken to surfacing and organizing for work on problems of older people, poor people, women, blacks, Indians, or other segments of a city's or state's variegated population. In the World Institute, the goal was to build a framework for continuing work which requires communication and cooperation that contravenes deeply reinforced cultural and political habits and value orientations. Laboratory methods are now used to deal with a variety of human difficulties and opportunities, and are capable of adaptation to a further variety in which applications have not yet been attempted.

A second difference has to do with variant emphases in programs on personal learning and on social changing. More personally focused programs are designed to create conditions for learning, and situationally focused programs are designed to stimulate and support the invention and testing of ways of changing social roles, norms, goals and cultural patterns where changes seem desirable. But a closer look at this difference shows that it is a difference in emphasis rather than a difference in kind. The personal learnings achieved in the human relations laboratory are achieved for use by participants in changing their behavior and interpersonal and group relations outside the laboratory. Learnings are not achieved only for use in the especially designed social environment of the laboratory. They are general learnings in the sense that participants may choose to use their learnings in changing their families, work settings, civic activities, or all of these. And though the other laboratory activities are designed to stimulate and guide changes in more specific shared, social situations in organizational, community, or international settings — they are also designed to support learnings by participating persons — learnings which will enable them to work more effectively in bringing about changes in these specific environments.

A third difference lies in the kinds of data collected, analyzed, and evaluated in various especially designed programs for learning and changing. Programs oriented toward personal and interpersonal changing elicit and utilize more data about personal subjective feelings than do programs oriented toward changing situations. In these latter programs, more objective and intersubjective data have to be collected, analyzed and utilized. But now, a closer look shows that affective, perceptual, aspirational-volitional (value) and cognitive data are used more or less integratively in all types of laboratory programs. It is *the mix* of such data that varies with the specific objectives of particular laboratory programs.

SIMILARITIES AMONG LABORATORY PROGRAMS

Two of the similarities that characterize various applications of laboratory method already have been revealed in probing the differences manifested in the five snapshot cases. One of these is the integration of personal learning and planned action for social improvement which all responsible laboratory programs seek to achieve. The second is its attempt to deal integratively with the affective, valuative, and cognitive, the inner and the outer, dimensions of behavioral, personal or social, change, rather than to segregate work on one or another of these dimensions.

A closely related earmark of laboratory learning and changing is its emphasis upon utilizing the participative experiences of those involved in a program as indispensable data in the learning or changing process. This calls for the gathering and analysis of data by participants about their processes of dealing with one another and about the quality of their relationships. Such data will not be forthcoming from people unless norms of open and trustful communication are developed within the laboratory environment. Hence, the emphasis on open and direct exchange among participants which is emphasized in all the cases examined. Such process data are no substitute for objective knowledge about situational factors or for technologies and methods for altering or modifying these factors. But programs of laboratory learning and changing attempt a melding and merging of "process" and "content" data in building a workable basis for planned changes in human behavior and human systems.

Another similarity revealed in the five snapshot cases is the importance which laboratory practitioners attach to the designing of conditions which support free participation by all concerned in a change program in setting directions, planning ways of moving in directions chosen, and in analyzing and evaluating relevant activities as these are undertaken and carried through. Design involves attention to *ecological* factors in the laboratory environment — the hollow square arrangement in the intergroup workshop, the small round tables in a common space in the Youth Institute, the absence of telephones and office paraphernalia in the industrial team-building sessions. Design also involves decisions about *macroscopic* human aspects of the program — about the various groupings of participants required by the program objectives, about the human resources required, and about preparatory and follow-up activities by staff and participants before and after salient events in the programming sequence. And design extends to more *microscopic interventions* in the ongoing, developing experiences of persons and groups involved — to objectify here-and-now processes and relationships, to widen the range of alternative paths of movement when participants find themselves confronted with dilemmas and choices, to link participants with appropriate resources as they discover needs for specific resources in their ongoing learning and work. It is the importance given to design which distinguishes the uses of laboratory method as one species of *planned* change.

Finally, all five cases involved the use of especially trained resource people to help groups of laboratory participants in meeting their various design problems effectively. Various names were used to designate the resource persons involved: laboratory practitioners, applied social scientists, facilitators, trainers, consultants. For the time, it is enough to note that laboratory programs normally require the services of members of a newly emerging practice-profession for optimum effectiveness.

This chapter has not provided a complete answer to the question in its title, What Is Laboratory Method? But it has illustrated a variety of uses of the method. And it has provided the reader with concrete cases in a range of applications which they can keep in mind as the discussion moves to a deeper probing of the method's conceptual and moral foundations.

FOOTNOTES AND REFERENCES

1. Of many descriptions and analyses of T Groups now in print, the most thorough treatment is to be found in Leland P. Bradford, Jack Gibb, and Kenneth D. Benne (Eds.), *T Group Theory and Laboratory Method*, Wiley, New York (1964). Also see Chapters 5, 6 and 12 in this book.

2. See Thomas J. Cottle, "Strategy for Change," *Saturday Review*, September 20, 1969, for a fuller account of a workshop similar to the one described briefly here. See also Chapter 15 in this book.

3. See W. Warner Burke and Harvey A. Hornstein, *The Social Technology of Organization Development*, NTL Learning Resources Corp., Inc., Fairfax, VA (1972), especially Section II, "Team Buildings," and Section III, "Managing Conflict." See also Chapter 18 in this book.

4. See Chapter 19 in this book.

5. The five snapshots, though not descriptions of actual events, are illustrative of many actual applications of laboratory method now assisted by trainers and consultants in various parts of the world. Examples of applications of laboratory method to the clarification and melioration of transnational problems by responsible persons from the nations concerned are unfortunately much fewer in number and more dubious in their effects. See Richard E. Walton, "A Problem-Solving Workshop on Border Conflicts in Eastern Africa," *The Journal of Applied Behavioral Science*, 7, pp. 453-489; and Martin Lakin, in collaboration with Jacob Lomrantz, and Morton A. Lieberman, *Arab and Jew in Israel*, NTL Institute of Applied Behavioral Science, Washington, D.C., 1969, for a description of two such experimental attempts. (These efforts are in contradistinction from participation by cross-national populations in residential laboratories where the focus is on personal growth and improved skills in interpersonal relations. Such cross-national laboratories are by no means uncommon and have been conducted in the Americas, Europe, Africa, and Australia with reportedly good effects. Cross-national laboratories frequently have also been conducted for the professional development of laboratory trainers and consultants from various nations.) For this reason, Snapshot Five, when compared with Snapshots One through Four, in a double sense, is imaginary.

CHAPTER 2

CONCEPTUAL AND MORAL FOUNDATIONS OF LABORATORY METHOD

Kenneth D. Benne

As Chapter 1 has made clear, laboratory method has developed concomitantly a methodology for the education of persons and their relationships and a methodology for effecting changes in human systems. It is thus at once an educational and a social-political innovation. As in the case of all developing social and educational inventions, it is difficult to say clearly within the fabric of social study and social practice where laboratory method ends and where some other methodology of re-education and of planned change in human systems begins. For, as laboratory method has spread from its first institutionalization in residential laboratory training programs, it has been influenced by developments in various disciplines of social science and in various professions of social practice, even as it has exercised reciprocal influence in return. As its proponents have sought to apply laboratory method in various institutional settings, outside the residential laboratory, and in various programs of change, development and action, the method has evolved into several distinct forms. These reflect both the changing needs and orientations of American culture and counterculture, and applications of new social knowledge and technology.

In brief, laboratory method has evolved since its beginning. Yet, through all the complexities of its social evolution, certain continuities and patterns of integrity have persisted. What are these distinctive characteristics which set off laboratory method from other methodologies of re-education and of planned change in human systems?

Since its novelty derives partly from a deliberate effort by its practitioners to bring into confluent and productive relationship elements of an industrialized and departmentalized culture whose participants operate typically in segregation, without effective dialogue each with the other, there is no single perspective in which the innovation can be adequately defined. Put positively, a rounded view of laboratory method requires placing it in six perspectives, which in our culture are often seen as the private property of differentiated research disciplines or practice professions, or of action leaders and managers in various institutions, but which practitioners of laboratory method have sought to bridge and integrate.

LABORATORY METHOD VIEWED IN MULTIPLE PERSPECTIVES

A Way of Learning

Perhaps most fundamentally, the method is a way by which people are helped to learn how to learn for themselves. It stands for experiential learning. The idea of learning through experience is, of course, no novel idea in the history of educational thought. But the idea has been constricted or distorted in its application to formal education by other dominant ideas, other often unexamined assumptions about teaching and learning. The first of these is the notion of education as the transmission of a cultural heritage to the immature and, by extension, to alienated and deviant members of a society. Those in charge of education who are knowledgeable about our culture, as it has come to be out of its past, and who occupy stable positions in its structures are assumed to know what learners most need to learn. Learning experiences are planned by those who know — the teachers — so that learners — usually children or young people, but also immigrants or other uneducated or "miseducated" adults or aliens — may acquire what the more experienced and established judge that they need to know. This view of learning and its management has several constricting influences on processes of experiential learning. First of all, legitimate learning outcomes are defined in advance of meeting and dealing with learners by the managers of learning processes. Responsible participation by learners in determining what they need to learn, in inventing or creating ways to pursue these learning goals, in assuming responsibility for managing the behavioral conditions of learning — motivational, affective, and emotional states as they contribute to or thwart learning, power and authority relations in the learning situation — is severely limited. The management of these conditions is assumed to be the responsibility of the teacher or the administrator or, perhaps, the school board or legislature. Where classroom learning is supplemented by extra-scholastic experiences — vocational, rehabilitative or civic — a similar relation usually operates between master and neophyte or experienced leader and inexperienced followers.

Practitioners of laboratory method, in contrast, envisage education and re-education as a process of personal and cultural renewal and reconstruction rather than as the transmission of a heritage from the past. This view requires a different relationship between "teacher" and "learners" and between "learners." The relationship sought is one of peer collaboration in reconstructive inquiry. "Teacher" and "learners" jointly determine learning needs and goals, and jointly assess the resources of "teacher" and "learners" and of needed outside resources in relation to these goals. Learning experiences are regarded as "experiments" designed to link creatively and effectively needs and available resources. As "experiments" the experiences are problematic; the outcomes cannot be fully known in advance. In evaluating the outcomes of learning experiences, processes of planning and execution are lifted into consciousness. The teacher's behavior, as it affects the learning environment, is evaluated along with the behaviors of other learners. Power and authority relations are observed, analyzed and redefined in the interest of more meaningful and effective learning. A major outcome of learning sought is self-knowledge and group knowledge about the processes of experiential learning and about ways of transferring such knowledge to other situations in which members are now involved or will be involved in the foreseeable future. Teachers and learners work to develop mutually helpful interrelationships and to develop interpersonal and group relations conducive to learning by all.

Laboratory method does not demean or dismiss cognitive or conceptual learning. Nor does it suggest that each learning group must start afresh on the task of conceptualizing and generalizing from its own limited experience without reference to accumulated knowledge and concepts. This point will be emphasized later in discussing laboratory method in the perspective of knowledge utilization. But practitioners of laboratory method do recommend strongly that learners relate their cognitive learnings to concomitant learnings in value orientation and skill in order to apply new knowledge and skill and newly chosen values in projects designed to confirm or disconfirm, to alter and improve, both concepts and values in the crucible of continuing action and interaction. The enervating and guilt-producing gaps between what we know and what we profess to value, on the one hand, and what we actually do on the other — gaps which all of us experience in our lives — led the inventors of laboratory method to emphasize that learners develop and practice a wide repertoire of action skills, in order to narrow the gap between inner intention and aspiration and outer behavior in social situations. It was this emphasis on the importance of skill development in building and rebuilding human relationships that led the innovators of laboratory method to attach the name "training" to its educational applications. Much formal education, particularly in its non-vocational forms, operates under the assumption that "schooling" stops short with "learning that" and "learning about" and does not support learners in developing motivation and skill to utilize understandings achieved "in school" in the improvement of overt action and behavior throughout their lives; more briefly, it neglects the integration of many "thats" with "hows" and "whys" so that the individual can experience greater congruence between his knowledge and values and their behavioral expression. The innovators of laboratory method in education took the risk of using the name "training" in order to underline the importance of skill development, even though "training" connotes to many people what proponents of laboratory method most seek to avoid — the mechanical routinization of skills acquired without conscious linkage to concomitantly developing understandings and value orientations achieved in processes of experiential learning.

Process as Content

The innovators of laboratory method in education thus emphasized understanding and skill in methods of instituting the conditions and processes of experiential learning in various associations and relationships of life as an important outcome of education. But they also emphasized the importance of experiential content, often neglected in formal education, as essential to the achievement of this outcome.

As an early publication expressed it —

> Effective membership in modern society demands participation by all citizens in a large and increasing number of interacting groups. If group functioning is to be intelligent and productive, members and leaders need to understand the dynamics of effective group . . . (deliberation) . . . and action and to . . . (become) . . . masters of the skills of effective member and leader functioning. . . . Typically, training in group leadership tends to take the form of passing on a limited number of empirical techniques for transmitting information or for group manipulation. Until we acquire experimentally grounded knowledge of . . . leader and member skills required for productive group . . .

> (deliberation) . . . and action and of the methods for training group personnel in these skills, we fail to release and develop the intelligence and productivity latent in our organized life.[1]

Experiential learning of group and interpersonal dynamics and of skills for changing and improving these, where change is needed, required bringing into the ambit of educational responsibility experiential content typically excluded, by unexamined assumption, from conscious and public attention in learning situations. How does one learn to collect data about the process side of group and member functioning? It requires awareness and sharing of feelings and immediate perceptions of what Schutz once called the interpersonal underworld of group and social life. Questions about control and domination, of dependence and counter-dependence, of intimacy and distance, of exclusion and inclusion must be put to the ongoing group and interpersonal experiences in which learners are personally and subjectively involved. And such questions can only be answered if feelings and immediate perceptions of self and others and of their relationships are surfaced, expressed, shared, reflected upon and interpreted. Accurate diagnosis of the functioning or malfunctioning of group and members is impossible without such data. And wise decisions about improvement of group and member malfunctioning are impossible without such accurate diagnoses.

Much of the affective, aspirational, and volitional content required for such learning is hard for many people to get into the open; to express. People are not ordinarily encouraged to express publicly feelings generated in their exchanges with others. In fact, powerful standards of etiquette and politeness coach them to inhibit the expression of "subjective" feelings in most situations of life, particularly in work, action, and school situations. The proper and efficient thing to do is to be diplomatic and to speak relevantly to the "objective" goal or task. These standards may be internalized so thoroughly that persons become unaware of their own feelings and immediate perceptions evoked in exchanges with other people and, in the same process, anesthetized to the feelings and immediate perceptions which their behavior evokes in others. We are so coached to focus attention on the objective goals and tasks of "learning" and "work" that awareness of process is inhibited and/or repressed. To gather the data needed for understanding and improving group and interpersonal processes, and, by extension, organizational and community processes, special conditions and methods of laboratory education had to be devised and tested.

Prominent among these conditions which practitioners of laboratory method have employed is the face-to-face group. As fears of open expression of feelings by group members, which does render the expresser vulnerable in competitive situations, are relaxed, as a climate of trust and openness is engendered in the group, members learn to attend to their own feelings and here-and-now perceptions and to express these more openly in relation to the actions and behaviors of others in the group. Data are thus provided concerning the process-reality of group and member (including trainer) functioning to be reflected upon and interpreted by the group. As the meanings of these data are interpreted, improvement and change goals for members and for the group can be identified and commitment by members to the advancement of these goals taken.

The face-to-face group thus becomes an important medium for the utilization of laboratory method. It can provide a support system for persons in learning to make public their own process data and to receive process data from others — data important for self-directed growth in social intelligence but data which are not usually made public in most social situations. The small group also can provide a feedback system which furnishes relatively undistorted data as an empirical base for personal and group change and improvement. An important function of the practitioner of laboratory method (teacher, trainer, process consultant) is to help persons build a group which provides at one and the same time a support system and the challenge of openly expressed feedback on the effects of one's own behavior on others in process-oriented exploration and inquiry.

A Way of Planned Change

The innovators of laboratory method were as much concerned with helping persons to develop skills and understandings relevant to the planning and achievement of changes in their social environments as they were in personal liberation and development. The maintenance and extension of insights and skills achieved by many participants in training situations in their continuing self-development outside the training situation depend on their ability to modify their social environment to support rather than to thwart and inhibit their functioning on a new level, in at least some of their important outside associations and relationships. Participants in training were thus expected to develop skills for changing the quality and character of the social systems in which they function outside of training as a necessary condition of continued personal growth.

It was thus a "natural" extension of laboratory methods beyond the residential training communities in which the methods were first innovated and developed into programs and projects of organizational and community development. Here the targets of change are larger human systems — institutions, organizations, communities. Many of the commitments include a commitment to participation and collaboration in the planning of change by all persons and groups affected by the change. An additional commitment is to the minimizing and reducing of power and status differentials as these inhibit the collection and use of data, relevant to locating areas of needed change and in inventing and trying out improvements, from all parts of the system, especially from low-status and minority parts. Practitioners of laboratory method try to convert conflicts of value and interest, as these are surfaced and faced, from win-lose polarizations into problems to be solved, preferably by creative compromise. Another commitment is to help participants provide an adequate and valid data base for the setting of change priorities. And the data base must include affective, attitudinal, and aspirational information from participants blended with relevant "objective" factual and technical information, as these enter the arena of planning and deliberation through various channels of specialized expertise.

Laboratory method thus extends to the invention, testing, and improvement of methodologies of social action and social changing as well as to the invention and improvement of methodologies for personal and interpersonal re-education and growth. And it seeks to link and to integrate the two kinds and levels of behavioral change in programs of personal-social development. Re-education becomes an important element in social action and change. And projects of social action assume responsibility for their educative and re-educative effects upon all persons involved in and affected by the action.

A Process of Cooperative Action Research

It was researches into personal, group and organizational behavior and dynamics, as well as awareness of unmet personal and social needs for learning and change, that stimulated innovators of laboratory method to invent and test the new formats and methodologies for learning and changing already described. They were aware of the gaps that typically exist in our society between the practitioners of basic social research, the practitioners of applied social science be they social workers, teachers, counselors or psychiatrists, clergymen, managers or action leaders, and the persons and groups who are suffering the effects of debilitating and dehumanizing social conditions and who are struggling, often ineffectually, to meliorate these conditions. How can these gaps be bridged? Part of the problem is to find ways of improving the tempo and quality of application and utilization of research-tested social and behavioral knowledge in informing and improving the life practices of persons and groups in various associational and institutional settings. This perspective on laboratory method will be discussed in the next section.

Perhaps more fundamental is the problem of infusing the value orientations and methods of cooperative inquiry into the practical efforts of human beings to understand their social and cultural environments and to modify these where changes are needed. Methods of cooperative inquiry have been developed and refined by basic researchers in relation to the specialized disciplines into which research efforts are divided.

Can professional practitioners along with their clients learn to utilize research methods as a way to understand the social problems which beset them and to build a valid knowledge base for projecting and testing solutions to these problems? The notion of action research, of research used by actors as a means of their own self-education and as a tool of social problem-solving is usually attributed to John Collier of the U.S. Bureau of Indian Affairs. Certainly, Kurt Lewin formulated the notion of action research more clearly and fully, and he and his associates advocated and practiced it in the context of inter-group and community relations in the early 1940s. Cooperative action research became a focal model of re-education and changing for the innovators of laboratory method. Such research requires collaborative relationships between persons trained in methods of social and psychological research, professional practitioners, and the clients of these practitioners. As an example, let us suppose the teachers and students in a school building are dissatisfied with the quality and quantity of learning that is going on in their building. They bring in a social researcher to help them understand what is going on in their situation to block and impede learning. A familiar way of using the outside resource is to have him do a study of the situation and make recommendations for its improvement. Such expert surveys have most often led to little or no change in the situation. A cooperative action research would require the research expert to enlist the teachers (practitioners) and students (clients) in jointly planning a study of their situation, jointly collecting data and processing the data collected (this task may in part be delegated to specialized researchers), jointly interpreting the research results and jointly formulating recommendations to themselves and taking commitments to try out the recommendations and evaluate their consequences as tried.

It is not difficult to see that such a model conjoins research, self re-education and cooperative action. The gaps between researcher, practitioner, and consumers or clients must be bridged if the effort is to be collaborative and if planned and knowledge-based changes are to occur and to be evaluated. Much work on the processes which inhibit and which support peer collaboration and teamwork between researcher, teachers, and students will be required. Feelings generated in the process will need to be surfaced, shared, and attended to. Conflicts of value and power will have to be faced, clarified, and resolved. Here, as elsewhere, the use of laboratory method requires attention to the "subjective" aspects of processes and relationships between the members of the working group or other social system, along with concern for valid, "objective," technical and factual information and knowledge about the situation being studied and changed.

Kurt Lewin believed that properly designed and conceptualized action researches could serve both the purposes of building and accumulating social-behavioral knowledge — purposes often thought to be well served only by the specialized efforts of basic researchers — and purposes of social re-education and of social action as well. This is a point still in controversy among practitioners of laboratory method, as well as others, and will be discussed later in this book. But that cooperative action research is possible and that it can be effective in improving social situations have been demonstrated by users of laboratory method in interpersonal, face-to-face group, organizational, and larger social settings, as we shall see.

A Process of Knowledge Utilization

We have emphasized before that part of the motivation of the innovators of laboratory method was to facilitate the utilization of research-tested social and behavioral knowledge by men and women of practice and of action. This was particularly true of knowledge of behavioral dynamics at various levels of human organization. Such knowledge, it was believed, if it can be internalized by men and women of practice and action, can assist them in making more accurate diagnoses of personal and social difficulties in which they are involved and in mobilizing more effectively their own and others' resources in meliorating these difficulties.

It has become a commonplace that industrialized societies have been more successful in applying knowledge accumulating from theorizing and researches in physics, chemistry, and biology than in applying knowledges from behavioral research. Practice professions of engineering have emerged to conduct the developmental study and experimentation required to translate new physical and biological knowledge into practical technologies and procedures and to scan sources of new knowledge in inventing effective solutions to practical problems. Resistances to the spread of "thing technologies" have arisen from the threats to customary human habits, values, and relationships which widespread installation of the new "thing technologies" entails. We have not been able to innovate the flexible and person-oriented human organization required to bring our burgeoning "thing technologies" under confident and competent human control.

Simplistic explanations of the humanly dangerous disproportion between accelerating applications of physical and biological sciences and faltering applications of social and behavioral sciences abound. And no doubt these explanations have some validity. Social and behavioral sciences are newer and have not developed knowledge of the same universal explanatory power and applicability as have the physical and biological sciences. "Give us more time," many social and behavioral scientists say. We have not, as a society, funded work in social and behavioral research anywhere to the extent that we have funded physical and biological research. "Give us more funding," many social and behavioral scientists say.

But part of the problem surely lies in the difference between the processes of applying and using social and behavioral knowledge in human action and practice and the processes of applying physical and biological knowledge in and to our non-human environment. The adoption and utilization of new knowledge of man and society by men and societies requires re-education in a more profound sense than does the adoption and utilization of new knowledge of the things and energies in our non-human environment. Men are identified with images of themselves and of the associational and normative structures which lend security and continuity to their lives. The beliefs by which they make sense of their existence and of their lives are complex syntheses of "knowledge," "value orientations," "wishes," and "aspirations." They maintain themselves in sanity by consensual validation of their perceptions and valuations of themselves and their environment against the perceptions and valuations of others, both friends and enemies.

New knowledge of person, group, society, and human culture can be internalized and utilized by men and women only as the new knowledge is chosen as promising to better meet their requirements for maintenance, continuity, and growth than do the knowledge components of their present belief systems. People must see a need for change in their belief systems before they can seriously entertain new knowledge of man and society alternative to the modes of explanation and interpretation which they are currently employing. They must acknowledge to themselves inconsistencies and discrepancies in their present ways of seeing and interpreting their phenomenal world. New sources of knowledge must become more credible and trustworthy to them than the customary sources of understanding against which they ordinarily validate their beliefs and perceptions. Persons, as Kurt Lewin has emphasized, find and accept new value orientations and new cognitive orientations as they find and accept membership in a new group with value and cognitive orientations different from those of other groups to which they now belong.

There is ordinarily a lack of opportunity in industrial societies for social scientists, members of the human practice professions, and clients of practice professionals to form groups in which they meet as peers and gain a first-hand sense of the needs and the resources each of the other. The sub-cultures of basic social researchers are relatively segregated from the sub-cultures of helping professionals — social workers, teachers, ministers, etc. And the sub-cultures of helping professionals are relatively segregated from the sub-cultures of at least some of their clients. This latter segregation has shown up dramatically in difficulties of middle class teachers and social workers in forming effective helping relationships with lower class clients from poverty areas of our society. The segregation is further complicated where racial differences compound sub-cultural class differences. The problem of utilizing the social knowledge validated by basic social researchers in social practice and in the life patterns of clients of social practitioners is in some part a problem of lack of effective human bridges between the segregated sub-cultures in which the principal parties to the utilization transaction live and think and value.

The problem is further complicated by the customary fragmentation of researches into social phenomena along disciplinary lines — psychology, sociology, anthropology, economics, politics, etc. A similar fragmentation exists among helping professionals. Practical social problems of people do not fit neatly into disciplinary or professional categories so far as the knowledge required for problem clarification and solution is concerned. The renovation or renewal of a malfunctioning school system, for example, does not present a psychological, sociological, economic, political, or spiritual problem to those who would solve it. It is a problem with psychological, sociological, economic, political, and spiritual dimensions to be reckoned with and dealt with simultaneously. The present organization of the social research disciplines does not make for ready retrieval of relevant and usable knowledges for the diagnosis and solution of practical or action problems, either by practice professionals or, with or without their assistance, by their clients, the "ultimate consumers" of the fruits, sweet or bitter, of new knowledge.

The innovators of laboratory method saw the need for human linkage and bridging between social scientists, practice professionals, and men and women of action as a central need in facilitating more ready and intelligent use of social science resources in the solution of practical problems.

The often-missing, linking, bridging human role which the innovators constructed, defined, and sought to train was that of "change agent." The change agent works to bring those with specially developed knowledge about change processes and those acquainted with system needs into collaborative relationships in order to convert the best relevant knowledge into the transformation of experienced aspiration, need or pain into a problem to be solved; into projections of and choices among alternative solutions to the problem; into the carrying of the chosen alternative into action; and into evaluating the consequences of the action. Change agents might be recruited from one or another of the social sciences, from one or another of the practice professions, from among men and women of action. His or her capacities, developed by training, must include the ability to sustain multiple loyalties and memberships with integrity, the ability to translate between the languages in which needs are expressed and the languages in which knowledge resources are ordinarily stated, the ability to help people translate conflicts into problems which may be jointly inquired into, and the ability to inquire into behavioral processes as well as objective aspects of situations, and to maintain the participant-observer role in tense situations. They must also develop the ability to maintain commitment to the values and methods of honest inquiry and the ability to work in team relationships with others whose specialized knowledge resources differ from, but complement, their own.

The trainer of the training group, the consultant to an organization or community in identifying, defining, and solving its problems, the "manager" of a cooperative action research program are some of the variant forms the change agent role may take.

In general, proponents of laboratory method have maintained that the problems of utilization of social knowledge can be solved only as men and women of knowledge and men and women of practice and action, with acknowledged needs for better knowledge of themselves and their situations than they now possess, can be brought together into processes of collaborative inquiry. Ordinarily, the facilitation of these processes requires the good offices of persons trained in bridging and linking hitherto segregated human systems — a role which we have called that of the "change agent."

A Way of Resocialization and Re-enculturation

A sixth and final perspective in which to assay the distinctive meaning of laboratory method is to view it as a process of resocialization or re-enculturation. Human organisms become persons and selves as they enter into membership in various associations and, in the process, internalize, make their own, the language, the standards, the thought-ways, value-ways, and behavior-ways, which prevail as a way of life in these associations. Much of this acquisition of ways of behaving, thinking and valuing occurs through non-conscious accommodation and conditioning of member responses to the modal ways of the groups in which developing persons seek and find membership. If and as the person develops his ability to think and choose for himself, he incorporates the cultural content of his social environment more critically and selectively, he creates his own distinctive value-system which permits him to exercise some measure of free and responsible control over the processes of his continuing socialization.

In a more or less "static" society, which relies for the most part upon tradition-direction in guiding its career in history, it is functional for much socialization to remain at the accommodative and conditioning level. In a rapidly changing society, in which unexamined traditions furnish no confident basis for choice, in which creative responses to novel conditions of life must be worked out, individually and collectively, as a condition of survival, people must assume greater responsibility for consciously and selectively directing the process of their own socialization. It is a corollary of this that continuing socialization and resocialization must occur throughout the lifetime of persons and that societies can no longer rely upon a fixed shaping of character in early socialization, on the assumption that the same character will enable a person to cope effectively with the vicissitudes of life throughout his career. A desirable consequence of helping persons to correct and modify the effects of early socialization which have become dysfunctional in coping with changing conditions, is to aid them in dealing more effectively with the conflicts and confusions which adult life now thrusts upon them. It is therapeutic in the sense that it seeks to correct and cure pathologies engendered in persons in some large part by faulty, constricting, and rigidifying, processes of early socialization. Professionals concerned with psychotherapy have found that properly guided experiences of persons in face-to-face groups are effective in helping them to identify and work through at least some pathologies engendered by dysfunctional early socialization.

While not denying the existence or importance of pathology in persons, proponents of laboratory method do not see their work with persons in groups as primarily therapeutic in nature. Their orientation is toward growth of persons and toward the prevention of pathology. They see their efforts as educational and re-educational in character rather than as curative of hang-ups engendered in past experience. Socializing processes do occur for members of any group in the life and work of which they become deeply involved. Proponents of laboratory method help members to become aware of these socializing processes in the groups and other human systems in which they are now involved or which they help to form for training purposes; they encourage members to become critical of these, to shape them freely and responsibly with due regard to the values and the growth needs of themselves and of other group members. They thus encourage members to learn the arts of managing the processes of their own continuing socialization, not alone in the training setting, but in other associations and relationships as well.

It is true that members faced with the task of building and managing a growth releasing and supporting environment for themselves will find clashes between novel demands upon their responses and patterns of response developed in their earlier socialization. The standards of the growth-releasing group, for example, may demand trustful openness about feelings and immediate perceptions, whereas earlier socialization has made a virtue of closedness and caution. The new situation may elicit autonomous responses from members where their early socialization made a virtue of authority-conforming or counter-conforming responses. Persons in a laboratory situation do review their early socializations relevantly to their functionality or dysfunctionality for maintaining an inquiry posture in an inter-dependent setting. And they do seek to work through changes in some of these or decide to accept them as valid and stable parts of themselves. Proponents of laboratory method recognize that many disabilities of persons revealed in their efforts to engage in cooperative inquiries into themselves and their situations represent not pathologies but rather lack of opportunity in the past to develop the personal and interpersonal skills and orientations which such efforts require. The "fault" lies often not in the inherent weakness of persons but in the method and design of educational processes which fail to support persons in using and developing the strengths required.

The extensions of laboratory method into organizational and community settings may be seen in part as efforts to produce mentally healthful environments in these larger human systems. A healthful organization is one that is aware of its socialization effects upon the persons who function in and through it. It is committed to involving these persons in converting growth-inhibiting patterns and structures into growth-releasing and supporting patterns and structures, both for the persons and for the organization. Its orientation toward mental health in such developmental work is, therefore, preventive rather than curative.

It would be false, of course, to claim that some persons do not reveal and discover personal pathologies while engaged in learning or change programs guided by the laboratory method. The responsibility of those who guide such programs is to help such persons to find therapeutic help in which the blemishes of faulty early socialization can, insofar as possible, be meliorated, if not healed.

The fact remains, however, that proponents of laboratory method seek to help persons become aware of socialization influences that play upon them in their collective lives and to become more free and responsible in guiding these socialization processes in the interest of their own continuing personal development and growth.

THE DYNAMICS OF EDUCATIONAL INNOVATION

We may gain further insight into the distinctive nature of the laboratory method of learning and changing by placing it in the perspective of the changing culture out of which it originally developed. Every educational and social innovation emerges from a set of cultural conditions with certain definable characteristics. First, the innovators perceive needs for learning and changing inadequately met by existing practices. Second, underlying these needs are cherished values seen as threatened in the drift of historical events or emergent values which are blocked in their actualization. These values assume a central role in shaping the new processes of re-education designed to give them renewed and augmented power. Third, new resources in knowledge, technology, and skill are seen as available, at least in embryo. Such conditions in American culture motivated the persons responsible for innovating the laboratory method.

Unmet Learning Needs of Contemporary Culture

Although most educational innovators have tended to turn to the practices of childhood or youth education to institutionalize their innovations, the founders of the training laboratory began with a venture in adult education. This is consistent with the laboratory emphasis upon finding ways to release and support continuing learning in all the relations and associations of life. The choice of adult education as a setting for introducing laboratory methods of learning into our society was further based on strategic considerations. The people now in control of educational and other institutions are adults. If they can experience and validate new ways of learning for themselves, they should be inclined to support rather than to resist similar opportunities for children and younger adults.

The founders of the first laboratory were thus concerned

about unmet learning and growth needs in the various organized associations of adult life, not just in formal education. They saw failure in meeting these needs as a dangerous condition in contemporary life.

> ... The development of the physical sciences and related technology thrusts upon all of us problems of individual and group relations of progressive complexity. The acceleration in number and complexity of such relational problems to be solved is increasingly disproportionate to our relatively slow advance in understanding and controlling the dynamics of individual and group behavior... Such skill and understanding can be developed only through the focus of research effort upon current pressing problems of human relations and of training individuals and groups in solving these problems. And such research (and training) can succeed only through the cooperative effort of social scientists, educators, and action leaders.[2]

Those who launched the laboratory movement, then, believed that individual persons are being compelled to change by inexorable pressures from application of knowledge from the natural sciences and related technologies with little, if any, preparation for handling changes, with sensitivity and effectiveness, in themselves and their relationships. Yet creative and collaborative adaptations are essential in achieving and maintaining personal and collective integrity and health in contemporary culture. This condition defines the basic area of unmet learning needs that the training laboratory was hopefully designed to meet.

The founders of the first laboratory saw the group as the link between the individual person and the larger social structure. They saw the group, therefore, as a medium for serving two sets of interrelated functions: 1) the re-education of the individual person toward greater integrity, greater understanding of himself and of the social conditions of his life, greater behavioral effectiveness in planning and achieving, along with others, changes both in himself and in his social environment; and 2) the facilitation of changes in the larger social structures upon which individual lives depend.

Can people learn to use groups for individual rehabilitation and for reconstruction of the social environment? And can groups be developed which are simultaneously alive to the needs of their members for growth as persons and to the needs of the social environment for reconstruction and improvement? The innovators of laboratory method answered "yes." The first laboratory was designed as a place where people might learn experimentally to develop groups to serve both purposes, and in the process, to become skilled in extending similar experimental efforts into nonlaboratory settings.

LABORATORY METHOD: DEFINITION AND REVIEW

To the founders of the laboratory, as already noted, part of the widespread disintegrity of personal and collective responses to changing conditions reflected a separation of three functions: action, research, and education. These functions must be integrated if social life generally is to become more supportive of continuing desirable learning and change. Decisions about social action are typically taken without the utilization of relevant findings and methodologies from social and behavioral research, while research efforts, though incidentally producing findings relevant to action choices, typically are undertaken without awareness of the knowledges needed by people who must take action. Where action leaders do employ competences in the social and behavioral sciences, they often make a limited and truncated use of them — often in the service of unexamined goals, values, and assumptions. And researchers, concerned with the violation of their own inherent values and goals, resist superficial, applied employment of their resources. How can researchers and action leaders be brought into significant relationships that do not violate but actually enhance the integrity and autonomy of each? The central need, as the laboratory founders saw it, is a confrontation, a dialectical interplay, and growing collaboration among action interests, research interests, and educational interests.

Since these interests are embodied in roles and the roles in persons, any adequate training community must bring into relationship persons representative of each. The training laboratory was designed not to set up a situation in which researchers could teach educators or in which educators could teach action leaders, but one in which each would come increasingly to value and to utilize the resources of the others. The immediate goal was deeper collaboration. A research goal was to learn more about ways in which this desired collaboration could be effected. The envisaged long-range goal was a growing methodology for effective collaboration between men and women of action, of research, and of education in a context of self-directed and self-correcting development and training. The parallel concomitant was the institutionalization of such a methodology in various segments of our organizational and community life.

How has the vision changed in a quarter century of experimentation with laboratory method? One change is a deeper vision of the problems of individual persons confronted by demands for change and adaptation which threaten their needs for autonomous growth as persons. Playing the "culture game" of achieving upward mobility in a society uncertain both of its future and of its roots produces individuals uncertain of their own identity. The re-educative task has deeper therapeutic dimensions than the founders of the laboratory realized, though they were not unaware that their conception of personal change through group experience led them into the borderland between education and therapy as traditionally institutionalized. Clarification of the therapeutic dimension of the educational task has come about through three sorts of influences. The first is through experimentation with training groups. In efforts to build a group of their own, participants were dealing with personal problems inadequately solved in the processes of their earlier socialization. Learnings about self became more prominent in the agenda of training groups through self-selection of learning emphases by participants. The second influence has come through the involvement of more clinically oriented professionals (psychiatrists and psychologists) within the growing network of professional trainers. The third influence has been from studies of social and organizational life outside the laboratory movement — many of which have been focused since 1947 upon the vicissitude of individuals in their questing for identity within a fragmented society. Closely related have been parallel developments in group therapy.

A second change has been a deepened awareness of the importance of formal, bureaucratic organization as a factor in achieving or failing to achieve the tasks of personal and social renewal. The eclipse of community in modern life has, in fact, stemmed from the depersonalization of human relationships as complex bureaucratic organization has extended into the provision of health, welfare, and educational services. The restoration of growth-sustaining and voluntary community to human relationships thus means, in part, efforts to rehumanize relationships within bureaucratic structures. This means the invention of new or revised models of organizational behavior as well as models of group and interpersonal behavior.

This dimension of the re-educative task of laboratory method has also stemmed from three kinds of influences. One is the introduction of laboratory method into the life and work of organizational managers and supervisors. This served to force problems of organizational behavior and its reconstruction upon the attention of trainers and consultants. Another influence has come from the incorporation of students of organizational behavior into the staffs of laboratory programs. Many of these "scientific" students of organizational life are also engaged as consultants to organizations concerning the better handling of changes. A third closely related influence has been the growth of studies of organizational life, outside the laboratory movement, which have highlighted the personal, interpersonal, group, and intergroup dimensions of life within bureaucracies.

A further change in the vision of unmet learning needs is not so much a change in social diagnosis as a growing realization of the limitations of the residential training laboratory as the way to meet these needs. From the first, laboratory trainers had been aware that the utilization of laboratory learnings by participants ideally required preparatory efforts within their ongoing social environments in order to create receptivity for changes there. It also ideally required supportive efforts of participants after training during a period of stabilizing behavioral changes in the home settings. The limitations upon early experimentation with these concomitants to laboratory experience were practical rather than ideological. Recently, important beginnings have been made in introducing laboratory methods into intra-organizational and intra-community programs of self-study and self-development. These efforts have further illuminated needs for learning and changing and have provided better evaluations of the place of laboratory methods in meeting them.

Values Threatened or Underdeveloped in Contemporary Practice and Action

Significant educational and social innovations are directed toward meeting needs for learning and changing in a society, but innovators are quickened in their efforts by concern with the fate of cherished values, traditional or newly emergent, perceived as threatened, or thwarted by the trend of historical events. Three sets of overlapping values were central in the concerns of the innovators of laboratory method: the values of science, of democracy, and of the helping relationship.

Concern for Science. Concern with the under-utilization of the social and behavioral sciences in practical affairs has already been underlined. More basic was the concern that the values implicit in science did not function potently in processes of problem solving and planning in practical settings. Science as a human enterprise has an implicit morality. It is this morality with its devotion to fact-finding and fact-facing, its commitment to free and open communication of findings and its pursuit of objectivity, which is widely neglected or rejected in processes of action-decision where efficiency, win-lose competition, and "tribal" defense and offense tend to dominate.

The innovators of the training laboratory felt that practical decision-making would gain in validity only if the moralities and methodologies of the scientific enterprise were more deeply infused into the moralities and methodologies of contemporary decision and action.

Concern for Democracy. Although verbally honored, democratic values as operational determiners of important processes of decision-making in organizational and community life in our society are widely neglected. Frequently, they are rejected as impractical or as threatening to power relations in the *status quo.* The innovators of laboratory method recognized very real difficulties in utilizing democratic processes. They believed that operational redefinition of democratic values to make them more relevant to conditions of contemporary life was demanded. Increasing size and complexity of units of interdependence bring increasingly complex problems for participative solutions by individuals and groups, and complexity requires expertness in its management. This factor combines with increasing remoteness from decision-making opportunities to remove the individual from responsible involvement in managing his own affairs. How can such involvement be restored and extended? The problem is partly re-educational in character.

> Democracy is an ideology which above all others demands that its practitioners be masters of skills of human relationship adequate to help groups of people make intelligent decisions concerning the changing problems that confront them. . . . Without appropriate and experimentally tested skills and methods for building effective cooperative relationships, democracy has no hands and feet.[3]

The innovators of laboratory method saw a large degree of coincidence between the democratic ethic and the scientific ethic. A reality orientation in facing difficulties and problems, an objectivity which extends to one's own assumptions, perspectives, and preferences as factors in problem solving, and a commitment to rational collaboration in problem definition and solution are obviously scientific in mood and temper, and they are also requirements of a democratic morality. The practical task was to design educational processes to help learners incorporate these values into their own processes of personal and collective decision making and problem solving.

Concern for the Values of the Helping Relationshp. The innovators of the training laboratory put great emphasis upon the importance of the helping professions.

> While an increase in tested human-relations skills and understandings is important to all members of a democratic society, it is of central importance for those whose job is to improve the learning, the maturity, and the productivity of others — educators, trainers, supervisors, social workers, and the like. . . . They are often blocked by typical resistance to the communication of problems and pertinent experience from level to level in a community or organization and from group to group. They are frustrated by the typically large areas of privacy that individuals have built. . . .

> Finally, they are blocked by a failure which they share with many others in our society — a failure to see that groups have their own immaturity and maturity as groups and that they require training as groups in improving their ways of thinking and producing.[4]

Values guide the efforts of a person in helping other persons, and values guide the receiver of help as well. Many of these find a common core in a joint commitment to the facilitation of learning and maturation in the client, whether the client is a person, a group, an organization, or a community.

The training laboratory was conceived originally as a place where helping relationships could be studied and improved. It was hoped that participants would be motivated to extend helping relationships into their associational lives beyond the laboratory. Some of the perceived blocks in contemporary culture to the spread of the helping relationship into action and practice settings have already been cited. Another block lies in the existing fragmentation among the helping professions themselves. The professions had emerged to help people caught in the conflicting demands for change and adaptation which industrialization and urbanization had thrust upon them. Typically, many helping professions, like social work and psychiatry, focused on helping people who had experienced "abnormal" difficulties in handling these conflicts. But in most helping professions, efforts were being made to reorient work toward prevention and away from a primary emphasis on therapy. What orientation might enable the helping professions to find common ground in their specialized efforts to help clients? The innovators of laboratory training found such an orientation in the generalized conception of the change agent — an agent committed to help others in improving their abilities to cope effectively with change and conflict.

An early report makes clear this commitment to finding a common ground in value and orientation for professional and volunteer helpers in our society.

> What is the common framework which helps the group worker, the public school supervisor, the personnel consultant in industry, the PTA president, the training officer in a government bureau, and others to see their special jobs as resources one to the other? The faculty believed, and laboratory experience confirmed the belief, that all of these helpers and trainers of other people can find common ground in the role of the "change agent." All . . . (helpers) . . . work to produce changes in the understandings, attitudes, and skills of the persons and groups with whom they work. All . . . (helpers) . . . must, for example, help persons to plan ways of solving problems, to evaluate

their plans as these are tried and tested, and so on. These helps to persons and groups require certain basic human relationship skills which can be identified, analyzed, and practiced.[5]

The training laboratory was thus designed to increase intelligent commitment to three sets of values beleaguered and inadequately utilized in contemporary society. It was these values, seen in interrelationship, that the laboratory innovators believed were best calculated to guide efforts to meet the unmet learning needs of a changing industrialized society. And these values have continued to guide the use of laboratory method during the quarter century of its development.

Resources for Linking Values and Needs

Where did the founders of the training laboratory seek resources to guide and inform their educational methodologies? They drew first on the resources of the academic disciplines and professional fields in which they had been trained and in which they were currently engaged in research and in teaching. Members of the training staff of the first laboratory were trained in social psychology, adult education, sociology, and the philosophy of education. In addition, the research staff had members trained in clinical psychology and in cultural anthropology. The staff drew also upon various fields of social practice.

Resources from the Social and Behavioral Sciences. The innovators of the training laboratory found encouragement in the shift in theorizing and research over a wide number of social and behavioral sciences from an emphasis upon "static" description and classification to an emphasis upon dynamics. The dynamic approach was seen as especially relevant in providing knowledge and concepts useful in diagnosing situations and in planning processes of change — processes with which laboratory methodology is centrally concerned. Much of the initial interest was in the developing field of group dynamics, with particular attention to the theoretical contributions of Kurt Lewin.

Theoretical and practical developments in action research methodology were of particular interest. As already noted, action research provided a model for utilizing scientific methodology in improving processes of practical problem solving. It also provided a model for inducing change by collaborative and scientific means.

Resources from Philosophy. Certain philosophic developments also were resources. Interest in democratic and scientific methodologies for increasing social intelligence pointed to the thinking of John Dewey and other American experimentalists as resources. Particularly useful were studies of the logic of practical judgment, as it operated in future-oriented planning and education, by R.

Bruce Raup and others, seeking an integration of democratic and scientific methods of policy and decision making. The kinship between this methodology and Lewin's theory of action research was noted.

Resources from Developments in Social Practice. The founders of the laboratory were aware of the several early attempts to use primary group processes as a means of re-education. They were aware of developments in group psychotherapy by S. R. Slavson, J. L. Moreno, and others, though they sought to differentiate training from psychotherapy. They were influenced also by Moreno's work in psychodrama and sociodrama, by the widening use of group discussion methods in adult education, and to some extent, by social group work.

Efforts, in workshops and work conferences, to design a total learning experience in which participation by members is a major vehicle of learning and planning were influential in shaping the format of the training laboratory.

Programs of leadership training developed in various organizations were seen as directed toward the learning needs with which the laboratory was also concerned. Criticisms of many such programs for their lack of grounding in the social and behavioral sciences and in a democratic ethic have already been noted.

These, then, were the resources, many of them in the pioneering stage, that staffs of early training laboratories saw as important. Other important resources have been brought in by the widening circle of scientists and practitioners who have joined in using laboratory method over the years. Two areas of research in the behavioral sciences, as previously noted, have come to loom larger in laboratory thinking and planning. These are the developing fields of organizational and individual behavior and dynamics. These influences have been mediated by increasing representation from these fields. In addition, studies of conflict and conflict resolution and of the dynamics of intergroup relations in organizational and community settings have been influential.

Later chapters will elaborate further the conceptual underpinnings of laboratory method in its variant forms and applications. A further elaboration of its value and moral orientation is in order here.

MORAL ORIENTATION OF LABORATORY METHOD

The laboratory method of learning and changing is by no means devoid of values. Nor do its proponents function without value commitments. The method incorporates values from the orientations of science, of democracy, and of processes of giving and receiving help, as already noted. Those who practice laboratory method share certain moral commitments. And yet they differ widely in the ultimate values they espouse as persons, the disciplines and professions through which they make a living and practice a vocation, and the life styles they express and enact. At any rate, this moral community indifference is an ideal among laboratory educators, an ideal sought, if not always attained, in their working relationships. And it is also an ideal, we believe, which practitioners of laboratory method, implicitly or explicitly, invite their clients to adopt as a standard, at least provisionally, and to evaluate, whether the context of application be one of training, consultation, or applied research.

Laboratory practitioners typically work with persons and human systems caught up in confusions and conflicts. And ordinarily these conflicts involve differences in values among contending "parties," whatever other clashing or dissonant factors may be involved. Conflicts often lead to polarization, in some degree, between and among contending or hostilely segregated parties. The "normal" behavior to be expected of those related to the conflict, as polarization deepens, is to take sides, to become partisan advocates of the purposes, rights and virtues of one side as over against those of the other(s).

Those who, like laboratory educators, try to avoid the role of partisan advocate in relation to the conflicts they are working with are not infrequently seen by those involved in the conflict as uncommitted people, as dehumanized persons or as witting or unwitting stooges for the "establishment," or as some combination of these far-from-savory roles and characters. Can laboratory educators maintain commitment to certain values at stake in a conflicted human situation and still maintain openness and objectivity in and toward it? And, if they can, should they? We will consider the question of possibility first and deal with the question of desirability later.

Actually, more than one kind of values is at stake in any conflicted human situation. One kind of value may be called substantive values. A community, for example, may be divided and in conflict over the legalization of the sale and use of marijuana. Substantive positions develop around the issue. Advocates of the removal of all legal restrictions on sale and use amass evidence and arguments concerning the harmlessness or the beneficence of marijuana, concerning the disrespect for law which maintenance of unenforceable laws, which try to regulate relatively harmless personal tastes, engenders, concerning the inequity and injustice of making criminals out of purveyors and users of marijuana as over against the legalization of the sale and use of alcohol and tobacco, which may be equally or more harmful to health, etc. Advocates of the maintenance of legal restrictions and sanctions amass evidence and arguments concerning the connection of its use with "graduation" to addiction to harmful drugs by the users, concerning alleged character deterioration associated with the use of drugs, etc. Advocates of various intermediate positions usually emerge.

Another kind of value at stake in such a situation may be called methodological values. These have to do with the ways in which such conflicts should be settled in making and remaking decisions or policies which are valid and mutually acceptable, at least ideally, to all parties to the conflict. There may be concern with the quality of the evidence used in settling the issue, its validity and its reliability. There may be concern with the inference processes by which meanings for action are derived from the evidence by various partisans. The human effects of the means of persuasion used — coercion, group pressures against the expression of minority opinions, exploitation of anxieties and fears, etc. — may be an object of concern. The quality of communication, of listening, of empathy between contending parties may be examined and pointed out as important in affecting the quality of the settlement reached. Concern may be generated that parties to the conflict do not learn anything from the conflict, do not invest imagination in creating solutions integrative of the substantive values in conflict and embodying new values created in the exchange, that energy is invested only in trying to impose rigid, prepared positions, one upon the other and destroying, not strengthening, whatever moral community has existed among the parties. And advocates of appropriate, relevant, and creative methodologies to be applied in and to controverted situations may and do appear along with advocates of various substantive positions.

Practitioners of laboratory method are methodological advocates with respect to the proper ways of settling confused, controverted, conflicting human situations. They work on the assumption that there is a close interconnection between the human quality of the means used and the human quality of the resolution attained. It is not true that they themselves have no substantive values with respect to the desirable ends of human action. The assumption is rather that they, along with all other persons, have such values. It is further assumed that persons involved now differ in their ultimate value orientations and will probably continue to do so. But laboratory practitioners do believe that differences in value orientation need not be a blemish upon and a threat to learningful common deliberation and action, if commitment to the use of methodologies which respect differences and employ them to enrich and improve common action can be attained and maintained by all parties in and through conflict situations.

The best safeguard to the continuation and enhancement of personal and sub-group differences within a society may well be the cultivation of common commitment to appropriate methodologies for dealing with social difficulties and issues. These must be methodologies which incorporate respect for differences, which build upon the expectation of open expression of articulated differences by all parties in the arena of public deliberation, which require the imaginative weaving of differences into the fabric of common policies and decisions reached, and which conceive of conflict resolution as potentially a process of mutual and desirable learning, re-education and change for all of those involved.

This is, of course, not a description of the way in which conflicts are typically resolved in contemporary society, whether at the personal, interpersonal, intergroup, or international levels of human organization. It is rather a normative position about effective and desirable conflict-resolution. The fact that moral commitments are often interpreted in terms of steadfast and unchanging substantive commitments to socially inherited and frequently unexamined or allegedly unexaminable value orientations does not lead validly to the conclusion that such an interpretation of moral commitments is morally right or viable for our historical period. It does set a vast re-educative task for those who define moral commitments in terms of the utilization of methods of conflict resolution which are designed to lead to intelligent and mutually acceptable resolutions to particular controverted situations and to a general building, strengthening, and widening of moral community in difference among the contending parties. This is the re-educative task to which proponents of laboratory method are committed.

Actually, every human person has both a substantive and a methodological character. He possesses more or less integrated and consciously criticized value orientations with respect to the ends and objects of human life and action. But he possesses also more or less integrated and consciously criticized value orientations concerning the ways in which he should deal with conflicts in himself, between himself and others, and between the group(s) to which he belongs and other groups. If the function of laboratory methods of learning and changing is to challenge and support persons and groups in examining their "methodological characters" and in refining and improving these toward greater relevance to and power in the choices and decisions with which contemporary life confronts men, this does not mean that the goal is to deprive men or groups of variegated substantive commitments or to destroy their commitments to differing personal ends in living. Improved methodological characters should rather lead men and women to develop various, ultimately unique substantive orientations which are yet more reality-oriented, more tuned to the demands of contemporary living, and more open to continuing re-education through exchanges and transactions with others.

Many cultural anthropologists speak of their way of learning cultures different from their own as participant observation. This implies that each anthropologist as a person is at once a participant and an observer. By extension, as each person becomes his own functioning anthropologist, he develops himself both as an observer and a participant. As participant, he enacts the substantive values which he has come to hold through his past processes of enculturation. As observer, he attends and responds to the different values and behaviors which others around him are enacting and in the same process becomes an observer and critic of his own behaviors and value orientations. And as he pursues his processes of observant participation he may hope to improve his skills, understandings, and commitments, both as observer and critic of and as participant in human life. This is another way of describing the interactive growth in methodological and substantive characters which the laboratory educator seeks to develop for himself and which he encourages others with whom he works to develop for themselves.

As already noted, the laboratory method derives its moral orientation from the value orientations of science, democracy, and of the "pedagogical" process, conceived of as a process of reciprocal giving and receiving of help in facilitating growth and learning within and between persons. To make sense of this derivation, "science" must be seen as, most basically, a process of inquiry into situations marked by conflicting knowledge claims. The goal of inquiry is to test variant knowledge claims with respect to whatever confused or conflicted matters of fact it is addressed. The values of science operate as an ethic of investigative conduct in the individual scientist and as norms of proper investigative conduct within the scientific group or community. Scientists cannot know in advance the outcome of a genuine inquiry. They can best guarantee the validity of the outcome by attending to the methods and processes by which the inquiry is pursued.

Similarly, democracy must be seen basically as a process by which persons and groups who differ in interests and orientations, seek, through exchange and deliberation, to attain uncoerced bases of common action to guide and control their common and public life. It is important that democracy not be identified with the political and economic institutions of any particular polity, American or otherwise, although this is a continual temptation in polarized conflicts among groups as each seeks to justify and exalt the righteousness of its traditional culture and, as a consequence, to exempt inadequate features of that tradition from open and internal examination and reconstructive criticism. We are using democracy as John Dewey once used the term "democratic" to characterize any society or group which is committed to becoming aware of and responsible for the effects of its actions upon the life and growth of persons affected by them. And this includes, of course, persons within the society as well as persons outside. Such a society or group strives to become more of a moral community, and less a collectivity in Martin Buber's meanings of those terms. As in the case of the scientific community of inquiry, a democratic community cannot know in advance whether its decisions and policies will actually enhance the life of various persons involved. It must expect "mistakes," surprises, unanticipated consequences. But it pays attention to the methods it employs in making its decisions and policies in terms of open communication and of full participation of interested persons and groups in its processes of deciding as the best guarantee of avoiding moral and political "mistakes" and of learning and self-correction through surprises and through unanticipated consequences of actions undertaken.

It is not too far fetched, in this view of "science" and "democracy," to see both as methods of re-education through which men seek to learn their way into an unknown future with the claims of valid knowledge and of moral growth of persons centrally in mind. It is, therefore, not alien to the enterprise of advancing the use of these methods in the practical affairs of men to see processes by which human beings receive help from each other as important to the enterprise. These processes have been lifted into consciousness and the values associated with their effectiveness identified in studies of pedagogy, counseling, and psychotherapy. Unfortunately, the processes of giving and receiving help in these relationships are often seen as somewhat less than reciprocal and mutual. The receiver of help tends to be identified with only one side of the relationship because of the relative ignorance, immaturity, distress, or alienation of the client when compared with the alleged or assumed knowledgeability, maturity, and "needlessness" of the helper. In processes by which men and women try jointly to learn their way into an unknown future, they meet more as peers, as equals in ignorance, immaturity, distress, and alienation. Exchanges in the helping relationship must, as a consequence, be more reciprocal and mutual. This is not to discount the importance of childhood education, counseling, or psychotherapy. It is rather to caution against taking the relationships in these uncritically as models for the relationships which ideally should come into being in processes of laboratory learning and changing. Nevertheless, the values identified in effective helping relationships can be used by users of laboratory method, if they are conceived reciprocally rather than in terms of a fixed and non-mutual relationship between helper and client. The values embodied in statements such as those of Carl Rogers concerning the conditions of an effective helping relationship — empathic understanding of the other, positive affective attitude toward the other, genuineness in expression (words coherent with inner feelings), and a match in intensity of affective expression in the exchange — have been incorporated in the norms, which should guide the use of laboratory method, that follow.

The moral orientation of proponents of laboratory method can be formulated more concretely in terms of norms that should be developed in processes of learning and changing. These represent an attempt to fuse the value orientations of science, democracy, and the helping relationship.

1. Processes of learning and changing should be experimental. Such processes are addressed to the clarification of a confused and conflicted present. They are aimed at developing more adequate ways of thinking about, valuing, and handling a future which by its very nature is partly unknown. Plans which emerge from transactions and deliberations in the present should be held provisionally as they are acted upon. Plans for continuing evaluation and revision, in the light of continuing experience in action, should be built into plans for action and re-education.

2. Processes of learning and changing should be collaborative. They should involve living persons with a stake in the outcome in responsible participation, in reciprocal and responsible influence and interpersuasion in reaching the decisions which do affect and will affect their lives. Now muted voices need to be articulated and strengthened. Those with powerful and fashionable voices should learn to speak less and listen more. Ultimately, each personal contribution is unique and common bases of action and evaluation are less adequate than they need be unless the widest possible range of personal contributions is woven into their fabric.

3. Processes of learning and changing should be oriented to the requirements of the confronting task and situation, not oriented to maintaining or augmenting the prestige and status systems participants trail with them as they enter into processes of learning and changing. This means that contributions to a process of learning and changing are to be judged by their relevance to the confronting problematic situation, not by the prestige, position, and credentials of the sources of contributions. This is not meant to deny the importance or the necessity of authority in processes of learning and changing. It means rather that authority relations need continually to be built and rebuilt in relation to the changing situations which people confront. The right to exercise authority does not rest on past achievements but on the cogency and relevance of contributions to the presently confronting situation.

This norm is most difficult to develop and maintain in exchanges in which some participants are "laymen" and others are "experts," in which some are young and some are old, in which some are of "majority" status and others of "minority" status. But it is in such exchanges that the norm most needs to be developed and applied.

4. Processes of learning and changing should be educational (and re-educational) for all participants. This may seem tautologous for processes of learning. But closer examination shows that it is not. Many learning situations are set up monologically — the students learn from the teacher; the teacher does not learn from the students. This norm prescribes dialogic processes of learning in which all learn and in which, ideally, each learns what he most needs to learn. In the learning situation each participant learns something different, whatever the core of common learning may be. In learning situations which employ laboratory method, this psychological fact is made into a virtue, not a blemish. Many changes in institutions and communities are "engineered" by those with greater power and prestige without attention to or responsibility for what participants learn in the process. This norm proscribes such "engineering."

Processes of learning and changing are re-educational when earlier enculturations of persons are brought up into consciousness and when persons develop a more adequate awareness of potentialities in themselves and in their environments which are inhibited from actualization by these previous enculturations. One of the important re-educative effects of desirable processes of learning and changing is an enlarged capacity in persons and groups participating to learn freshly and to revise old learnings more readily and wisely in future situations; in short, as they learn how to learn and to relearn for themselves.

5. Processes of learning and changing should make full use of available relevant and validated information and experience. Laboratory methods of learning and changing emphasize the importance of using valid information as a basis of decisions and action policies. This includes the use of relevant, objective, technical, and factual knowledge. But it includes also relevant information about the subjective and personal states of the persons and groups participating — feelings, attitudes, aspirations. The development of meaningful and rational responses in and to human situations requires a blending and integration of "objective" and "subjective" information; of public and personal knowledge.

6. Processes of learning and changing should be anti-individualistic but deeply respectful of personal and group uniqueness and identity. To understand this norm, two ideas and ideals of personal maturity need to be contrasted. The individual-

istic idea and ideal, still prominent in liberal cultures, envisage human maturity in terms of individual independence and self-sufficiency, in terms of freedom from responsibility for the welfare and growth of other persons. The communal idea and ideal conceives of maturity in terms of autonomous personal functioning in interdependence with other autonomous persons, in terms of a free assumption of responsibility to give and take with others in the service of mutual personal and group development. The latter idea and ideal seem more consistent with what we have come to know of the social development of persons. They seem also more conducive to the task of building moral community within and among dangerously dehumanized collectivities which characterize life in contemporary societies.

7. Processes of learning and changing should be self-evaluative, self-correcting, and self-renewing. What is known about the release of human potentialities for self-directed learning and changing is only a fraction of what is still to be discovered and invented. Ideally, every program of training or planned changing, involving as it does new people and new situations, presents an opportunity for gaining new knowledge and for inventing and testing new technologies. But such accumulation of refined insights, concepts, and methods depends upon building self-critical evaluation into every program. And self-evaluation and self-criticism should extend beyond the cognitive and technological underpinnings of laboratory method. It should extend to the implicit and explicit value orientations which guide its use and application. The morality of laboratory method, as defined by the normative principles formulated here, is not a fixed morality. It represents in part an induction from experiences with laboratory method in various settings to date, though indeed it draws on moral wisdoms derived from man's long cultural history as well. Self-evaluation should attend to the revision and reconstruction of these principles, as experience proves revision and reconstruction to be necessary. Only as continuing self-evaluation is directed to the cognitive, technological, axiological and moral dimensions of laboratory method can self-renewal of the method and of the persons, groups, and larger human systems that accept it as a way of planning, learning and living into the future become a rational hope, if never a certainty.

FOOTNOTES AND REFERENCES

1. Faculty of the Training Laboratory in Group Development, "A Laboratory in Educational Dynamics," *School and Society. 66,* p. 475 (December 20, 1947).

2. *Ibid.*, pp. 475-476.

3. *Ibid.*, p. 475.

4. *Ibid.*, p. 476.

5. Kenneth D. Benne, "Principles of Training Method," *The Group, 10,* 2, p. 17 (January, 1948).

CHAPTER 3

A RESEARCH PERSPECTIVE ON THE LABORATORY METHOD*

Jack R. Gibb

The laboratory method is a process of inquiry, a continuing search for more effective ways of changing and learning. It is a self conscious effort to integrate research with training and action. In one sense, the laboratory method *is* research.

Research is a fusion of three highly interrelated processes: observation and measurement; conceptualization and theory building; and engineering application and test. Development of such research is a continuing process of refinement of these processes of observation, theorizing, and application. It is particularly clear in training and social action that each of these three interdependent processes feeds and derives meaning from the others. Observation and measurement, guided by well-formulated hypotheses, derived, in turn, from socially-significant "engineering" problems, become highly functional. Theory, the propositions of which are tested in the laboratory and tried out in the factory and the home, is increasingly meaningful. Business management and child rearing become progressively more functional as practices are tested in the laboratory, generalized, and reformulated as new data from more refined observations are available.

The laboratory method attempts in various ways to integrate research into learning and action. Each participant, for instance, can be his own researcher. Each is his own observer, theorist, and engineer. Each gathers data from his own internal and external

---

*Because of its length, the bibliography for this chapter has been placed near the end of the book as Appendix A. References in the text of the chapter are to selected items in this bibliography.

environment, processes the data, formulates hypotheses about his own effectiveness, builds his own mini-theories, and tries out new behaviors, roles, or life styles. Laboratory training provides a climate wherein learners become more aware of these processes and carry them out more effectively.

This quest can become interdependent and cooperative. Early attempts to bring these processes to awareness in a group setting engendered great excitement and fresh theory in the early days at Bethel. Each group gathered formal and informal data in a variety of ways on member behavior and on group processes, had observers feed back the observed data to the group, discussed the data at great length, formulated hypotheses about group action, tried out action experiments upon itself, sometimes in collaboration with other groups, and discussed theories that would integrate in some way their continuing experiences.

This model of the individual or the group being its own researcher is, as is pointed out in Chapter 2, a core ingredient of the laboratory method. It has been extended to action and work groups, larger social systems, and to individuals in organizations. This extension to other systems is discussed later in this chapter.

A LOOK AT RESEARCH TRENDS

The early studies (Durham and Gibb, 1960; Stock, 1964) examined aspects of these processes of the individual or the group being a "research" system: stability and determinants of first impressions (Kelley, 1948), the integration of feelings and emotionality into group action and group work (Stock and Ben-Zeev, 1958), feedback processes, changes in diagnostic sensitivity, role-taking, experimenting with new behavior, and the perception of power and benefit (Livingston, 1951).

From the first, however, efforts were made by teams of researchers to engage in more formal processes of observation and data gathering; hypothesis testing and theory building; and tryouts of the new models in industry, school systems, and other social organizations. In an effort to examine the development of the laboratory method from this kind of research perspective, the author collected over 2,000 manuscripts, informal and formal, of a highly diverse nature, but all bearing upon efforts to measure, theorize upon, or make an engineering test of laboratory learnings. The material on theory varies from hunches and speculations to more formal theory. The material on applications is often discursive and anecdotal, but is highly informative and of considerable relevance to both theorists and experimenters.

Although the laboratory method applies to all systems (intrapersonal, interpersonal, group, inter-group, institutional, and community) and the materials refer to each system level, there is an expected heavy concentration on the small group. Because of this concentration, and because it is considerably easier to differentiate "laboratory method" from other methods in small-group research than in research on individuals and institutions, for example, the decision was made to restrict the review of research to the small group.

For this chapter the author was especially interested in studies evaluating effectiveness. A group of studies was selected which evaluated "laboratory training" or some aspect or variation such as sensitivity training, process-oriented organizational development, encounter group programs, or a program of which the primary element was a "T group." Included were studies which had quantitative data relevant to the tested hypothesis, and which were available in English in a form such as a doctoral dissertation, book, or journal article. Excluded, due to the purpose of the survey, were (a) many studies of laboratory-method groups; studies not designed specifically to evaluate training outcomes, but designed primarily to illuminate processes in the group or relationships between intra-group variables (such studies were included, for instance, in the Stock, 1964, review of T group research); (b) studies of groups that were not strictly "laboratory method" groups (such as therapy, counseling, rehabilitation, didactic, in structional, etc.); (c) master's theses; and (d) studies published in journals that were not readily available to most readers of this book. It is to be noted that this process excludes from the list a great number of studies which obviously are highly relevant to evaluation of training outcomes, particularly those testing hypotheses about training-related intra-group dynamics. Restricting the list was necessary because of the great expansion of the research literature. Included in the list were a few studies that were exceptions to these criteria, but added in each case where the study was considered especially relevant to an issue under discussion. The 344 studies thus included are listed in Appendix A. This list provides an adequate bibliography of research evaluating the effects of the laboratory method during the twenty-five-year period from 1947 through 1972. Also included in the list of references are twelve additional research-related items referred to in the text of the chapter.

This chapter will present a research perspective on the labora tory method, relying heavily on a survey of these 344 studies, and comparing these studies at times with the larger body of more impressionistic and clinical literature.

A pronounced acceleration of research has occurred during the past twenty-five years, with an especially noticeable increase in the

Table 1. Research Studies on the Effects of the Laboratory Method, During the Period 1947-1972

Years	*Doctoral Dissertations*	*Other Studies*	*Total*
1947-48	1	0	1
1949-50	0	0	0
1951-52	3	2	5
1953-54	0	2	2
1955-56	2	3	5
1957-58	4	5	9
1959-60	2	2	4
1961-62	2	6	8
1963-64	3	8	11
1965-66	10	20	30
1967-68	22	15	37
1969-70	83	27	110
1971-72	75	47	122
Totals	206	138	344

past five years. Table 1 presents a tabulation of the number of doctoral dissertations and the number of other research studies performed in each two-year period from 1947 through 1972.

There is a continuing improvement in design and overall quality. The earlier studies were frequently and justifiably criticized for methodological limitations (See, for instance, Campbell and Dunnette, 1968). It is admittedly difficult to achieve rigor of design in view of the familiar practical problems in such research, but many problems can be solved with ingenuity and design skill (Harrison, 1971). Some persistent problems are bothersome. One of the more limiting aspects of current studies is the lack of attention to representative design. For instance, it is common to provide a sample of several hundred participants (often more than enough to make reliable measures) and then to "sample" only one or perhaps two trainers for a particular method or condition, or "sample" one school system, company, or church. Presumably there may be as many individual differences in trainers as there are in participants, or in companies as there are in workers. Some of the studies suggest that trainer difference may be greater than method difference (as measured by effects produced). Other studies clearly indicate a powerful effect of the macro-environment in the institutions and a suggestion that these differences between systems may be very large.

The laboratory method of group training was developed with heterogeneous adult groups in "cultural island" settings. Thirty-one of the studies reported here have been done in such settings. A dramatic development is the widespread use of the method with diverse populations and for multiple purposes. One hundred and eighty-seven studies have occurred in an educational institution, nine of which were performed with high school students, 130 with college undergraduates, and forty-eight with graduate students. The groups have often been relatively homogeneous (for example, gifted female high school students, counseling trainees). There have been fifty-two studies in a business setting (for example, senior executives, demoted field sales managers, restaurant employees); twenty-seven in a health and correctional agency setting (for example, diabetics, interns, police officers, honor camp inmates); twenty-four with educators (for example, administrators, black teachers, counseling staff); and twenty-three in religious settings (for example, Catholic nuns, religious lay leaders, seminary members). While the populations used have been highly diverse, there is still a heavy concentration on middle class, managerial, and professional individuals.

In addition to positive contributions to the understanding of the training processes, the research is likely to have had considerable and ancillary social change impact. Most of the studies were performed in connection with an action program: pre-professional training for teachers, counselors, therapists, social workers, or business managers; social action programs designed to reduce prejudice, improve race relations, or raise women's awareness; in-service professional training for managers, judges, teachers, or priests; training for interns in group leadership in a wide variety of disciplinary backgrounds, and a host of other programs with presumably wide impacts often with large numbers of groups. The majority of the programs (with a few reported exceptions) had participants most of whom perceived the training to be highly effective (whether or not the other measures showed significant change).

An examination of the wide variety of informal materials indicates that there is likely to be far more unpublished than published research, and that the studies surveyed here describe only a small part of the research on the laboratory method. A further indication of probable impact is the large number of experimental subjects participating in the 187 studies in educational institutions. A surprising number of these subjects were pre-professionals engaged in programs preparing them to make professional use of the laboratory method in training, consulting, counseling, or teaching (cf. the discussion of training of laboratory practitioners in Chapter 21), and thus the impact is likely to accelerate.

The range of interdisciplinary sponsorship of research is indicated from an analysis of the doctoral dissertations in the sample. Dissertations were produced in eighty-seven different universities, widely spread geographically. From four to eleven dissertations come from each of the following: Universities of Chicago, Florida, Michigan, Missouri, and Texas, Boston University, Case, East Texas State, George Peabody, New York University, Purdue, University of California, Los Angeles, United States International University, and the University of Southern California.

Dissertations come from a variety of disciplines; frequently from interdisciplinary programs. The heaviest concentration is in the fields of psychology and counseling, with a wide variety of specialties in psychology represented: industrial, educational, social, clinical, counseling, general, and experimental. Other dissertations come from such fields as social work, education, economics, psychiatry, business administration, nursing, human development, guidance, educational administration, health sciences, adult education, home economics, speech, and higher education. This trend to broaden the base of research is likely to increase the diversity and hopefully, in time, to lead to more cross-fertilization in improved theory and methodology, and probably to increase the range of applicability of the findings.

A LOOK AT THE DATA

The substantive data in the studies are conflicting and difficult to interpret, and there is a vast range in the quality of the research. One source of ambiguity is the variation in what constitutes the independent variable. Analysis of the available protocols or material describing the intervention or training method made possible the selection of studies which use as an independent variable a "laboratory method" intervention. However, several studies clearly corroborate a finding from the therapy research literature, in that the behavior of the trainer or intervener may be very different from the theory that he describes. The following variables seem to make major contributions to the variance: the macroenvironment in which the intervention occurs, the behavior of the leader or consultant, the length of the training, the group state, the amount of functional feedback, the amount of affective experiencing, and perhaps the technique or method used. A contribution of the studies to date is that investigators are now more able to create economical and productive research designs that will pertain to relevant questions. A key indicator of progress in research is progressive refinement in the kinds of questions asked.

There has been progress in measurement of relevant variables. Analysis reveals many expected problems. Over 300 different measures were made of dependent variables, including standardized tests, specially constructed instruments, Q-sorts, rating scales, behavioral samples, peer ratings, observer codings, and interviews. The Personal Orientation Inventory (POI) was used in twenty-seven of the studies, discriminating between experimental and control groups in thirteen of the studies. The Tennessee Self-Concept Scale was used in twenty-two studies, showing positive changes in favor of the laboratory groups in nine. FIRO–B was used in twenty-one studies, showing positive changes in twelve. These were by far the most commonly used tests.

With few exceptions, studies concentrated on proximal variables and internal measures. A few studies, discussed later in the chapter, attempted measurements of changes back on the job or in the organization.

Studies reported positive changes on a wide variety of dependent variables, such as: increases in expressed warmth, self acceptance, internal control, risk taking, empathy, expressed caring, interpersonal sensitivity, problem solving skills, expressiveness, openness, democratic behavior, trust, number of innovations, and genuineness; and decreases in anxiety, rigidity, racial prejudice, discomfort with feelings, dogmatism, alienation, and even "unnecessary" visits to the physician. The most frequent variable measured, by far, was self-acceptance, used as a dependent variable forty-one times, measured variously and showing positive changes in twenty-one studies, and no change in twenty others.

A number of attempts have been made to define variables more precisely and to improve the measurement process. Trust, for instance, seen as a significant mediating and leverage variable, has been examined critically and systematically compared with other variables by Kegan (1971), factor analyzed by Leon (1972), and used as a variable in several of the studies, shown to change under some conditions and not under others. Examples of promising approaches to the measurement problem are those of Simon and Agazarian (1967) with their SAVI model, Hill (1973) with the interaction matrix, which was used in several of the studies, and Bebout and Gordon (1972) with a long-range program of examining measures in the context of other measures, and in relation to persistent trends.

It seems clear that laboratory methods under some conditions do produce changes in individuals. The question in that form (does the laboratory method produce changes?) probably is no longer an interesting research question. The field now has moved to more productive arenas of inquiry: how effective is the laboratory method relative to alternative experiential methods in producing comparable change in individuals and institutions? What are the mechanisms which mediate the change and the learning? What are the critical training behaviors that are associated with what changes? What proximal changes are associated with changes on the job and in the home?

One hundred and twenty-seven studies compare sensitivity training with a group that had no treatment. Of these, one hundred two studies found significant differences favoring the training group on some measures. Another twenty-one studies found no differences. Three studies found that the training group did significantly less well on the measures than the control. Interpretation of individual studies is often difficult. Obtained differences may be artifacts such as test wisdom, regression toward the mean, random variations in test scores, rater bias, and the like. It is likely that laboratory training does produce changes (if the number of cases is large enough and the measure is sufficiently precise, any "event" is likely to produce change of some magnitude). The changes may not be of psychological or social significance. Not getting differences may be due to no "real" difference between conditions, insufficient time in training, lack of competence in the trainers, insensitive measures, measurement of the wrong variables, or a host of other factors. There are a number of clues in the no-difference studies which give information to future researchers. Space in the chapter allows some discussion of the variables that seem to contribute to the obtained differences. There is not sufficient space to analyze individual studies. This has been done by the author and by several other reviewers cited in the bibliography.

The studies reveal changes that may be interpreted as negative. The laboratory method produces more affect than most other forms of education. This creates some risk. The research shows that some participants, following training, report less tendency to disclose (Walker, et al., 1972), increased irritability on the job and in the family, increased reaction to authority (Gamez, 1970), less conformity to role in the organization, reduced feelings of confidence (DeMichele, 1966), more requests for therapy (Lieberman, et al., 1972), increased defensiveness (Reddy, 1970; Mindes, 1970), and unrealistically increased levels of aspiration (Gibb and Gibb, 1952). The evidence is far from clear, but studies suggest that these disruptive effects may be due to such specific aspects of the training as the following: intensive feedback at inappropriate early stages of the group, a training period that is too brief, too little structure especially at early stages of the group, a leader style that is too tightly controlling, or certain dysfunctional compositional groupings.

Too little research is available on the extreme effects of training. The informal literature and the clinical reports cite many instances of extremely positive changes: peak experiences (Armor, 1969), enduring changes in life style, greater creativity, new stages of self-actualization, greatly increased organizational productivity, and the like. Unfortunately, these important effects, very likely true in part, and very likely exaggerated in part, have not been carefully studied. The informal literature, rumor mills, and clinical reports also contain instances of extremely negative changes: psychotic episodes, divorces, job losses, suicides, and so on. A great deal of attention has been given by professional associations and organizations (National Training Laboratories, American Psychiatric Association, the American Episcopal Church, et al.) to understanding and evaluating these reports. We have very little good research evidence. It is not likely that dramatic negative or positive changes (psychosis, enduring changes in life style) are produced by the five- to fifty-hour experiences (usually twelve to twenty hours) studied in the references cited, but it is possible that these experiences trigger (or may be seen by the participant as triggering) behavior or attitudes that have built up from previous experiences. The available research gives us some clues. A recent study reports that college students who volunteer for "West Coast" encounter groups (reputed to be quasi-therapeutic in contrast to the more process- and skill-oriented "East Coast" T groups) show, following the encounter groups, a high percentage of disturbance

(Lieberman et al., 1972). It is not likely that similar disturbance follows the process-oriented training given, for instance, to managers volunteering for management development programs. In a study of tension induced by T groups a recent analysis showed that the pre- and post-tests aroused more anxiety as measured by their scales than did the T groups (Johnson et al., 1973). Preliminary data being gathered on the negative effects of sensitivity training compared with the negative effects of exposure to such "treatments" as graduate school, competitive athletics, marriage, adoption, residence in a home for the aged, simulated police roles, depth therapy, and foster homes may shed some light on the mediating mechanisms for trauma and/or change. Lubin and Zuckerman (1969) provide a suggestive model for studying the issues. They find that stress level in the T group does not reach a "deviant" level, though more intensive experiences (perceptual isolation studies) do. More data of this kind would be useful.

RESEARCH ON TRAINER OPTIONS

Leader style is examined directly by eighteen studies. The clearest evidence, corroborating the studies of therapist behavior, relates to the amount of support, warmth, or caring that the leader shows. Warmth and supportive behavior seem to lead to greater learning and greater positive change.

The following studies provide heuristic but inconclusive data relating training outcomes to leader self-concept (Mates, 1972), leader tendencies to reward and punish (Bolman, 1971), trainer attractiveness (Cooper, 1969), leader being process-oriented versus member-oriented (Pino, 1969), and leader tendencies to self-disclose (Culbert, 1968).

How much structure and what kind of structure to provide are key questions that have confronted laboratory trainers from the beginning. The T group itself is a relatively unstructured intervention, and is described as such in the research studies. The thirty-six studies that compare the laboratory method with a more structured classroom group (for example, didactic groups, discussions) in human relations are relevant. Of course, the comparison groups also are more content-centered (as contrasted with process-centered), as well as contaminated with other variables. In seventeen of the studies, the laboratory methods produced significantly greater change than did the didactic/structured controls. In three cases neither improved. In seven cases both improved. In three cases the structured/didactic conditions performed better on outcomes related to the content of the course. The unstructured groups seemed clearly superior to the structured groups when measured on the kinds of outcomes described above. Whether the superiority is due to unstructure, process-centering, feedback or other variables is indeterminable. Data on these issues are presented later in the chapter.

Twenty-two studies compared unstructured laboratory training with a relatively more structured experiential comparison group. Here the differences are less clear, suggesting again that some kinds of structuring are more productive for certain purposes than the unstructured laboratory group. Thus, interaction analysis training (Nye, 1971), role playing (Shapiro, 1970), and a communication skills experience (Shilling, 1970) were each significantly superior to the laboratory groups in generating outcomes related to the training. In ten of the studies, the unstructured laboratory groups out-performed the more structured groups; in five cases, the more structured groups were superior; in four cases, neither group showed significant gains in the outcomes measured; and in three cases, both groups performed about equally well.

Several studies indicate decrements when the structuring is too rigid or the leader is seen as too controlling in administering the structure. Structured leadership in the early stages may cause less resistance (Lundgren, 1971), and better decision-making (Tompkins, 1972). Reducing structure has been found to lead to increased problem-solving ability (Easton, 1971), and increased feeling expression (Hull, 1971).

The studies of programmed training are relevant here. There are thirty-eight in which some kind of leaderlessness is studied. Twenty-one studies used the programmed Encountertapes. The other studies used some other form of programming or unprogrammed groups without leaders present (Berlin, 1964; Blake and Mouton, 1966; Rothaus, 1964). The implications for structuring, as such, are often not clear. In many cases the Encountertape groups, because they presumably follow taped instructions (protocols indicate that participants do not always follow the instructions), may be more structured than the control groups.

When Encountertapes were compared with leader-led groups, the leader-led groups performed better in a majority of the studies. In some cases (notably, Davies, 1970; Leiterman, 1970; and Rudman, 1970) the Encountertapes produce results significantly better than the leader-led groups. Impressive is the fact that groups without leaders physically present show some of the same gains that leader-led groups show, outperform leader-led groups on occasion, and usually show fewer decrements or negative outcomes.

There is some evidence that neither tapes nor instruments are necessary in leaderless groups to produce significant effects (Byrd, 1970; La Boon, 1971; Pressman, 1970), and that low structuring may be possible even for pre-structured outcomes (Brenner, 1971).

The amount of time spent in training in the experimental conditions in the studies varied from five minutes to about sixty hours (it is often not possible to find total time data from the report). A surprising number of studies used from one to twelve hours of total training time, a time considered to be too brief for their purposes by the experimenters themselves. This is especially brief when one considers that in the 1950s a standard laboratory-training session lasted up to four weeks, with as much as one hundred fifty hours spent in various groups.

A tabulation of the studies by length of time in session yields no clear trends. Only two of the studies attack the problem of duration directly. Bunker and Knowles (1967) show that three weeks of training were superior to two weeks of training, particularly when overt behavioral changes are measured. Bramson (1969), comparing three-day, five-day, and eight-day sessions, found little difference, but did find that loss of sensitivity was less after eight-day than after three-day sessions. In light of the probable significance of this variable it is surprising that so little research has been done.

How the time is spaced has been the subject of several investigations. Only one of the five studies that have compared massed or continuous sessions with spaced (weekly or bi-weekly) sessions show any differences between treatments and this study (Bare and Mitchell, 1972) shows slight differences in favor of a combination condition (five two-hour sessions weekly and a ten-hour weekend). Eight studies use marathon sessions (a massed condition) as a treatment in a laboratory setting, but none compares these with a spaced comparison group. Only three of the studies show differences in comparing marathon sessions with no-treatment controls. There is no convincing evidence that the marathon format is an economical design in a training context. In the light of the widespread opinion that the marathon format is a powerful design, there is great need for well-designed studies comparing, for instance, twenty-four or thirty training hours massed for a weekend with a comparable number of hours spread over several weeks.

Of considerable interest is the question whether changes persist over long periods of time. Studies were analyzed for follow-up data and showed few data that were possible to interpret meaningfully. A widespread assumption is that effects of laboratory training persist only briefly and that decrements are great. The studies provide little relevant data. About a third of the studies make follow-up measurements. Most of these measurements were made from one week to six months following training, with only a few studies making measurements after six months. Most of the studies that show significant post-training differences found similar differences occurring in the one-week to six-month follow-up. Four studies found that differences also persisted in the no-treatment control groups. If there are psychologically significant changes, do they persist long enough to have effects two to five years later? What is the drop-off rate? Is it too much to ask of short-term experiences of one to twenty hours (training time of most of the studies) that they produce enduring changes? Are booster shots required? Obvious difficulties stand in the way of significant long-range follow-up studies, but they are greatly needed.

Some attention has been directed toward group composition dynamics and effects. Early training laboratory groups were heterogeneous. Almost all of the research described here has been performed on heterogeneous groups to which members have been randomly assigned. Considerable homogeneity often occurs (for example, all diabetics; all black female sophomores; all counseling interns), but there is usually no way of assessing the effect of such homogeneity. Experimental attempts to produce homogeneity and compare it with heterogeneity have used a number of variables: work-oriented versus person-oriented members (Harrison and Lubin, 1965), predisposition to a Bionic modality (Lieberman, 1958d), high- or low-trust on basis of the Rotter test (Piper, 1972), and FIRO-B predispositions (several studies). Results are heuristic and inconclusive, but strongly suggest that compatible groups may outperform incompatible groups on selected measures, that group atmospheres are influenced by composition, and that there are individual differences in reactions to the homogeneity. Powers' data (1965) show that differential effects may be produced by trainer variables.

An apparently profitable avenue of research is opened up by investigators who systematically mix (or measure) composition and then relate composition to group states or to differential outcomes: liberals and conservatives (Harpel, 1970); high-anxiety and low-anxiety subjects (Cherlin, 1967); high barrier (well integrated body image) and low-barrier patients (Cleveland and Morton, 1962); black machine operators in groups with their white supervisors (Joure et al., 1971); and various other racial, national, and sex groupings. Results are suggestive and inconclusive, but open the door to a number of promising leads to research.

IMPACT ON THEORY

An encouraging trend shows that research is becoming more theory-based and more appropriately designed toward determining mechanisms underlying the differential effects of the groups. Among the mechanisms proposed by the researchers as a primary factor are: quality and amount of feedback; therapeutic qualities or behaviors of leaders, members, or relationships; group development stages; formation of trust; experiencing and sharing of affect in an interactive situation; development of self-esteem; cognitive integration of the experience; and reciprocal disclosure. Each of these formal or informal orientations has led to differential treatment in design of studies, choice of measures of dependent variables, selection of comparison groups, analysis of data, and interpretation of results. In some cases studies have progressively built upon each other, and that data collection has led to reformulation of both theory and of engineering application.

Space permits a few illustrative examples. Fourteen studies analyzed the feedback process. Four compared a video-tape feedback condition with a standard T group. The video-tape condition did in some cases differ significantly from the control conditions in producing greater change in some aspects of self-concept, but not in other cases. Egelhoff (1970) related feedback theory to dissonance theory and partially confirmed the hypotheses. There is considerable support to the hypothesis that greater feedback produces greater change in participants (French et al., 1966; Lippitt, 1959; Kolb et al., 1968). Analyses of the data of the studies give significant cues as to the nature of feedback that is perceived as helpful by the participant, and/or conducive to change in behavior.

The group itself became a focus of research attention as the laboratory method evolved (Durham and Gibb, 1960; Stock, 1964), and continuing efforts have been made to find stages or significant sequences that occur at similar times in various kinds of groups. This search, though seductive, has not been very successful. Groups differ widely. There seems to be little consistency in the trends found in groups under varying conditions (Lubin and Zuckerman, 1967, for instance). Some beginnings have been made in providing data at various intervals in the development of a group: rated level of trust (Draeger, 1968); predictable shifts in mood (Bass, 1962); sequence of group themes (Liebowitz et al., 1972), process movement (Meador, 1971); development of Tuckman's stages (Runkel et al., 1971); and type of work and emotionality (Stock and Ben-Zeev, 1958). Three of the more promising approaches are those by Dunphy (1968), whose model features phases that are influenced by emergent role specialists;

Mann (1966), who builds a stage model focused upon member-trainer relationships; and Glidewell, who describes in Chapter 6 a systematic developmental analysis of group processes along lines suggested by a social-psychological research perspective.

Considerable research bears upon or has been generated to test the Gibb fear-trust TORI model. For example, Friedlander (1970) provides evidence that groups that have reached high trust prior to training reach higher degrees of group effectiveness than groups reaching less trust prior to training. Trust proved to be a better predictor of group accomplishment than any other measure. However, trust did not increase during training. Rutan (1971) demonstrated a significant correlation between an increase in trust and an increase in self-acceptance, but did not find an increase in trust following training. Clarke (1971) found trust increased with training, under special conditions. Leon (1972), devising a Trust Questionnaire based on the theory, found that the Own Trust score did not significantly change following T group training, but that the Mean Trust score did. A factor analysis of the trust instrument showed four distinct factors: openness in relating, egostrength, immaturity, and acceptance of self. Garner (1970), making several predictions from the theory, found only partial support. Program designs derived from the theory show statistically significant gains in predicted directions in a college setting (Seashore, 1955; Gibb & Gibb, 1952), and in a community-building experience (La Boon, 1971; Pressman, 1970).

RESEARCH IN THE ORGANIZATIONAL SETTING

Some evidence, and a considerable amount of professional opinion, indicates that the duration of effects of training is greatly influenced by the macro-environment. Twenty-six studies report attempts to apply the laboratory method directly in the educational, industrial, religious, or health organization setting. One approach has been simply to give laboratory training to groups of members of the same organization. These attempts have met with mixed success. Taylor (1967) reports positive changes following training within a company on both individual variables and organizational variables. Zenger (1967) reports positive perceptual and productivity changes with supervisors in the same company. Shaevitz and Barr (1972) report some changes in a study using encounter groups in a religious order. Kernan (1963) reports no significant differences in a study of engineering supervisors. Keutzer et al. (1971) report positive outcomes in training workshops with the entire staffs of two high schools.

Bowers (1973) confirms the growing impression that this

simple approach is minimally effective. He reports a study of twenty-three organizations in which laboratory training, presumably performed as an intervention method in relative isolation from an ongoing consultation-action program, was associated with declines on measures of organizational functioning, whereas survey feedback and interpersonal process consultation, for instance, were associated with statistically significant changes on a majority of measures.

Recent consultant-researchers have taken an alternative approach, focusing on the total organization as the target of change, working with organizational-health variables, system concepts, and long-range, theory-based, integrated efforts. Some of the studies show convincing change data (for example, Friedlander, 1968), and others clearly show no significant change on the variables measured (for example, Benedict et al., 1967). The following are illustrative examples of this organizational approach. Golembiewski et al. (1967) present a multi-level, interdepartmental model emphasizing confronting organization members with perceptual data. Benedict et al. (1967) describe a "clinical" hypotheses. The Dyer et al. (1970) study concentrates on the improvement of the model of training itself and the theory-based integration of the model into the processes of the industrial organization. The Management Grid approach has been extended to a wide range of organizational settings (for example, Greiner, 1965; Blake and Mouton, 1966). Schmuck et al. (1969) show how a series of integrated interventions can be applied to an educational setting. Brown (1972) emphasizes an integration of research and action around information exchange in a school system. Friedlander (1968) suggests that the key to organic change is the amount and quality of pre-training and post-training consulting rather than the trainer role or differences in the training itself. Gibb has developed an approach to organizations which involves a series of integrated organization-focused experiences of which one is a three- to ten-day session in which total organizational units of fifty to three hundred members can have confrontation and information-sharing experiences (La Boon, 1971; Pressman, 1970).

This surprisingly large body of research is limited in many ways and is subject to the vagaries that perhaps necessarily accompany low budget research in practical settings with the meager body of available theory and the low-precision measuring tools. It is, however, considerably better than the author imagined prior to his intensive review. There are many highly suggestive leads for research and many implications for the practitioner. Further implications of the studies for trainers, group leaders, and consultants are spelled out in greater detail in another publication (Gibb, 1974).

CHAPTER 4

THE LABORATORY METHOD IN IDEOLOGICAL PERSPECTIVE

Kenneth D. Benne

As laboratory methods have been applied in various institutional settings, as they have penetrated defended "territories," staked out by various groups of practitioners and researchers, they have attracted criticisms written from various points of view. Some of the critics of laboratory practice have been researchers in disciplines of social and behavioral science. Such critics have addressed themselves to the cognitive inadequacies of laboratory method. These criticisms have been noted and responded to in the preceding chapter.

But other criticisms have come from proponents of alternative modes of social practice and social action. Modes of action and practice, although they incorporate claims to correct knowledge in their rationales, are guided also by value orientations. These are necessary to enable activists and practitioners to make judgments about what needs to be changed in the lives of people and about goals of improved life for people toward which their efforts should be directed. Rationales for modes of social action and practice are thus belief systems, incorporating claims to knowledge about man and society interwoven with value orientations about what man and society should be. And the rationales also incorporate beliefs about effective means of changing existing patterns and conditions of living toward "better" ones. Such rationales provide *ideological* perspectives from which the ideology and practice of laboratory method have been and are being criticized.[1]

As the editors planned this book, we decided that a rounded presentation of laboratory method should include criticisms by critics broadly representative of currently influential alternative modes of social practice and social action, along with the responses of a laboratory practitioner and ideologist to these criticisms. We asked for a critique from Prof. Leonard Krasner, a leading "behavior modificationist," since we recognize the scope and vitality of current efforts to effect behavioral changes through the application of ideas originating in the work of B. F. Skinner. And we solicited a comment from Prof. Harry Levinson who works out of a psychoanalytical orientation. We asked Prof. Howard Zinn, a student of national and world politics and a recognized ideologist of the civil rights movement and the "new left" in America, for a comment and critique. Krasner, Levinson and Zinn all received a draft copy of Chapter 2, an extended statement of the *ideological* perspective of laboratory method. Their comments and criticisms are addressed to that statement. Max Pages, author of Chapter 17, solicited a critique of that chapter from Prof. John Southgate, an English colleague of his in conducting laboratory programs, who works out of a Marxist orientation. When the editors read Southgate's comment, we gained the permission of Pages and Southgate to include his critique in this more general assemblage of criticisms. Readers may wish to read Chapter 17 before reading Prof. Southgate's comment.[2]

The four criticisms fall into two kinds of orientations. Krasner and Levinson are applied psychologists. Whatever the scope of the particular organizational or social problem which might mobilize their change-agent efforts, the immediate target of change is for each of them the individual human organism. Their change efforts thus fall within the ambit of *social practice*, as usually defined in our individualistic culture. On the other hand, Zinn and Southgate work out of political orientations. Their chosen change efforts are directed toward changes in social institutions, more particularly toward changes in the power relations between groups and classes of people in contemporary society. We will first present the comments by Prof. Krasner and Prof. Levinson and my response to these. We will next present the comments by Prof. Zinn and Prof. Southgate with my responses to their criticisms.

COMMENTS ON THE LABORATORY METHOD
By Leonard Krasner

My task is to comment on "The Laboratory Method" from the "behavior modification" viewpoint. I would prefer to give my reactions as an individual psychologist who identifies with behavior modification rather than as a spokesman for a point of view. The label of "behavior modification" now encompasses such a wide range of views as to the most useful ways of conceptualizing human behavior and methods of modifying it, that it would be difficult for anyone to be its representative.

My impression is that there are a considerable degree of overlap and points of articulation between "behavior modification," as I conceive of it, and the "laboratory method" as discussed in this chapter. There are also some sharp, and perhaps crucial, differences between the two approaches.

In order to pursue adequately the similarities and differences between these two concepts of human behavior, both would have to be carefully defined and put in historical perspective with specific illustrations cited. This is clearly too comprehensive a task for a brief critique. I will, therefore, limit my comments to impressions without the necessary documentation.

The most striking similarity is that both orientations can be classified as social movements. They both aim to change individual behavior and society more generally, to bring about a "better world." This means a considerable amount of "religious" fervor among their adherents, of desire to influence others and to "spread the word," as well as a strong belief in the desirability and efficacy of their procedures. Both see a close linkage between the behavior of their adherents and ethical and moral values.

Both movements are based on basic principles derived from the psychology laboratory as enhanced by clinical and social observations. Both reconceptualize the mode of helping people in terms of an educational process rather than a psychotherapeutic one. This means that they are both involved in training "social change agents" to train other individuals to learn how to control their own behavior, and to influence others. In effect then, both are training for more effective living in the sense that they are striving for better interpersonal relationships and for social institutions that are supportive rather than repressive of human beings. They both can thus be labeled as "utopian" in a positive, social reform sense.

A further major similarity is the belief of adherents of both movements in the desirability of breaking the barriers between the concepts of *research* and of *application*, arguing that these can and should be conceived of as one process. Both attempt to lower the forbidding barriers between so-called scientific disciplines in their focus on using whatever data are relevant for changing and improving human behavior, irrespective of who generates these data.

However, these similarities should not obscure very real differences. Perhaps the most important of these is the implicit model of human behavior which each utilizes. The laboratory method still appears to be working within a modified psychodynamic approach which conceives the locus or wellspring of human behavior as being *within* the individual. This is evidenced in part by the many references to the desirability of fostering or releasing "growth" within the individual. The laboratory method also seems to accept the medical or disease model of deviant behavior which conceives such behavior in terms of pathology, mental illness, and mental health. Admittedly, the proponents of the laboratory method argue that they are working with people who are "well" or healthy, but they do not eschew the mental health model itself. In contrast, many of the behavior modification adherents attempt to present an alternative social learning model based on a socio-psychological view of man which does not accept the notion of unique development for behavior labeled as deviant or sick. A major element in this alternative model is that the locus of the change is *environmental*, or situational, not intrapersonal. From such differences in model, differences in change procedures follow.

The laboratory method focuses on change in specially designed group situations divorced from or away from the individual's "real" social life. In effect, a miniature society is set up in part on the rationale that behavior influenced in this new society will carry over to the individual's life outside. Yet every environment is as real as any other, and new problems, interactions, and ways of relating develop in these situations which *may or may not* be related to the world in which the individual must function daily.

In contrast, the behavior modifiers focus on helping individuals in their own environment so that the individual may learn to control this environment in a more satisfactory manner. Put in concrete terms, the behavior modifier is more likely to observe behavior and attempt to train people directly in the school, home, hospital, clinic, industrial setting, etc., rather than in a separate environment.

This is not to argue that meetings in group settings are not useful or desirable social goals in and of themselves. But to help people live more effectively in the world they inhabit, it can be argued that they should be trained to deal with very real difficulties and problems in their world rather than worrying about whether behavior in one setting, with its special situational circumstances, will generalize to another very different environmental setting. If one believes that human behavior is situation specific, in contrast to determination by ubiquitous personality traits, then the focus of one's efforts is to bring about change in the real life situations in which human beings find themselves rather than to create a separate laboratory society.

CRITIQUE OF LABORATORY METHOD

By Harry Levinson

Cognitive learning involves facts and figures, concepts, interrelationships, and the internal road map of life experiences which constitutes the context for behavior. Emotional learning involves awareness of our own feelings, increasing sensitivity to the feelings of others, and particular grasp of the nuances of interpersonal and group situations.

There is always an emotional component in all cognitive learning. Our feelings about what we are learning, the people who teach us, and the context in which we learn influence heavily whether we do indeed learn, how much of what we learn we retain, and how well we are able to use what we learn. Despite the fact that men have known for centuries that how one feels affects what and how he learns, such considerations have been largely ignored in most school systems, regardless of country or level of education. As a result, cognitive learning has become a drudge for many, and significant numbers of children as well as adults have withdrawn from such learning situations. This onesidedness about the acquisition and transmission of knowledge derives from socio-cultural values which emphasize the repression of feelings and the development of elaborate ritualized modes of behavior to foster that repression. People in almost all cultures learn to memorize certain modes of behavior and to forget other impulses, to act as if the cultural norms were the same as the underlying wishes and impulses. As a result, in many cultures, including our own, it is difficult for people to know how they themselves really feel, how other people really feel, to know what is true and what is untrue in human relations, to trust other people and even, indeed, for a person to trust one's self to express those feelings of which he is aware.

Given this state of affairs, those who are concerned with establishing their own genuineness seek to ascertain their basic feelings, usually after some pain or failure has occurred which makes it clear to them they are acting on invalid assumptions. The fundamental method for doing this, in its contemporary form, is psychotherapy or psychoanalysis, derived originally from Freud. Ideally, these two processes lead to insights about those sources of maladaptive behavior that occurred in the course of one's growth and development and lie in repressed conflict. The assumption on which these processes operate is that when one has obtained insight into his own unconscious motivation, he will no longer respond maladaptively by reading repressed past conflicts into present situations.

In its original form, psychoanalysis leaned heavily on making possible the expression of unconscious feelings on the assumption that such expression would undo the maladaptive behavior that was caused by the repression of sexual and aggressive impulses. However, in the course of the evolution of psychoanalysis as a treatment method, it became clear to psychoanalytic practitioners that the mere expression of feelings was not enough. In addition, the therapist or analyst had to recognize and deal with the patient's resistance to making use of the information he discovered about himself. Finally, attention had to be given to the maladaptive defensive behavior which the person maintained in order to sustain his psychological equilibrium. That is, he had to learn how to control the expression of his impulses more adaptively. Thus, in contemporary psychoanalytic practice based on the psychoanalytic conceptions, much of the therapeutic effort has shifted from catharsis to interpreting resistances and examining defenses as well as understanding transference reactions (that is, the reactions of the patient to the therapist when in the patient's mind the therapist symbolically represents other figures from his past) and to helping the person evolve new adaptive modes.

Psychoanalysis and psychotherapy are not the only methods of emotional learning. A classic method has been the experience of intense relationship to an ideology which in turn makes it possible for people to identify with models and images. Most notably this occurs in religious conversion that leads to identification with saintly or heroic figures, a wish to emulate them in behavior and a dedication to the example they have set. Such emotional learning often brings new inspiration, dedicated motivation, and greater equanimity to many people. It is one of the major means by which the cultural heritage is transmitted.

Another more contemporary mode of emotional learning is that of group process, in which people coming into an unstructured situation together, talk with each other about their common task of forming a group and, in the process of struggling toward that end, how they feel about each other. In the course of their encounters, they see vividly how they are affected by others and how they in turn affect others. Having been confronted in a situation free of the usual emotional supports, and often unable to deny this confrontation, their guilt and inadequacy is mobilized and they seek to undo their modes of behavior and to replace them by behavior which is more conducive to effective accomplishment of mutually shared tasks. Frequently, in the course of such experiences, they develop warm, affectionate, and trusting relationships with others with whom they have shared experiences and who have understood and empathized with their psycho-social dilemmas.

It is the last experience which is referred to in this volume as the Laboratory Method. This method has made significant contributions to the understanding of group processes by heightening sensitivity to the manner in which feelings affect behavior, and in which struggles for position, power, control, and alliance take place in groups. The method has spread around the world, as a new religion for some and a dangerous threat to psychological equilibrium for others. Many in between have learned the importance of trusting and supportive behavior to counteract the "as if" behavior more characteristic of life in contemporary society.

However, the Laboratory Method suffers from a number of serious handicaps. First, and most fundamental, it is without a theory of individual personality. That is, it has no theory about feelings except that they should be expressed. Although its adherents and practitioners include among their number psychiatrists and psychologists, the method itself does not assume an individual personality theory. This is indeed a puzzling paradox, for the writers of this volume argue that they take information from the behavioral sciences, the social sciences, philosophy, the liberal arts, and elsewhere, and integrate them into a value system that they practice. It is curious that a method devoted to learning more about one's own feelings, the feelings of others, and understanding the feelings which lie behind the many forms of behavior should have such a powerful scotoma about the need to know in depth a systematic theory of individual motivation (feelings). Despite much discussion of emotional learning, mental health, insight, sensitivity, conflict resolution, and so on, nowhere is there a statement about individual motivation or the assumptions about personality functioning upon which learning inevitably must be based.

Several consequences follow from this gap. The first is that because there is no systematic theory of personality, there is a good deal of seeming glibness about the discussion of experiential learning. Thus, it is too easy to toss aside cognitive learning as unimportant or at least to keep writing as if it were unimportant. Second, because trainers are not required to know anything about the motivation of individuals, or to understand their psychological equilibrium-maintaining activity, the movement has attracted to its ranks all kinds of people who become trainers with inadequate training themselves. The consequence of this is that some people have been unnecessarily hurt psychologically in the course of such laboratory experiences and others have been sadistically exploited. Still others have been victimized by trainers whose gratifications have come from striking their psychological hands deeply into the psychological bowels of other peoples' experiences and manipulating those people for the gratifications that derive from having power over others and being able to peer unabashedly into their psychological insides.

From this gap, which has never been closed, have come a wide range of other anti-intellectual techniques — those which aver no need for a conceptual structure either to guide or understand their process. The wide-ranging, uncontrolled gamut of encounter groups, marathons, and similar activities have their roots in the conception that people need only to get together and to spill their emotional intestines and their problems will be resolved. Few of the proponents of experiential learning seem to have heard of psychoanalytic experience, let alone to have learned from it.

While the laboratory method, as described herein, adheres to a democratic value system and an ethic which endorses the capacity of people to better their own lives, there is no code of ethics for the practice of T group trainers. There is no mode of selecting people to participate — indeed there cannot be — nor is there even an adequate mode of selecting, screening, and supervising trainers. In all fairness, it should be said that the clinical disciplines do not do an adequate job of screening potential psychiatrists and psychologists, but at least they are bound by codes of ethics, board examinations, and supervision in the course of extended training.

Furthermore, the laboratory method assumes unequivocally that the fact that people experience catharsis is in itself always therapeutic and that feedback about one's behavior will be sufficient to bring about behavioral change in most cases. These two assumptions deny what psychoanalytic psychology learned a long time ago about the limits of catharsis, the importance of dealing with resistances and transference and the importance of unconcious motivation. One could not fault the laboratory movement if it specified that it dealt only in the conscious, only in cathartic expression, and only in the feedback of the impact of one's behavior on others; if it said that there was a wide range of behavior with which it could not and did not deal, and that that fraction with which it did deal was only a small part of the forces that operated to make people behave as they did. However, nothing like such qualifications are publicly stated, though privately more sophisticated trainers agree.

If the adherents of the laboratory movement had done just that and had concentrated heavily on the training of trainers who themselves were aware of their limitations, then there would be little to criticize. Instead, as the movement has concentrated more and more on growth of individuals, the lack of a personality theory, the lack of skill among trainers, the lack of their ability to deal with resistances and transferences, and the pain caused when the people's defenses are unwittingly or unknowingly disrupted has made many people like myself uneasy.

When adherents of the laboratory method speak about being a

bridge between psychotherapists and educators, between social scientists who are researchers and those who are problem-solvers, one has to ask how much they know about the various disciplines they are trying to bridge and whether the mere encouragement to openness and confrontation is sufficient to build the kinds of integrated bridges of which they speak. For example, how is one to reconcile the claim that the laboratory method intends to do much for mental health when its concept of mental health is not rooted in a theory of personality that has meaning to specialists who deal professionally with mental health and mental illness?

The issue of offering the method as a panacea is reflected in the fact that there is no discussion of the failures of the laboratory method. Certainly no method can work all the time in all circumstances. Yet there is no differentiation of when it has worked and when it has not, when it has been more successful and when it has been less successful, when one should use it and when one should not. The reader is led to believe that it is always applicable in all circumstances to all problems.

There is much talk about fostering growth as the way to mental health. There is no talk about supporting defenses. How are people helped to understand situations in which they should not be open and act accordingly to protect themselves? There is much talk about making people less dependent, but there is no discussion of the wisdom of creating structures for dependent people which will permit them to be comfortably dependent. I, and I am sure many others who work with organizations, encounter many people of limited competence, skill, ambition, interest, and capacity for abstraction. Often such people merely want to have a safe occupational haven where they can be sure of a reasonable income and economic security. But in T group circles, such dependency is bad by definition. The same failure to understand the psychological phenomena with which laboratory adherents deal occurs with respect to differentiating among people who have not had the opportunity to learn interpersonal skills as contrasted with those who have psychological pathology. How one can make such a distinction with no clinical training and no theory of personality is a question to be pondered. Although the method is not supposed to help those with pathology, there is no theory by which to recognize pathology, there is no skill in its recognition and no training in dealing with it. There is much discussion of the importance of the helping professions and being aligned with the helping professions, indeed of being a helper, but one sees no evidence of significant training in the laboratory movement which would make trainers members of the helping profession or even sufficiently skilled in their understanding of the respective helping professions to facilitate what they are doing.

Everyone who is experienced in working in and with organizations knows that organizations frequently need someone who will give them active leadership, someone who will take charge, someone who will bring expertise and knowledge and give direction. However, such authoritative guidance is proscribed by the laboratory method, as described here, as a form of social engineering in which the elite make decisions for and about the less elite. Whatever may be intended, what comes through is an excruciating naivete. Perhaps that fits with another observation: Why is it that so many change efforts greeted with great enthusiasm in the vanguard of the movement have fallen by the wayside? I suspect it is because of a failure to understand the meaning of power, together with the other issues I have raised.

I do not mean to imply by raising this question that the movement is a failure. Rather, I suggest that arising out of the academic community without an adequate conception of personality, without an ethic, without recognition of the need for formal training, without appropriately modest assertion about what it can do, without adequate controls over the practices of its adherents, without differentiation of function and application, the laboratory method has overreached itself and now has so often become dissipated into such a variety of activities, all of which have the same name, that one no longer really knows what the laboratory method is, or indeed, what it could become.

RESPONSES TO KRASNER AND LEVINSON

Prof. Krasner is quite right in ascribing to the rapid spread of both "laboratory" and "behavior modification" approaches to changing human behavior the characteristics of social movements. And I agree with him further in his observation that both depend on education and re-education as major elements in their strategies and hopes for achieving improvements in individuals and societies. Their chosen methods of re-education are, in some large part, derivations from psychological and social research and experimentation. This is in contrast to the principal bases of rationales for therapy and for school education. Therapeutic rationales have been customarily derived from clinical observations of pathological subjects in treatment and therapeutic settings. And educational principles tend to rest on rationalizations and refinements of learning processes within programs of schooling as currently institutionalized.

The devoted espousal of novel methods of education by both laboratory practitioners and behavior modificationists has, as a result, tended to mobilize resistances to their use among devotees of established methods of schooling. And their focal concern with application of knowledge and their consequent disrespect for disciplinary boundaries in traditional research into human affairs have evoked "startle reactions" to both among "pure" researchers working within the traditional boundary lines of disciplines. Their "brash" extension of re-educative efforts into the no-man's land between "therapeutic" and "educational" practice, as traditionally defined, has also evoked more or less harsh attacks from established therapeutic professions and professionals. Dr. Levinson's comment shows some of this attack mentality, though it is much milder and more rational than many such attacks have been.

So I concur in Dr. Krasner's placing of "laboratory method" along with "behavior modification" within the perspective of the sociology of knowledge, as "utopian" social movements. He goes on to chide practitioners of laboratory method for not eschewing more completely than typically they have done the medical model of re-education in which re-education is equated with the treatment of those who exhibit pathological or deviant behavior by techniques known only to expert practitioners. Dr. Krasner, I am sure, believes that rejection of the medical model would serve to "free" the social movement of laboratory practice from the trammels of the traditional therapeutic professions. But such rejection would also work against effective bridging between the new profession of laboratory practice, which is emerging within the social movement, and traditional professions of psychiatry, social work and other health professions. All of these professions have much to learn from one another. So I favor a process of professionalization of laboratory practice which will bring badly needed quality control into the work of its practitioners, but which will preserve the values to which it has given rise. Prominent among these values explicit or implicit in the social movement are: the granting of higher priority to the release of growth and renewal in human lives than to the melioration and correction of pathology as the goal of re-education; breaking through the hardened lines of established professionalizations and stimulating more teamwork among professionals and paraprofessionals in meliorating personal and social difficulties; and restoring importance and dignity to volunteer effort, in collaboration with various professionals, in the diagnosis and solution of human problems.

Prof. Levinson does not see laboratory practice as it has evolved as a social movement, but rather as a misguided profession. So he tends to be unaware of the values of the movement named above and highly aware of the admittedly bad results which have accompanied the Topsy-like expansion of laboratory practice as a social movement. The movement has attracted many people who are more distinguished for their missionary zeal than for their understanding of the complexities of human behavior, for their competence in stimulating and guiding persons in trying to change the patterns of their lives, or for their ethical scruples in offering and giving help to others. Such people have sometimes abstracted gimmicks from the developing technology of laboratory practice with limited awareness of their conceptual underpinnings and have offered these as panaceas to people in quandaries without adequate diagnosis of the persons and groups whom they promise to help. Traditional schooling has tended to neglect the affective dimensions of all learning and to focus myopically on its cognitive and intellectual dimensions — a neglect and myopia which Prof. Levinson affirms along with thoughtful laboratory practitioners. Some zealous practitioners of laboratory method have neglected or rejected the cognitive and intellectual dimensions of learning and have focused myopically upon its affective dimensions. Such an anti-intellectual emphasis I deplore along with Prof. Levinson.

Such distortions of valid laboratory practice have come not alone from zealous devotees of its professed values. They have come also from some who have sought quick financial gain from shoddy and oversold offerings of "sensitivity training," "encounter groups," or "group therapy for normals" to alienated, lost, and lonely persons who abound in our bureaucratized and non-communal society.

I would say nothing to detract from Prof. Levinson's criticism of the excesses to which unprofessional applications of laboratory method have sometimes led. Most researches on the effects of such practice show little of the personality damage to participants which Prof. Levinson seems to fear. I agree that even that little is reprehensible. But the building up in people of false hopes for simple cures to complex difficulties and the discrediting of responsible efforts to apply, extend, and improve laboratory practice are, in my judgment, even more deplorable effects.

So I agree with Prof. Levinson that laboratory practice needs professionalization. And professionalization means, as he suggests, more adequate programs for practitioner-training, more adequately formulated, publicized, and enforced codes of ethics, and more adequate professional organizations to support effective measures of quality control within the social movement which has grown around laboratory practice. What Prof. Levinson seems *not* to realize is the fact of the early and continuing efforts by laboratory practitioners along all of these lines. I need not outline here the history of these efforts, nor give an account of the present admittedly inadequate state of development of the emerging profession of laboratory practice. Chapters 20, 21, and 22 offer descriptions of this history and of the current state of professional training, ethics, and organization among laboratory practitioners. I hope Prof. Levinson will read these chapters and provide further helpful criticism on the basis of the information which they provide.

Prof. Levinson attributes many of the inadequacies of laboratory practice to its lack of a defensible theory of personality. This criticism no doubt reflects a dominant assumption of his own chosen brand of social practice. The principal unifying conceptual basis of psychoanalysis and of psychoanalytic therapy is a theory of personality development and dynamics. "Real" change for the psychoanalyst is change in personality. Laboratory practitioners do not share this assumption about what change is "real." Their common focus is in a methodology of collaborative and self-directed learning in which renovation of patterns of behavior, of relationship, of role, of social and normative structures can be accomplished by people, and limits of changeability discovered and accepted. Personality factors are only one of the kinds of factors involved in such changes or in setting limits to change. Group, organizational, cultural, political (macro system) variables are no less or no more "real" than personality variables in changing so conceived, in upsetting existing behavioral equilibria or in stabilizing new ones.

This view of changing (and learning) does not imply that working concepts about personality are unimportant to laboratory practitioners. Effective practitioners do and must have such working concepts. Actually, there is no one theory of personality common to all practitioners. Their group includes persons who call themselves Freudians, Rogerians, Adlerians, existentialists, Maslovians, behaviorists, humanists, Reichians and, no doubt, other names as well. This variety, so far as their dominant concepts of personality are concerned, has proved no insurmountable detriment to their collaborative work in team relationships. In fact, most laboratory practitioners would, I believe, consider this variety an advantage, a source of mutual enrichment, and a deterrent to cultism. Their basis of community does not lie in a shared, substantive theory of personality or of groups, organizations, cultures, or societies. Their basis of community is, rather, in a methodology for stimulating, supporting, and guiding human systems in achieving self-directed and collaborative changes in the patterns of their lives, as Chapter 2 has tried to make clear. Various concepts of personality, not just one, are used as resources, as they are found useful in applications of the methodology.

If Dr. Levinson believes that laboratory practitioners lack commitment to *a* theory of personality, Prof. Krasner chides them for making too much in their thinking and practice of "the psyche" as "the locus or wellspring of human behavior." If "the psyche" tends to preempt the place of environmental factors in the arena of human change for psychoanalytic change agents, the opposite pre-emption takes place in the thinking and practice of behavior modificationists. For them, "the locus of change is environmental, or situational, not intrapersonal." Again, as in the case of the psychoanalytic view but with a contrary emphasis, the question is an ontological question, not a psychological one: "What is *real* change?" And the answer, from the point of view of laboratory practice, has already been given. The answer is in part an empirical one. Within the field of forces that determine behavior and behavioral change, do personality variables exercise influence along with environmental variables? Is behavior entirely "situation specific," as Prof. Krasner believes? Or do generalized ideas, attitudes, values, and commitments of persons operate, along with situational factors, to lend an integrity, a pervasive quality of coherence to persons' lives in and through various situations? I believe that there is strong empirical evidence, qualitative evidence in some large part, that persons do, within limits to be sure, shape their careers through their own decisions and actions. The shaping is more coherent and consistent if persons are conscious about who they are and who they aspire to be. The effort of laboratory practice to encourage persons to become more conscious of and more responsbile for themselves as moral agents in processes of change is built upon this empirical fact.

But the second part of the question is not so much empirical as moral. *Should* persons be encouraged to become more aware of themselves, more deliberately responsible for the effects of their own choices upon themselves and upon others, more committed to using and enlarging their margins of freedom in building an environment of people and things more supportive of their aspirations and value commitments? Laboratory practitioners answer this moral question affirmatively. Behavioral modificationists, because of their differing ontology as to what is "real" change and what is "real" in change, are not so likely to attach importance to this question in self-criticism of their own change efforts and in their encouragement of participants in change programs continually to raise this question in their own self-criticisms.

Prof. Krasner raises the question of whether laboratory practitioners are unnecessarily committed to a "cultural island" approach to changing. This means withdrawing participants into a place for learning away from the pressures of their home and jobs to build a community with norms different in some respects from the norms operating in their back-home situations. He correctly points out that such training raises difficulties for participants in transferring learnings from the "cultural island" of training to the mainland of their ongoing everyday lives. Transfer problems are reduced, if not eliminated, in training near or on "the job." Laboratory practice did, in its early commitment to residential laboratories, rely heavily on creating "cultural islands" for training. As it has developed, training and consultation have been brought nearer to the back-home situations of clients and have been focused more on situational difficulties and problems. This is true in the growth of organizational and community development programs as we shall see later in this book.

But can or should such developmental programs dispense entirely with experiences "in specifically designed programs divorced from or away from the individual's 'real' social life?" I believe that such experiences cannot and should not be dispensed with for at least some participants in change programs. I have three reasons for this belief. First, persons embedded in the "real" life situations of our society have often lost any clear images of themselves or are operating, with pain and loss of creativity, with self-images which are contrary to what they usually do and are required to do in their situations. Recovery of a relatively undistorted image of self can be attained more readily in specially designed programs where participants are not playing for keeps, than within the conformity pressures and expectations of back home settings, where self-experimentation is a dangerous and high risk activity. Second, persons enmeshed in situational pressures often are blind to paths of action alternative to those which they are now taking to no good or to unsatisfactory effect. Specially designed programs can help them discover and create new images of potentiality in their situations and new images of personal or joint action for themselves in their back-home situations. Third, integral learning requires special conditions which are often not present in "real" life situations. Learning communities can be built which embody these required conditions and permit participants to experience how to learn and to go on learning. This does require work on transfer of learnings, on how to build opportunities for continuing learning within the institutional framework of their lives back home. But the work is worth the cost, in the view of most laboratory practitioners.

I have emphasized the differences between Prof. Krasner's and Prof. Levinson's positions as these are revealed in their criticisms of laboratory practice. But, in an important sense, their positions are similar as over against the position of laboratory practitioners. Both approach situations of change with prior conceptions of what realities are to be found there, realities which are relevant to the effecting of *real* change. Thus, for Prof. Levinson, personalities are the really *real* targets of a change worthy of the name. And for

Prof. Krasner, environmental factors are the really *real* factors to be manipulated in effecting behavioral changes. Both ascribe reality to the objects of knowledge that emanate from particular substantive inquiries into the nature of man.

As I understand the approach of laboratory practitioners, they make no such prior assumptions about which subject matters, derived from studies of human situations, reveal the *reality* of those situations. Men have personalities. Their behavior is influenced by environmental factors. Men live in and through various systems and structures. And these have political, economic, and normative aspects. The concepts of any positive discipline are instruments for probing the experiential realities of human situations in their holistic complexity. The concepts do not give us pictures of the human reality. Laboratory practitioners try, not always successfully, to avoid the fallacy of misplaced concreteness so far as the concepts of any or all scientific disciplines are concerned.

They do not always avoid the flabby eclecticism which is the danger lurking in their preference for a holistic approach to the study and the changing of human situations. They try to save themselves from this danger by finding community in a methodology of inquiry and experimentation and in the values which undergird the methodology. No *individual* practitioner can incorporate all the knowledge from various specialized disciplines and professions which *may* have resources useful in diagnosing and dealing with diverse human situations. Laboratory practitioners do not pretend to such universal knowledge. They recognize the consequent need for teamwork among disciplines and professions in diagnosing and dealing with the human problems that confront us as persons and societies. They attach great importance to the conditions and processes of effective teamwork. I would like to have both Prof. Levinson and Prof. Krasner on my team.

COMMENTS ON "LABORATORY METHOD"
By Howard Zinn

The spirit behind laboratory learning is admirable: seeing education "as a process of personal and cultural renewal" rather than as a mechanical transmission of a limited culture; insisting that learning include action, that the techniques of research be joined to techniques of action; that face-to-face contact and emotion give immediacy to what otherwise would be traditional abstract learning.

It does present the danger, as the authors themselves recognize, of having personal problems and a focus on individual development crowd out larger questions of social change, as intense personal concerns have a tendency to do. Verbal recognition of this danger will never solve it, by itself, so long as the environment of the group remains dominated by its small-scale, face-to-face encounters. Only a constant breaking-up of the closed solidity of the group by forcing it to encounter the outside world will ensure that the personal is kept in its important but properly small place.

One premise of the method seems to me unjustified: that "conflicts of value and interest" can be turned "from win-lose polarizations into problems to be solved, preferably by creative compromise." Granted that this is true in many situations, where compromise can both move social change onto the next level, and prevent conflict which is debilitating and counterproductive to those whose condition needs to be changed. But there are other situations where differences in interest are so basic that no compromise is possible short of acquiescence either to the *status quo* or to token reforms. In such cases, creative conflict can push the boundaries of possibility far beyond what a mood of compromise can accomplish. In the end, *after* the conflict, there is always some compromise; social situations, except in cases of total revolution, are not resolved by unconditional surrender. But there is a crucial difference in the level at which the final compromise rests, depending on how much conflict there has been in the interim. "Slavery, Sir," Garrison once said, "will not be overthrown without excitement, a most tremendous excitement." And so it is with most important issues in society where vested interests in property and power face the indignation of those without those resources.

An important distinction must be made. There are contending groups whose interest is ultimately similar (like low-income blacks and low-income whites; like men and women; like the cannon fodder of all countries) — where information, communication, contact, can erode differences; where compromises can be worked out to create unity against the larger common foe. But that foe is often real, and unmovable by compromise, but only by power and persistence. In short, not *all* people can be united happily on the basis of reasonable discussion and compromise, even though we want to carry discussion far enough to make sure we have stripped off as much as we can to lighten the core of trouble.

The method tries to bring together basic researchers, appliers of research, and suffering groups. To make believable the interest in gaining the participation of the third element, a stronger effort will be required than is suggested by the tone of the authors. The customary situation is where some symbolic representatives (blacks, workers, tenants, etc.) are invited into a situation dominated by intellectuals and social workers. A true laboratory method would reverse the balance, and give enough weight to the "clients" to make sure that the urgency of their need is, yes *organized*, but not *diminished*, by the professionals.

The laboratory method — taking note of Kurt Lewin's point — talks of support for the building of "new value orientations and new cognitive orientations" as a result of membership in a group different from traditional groupings. It should be emphasized, I believe, that "membership" is not enough, that the action taken by the group is the crucial element. Furthermore, and this is a point which can hardly be exaggerated: the action needs to win, from time to time, either materially or symbolically, in order to give members of the group a feeling for the possibility of victory through group action. One of the most powerful psychic deterrents to change is the sense of powerlessness, because of the limits of what an individual can do, and because of the failures of so many groups which have attempted change. Setting realistic goals (which everyone understands to be limited, but which are steps toward larger objectives) and working hard enough, skillfully enough to achieve them can give that confidence in group effort which we all need, in a social system which repeatedly reminds us of our impotence.

The method's criticism of disciplinary segregation is very important and very true. The diligent pursuit of a real problem will be the most important evidence of the obstructive character of disciplinary lines. And the most important kind of segregation is, as the report notes, that which separates action, research, and education.

I am worried about the interpretation of "the values of science" and the "implicity morality" of science, when this is defined as "devotion to fact-finding and fact-facing . . . and its pursuit of objectivity." Perhaps this is so abstract that I have misunderstood it, but it comes too uncomfortably close to the traditional emphasis on "value-free" social science to be consistent with the *change* aim which is crucial to the laboratory method. The "implicity morality" in science is not in objectivity, not in any methodological principle, I would hope, but in the improvement of the human condition. (Perhaps the authors and I have here a problem in communication rather than a deep schism in values, and it can be worked out by a change-agent gifted in translation!)

I am troubled, once more, by the statement that "differences in value orientation need not be a blemish upon and a threat to learningful common deliberation and action, if commitment to the use of methodologies which respect differences and employ them to enrich and improve common action can be attained. . . ." This seems to indicate that value-differences can be overcome by methodological agreement. If a landlord seeks maximum profit, and a tenant minimum rent; if a political leader seeks absolute power, and his constituents want power of their own; if a judge wants to put offenders in prison, and others want to empty the prisons to force us to change the society and make prisons unnecessary — we have here such deep value-conflicts that they cannot be solved by any methodology, only by the substantive fact of the power of organized action groups.

Perhaps I am misreading the point, because here — as in so much of the explanation of laboratory method — the ideas are expressed in the abstract, without concrete examples to clarify their meaning. But I suspect not, when I read about "methods of conflict resolution which are designed to lead to intelligent and mutually acceptable resolutions" and that "This is the re-educative task to which proponents of laboratory method are committed." Now, suddenly, that triple entity of education-research-action has given way to an emphasis on the "re-educative task." Yes, but in a world of such sharp value differences that "intelligent and mutually acceptable resolutions" cannot come without conflict, the re-education necessarily comes through conflict. Agreed, a conflict informed by research, and taking advantage of whatever possibilities for persuasion and compromise there are. But it is to each to drift into the customary emphasis on moral education rather than the harder path of organization and struggle.

It seems that I am siding with Reinhold Niebuhr's emphasis on power and conflict in his *Moral Man and Immoral Society*,[1] rather than with John Dewey's emphasis on rational persuasion in *Liberalism and Social Action.*[2]

A SHORT COMMENTARY ON "THE FLEXIBLE STRUCTURES LABORATORY"

By John Southgate

The essence of Max's analysis is shown in his last paragraph. He sees social change as a *contradictory process* and provides a dialectical analysis of a specific laboratory[1] and uses this to generalize about other matters. I will add some comments in the same manner with illustrations from another laboratory.[2]

One unusual feature of Max's article is the way he sees the laboratory as an analogy of the history and future development of capitalism! Most laboratories are concerned with some kind of individual change or at the most provide experiential analogies of the family, an organization or some inter-group phenomenon. I am convinced that the former analysis is useful; I have been engaged in other labs where events provided material for such an approach, albeit with somewhat different outcomes.

An assumption is, therefore, that it is worthwhile to examine the internal contradictions in these situations and to generalize. Of course, at some point, it is absolutely necessary to look at the external contradictions; such as the role of staff and participants vis-a-vis parent-organizations, the class nature of the activity, where the activity fits into the general productive functions and so on. If this is not done, then, indeed, behavioral scientists will never come to understand the mystifying and conservative functions in which they are unconsciously (?) engaged.

For those who have not experienced this kind of laboratory, I recommend comparing some of the descriptions by Max of the "Gauchists" with Sartre's descriptions of 'Groups-in-fusion' in his *Critique de la raison dialectique.*[3] Sartre's material is, of course, derived from historical sources from the French Revolution onward. Max describes, in essence, similar phenomena. I agree with him that from studying the dynamics of groups in some labs, we can gain a degree of insight into social reality.

If you think of the "trainers" as an analogy of the "ruling class" of a structure, then you could describe the developing processes in various stages. At the beginning, you have a sort of "monarchy" with passive acceptance by the "under-privileged." Only minor decisions are contested; the emotionality is parent-child-like[4] and the primary task, the ideology and certainly the "forces and relations of production," that is, the economic and psychological ownership is clearly with the ruling class.

The "unionist" period is distinguished in the power structure by negotiations over moderately important decisions along with a move toward an adult-like emotionality. It is not until the arrival of the "Gauchists" on the scene that there is any serious challenge to the ruling class; that important decisions are contested. There is an influential counter-ideology and a more aggressive emotionality but, even so, the ownership remains firmly in the hands of the ruling class.

So far, in a simplified form, we do have a rough approximation to historical development. If the analogy holds, then the next part of the laboratory gives us a glimpse of a possible future. So what happens?

The change came with the "chaos." (I see this as an analogy of a time of revolution and its aftermath). This was a period where the ownership was challenged and changed and a whole new way of living emerges. New contradictions arose that were powerful and salient for everyone. In Karl Marx's terms, you had a society trying to live in terms of use-values (that is, need-values) rather than exchange-value. The psychological problems of really standing up for what you *want*, what you *desire*, produced many contradictions; primarily the problem is being psychologically strong enough to push your needs and at the same time to accept some kind of collective resolution of the competing needs within the group. At the moment of writing, there is an "occupation" of students in the polytechnic where I work. When they set up an "alternative education" program, they were faced with a similar situation. Students tended to be passive, and still look for "experts" to run things and give lectures. There was reluctance to say "I want to learn this or that," or to organize in a self-directed manner. After some discussion, we organized a "wall-paper" and produced a program based upon it. The contradiction was only partly overcome.

The period described as the "ultimate phase of the laboratory" is also rather like the "withering away of the state" as envisaged by Marx, although this is stretching the analogy, to say the least. Arguing by analogy is, of course, problematic. Even within this unique, particular laboratory, there are some glaring differences from the "real world." For example: you have a "ruling class" that actually wanted (or was reasonably willing) to liquidate itself; this was dramatically illustrated by Max's willingness to be driven out of his own organization rather than stop the developments produced from the laboratory. Historically, it is a truism that no ruling class has ever given up its power voluntarily; it has always had to be forced to give up its power.

It is possible, however, to examine this problem in a laboratory setting. Max Pages and I were involved in such a lab and I will briefly use it in an illustration. (I will call this lab "the Charbonnier lab"). In this case, the analogy only took us as far as the "present day." We had developments which I have characterized as analogies of the formation of the "family," "tribalism," "early capitalism," "left reformism," and finally, a revolutionary period — which in spite of strenuous efforts *ended in failure.* I do think that we had a closer simulation, however, to present society than was the case with Max's "flexible-structures" lab. I think this because we were finally stuck in a situation that I call "repressive-tolerance," after Marcuse.[6]

It is important to understand this phenomenon because, on the one hand, this is the major problem in western capitalism (direct repression being more the case in the east) and, on the other hand, nearly all the work of behavioral scientists, no matter how apparently radical, is itself a part of this repressive-tolerance structure (including, of course, the work that I do, this article, and the book you are reading at this moment).

I use the expression "repressive-tolerance" to mean a social situation where the under-privileged members are apparently free to change or control the power structure; the reality, however, is that the ruling class is maintained by a variety of ideological, emotional and control mechanisms; and also by mystification of the primary task goals and the ownership structure.[7] All members of the system consciously or unconsciously collude in maintaining this status-quo. There may very well be an ideology of "freedom of the individual," but in reality, the major and important decisions are taken by members of the ruling class in accordance with their task-goals. The emotionality mechanisms operate in defense of ruling-class interests; the under-privileged groups may experience dependent or counter-dependent feelings deriving from a parent-child modality. Alternatively, there can be a flight into emotionality, warmth, affection, closeness, or sexuality. Another possibility is a flight into scapegoating or other projections upon symbols.

A specific form of emotional structure common to "repressive-tolerance" is what Sartre calls "seriality."[9] Briefly, this is where persons are connected by some object or objective, and yet have no relation to each other, and no control over the process. Examples would be a bus queue, those watching a TV program, members of a market, and the like. Each member is "merely one in a series."

All praxis[10] to change the system is contained and deflected so that it does not really threaten the fundamental structure of the social system. In a repressive-tolerance situation (as opposed to a directly repressive situation) there is little necessity to use open coercion. Mechanisms associated with competition, emotionality, and ideology (especially control of communication/education media) allow all such praxis to be "tolerated."

I have defined the classic repressive-tolerance situation. The "Charbonnier lab" proved to be almost a textbook example. The lab was a "large group" consisting of ninety people from ten countries.[11] We lived together for ten days without formal structure. On the last day, after many attempts to "take over the means of production" (the staff's fees and rights), we entered a period that was rather like a sort of madness. Each time I read my diary, I recall the drama of the event and find that words cannot convey the atmosphere and feelings. I have never experienced such a dramatic demonstration of alienation. People talked about "shadows." They said how powerless they felt; and some of the "shadows" started to speak and say that they had never felt so alienated. There were many inputs of this kind and many arguments; they argued that this situation was because of "the staff," or "we hadn't tried to love each other enough," or "we couldn't communicate," or "it was language," or "it was mystical," or "it was madness." And madness was talked about (and

Laing used in explanation).[12] I felt at the time that here in front of me was a film that encapsulated the madness of the social structures in which we live and which we have internalized. As the "shadows" started to stand up and speak (often for the first time), I had a picture of the literally, millions of "shadows" who also are without power and alienated.

The classic repressive-tolerance structure is a terrible paradox. It is an inert-process of the most invidious kind, because no one, literally no one, in the system desires the situation to continue.[13] All of us, staff and participant alike, wanted to change the repression — and yet we were powerless to do so.

Of course, in theory, the staff could have "given up" its fees and rights and thus removed the fundamental structural reason for the situation, that is, the ownership of the "means and relations of production" (a very paternalist action!). We refused to give our fees to an "amorphous group with no specific external goals." But even if we had done this, then we would have merely brought up another contradiction — the "repressive-tolerance" ruling class once again would retain psychological and ideological control. What then should the solution have been?

I had a view, prior to the lab, that the solution was for the under-privileged members to engage in common praxis.[14] I still hold this view. Like Max, I believe that radical change has to come from "below." However, the manner of doing this is important; individual actions do not succeed. It is necessary for groups to form together in a collective, with the goal of converting the whole community toward a cooperative goal, where capital — both economic and psychological — is shared.

With this perspective, a number of us tried to engage in common praxis and set up some kind of soviet.[15] From time to time, our actions would meet with success, we would push the community, and then find that the system would overwhelm us. Our main ideological weakness was connected with the equivalent of "communication media" in this situation. The main communication means was the spoken word, and "process-comment" was the norm. Thus, every time we pushed for actions or decisions, this was defeated by endless process-comment ranging from "unconscious forces" to "leadership struggles" and much else.

Another problem is that participants often find it "unthinkable" to challenge the rights of the staff and sponsoring institution, especially over economic goals. In the "real world," many workers and under-privileged also find it "unthinkable." The ruling class, both in the lab and in the world, depend upon such rights for their life-styles, economic, and psychological security. Only the kind of "chaos" described by Max can act to provide a real challenge to such assumptions.

General Comments and Conclusions

Max found that the flexible-structures lab could not be tolerated by his parent-organization. I suspect that the one I have just described also would not be tolerated by the typical institutions which sponsor laboratory-style learning. After this last event, a number of people, including staff members with international reputations, found that they had to re-think their whole political position. In different ways, they came to realize that, by itself, the whole of laboratory work, is a mere tinkering with the system for a small privileged group, which in the long run is not going to make fundamental changes in social structures.

What is more, the typical trainer behavior, in this situation, can be seen very clearly to be about *relations as they are now, reified and mystified.* However, I do think that this kind of laboratory is very worthwhile; I think it demonstrates the logical conclusion of laboratory education and points to the end of its usefulness in its present form. In my view, its future can only be in a political context working directly with the working class and the under-privileged.

In conclusion, I want to outline a brief analysis of the contradictions that have led to my prediction that we are now at the end of the "laboratory" movement in its present form.

From about the end of the war, a whole movement has arisen in the fields of clinical psychology and philosophy based upon an ideology of freedom. Its roots lie in the existential tradition and have permeated into the avant-garde of management, clinical practice, and, latterly, the "growth movement." The *theories* imply complete participation and freedom. The relative boom of western capitalism has allowed small groups of elite people (managers, organizational development specialists, middle class intelligentsia) to have the benefits of practices based upon such theories. I refer to T Groups, encounter groups, and much of the "business" of advanced behavioral science. In addition, there was a necessity for the social system to do this kind of thing. The task structure has become so complex in our modern technology that the experts and technologists have to cooperate and work in groups. The traditional authoritarian power structure and emotionality, although all right for most shop-floor situations, was inconsistent with this development. Thus, practitioners and academics have combined to work and develop this area. The two labs described in this article are outcomes, children of this movement, so to speak.

The universal contradiction is *that there is now a complete divorce between the theory and the practice of the behavioral scientists.* The *theory* is for total participation, freedom, and self actualization. The *practice* is that the few benefactors are a small privileged group whilst the majority live in conditions of either direct repression or repressive-tolerance.

Hegel argued that each new generation, in a concentrated fashion, has to learn about and catch up with the whole of previous history. Anyone who is new to this field can use this book to "catch up" and, I hope, take part in labs similar to the ones described by Max and myself. However, it is my view that the reader, whether just starting or well-established, has only two basic paths open to him in this day and age. The first is to become part of the représsive-tolerance structure, and to do some good work in the less important areas of capitalism and help maintain a few privileged people. The other alternative is to work politically and collectively toward overthrowing repressive-tolerance and the madness and meaninglessness that is involved.

The reality of the world is more frightening than the most devastating laboratory. In the two labs described, two-thirds of the population were *not* starving or subject to incredible violence. Even without this, it was obvious that despite the affluence of our "advanced" world, such a system leads to a psychology that borders upon madness.

I think that everyone in this field should aim to cease being part of the problem, and become part of the solution.

RESPONSE TO ZINN AND SOUTHGATE

The criticisms of laboratory method by Prof. Zinn and Prof. Southgate are of a sort quite different from those raised by our psychologically-oriented critics. The former address their criticisms to claims for the efficacy of laboratory method in changing social institutions, not with claims for its efficacy as a means in stimulating and supporting increased personal awareness or in modifying interpersonal relations. More particularly, Prof. Zinn and Prof. Southgate express doubts about the efficacy of laboratory method to alter significantly power relations within our capitalist society and raise questions about the stance of laboratory practitioners toward the uses of intergroup conflict in achieving social changes.

I will deal first with the comments by Prof. Zinn. He believes that "the premise" of laboratory practice that "conflicts of value and interest" can be turned "from win-lose polarizations into problems to be solved, preferably by creative compromise," is unjustified. I hope that Prof. Zinn realizes that this premise is a conditional one for most, if not all, laboratory practitioners. The resolution of polarized conflicts in interest requires conditions of free and open exchange between all parties to a conflict and a shared hope that a mutually satisfactory resolution can be created by joint effort. These conditions do not come into being "naturally," or by letting history take its course. They develop only through strenuous efforts and usually require the help of "third parties" mutually acceptable to all conflicting parties. Moreover, such "third parties" ordinarily require special training in ways of building the required conditions of creative compromise already noted, necessarily with the collaboration of the conflicting parties.

Since the premise is conditional, no laboratory practitioner could logically predict from it that there are not situations which can only be settled by a power struggle, in which the more powerful party coerces the less powerful into compliance. But unless the counter-premise is held unconditionally, the opposite prediction is also open to question. I hope that Prof. Zinn does not hold his counter-premise as an unconditional or absolute one. If he does not, perhaps he and I can agree that the amenability of conflict situations to attempts to establish the conditions required by laboratory methods in their resolution is an empirical question, not one to be settled by dogmatic assumption.

And if Prof. Zinn agrees further that the human costs of power-coercive resolutions of unmediated intergroup conflicts are excruciatingly high in our increasingly interdependent world society, he may also agree that widespread re-educative efforts to establish the conditions that make collaborative resolutions of conflicts more likely are worth investing in, psychologically and economically. Actually, power-coercive settlings of intergroup conflicts seldom, if ever, in themselves solve the problems at stake in a conflict. These remain to be resolved by more rational, collaborative, and re-educative methods, if at all, after the cessation of hostilities, as Prof. Zinn has noted. And most settlements of conflicts by win-lose struggles prejudice the use of problem-solving methods after a truce is attained and are notoriously unstable. Energies of the defeated tend to flow into various forms of continuing resistance against the victors. And the energies of the victors tend to go into policing the settlement, into attempts to enforce compliance on the part of the defeated. There is little if any confluence or synergy of the energies of the conflicting parties into the joint creation of a mutually satisfactory resolution of the conflict. If the above is true, and I believe that it is, the quest for effective methods of synergistic resolution of human conflicts, of which laboratory practice is one, is a quest worthy of contemporary support.

Actually, Prof. Zinn may have misread the position of laboratory practitioners with respect to the uses of human conflict. I would agree fully with him that "creative conflict can push the boundaries of possibility far beyond what a mood of compromise can accomplish." Laboratory practice does not seek to reject or suppress conflicts. Rather, it seeks to bring conflicts into the open, to strip conflicts of their unrealistic and dehumanizing elements of fantasy and projection, to use the realistic conflict as it is mutually understood to stimulate the creation of new paths of resolution which lift up the conflicting values into an envisioned synthesis that would be impossible of achievement without the conflict and without joint effort by the conflicting parties. Perhaps Prof. Zinn read the *compromise* part of the resolution preferred by laboratory practitioners without emphasizing the *creative* compromises to which they, in practice, aspire. The goal of most laboratory practitioners is not to resolve conflicts, in the sense of eliminating them, but rather to manage them toward mutually acceptable outcomes with conflicts persisting, just as differences persist, among persons and groups.

I am glad that Prof. Zinn recognizes that laboratory methods can be used within contending parties to build community and strength on either or both sides of a massive and continuing conflict. One condition of effective use of laboratory methods in managing conflict is a comparative equality of power among the contending parties. And building community within a group is a way of increasing its actual and self-perceived power. As an example, I, along with colleagues, have used laboratory methods to create trust, to reduce wasteful leadership struggles, to build a common sense of destiny among citizens, black and white, in an urban poverty area. This is one way at least of moving beyond the sense of powerlessness, which, as Prof. Zinn points out, is a major deterrent of effective social action. At the same time, with the full knowledge of both citizens and police that we were working with both sides of the conflict, my colleagues and I worked with the police of the area, creating trust there, obviating status differentials, building "ego strength" in the police group. When the citizens and police came together, they were able to join their real conflicts openly and to create resolutions for some of the problems implicit in these conflicts. The strength provided by the "community-building" efforts on both sides of the conflict made possible this joint facing up to the conflict and the invention of viable resolutions, more or less satisfactory to both. Laboratory methods when used to convert a mass of "oppressed" people into a collaborative, informed, and committed group can increase their effectiveness in serving their interests. I also believe that laboratory methods used with an "oppressor" group in resolving its problems of latent guilt, and inner problems of membership and leadership will make it more amenable to working out creative compromises with an "oppressed" group, similarly trained, when they join conflict, with the help of mutually trusted change agents. And this is true even if the compromise solution involves some loss of customary power on the part of the "oppressor" group. I suspect that Prof. Southgate would disagree with me here and would appeal, as he does in his critique, to the "truism that no ruling class has ever given up its power voluntarily" to confute me. I have had enough experiences like the one outlined above to sustain me in my belief.

But let me respond to one more point made by Prof. Zinn before dealing directly with Prof. Southgate's critique. This is a point with respect to the morality of science which I argued in Chapter 2 had been incorporated into the morality of laboratory method. Prof. Zinn comments that the emphasis on "objectivity" as a value in scientific morality "comes too uncomfortably close to the traditional emphasis on 'value-free' social science to be consistent with the change aim . . . (of) . . . laboratory method." Perhaps Prof. Zinn is confusing "objectivity" with "neutrality." An applied social scientist cannot be neutral with respect to the conflicts in a social system into which he chooses to intervene. He acts on his values as any person does when he acts. But he can be committed to being objective about his own values and about competing values in the situation in the very interest of effective action. "Being objective" means being aware of and articulate about his own value positions and motivations and, indeed, being aware of and articulate about competing value positions. He cannot serve his values best without being as aware and articulate as he possibly can be. I hope this clears up some of the difference between Prof. Zinn and me. I suspect he would still object to the priority of methodological advocacy over substantive advocacy which I recommend to change agents. Yet, I hope he agrees that it is better for us to be aware of and articulate about this difference than to be unaware of and inarticulate about it.

Laboratory practitioners should be grateful to Prof. Southgate in his comment and to Prof. Pages in Chapter 17 for their innovative use of human relations laboratories to provide staff and participants with a first-hand experience of processes and stages of historical development. Experiences in laboratories are subject to various interpretations, each valid in its own right. Categories of interpretation of laboratory experiences have traditionally been drawn from the psychology and sociology of persons, interpersonal relations, groups, organizations, and local communities. Prof. Southgate and Prof. Pages have chosen to interpret laboratory experiences in political, economic, and historical terms. Of course, of necessity, they needed to work out a design which produced data amenable to such interpretations. Indeed, the experiences in the laboratory were analogies of the dramas of political and economic history as these develop on a national or international stage. But participants capable of analogical thinking must have left these laboratories with a vivid new consciousness of actual historical processes moving in and around them and with new options with respect to the investment of their own energies in these processes.

While I applaud Prof. Southgate, Prof. Pages and their colleagues for their innovative use of laboratory experience, I find difficulty in accepting Prof. Southgate's pessimistic conclusions with respect to the uses and usefulness of laboratory method in our contemporary period of history.

My major difficulty comes with the adequacy of the analogy from which, at least in part, Prof. Southgate's pessimistic conclusions about laboratory method are drawn. Whatever else a training laboratory offers to its participants, it offers the services of professionals who can help participants objectify and learn from the experienced events of their laboratory life. While the trainers must become, in some degree, participants in order to understand "from the inside" the experiences they help participants, less experienced than they in laboratory methods, to learn from, they must remain in some measure observers, in order to fulfill their training function adequately. Of course, they enlist participants in becoming observer-participants and in sharing the training functions as the laboratory develops. But they must remain available to help objectify involving emotional experiences which so fully engage participants that "third party" help in producing learning out of the experiences becomes essential.

I have difficulty with drawing conclusions about the inefficacy of laboratory methods from experience in a laboratory in which the trainers became so involved in acting out the role of the "ruling class" that they also became unavailable to help the "proletarian" participants to understand what was going on in and around them and to develop cohesiveness and strength to reorganize the situation toward fuller, *not idealistically full*, satisfaction of their thwarted interests. A laboratory is designed to help participants acquire a clearer, less distorted consciousness of the laboratory situation, and by analogy of their extra-laboratory situations as well. But it is also designed to help participants to invent and try out skills for dealing with situations which their new consciousness has enabled them to diagnose more accurately and adequately. Such learnings do not come "naturally" but ordinarily require the resources of persons skilled in helping to develop the conditions without which exploratory invention and experimentations will not occur. This is true whether the repressive climate to be altered is one of direct tyranny or of repressive tolerance.

Prof. Southgate's apparent theory of learning seems to me open to serious question. Many people have learned habits of uncritical followership under conditions of "repressive tolerance," which are all too prevalent in bureaucratized industrial societies. When such habits of uncritical dependence for direction from remote and obfuscating managers of the system are unmasked for participants in a laboratory, such as the Charbonnier laboratory which Prof. Southgate describes, isn't it too much to expect that participants will spontaneously begin to enact alternative habits of action which responsible self-direction, personal, and communal, require? Such an expectation seems more consistent with an "idealistic" Rousseauism than with a realistic, dialectical view of human history. The unmasking is a first step in a deliberate process of unlearning old habits and beginning to learn new ones more appropriate to self-direction and communal democracy. In this learning, they will need to depend on others to help them take experimental, behavioral steps toward autonomy and interdependence. Helpers committed to the development of greater autonomy and interdependence in those whom they seek to help must accept some dependence on their direction as incremental (not serial) movements toward the development of the skills required for more fully autonomous functioning. These are achieved and integrated into the persons of learners and into the norms of the groups in which they work. To will the ends of new learning without accepting responsibility for the always arduous and ordinarily stepwise processes of relearning and learning anew is to invite failure and woo despair. The motivations for reeducation must come "from below" as Prof. Southgate uses this expression. But motivation and consciousness require concepts and skills to implement the learning process. And these are part of the cultural conserve mediated to learners through their trainers and helpers. In hoping, undialectically, for spontaneous generation of new forms of social life, soviets or otherwise, to save us, I wonder if Prof. Southgate has not himself blurred the distinction between process and praxis, a distinction, which, I agree with him, is often confused in the training world.

Repressive conditions outside the laboratory, as in the laboratory, will not be changed without the services of change agents who can help embattled or regressed people invent, develop, and test alternative, less repressive, conditions of life for themselves. And laboratory methods remain one of our best hopes for the development of more such change agents. We should not be defeated by truisms, held dogmatically, "that no ruling class has ever given up its power voluntarily." I find a restatement of the truism "more nearly true" than Prof. Southgate's statement of it. "No ruling class, without help in seeing advantages in a redistribution of power, in order to achieve a better state of affairs, jointly envisioned in open and sustained communications with those with conflicting interests, has voluntarily agreed to a redistribution of power." This is, of course, a conditional statement. And, important in these conditions, is the availability of helpers skilled in releasing communication across lines of conflicting interests and unequally distributed power. The hope in laboratory method lies in its promise to develop such helpers and to make their services available to parties on *all* sides of the conflicts that now threaten human survival. There is no certainty in the promise. But there is a hope which I wish that Prof. Southgate might share.

FOOTNOTES AND REFERENCES

A. In Benne's Response

1. Ideology is used here as a name for belief systems which serve as guiding rationales for various modes of social practice, social action, and social praxis. Praxis refers to deliberate attempts to change and transform one established preconscious process or another. Social practice refers to processes of helping people, processes which are ordinarily under the management of professions and professionals. Social action as deliberate effort to solve social problems, though it overlaps some forms of social practice, is ordinarily led by "volunteer" leaders, rather than by trained professionals, although programs of social action may employ the services of various professionals. Applications of laboratory method cut across the conventional boundaries which demarcate social practice, social action, and social praxis. As a result, it has attracted criticism from actionists, professional practitioners, and ideologues of other social movements.

In speaking of "ideology," we do not follow the usage of Karl Mannheim who limited "ideology" to world views that are conservative in intent and effect. We include Utopian along with conservative social perspectives in our usage. Nor do we limit "ideology" to idea systems that are designed and used as weapons in social and political struggles, particularly class struggles, as Max Lerner, Daniel Bell, and others have done.

2. Leonard Krasner is professor of psychology in the State University of New York at Stony Brook. Harry Levinson is a professor at the Graduate School of Business Administration, Harvard University, in Cambridge, Massachusetts. Howard Zinn is professor of political science, in Boston University, at Boston, Massachusetts. John Southgate is a member of the faculty of the Polytechnic of North London in England.

B. In Zinn's Comment

1. Reinhold Niebuhr, *Moral Man in Immoral Society*, Scribners, New York, 1932.

2. John Dewey, *Liberalism and Social Action*, G. P. Putnam's and Sons, New York, 1935.

C. In Southgate's Comment

1. Explaining the nature of dialectical thinking would require a whole article. A good introduction can be found in Aaron Esterson, *The Leaves of*

Spring, Pelican Books, 1970. A set of "Teaching Cards" by John Southgate is published by the Applied Behavioral Science Division, Polytechnic of North London, 1972. See also John Southgate, *Dialectical Peer Counseling*, Polytechnic of North London, 1963.

2. This laboratory was held in Charbonnier, France in April, 1972. It was sponsored by E. I. T., Laboratoire de Changement Sociale, and Applied Behavioural Science Division, Polytechnic of North London.

3. Jean-Paul Sartre, *Critique de la Raison Dialectique*, Tome 1, Editions Gallimard, Paris, 1960.

4. I use these terms "parent," "child," and "adult," in the usage of transactional analysis. See Eric Berne, *Games People Play*, Grove Press, New York, 1964.

5. Unpublished Ms., "The Charbonnier Lab," by John Southgate. Also available in John Southgate, *The Living Dialectic of You, Me and We*, 1972.

6. See R. I. Wolf, Barrington Moore, Jr., and Herbert Marcuse, *A Critique of Pure Tolerance*, Jonathan Cape, London, 1969.

7. By primary task goals I mean the most important decisions upon which all other decisions in the system depend. For example, "to maximize long term profits" would be the primary task goal of a commercial company.

8. See Reimut Reiche, "Sexuality and Class Struggle," NLB, 1970, especially regarding "repressive sublimation."

9. See Wilhelm Reich, *The Mass Psychology of Fascism*, Farrar, Straus and Giroux, New York, 1970. Sartre's concept of a "manipulated serial" is also relevant. A description in English can be found in Wilfrid Desan, *The Marxism of Jean-Paul Sartre*, Doubleday, Anchor Books, Garden City, New York, 1966.

10. "Praxis" is defined in contradistinction to "process." This important distinction is often confused in the training world. "Process" means a series of events that continue without the conscious control of those concerned; it "happens." "Praxis" is conscious action taken to change or transform a "process." Examples of "processes" are the "games" described by Berne, *op cit*, a market, international trade, etc.

11. By "large group" I mean from about 15 upwards; it is hardly possible to work on the kind of dynamics described in the article with a group smaller than 15. In fact, groups of 30 or more are preferable.

12. R. D. Laing, *The Politics of Experience*, Penguin Books, Hammondsworth, England, 1967.

13. "Inert Process" is a Sartrean term.

14. "Common praxis" is that of a group as opposed to "individual praxis."

15. By "soviet" I refer to the kind of spontaneous organizations that arose in USSR from 1917 until their complete degeneration in the late 1920's and to similar events in Bavaria and Turin during that period and the later soviets in Spain during the Civil War, Hungary in 1956 and elsewhere.

16. "Universal contradictions" refer to those that apply to large social structures or societies.

PART II

CONCEPTUAL AND METHODOLOGICAL PERSPECTIVES

PART II

INTRODUCTION

The focus of Parts III and IV are on the applications of laboratory theory and method to personal, group, organization, and community development.

This part presents a series of more generic analyses of the conceptual underpinnings and methodological perspectives of laboratory practice. These cut across the focus of laboratory method on different levels of human organization. They explore in greater detail some of the dimensions suggested by Kenneth Benne and Jack Gibb in Chapters 2 and 3.

In Chapter 5, Leland Bradford looks in detail at the participative learning process and the personal involvement, interpersonal transactions, and group functions which support learning about self and others. He begins an analysis of the types of intervention by the laboratory practitioner which serve to facilitate such learning. Chapter 11 probes this area of intervention strategy and style more deeply. In preparing Chapter 11, the editors elicited statements about intervention goals, decisions, and strategies from a sample of their colleagues as well as from themselves. The analysis and interpretation of these responses provide an unusual opportunity to probe and clarify the different behavioral styles, value postures, and decision processes of a range of successful senior professionals.

Underlying the concepts of laboratory education and the action assumptions of laboratory educators is a large volume of research and theory — psychological, socio-psychological, and sociological. Kurt Lewin's attempt to blend these strands in the study of small group process and structure, which he called group dynamics, was the stimulus for an explosion of socio-psychological studies of group life and interpersonal relations. In Chapter 6, Jack Glidewell has performed a unique service by organizing many strands of this research and connecting them to important issues in training applications of laboratory method.

The process of "learning human relations" has been ignored in most formal research programs on human learning. Trainers and consultants have had to confront the problems of learning and of resistance to learning continuously, and they have had to develop their own operational guidelines for what conditions and interventions promote learning and change. In Chapter 7, Ronald Lippitt makes an effort to conceptualize the learning process in laboratory education as a process of stimulating and supporting internal linkages between different psychological functions such as knowing, valuing, intending, perceiving, and acting. The conditions of laboratory education described by Bradford are viewed in this chapter as providing individual learners with opportunities to make such linkages or "learning closures."

One of the most valued resources of successful laboratory educators is competence and creativity in designing appropriate learning activities, sequences, and programs for many different learner groups, settings, and purposes. There is very little professional literature on the parameters and skills of designing participative learning sequences. In Chapter 8, Ronald Lippitt and Eva Schindler-Rainman have attempted to summarize and conceptualize an approach to designing for learning which has developed out of their modules for trainers on designing for participative learning, offered in NTL Institute Learning Community Programs, and in advanced training programs at the University of Michigan and the University of California.

Two of the learning outcomes, among others, sought in most laboratory education programs are: (1) an increase in sensitivity to or awareness of self, others, and interpersonal and group processes; and (2) an increase in the perceptual and behavioral skills of receiving input from the behaviors of others and behaving effectively toward others to express validly one's feelings, intentions, and goals. In Chapter 9, Schindler-Rainman and Lippitt point out that in laboratory learning programs, awareness and skill learnings may be focused on the improvement of work productivity as a participant in problem-solving tasks and/or on growth in process sensitivity in the expression of feelings and in interpersonal behavior. They have attempted a conceptual framework for the many types of exercises and activities which laboratory trainers have invented to help facilitate such learning goals.

One of the "trademarks" of laboratory education has been a focus on the "here-and-now" as contrasted with the "there-and-then," on the dynamics of the present life situation as contrasted with intensive exploration and reconstruction of the past. But one key aspect of the here-and-now life space, as Kurt Lewin pointed out, is the psychological time perspective toward the future. Increasingly, laboratory educators are becoming impressed with the significance of personal and group goal setting and planning, with the generation of hope and a sense of potency and commitment, engaging clients in defining directions for their desired growth and accomplishment. In Chapter 10, Herbert Shepard has eloquently expressed the importance of this future orientation and has presented several laboratory activities to facilitate creative risk-taking steps into the future. Another recent publication by Fox, Lippitt, and Schindler-Rainman on the projection of images of potentiality provides additional training designs and methods.[1]

Another area of laboratory education which has developed rapidly in recent years is that of value clarification, confrontation, and inquiry. During the early years of laboratory training, the strong focus on socio-emotional processes tended to neglect value orientations and attitudes and goal setting. More recent developments, such as the Clarification Group reported by Birnbaum in Chapter 15, and the development of value dialogue, value clarification, and value confrontation designs by many trainers, are demonstrating the important interactions between the affective, cognitive, and evaluative aspects of laboratory learning. The value dimension of changing and reorientation in laboratory programs is touched on in many of the chapters in this book. We regret that space considerations have kept us from including a chapter which focused on this important and sometimes neglected dimension of behavior and learning.

The first two parts of this volume illustrate some of the important dimensions of development — conceptually and operationally — of laboratory practice since *T Group Theory and Laboratory Method* was published in 1964.[2] There is much to be done in making more of the conceptual linkages to other areas in the behavioral sciences, following the model of Glidewell's efforts. The work on educational design needs to be complemented by a similar effort in the utilization of multi-media resource materials in training. Much more work is needed on the theory and technology of combining laboratory work focused on task group productivity and on process group learning. The work on intervention theory is still in an early stage of development as laboratory educators seek to achieve a simultaneous orientation to several "levels" of human organization — the intra-psychic individual, the person-member, the small group, the organization, and the inter-system contexts of neighborhood, community, and macro-social systems. Achieving such a multi-level sensitivity will trigger a great leap forward in intervention sophistication and helpfulness. There is still much work to be done. But much progress has been made.

FOOTNOTES AND REFERENCES

1. Fox, R.; Lippitt, R.; and Schindler-Rainman, E.; *Toward a Human Society: Images of Potentiality*, Learning Resources Corporation, Fairfax, Va., 1973.

2. Bradford, L. P.; Gibb, J.; and Benne, K. (Eds.); *T Group Theory and Laboratory Method*, Wiley, New York, 1964.

CHAPTER 5

CREATING A LEARNING ENVIRONMENT

Leland P. Bradford

Learning is seldom easy, particularly learning about one's own behavior. This is true in a group devoted to learning and relearning about human behavior like a T Group. But it is true also in a classroom, in whatever subject, where individual learnings often unknown to the teacher are experienced by the students. These may be in the areas of self-confidence, self-worth, expectations of future failures or successes, along with learnings about the subject. Learning isn't easy in a task group where factors of communication, rivalry, hidden agenda, and inter-personal relations are as dominant as task issues; or in a team-building situation in a company, school, community, or governmental organization where fears of the boss or leader, or competition among members, block better interrelationships and intra-group behavior; or in a two-party meeting or confrontation.

Therefore, this chapter will attempt to indicate and illustrate the process and component parts of the building of a learning environment for a wide variety of learning and work situations on both micro and macro levels. The chapter will also relate this process to the principles of laboratory education which are basic to the creation of an effective learning environment and successful learning outcomes. This chapter will further identify many of the activities a trainer, teacher, consultant, volunteer leader, manager, or group member can engage in to facilitate successful learning or productive problem-solving.

The emphasis of the chapter will be on the training group (T Group) as the clearest way of illustrating the creation of a learning climate. Examples from other types of groups will be utilized to indicate the uses of laboratory method in settings other than T Groups.

POTENTIAL LEARNING

There are many potential learnings for the participants in a T Group. One may learn greater self-awareness, which includes clearer understanding of one's own motives and feelings, a clearer sense of identity, of self-worth, of one's own competencies and limitations. One may learn about the consequences of his behavior on others and on a group. One may learn the differences between his intentions and behavior, and between his behavior and his real motivations. One may learn how his behavior can come to be more congruent with his feelings and thus communicate with less distortion. One may learn about his distortions of others' communications, his tendency to stereotype and misjudge others. One may learn skills of intervening in a group situation and interacting with another in such a way that the other can respond authentically and helpfully. One may learn to listen more carefully to others and to accept others more fully.

Secondly, the learner may gain understanding about the motives, feelings, and behavior of others. He may learn to disapprove of the other's behavior without rejecting him as a person.

Thirdly, he may learn much about group formation, movement, and development. He may learn to diagnose group problems both on the task level and the emotional level. He may come to recognize hidden agenda on which he and others are working, and how these may more readily be brought to the surface. He may learn the various task and maintenance roles, both of equal importance, that are needed at crucial moments in the group, so that it may be productive on the task level, and may keep the group in good working order on the maintenance and growth level.

Fourth, the participant may gain understanding of the consequences of conflict between groups, and how such conflicts can be utilized constructively.

Finally, he may learn how to help others and receive help from others who are his peers. If he can learn this, he has discovered a possible way in which he can continue to learn from many of his human contacts in the future.

But these learnings are hard to reach. Each of us has defenses. Without defenses, we would be hard put to survive psychologically or physically. The problem is that we tend to be over-defensive. We leap to our ramparts at the slightest perception of attack. We have built a self-image, never wholly correct, that we wish others to accept. When any comment seems to undermine this self-image, we rush to shore up the dike. We endeavor to frame our behavior in a way that is congruent with the image we wish to believe and have others believe. We reject stray thoughts that cast doubt on this image. We rationalize. What we often don't recognize is that the behavior we think or hope expresses this image, does just the opposite. It reveals parts of ourselves we prefer neither to believe nor reveal.

On the other hand, the recipient of our behavior has observations and reactions, but no way to tell us what he has seen and experienced without risking defensiveness in response and the charge that he is violating social norms of polite behavior. Only when his self-image is attacked by the behavior of the other is he likely to respond with his observations and reactions, but often with the distortions that accompany defensiveness. With neither the skills of reporting to the other nor the signals from the other that the response will be heard without great defensiveness, nor fear of violation of cultural norms, the recipient of a behavior either withdraws, makes some innocuous response, or perhaps a distorted or hostile one. Thus, no learning takes place for either party.

What is true for individual learning through interaction, may be equally true for work groups whose members are overly threatened and defensive about any feedback about their patterns of group behavior or leadership. Examples are two groups in conflict within an organization, both denying the conflict or blaming the other in self-defense; or of two or more community organizations meeting on what should be a common issue, but each defending the part it has played in the past; or of a teacher concerned about classroom leadership behavior; or of two different racial groups meeting to solve an inter-racial issue and with each group blaming the other.

Here is the crux of the learning process in a problem-solving situation. At least six conditions need to exist before change, productivity, and learning will take place.

1. Reduction of fear that they — individuals, sub-group, group, or organizations — will be destructively hurt.
2. Willingness to expose behavior more than is usually done. This includes feelings usually hidden, but nevertheless interpreted wrongly by others.
3. Trust. This may be defined as belief that the other's comments and responses are meant to be helpful and are authentically as the "other" sees and feels one's behavior. With trust, comes a sense of support; that the "others" honestly are trying to support the individual in successful behavior, in trying new behavior, and in perceiving events

and others with less distortion.

4. The hearing of feedback about one's behavior, thoughtfully considering it, but not necessarily automatically accepting it — all without over-defensiveness.
5. Giving feedback to the others (which may mean a group, organization, community, or other social system) in a way that is a true picture of what is observed and felt, but in a way that enables the "others" to respond non-defensively and congruently with their reactions.
6. Planning the use of learning and change, and of helping others to change. Unless there is planned follow-up for the maintenance and try-out of new learning and ideas for change, and for continued learning and further change, there is likely to be regression to former kinds of behavior.

The creating of a learning and changing environment is a difficult one, and takes the combined willingness, cooperation, and energy of all involved. This means trainer, teacher, change agent, consultant, manager, volunteer leader, helper, and all others who compose the two-party, group, or organization systems. It means the reduction of fear and anxiety about exposure, development of openness, trust and support, and the constructive use of feedback, as previously discussed.

While this creation often occurs gradually and reluctantly, it is best illustrated in the T Group. The T Group is itself one complex application of laboratory method. While this method is described generally in Chapter 2, its parts are mentioned again here, so that the development of a T Group may be better understood.

THE T GROUP

Thus far, it should be evident that learning in the areas of individual, group, organizational or community behavior, requires risk-taking. The individual, group, or organization must risk exhibiting behavior that is normally thought to be kept hidden behind a smooth facade and is seldom commented upon by those observing the behavior. There is risk-taking to one's self-image to receive openly expressed reactions to one's behavior. For such risk-taking to occur, fear of loss of status, respect, acceptance, position, and influence needs to be reduced.

The T Group is so constructed that a climate to reduce fear and encourage risk-taking is gradually created as part of the process of building a group whose product is some or all of the learnings already identified. So the creation of a learning or work climate and the construction of a group for learning and working go hand in hand. Some of the methods used in the T Group in creating a climate for learning apply to many other situations to be described later in this chapter.

The Initial Ambiguous Situation. The T Group releases an enormous amount of individual energy and emotional involvement. Almost like flies attracted to fly paper until they are inevitably trapped, so do participants in a T Group, no matter what their initial plan, become deeply involved and thus drained, but emotionally exhilarated, as a result of the emotional energy they expend. The outside world becomes quickly diminished in importance. T Group members continue their discussions in recreational and meal periods and often far into the night. Amazingly, members seldom leave a T Group, even if sometimes it is painful. Whether leaving would be a sign of defeat, a blow to self-image, they have increasing concern for the group, or whether their personal involvement is too great is unclear.

It takes considerable involvement and expenditure of energy for learning, and particularly relearning to take place in the area of personal behavior, beliefs, actions, perceptions, and values. To relearn is to unlearn, or to give up tightly held beliefs. Thus, there is the need for high involvement and expenditure of emotional energy if effective learning is to take place.

The T Group begins with an ambiguous and largely unstructured start. The trainer says, in various ways, that he hopes that the group members will learn from their experiences together, and that he does not intend to lead or direct the group, but will try to find ways of being helpful at appropriate times, as he hopes they will. This violation of previous experiences as to how groups are led produces stress concerning individual identity and group survival. While identity stress is high (Where is my place in this group? Will I be accepted? Will I have influence?), the early remarks generally deal with concern for group survival. Is the trainer testing us? Will he lead us if we flounder? If he won't lead us, who will? How would he do it? Do we want him to?

There is uncertainty and unclarity about the goal. Even if the goal were clear, there is greater unclarity about how the group goes about the task. Even though by this time most people have read or heard about the T Group, and even if the opening session of the laboratory has demonstrated briefly how a small group might form, there is still hesitancy on the part of members.

The question of group survival, if not uppermost in the minds of most members, at least can be talked about, rather than the uncertainty that each member has about what will happen to him. So the unclear, unstructured opening by the trainer has created an ambiguous situation creating tension in the participants. This tension requires energy expenditure to try to reduce the tension.

This energy expenditure provides the fuel to run the group.

The Personal Identity Crisis and Group Survival Stress. The problems of acceptance and influence of group members have been described. What should I conceal and what reveal? What can hurt? Who will be friendly and who hostile?

On a group level, how can a group meet so closely for two weeks with no clear task, no leader, no procedures? What conflicts will emerge? How will they be handled? How do I react to conflict? Do I want a leader and, if so, whom? Do I want to be the leader? Can we do without a leader?

These are some of the problems facing the participants and the group as a whole as they struggle to find a way of becoming a group acceptable to all. How can the reticence of some and the dominance of others be brought to a comfortable medium?

The group usually tests the trainer to see if he will tell them what to do. When he does not respond, or if he does, it is to state again that he will not serve as leader, some participant usually jumps in with a suggestion as to what to do. It may be to introduce himself, which he claims is the normal thing to do. (Here is where trainer-intervention often can be helpful, as will be described later). The group may grab this suggestion, only to be left at the end of the introductions with the same problem of determining a common goal and a method of acquiring one. Someone else may jump in with a suggestion, far removed from learning about one's own and the group's behavior. This suggestion usually dies quietly on the table or the middle of the room because of lack of interest upon the part of the others, or because others perceive the suggestion as a ploy for leadership. No reasons are usually given for the rejection of a suggestion, leaving the individual uncertain as to whether or not he is being rejected.

Role and Intervention Uncertainty. One reason that interventions often are not responded to is because no pattern of intervention has been created by the group. In this group, how does one express disapproval of a statement? How would it be received? What would be the consequences? Until some acceptable way of response is decided upon, there is a tendency for individuals to remain silent and let a suggestion "plop" on the table or floor.

Again, no one is certain as to what roles are needed to keep the group moving, or how others would perceive one's effort to aid the group. So helpful statements to individuals or the group are not made, leading to misperceptions, lack of group movement, and individual withdrawal. The group still faces the task of discovering role needs on task and maintenance levels and of clarifying these roles and making it acceptable for anyone to fill a needed role without his motives being misperceived.

Equally, interventions need to be tested in terms of risk-taking and helpfulness. Individuals need to learn that an intervention that doesn't move the group or hit the target is no reflection on them. In fact, their intervention may trigger a more effective intervention from another.

The Development of Group Norms. Norms of behavior for individuals and the group are like the scaffolding of a building. In the group, and from experience, they are gradually discovered or created. One of the early norms for most groups is that one doesn't need to shout to be heard, so the decibels reduce. Another is that each person is to be really listened to, and not cut off by an interruption. Another may deal with the matter of "air-time"; while not clocked or made even, each person has a right to speak, but not at a duration that takes that right away from others. Still another deals with the problem of differences and conflict — that these differences can be talked and worked through and that differences of opinion should not bring enduring dislike between individuals. Another may treat with interventions — the difference between those that are helpful and those that are destructive. (Again, as will be discussed, trainer interventions may do much to aid a group in recognizing and accepting a norm they have just created from an incident of their own making). Another norm that builds a bit later is the discovery that someone can be angry at another's behavior, and express it, without really being continuously angry at the person, or judging him. Participants come to believe in the norm that a relationship belongs to both parties and each has equal responsibility to repair it.

Self-Investment and Responsible Participation. Each individual takes membership in the group in different ways. Some do it trying in varying, and often ineffective ways, to keep the group moving or by steering it in what they hope is the proper direction. They usually enter early and are the first to be bombarded by feedback. If they accept the feedback with some grace, they become accepted as members. Others enter by indicating willingness to expose their behavior in areas where they wish to learn, show agreement to be an authentic mirror for others as they hope others will be for them. Others join through indicating care and concern for others. Another may receive membership by endeavoring to help the group look at itself and see how it is evading its learning task.

Each successful membership entrance somehow makes it easier for someone else to enter. Members enter, as they do a club, when the value seems greater than the cost. Interestingly, as each member joins, another norm is often constructed. Often a crisis in the group of a competition with another group enhances the speed with which participants join.

Taking membership in a group such as a T Group brings a sense of responsibility for the improvement and growth of the group. Out of this responsibility can come many learnings — that group goals comprise the goals of all and must meet the needs of all — that even in a task group the leader is wise if he checks to see if the agenda or group goal is equally clear and means the same thing to all members. He may learn that a group capable of concentrated effort is not born quickly or established by fiat, but a group really forms when members feel accepted, feel they can exert some influence, and feel they will not be damaged by cooperation. He may learn the many different task and maintenance roles necessary for group productivity, and he may learn both to be more diagnostic about group problems on all levels, and how to develop designs that might help to unravel the problem. He may learn to recognize and value different resources in the group and how to help more reticent persons share their resources with the group.

Collaboration and Meaningful Feedback. The mechanism for improvement of individual behavior, motivation, beliefs, values, and judgments of others; of group operation and intra- and intergroup conflict is that of feedback.

Feedback, very simply, is the collection and use of information through the reporting of the observations and feelings of those witnessing or receiving the data; through observation and feeling reactions to a simulated exercise or role playing scene; through information collected by outside observers such as a consultant or other observer; and through other data collection devices such as interviews and questionnaire reports. These data, in whatever form collected are reported, or fedback, to the individual, group, organization, community forum, task group, or committee from which the behavior emanates and to whom the data are relevant. Hopefully, the feedback of the data will be heard clearly, without distortion or ascribing of ulterior motives or over-defensiveness by the individual or other system receiving the information; will be considered carefully; and, if appropriate, will be used for change or learning not only by the person or persons toward whom the feedback is directed, but often by others witnessing or participating in the situation, who may quietly apply the feedback to some situation of their own.

Electronically, feedback is a term used to garner physical data from a target to redirect the pathway of a missile, or information from the temperature of a room to turn a furnace on or off. In the pre-beginnings of NTL, it was considered, at least by those involved, that feedback as a concept and method could be used by human and social systems for learning and changing, rather than only in the correction of direction or turning off and on of a mechanism with preset and unchangeable purpose and structure. Unless the recipients of behavior, whether one person, a group, or a larger social system, feed back their observational and feeling reactions constructively and authentically and with the motivation to be helpful, there are few effective ways in which the initiator or initiators of behavior causing the feedback can gain accurate knowledge of what happened to their behavior. They may judge they have been rejected and so they may withdraw or repeat the same behavior more vehemently. Or they may judge, incorrectly, that they are incompetent and so they withhold later important information.

Without adequate feedback, there is less opportunity for an adequate diagnosis of the situation to be made. Without an adequate diagnosis, it is difficult for the group, the larger system, the trainer, teacher, consultant, change-agent, or group to suggest a design or the construction of a norm that will move the learning-changing situation forward.

There are three aspects necessary for effective feedback. First, the individual, group, or larger system must be willing to be open in disclosing the behavior of self and others and problems of intra- and inter-group behavior which are holding up the system. Unless this occurs, there is little opportunity for feedback to be made (unless, of course, the intervention of the trainer or consultant is that he feels no one is leveling or being open, which may stimulate further openness). If no diagnosis of the need and direction of change is possible, it is difficult to create designs for improvement. Part of this aspect is the need for the recipient or recipients of feedback to listen, reduce defensiveness, and consider the helpfulness and accuracy of the feedback.

Second, the feedback must be congruent with what the recipient of the behavior observes and feels. If it is supportive in a phony way; if it is given with destructive motives; and if it contains self-serving motives, it will usually be perceived as false and further feedback from that person or group will be distrusted.

Frequently, unless the trainer is skilled, knowledgeable and ethical, some individuals will quickly perceive that feedback is a wonderful way for them to vent all of their spleen and hostility under the guise of being helpful. Feedback from a number of persons, underscored by observational data, can be a safeguard against such scapegoating feedback.

The third major aspect of feedback is that it needs to be non-judgmental. This means that the individual or group reports back observations and feelings he has with no effort to ascribe motives or judgments to the person whose behavior he has received. He merely reports to the other in a helpful tone, how he feels and the consequences on him of the other's behavior with the assumption that the other has not realized them. In essence, he holds a mirror up, helping the other see himself as he is seen and heard by others. For example: "When you speak in a loud voice, I feel uncomfortable and not certain how I respond. This may be my problem, but I thought it might be helpful to you to know how I felt," versus "Your loud voice shuts me up and damages the group."

Feedback should be congruent with observation and feeling and be non-judgmental. Yet, congruent and non-judgmental feedback is not enough. Feedback should enable the other to respond congruently, non-judgmentally, and helpfully and with evidence he has wisely heard the original feedback. Hopefully, such non-judgmental response to feedback may open a dialogue helpful to both and to others observing. For example: "I have no feeling that you meant to, but your last sentence left me at a loss as to what I might do. Would you try again to help me?" Response: "That really wasn't my intention as far as I can tell. Please tell me what there was in the last sentence that didn't ring right to you." Obviously, such a dialogue could lead into problems of communication between persons, depending on the assumptions and perceptual screen each has, and how communication can usually be straightened out, and the need to do so.

As trust and openness develops in a group, and individuals realize they can gain much knowledge helpful to them, they pour more energy into the group. Thus, the initial energy generated by anxiety is now generated by satisfaction in learning.

Trying Out New Behavior With Support. As a group develops trust in each other and openness, individuals find mannerisms of behavior that they were unaware of and which no one cared enough or dared to risk telling them about. These may well be blind spots for the individual, but are mannerisms easily corrected. In one of NTL's Presidents' Conferences, the president of a large multi-national company always said three times in one sentence what he needed to say only once. After some short discussion of the extent that this caused other persons' minds to wander, he asked for help. We had invented the term "box-car" to describe his behavior. He would try to shorten his sentences, but when he forgot and regressed, it was sufficient for someone in the group to say, "——, you're box-carring again," and he would thank the individual and try again to speak in shorter sentences.

In many groups, there are those who are too reticent, who

need encouragement and support to speak out more frequently, as well as those who are unaware that they interrupt others in their anxiety to speak, or those who tend to monopolize the conversation.

These are all behaviors, usually lying in the blind spot of individuals which, once aware of, they are glad to correct and seek the support of others in making changes in their behavior.

Other areas of more serious import: fear of risk-taking, unwillingness to listen to others, stereotyping, judgmental behavior can also partly be changed by the individual if he shows he is eager to change and willingly takes feedback when he regresses. Thus, trying out, or practicing new behavior, can come when a group has learned to use the feedback mechanism wisely. Frequently, role-playing, where an individual can practice being different without the embarrassment of failure in a real situation, is helpful.

Planning to Maintain Learning. Toward the end of a T Group, anxiety begins to increase as to how the members are going to maintain and use their learnings back home. They recognize that their peers, superiors, and subordinates in the hierarchical organizations in which many of them work will be waiting with suspicion as to what they will do differently. One of the first places they generally plan to try out new learning and seek support is in their homes, particularly with their wives. Only gradually will they plan changes in their work life. It is generally recognized that their behavior will communicate more than their words.

Those who will return to teaching or consulting see a little greater freedom to be different, but even here they recognize the need to seek support from others in order to maintain different behavior. The problem of transfer of learning is difficult, particularly where there is re-education of old behaviors to which associates have become accustomed.

One example which has great meaning for the problem of new knowledge lies in an incident that occurred about twenty years ago. NTL had brought its first European team from Austria for training in the laboratory method and for training Austrians as trainers. After a number of months spent in the United States, a three-day final seminar was held to deal with their return home. For two days, the same role-played scene was held. Essentially, each of the Austrians played returning to Vienna and being greeted by his boss with some such statements: "I see you're back. I hope you had a good time in America." The question was what was meant by this welcome. Was he missed? Was he ruined by the Americans? Did he still feel like an Austrian? What changes would he try to make?

As a result of this scene, played again and again, each Austrian decided to put his new purchases in the bottom of his trunk and not wear them for awhile; to show pictures of American slums rather than American skyscrapers; to say as little as possible about his learnings, but when he felt certain he was accepted again as an Austrian, gradually, to make some suggestions for change. Those members of the team who wanted to continue in this area, found this process of reestablishment highly successful as the first move upon return.

THE INTERVENTIONS OF THE TRAINER

The trainer plays an important part in the group, as does the consultant or change-agent. But even the most experienced and competent trainers vary to a considerable degree in the interventions they make, when they make them, on what basis or theory, how frequently, and to whom. Trainers vary as to how they interpret the laboratory method, whom they perceive as targets of learning, how active they should be. Because of no "right" way, this part of the chapter can be written only as I perceive and have experienced the trainer role. Others, either within this book as evidenced in the chapter on Intervention Theory, or in other chapters describing different approaches to training, or in other books and articles have described other approaches.

The trainer, whose role is to help the group help itself, must depend on diagnoses based on data he collects from observation of behavior, feelings in himself he is trained to recognize, and data collected by the group to help him determine what interventions and suggestions he should make. He needs always to be ready to test his interventions with others in the group, and accept feedback without defensiveness, whether or not his intervention was correct. Following are thirteen areas where I find that I made interventions, generally to model some appropriate behavior; to report observational data that the group could use, but which no one else had reported; express my own feelings in as authentic a way as I could; bring to the group's conscious awareness norms they have created. I may not intervene in all groups at each of these points, and there may be other points where the data indicate the need for an intervention.

Direction Setting. I tend to start a group with a statement of expectation. I usually say, "I believe we are here to learn all we can and all we wish to about ourselves, others, group formation, and development. We will be together for much of the next ____ days. Further, it is my belief that we can learn most effectively by examining what goes on within the four walls of this room and by looking at our own behavior. I do not intend to lead or direct the group, but I do plan to be as helpful as I can appropriately for our learning together. This group belongs to all of us."

While this goal is clear to me, I also know that it is unclear and ambiguous to the participants. I know, also, even though something like this has been said in the opening session, that few have heard what I said because of their anxiety. However, I believe this is an honest and authentic statement for me to make about my role. I have both modeled openness and indicated that I owned, and was responsible, for my share of the group — that the group belongs to everyone. I feel that my statement makes it possible for me to interact in a transactional way with other group members later.

With no different response from me, although I am often tested, members make various suggestions as to how the group should begin, most of which are met by dead silence because members have not discovered the "appropriate" pattern of response or intervention. Someone usually suggests that persons introduce themselves. This is usually accepted as the customary thing to do, so individuals in turn introduce themselves by naming the organization in which they work, their job title, and the number of people they control. If I am sitting beyond the middle of the circle from the person who started the introductions, and if no one else has intervened, I may say, when my turn comes, that I really learned very little about the persons who have introduced themselves in terms of what I'd like to know, considering that we are to be together so long. I say that I have learned quite a bit about the jobs people have, but little about them. I add that this knowledge forced me to be careful not to stereotype them in terms of the jobs they held. I end by asking if others have felt as I did.

Before those who say anything, who I suspect feel somewhat as I do, others jump in to deny hotly my statement. They say they have learned a lot from learning where people come from and what they do. I forbear to answer because I have no evidence they are incorrect. Furthermore, I have laid a seed which I believe will later be picked up.

If my turn comes earlier in the introduction process, I introduce myself in terms of how I feel about myself, what I find enjoyable in life, the things about myself and others I still wish to learn about, and my family. This intervention often brings the round of introductions to a pause while people discuss what is really desirable to know about others, that by giving only name, rank, and serial number, people are keeping others at a distance. After such a discussion, introductions continue, but on a more sober, less self-serving basis, and the group has learned more than they realize about tendencies to hide behind a facade, and what might really be useful to know about a person.

Helping the Group in the Diagnosis of a Group Problem. There are often points in the group process where a person or event seems to immobilize the group from handling the situation. The trainer, obviously, doesn't rush in to save the group. However, if he recognizes after a period of time that the group needs a model in order to form a norm so that it can handle other problems, he may make an intervention. In a particular group, one large, loud-spoken individual had managed to dominate the group to a point where hardly anyone dared speak, and no one knew how to handle the situation. After waiting for some time for the group to do something, the trainer finally made an intervention. He said,"I've been wondering for some time (seeking data) if other members feel as I do, that Joe has been taking a great amount of the group's time. It may well be that Joe hasn't been conscious of this because no one of us has helped him to realize it. It is not a matter of blaming Joe. Rather it is a question as to why someone did not help him as well as the group. Does anyone have any hunch as to why we did not?"

After Joe had rather defensively explained his actions, gradually people spoke up. A discussion led to the disclosure that everyone waited for someone else to act, that Joe was a rather formidable person physically and vocally, that members were not certain what the ground rules were, and that they expected the trainer to control the group. The trainer laughed and said he was almost sorry he had said anything, because it was a group problem. At the same time, he said that he felt he owned a very small part of the group, like everyone else, and he had been wanting to hear others speak. After some group discussion, intermingled with both defensive and apologetic statements from Joe, there grew a norm about air-time, a concept about helping others talk, and beginning learnings about how to give feedback without arousing over-defensiveness and antagonism. At the end, Joe sort of growled that he guessed this had been one of his problems for a long time, and it was a good thing to get this aired early in the group.

Bringing to the Group's Attention a Situation whose Solution Helped to Create a Group Norm. Usually, there are one or two persons who say nothing the first day or two. Finally, someone tries to bring the persons into the conversation. Often this effort, however well intentioned, may be ineptly and punishingly done. This is where a trainer can collect data about how the silent members felt and how the group felt. He often finds a silent member felt very embarrassed to be called upon at that moment, but that the group was feeling more and more uncomfortable at the silence. Other group members did not know whether the silent member did not like the group, had been hurt by some incident, or just felt superior to everyone else. This pluralistic ignorance was shocking to the group. They became aware of how many buried thoughts and feelings were floating around the group. If many of these thoughts could be shared, they said, everyone would be helped.

After this was talked through, the trainer reopened the conversation as to how a silent member could be invited into the group without punishing or embarrassing him. Suggestions began to be made that the silent member could be asked if he wanted to say anything then, that the group wanted his resources, that they wanted him to feel comfortable. One member said that if everyone was more sensitive to others, they might note a gesture such as a half-opened mouth, a shifting forward that should tell them that individual really wanted to come in, but needed help in doing so. Thus, the role of a gate-keeper — one who helped a more reticent person enter a noisy discussion, was identified.

Assisting the Group to Become Aware of Norms They Have Created. Often, somewhere during the middle of the total sessions, some member in a group will express amazement at how far they have gone as a group, how well they know each other in so short a time — better, someone will say, than they know people back home with whom they have worked for years. This is an excellent place where a question on my part continues a discussion as to how we got this way. The group begins to look at the peaks in their history and I can ask what norm or building structure they created or agreed upon at each peak, whether it was acceptance of each other, finding and using each other's resources, being sensitive to each other's needs, giving adequate air-time to each, or whatever the norm may be. This fairly deep and prolonged analysis of where they started and where and how they have come to the present usually gives most members considerable insight into how groups form and grow. They think of their groups back home and recognize how feedback, carefully given to individuals and the group, can vastly improve their communication and their working more closely with others. They often recall the crisis points in the group back home that have been carefully avoided, so no improvement took place in member or group.

Aiding an Individual to Bring Forth Feelings he has only Partially Expressed. Often a member will express a feeling or an incident very partially, such as putting a toe in the water to see if one should venture further. This is where a member, if possible, or the trainer can carefully help the individual express more of what he is feeling. Non-directive re-expression of the feeling by someone else, a carefully worded and supportive question, a statement that we feel the person has more to say which we would like to hear — and perhaps need to hear for the sake of the group, may encourage the individual to open up more of his feelings or thoughts. Often the expression of feeling can release feelings on the part of another. Certainly, the expression of feeling on the part of one person should usually be checked around the group to collect data about the extent this feeling is shared.

Serving as a Model in Improving the Communication System in the Group. There are usually obvious cues, either non-verbal or verbal, that an intervention has been misheard or not heard in the group. If no member recognizes this or does nothing about it (and the trainer needs always to wait a few moments to see if a member does comment), the trainer can model how a group may improve its communication among its members. First, he may collect data around the group as to how the intervention was heard, explaining that he was not clear what was meant himself. Generally, the data will indicate a surprising number of different interpretations, and even some data showing a few members were not listening. The data collection itself becomes extremely meaningful to the group. Members realize that they may often have been misheard, but did not know it. They are surprised at many different motivational interpretations that were placed on the intervention, but never fedback to the intervener. They begin to understand how one misinterpretation can lead to a further string of misinterpretations. And they understand why ten persons can leave a meeting with almost ten different understandings as to what was decided.

At this point, the trainer can model various ways in which a group can improve its communication, varying from the day's practice of having someone repeat back what he has heard until there is clarity that what is heard coincides with what is said, to feedback about what the listeners heard and what they thought the other meant by making the interpretation at that time, to the uncovering of hidden purposes, to skill in using communicative words. Individuals come to see that often garbled interventions represent some form of ambivalence in the speaker. At the very least, group members are more conscious of the importance of clearing their communication system.

Intervening with Own Feelings, Observations, and Experiences. For me to be authentic and to model authentic behavior for others, I have no hesitation in infrequent crucial situations to express firmly my own feelings, whether of hostility, pleasure, or affection. I expect reactions and feedback, and I am prepared to accept them and consider their correctness and value to what I value as me. I do try to express myself in ways that others can feel equally free to express themselves. Similarly, I feel free, from time to time, to express my observations. I have watched individuals with fists clenched, arms taut, and perspiration on their faces deny that they are having any feelings. I comment on the body signals so clearly shown to all, ask the individuals how they could have no feelings if their bodies were so tense, and invite them to talk about what they are really feeling inside. Members learn that feelings are legitimate facts, that they are always dealing with their whole selves, and that denial of one's feelings is to present to themselves and others only half the data.

Sometimes a report of some incident in my past serves to unlock doors for others. I have noticed in groups of top male executives that masculinity is highly prized. If I mention a health problem I may have had in the past, a dam seems to burst and member after member tells of some serious illness or handicap they have had to compensate for. And their telling seems to release considerable tension in them.

These interventions by the trainer, if overdone or not done at an appropriate moment, may readily increase any dependency present. However, with intuitive feelings and some diagnostic evidence of appropriateness, I find such interventions serve to increase the transactional nature of the group and to reduce dependency.

Confronting a Member Where Confrontation is Necessary. Sometimes it may be necessary for the trainer to confront expressions of hostility by a member who is seeking a fight with the trainer. Usually, I can deal with such an event by calmly asking the individual what I have done to create these feelings in him. Sometimes this is not sufficient. One example stands out in my mind. In one T Group in which I was working with a favorite co-trainer who was himself Jewish, a member, also Jewish, showed from the beginning of the group quite extreme hostility to me and extreme laudatory responses to the other trainer. After several softer efforts to break through this situation failed, I confronted him in a much louder voice than I usually use. I said, "I feel you think I am prejudiced against you because you are Jewish. I feel you are prejudiced against me because I am not. Now, let's talk this through so we can all work as a group." He, and much of the group, were shocked by the vehemence of my voice, but we did talk. As a member of a minority group long accustomed to being prejudiced against, it was a learningful shock to him to discover he could have prejudice against others. Our confrontation left us in good communication for the rest of the session, and beyond, was extremely learningful to him and to others.

Suggesting the Use of Data Collecting Methods where Desirable. No matter how open a group becomes, there is always hesitation in securing verbal data about how everybody feels concerning the group. Conformity pressure in any group, no matter how open, causes some people to "go along with the majority." In many groups, short Post-Meeting Reaction Sheets, each with a few questions, are used, with data sorted and presented back to the group for discussion. Or individual diagnoses can be written on paper, mixed up and read to the group.

There are a variety of simple data-collection devices that are written rather than verbally given that help a group. The trainer can suggest these when there is obvious evidence that true feelings are not coming out. He may even remind the group, if they come to a somewhat similar situation to one faced before, that they tried a certain solution that might work again.

Suggesting Experiential Designs such as Role-Playing, Verbal, Non-Verbal, or Body Exercises to Help a Group Increase its Learning. From time to time, but not too frequently, trainers may find it desirable to suggest an experiential exercise to deepen learning. If used too often, such predesigned exercises may create dependency and reduce learning from the exercises. Sometimes role-playing can enable an individual to see just how his behavior comes across to others, particularly if he plays the role of recipient of his customary behavior. A non-verbal or body exercise may deepen the members' self-awareness of themselves as whole persons with sensory experiences, feelings as well as thoughts, and so widen their horizon about themselves.

Helping Group Members or a Member Control Feedback when it is becoming Clearly Destructive or Over-Sufficient. Because feedback requires both sensitivity and skill, a group may need help in learning how to give feedback that is both laudatory and supportive as well as corrective. Usually, a group is far more cautious of giving hurt to a member, and so frequently shortens the learning for the individual. But sometimes a group or group member may be carried away by intensity of feelings, move into judgmental feedback, or fail to observe that the individual is not hearing any more. Because giving as well as receiving feedback is so sensitive and delicate a skill, it is certainly proper for the trainer to model more appropriate ways of giving feedback. He may help the person giving feedback learn what his behavior seems to be creating. A soft sentence to the individual receiving feedback, such as, "Do you need time now to think about what we have said?" Or, "I am feeling that you may have heard all you wish today. Do you feel that way also?" Or to the feedbacker, "Looking at Joe (the recipient), I am feeling that he has all he can chew over for now. Have you noticed that he does not seem to be listening as intently." Or, "I felt that your last sentence sort of judged Joe, rather than helped him. I wonder if others feel the same way? Let us ask Joe how he felt." In one sentence, I tried to help the feedbacker pause, mentioned only one sentence, thus implying no judgment of the rest of his feedback, asked for validating data from other members and particularly from Joe, who probably had the deepest feeling and perhaps the most valid data.

There may be times when the trainer needs to say to the group, "I feel we have given Joe enough feedback for the moment. Like every one of us, he needs time to mull over what he has already heard."

There are times, also, when feedback to an individual is necessary for the group and may need to be given fairly bluntly. An example: "Jim, I am going to test my feelings with the other members of the group, but I am feeling angry as one member of this group, because you seem to persist in using all the group time for your own purposes, even after a member or members have called you on this, and other members have been rejected after trying to help you with what you describe as your problem. This leads me to wonder whether you are seeking help, or exactly what your intentions are. You could help me not to feel angry if you could help me understand what you wish of us."

Helping an Individual or Group Overcome Over-defensiveness. It is natural and to be expected that in the beginning of a T Group, many members, and the group as a whole, with anxiety about what will happen, keep defenses very high. Individuals can only decrease defensiveness as they improve the depth and authenticity of their communication with each other, and thus, their trust in each other. The reduction of defensiveness comes slowly and gradually. The trainer has a part to play in helping members recognize defensiveness when it appears. As an example, let us suppose the following. The trainer has given a very small piece of observational and feeling feedback to a participant. The participant has responded quickly, saying that his behavior was not as described and that the trainer should not feel as he did. The trainer responds, "You seemed to answer me very quickly, so much so that I don't know how much thought you gave to what I said. Also, no one can really tell anyone else how they ought to feel. How each person feels is how he feels. But my real problem in which you can help me is this. I must have been clumsy in offering you the knowledge of what I saw and how I felt, hoping that it would be helpful to you to know. How could I have been open and helpful to you without arousing your defenses?" The trainer hoped the other would ask what he had done to appear defensive because he was not aware of being so. In this case, the other did not ask the question, but it was not long before members of the group began to discuss defensiveness, saying they usually did not recognize it in themselves, although they could observe it in others. Before long in the group, a norm developed that individuals could gently remind someone else that he, the individual, felt the other to be somewhat defensive. The group also discussed three other points about defensiveness. First, that sometimes a person recognized that he had responded ineptly and wanted to try again to communicate. Second, that everybody had, and needed, defenses and others should have tolerance for each other. And third, that being defensive really cut one off from learning much, both because one really did not think about and consider feedback which could have great learning value, and because others stopped giving any feedback. So the concept of helpful feedback and their individual ability to learn and grow through feedback became the central learning core of the group. As they practiced, with some help from the trainer, they gained skill in a very important art.

Watching for Signs of undue stress or inability to cope with stress in a member; Helping the group help others cope with stress that the individual can handle, and Helping the group handle its problems of guilt when a member copes with his stress in unexpected ways. Becoming more aware of oneself, like any fundamental learning in human behavior and relations to others, is never easy and is frequently painful. Each of us wishes to be liked, accepted, approved of; to have influence and to make contributions. Each of us also faces the problems of liking oneself, and particularly, of having a sense of self-worth. Our hope is that our sense of self-worth, to the extent that we own it, is realistic and accepted by others. Because we so seldom are certain in this life of loneliness and distrust, we hesitate to reveal much of ourselves to others because we fear that self-exposure will bring pain to our image we hope to maintain. Learning about others' feelings and observations of our behavior can be stressful in lesser or greater degrees. Most of us can cope with stress. A few cannot, and they should not enter a learning group. Unfortunately, the inability to cope adequately is seldom known ahead of time by the trainer, and sometimes not by the person himself. Thus, any competent trainer must be clinically aware of evidences of such incapability, rare as it is. He must be able to help the individual, to refer him for competent counseling, and, in some cases, ask him to withdraw from the group. These are rare occasions. What is not so rare, but still uncommon, is for a person to cope with momentarily unbearable stress by bursting into tears, running from the room, pulling back from the circle, burying his head in his arms, all of which may be healthy coping mechanisms. Two problems exist, however, and they require trainer intervention. The person using these unexpected and not socially customary coping responses may feel guilt at what he perceives as weakness rather than as appropriate coping response. The second problem lies in the shock and guilt felt by the group.

If the individual who bursts into tears stays in the room, the first thing the trainer can do is to remain calm, both for the sake of the individual and the group. A reassuring statement, such as, "Tears are a wonderful way of relieving tension, and those of us who can cry when we feel stress are very lucky. It is too bad so many men were brainwashed when they were small children, so they find it difficult to cry now that they are adults. So Sarah is very fortunate to have this release." The trainer may wish to walk across the room to give a hug and a gesture of comfort to Sarah. He then suggests that the group go on with its work while Sarah enjoys the release of her weeping.

Later, the trainer may make a point of talking with Sarah to make sure that she feels no guilt but is conscious of the caring of members, to check what learning took place to reassure himself that Sarah now feels better about coping with any further tension that may arise.

If the person runs out of the room, the trainer's first responsibility is with the group to allay fear and guilt feelings, to talk about the incident so that members see it was not a shattering intervention that caused the situation. He can reflect that different people have different ways of handling situations, and for some, a sentence or a situation recalls for the individual some difficult event in the past the individual cannot yet talk about, even to himself, and so goes away to recover composure. In every group in which I have witnessed this, and there have been few incidents indeed, someone offers to go find the person to make sure she is all right, and the group members breathe sighs of relief but do sit tensely until their emissary returns to report that all is fine, that the person recalled a tragic incident earlier in life that could only be faced alone. Later, of course, the trainer may make a check of the person or report the incident to the counselor of the training community.

For the person who may bury his head in his hands, and after someone may ask if he is feeling ill and receives a negative shake of the head, the trainer may again respond by speaking of the different ways people have of coping with situations, of withdrawing from the group momentarily to think through the implications of a recent statement or event for him.

The trainer recognizes that many an emotional explosion is a measure of some very valuable learning for the person. One of the important learnings from a T Group for many persons is the realization and acceptance that people have different ways of behaving, of coping, of reacting and feeling, and that acceptance rather than stereotyping and judging is a better way of relating to people.

WIDESPREAD USES OF THE LABORATORY METHOD

As mentioned before, the laboratory method is applicable wherever human and social behavior is present, and wherever learning, problem-solving, decision making, conversation, and communication is the pattern of work. This chapter has endeavored to illustrate the laboratory method thus far by describing the creating of a learning environment in a learning group. Now, I will attempt, by a few examples, to illustrate its spread to other settings. These examples obviously are only a few among the very many that could be given.

Two-Person Situation. We have recently moved to a new community, one where the laboratory method is unknown except for a few lurid magazine articles describing training programs in Sensitivity Training conducted by incompetent and unethical trainers. I have faced the problem of finding and selecting those I would like as friends, and of helping to create the climate that would enable our friendships to be more than superficial. With the situation as it was, I felt more responsibility rested on me. One friend in question is a retired M.D. For awhile, in our golf games, we humorously called each other Doctor, keeping our relationship on a pleasant, but not too close, level. Once in awhile, I would ask him a medical question. He would always describe more than I could understand. This seemed a place where careful feedback would help us. One day I said, "Phil, when I ask you a medical question, you always tell me more than I can understand. But I feel very good that you assume that I do understand. You leave me with a great sense of dignity and self-importance. I wanted to let you know how I felt." Without going into our extended conversation, we now compare cases from both a medical and psychological basis. He has read much of our previous T Group book, and so our discussions go both ways, with a much closer relationship.

This episode illustrates the importance and value of creating a climate in which deeper and richer communication can take place. It is safer for each person to play the pleasant, casual game. In this situation, I needed to judge from his willingness to describe so much medical information, both his interest in his subject, his loneliness in having few other medical doctors around to talk to, and his respect and basic liking for me. Given those cues, I could give him feedback that said exactly how I felt, recognized his interest in talking about his field, and still was supportive and congratulatory and asked for more of the same behavior from him. My feedback created a new level of response from him. The essence of this point was that my feedback needed to be congruent with my feelings and specific about his behavior.

Third-Party Relationship. In one company with which I consulted for awhile, the top team finally convinced the president that an executive vice-president should be appointed. He had resisted the idea for some time. Finally, he agreed, and with their help, chose the logical person for the job. It was clear to me as an observer, however, that trouble lay ahead, because I felt certain the president was not really ready to give the new executive vice-president the authority and responsibility be expected. I suggested that the three of us spend a day together talking about perceptions and expectations. I offered to serve as a bridge between them when communication became snarled. After a day in which I was able, as I would as a trainer, to help each see where he was not listening to the other, where he was not clearly communicating his expectations, where he was not being open, the result was of a clearer understanding of responsibilities, expectations, and boundaries. This episode again described the creating of trust in me as a consultant, in the process of looking below the superficial levels of communication, of working on the usually unshared perceptions and expectations that often clutter up communication between individuals.

Team-Building. In this company, there were problems at the top level. The president met separately with two sets of vice-presidents, and the communication between the sets was naturally poor. We agreed to meet for a number of two- or three-day sessions spread over a number of months, after I had had a chance to interview not only the president and all vice-presidents, but a sampling of persons immediately below the vice-presidents.

At our first meeting, after reporting back the essence of my interviews, I stated my expectations, my perception of my contract with the company, and the way I proposed to work. I stated that I believed I was working for the company, not for the president, who may have originally brought me in. I said that it was my belief that every member of the group, president, and all vice-presidents, owned the group and the company to almost the same extent psychologically. It is not the president's company, but the team's company. I said I perceived our task was to examine and try to remove some of the blocks to team functioning. I said, finally, that I would help in their identification of problems, in communicating openly about them, but that I did not have the answers to their problems.

In this case, the interview data reported indicated a number of problems: reluctance of the president to delegate certain responsibilities, rivalry between line and staff vice-presidents and no effort to communicate effectively between them, competition for power, confusion over the reward system, each vice-president feeling responsibility for his division, but not for the company as a whole. The president, who was having a rough time in the meeting (as I had warned him he might), finally "invited" everyone to feel a sense of concern for the whole company. He had felt he was the only one who cared, while the others felt they were not allowed to care.

By working on interpersonal problems, authority issues, intragroup ways of working, meetings they could have before our next team-building meeting, the group finally coalesced. Individuals verbally expressed, and showed by their actions, a greater concern for the company. The president was seen as more approachable, and his ability to take feedback from his vice-presidents (a skill and an attitude I worked on with him privately) did much to develop the teamness necessary for cooperation among divisions.

This example illustrates a number of examples described as occurring in a T Group, and mentioned as basic elements of the Laboratory method. Data collection, feedback to those supplying the data, the role of consultant (like trainer) in developing a contract for his behavior that indicated helpfulness but left the group with the problems of further data collection and problem solution and action, the setting in which the expectation of the development of a team brought forth many different perceptions, expectations, and anxieties to be shared and solved; all were examples of transactional efforts to improve relationships so that work could improve.

Task-Group. In my experience, the procedure in working with a task or work group has many similarities to working on team-building. Here, however, it is my role, as I perceive it, to help straighten out miscommunication where noted, to help bring to the surface hidden agenda held by individuals, and to suggest task roles not being filled, such as insufficient information, the use of critical questions, and efforts to build bridges between suggestions.

This example is in a sense the reverse of the former. Instead of the team jointly seeking interpersonal blocks to productivity, laboratory methods of data collection, feedback, and diagnosis were directed toward unraveling task functions not being fulfilled at the appropriate time for effective decision-making.

A State Organization. This particular state organization was an old one. There were local chapters in most of the towns and cities in the state. In time, a kind of bureaucracy had grown. Many of the same kinds of people were elected on the local level and also on the state level. Most members in the past had joined because they thought they ought to. Now, membership was beginning to fall off. I was asked to come in for a day to help the state and local officers look at their leadership. There was not the time for observation and data collection that I would have wished, but I was able to use half the morning in having small groups make two lists: one, a list of problems they faced in leading meetings in their home towns, and the second, a list of the irresponsibilities they thought members showed (and for which they blamed them). After a coffee break, these lists were copied on newsprint and stuck around the wall with masking tape. People went from sheet to sheet marveling at the similarity of problems. The next step provided a different kind of data collection. A number of volunteers were sought to enter into a role-playing scene of a committee discussing how to involve more members. The role-played scene was held in the center of the room. The rest of the audience, divided into observational teams, surrounded the role-players. One team observed the leader, another the extent to which group members contributed, and how evenly. Other observational teams observed the way solutions were arrived at, and the quality of the decisions. Thus, data were being collected from their own behavior on both task and group process levels.

After all the teams had reported their observations and I had written the salient points on two sheets of newsprint, one for reactions to the suggestions and one for the way the leader conducted the meeting, a long discussion was held.

By this time, much of the day was finished, but there was still time for more work. The audience divided again into small groups, according to size of the community they represented, and discussed ways in which they could involve members more actively in the work of their local chapters. They also shared what they had each personally learned about how to lead a group.

While this was far from sufficient time to train all the leaders, the day did shake audience members up to a considerable extent. I was able to recommend a few nearby trainers to help those chapters who now eagerly wanted to continue in the improvement of their organization.

This example illustrates the extent to which, even with so short a time, methods of experiential learning, data collection and use, observation of own behavior, and planning for action back home can be carried fairly far in one day, insufficient as this is.

An International Conference. Those who have suffered through international conferences where several languages are spoken and where interpreters either have to try to convey the substance of long speeches through ear-phones, or where there is no simultaneous translation, making any speech incredibly long as the speaker has to pause every few minutes while an interpreter translates what he has said, can understand the problems faced in using laboratory methods in conducting a participative international conference.

In this particular conference, where around two hundred persons came from quite a few countries, we had evidence as to who was coming, some time before the conference was held. By questionnaire, written in four different languages, we had information as to the maximum number of languages that had to be considered (many had indicated ability in more than one language). We had information as to the three most pressing problems faced by each person. From this we were able to form a series of problems, about eight in number, and again find by correspondence the first, second, or third choice of a group for each individual.

A previous conference had just ended in the hall we had at our disposal. That conference had used four long rows of tables extending out from a platform, and with chairs at each side of the rows of tables. There was not time to clear the room for our first session, so we merely took away every fourth chair, thus leaving little clusters of chairs — three facing three. As participants arrived and seated themselves, we asked them first to get acquainted with the five others in their cluster, whether or not they spoke the same language. From the rostrum, which we had to use the first night, we explained how the conference would work, as well as hearing a short substantive talk.

By the next morning, we had arranged fifteen tables in the form of a U, but distant enough from each other so that noise would not interfere. Near each table was a stand-up microphone. Each table contained persons who spoke a single language. (English, French, and Spanish were the only languages needed.) Each table had at least one person who also could speak English. Each table was assigned two of the eight basic problems to work on for the conference. At the top of the U were fifteen chairs set at a slant facing one chair for the interrogator. At periodic intervals, each table would send a representative to the front, and the trained interrogator would expeditiously ascertain where the groups were and what problems or tentative solutions had been reached. Any table could also use its microphone to ask questions, clarify, or raise objections to a solution. Then, the representatives would return to the groups which now had knowledge of what the other groups were thinking.

During the two days of the conference, with the participation of all, with periodic collection and sharing of data about progress, recommendations and plans for action came from the conference.

The laboratory method of learning and changing can, as this example illustrates, be used with larger groups and particularly international situations and across language barriers. From the beginning through questionnaire and correspondence, to a more intimate way of getting acquainted, to the imaginative use of space, small grouping, intercommunication among groups as to direction and progress through open interrogation of group representatives — all of these helped to create a truly participative and learningful climate.

SUMMARY

This chapter has attempted to illustrate the utilization of the laboratory method of learning and changing applied in many settings to develop understanding or insight into the behavior of individuals, groups, and organizations. It has concentrated on the T Group as the clearest example of how a trainer (or teacher, consultant, change-agent, manager, member) can assist in creating a climate for experiential, participative learning. But it has also illustrated the applicability of the same principles and methods to various other types of groups and settings.

BIBLIOGRAPHY

1. Bradford, L. P.; Gibb, J. R.; and Benne, K. D. (Eds.); *T Group Theory and Laboratory Method,* Wiley, N. Y., 1964.

2. Dyer, William G. (Ed.), *Modern Theory and Method in Group Training,* Van Nostrand Reinhold Co., N. Y., 1972.

3. Golembiewski, Robert T.; and Blumberg, Arthur; *Sensitivity Training and the Laboratory Approach.* F. E. Peacock, Itasca, Ill., 1970.

4. Lakin, Martin, *Interpersonal Counter-Theory and Practice in Sensitivity Training.* McGraw-Hill, N. Y., 1972.

5. Mann, Richard D., *Interpersonal Styles and Group Development.* Wiley, N. Y., 1967.

6. Rogers, Carl, *Carl Rogers on Encounter Groups.* Harper Row, N. Y., 1970.

7. Schein, Edgar H.; and Bennis, Warren G. *Personal and Organizational Change Through Group Methods,* Wiley, N. Y., 1965.

CHAPTER 6

A SOCIAL PSYCHOLOGY OF LABORATORY TRAINING*

John C. Glidewell

In general, a social psychologist undertakes to create knowledge about the processes and structures by which social systems influence, and are influenced by, individuals. A laboratory trainer undertakes to intervene into the structure and processes of system-individual influences in the interest of training the individual toward the goals of self-awareness, authenticity, sensitivity to the feelings of others, and skill in collaborative, experimental action to solve social problems. A social psychologist of laboratory training ought to undertake to create some knowledge about the nature of the particular interventions into the structures and processes of system-individual influences commonly employed in laboratory training. Accordingly, I propose to review (1) some of the empirical observations made by students of laboratory training processes and settings, (2) some of the empirical findings of social psychology which I would judge to be relevant to or parallel to laboratory training processes and settings, and (3) some theoretical propositions by which one may explain the findings and observations reported.

CONCEPTUAL FRAMEWORK

Following are three groups of concepts stated in quite abstract form. One group concerns the nature of individual motivation; one

*Because of its length, the bibliography for this chapter has been placed near the end of the book as Appendix B. References in the text of the chapter are to selected items in this bibliography.

the nature of social systems; and one the nature of individual-system interactions. These concepts will later be made more concrete, but for now they are set forth abstractly as an orienting background.

The human individual has two needs of special social relevance: (1) effectance needs and (2) affection needs. Effectance needs (conceived here largely after the ideas of White[139]) involve the motivation to cope with one's environment with some foresight and influence. They lead to the development of competence and specialization, and they contribute to a sense of special identity, self-esteem, and psychological security. Effectance motives also lead to conflicts between dominance and submission and to preoccupations about social status and social power.

Affection needs involve motivation to engage in emotionally positive human relations with some dignity and joy. They lead to supportive friendships and particular intimate pairings, and they also contribute to a sense of special identity, self-esteem, and psychological security. Affection motives, in addition, lead to conflicts between love and hate and to preoccupations about social acceptance and social inclusion.

Individuals also develop schemata (conceived here largely after Piaget)[109] or habitual ways of thinking and acting in accord with the demands and possibilities of environmental situations. Schemata are, for the individual, the best learned ways of offering and receiving resources, ways leading in the past to some effectance and affection.

A social system is an arrangement of social components engaged in the exchange and modification of resources in accord with some discernible set of expectations. The exchange of resources is both with the environment and among the components. A component can be a person, a dyad, a group, or other larger sub-system. Resources include objects, motives, feelings, ideas, and skills. Expectations are shared schemata, discernible if not in fact discerned.

The individual-system interaction (resource exchange) is characterized by some degree of complementarity, reciprocity, assimilation, accommodation, and development. Complementarity is the degree to which the resource supplied enables a functional completion of some resources already available to the recipient. If I have pen but no ink and you supply ink, the exchange completes my resources for the function of writing. If both of us come to believe that you have a *duty* to supply ink to me and I have a right to receive it, we have developed a *norm* of complementarity.

Reciprocity is the degree of equity of an exchange, using Gouldner's[64] conception. If I accept your ink and supply nothing in return, there is no reciprocity. If, however, you have no pen and

I supply one, that exchange, together with the first, approaches reciprocity to the extent that the pen and ink are equitably (not equally) valued on some shared standard of comparison. To the extent that we agree how much and what kind of resources make an equitable exchange, we have developed a *norm* of reciprocity.

Again, following Piaget, assimilation is the process by which the expectations of others can be fitted to one of an actor's own schemata — his best learned ways of offering and receiving resources. Accommodation is the process of modifying a schema of an actor to fit some novel or apparently incongruous expectations of others.

Following von Bertalanffy[11] on biological systems and Katz and Kahn[74] on social organizations, the stable repetition of patterns of activities in social systems is conceived as composed of inputs of energy from the environment, transformation of energy within the system, and outputs of energy from the system to its environment. Inputs from the environment may be considered the "investment" of the environment in the system, and the output to the environment, the "return" on that investment. Dependent upon expectations of reciprocity, output must be seen to have a value equitable to input. There is a general trend in social systems to maximize the ratio of input to output and to store energy. There is thus incentive to transform resources during their processing within the system so as to make the resources more useful, more timely, or better located for the environment, and thus to add to their value. This added value returned to the environment reciprocates the value of the resources received and absorbed within the system. Value is a changing social concept, and thus some systems may be privileged and others deprived in the exchange with the environment. I shall argue that, in the short run, social systems engaged in laboratory training are privileged.

Understanding that such abstractions as the foregoing must be connected to more concrete referents, they will be applied, expanded, and further explained as an attempt is made to explicate the nature of the psycho-social aspects of laboratory training.

THE LABORATORY AND ITS ENVIRONMENT

In a very general sense, laboratory training is conducted in an open social system engaged in an exchange of resources with its environment. Specifically, however, most training laboratory members, along with those persons in their environment, have special expectations (shared schemata) which limit the exchange of resources between the laboratory and its environment.

It was Lewin's[88] idea that environmental forces maintained a steady state in attitudes of individuals, and therefore such "unfreezing" of the steady state as a training laboratory required would be possible only in the confines of a separated "cultural island" where the demands of one's usual social duties could be partly suspended. Years later, even when no such isolation was sought, it was observed that after the first days of training, the rate of communication with the environment dropped almost to zero, and a distinct sense of isolation and some suspension of convention were regularly reported. The discontinuity between the laboratory and its environment was also noted in observation that the use of newly developed competencies were applied with difficulty or not at all, on first return to the environment.[28/34] Special linkages were necessary to transfer the skills from the laboratory to the environment.[1/92]

It seems reasonable to say that the exchanges between educational organizations and their environment are probably characterized by (1) an excess of inputs over outputs in the short run, a temporary suspension of duties to the parent system, (2) intense involvement in internal activities, (3) low communication output to the environment, and (4) a discontinuity in the immediate use of newly acquired skills by members on return to the environment.

Excessive *inputs* to educational organizations have been noted by most students of educational sub-systems; for example, Charters,[30] Callahan,[27] Bidwell,[12] Miles,[103] Lake & Callahan.[82] Indeed, the vulnerability of the school to excessive environmental inputs has been more emphasized than the right of the school to an excess of inputs over outputs. On the other hand, low or indeterminate *output* has not been specifically emphasized. Bidwell does emphasize that the prime objective (desired output) of the school is the long-term preparation of young persons for adult status. He also emphasizes that immediate satisfaction (immediate outputs desired) are not generally prime objectives.

A number of social scientists have found evidence of the intensity of attention to the internal processes of educational systems, especially the classical studies of Waller,[138] Gordon,[63] and Coleman,[33] and most recently, Lortie.[94] It is striking that the attempts at organizational development in schools reported by various social scientists in the volume by Schmuck and Miles[119] concentrate quite exclusively on modifying the internal processing (transformation or throughput) within schools as social systems. Perhaps the most clear and compelling evidence of the sparse immediate output from educational sub-systems lies in the everyday experience of the millions of parents who have asked their child, "What did you do at school today?"

My explanatory proposition involves the idea that laboratory training shares a specific special status with all educational sub-systems, probably in all societies. I think one will find, in all societies in which training is done outside primary groups, that the induction of new competencies is undertaken by interaction in temporary sub-systems that receive considerably greater input from the environment than they return output to the environment. The fact that such educational sub-systems are accorded the right to receive more resources than they have the duty to return (a special norm of reciprocity) appears to be based on: (1) the limiting of individual tenure in such systems to childhood or to quite limited time periods; (2) the belief that educational sub-systems should be more vulnerable to the environment than vice versa; (3) the belief that the relevant return on the investments in such sub-systems is to be realized in the remote future.

A related proposition is that the educational sub-system is a special case of the use of temporary systems for tension management. There are many examples of temporary systems: committees, task forces, new product development teams, classrooms, Olympic teams, and doctor-patient dyads, for example. Each such temporary system has some special functions and structures, but all have special properties that make them good instruments for tension management — not tension elimination, just tension management. Resources exchange is faster and transformation is faster. For short periods, people will submit to discomforts to which they would not submit for long periods. Mistakes made in temporary circumstances have less extensive consequences. As noted by Miles,[101] people will take greater risks, examine more alternatives, conduct more experiments, question more norms, and confront more threats in temporary social systems than in long-lasting ones. (For a more complete discussion, see Glidewell.[59/61])

In summary, the training laboratory is a special case of the more general tension-managing, temporary educational sub-systems which are accorded the right (and the vulnerability) to receive more resources from the environment than they have the duty to return to the environment in the short run. In addition, the temporary discontinuity necessitates extensive assimilation and accommodation before the long run outputs are functional.

While it is often hard to do, these relationships between laboratory training and its environment must be kept in mind as attention shifts to the internal processes of laboratory training groups.

THE DEVELOPMENT OF INTERNAL PROCESSES

In the discussion to follow, a T group will be assumed to be a group of about eight to fourteen strangers, not *passant* but temporary, who come from widely different backgrounds and are heterogeneous in age, sex, race, social class, and ethnic identification. It is also assumed that the members differ considerably in the amount and content of the information each has received concerning what sort of behavior is to be expected of a T group member.

Another assumption is that, individually heterogeneous though they may be, the members of the T group are from the same broad culture, so that they have a common language, similar dress codes, dietary customs, and similar beliefs about the perfectibility of man, the influenceability of nature, the allocation of time, and the value of risk-taking.

In fact, not all T groups are composed of heterogeneous strangers from the same broad culture, but this analysis will start from that assumption. Variations from such conditions can be examined later.

An additional and somewhat non-conventional assumption is made. While the decision to join the T group is voluntary for some, involuntary for others, once begun, T group membership becomes compelling to the point that it is almost involuntary. While there are no explicit sanctions against withdrawing from a T group, the implicit ones are painful. The members feel that to withdraw is to show some particularly embarrassing defect of character or personality. It would be most informative to analyze how and why such an assumption is tenable, but for present purposes it remains simply an assumption. Lieberman, Yalom, and Miles[91] found a 10% dropout rate scattered irregularly over twelve of seventeen groups of college students especially recruited for a non-residential, transient situation. In usual residential laboratories, dropouts are considerably more rare. The assumption is maintained, however, in the face of the fact that dropouts do occur.

Conceptually, the temporal processes of developing systems appear in cycles. The inclusion, attraction, involvement, and commitment necessary to the sharing of schemata of explicit rights and duties or of implicit expectations are regularly repeated as social systems generate conflicts of control and support. First, there is a process of prudent exploration of the possible resources available and a developing consensus on the inclusion of the resources. Then there is a "shift to risk" of confusion or embarrassment while negotiating, openly or in disguise, the terms of commitment and some provisional trials of actual resource interchange. As the provisional trials yield rewards — become complementary and reciprocal — commitment is generated. As commitment develops, the resource interchanges take on dependable patterns, and members become differentiated in activity levels, interpersonal attraction, perceived competence, and social power. Commitment always, however, has within it some forces for change. There is always at least a little residual conflict — at least a little doubt about whether the terms of interchange are in fact just or realistic. Further, over time, the value of repeatedly received rewards decreases as a satiation process. Still further, new resources appear — perceptually and factually — and old resources disappear (are used up, work out, migrate). Regularity also produces some plain boredom. Motivation to novelty is strong enough in most people that extended regularity, however productive, gets boring. The result of all these forces is that somebody does something unexpected.

Most T groups are especially adaptable systems. One state of commitment is barely established before it is disrupted. Indeed, it may be inappropriate to say that resource interchanges in a T group ever take on a regular systematic character for very long periods of time. While, to the participants, there are almost intolerably long periods of frustration and inactivity, relative to most learning systems, cycling and re-negotiation in a T group are rapid and diverse.

I shall propose that the most visible phases of the recurrent cycle are (1) prudent exploration at the beginning and following each disruption, and (2) the shift to risk of confusion and embarrassment by taking some position or making some commitment about an issue of certain significance and uncertain outcome. Sometimes the shift to risk concerns one issue, sometimes another. The most common issues are conceived to be (1) flight and fight, that is, the conflict between a climate of protective evasion and a climate of direct confrontation, (2) dependency and autonomy, that is, the conflict between a climate of secure conformity and a climate of insecure independence, and (3) distance and closeness, that is, the conflict between a climate of distant social contact and a climate of close personal intimacy.

Initial Climate: Prudent Exploration

The initiation of any *new* relationship requires one to begin interaction with minimal and fragmented information concerning the nature of the new system and its promise of future effectance and affection. The resources available, the components involved, the expectations in effect — all are vague and fragmentally represented. Existing research gives a reasonably clear specification of the behavior consequent to such minimum and fragmentary information. The participant emits the behavior that in his experience: (1) has been most closely associated with the fragments of information currently available, and thus easiest to assimilate to his existing schemata and easiest to produce; and (2) has been most often "correct."

Consider a simple demonstration of the perceptual processes involved. Suppose you saw a word flashed on a screen so quickly that you could perceive only "WH__E." You could see that there were five letters, but you missed the two middle ones. What was your first impression of the word, "WH__E"? Most likely, it was "WHERE" or "WHILE." "WHERE" is the most common of the words that fit, and therefore the most easily assimilated to the fragment, "WH__E." It is thus easy to produce and most likely to be "correct." Note that there are several possible words that fit, but both intuitively and statistically the most common word in the language usage is the one most likely to be actually on the screen.

Note also that one possible word is "WHORE," a word still taboo for many people. Did it come to mind before you read the last sentence? If it did not, was that because it was taboo or simply because you have not used it as frequently as the word you did think of? Thus, "WHORE" was not as strongly associated with the fragment, and being infrequent, not as likely to be correct.

Under conditions of situational ambiguity and free choice of response to the ambiguity, the effects of frequency of prior association and regularity of prior rewards (two variables themselves positively correlated) have overcome even highly aroused motives and drives. The following studies, while quite specific to visual perception and verbal behavior, are illustrative of a considerable body of empirical research in the laboratory and in the field.

Lazarus, Yousem, and Arenberg,[85] following the pioneering work of Levine, Chein, and Murphy[86] studied the effects of hunger on the responses to ambiguous stimuli, in this case, slides presented for only a fraction of a second, allowing only blurred fragments of the picture to be perceived. Some slides contained food objects, others non-food objects. These fragmentary and blurred visual stimuli are analogous to the minimal and fragmentary information available to the participant at the initiation of a T group.

The slides were shown to subjects who had been deprived of food for varying lengths of time, and, thus, felt hunger of varying intensity. As in other similar experiments, after *longer* periods of deprivation, hunger *did not* affect the responses. Recognition of the stimuli was more determined by familiarity, that is, the frequency with which the object had been seen and correctly named in the past. Ambiguity thus elicited the best learned and most often approved schemata, even overriding conditions of a strong hunger drive.

Confidence in the interpretation was increased by the work of Brozek, Guetzkow, and Baldwin.[23] They analyzed word associations, dreams, and descriptions of ink blots of a group of persons who volunteered to maintain a semi-starvation diet for six months. They found little or no effect of increased food deprivation on word associations, the content of dreams, or responses to ink blots. Again, the main effects upon responses to ambiguous situations were the strengths of past learnings rather than current deprivations. For example, the most common response to "man" was "woman," to "light" was "dark," and so forth. It is reasonable to conclude that ambiguous situations call out the most familiar perceptual schemata and in consequence the strongest associations, best learned skills, and most widely approved behavior (broadest social stereotypes) available to the participant. This behavior is appropriately described by T group observers as "safe" or "cautious" or "restrained." In Bradford's words, ". . . discussion usually wanders in apparent aimlessness from descriptions of events back home to discussions of abstract or harmless topics. . ." (Bradford,[18] p. 197). Miles[99] interpreted the initial behavior to be a process of interpersonal exploration and testing of the situation; Herbert and Trist[69] perceived the process as orientation to the trainer (consultant); Bennis and Shepard[10] saw the process as quick acceptance and of dependence on conventional structure and arbitrary norms; Bales,[4] and Strodtbeck,[6] observing leaderless groups, found a major emphasis on seeking and giving orientation.

I propose that assimilation takes priority over accommodation, and that until some attempt is made to fit new situations into old schemata, little or no attempt will be made to modify old schemata to fit new situations — to accommodate. Accordingly, a new T group, like most new groups, will find its members beginning with a series of offers of the most palpable social stereotypes in exchange for minimal social approval. But first meetings also show high levels of anxiousness and dependency. If the participants behave cautiously, it must be because each anticipates some impending pain, the genesis of "fear and facade."[57]

One of the most dramatic and productive controversies of the psychology of perception has been the set of arguments for and against the proposition that human beings either simply fail to perceive painful stimuli or distort such stimuli so as to preclude the pain. In the "WH_E" demonstration, *where* and *while* are more often given than *whore*. Is that because saying the taboo word is painful?

McGinnies[98] flashed a series of eighteen words on a screen, first so quickly that it was not possible to see even a fragment, then gradually for longer exposures until it was easy to recognize the words. In all presentations, the observers were asked to report a best guess about what the word was. At the same time, McGinnies recorded the observers' galvanic skin response, an involuntary response to emotional arousal. The experiment showed that (1) the taboo words had to be exposed longer to be recognized, (2) the incorrect guesses for taboo words were less similar to the actual words than were incorrect guesses for neutral words, and (3) most dramatically, galvanic skin responses appeared even when taboo words were exposed so quickly that the observer did not report recognizing them. The findings lead one to believe that a person can avoid or distort a stimulus before he is conscious of what the stimulus is. How does one know to avoid it?

Further work showed that many subjects in fact perceived the taboo words but, anticipating embarrassment, felt constrained not to report them until they were quite certain they were acceptable in that situation.[110/141] In the same way, members of a new T group see things that arouse anticipation of embarrassment, but they do not report those perceptions until they are quite sure that the perceptions will be acceptable in that situation. Another finding of relevance to new T groups is that, in the experiments, once it was established by precedent or by instruction that the taboo was to be suspended in the experimental situation, the delay and distortion appeared only rarely.[14/52/77/81/144]

The work of Dulaney[43] has special application to the initiation of T groups. He showed that avoidance learning can produce a special sensitivity, making people see threatening percepts *more* quickly. When in prior experience, on having seen some threatening percept, it had been possible to take some *action* to avoid the impending pain, a special sensitivity developed, leading the person to see such threatening percepts *more* quickly than neutral ones. Clearly, the percept became a cue to take action to avoid impending pain, and the special sensitivity was rewarded by pain avoidance. Dulaney, as well as Eriksen and Browne,[46] also showed that when, following a threatening percept, it was *not* possible to take action to avoid pain, the percept was recognized *less* quickly. Following an analogous line of reasoning, one would expect that, in first meetings of T groups, the members would quite quickly perceive but not mention cues which trigger an avoidance action schema and be slow to perceive and fail to act on cues that were assimilated to a schema of unavoidable pain.

In summary, the experimental findings of social psychology, taken together with the observation of the initiation of T groups, lead, in my view, to the proposition that the initiation of a T group presents the participants with minimal and fragmented information about the situation and its promise of rewards — effectance or affection. The strangeness induces expectations of impending failures of effectance (confusion) and failures of affection (embarrassment). Such a situation calls out overly quick assimilation in the individual, forcing a tenuous fit of the perceived fragments to well established individual schemata, producing behavior which (1) has been most closely associated with the fragments of information available, (2) has been most widely approved, (3) has been effective in avoiding confusion and embarrassment, (4) involves special sensitivity to, but no mention of, cues to act to avoid confusion and embarrassment, and (5) involves denial or distortion of cues signaling unavoidable confusion and embarrassment.

The Climate of Involvement: The Shift to Risk

Threaded all through the foregoing sections is the concept of risk, and more specifically the risk of frustrating two basic motives, effectance and affection. The risk of failure of effectance has been called the risk of confusion, and the risk of failure of affection has been called the risk of embarrassment. The phenomenon now to be analyzed is the shift from prudent exploration to risk of confusion or embarrassment.

Stimulated by the work of Stoner,[125] an increasing number of social psychologists have investigated the processes involved when a person's willingness to take risky actions (or recommend them to others) increases significantly after having participated in a discussion of the problem in a small group. The consensual group decision is more risky than the mean of the pre-discussion individual decisions; and, comparing individual decisions only, the mean of the post-discussion individual decisions is more risky than the mean of the pre-discussion individual decisions. This phenomenon has become known as the "risky shift phenomenon."

The phenomenon has been widely found: with management trainees at MIT,[125] with senior executives,[97] with undergraduates,[136] with industrial supervisors,[115] with professional practitioners,[122] and with grade school children.[79] The shift may well be international in that it has appeared in Israel,[114] in England,[7/51] in France,[80] in Germany[84] and in Canada.[132] The increase in risk-taking has been found after discussion with and without consensus; it has been found where there were no real outcomes to the subjects and where real monetary rewards were gained or lost and where the subjects expected to avoid physically painful consequences.[135] It is fair to conclude that the "risky shift" is quite general.

The work has forced attention to explaining how a new group moves from a cautious, flighty, conservatism to a risky exploration of uncertain consequences. A number of scholars have evaluated the competing explanations: Brown,[22] Kogan and Wallach, [78] Kelly and Thibaut,[75] Dion, et al.,[42] Clark,[31] Pruit,[111] and Vinokur.[134] It is consistent with all prior evaluations to say that somehow involved in the process of the shift to risk are: (1) the influence of some broad cultural value on risk or caution, (2) an initial pluralistic ignorance[118] leading the participants erroneously to believe themselves to be nearer the valued end of the risk-caution continuum than most others, (3) the introduction of information to show that many participants are, compared to others, less risky (or cautious) than they first believed (a disconfirmation phenomenon), (4) a change of individual position by low-risk participants in order to maintain the self-perception of favoring the culturally valued alternative (an accommodation phenomenon), (5) an enhancement of the valued end of the continuum due to the ready availability of well-earned rhetoric to communicate those values, and (6) a reduction of uncertainty about the problem and confidence in one's new opinion. Following is a condensed statement of the evidence relevant to the six processes listed.

The value explanation holds that, given uncertainty about the value of the reward for action and given some kinds of problems, risk-taking is positively valued in Western culture at least, and that, given other kinds of problems, cautious behavior is positively valued. Based upon my interpretation of the work of Nordhy, (sic),[106] Rabow, et al.,[113] Madaras and Ben,[96] Chandler and Rabow,[29] Levinger and Schneider,[87] and Fraser, et al.,[51] risk-taking is valued in problems involving processes believed to be reversible, such as economic, intellectual, and educational processes; and cautious behavior is positively valued in problems involving processes believed to be irreversible, such as marriage, pregnancy, and loss of life. There may be, however, some force exerted by a generalized value on risk, acting in all types of problems. Generally, cautious shifts have not been as extensive as risky shifts, and, as Fraser and his colleagues have suggested, [51] even when the cautious end of the continuum is valued, there is a counteracting force from the more generalized value on risk. The counterforce reduces the cautious shift in extent.

The uncertainty of the value of the reward for taking action is probably critical. As illustrated in the experiment of Zajonc, et al.,[143] where there is a clear and calculable outcome for each stake and level of risk, high risks are valued only when they produce favorable returns on investments. When participants know the exact stake and the exact return, they simply calculate the odds necessary to bring a profit.

In the application of this research to T groups, two of the previously stated assumptions are important: (1) that the members, heterogeneous as they may be in ethnic or socio-economic background, are from the same broad culture, so that they value the same end of the risk-caution continuum; and (2) that the group is composed of strangers, not *passant* but temporary, so that any process involved is short-term, and thus, if not reversible, clearly not permanently binding.

As the group begins, most members believe that they are greater risk-takers than most others, including other group members, as demonstrated first by Hinds,[70] then Pruit and Teger,[112] Wallach and Wing,[137] and Levinger and Schneider.[87] The interpretation is that, given uncertainty about the value of the rewards for action, people generally tend to see themselves as in a position more toward the valued end of the continuum than most others. The value being on risk-taking, the perception of the self will tend to be "more risky than most." The fact is, however, that the group members attribute greater caution to the group than is valid. Some of the members, therefore, are *relatively* less risky than they think.

Once the members make public their risk preferences, and particularly when several members perform acts making them clearly vulnerable to confusion or embarrassment, some of the other members become aware that their perception of themselves as risk-takers is called into question. Their original positions or their actions to that point are more cautious, relative to the actions of others, than they believed. This discovery sets up an imbalance or incongruity for those who thought themselves to be more bold than the current information proved them to be.

In Heider's construction,[68] the participant finds himself firmly if temporarily associated with a group, the group he discovers favors risk (more risk than he thought) while he by misjudgment has favored caution. According to balance theory, the set of relationships is unstable. The participant finds himself under pressure to (1) disassociate himself from the group, generally a most costly action, even in an *ad hoc* experimental group; (2) moderate the risks taken by others, generally in opposition to the pressure of his values; or (3) increase his own risk-taking. The most likely outcome is an increase in the risk-taking of most participants, for example, Miles,[100/102] Bunker,[24] Harrison,[66] Valiquet.[131]

Balance theory thus accounts for changes in those members who underestimated the risk-taking norm, but it would predict a balanced set and no change for those whose original position or early actions showed high risk. The experimental data show, however, that even initially risky participants tended to shift to more risk.[132] While the shift of the initially risky was not as great as that of the initially cautious, the fact of their shift requires additional explanation.

Given that the cultural value is on risk-taking, the most familiar and best learned rhetoric is that urging the valued alternative, risk. Brown[22] first pointed out that a certain kind of rhetoric was regularly produced in the group discussions of risk problems. The language of the dynamic spirit of adventure produces more active, dramatic, and exciting possibilities than does the static voice of caution. The richer rhetoric should provide *any* proponent of risk-taking with a persuasiveness which would influence both the originally risky and the originally cautious participants toward increased risk-taking. Indeed, initially risky participants may be influenced by their *own* rhetoric to increase the risk involved in their individual actions as demonstrated by Festinger & Carlsmith;[49] Brehm;[21] Cohen;[32] Hovland, Janis, and Kelley.[73]

Evidence that the power of the rhetoric of risk is greater than the power of the rhetoric of caution appears to be confined to Brown's[22] report of Nordhy's[106] content analysis of twelve discussions by Stoner's[125] subjects. The analysis revealed a greater *number* of speech segments favoring the direction in which the group shifted than favoring the other direction. The content analysis did not include an assessment of the expressive quality or eloquence of the speech segments. The explanation based upon the power of the rhetoric of risk has plausibility and seems especially applicable to the folklore of risk which surrounds laboratory training, but more systematic empirical evidence of its validity is needed.

Bateson[7] has proposed that some form of uncertainty reduction is necessary to the risky shift. Although I do not argue against the notion that confident people take greater risks, I can find little support for the proposition that increased confidence is a necessary condition for a *shift* to greater risk-taking. I do want to argue that a shift to taking greater risks (or even recommending them) is *followed by* reduction of uncertainty. The reasoning is that (1) pluralistic ignorance (Schank)[118] has been dispelled and new experience (or just information) has shown the position of the real group norm (a consensual validation process has been completed), (2) for those participants who are motivated to equal or exceed that norm, the cultural value has been concretely specified (in the sense that Brown said Parsons meant) (Brown,[22] p. 702), that is, the participant knows just what kind and degree of risky behavior is required to make one an object of generalized respect, (3) enough participants have recommended or actually taken risks to provide a sample of outcomes by which to generalize to other actions at other times, and (4) there has been enough time to resolve any post-decision dissonance existing in those who did take risky positions publicly.

The primary data supporting this position that the shift to risk is followed by reduction of uncertainty is the almost universal finding that (1) individual decisions following a risky shift in a group decision also show a risky shift and, (2) the typical resolution of a post-decision dissonance takes the form of increasing the value attached to the chosen alternative. Thus, risky behavior, once chosen and performed, will be even more highly valued than before the risk was taken.

Given the foregoing data and theory, I propose that the key explanatory concept is *disconfirmation.* The many schemata with which an individual enters a T group include strong, well-learned ones, having much confidence invested from confirming experiences, and weak, not so well-learned ones, having much doubt invested from disconfirming experiences. New disconfirmations unsettle both strong and weak schemata, but unsettling strong ones requires more frequent or more intense disconfirmations.

Disconfirmation, even of weak schemata, is confusing and embarrassing, and it unsettles percepts and concepts. Eventually, it leads even the most defensive to try some new way of perceiving one's environment, physical or social. One seeks a new view of a reversible image or a new view of being helpful. This perceptual shifting is called decentration by Piaget.[108] It involves a shift of attention from the accustomed central aspect of a situation to other aspects less customarily attended. Disconfirmation is also motivating; it leads one to intervene in one's environment in an attempt to produce predictable reactions; a shift to risk. The unsettling of percepts and concepts, the decentration, and the production of newly predictable reactions to intervention — all lead to new percepts, concepts, and then new schemata, in a word, accommodation. "The gains by participants were primarily predicted by variables connected with actual participation. . . unfreezing, active involvement, and reception of feedback." (Miles,[102] pp. 241-242.)

The shift to risk, then, is a response to disconfirmation of schemata, an unsettling of percepts, the decentering of attention to physical or social objects, the grasping of new viewpoints, and the active shift itself is a trial intervention in a search for newly predictable responses.

Such trial interventions can be seen as negotiations among participants to find resource exchanges which will produce the complementarity enabling of new functions and the reciprocal equity in the distribution of the effectance and affection generated by the new functions. Negotiation by trial intervention is often unsuccessful, and, thus, it entails risk of confusion or embarrassment. A shift to the risk of expression of affection may begin a shift to a climate of intimacy, probably the most acutely felt risk. A shift to the risk of expressing hostility may begin a shift to a climate of conflict, probably less threatening than intimacy.

The Climate of Conflict: Psycho-Social Negotiation

"What then gives rise to the need for verification? Surely it must be the shock of our thought coming into contact with that of others, which produces doubt and the desire to prove . . ." (Piaget,[107] p. 204). In any group, each member has an extensive repertoire of resources (objects, motives, feelings, ideas, skills), and each repertoire is unique. To develop jointly satisfactory outcomes of effectance and affection, the members must locate the particular exchanges which each will believe are complementary and reciprocal. A dyad in which each member had only ten resources available must choose from a hundred possible combinations. A group of eight members, each with only ten resources available, must choose from a hundred million combinations. Clearly, no such number of alternatives can be considered; previously developed schemata — imported expectations — adaptively limit the range of resource exchanges attempted. Such previously developed schemata are often disconfirmed in new situations. What one member believes are mutual expectations turn out to be conflicting expectations. People do unexpected things. One can ignore or distort the choice points for only a limited time (Glidewell[60]).

To most human beings, violations of expectations are broken promises. To break a promise is both reprehensible and annoying. While no explicit, current promise has been made in a new group, the well-learned schemata of each member lead him to be confident that "everybody knows" what to expect. For a simple example, everybody expects courtesy. When expectations are not met, as is inevitable in any complex exploration of human resources, each member perceives the others to be breaking promises and interfering with his outcomes. These constructs lead to a definition of social conflicts: a process by which each of two or more antagonists interferes with the outcomes of the others, usually accompanied by hostility.

Typical of the many experiments is the ingenious work of Morton Deutsch.[37/38] During the 1960s he and his colleagues mounted a series of experiments with the "Acme-Bolt Trucking Game." Each participant operated a fleet of imaginary trucks (lights on a board) and received payment for transporting a "load" from origin point to destination. His expense was based on the time elapsed from departure to arrival. Each player might take a long route (and lose money) or a short route (and risk a deadlock with another player on a one lane road). A number of variations were made: in the communication allowed, in the opportunities to interfere with the acts of others (by closing barriers on the routes), in announcing an irrevocable commitment to an action, in awareness of the intentions of others.[39/40/41] The findings confirmed the work of others[36/93/133] in showing that reduced communication inhibited trust and compromise; that consistency in strategy increased trust, shifts in strategy decreased it; that greater opportunities for interference reduced the sum of the payoff to the two players; and that irrevocable commitment to action also reduced the sum of the payoffs.

Opportunities for communication were powerful. If one subject could talk with another, his attribution of intent was more realistic; he had more opportunity to understand the other's schema. With communication, some explicit mutual expectations (joint schemata) could be and were contracted.[47/126/127] The experiments usually ended with simple "turn-taking" structures or individual action followed by some redistribution of group total outcomes. Their findings rarely extended past the first modifications in the simple structures. The experiments shed little light on the new conflicts that arise from frustrations with taking turns or compromising for moderate outcomes.

In a T group, the schema most often and most dramatically disconfirmed is the participants' structure of the trainer-member relationship. It makes a good arena in which to seek an explanation of the climate of conflict and the development of the psychosocial negotiations involved.

While the T group is similar to all new groups in its strangeness and fragmented information, it has one particular ambiguity. The role of the best informed and most experienced person is enigmatic. The trainer is the one person who has had extensive experience in T group. He would, in the customary instructional group, be expected to make his knowledge and experience available to others, and thereby demonstrate and validate the competence base of his status. In fact, typically he *does* identify himself as the trainer and therefore the one person with institutionally legitimized status, with some form of special competence, and with an obligation to value the welfare of the group, as reported by Bradford,[18] Benne,[8] Bennis,[9] Whitman.[140]

The actions of the trainer, however, do not include any prescriptions, instructions, or recommendations specific to coping with the anxiousness manifest early in the group's activities.

Indeed, when specifically asked for instructions or recommendations, he offers some unexpected alternative comment or some counter-request. He or she may explicitly refuse to comply with requests for instructions. Almost all observers of T groups, with the possible exception of Horwitz,[72] have perceived the "authority vacuum" to be a major force acting to induce a shift to risk in dealing with the role of the trainer.

The immediate emotional reaction to the conflict by the participants is righteous indignation. The more dependent participants resent the "irresponsibility" of the leader. The more counter-dependent participants resent the leader's "creation" of the anxiousness felt by the members. Those less concerned about dependency resent the preoccupation of the others with the behavior of the trainer.

As the trainer continues to offer behavior incongruent with the members' expectations, interventions to establish a clear set of authority relationships become more intense. The participants employ most of the classical coping efforts. Some withdraw. While physically leaving the group is too costly, remaining without participating is readily available. Some try to coerce the trainer to offer instructions by accusing him of irresponsible or unethical behavior. The tactic most difficult for the trainer is the participant's withdrawal of respect for the trainer. A trainer with strong status needs finds this form of manifest group-trainer conflict most distressing.

Underlying these emotional activities is a powerful schema: a simple power structure. The trainer in the schema gives clear instructions and explanations, indeed he has a *duty* to. Accordingly, the participant has a *right* to receive such instructions and explanations. The trainer expects conformity to his instructions and efforts to understand his explanations; indeed, he has a *right* to such acceptance and the participant has a *duty* to supply such acceptance. Conformity and effort are usually considered insufficient to compensate for the expertise invested in the instructions and explanations, and participants also supply money.

Trainer	*Participant*
Duty: Supply clear instructions and explanations	**Right:** to receive clear instructions and explanations
Right: to receive conformity and effort to understand — plush cash in payment	**Duty:** to supply conformity and effort to understand — plus cash in payment

This simple structure has a long and honorable social history as a fair exchange in teaching or training, in which the expertise of one person is made available to others. Clearly, the expert has "expert" power as defined by French and Raven,[53] but equally clear, the other (learner) has "legitimate" power to demand clear and effective instructions and explanations. The apparent (but not real) abdication of power by the trainer disrupts the simple structure. The trainer does not exercise his power to exact conformity to his instructions. What is more disruptive is that this trainer behavior dissolves the *legitimate power of the participant* to demand clear instructions and explanations from the trainer.

The disruption also dissolves a less apparent but critical *indirect* participant power. Within the schema of the simple structure, each participant may potentially exert great influence on other participants through the trainer — greater influence than he could exert directly. If the trainer accepts his duties under the simple structure, he can offer little resistance to one participant's demand for proper instructions to all participants, and those trainer instructions require greater conformity from other participants than any direct influence attempt by the one participant. As Freud[54] pointed out, a group member increases his influence over other members by identification with the leader. Thus, both the direct influence of the participant on the trainer and the indirect influence of the participant on other participants is disrupted by the trainer's unexpected behavior. The central position of the trainer in this assumed simple structure makes his disruptive behavior particularly disorganizing.

The resentment toward the trainer often leads a participant to seek alternative sources of guidance. Because leaving the group is excessively costly, the available alternative sources of guidance lie in the other participants. Thus, any participant with motives toward dominance may find himself moving to provide such an alternative to the trainer. At the point of such a move, the participants find themselves confronted with what is often perceived as a classic power struggle. Underlying the struggle is the varying but pervasive effectance motives of the individuals and a fundamental paradox of social integration. "What poses the paradox of social integration . . . is that the impressive qualities that make a person a particularly attractive and valuable group member also constitute a status threat to the rest," (Blau,[15] pp. 43-45). Blau's explanation gives a great deal of attention to the pressure exerted by the cognitive schema of simple power structure and the response of the individual who is motivated to demonstrate his competence, to exercise influence, and to withhold deference to others. Usually, there are participants with other motives, as Schutz,[120] Aronoff and Messe,[2] and Lieberman, Yalom, and Miles[91] have demonstrated. For example, a person with strong dependency feelings and strong motives toward psychological safety, would react to the challenge of individual claims in the competitive situation with reluctance to take initiative or to display his competence or otherwise to take the risk of being confused or embarrassed, and thus discredited. The heterogeneity of the group membership, therefore, enables some members to compete for status and esteem while others supply status and esteem, but do not themselves bid for it.

For the participant with great safety needs, the situation often calls forth behavior quite the opposite of bids for status; the participant displays his weaknesses. As the others sympathize with his misfortunes or are reassured by his self-depreciation, they are attracted to him by the implied appeal for acceptance and relief from status threat. The differentiation into a simple structure is the consequence of the existence of one person with esteem needs and many persons with safety needs. But in the counter-dependent T group, there usually are a number of persons with esteem needs, and each tends to interfere with the other's outcomes by withholding esteem. This situation requires a more complex power structure.

One of the important outcomes of the researches by Thelen and his colleagues[124] was the identification of an emotional culture in which fight was used to deny dependency. The participants persisted in fighting with each other for the control of the group, a persistence so extreme as to indicate a denial of underlying feelings of dependency. In the course of a study of problem-solving groups, [58] several such emotional cultures[13] were manifested by reports of the participants on questionnaires, sentence completion tests, and content analysis of the products (problem-solutions) of the groups.

The counter-dependent groups

> employed the fight modality to suppress their strong valency to dependency (as shown by responses to the sentence completion test) . . . to make use of or even give attention to the ideas of the leader. [The members reported that] they were much more inclined to show off their own ideas than to integrate several ideas into a problem situation. They engaged in frequent arguments, seeming to be more interested in winning a debate than in reaching an agreement. First one member dominated the group; then another. Their opinions flowed freely, but as a group, they rejected opinions, demanded authoritative contributions, but accepted little or nothing as authoritative. There was a steady flow of ideas, but, while many ideas were produced, they were often in conflict.

The persistence of such a power conflict leads to the question of whether the conflict serves any psycho-social function. In his remarkable set of essays on conflict, Georg Simmel[123] proposed that "contradiction and conflict not only precede unity, but are operative in it at every moment of its existence," (p. 23). In his elaboration upon Simmel's ideas, Lewis Coser[35] asked, "If conflict unites, what tears apart?" (p.73). Coser answered his question by proposing some conditions leading to disruptive conflict and other conditions leading to unifying conflict. He proposed that conflict was disruptive in groups with close, intimate relations, diffuse functions, high emotionality, unchanging status structures, assigned status, and some legitimized inequities in rewards. In such groups, conflict was especially disruptive if it was conflict over the core values and reasons for existence of the group. On the other hand, he proposed, conflict is unifying in groups with distant, loose relations, specific functions, low emotionality, flexible status structures, achieved status, and no legitimized inequities. Further, conflict was more likely to be unifying if it was a conflict over peripheral values or over means of achieving the agreed-upon ends of the group.

Most T groups, after a few meetings, can be characterized as showing high emotionality, close relations, and diffuse functions. Thus, there is danger of disruption from conflict. On the other hand, T groups also show achieved status in a flexible structure and do not consider inequities in individual outcomes to be legitimate. This second set of characteristics would lead to unification from conflict. In addition, the danger of serious disruption from conflict is mitigated by the fact that the intimacy has a special character, which while strongly felt, does not produce the long-term binding commitments for support that are common to the family group which Coser had in mind. Accordingly, based on his theory, one might predict that overt conflict would, in spite of the high emotionality and diffuse functions, contribute to and be a part of the development of unity in the pattern of resource exchanges and the feeling of solidarity in the members of a T group. If so, just how does it happen?

Consider first the instrumental outputs of a conflict over power. Each aspirant to power finds himself challenged to defend and strengthen the validity of his point of view. Accordingly, he develops and tries to present as varied a support for his opinions or proposals as he can muster. This is a significant shift in the basis for verification from "authority," that is, from the position of the person advancing an opinion, to "plausibility," that is, to the basis in knowledge or observation of others. It represents the beginning of a shift from legitimate power, based on institutional position, to competence power, based on some form of expertise.

Of significance also, is the wide range of ideas produced even if not much considered. The climate of prudence restricts the extent of the repertoire of resources considered relevant (potentially complementary and reciprocal). The climate of conflict extends the repertoire of resources considered relevant.

The expressive outputs of conflict also contribute to its developmental functions. As conflict accelerates, psychological safety is steadily more precarious. Such heterogeneous groups as T groups include some members with strong needs for psychological safety. Those members are regularly shifting from fight to flight. They change the subject, make a joke, call for a recess, or make overly intellectual analyses of problems. Such acts temporarily relieve tension, and such tension-relief allows for some relaxation in the defensive posture of the antagonists. Such relaxation may extend the receptivity of the antagonists so that each becomes aware of the divergent ideas of others.

Conflict fundamentally requires that each antagonist interfere with the outcomes of others; it is therefore quite costly. In its most extreme forms, the antagonists invest more energy in reducing the outcomes of others than in increasing their own outcomes, and the total outcome is negative. There is a limit to how long the antagonists can continue to suffer losses. It is the cost of conflict which is its primary limiting factor.

As costs mount, collective outcomes are reduced, the group experiences no progress, and breaks appear in the vicious cycle of mutual attack. As the breaks in the conflict appear, a few members offer support to one another, support of an opinion, of an action, of a proposal, even support of the self-disclosure involved in the active fight behavior of the more competitive antagonists. Such support provides the beginning of shared regard; the recognition of the wide range of divergent ideas; the extension of the resources potentially complementary and reciprocal; a beginning of awareness that varied and complex resources are needed. The extended repertoire of explicit resources is brought into active consideration; assimilation to old schemata is more and more difficult; the conditions for modification of old schemata are excellent. Accommodations appear, at first in awkward fragments, and then in coordinated actions.

Empirical work is sparse, but that which exists supports these proposals. Blau[16] found that agents in a government office *could* benefit from an action that reduced outcomes of the total group, and thereby could take an exploitive action. If, however, *all* the agents took the exploitive action, no one benefited (subordination vs. impasse). The norms of the agency constrained the agents to sacrifice a possible personal advantage for the advantage of the group. Explicit approval of conforming to such norms added to the relative value of subordination to group norms by adding approval and respect to the inherent outcomes from the exchange governed by the normative control. In addition, Thibaut and Faucheux[127] found that inequities in outcomes (allowing exploitation by one member of a dyad) led to "contractual" norms, limiting the degree of exploitation possible. It seems reasonable to conclude that the costs of conflict — experienced or anticipated — lead to norms limiting exploitation and enhancing common group outcomes. Normative control, thus, becomes attractive.

The foundation of the attraction-based power appears to be the attraction and trust which is developed from the experience of normative control — shared personal sacrifice in the interest of the group. When each participant has felt the benefits of others' sacrifice of personal outcomes for the common group outcomes, a sense of trust and a feeling of camaraderie develop. The solidarity is similar to that of soldiers surviving combat or victims surviving a disaster by the self-sacrificing efforts of many members. Thus, trust, more than competence, becomes the basis for influence. Mutual regard and peer relations become the new theme of the group. Power struggles become passé.

The Climate of Solidarity: Psycho-Social Reassurance

If the climate of conflict can be generated by counter-dependency, the climate of solidarity can be generated by counter-hostility. If conflict brings disconfirmation of discrepant schemata, solidarity brings confirmation of shared schemata.

Melvin Feffer[48] asked a variety of persons to make up a story about an ambiguous scene. When they had completed the story, he asked each to re-tell the story several times, each time from the viewpoint of a different one of the characters included in the first story. He analyzed these stories to bring out the extent of social decentering. Some people rigidly maintained the original viewpoint, while trying but failing to shift to the perspective of a different character. Some told discontinuous or contradictory stories as they shifted to the perspective of a different character. Some people achieved a synthesis of the number of different viewpoints.

Feffer found an increase in social decentering with age in children from six to thirteen. He also found, in college students, that ability to decenter was associated with success in the "Password" game. The game requires each partner in a pair to guess a word known to his partner, using as cues the one-word associations of the partner. In general, the capacity to take the viewpoints of the other persons is critical to the process of accommodating one's schemata to fit data from novel social experiences. I shall argue that a climate of solidarity is one necessary condition to learning how to take the viewpoint of others. In the first place, a climate of solidarity provides one with viewpoints sufficiently similar to make such social decentering easy. But more important, it provides the consensual validation and mutual support needed to confront the real individual differences which also provide a basis — as I shall explain — for a solidarity based upon mutual aid.

The first step in the argument is simply to point out the fact that sheer proximity generates attraction and interaction. Similarity of personal characteristics also generates attraction and interaction. The social interaction thus generated exerts a powerful force toward agreement and homogeneity of perception, attitude, and behavior. The seminal work of Sherif,[121] Asch,[3] Schachter,[117] and Newcomb,[104/105] has often been cited. Both theorists and empiricists have confirmed these homogenizing effects of proximity, similarity, and interaction: Lundberg and Beazley[95] on a college campus; Festinger, Schachter, and Back[50] in a housing unit; Gullahorn[65] in a corporation office; Newcomb[105] in a student rooming house; and Kendall[76] in a medical school.

Social solidarity is generated by, and in turn generates, homogeneity of tastes, attitudes, dress, sympathy, liking, and trust. In a sense, a climate of solidarity is the overt manifestation of the underlying quest for trust, as has been analyzed in detail by Gibb.[56] The climate of solidarity in a T group emphasizes similarities of all sorts: motives ("We're all here to learn"), feelings ("All of us really like each other"), beliefs ("We think alike about basic issues"), skills or lack of them ("Everybody has problems of communication").

One would expect powerful social influences on self-perception. In a carefully developed analysis of the stability of self-perception in interpersonal interaction, Secord and Backman[116] have made a convincing argument, reasonably supported by empirical observation and experiment, that a person is an active agent in seeking, inducing, and imaginatively constructing a congruence between his perception of himself and his belief about how others perceive him. Both assimilation of new data to old percepts and accommodation of old percepts to new data are involved, but an attempt to see one's self as others see one, an attempt to take the viewpoint of others, is an indispensable component of the maintenance of self-consistency.

Solidarity, however, can be based on differences. Laken,[83] Thibaut and Kelley,[128] Homans,[71] and Blau[15] have elaborated upon the concept of exchange contained in Durkheim's[45] explanations of solidarity based on complementary differences. In fact, the homogenizing effects of a climate of solidarity are as overstated as is the similarity of the participants in such a climate. One of the closest of social ties is generated by a complementary interchange of resources. Each participant, because of his different resources, supplies another with motives, feelings, or skills which the other could not supply for himself; esteem motives in exchange for safety motives, supportive affection in exchange for prudent apprehension, instrumental skills in exchange for expressive skills. But the demands of the climate emphasize the homogeneity, de-emphasize or indeed deny the complementary heterogeneity.

As Brown[22] pointed out, there are some inherent conflicts between solidarity and status. Solidarity emphasizes similarities and status emphasizes differences. Accordingly, in a climate of solidarity, differences in status, power, and competence are left implicit or overtly denied. Friedlander,[55] in interpreting factors emerging from an analysis of a questionnaire about interaction in a T group, found that most items on a factor reflecting trust were negative: "There is a destructive competitiveness among the members of the group. . . . Others in the group are reluctant to sacrifice ideas so that the group may agree." Trust was evidenced by a *negative* response to such items. It thus appeared that the participants defined trust by what it was not, and trust was *not* differences in competences among participants. The one positive item was simply and generally stated, "There is trust and confidence in each other among the members of the group."

All the students of T groups whose work was reviewed included some account of a time (albeit sometimes quite short) when the primary activity was some expression of mutual support, interpersonal attraction, group solidarity, and loyalty of the individual to the group. Concurrently, the participants avoided conflict, denied hostility, and tolerated wide variations in individual behavior so long as the behavior did not endanger the solidarity of the group.

When it follows resolution of conflict, solidarity can be generated by a communicated joint personal sacrifice in the interest of the group (Bonachich,[17]). When it follows prudent exploration, solidarity can be generated by a need for establishing shared expectations of valued outcomes — a basis for confirming the importance of the group to the individual.

Thelen and Dickerman[129] observed a "love feast" of mutual affection, Miles[99] reported a phase of group cohesion and individual identification with the group, Hearn[67] identified a stage of group solidarity and support, Bradford and Mallinson[19] described a period of reorganization and repair following conflict. According to Tuckman,[130] "While the social function of the . . . stage is to cause a unique and cohesive group to emerge, the task function is to attempt to use this new structure as a vehicle for discovering personal relations and emotions by communicating heretofore private feelings," (p. 390). Burke and Bennis[26] found, over time, T groups, increased congruence of a participant's perception of himself and the perception of him by other participants. Both perceptions changed, but perceptions of others more than perception of self.

I shall propose, as I have elsewhere,[62] that a necessary condition for the accommodation of old schemata to new data is a secure basis of self-esteem, a kind of platform of schemata providing for assimilation of experience to core percepts of self in relation to others. Social order is generated by shared expectations — shared schemata for predicting valued outcomes. It is a necessary condition for predicting consequences of one's actions; it is *the* basis for social foresight and personal security. The climate of solidarity provides this core of personal security around which vital schemata can be disconfirmed and experiments with new behavior can be mounted.

To generalize a bit further, a climate of solidarity is based upon a sense of mutual trust and dependability. I think that dependability is the key connection between social order and personal security. Security comes from experience — experience showing that others are committed to the agreements they have made to the goals of the system. Commitment is shown by doing the things one is expected to do at the time, in the place, and in the manner expected; in a word, by conformity.

Commitment which is nothing more than conformity results in a very rigid system, and security has a high cost in dependency. Commitment also means doing *unexpected* things that one believes will turn out to be good — to improve the accommodation between the individual and the system — to move the system further towards its ultimate goals. Confidence that psycho-social experiments will yield valued returns, and willingness to participate in such experiments, is a form of commitment. It is, however, a less rigid basis for social commitment and personal security.

Within a rigid system or a flexible one, solidarity emphasizes similarity, and the dynamic for change inherent in the climate of solidarity is the energy invested in the avoidance, denial, and disguise of individual differences. Eventually, a limit is reached, and the differences as well as the similarities are perceived. Interpersonal aversion is seen as well as interpersonal attraction. Somebody does something unexpected. Again social change is generated, the group re-cycles, and a new climate of prudent exploration begins the process of re-negotiation of rights and duties.

The Climate of Work: Psycho-social Tension Management

Coordinate with the two fundamental needs for effectance and affection are two fundamental requirements of coordinated individual actions: social control and social support. Underlying the individual motives and the social requirements are fundamental conflicts. Effectance may reduce affection; control may reduce support. Social organization in general is some sort of compromise whereby interdependent individuals sacrifice one for the other: effectance for affection, and *vice versa*; control for support, and *vice versa.*

The norms of complementarity and reciprocity take the forms of felt demands from, or obligations to, one's fellows: one must offer some resource "A" (praise, criticism) at the time "A" (following a well-meant blunder) to person "A" (a friendly blunderer). These demands, however, are often in conflict. Does one offer praise, and risk the repetition of the well-meant blunder? Does one offer criticism and risk despair or evasion? Sometimes one's most effective and discerning contributions avail nothing simply because they cannot be heard. So sometimes one's most humane consideration avails nothing because blunders are reinforced and repeated. Effectance and affection needs are thus often in conflict.

Similarly, there are conflicting group demands for both short-term outcomes (that is, peace) and long-term outcomes (resolution of real issues); for spontaneity and for foresight; for openness and for consideration. Such conflicts create tensions in the system and psycho-social climates evolve to facilitate one demand while suppressing risk, risk suppressing prudence; control suppressing support, support suppressing control.

In some groups, one can trace the social compromise through repeated cycles of prudence and risk, of control and support. Each phase of the cycle sets out a demand for what the last phase suppressed. Such cycling of conflicting demands, I propose, is one fundamental form of tension management.

By the term, tension management, I mean some social process or structure which enables a social system to continue its work while under tension from conflicting demands. By work I mean the continuing input, exchange, transformation, absorption, and output of resources. A climate of conflict enables some progress toward accommodation of disconfirmed schemata about the exchange and transformation of hostile feelings, but it suppresses affection. A climate of solidarity enables progress toward accommodation of disconfirmed schemata about the exchange and transformation of affectionate feelings, but it suppresses hostility. Movement through cycles of psycho-social climates *enables* more resources to be exchanged and transformed. Even though tension management devices do not directly accomplish any conflict resolution, they do enable the work which is a necessary if not sufficient condition for conflict resolution.

Cycling is a social *process* for tension management; a temporary social system is a social *structure* for tension management. The temporary nature of the T group is itself a tension management device. Significant modifications of self-awareness are full of intra-personal conflict and are thus tension producing. A temporary system limits the duration of such tensions. As indicated at the outset of this article, for short periods of time, people will submit to more discomfort, take greater risks, conduct more experiments, confront more threats, express more affection. The reason is clear. The consequences are less extensive. When the system is disbanded, one may choose to continue or discontinue any innovation in personal style, any new schemata of interpersonal relationships. The main point is that cycling and temporary systems, both time variations, are tension management devices, necessary if not sufficient for a climate of work. As groups move through various psycho-social climates, a variety of tension management methods evolve and may become incorporated into the shared schemata about the rights and duties of the member roles.

In a new group, and, therefore, often a part of a climate of prudent exploration, pairing is a common tension management device. The essence of pairing is simplification. In the confusion and embarrassment of coping with a strange situation, it helps to take recourse to the simplest of social systems: the pair. Further, pairs are more supportive, allow but do not demand more individual activity, and can be more intimate in privileged communication of embarrassing feelings or confusing ideas.

In a climate of conflict, gamesmanship is developed as a tension management device. One way to cope with the destructive aspects of fights is to pretend that the fight is a game. It is not an accident that much of the theory of interpersonal and intergroup conflict is couched in the form of a theory of games. In the face of a sure expectation that a group *must* evaluate its work, and thus *must* criticize its members' actions, the demand can be given the form of a non-serious game. Thus, critical attacks are possible in spite of the real tensions created by the conflicting demands for both attack and support. "Leveling is the name of the game," in a climate of conflict.

In a climate of solidarity, special supportive roles are discovered and developed. Considering that T groups, like most groups, must confront members with experiences disconfirming individual schemata, the members go through periods of confusion and embarrassment when the inherent conflicts of the group become the personal conflicts of the individual. At such times, members seek some short-term special affection, support, and reassurance about the possibility of more gratifying long-term outcomes. By personality or by the strength of the demand, special supportive roles are taken. Sometimes individuals find the role rewarding and become "group counselors." Sometimes individuals not usually drawn to the role by temperament perform it intermittently when it is clear that nobody else can perform their role. The slow but relentless power of this demand was shown in Lieberman's observation[89] of a group from which persons drawn by personality to supportive roles had been excluded. Such supportive roles — in helping dyads and helping triads — represent another form of tension management, enabling continuation, under stress, of work — disconfirmation of old schemata and accommodation of the old schemata to newly seen possibilities of resource exchange and modification. I have given special attention to such helping subsystems in a previous paper.[62]

The most sophisticated form of tension management is a flexible, complex social structure. In more enduring social organizations, the conception of development involved increases in size, as measured in number of people or quantity of output; increases in wealth, as measured by the quantity of resources owned or controlled; increases in autonomy, as measured by independence of environmental changes; and increases in adaptability to both internal and external changes. In a small, temporary T group, isolated from its environment, the concept of development involves increases in the proportion of resources of individual members that are included, involved, and committed to exchange and modification. Such a form of development requires frequent modification of expectations — accommodation of shared schemata to new ideas about what are complementary and reciprocal exchanges. Such flexibility requires sensitivity to subtle cues about expectations.

Duncan[44] has reported a remarkable study which explicates the common use of subtle cues, of which the participants are often unaware. The fact that participants usually take turns in speaking is commonplace, but few participants are aware of just how one knows it is his turn. Duncan made videotape recordings of nineteen minutes of two interviews of two participants each. He made a detailed, written account of segmental phonemes, intonation, pitch, juncture, intensity, and body movements of each participant (work requiring the better part of two academic years). The quite comprehensive analysis identified six turn-taking cues: (1) rise or fall of pitch, (2) drawl on a final or stressed syllable, (3) termination of any hand gesticulation or relaxation of a tensed hand position, (4) appearance of a stereotyped expression such as "or something," "you know," and "like that," (5) drop in loudness, and (6) completion of a grammatical clause. While the appearance of one cue was not enough to insure smooth turn-taking, the appearance of one or more cues was followed by a smooth turn-taking (no simultaneous speaking) in eighty-one of eighty-eight observations — 93% of the time. Thus, subtle, extremely subtle, cues account for the distribution of "air time" in a dyad with remarkable regularity but little awareness.

In a similar fashion, experienced T group participants develop implicit consensus on cues for expected actions which influence much behavior, even though the participants often are not aware that such influences exist. By the usual definition of norms — explicit agreements about how members should behave — such influences are not norms. They are not explicitly agreed upon. They are, however, discernible if not discerned expectations. As with cues for taking turns in speaking, the subtle cues are usually multiple and flexible. In Duncan's work, the appearance of multiple yielding cues did not automatically result in an attempt to speak by the listener. It simply insured that, if he did attempt to speak, he would not be interrupted. Given even five or six yielding cues, the listener chose to speak only half the time. Considerable individual discretion was involved. Similarly, in a complex psycho-social structure, considerable individual discretion, and thereby considerable flexibility, is involved.

Attempts to define and specify the dimensions of psycho-social structure have been consistent in retrospect; for example, in the findings of Bales,[5] Newcomb[105] and Willard and Strodtbeck.[142] The findings converge on activity and interpersonal attraction, and perceive competence as significant dimensions of psycho-social structure in small groups. Social power is a derivative of activity, attraction, and competence, either directly or through the specification of roles and positions. In a more flexible and complex psycho-social structure, less attention is given to social power as simply power, and more attention is given to its sources in activity, interpersonal competence and interpersonal attraction.

Because the complex structure is based upon subtle cues of which participants are often not aware, the risk-taking of the individual in the T group is often quite different from his actions elsewhere. The output to society — "transfer of training" — from the T group to other settings is disjunctive and difficult. The transfer is often easier to an intimate, close, simple social system (such as a pair), because the simplicity and intimacy allow for attention to subtle cues. A participant may say, "The T group had a profound effect upon my personal life, but little effect on my work life." The difference is in the opportunity for and the *legitimacy* of attention to subtle cues. As demonstrated by Bunker and Knowles,[25] when T groups continue over longer periods (within some unspecified limits), the discontinuity is less abrupt and the transfer is more extensive. The longer time limit allows for a more clear and explicit awareness of the subtle cues and the complex social structure. Application to even a repressive social organization is possible when the key still is awareness of the subtle cues that appear in both T groups and the repressive organizations.

In summary, coping realistically with the conflicts inherent in both life and T groups requires tension management processes and structures such as cycling and pacing, pairing and counseling, gamesmanship and non-serious interaction. The most sophisticated form of tension management is a flexible, complex social structure, based upon activity, attraction, and competence, and adaptable to a wide variety of social functions.

SUMMARY STATEMENT

The training laboratory is a special case of the more general tension-managing, educational, temporary social systems which are accorded the right (and the vulnerability) to receive more resources from the environment than they have the duty to return in the short run. Such systems generate experiences which confirm and disconfirm existing schemata, focus intensively on internal processes, and manage high levels of tension often connected with the process of decentration — the shifting of attention to new aspects of interpersonal relations.

The initiation of a T group presents the participants with minimal and fragmented information about the situation and its promise of rewards — effectance or affection. The strangeness induces expectations of impending confusion and embarrassment. Such a situation calls out overly quick assimilation in the individual, forcing a tenuous congruence of the perceived fragments with well established schemata, specifically, producing behavior which (1) has been previously most closely associated with the fragments of information available, (2) has been most widely approved, and (3) has been effective in avoiding confusion and embarrassment.

Such a prudent activity, however, denies, distorts, or disguises some motives, feelings, ideas, and skills. The accumulation of such discordant data eventually generates disconfirmation of existing schemata. Participants experience an unsettling of percepts, a decentering of attention from one central aspect to a new central aspect, a shift to a risk of confusion or embarrassment. The decentration generates provisional changes in impressions of personality, in beliefs about the rights and duties of group members, and in patterns of resource exchange (interaction). The risky provisional new actions are often unsuccessful in inducing expected responses; many participants find their expected outcomes interfered with by the actions of others. The shift generates a climate necessary to experiment with the problem for which the group has the best resources; that is, conflict for a group with skills in negotiation, and awkwardnesses with affection, solidarity for a group with skills in personal support, and awkwardnesses with negotiation.

The climate conflict often takes the form of the classical problem of social control. If all participants interfere with the outcomes of all others, all lose effectance. An impasse results. If some participants provide resources, but receive none, exploitation arises. Critical and hostile interpersonal perceptions are exchanged. Decentration is from unidimensional power to multidimensional power. Peer relations with exactly equal power grow attractive, but are seen to be unrealistic. The most rewarding solution is normative control, allowing temporary subordination to a participant with especially valued resources or especially poignant needs, but contractually precluding exploitation and requiring sacrifice of individual advantage in the group interest.

The shared experiences of personal sacrifice in the interest of the group often lead to a sense of mutual trust and solidarity. The experiences of personal sacrifice also generate a consensual validation of schemata about the rights and duties of T group members, with little differentiation among members, adding to a feeling of camaraderie and identification with the group. With respect to skills, persons with a similar level of skill engage in social comparison processes and supportive interpersonal perceptions are exchanged. If the comparisons yield non-supportive impressions, they tend to be denied, suppressed, or disguised. The schema of personal sacrifice, solidarity, and consensual decision-making are confirmed. As mutual aid is needed from different participants, attraction based on individual differentiation appears. The participants see more clearly the conflicts inherent in the needs to influence and effect one's environment and the needs for love and affection, the conflicts inherent in the requirements for social order and the requirements for social support. Conflict and consensus, prudence and risk, are generated in shorter cycles.

Coping realistically with the conflicts requires tension management processes and structures such as cycling and pacing, pairing and counseling, gamesmanship and non-serious interaction. The most sophisticated form of tension management is a flexible, complex social structure. Based upon subtle cues not usually explicit in the group, a system of linked triads is developed. The form of the linked triads remains stable while the individuals move in and out of the particular positions. The flexibility of the structure allows for changes as schemata are disconfirmed and social decentration occurs. Accommodation occurs and the participants develop new schemata concerning the exchange of resources, the rights and duties of particular member roles and particular members, and the complementarity and reciprocity of resource exchange. Where T groups last long enough for the subtle cues and complex structure to become explicit, the continuity of personal style from T group to work group is enhanced.

Given minimal time, enough cycling of prudence and risk, conflict and consensus, and adequate tension management, the experiences of the participant may generate in him greater self-awareness, a more unflinching authenticity, a keener sensitivity to the feelings of others, and sharper skills in collaborative, experimental inquiry into social problems.

CHAPTER 7

LINKAGE PROBLEMS AND PROCESSES IN LABORATORY EDUCATION

Ronald O. Lippitt

The impetus and support of successful learning and changing comes from two sources: (1) from functional connections between the learning system (person or group) and needed resources and opportunities; and (2) from stimulation of linkages within the learning system between those functions which need to be linked in order for an integrated learning closure or action closure to come about. In other words, the learner or learning system needs to be related to and make use of a teacher, or change agent, or resource materials, or demonstration activity, or some other stimulus input to help activate and give direction to an internal change process; and within the learning system new functional connections need to be brought about between new knowledge, existing or new goals and values, needs and intentions to act, and a repertoire of behaviors appropriate to give action closure, that is, to actualize in behavior the outcomes and implications of the internal linkages. Only recently have the processes of knowledge utilization become the focus for active programs for research and conceptualization.[1]

In this chapter, I will examine some of the learning issues involved in connecting the learner with outside sources of stimulation, and in supporting the internal aspects of the learning process. Then I will suggest ways in which the laboratory method can provide a conceptual and practical basis for supporting the needed linkages and the integration of the external and internal linkage processes which are involved.

ISSUES OF ALIENATION FROM OUTSIDE RESOURCES FOR LEARNING AND CHANGING

Many different technicians and scholars are involved in retrieving, summarizing, coding, and storing the great flow of knowledge in the many fields of research and scholarship. Computerized clearinghouses and microfilm libraries are growing in abundance, and the magnitude of budgets and personnel required to cope with the increasing quantity of new knowledge resources is also on the increase.

From the point of view of the potential learner-user, there are a number of problems. The knowledge is coded and stored in categories that seem unconnected with the learner's information needs. Storage centers are geographically distant, and the procedures for making connections with them are unclear or absent.

Often the librarian-technician role seems to be a protective one toward the stored knowledge. There seems to be less orientation toward initiating service than there does toward protecting the warehouse and refining the storage operation.

Also, would-be learner-users have a sense of immediacy about their retrieval needs. They want the knowledge *now* because they are confronted with the need for it now. They have not been trained to plan for their knowledge utilization needs, and they have not learned appropriate search skills for using human resources or documentary knowledge resources.

The knowledge which is presented in organized fashion by teachers, using textbooks and other resource materials, creates or confronts feelings of irrelevance in the learners, or fails to stimulate a need to use, or to seek. The past learning experiences of many learners have resulted in a deep sense of alienation from knowledge sources and knowledge carriers. There is a sense of distrust of the relevance of the opportunities offered, and a rejection of the teaching roles which are established to provide linkage between knowledge resources and the needs and interests of potential learners. As I will show later in this chapter, laboratory methodology attempts to facilitate linkages between learners and external resource opportunities in three different ways:

1. By designing learning sequences which confront the learner or learning group with problems to cope with and which stimulate a need to search for internal and external resources. The confrontation-search laboratory is illustrative of this approach to motivating the learner to seek connections to resources.

2. By initiating efforts to make knowledge resources visible, available, and usable. Some new multi-media resource units are attempts to provide this type of initiative, as are the orientation efforts of some of the clearinghouse centers.

3. By the trainer-consultant taking an active "third party role" to bring about linkage between learner-users and appropriate resource materials. The knowledge derivation and utilization work conference is one example of such a laboratory design.

ISSUES OF NON-LINKAGE OR DYSFUNCTIONAL LINKAGE WITHIN THE LEARNING SYSTEM

In Chapter 2, we referred to "the enervating and guilt-producing gaps between what we know, what we profess to value, and what we actually do." One of the intentions of the laboratory method of learning, we said, is "to narrow the gap between inner intentions and aspirations, and outer behavior in action situations." Much educational effort, we said, "stops short with learning what" and "learning about" and does not support learners in developing the motivation, intentions, and skills to utilize understandings for the activation and improvement of overt behavior.

It was also emphasized that learning as a process of incorporation and utilization of new knowledge is a dynamic process which goes on at several levels of human systems: (1) at the level of the individual person system; (2) at the level of the small face-to-face group system as the unit of learning and change; (3) at the level of macro-systems such as organizations and communities. The change agent who is concerned about supporting an integral process of learning-change at any or all of these levels must be concerned about creating conditions of learning which will facilitate and support linkage, within the system, between the functions of *knowing, valuing, intending,* and *acting.* In most cases, the change agent must also be concerned about the transfer of learned behaviors *from one life or action situation to another* and *from one time to another.* Let's look at some of the typical issues of premature closure and inadequate linkage that are likely to occur in most learning and change processes.

"I learned what she asked."

"My learning is completed. I can say it back to her, and that proves to her that I know it, and that's what counts." The closure of learning is to meet the teacher's expectations. We also find this externally oriented criterion of relevance at the level of the small group. The appointed committee carries out a fact-finding job to meet the requests and needs of the administrator in the organization or the community. This process of mobilizing knowledge often occurs with a survey data collection activity, requested by the administrator or activated by the city planning office. Premature closure takes place with the writing up and "handing in" of the report. The typical result of this process at all levels is a sense of futility about the learning effort, a sense of irrelevance of the acquired knowledge, and a lack of any sense of in interest or commitment to do anything about the implications of the facts which were learned.

"I'm Fuller Than I Was."

Frequently, self-motivated learning has the aim of satisfying momentary curiosity or a need to "learn as much as I can about things." Idle, undisciplined, self-indulging needs to acquire information are often self-satisfying and action-defeating. There is no impetus to go beyond knowing. The satisfaction and the closure are in adding to a storehouse of personal knowledge, and enhancing a self-image of "knower." In talking about his college days in intellectual liberal circles in a foreign university, a colleague said, "There was no problem of the world we could not settle over a coffee table any afternoon, but there was certainly no implication that we should ever consider doing anything about anything." In many organizations, the files of administrators and the shelves of the research departments are bulging with facts and figures about the organization. There is great pride in having "a complete set of data" or of having "a complete set of records." This pride often represents a pre-action closure.

"That Would Be A Good Thing To Do."

Sometimes the learner or learning group inches a step toward utilization of information when they derive a general implication and a value judgment. Perhaps the information is an interesting piece of knowledge about a program of activity elsewhere. This may activate the value judgment, "It would be good to have that kind of thing going on in our organization or our community." Perhaps the information is about some of the causes of race prejudice or conflict. The learner may do some integrative thinking and emerge with a value judgment that that kind of prejudice ought to be prevented, or in those kinds of conflict, it would be a good thing to have a mediator. Sometimes this "closure through value judgment" takes the form of perceptive criticism — seeing through "their" arguments, understanding what is wrong with the way "they" do things, or astutely judging the ways things ought to be done, instead of the way they are being done. But this move from an informational or analytic mode of thinking to an evaluative mode is still far removed from any activation of the learner to utilize the knowledge personally. What ought to be done, or what "they" ought to do, is a safe closure which keeps the action removed from self and from the risks of action.

"I'm Going To Do That Sometime."

Sometimes the new knowledge may activate personal intention-setting. Sometimes the group or the organization may arrive at some decisions that it is going to make some changes sometime in the way it operates, or it's going to pursue a new goal priority sometime in the future. The establishing of this linkage between knowledge, evaluation, and intention to act "sometime" is a very significant step in a total learning process. In the majority of cases, this process ends up as premature closure because there is no definite linkage to what Lewin would call the motoric or concrete action-taking aspects of the person or the group or the organization. It is often self rewarding, or a source of approbation from others, to formulate and announce such good intentions. But as our folk wisdom says, "The way to Hell is paved with good intentions." The tremendous loss of human resources in unactualized intentions was the source of some of the deepest concerns leading to the re-examination of the learning process in the development of laboratory learning methodology. It has been very astutely observed that because we have the advantage of internal observation, we can give ourselves credit for good intentions while those outside of us who interact with us must depend on observations of our behavior and, therefore, tend to give credit and evaluation on the basis of our behaviors rather than our intentions. These two different frames of reference lead to many circular processes of misunderstanding, miscommunication, righteous indignation, hurt feelings, and disappointments. Feeling complacent or satisfied about having a good intention is probably the most pervasive premature closure in the total process of learning and the utilization of learning.

"We Have A Very Good Way Of Doing It."

In organizational development work, we often find that the organizational leaders have developed a self-image of high satisfaction with current procedures and structures. This "self satisfaction image" prevents new information and images of action from becoming connected to action. There is a premature closure of "we do that adequately already."

"If I Can't Do It Just Right, I Shouldn't Try."

The "image of perfection" is another of the frequent blockers of linkage between goal images and action efforts. It is natural and desirable for anyone with ideals and significant goals to perceive desired outcomes and levels of performance which are well beyond the present situation and present level of skills. But to use this discrepancy as a rationale for inaction rather than as a source of challenge is often a defensive maneuver to avoid the commitment and energy of intention-behavior linkage and of work on first steps and skill development.

"They Wouldn't Approve Or Support."

The non-tested assumption that external authority forces or coalitions of power would reject or resist the relevant action is one of the most frequent preventers of linkage between a valued action and an actualization effort. One of our most frequent action-supporting interventions in laboratory education situations is to help a person or group face the fact that they are making untested assumptions about "what they (the authorities) would think and do," and to help plan steps of involvement and tryout which will test such assumptions. More often than not, the assumption proves invalid, or the negative attitude is changeable with appropriate information-giving and strategies of involvement.

"I've Got To Act Right Now."

There are some learners and action-takers for whom it is intolerable to formulate an intention without immediately acting upon it. If one has decided something is "a good thing to do," and has formulated the intention to do it, then this decision validates the action-taking. This type of internal impulse-freedom and impulse-validation represents a different kind of premature closure — premature in the sense that the process of knowledge-utilization stops short of considering the strategy and skills required for action-taking. To take action because it feels necessary to the self, without scanning for data from the reality situation, and without mobilizing or developing skilled action, is a self-indulging closure which may do a great disservice both to the self, others, and to the goals which are the target for action. One support for this premature closure is the widespread idea that "doing what comes naturally is best," or "being spontaneous" is better than planning for action. From our observations, it seems clear that at both the individual and the group level, "doing what comes naturally" tends to be more self-serving than other-serving, tends to be insensitive to the needs and resistances of others, and, therefore, tends quite often to be self-defeating as a change effort.

"Part Of Me (Us) Doesn't Want To Learn Or Change."

Another typical source of internal disconnection is the state of ambivalence in which we have several parts of the self or group thinking and feeling differently and pushing toward different directions of action and avoiding communication between the parts. This may result in personal or group polarizations too difficult and painful to deal with. Therefore, new knowledge input from a teaching, training, or consulting relationship may be supporting and activating one part of the self or system, resulting in the mobilization of other parts to disrupt the linkage to action. It is an even more difficult issue when internalized repression has resulted in part of the self becoming disconnected from the rest of the self and unavailable as a resource or as participant in the learning and action-taking process.

Turning to experience with larger learning systems, such as groups and organizations, we can identify similar issues of dysfunctional linkage or non-linkage between parts of the system involved in the learning and change process. For example, differences in role, status, race, sex, and position in organizational structure may function as barriers to communication, and to the diffusion and use of new knowledge, values, or action plans. Barriers of distrust between persons or units may function so as to prevent linkage, or linkage may remain at such a superficial level of communication and cooperation that no real consideration or cooperation about change can take place. We are familiar with the ways in which "turfdom protectiveness" prevents coordination linkages and collaboration. All of the protection process can function to prevent receiving or utilization of new knowledge or new goals, policies, and programs.

LABORATORY METHODOLOGY AS SUPPORTIVE OF LINKAGES FOR ACTION AND CHANGE

Facilitating Linkages Between the Learning System and the Resource Environment

One of the first challenges for every consultant-trainer is the working through of a mutually acceptable contract with the client which defines a working relationship of the client to the trainer *as a part* of the resource environment. Some of the most important skills of the trainer or consultant are those of establishing the credibility and relevance of self as a needed, helping resource. The techniques of entry and of start-up, and of developing a voluntary learning contract, are core aspects of laboratory methodology. Sometimes one of the interesting and important aspects of entry technique and contract development is the designing and conducting of "micro-experiences" which permit the client system to have a participative experience to see what it will be like if a decision is made to enter into a learning relationship with the trainer.

Another important laboratory education design for stimulating motivated linkage of the learner to external resources is the *confrontation and search laboratory* design developed by Irvine Millgate at Xicom Laboratories. The central idea of this procedure is that individuals or small learning groups begin with a confrontation experience in which they must cope by behavioral response with brief, video-taped episodes which come from their own typical life situations and require a response of "What do I do or say now?" Knowing that there will be additional opportunities to try the confrontation situations again, the learners are given access to a search library where various types of resources are available to help them develop the knowledge and skills needed to improve their performance for the second and subsequent coping efforts. These resources may include a library of tapes of the behaviors of others who have coped effectively with the situation, also technical literature, expert consultants available for discussion, and roundtable discussions with peers who have also "taken the confrontation" and are planning work on improving their next performance. Under these conditions, there is a very focused and highly motivated utilization of reading materials and other resources.

Another design for linkage to resources, which is being used increasingly in laboratory work, is the "exchange of practices" procedure which makes it possible for learners to be parts of the resource environments for each other by using a structured group interview procedure to interview each other as informants, documenting on ditto masters the detailed description of successful innovative practice so that all practices can be duplicated and made available to all members of the learning group. The trainer has a very crucial role in providing the techniques of effective communication linkage between the peer learners, and helping to overcome the restraints to freely communicating.

We mentioned earlier the difficulties of retrieval of relevant knowledge at the time it is needed. A number of laboratory educators have been experimenting with on-the-spot conference telephone calls with resource centers and resource persons at the time when retrieval of information is needed in a lab design. Using an inexpensive telephone amplifier box makes it possible for a group of learners to conduct the telephone interviews with the distant resource person or persons.

Another procedure is for the members of learning groups to take responsibility for dividing up the labor of interviewing, going out to interview needed resource persons, and making tapes to bring back and include in a resource library.

Another procedure is to make careful preparation for the use of an invited resource person who receives briefing ahead of time about the areas in which his information is needed. The group may have prepared for the conference situation by developing a group interview schedule.

Perhaps one of the most neglected areas of linking learners to external resources is the providing of specific participative practice in arriving at derivations and implications from written resource materials. It is remarkable, but understandable, how little most learners use the reading of research reports and other informational input as a basis for deriving implications for decision-making and action-taking. Procedures for conducting sessions on deriving implications for action from research generalizations and theory propositions can be an important part of laboratory learning designs. Interesting designs have also been developed for retrieval periods in which all members of the learning group take time to delve into and scan selected items in a resource library in order to make reports to each other on relevant findings, and to practice converting readings into implications for their own behavioral experimentation. This is an area of laboratory education where a great deal of innovative experimentation is needed in order that the interpersonal interaction processes of the learning group can be enriched and informed by the effective utilization of external resource persons and materials.

These are just a few examples of the challenges facing laboratory educators in giving leadership to one of the most important aspects of the learning and changing process, that of facilitating connection with and utilization of the many resource opportunities in the immediate and extended environment of the learning group, including the effective use of themselves as resources and linkers to other resources.

Facilitating Linkages For Learning and Change Within the Person Or Group

Perhaps an even more difficult and important role for the laboratory educator is in providing a supportive relationship and appropriate learning designs for bringing about effective integrative linkages between the different internal functions of the system; linkages which are necessary for adequate learning closures to be achieved. The trainer or consultant must become a collaborator with the learner in helping provide the support and stimulating commitment. The learner must be helped "really to put my intentions into action," "really to carry through on my ideas," "really to look at whether my behaviors are in line with my values," "really to work on living up to what I've decided I want to do and be." So the strategies of internal system support for learning work are at the core of the skills and methods of the laboratory educator.

The diagram below illustrates the types of internal functions within a person or group system which usually need to be linked in some way by laboratory learning activities if knowledge and intentions are actually to be converted into skilled behavior output. One way to look at a design for learning is to assess which internal linkages will be created or supported by the specific micro-design in the learning or problem-solving sequence.

PARTS OF LEARNING PROCESS INSIDE THE LEARNER OR LEARINNG SYSTEM

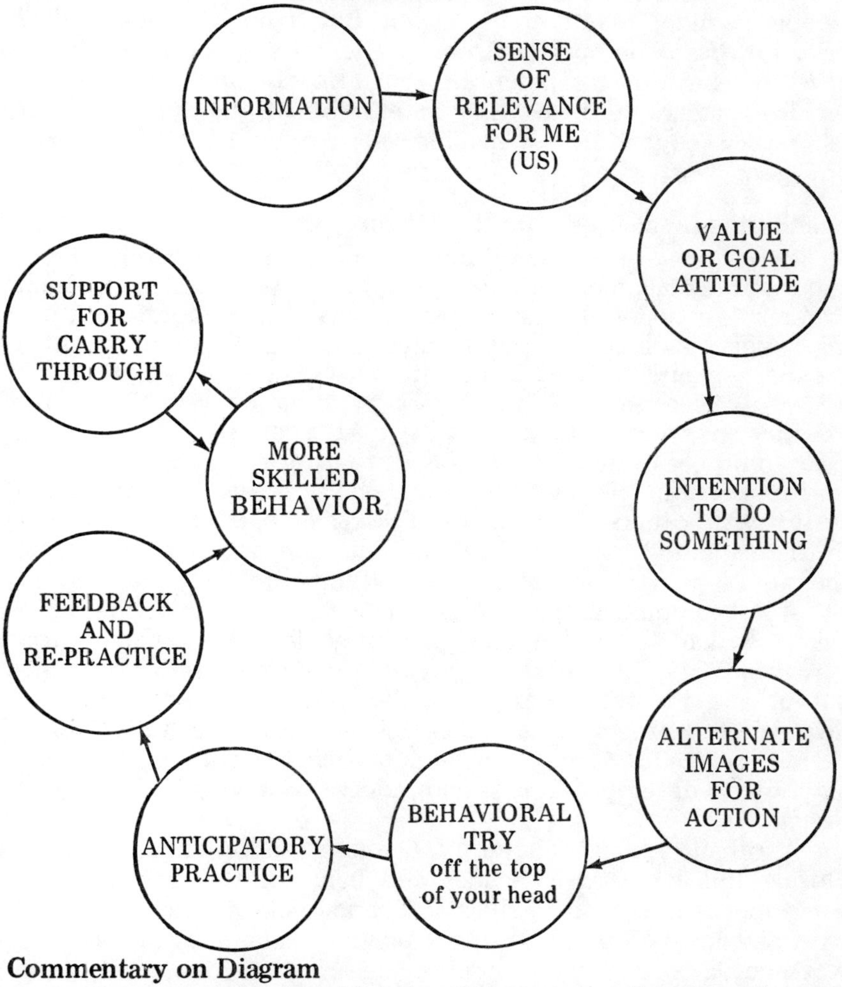

Commentary on Diagram

One of the ingredients inside of us that has to get linked somehow to behavior is some kind of cognitive content; *information* or *knowledge* it is often called. A second ingredient is a belief that the bit of information has *relevance* for the self. The sense of relevance may be connected to or help generate a *goal* or a *value* or *belief.* And often, a *goal* or *value* helps generate an *intention* and *commitment to act* — at this point the internal processes of the self are sneaking up on action, but we still have no guarantee that ideas will be converted into overt action.

The next linkage in internal movement toward successful action is whether or not the learner has *alternative images* of possible action. So often good intentions get blocked through not having alternative images. We have only one image of doing it and that has to be the right way because that's all we can see. So frequently this impulse to act comes out as *unpracticed* or undeveloped, crude, *first draft behavior.* But it may become *skilled behavior*, based on consideration of alternatives, and *practiced* to develop behavioral competence through *revision and repractice.*

The paragraphs below illustrate some of the approaches of laboratory education to helping learners with these internal linkages.

Facilitating Linkages Within the Person

This is one of the much needed supports for reflective thinking and internal dialogue. Various applications have been made of John Rickman's concept of "the internal society." The laboratory learning design may include periodic internal dialogue sessions in which the participants each write an internal dialogue in script of the different voices they can identify in "internal conversations"; for example, between those aspects of self that are in favor of taking risks and those in favor of caution, or the voices that take different positions within the self, concerning the posture of openness and trust toward others. This process of internal observation is difficult in the beginning for many learners, but soon proves to be one of the most supportive aspects of the learning process.

Another important internal linkage support is to help the learner articulate connections between goals and alternative ideas for action. The "image of potentiality" exercise developed by this author and his colleagues is one illustration of a procedure for helping the learner project himself into the future, to articulate desired outcomes of his efforts, and then to return to the here-and-now to develop strategies and tactics for moving in the desired directions.

Another type of laboratory learning session focuses on exploring linkage between values and behavior patterns. Discrepancies between personal values and actual behaviors are identified with the help of peers, and role-playing techniques are used to work on developing the desired linkages, with feedback help from fellow learners.

Probably one of the most important and under-used aspects of laboratory learning methodology is supporting linkage between intentions and action by providing skill practice opportunities where one is trying out new behavior patterns in situations of "Not playing for keeps," and receiving guiding feedback for purposes of re-practice in developing a repertoire of behavioral skills to more adequately represent one's internal goals, values, and intentions in action. The techniques of this approach are developed in Chapter 9.

Supporting Linkage and Integration Between Persons Within the Learning and Action System

Typically, there is much collusion to maintain non-linkage among members of the same group or organization; a collusion of non-shared information about each other's interests, skills, values, and resources. Stimulating the flow and use of such information is a challenge for laboratory educators. One design for facilitating such communication involves having the members of the group pair and interview each other, using an interview schedule which may include such questions as "what most turns you off and turns you on?" touching on interests, skills, and successful practices that one could share with others. The interview data are written with a felt-tip pen on a manila folder hanging around the neck of the interviewee, so that as soon as the interviews are finished, there can be a "milling period" where people have a legitimized opportunity to read the data about each other. Later, these folders may be put on the wall and used as a resource directory during subsequent meetings of the groups.

Many trainers use a variety of listening exercises to help the members of a group or a staff develop the unused skills of listening to each other and using what has been heard as the basis for continuing dialogue.

Another type of design focuses on legitimizing and supporting conversation about value positions which are usually left unexplored. In one such procedure, all members of the group check individually on a four or six-point scale of agreement-to-disagreement their response to a given value statement. They then walk to those scale positions as identified by cards on the wall or the floor so that public value position-taking is legitimized. Groups are then formed which, in order to be "good groups," must be made up of persons from the different value positions. Value dialogues begin with the aim of influencing each other and listening to each other. "Stop sessions" in the group discussion are called periodically to look at the kind of balance that the individual members in the group are achieving between articulating one's own value position and listening to those of others. Groups of six to ten explore various new integrations and creative compromises which emerge from such discussions.

Perhaps one of the most important kinds of linkages between persons in achieving collaborative problem-solving and learning activity is the asking for and using of feedback. A great many different designs have been developed by trainers and consultants to support and make legitimate the asking for feedback among members of a group. They work toward free and open giving of feedback about the effects of the other persons' behavior, and give support for using feedback in setting up personal experiments in risk-taking to try out new patterns of behavior suggested and implied by the feedback that has been received. In such situations, we can recognize that two kinds of learning are going on. One level is process learning in which individuals are acquiring new knowledge about themselves and their impact on others, and being helped to convert that knowledge into implications for personal action and action tryouts. At the second level, work is focused on achieving more effective working connections between the members, so that the group can work more productively on the group tasks of using external resources, making decisions and plans, and working efficiently toward group goals.

Another type of support for interpersonal linkage helps members to put themselves in each other's shoes by the use of role-reversal and alter-ego role-playing techniques. Through such procedures, members can be helped to develop sensitive awareness of each other's feelings and positions, and to use this empathy as a base for deeper levels of interpersonal collaboration.

In many group consultation situations, the consultant discovers the existence of polarized clique and sub-groups, and provides a crucial linking service to permit group development and group action.

Facilitating Linkage Between Sub-Systems and Between Systems

Later chapters (19 and 20) focus on the techniques of organization and community development which utilize a variety of laboratory education approaches to bring about linkage and integration between departments or sections of an organization or between the agencies and populations of a community. At this point, we want to emphasize that the goal of the laboratory educator, at all levels of client systems from the personal or interpersonal context to the group or agency or community context, involves the generic task of helping the client system develop the linkages, integrations, and coordinations needed to function as a learning system in working with a trainer-consultant on challenges of confronting, internalizing, and utilizing new resources in order to function more effectively in achieving desired goals. In working with large systems, very frequently the change agent must utilize designs to "mix up" the population in order to open up communication between professionals and volunteers, between administrators and workers, between old and young, between races, between sexes, and between representatives from different types of agencies and organizations. The function of the change agent as a third party convener, linker, and trusted message carrier becomes crucial in working with a macro-system.

THE LABORATORY METHOD AS STIMULUS AND SUPPORT FOR THE APPLICATION OF LEARNING AND CHANGE TO OTHER SETTINGS AND TIMES

Even the most thorough and creative designs for integrative learning often fall short of the necessary support for successful transfer of learnings to other situations and later times. Systematic follow-up evaluations of residential laboratory training have usually discovered a great loss of functional learning and behavioral change from the end of the learning activity to performance in various back home operating situations. All of the perceived expectations of on-the-job peers to "keep on being who and what you've been," the fear of risk in trying out new styles of behavior, and the sense of awkwardness that goes with innovating a new pattern of behavior, all function as constraints to the application of learnings. As one teacher put it, "Over 80% of what I learned in summer workshops disappears the first day I face the risk of using those learnings in my own school building and in my own school room." The developers of laboratory education methods have been challenged from the beginning to discover effective ways of bridging or linking learning situations and action situations between the here-and-now learning context and the there-and-then application settings. Here are several of the types of designs which have been developed to support transfer and application.

The Cross-Situation Team. With greater and greater frequency, laboratory programs recruit and work with "back home teams." In other words, individuals come not as singleton learners, but as members of organization or community teams, who, as they develop the skills of collaboration through laboratory training, and as they develop mutual commitments to back home action, provide a major bridging support for each other. This is a great asset to the back-home setting which has a much better chance of "getting its money's worth" as a result of a training program because of the support team which is helping maintain a carry-over and continuity of the learning activity.

On-The-Job Focus of Learning Tasks. The tradition of some laboratory designs is to focus only on data from the life situations generated in the process of the here-and-now laboratory activity. But in order to facilitate transfer of insight and action to the back home life situations, other laboratory designs provide for a mix between a study of the here-and-now laboratory situations and the there-and-then life situations. For example, the laboratory participants working in trios may help each other identify critical episodes back home which they would like help in diagnosing and coping with in the laboratory. Using each other as role-playing resources, they create these critical episodes on cassette tapes and use them to play to fellow learners, to brainstorm alternative ways of coping, or to discuss diagnostic possibilities. This type of activity provides an opportunity to integrate the learnings which have been derived from the here-and-now process experiences in the laboratory with the on-the-job life situations.

Anticipatory Rehearsal. Many laboratory designs provide opportunities for the learners to project goals for change which they would like to initiate in their back home situations. Then with consultation from each other, and from the trainers, they plan the steps of action needed to implement the change goal. Then, using role-playing techniques, the participants provide each other with the opportunity to practice the first steps of action which they anticipate when they return home. They brief each other to take the roles of the administrators or colleagues or whomever they anticipate interacting with in their first steps of action-taking. This type of anticipatory tryout, with opportunity to receive feedback and to re-practice, has been evaluated by many learners as one of the most helpful supports for the transfer of learning to back home settings.

Follow-Up Support. In some laboratory learning situations, the participants and the staff plan specific follow-up designs. These may include plans for communication by telephone or tape at specific intervals, or there may be deadlines for reports to be put together as a newsletter, or there may be specific plans for participants who live near each other to get together on a periodic basis for support and continuing stimulation.

Sequential Designs and Interim Tasks. More and more frequently, laboratory learning designs are organized as a sequential series of sessions. In one current design, the community teams meet for a team development and action-planning laboratory two days every two months for a year. In another design, there is a three-day start-up followed by a one-day session a month later, and then another final two-day session a month after that. There are two sources of support for application in such sequential designs. One support comes from the commitment to interim tasks that will be tried out during the period between sessions. This provides much support for experimental tries and for bringing experience back to a subsequent session for further diagnosis, consultation, and further strategy-planning with peers and trainers. The second type of support comes from the fact of the subsequent session which provides an opportunity to focus on further knowledges and skills which are needed, after there has been a clear identification of exactly what kinds of resources are most needed to carry learning through successful application.

The common theme of all these laboratory designs, and many other similar ones, is the effort to provide support to the learner for linkage between the learning situation and the variety of application situations where goals, values, attitudes, intentions, and behaviors must be successfully "carried over" and applied if the learning is to have a successful closure in reality.

LEARNING TO LEARN AS LINKAGE LEARNING

One of the most basic tenets of laboratory learning as it has been discussed in the previous chapters is the focus on helping the learner (or learners) become aware of and skilled in the utilization of a self-initiated continuing learning methodology for himself (or for themselves as a group or organization). Laboratory educators attempt to help learners internalize a learning-to-learn conceptual framework and methodology and motivation through sharing at all stages the design of the learning activity, through helping the learners become increasingly involved in designing their own learning experiments and through increasingly encouraging learners to individualize their own learning activities. In one recent laboratory, participants brainstormed some twenty-five different ways they might take initiative to secure and maintain their own support systems back home to insure their own continuing growth activity. They recognized that something is needed beyond commitment and good intentions. They recognized that all of them, as learners, needed to develop procedures, relationships, situations, time schedules, deadlines, to insure their own continuing self-renewal efforts as persons and as larger social systems. Probably the internalizing of the designs and skills for one's own learning activity, and the taking of initiative to design and implement support systems for one's continued learning and application of learning, represent the two most significant and pervasive supports for transfer and application of learning. In organizations and communities, the mechanisms of continuing self-renewal include designs for periodic evaluation, effective research and development units, long-range planning teams, manpower development programs, and effective use of outside resource persons.

THE LEARNING LINKER AS A METHODOLOGICAL ADVOCATE

There is much discussion among laboratory educators about the goal of "installing mechanisms of self-renewal" in client systems as a part of the job of being a temporary helper who is able to terminate a relationship with a client system which has achieved the ability to continue the learning and development process for itself. In practice, this means that the trainer-consultant takes a value position of being an active advocate for the development of "methodological resources" within the learner system. In other words, the consultant actively initiates efforts to teach the skills of learning to learn in individual learners; and at the organizational level attempts to get the client system to install continuing action-research mechanisms which have the responsibility for scanning for new knowledge, retrieving feedback data from within the system, creating procedures for facilitating, internalizing, and using such information as a basis for revision of goals, development of new program emphases, and re-organization of structures to adapt to changes in the environment and the task. A central purpose of every laboratory educator is to help learners and learning systems achieve the motivations and resources to: (1) link continuously to their resource environment; and (2) promote and facilitate continuously internal linkages that support the full and effective utilization of external and internal resources.

FOOTNOTES AND REFERENCES

1. Ronald Havelock and Ronald Lippitt, "Needed Research on Research Utilization"; Working Paper, Institute for Social Research, CRUSK, University of Michigan, Ann Arbor, Michigan.

2. R. Olson and I. Millgate.

3. Robert Fox and Ronald Lippitt, "Identifying, Documenting, Evaluating, And Sharing Innovative Classroom Practices," Working Paper, Institute for Social Research, CRUSK, University of Michigan, Ann Arbor, Michigan.

4. Ronald Lippitt, "The Research Utilization Conference: An Illustrative Model," Working Paper, Institute for Social Research, University of Michigan, Ann Arbor, Michigan.

5. Adapted from paper presented by Ronald Lippitt and Eva Schindler-Rainman to Long Beach State University Seminar, May, 1972-73.

6. Robert Fox, Ronald Lippitt, and Eva Schindler-Rainman, *Toward a Humane Society: Images of Potentiality*, Learning Resources Corporation, Fairfax, Virginia, 1973.

7. Ronald Lippitt and Eva Schindler-Rainman, *Team Training for Community Change: Concepts, Goals, Strategies and Skills.* University of California, University Extension, Riverside, California, 1972.

8. *Ibid.*

CHAPTER 8

DESIGNING FOR PARTICIPATIVE LEARNING AND CHANGING

Ronald O. Lippitt and Eva Schindler-Rainman

Planning for the mobilization and use of all the resources which will facilitate learning and problem solving is the focus of the design task. The challenge for the laboratory educator is to ensure an effective blend of utilization of human, material, and situational resources in order to facilitate the participative involvement of client-learners in an optimal learning process. Our examination of this area of professional practice has led us to formulate the following basic assumptions as guidelines for designing laboratory learning programs and sequences.

BASIC ASSUMPTIONS FOR THE DESIGNER OF LABORATORY LEARNING

1. Planning for any professional helping relationship with a client system is an ethical responsibility of trainers and consultants.
2. Each training event or consulting contact should be planned for the particular group with its specific learning needs and problem-solving confrontations in mind.
3. Helping the client articulate and clarify his own values, goals, and needs for help is a responsibility of the designer.
4. Planning for the most facilitative arrangement of the physical environment of the interaction situation with the client is a part of designing the laboratory education experience.
5. Identifying the available resources (budget, physical setting, personnel) is an important responsibility of the designer.

6. Designing for utilization, or potential utilization, of helping resources other than the self (for example, other persons, materials) is a responsibility of the trainer-consultant.

7. Designing to optimize participative involvement of the client and to ensure two-way influence in goal-setting, contract-defining, and problem-solving work is a responsibility of the trainer-consultant.

8. Designing to help the client achieve methodological skills of inquiry, problem-solving, and self-initiated change and self-renewal is a core responsibility of the designer.

9. Designing to make one's own role as a helper progressively unnecessary and to prevent dysfunctional dependency is a responsibility.

10. One important feature of any design is its provision for flexibility, for openness to redesign on the basis of data from the ongoing helping process.

THE VARIETY OF CONTEXTS FOR DESIGNING PARTICIPATIVE LEARNING

The developer of learning and problem-solving designs must consider a variety of dimensions of the learning situation; for example, the purpose, characteristics of the learners, size of the group, and length of time available. There is space here for only a brief summary of some of these factors.

Types of Purposes of the Learning Activity

The purposes might include the following:

1. Improvement of ongoing task work. An example of this might be the ongoing work of a staff of an agency or an organization that meet regularly and have both decision-making and information types of meetings in order to carry on their work.

2. Development of new personal role skills. For example, the training of persons who have been elected to a new office, such as that of a Board of Education member, or Chairman of a Committee, or Board of Directors. These people need to learn their new roles and often take very special courses in order to learn them. Or, it may be that someone has a promotion from one job to another, so that he may need to learn training or consulting skills, which he has not needed before.

3. Personal development may be the purpose of a learning-teaching activity. This purpose may include such foci as "Personal Growth," "Insight Building," and "Understanding of Self."

4. Process work on group problems. This is a very common purpose. It includes such things as process observation of ongoing

work in a group. This may include stop sessions for the group to look at its work and diagnose how it could improve, and it may include observation by a trainer or consultant to help a group look at its work, how it is doing it, what things are helping the process, what things are hindering it, and then helping the group to look at how to improve its work.

5. New process skills for a system. This might include a series of meetings to improve the communication between departments as well as vertical communication from the executive to the worker and back again.

6. Conflict resolution or crisis-coping. Often, these days, the purpose of a series of meetings is to help a group or system deal with conflict or crisis. This may be between consumer and provider, or it may be conflict between different racial or ethnic groups, or it may be a conflict that is intergenerational.

7. The development of collaboration. An example of this might be a request by several community agencies for a series of meetings between all of the agencies in a particular field, or with a particular interest, to learn how to collaborate. For example, it might be all the agencies in the community that would like to collaborate in improving the education of the young.

8. Trend analysis and future planning. Here, the purpose may be to help a group look at future trends and to derive from these trends implications for new goals and current action priorities.

9. Information getting. This often calls for a design to facilitate effective information seeking and input. There may be information needed by a group on new policies, or on new tax laws, or new findings from research (for example, in the medical field) that will affect practice and action.

10. Inspiration and motivation. Sometimes the purpose is one of trying to inspire a group to do something or to think about something. Often this is true of religious services.

11. Research derivation. This may be a need to retrieve research findings in a particular field, to analyze them, think about them, and to derive the implications for action plans and programs.

These are some of the typical purposes for which short or long-term designs for learning and action are needed.

Types of Client Population

There are many ways to differentiate types of learner groups. Here are several ways that are often important in designing:

1. Strangers, that is, a population of participants who are strangers to each other, from different systems, different organizations, or geographic areas. Strangers may consist of a group, such as going to an institute to which the public is invited. They

may be a stratified group; for example, inter-agency peers, or a vertically stratified group. They may be a heterogeneous group, very mixed in terms of age and race, sex and socio-economic backgrounds. Or they could be a homogeneous group; that is, they may all be male, or they might all be consultants, or all women interested in women's liberation, or a group of sixth-graders.

2. Another type of client population is the continuing small group with which one works on a continuing basis. This might be a classroom group, a staff group, or a community planning group that is a sub-group of the community council.

3. There are also continuing large groups that are made up of representatives from a variety of organizations and systems. Or they may be representatives from within one system. These groups could be inter-agency or inter-departmental in composition, or they might be a large group from one department or one agency.

Size of Meetings

Another variable to be considered when designing is the size of the meeting or the size of the group for which one is designing. Size might vary as follows, which makes a great difference in the job of designing.

1. The one-to-one interaction, which may take place through interviews or discussions.

2. A three-to-fifteen person, small group such as committees and commissions. Members might be drawn from one organization or from several organizations.

3. A fifteen-to-thirty person, middle-sized group such as a Board of Directors, a classroom group, or staff groups. These may be horizontal or vertical groups, and again may be recruited from one or from several organizations.

4. Thirty to fifty persons. These larger groups may be the kinds of groups found at annual meetings, in workshops, advisory boards of various kinds, or city commissions.

5. Fifty people or more. Examples of such a population might be all the employees of a company, some institutes, or regional, state, or local meetings.

6. Five hundred to thousands of people. For such a large group, the design problems are entirely different. Examples are a statewide meeting of the PTA, or a national meeting of the American Society of Training Directors.

The size of the training population has much to do not only with the physical ecology requirements, but also with the kinds and amounts of resources needed and the kinds of designs that are appropriate.

Types of Contact

There are a variety of ways in which people and meetings come together, all of which call for different types of designs.

1. The micro experience. This is a two-to-three hour experience in which participants are given a kind of see-ahead view of what might happen if they were to participate in a longer workshop.
2. Staff events, lasting from one-and-a-quarter to two hours.
3. One day drive-in events, where people are able to come to a one day workshop and drive home at the end of the day. Typically, these last from nine to 3:30 p.m. or thereabouts.
4. Two to two-and-one-half days residential events.
5. One week workshops or laboratories.
6. Two or more weeks for a residential or non-residential workshop or laboratory.
7. Annual meetings, conventions, or conferences.
8. Telephone conferences.
9. Two or three phase residential designs, where there may be a three day start-up design, and then people go home and work on a project, and come back for three or more days, and again an interim period, and again some more time together.

Any of the above types of contacts might be designed with follow-up support or without, depending on the contract that is made.

TYPES OF DESIGN PLANNING PATTERNS

There are a variety of ways in which designs can be developed, the most typical in our experience are:

1. The diagnostic briefing by an inside person or committee of an outside person or trainer. This is then followed by the trainer-consultant offering a design that he has either developed at the meeting with the group or away from the group. But, whichever way he develops it, he would bring it back to check it out with the persons who briefed him.
2. Or there might be an inside-outside design team, an outside trainer-consultant or consultants working with several people from the inside, as a planning committee. They develop together the purpose and the ingredients, the timing and the design of the session.
3. Or, the outside trainer might develop the design and use the inside team to check the plan. Often in this pattern, the outside-inside team also carries out the design together in some agreed-upon way.
4. A joint team serving as both designers and leaders of the

learning event. From the very beginning, the outside trainer-consultant teams up with other persons from inside.

Types of Sequential Design Patterns

Most learning designs require some type of plan for a sequence of work. Here are a few of the most frequent patterns:

1. The one day pattern in which there is no planned follow-up. The event begins and ends in a one-time setting.

2. A start-up event of one, two, or three days, with an interim period and then other days of work. This has been found to be a very helpful pattern for ongoing classes, where students have an opportunity to begin work on a project of their own, and then have time to work on it away from class, and then come back for support, evaluation, and additional information.

3. A start-up event, followed by a home site session which is then followed by another get-together. Sometimes groups will start up at a conference center or hotel or away from home, and then have a session back in their own bailiwick, and after the on-site session, they get back together off-site to discuss and practice.

4. Another pattern may be an in-service series where there is an agreement that there will be from five to eight sessions dealing with particular types of problems.

5. There are courses which may run from four to typically fifteen weeks.

6. Another pattern is continuing or periodic consultation by one or more trainer-consultants with the particular client system.

7. There may be a series of telephone, tape, and newsletter contacts between actual meetings, or sometimes in lieu of face-to-face meetings.

All of these are continuity contexts for designing, and all of them need to be taken into consideration depending on the particular design task at hand. Different contexts require different designs and different adaptations. Information about the context for which one is designing is perhaps the most important diagnostic data one has to gather in order to be able to enter into a realistic contract with the client population.

Levels of Designing for Laboratory Education Activity

We have identified four types or levels of decisions in creating a design for helping with learning or problem solving. All four types of decisions are made by the designer no matter whether he or she is planning a laboratory, a staff institute, a consultation session, or a convention. Some of the specific decisions will be explored in more depth as we look later at an illustrative design. Here we wish to identify the four "levels" of design decisions:

1. Decisions about arranging and using the physical setting facilities and equipment to facilitate effective involvement and interaction.

A designer must find out what the available space is before working on the design, or must make decisions about the space and special arrangements which are needed in order to make a particular design feasible. Is the space large enough for the number of people who will be working in it? Is there enough space between tables so that work groups will not interfere with each other? Are the heating, acoustic, and lighting facilities adequate? Also, decisions must be made about design of individual nurturance and maintenance. For example, are the restroom facilities adequate in location and number? Can coffee and tea be available when needed? How adequate are the quality of the food and the efficiency of service?

A checklist of needed equipment and tools also is important. Will a loudspeaker be needed? If so, is good equipment available? Is audio-visual equipment needed? What about the supply of newsprint, easels, felt pens, and other tools for communication?

Often the trainer-consultant also needs to influence decisions about the actual location of the training or consultation activity. Should participants be able to get away from the office or the city? Are there advantages in staying closer to the context of day-to-day work, making provisions for isolation within that context? What are the advantages and disadvantages of a residential *versus* a commuting situation? Are some of the participants who are needed excluded by time, distance, and expense?

Such a checklist of questions to explore and decisions to make about the resource environment is a critical resource for the designer of laboratory education programs and activities.

2. Decisions about the macro-design of the learning activity.

These are the decisions about the overall goals and sequence of the learning activities. There are such questions as: What kinds of activities would be most appropriate for morning work or evening work? What is the appropriate amount of work in a day, as balanced with recreation and rest time? What would be the most appropriate groupings for the participants, to facilitate the objectives of the total learning activity? This level of decision making might be thought of as the level of "curriculum decisions," as contrasted to "lesson plans."

3. The third level of decision making has to do with the micro-designs, or modules of activity which make up the overall sequence of the macro-design.

What kinds of skill and practice exercise should be used and what should be the design? What design should there be for participation in information input sessions? What is the most effective plan for using the film? How should the first half hour as people enter the room be designed?

4. Decisions about intervention strategy and specific interventions are the fourth level of design thinking and planning.

What is the best way to legitimize getting problems expressed? Should the trainer model openness or leave it up to them? How can the trainer offer ideas and resources without creating dependency? Is it better to intervene in the conflict now or let things develop further?

The trainer or consultant is making a continuous flow of such decisions to intervene or not to intervene during the process of interaction between the learners or clients. A rather important part of competent professional practice is the anticipatory thinking through of such decisions in regard to particular individuals and groups, and a clarification for self of ideas about appropriate help strategies.

We will illustrate these four levels of designing and of decision making in the next sections of the chapter.

Data Needed for Design Planning and Decision Making

Design thinking must start with an effort to understand the situation and the needs and expectations of the client group. Often there is a temptation for the trainer or consultant to start with "what's in my repertoire" that would probably work well with "them." This often results in a "gimmicky" design full of seductively interesting activity which has not been derived from or related concretely to the needs of the client population. One help for the designer is a systematic procedure for summarizing the data needed to create a design or plan for consultation or training. The scheme presented below has proved of great value in the development of learning designs for many different kinds of populations and purposes, during several years of use by several trainer-consultants, including the co-authors. It is presented here filled out for a sample population. In practice, we use mimeograph blanks to fill in as data are collected and summarized.

Some Important Decisions and Issues in Design Development

The process of pre-planning which is being described is certainly not an armchair activity carried out by a trainer or consultant in isolation. Often, fact finding and interaction with clients is required, although sometimes this must happen by phone, through the mail, or in the first stages of the training activity. Here are several of the critical directions of inquiry and decision making which seem to us important in these early stages of designing:

ILLUSTRATIVE DESIGN CHART I
Summary Sheet for Design Planning

About the Client Group — Characteristics, Needs, Expectations, Contract	Desired Outcomes	Possible Ingredients Activities Methods	Needed Facilities Resources Equipment Layout
25 trainer-consultants, want professional skill help as trainers	Increased competence in designing	Practice in designing for different types of clients and situations	Room with work tables for 4-5-6 cassette tape recorders and tapes
About ½ internal organization consultants & trainers	Ability to do diagnostic "scouting" & contract development	Simulations of diagnostic inquiry of several types of client situations	Coffee-tea setup side of room all the time
18 males 7 females	Increased skill in making process interventions	Share diagnostic tools	2 easels for newsprint
Great range of academic training and experiences	Ability to conduct skill practice & interpersonal awareness excercises	Cassette tape skill practice design on contract development	Supply of newsprint, magic markers, felt-tip pens, overhead projector, ditto machine and ditto masters
2½ day residential start-up and 2 more times after 3 months interim period	Ability to create & use feedback and evaluation tools	Variety of process stop-sessions	Buffet lunch arrangement
Expect some kind of "certificate of competence"	Development of implementation of back-home training design	Time to work on back-home design with consultation	Cocktail hour
See individual data sheets for types of consulting and training experiences	Development of personal plan for continuing professional growth	Workshop on evaluation & feedback	Name tags
		Develop back-home designs with consultation	Telephone amplifier box
		Telephone support consultation	
		Possible learnings back-home	

1. Who should be involved in the designing? When?

In a client system that is being worked with, it is important that appropriate insiders be involved as helpers in fact finding, as informants, and as reactors to tentative ideas about design outcomes, methods, and activities. If a special population is being worked with, such as representatives of a variety of agencies or organizations of a community, it is important to stimulate the development of an ad hoc committee of representative linkers who can collaborate in the early stages of design thinking. If a population of strangers will be arriving for a training event, it is important to explore the kinds of data which can be secured in advance about their needs and interests, and to design a start-up activity which will provide opportunities for the participants to share the kinds of data and orientations which can influence and modify a tentative design. You may discover that even when it is difficult to have any advance communications with clients, it is usually quite possible to get information about who is coming and the kinds of occupational roles they play, sex, age, etc., and to actually have a staff team spend a period of "role playing the participants," and brainstorming all the ideas the staff can generate about the probable sub-group differences, varieties of interest, expectations, and development needs which the client may have. This is a great help in keeping the staff "on the beam" in thinking about appropriate tentative design activities and sequences. It is also important to share with participants in the beginning of the working relationship, the types of efforts the staff have made to collect data or to project themselves into the situations of the participants in trying to be sensitive designers of relevant learning activities and work sessions.

2. How much pre-planning? What provisions for revision of design?

Some trainers and consultants believe that an "emergency design" in which little preplanning is done is the most appropriate working relationship with the client system. It is our belief that the contract to be a professional helper includes the responsibility to prepare in every feasible way for a productive working relationship and an effective start-up of that relationship. Unless appropriate anticipatory work is done, the trainer or consultant is not able to think through the types of resource material which will be needed and the types of diagnostic questions which will need to be explored. As we have indicated, such advance planning needs to be regarded as tentative and shared with the participants as a basis for modification and progressive development of the learning design. One of the important aspects of a creative design is that it has in it regular periods for the securing of feedback about reactions to the learning activities, and procedures for sharing influence in the projecting of desirable changes of design.

3. How much individualization of learning activities is needed? What kinds of options should be provided?

Every learning group or client population is composed of individuals with different needs, expectations, and readiness for learning or for work. It is critical that the designers of laboratory learning activities identify these differences between individuals and the different sub-groups which make up the population. One of the challenges of thinking about desired outcomes is to clarify what differences there might be in desirable outcomes for different individuals or sub-groups; to try to be creative about the kinds of individual differences in style of learning and patterns of participation which can be provided for in the design; the types of sub-groupings that can be designed for with different options for their activities. Even though the staff might be small and the group quite large, it is feasible to develop many designs for individualization of learning activities.

4. How much time will be needed? Or how much time is available?

One of the frequent traps for trainers and consultants is to become committed to certain important outcomes in terms of information, skill development, and planning which cannot be realistically accomplished in the time which has been committed by the client population. In the early negotiations of contract (or this may be in the writing of a brochure for a laboratory), it is crucial for the laboratory educator to force himself to be realistic about the time needed to achieve certain goals, or the goals which are feasible to accomplish with a given amount of available time. Such realities often become apparent when a design chart is developed with an estimate of the time needed for the achievement of the various goals.

5. What kinds of continuities are needed? What are the potentialities for supportive follow-up?

One of the most frequent weaknesses is the one-shot characteristic of many training activities. Most significant laboratory learning objectives require some type of supportive continuity of learning activity to stimulate and support the necessary transfer of learnings and application of learnings to the various life situations of the participants. The intensive learning experience may effectively open the clients to new learnings, stimulate new motivations and intentions, and develop significant insights about self or one's life situation. But the evidence from research is that such significant start-up experiences do not carry through to significant transfer and application in most cases, unless the design includes a continuity of support. Such designs for continuity may include interim periods of work and subsequent laboratory sessions such as in the illustrative design in this chapter, or there may be plans for the development of back home teams with a design for continuing team meetings, or there may be designs for follow-up support through a distance, such as telephone and tape, or a wide variety of other possible continuities. The key confronting question for the trainer or consultant is what kind of design for continuity is appropriate, and what kind of commitment is he ready to make?

6. What kind of staffing is needed?

Every designer of a laboratory learning or problem-solving activity must face the question of what types of human resources are needed to carry through the types of activities required to achieve the desired outcomes which have been developed with the particular client population? What kind of division of labor will be needed in a staff team? What variety of skills will be required? Will special resource persons be needed for short times to supplement the knowledge and resources of the designers? Some very creative designs call for the securing of taped responses to key questions from resource persons at a distance, or the setting up of telephone conferences to achieve certain kinds of technical information. There are many creative ways of facing the questions about the matching of needed human resources to the needs and expectations of a particular client population and type of work to be done.

7. What ecology is needed to facilitate the learning design?

In the early years of laboratory learning programs, much emphasis was placed on a "cultural island" removed from all the pressures and distractions of ongoing work and life situations. As the applications of laboratory learning have extended to many other populations and learning objectives, many additional criteria for the selection of an effective learning ecology have been clarified. For example, the laboratory design may include the requirement of collecting data or testing out plans in the reality of situations of the community as part of the design, and, therefore, it may be important for the program to be located near or in a large community. The requirement of a particular organizational population may be that only limited time blocks are available, but on a regular basis, so that it may be most efficient to create a limited "cultural island" within the office building or nearby. There are many new creative designs that balance the needs for freedom from distraction and the importance of being able to interact with the reality context of daily work or other aspects of life situations. The support for transfer and application is a critical requirement, as well as the need for periods of freedom from involvement in these other aspects of life situations.

These are a few of the decision challenges which must be

coped with by creative designers of laboratory education programs. With these in mind, let's return to our case illustration, and look at a second design tool which helps the designer move from his summary sheet of background information to the constructing of a macro-design for the training or the consulting sequence. The illustration in Chart II summarizes the flow of four phases of a macro-design, with an attempt to provide enough detail to illustrate the way in which this tool has been used in designing laboratory learning programs.

Macro-Design Interim Phase II

By the end of the two and one-half day start-up, we expect that each participant will have developed and tested by consultation with staff and peers a design for a training event or consultation sequence, or action start-up, to be implemented during the next two months.

The staff commits two evening periods for telephone or tape consultation which is included in the total tuition fee. An appointment schedule is made for half-hour periods on the phone with the staff (using phone amplifier box) or a half-hour for the staff to respond to a tape or list of questions which have been sent in.

Macro-Design Phase III — Second Residential Period

The two-day follow-up, two months after the first period, is planned for with the design charts presented above. The two days focus on "clinic sessions" on innovations and issues from the interim experiences, and skill practice of critical dilemmas or confrontations which have been identified. Work is done on ethical issues, professional standards, and development of a personal plan for continuing professional growth. The group decides on a follow-up newsletter to exchange practices.

Macro-Design Phase IV — Follow-Up Support And Evaluation

As agreed on, the staff distributes analyses and summarizes a follow-up evaluation of the program and its impact six months after Phase III. One of the participants collects and duplicates the contributions to the newsletter.

Some Additional Design Decisions

In reviewing the decisions made by the designers in planning, and carrying through the design illustrated in Chart II, we have identified a number of key decisions which would be generic to most laboratory learning designs.

1. What kind of design for start-up involvement will provide an effective entry into the learning situation?

One response to this question is illustrated in the

ILLUSTRATIVE DESIGN CHART II: MACRO-DESIGN FOR TRAINING SEQUENCE

Residential Phase (2½ days)

Purpose: To work on development of design to introduce an educational innovation in back-home system, and to create a back-home action plan with commitment to skill development to implement during three-month interim period.

Time	*Activity*	*Method*	*Who's Responsible*	*Setup Facilities Equipment Resources*
1:30 - 2:00	Individualized start-up entry providing data about special skills, needs, expectations	Sheet on wall with name on; briefing sheet of questions to respond to on sheet	Ron put up sheets; Eva do brief. Sheet on easel at door	Newsprint, tape, felt-tip pens, name tags
2:00 - 2:30	Milling—reading each other's sheets, discussing observations	Brief to read & share observations on "Who we are"—differences and similarities	Trainers support & model the activity	Masking tape around on wall to put up sheets
2:30 - 4:30	Practice designing, choosing a case situation for designing from several options. Design teams work one 10-minute stop session to look at team process	Form design team trios of own choice. Input by staff on designing. Each team to produce design & list of design decisions	Trainers model the task for a few minutes on newsprint in front of room	Optimal cases on ditto for teams to read & choose
4:30 - 5:15	Clinic on designs & design decisions. Summary report out last ten minutes	Designs for same case side by side on wall, staff lead critique with participants in 2 groups of 12 moving from case to case	Each trainer lead a clinic group	Two different walls for the two sets of designs

Time	*Activity*	*Method*	*Who's Responsible*	*Setup Facilities Equipment Resources*
5:15 - 7:30	Social hour, dinner	Suggestions of getting acquainted with those you know least or want to probe as resources from wall	Trainers eat together & review observations as relevant to any changes in evening design	Small tables to eat together
7:30 - 9:00	Skill practice on critical intervention decisions & behavior skills. General session reports on skill point discoveries & issues	Afternoon design teams create critical intervention confrontations on cassette tapes by role-play episodes which stop at critical "What should I do now" point. Tapes used for brainstorming alternatives. Skill practice of selected alternatives. Develop criteria for choice	Trainers model procedure for 5 mins. then move around to support groups as they work	Enough cassette recorders supply of cassette spaces for trios to record
9:00 - 9:15	Feedback to staff, review of tentative design for tomorrow	Fill out feedback sheet. Group interview by staff to interpret data. Presentation of design plan for critique & modification if needed	Eva lead. Ron record data on newsprint	

The next 2 days were tentatively pre-planned in similar fashion and modified as feedback and discovery of emergent needs guided modifications of the design. The criteria for flexibility and choice between alternatives are much clearer when there is a plan to change from, as contrasted to a "play it by ear" philosophy.

micro-design presentation in the next section.

2. What kind of contract development and clarification process is desirable?

Very frequently, a planning group is not ready to participate vigorously in contract development until they have had enough warm-up experience to feel confident and competent. In other situations, contract development work has begun in the early stages of planning and final negotiations are appropriate at the time of the start-up laboratory learning activities.

3. What are the best continuities for the work sequences?

This includes questions of whether the sequence of learning or problem solving can best start with informational input, or with a confronting case situation, or with interpersonal process work, or with a value inquiry. The confrontation and search design developed by Millgate and his associates at Xicom starts with a confronting behavior situation to be coped with, and the exploration of reading resources, followed by another behavioral try. Other sequences start with conceptual information input from which are derived participative activities which move to skill practice. The variety of patterns emphasizes more deductive or more inductive start-ups and sequences. It is important for the designer to clarify what the preferred sequence is for the specific learning purpose. The effective handling of the transition from one type of learning activity to another is another challenging decision area.

4. When are the appropriate times for which kinds of work?

Most trainers and consultants, from their experience in working with clients, have discovered certain types of activities are good "morning work," other types of activities to mobilize the post-lunch period or the late afternoon time, and still other activities more appropriate for evening sessions. Any successful design must face such decisions about timing.

5. What timing for work and relaxation?

Another question of timing has to do with the total workload that is appropriate for a day, three days, a week, and the best timing for relaxation, free time, the lunch break, the best starting time in the morning, etc. There are very important regional and cultural differences in style of life that must be taken into account, as well as the intensity of the work, the nature of the emotional investment, and the comfort of the physical space. It is unfortunately true that most designers over-schedule the work time in the early phases of the design, leading to a gradient of fatigue, rather than providing for a design which facilitates increasing enthusiasm and motivation as the learning program develops.

6. The timing of process work interventions and task work interventions.

In laboratory learning, designs where the primary focus is on process learning, such as personal growth laboratories or T group programs, it is important for the designer to make decisions as to where opportunities for task work should be provided in the sequence, so that the personal insights and process learnings can be applied experimentally in work tryout situations before the laboratory period is over. If the focus of the laboratory learning sequence is primarily on problem solving, task work, skill development, or team development, then the designer needs to make decisions about the most appropriate timing for "process stop sessions" to help the participants reflect on the interpersonal and group processes involved in the work, and to generate insights about ways of improving productivity through paying attention to process.

7. How does support of personal integration work?

In almost every laboratory learning design, the participant engages in quite a wide variety of learning activities, usually in a variety of groupings. Very often designers tend to neglect to set aside appropriate time and support for "alone time work" on the synthesizing and integrating of the experiences into meaningful personal generalizations and insights and plans for application. It is very important for designers to think through the most effective ways of helping each participant personally to integrate his learnings.

8. What are the best ways to support applicatron and transfer and provide an appropriate termination experience?

It was traditional for some years for laboratory designs to devote a final period of the laboratory to "back home application." This was clearly an inappropriate amount of emphasis and timing to provide the support necessary for transfer of learnings. There is research evidence to support the idea that creative transfer is most likely to happen if the here-and-now learning situation and the then-and-there application situation are both maintained psychologically as "overlapping situations" in the life space of a learner. Therefore, it is very important for the designer of laboratory learning sequences to think through effective strategies of providing opportunities to work on application and transfer of learnings and to provide for psychologically open-ended rather than "terminal" closures in the learning program. The decisions about this strategy of support and transfer are perhaps even more critical than the design decisions about entry and start-up. Both aspects of designing are among the most important in the repertoire of the laboratory educator.

With this orientation to the macro-design level of decision making, we are ready to move on and look at micro-designing, or the development of the specific modules of the laboratory learning program.

Types of Foci in Micro-Design

The focus of micro-designs is on either a single short period training activity or in support of a larger macro-design. Here are some typical micro-design modules within a macro-design for training.

1. A start-up and entry orientation unit.

   This is the process whereby the consultant-trainer designs how a particular meeting will begin and how participants will be involved in that beginning.

2. A contract development and clarification unit.

   Included here is the whole question of the contract with the client or clients, and how it will be carried out. In the case of a one-time two and one-half hour meeting, this contract may be part of start-up and entry.

3. Information input and conceptual resource designs.

   Often it is necessary to design for units of information giving. This may be done verbally by one person or several persons. It may be done through a taped input, either video or audio tape. Or, it may be done through a confrontation search design, where the participants are confronted with an episode and have to search for the answers in order to get their information.

4. A process sensitivity module.

   This may focus on intra-personal, inter-personal, or inter-group processes.

5. Skill development units, where the focus is on helping the participants learn a particular skill, like listening or leading a meeting.

6. Value confrontation and dialogue units, where the emphasis is on pluralism, an opportunity for participants to become aware of a variety of points of views and values, and a chance to increase their understanding of that variety through confrontation, negotiation, creative compromise, and other designs.

7. Goal setting and decision making modules. Often it is the purpose of a micro-design to help participants set goals and decide how to begin to work on them.

8. Feedback and the utilization of feedback micro-designs. A stop session, for example, after an hour of a two-hour meeting, can give people feedback on the way they are doing and on some of their process hangups. Before the next half-hour is over, there can be feedback on the feedback, and suggestions on how the information can be utilized to improve the process of a group.

9. Diagnostic work units, including such procedures as force-field analysis, and internal dialogue in which the participant listens

to all the kinds of voices, attitudes, and feelings within himself and writes a dialogue between these voices in relation to a particular situation, for example, whether or not to risk a new way of doing things.

10. Action planning, commitment, and application modules, where the participants are helped to plan action in a way that gets them committed, tests feasibility, and clarifies next steps, so that after the unit, they can continue with the action planning they have begun during the session.

11. Support designs. These may be designs that support beginnings taken during the meeting, but continue after the meeting. This could include taped conversations with the trainers, telephone follow-up, personal consultation. It may be support between the participants that is designed in as a micro-unit.

12. Anticipatory skill practice units, which provide an opportunity to practice skills needed to take actions which are planned and anticipated.

13. Exchange of practice designs, where there is an opportunity for participants interested in creating new practices to exchange these practices in a way that allows them to adapt the practices of another. For example, a group of third grade teachers might meet to exchange practices on how to help un-turned on third graders to learn how to read. They can do a group interview in such a way that they can utilize each other's innovative practices in that area.

CRITICAL DESIGN DECISIONS AND DILEMMAS

Before, during, and after micro-designing, there are a variety of decisions that need to be made and a number of dilemmas that the designer typically faces.

1. Deciding on appropriate briefing techniques, how to brief the participants at the beginning of an event, and/or during that event, so they can participate fully and knowledgeably.

2. Selecting support materials, what kinds of materials to have ready; how much of any given material will be needed; and when to hand it out. These materials may include everything from short articles to newsprint, masking tape, pens, and audio tapes. They include all those materials needed to support the activities of participants in a particular design.

3. What are participant options? What are the kinds of options that should be open to the participants, so that they may be able to choose one activity over another? Or should there be any options at all? Sometimes it is necessary for the total group to do the same things so that they can learn through comparing

their data.

4. Decisions about time and timing, including such decisions as how long something should take, whether or not to let it run longer when the group seems to need more time, and also, how to allow for the different rates of speed of learning and participation. The other thing that comes in here is what kinds of activities to put at the beginning or toward the end of a design, or the afternoon as different from the evening session.

5. Stop sessions for process review. When should one have a stop session for the group to look at its process and consider how to improve its productivity? The timing of these stop sessions is very critical, and one has to make the decision whether or not in a micro-design such a session will help or hinder the task work.

6. Transitions are another decision dilemma, because one has to decide on how to move from one activity to another in a connected way, rather than there being a series of short staccato events.

7. Time for review and integration. Such times are needed in order for the group to know where they are, why they are doing what they are doing, and in order to move on.

8. How to present clarity of rationale at the beginning is important, so that the group knows why they are doing what they are doing, and has a chance to question that rationale if they want to.

9. Staff roles. There has to be a decision made as to what will be the role of the staff members at the beginning and during the activities. Will they be giving input? Or will they act as consultants and rovers in order to help participants? Or will they be available for questions? The role needs to be clear to the staff, and shared with the participants.

10. Physical space and layout. Decisions must be made on how the physical space that is available is to be used, i.e., it is important if one has many table groups participating to be sure that each of these tables is an island to itself, if people are to hear one another and work comfortably in that kind of a set-up. Also, this includes looking at the problems of microphone facilities, plugs for tape recorders, and the availability of coffee and other beverages throughout the meeting at the side of the room, so that one does not have to take a coffee break. The physical ecology is terribly important to the smooth handling of a micro-design.

11. Dealing with initial dependencies. Often groups become very dependent on the trainer, particularly when they think there is only a short time together. It is important to very quickly clarify in the contract that in order to get something from the meeting, they all need to participate as actively as possible with the trainer-consultant being available to help them when needed.

12. Endings. Not only when to end, but what to make the last activity, and how to tie up the micro-design in a way that people can walk away, ready for next steps to be taken on their own.

Illustrative Micro-Design

Since the micro-design may very well be part of the sequence of a macro-design, we shall use an example of a design, the purpose of which is to transmit information about societal trends that have implications for the participants. This is a conceptual input session that lasts approximately two and one-half hours. The session is a part of a macro-design for approximately one hundred people, who are teams from community agencies working on a community diagnosis and action plan over a series of six meetings.

The first meeting, after getting acquainted and getting clear on the purpose of their series and the general agenda, now sets the tone by looking at the kind of societal trends that affect the communities in which these people work.

ROLES OF THE DESIGNERS

The designer-consultant-trainer assumes many roles in the designing of participative learning and change experiences. Often these roles are not simultaneous, and certainly most designer-consultants-trainers are not equally skilled at all of them. But sooner or later, these are the kinds of roles that are necessary for the movement of participants in their participatory learning experiences. Sometimes trainer-consultants find that they need additional people to help them because they cannot assume some of these roles as skillfully as can others. The roles include those of:

1. Planner. Planner-designer of the learning-experience.

2. Contract initiator. Often the trainer-consultant has to initiate discussion about contract, even though the first request for his services may not have been initiated by him but by the client.

3. Teacher. At some point in the design the trainer does become a teacher for short periods of time.

4. Team leader and builder. It is the task of the trainer-consultant to be the leader of either a team of staff people, or sometimes it is a team of inside-outside consultants, and, as he leads the team, he tries to build it, that is to mold it into a working group that can maximize the learning of the participants.

5. Resource finder. It is the job of the trainer-consultant to find the necessary resources. These include human resources, such as table leaders and recorders, or projectionists, etc., as well as material resources. This may include everything from microphones, tape recorders and equipment, to newsprint, masking

ILLUSTRATIVE DESIGN — MICRO — CHART III

Purpose: To help participants understand the future societal trends affecting their communities now.
Number of Participants: 100 — men and women — 20 to 63 years of age, in teams of three or more from some agencies.
Time available: Approximately 2½ hours — 9:30 a.m. to 12:15 p.m.

Time	*Activity*	*Method*	*Who's Responsible*	*Facilities-Resources*
9:00 to 9:30 a.m.	Registration—Assignment to tables Coffee and tea available	Individual hosting and greeting by planning committee members	Registration and planning committee	Four tables, 16 chairs, name tags, pins, pens, registration folders, coffee, tea, cream, sugar, cups, spoons, available all morning
9:30 to 9:45 a.m.	Greetings—overview of entire sequence, overview of today's plan with rationale. Questions for clarification	Dialogue with overhead projector. Total group participation	Inside trainer and outside trainer-consultant	Ten tables for ten persons each. Numbers on tables, newsprint on tables, large felt pens (2/table) masking tape, overhead projector, transparencies, special pens, extension cord.
9:45 to 10:00 a.m.	"Major Societal Trends Affecting Community Work and Workers" Introduction to our work on trends	Lecturette in 6 pieces. After each trend is presented there is discussion of implications	Outside trainer-consultant with table group leaders	Hand-out materials on trends
10:00 to 10:15 a.m.	Presentation of Trend 1. Discussion of this trend	Lecturette, table groups discuss implications for them	Trainer-consultant table groups	Newsprint and own materials to write on
10:15 to 10:30 a.m.	Report out	Table leaders report one implication they have discussed	Trainer-consultant	Implications listed on newsprint, 4 mikes around the room

Time	*Activity*	*Method*	*Who's Responsible*	*Facilities-Resources*
10:30 to 10:50 a.m.	Presentation of Trends 2 & 3. Discussion	Table discussion around what agencies or organizations might have to do differently	Trainer-consultant	Newsprint, pens
10:50 to 10:55 a.m.	Trend 4		Trainer-consultant	Newsprint, pens
10:55 to 11:10 a.m.	Table participation after instructions in rules for brainstorming	They brainstorm & record on newsprint all the possible implications of this trend	Table groups	Newsprint, pens
11:15 to 11:20 a.m.	Trends 5 and 6		Inside trainer	
11:20 to 11:30 a.m.	Total group involvement	People call out implications and they are put on the overhead projector	Trainer-consultant	
11:30 to 11:50 a.m.	Pulling together action ideas from implications. Trainer-consultant visits each table	List *all* the action ideas by teams (individual work together). Star those to start on	Trainer-consultant leads	List action ideas on sheets of newsprint and hang on wall
11:50 to noon	Summary of major action ideas	Lecturette	Inside trainer	
Noon to 12:15 p.m.	Perusal of reports on wall	Walk about as they go to lunch and see action ideas of other teams		Wall exhibit

tape, and pens. Often this includes the name tags as well as the beverages that are necessary, or the food, if this is part of the meeting.

6. Continuity provider. It is necessary to provide continuity for the participants. Often this is done through verbal input; sometimes through a question period, or through instructions on an overhead projector.

7. Consultant. The trainer-designer-consultant may act as consultant to individuals or groups throughout the time of the micro-design. He may do this by wandering and offering consultation, or it may be done because participants ask for consultation, or it may be a mixture of both.

8. At-the-elbow supporter. Often the trainer needs to be available to recognize the efforts of participants and to support such effort by simply recognizing and being positive to individuals and groups who are working on some particular task.

9. Leader of sessions or pieces thereof. It may be necessary for the consultant to give directions and to lead the beginnings of the pieces of the micro-design.

10. Input. This is when the consultant actually gives a lecture or offers information in a verbal way to the group.

11. Molder of design to outcomes. It is the job of the consultant-trainer to be sure that the design is tailored in such a way that the outcomes that are desired happen.

12. Process intervener. The consultant decides when and how such interventions need to be made. It may be done verbally, or more likely, through stop sessions with little printed slips suggesting a particular way of processing to the various small groups or to the group with which he is working.

13. Blockage identifier or "hangup" identifier. It is often the job of the consultant to identify where blocks are, and to help participants overcome these blocks.

CONCLUDING COMMENTS

We have attempted in this chapter to identify some of the major functions and roles of the laboratory educator as a designer of learning sessions, sequences, and programs.

In addition, we have provided a framework of dimensions of the design task, and illustrations of the use of tools for designing. Finally, we have identified key decisions of designing, at four levels of decision-making — learning environment decisions, macro-design decisions, micro-design decisions, and intervention decisions.

CHAPTER 9

AWARENESS LEARNING AND SKILL DEVELOPMENT

Eva Schindler-Rainman and Ronald O. Lippitt

In Chapter 6, we identified a variety of areas of content that often are focused on in laboratory education designs; for example, values, concepts, theories, emotions and feelings, skills, awareness, goals, and back home plans. In this chapter we discuss two complementary core areas of laboratory training, namely, the development of awareness and the development of skills. We believe the concepts and designs for helping with these two areas of learning give us a good opportunity to review and articulate some methods of laboratory education which combine structured learning opportunities with a concern for the unique learning needs of individual or group clients.

We will focus first on the concepts and methods of awareness learning. We will focus next on the concepts and methods of skill development. We will then discuss the linkage between these two types of learning, and finally we will suggest ways in which these two types of learning objectives and activities fit into the larger context of designs for laboratory education.

A CONCEPTUAL NOTE ON AWARENESS AND SKILL

Kurt Lewin defined the "motoric functions" of the person or group as composed of two aspects: (1) the output or behavioral functions of doing, of action; and (2) the input reception functions of perceiving — seeing, hearing, sensing. We will refer to skill as the achieving of excellence of functioning in both of these functions of action and reception, of output and input transactions between the system and its environment.

We have defined awareness as a number of inside-the-system processes which determine the nature and quality of the use of the input mediated to the system by the perceptual motoric. Awareness also influences the nature of the guidance and direction given to the system output or action motoric. The internal values, goals, needs, knowledge — to the degree that they are available as awareness — provide resources and guidance in the processing of incoming data and in directing the perceptual search for relevant input. The internal state of awareness also includes the goals, intentions, and means-end images which activate and guide behavioral output. The sensitivity, sophistication, or excellence of the quality of awareness thus greatly influences behavior. Also, the level of skill of the perceptual functions and behavioral repertoire will determine how well awareness is supplied with external data, and how sensitively the repertoire of behaviors represents the goals, values, and intentions of the person or group.

It follows from this conception that a learning program (such as many of those in our educational system) which places major emphasis on awareness development may generate great frustration if the behavioral skills to actualize the awareness in human action and interaction are missing. And a training program which focuses just on skill development may result in efficient but "inhumane" behavioral competence which lacks the guidance and sensitivity of highly developed goals and values.

So the two sections of this chapter are actually complementary and interdependent.

AWARENESS LEARNING

As one looks at the function of awareness and the process of awareness learning it becomes clear that this process involves awareness of the self, that is, sensitivity to the internal society or internal voices interacting within the self, and also awareness of one's own physiological and psychological functionings. It includes further the ability to sense whether one is feeling well or not, worthy or unworthy, being liked or not, feeling happy or not, feeling secure or not.

Awareness also involves relationship between the self and one other or several others. Included here are such feelings as empathy. These relationships may be of a long standing personal nature, and may include both a present and past time perspective. Or the relationship may be a short term contact, either personal or professional, or just a happenstance, temporary contact. Or the relationship may involve an ongoing relationship, such as a love relationship between members of a family or love relationships between consenting persons. Relationships with another or others may be long-standing, short-term, or ongoing. They may be of a deep, meaningful personal nature, or of a superficial, impersonal, temporary nature, or they may be deeply personal and temporary. So both time and feeling perspectives are important aspects of awareness.

Another kind of awareness of relationship is between the person and the larger environment. This larger environment may be the immediate environment of a person, such as home, garden, and community. Or it may be a remote and larger environment, such as the state, the nation, or the total world. The larger environment may include the cultural environment — art, music, drama, prose, poetry, dance, nature and all of the surroundings of trees, mountains, streams, rivers, sunup and sundown; ecology — noise, crowds, or their opposites; the economic and political arenas; the welfare, health, recreation, and public safety arenas. Awareness of the larger environment may be in terms of geography or in terms of such functional communities as those mentioned above.

There are many different levels of awareness and ways of relating to these different environments. Both we and the situations we are in are always changing. Therefore, awareness needs to change, too. For instance, in a person's relation to himself, he may have a variety of self-images, including insights into his limitations, as well as his strengths and abilities; insight into potency and competency; into prejudices; or into his hopes, aspirations, and goals. Relationships with others may be relationships of love, friendship, hate, reciprocity, non-caring, dependence, independence, complementarity, support, non-support. In brief, one's relationships with others, near and far, display a large variety of characteristics, and one's awareness of these varies tremendously.

Some Dimensions of Awareness

Becoming aware surely includes arousal, meaning to stir up, excite, or stimulate. This may happen through a variety of learning activities: for example, confrontation, activation, model presentation, comparison, and exhortation. The learning media may include films, audio and video tape, records, sounds of music or other sounds, poetry, noise, non-verbal activities, dance, odor, and touch. The sensory modalities involved in awareness and becoming aware include seeing, hearing, touching, smelling, and kinesthetic sensing. The objects of awareness may be the self, other, others, groups, social systems, and the larger environment.

In another dimension, awareness may involve the *attribution of feelings aroused* by an object in nature or art toward the object itself, as when one speaks of a painting full of love. Or awareness may be understandings so intimate that the feelings, thoughts, and motives of one are readily comprehended by another.

Awareness may involve reflection and thinking deeply and seriously. This is usually an activity of the self for the self. But often the source of awareness is communication and exchange of feelings and perceptions between the self and one other, several others, or the larger environment. It usually includes both verbal and non-verbal communications. Projecting future images is another kind of awareness which is very important for personal functioning. This really means projecting a plan for an anticipated course of action. One can project aspirations, hopes, fears, apprehensions, expectations.

Why Awareness Learning is Part of Laboratory Education

There are many reasons to learn how to enrich life or the quality of life through becoming more aware. These may include the wish for a better knowledge of self, or the wish for more data of a whole variety of kinds about oneself and others, and about the larger world. Or one may wish for a more sensitive use of self in a variety of interpersonal situations. Other reasons for awareness learning include the possibility of an enriched self-view and enjoyment of and sensitivity to the world around us — people, nature, things, happenings. It is possible to enhance greatly people's sensitivity to their environments. Learning may also enlarge one's ability to cope with confrontations, self-doubts, limitations, or with challenges in life. Or it may free one to learn of one's needs for support of all varieties.

This kind of learning can increase one's ability to relate to others in one-to-one, small group, and large group situations. The wish to improve one's relationships with others is the motivation for many to participate in awareness learning. Also, awareness learning may be used to increase one's sense of interdependence with a larger surrounding.

Where Does Awareness Learning Fit Into the Personal and Social Problem-Solving Process?

An interesting fact about awareness, or becoming aware, is that it provides the possibility of *integrating knowledge and feeling, or content and process.* Such integration is necessary if one is to have a functional understanding of the complexity of personal and social problem-solving processes. Further, increased awareness may enable the participant to retrieve and *blend happenings of past, present, and future,* which will enhance sensitivity to the complexity of time frames. Increased awareness enables the learner to improve his perceptiveness and his verbal and non-verbal communications, and enriches his comprehension of the resources of self and understanding of the resources of others. This enables a person to utilize his own and others' resources better. In working with groups, increased awareness should help trainer and participants to be more sensitive to both individual and group processes, to the cues, symbols, and signs of communication between members of a group or an organization.

Increased awareness can make clearer the feelings and emotions that help or hinder task-focused problem-solving. The forces that help or hinder problem-solving become much clearer as one becomes more sensitively aware of all of the dynamics of the situation. For laboratory educators, increased awareness of self, others, and the larger environment allows for a more conscious use of self. This means that the self can be used as a professional tool, rather than to rely on actions stemming from an unexamined intuitive base. It is helpful to distinguish process sensitivity or awareness, and task- or work-centered awareness. Laboratory education needs to focus on the enhancement of both kinds of awareness.

The Activation of Task and Process Awareness

In order to be motivated to enhance one's awareness, the activity must be legitimized as part of a participative learning program important to both the trainer and the participants. It is part and parcel of a trainer's design to help participants become aware of themselves, others, and the larger environment, particularly in relation to whatever the content and purpose of a given learning activity may be. One of the ways by which this can be done is through taking the roles of others in order to understand their feelings and motivations, thereby enhancing one's own ability to diagnose, plan, treat, and evaluate. Learning activities should also increase a learner's ability to be self-evaluative, self-critical, and self-helping, as he is helped to develop the values, skills, and tools that support these functions. When awareness is activated, it is possible to participate in third party dialogue and to help others become aware of their feelings about the process issues as well as the task issues that confront them. Also, the learner may be helped to achieve more awareness of causal connections between goals and means and to perceive more alternative paths of action for himself than he is now able to perceive.

ILLUSTRATIVE AWARENESS–LEARNING ACTIVITIES

Types of Task-Centered Awareness

As trainers design laboratory education programs, with various outcome objectives and with different types of client groups, it is important to be sensitive to the different "clusters of awareness" which may be important foci for learning activities. In Chart 1A the left hand columns suggest what seem to us to be some of these types of awareness.

Types of Process-Centered Awareness

In Chart 1B we have summarized what seem to be some of the important areas of sensitivity to relationships within the self or between persons which need to be acquired in order that individuals may be able to relate to each other, interact with each other, and to collaborate with each other sensitively in the process of pursuing goals or seeking personal security and growth. Here are seven clusters of process-awareness which seem important to us.

CHART 1A
TASK-CENTERED LEARNING MATRIX

Type of Awareness	*Examples of Awareness*	*System Level*	*Awareness Level*	*Illustrative Awareness Learning Activities*
1. Resources	Location Interrelation Availability Content	Intra-person Inter-person Group Inter-group Organization Community Macro-System	—Self —Others —Surroundings —From no awareness to total awareness	Own resource inventory Human resource directories One person interviews Group interviews Exchange of practices Using storage systems

Type of Aware-ness	*Examples of Aware-ness*	*System Level*	*Aware-ness Level*	*Illustrative Aware-ness Learning Activities*
2. Oppor-tunities and Options	Location Relevance Support	Intra-person Inter-person Group Inter-group Organization Community Macro-System	—Self —Others —Surround-ings —From no awareness to total awareness	Brainstorming Imaging alternatives Observation Sub-groups Alternative inter-pretations
3. Goal Rele-vancy Crite-ria Values	—Reward value —Potential risks —Degree of consensus	Intra-person Inter-person Group Inter-group Organization Community Macro-System	—Self —Others —Surround-ings —From no awareness to total awareness	Forcefield analysis Value Clarification
4. Action Alter-natives	Feasibility Difficulty Legitimacy	Intra-person Inter-person Group Inter-group Organization Community Macro-System	—Self —Others —Surround-ings —From no awareness to total awareness	Brainstorming Role-playing Pilot testing or tryout Creative thinking exercises
5. Latent Con-cealed Uncon-scious Re-pressed	Hidden agenda Organization Defenses Guilt	Intra-person Inter-person Group Inter-group Organization Community Macro-System	—Self —Others —Surround-ings —From no awareness to total awareness	Internal dialogue Significant others Non-verbal techniques Johari Window Montages
6. Goal Means Con-nection	—Magical thinking —Side effects	Intra-person Inter-person Group Inter-group Organization Community Macro-System	—Self —Others —Surround-ings —From no awareness to total awareness	Action derivations Consequence analysis Consequence brainstorm Creating thinking techniques

Type of Awareness	*Examples of Awareness*	*System Level*	*Awareness Level*	*Illustrative Awareness Learning Activities*
7. Path Sequences	—What are first steps? —How long?	Intra-person Inter-person Group Inter-group Organization Community Macro-System	—Self —Others —Surroundings —From no awareness to total awareness	Paths of progress PERT charting Diagnosis Verbal and non-verbal
8. Interdependence of different goals, needs and means	Competition Compromise Potential Complementary	Intra-person Inter-person Group Inter-group Organization Community Macro-System	—Self —Others —Surroundings —From no awareness to total awareness	Brainstorm connections Use films Value dialogue Significant connector conversations Life planning techniques Collaboration simulation game

CHART 1B
PROCESS-CENTERED AWARENESS LEARNING MATRIX

Type of Awareness	*Examples of Awareness*	*System Level*	*Awareness Level*	*Illustrative Awareness Learning Activities*
1. Feelings about self and others	Love Respect Trust Distrust	Intra-person Inter-person Group Inter-group Organization Community Macro-System	—Self —Others —Surroundings —From no awareness to total awareness	Non-verbal movement Trust exercises Brown bag Paired interviews T-group Gestalt "hot seat"
2. Feelings about things, nature, etc.	Beauty Movement Shape	Intra-person Inter-person Group Inter-group Organization Community Macro-System	—Self —Others —Surroundings —From no awareness to total awareness	Guided observation Braille trail Multi-media experience Trust walk Nature walk Non-verbal touch technique

Type of Awareness	*Examples of Awareness*	*System Level*	*Awareness Level*	*Illustrative Awareness Learning Activities*
3. Feelings from	From self From others	Intra-person Inter-person Group Inter-group Organization Community Macro-System	—Self —Others —Surroundings —From no awareness to total awareness	Internal dialogue Breathing and relaxation Non-verbal communication Projective techniques Mirroring T-group
4. Feeling into	Needs of others Fate of others	Intra-person Inter-person Group Inter-group Organization Community Macro-System	—Self —Others —Surroundings —From no awareness to total awareness	Role-reversal Movement Film Alter ego role play Listening games Music or other sounds
5. Feeling a part of	Common fate Bigger focus	Intra-person Inter-person Group Inter-group Organization Community Macro-System	—Self —Others —Surroundings —From no awareness to total awareness	Group merging non-verbals Problem-solving Trend implication discussions Films Slide-tape presentations
6. Interdependence	Effects of own actions Interrelation of decisions	Intra-person Inter-person Group Inter-group Organization Community Macro-System	—Self —Others —Surroundings —From no awareness to total awareness	Team-building exercises Trust exercises Erector set games Simulated tasks Non-verbal turfdom technique
7. Causal connections Interrelations	Circular process Feelings of hostility Reciprocation	Intra-person Inter-person Group Inter-group Organization Community Macro-System	—Self —Others —Surroundings —From no awareness to total awareness	Interdependence games Role play Brainstorm causal connections Self inquiry "The vicious circle package"

The Learning of Task-Centered Awareness

It is not possible here to present a comprehensive "how to do it" manual of awareness designs. The design chapter offers ideas on how to design such activities. Here we offer some illustrations of learning activities that can help to expand the awareness of client-participants.

1. *Resource Awareness.* In order to increase the client-participant's awareness of human resources, it is possible to: help him/her develop an explicit listing of his own resources; develop a directory of resources of other relevant individuals and groups; do person-to-person interviews to discover resources — skills, knowledge, etc.; hold an exchange of practice session where practitioners using a group interview schedule, exchange information about innovative practices and become aware of alternative practices; have some training sessions on the presence and use of storage systems and clearing houses (like the ERIC system).

2. *Opportunities and Options.* One of the traps in most problem-solving activities is the limited perspective of the participants on the range of opportunities and options which are open to them. Some possibilities: brainstorm all the ways to do something; imagining a situation six months, one year, three years hence and "seeing" and listening in present tense all the things happening that please one; observation of a variety of people in a variety of situations; asking sub-groups to look for and list a variety of ways to do things, and pooling their findings; encouraging alternative interpretations without judging them at the point of their being offered.

3. *Awareness of Goal Relevancy Criteria.* In order to enrich a more aware choice of goal or goals it is possible to use: force-field analysis to become aware of the helps and blocks in the field of goal setting and reaching; value clarification dialogue pushes awareness of different value stances rather than consensus.

4. *Awareness of Action Alternatives.* Awareness of action alternatives is important if the client-participant is to be aware of a variety of action possibilities we have used: anticipatory role-playing to become aware of behavior possibilities before doing them in the real situation; trying out various actions in the pilot testing sense to become aware of reactions as well as alternative possibilities; creative think exercises to push out the boundaries of awareness inhibitors such as thinking through and listing all the consequences if all laws were removed from society — or the unusual user test.

5. *Awareness of Latent, Concealed, Unconscious, Repressed Facts.* Developing an awareness of hidden agenda and of the defensive collusions within self, selves, and organizations as well as inhibited needs and motives is a crucial area for developing

diagnostic awareness.

This is a hard area to work on, but it is possible to become more aware through such methods as: internal dialogue where one writes a conversation between the various voices within the self, about some particular issue such as whether or not to participate in an awareness laboratory; besides an internal committee or internal voices all of us carry the voices, structures, advice of the significant others (lover, mother, father, friend, child, teacher, etc.) in our lives. As one makes choices or decisions, it is possible to become aware of who is affecting one as well as how the significant other influences us; a variety of non-verbal methods combined with verbal soliloquy or dialogue is available; the Johari Window is designed to help one look at things I am aware of and you are not; things we are both aware of; things you are aware of and I'm not; things neither of us have access to; montages that picture one's feelings or the characteristics of a group.

6. *Awareness of Goal-Means Connections.* A clear grasp of the connection between desired goals and thought about means is an important aspect of problem-solving sensitivity. These can be achieved through: looking at and analyzing a series of alternative actions and deriving a whole variety of outcomes; seeing all the consequences of any given action; brainstorming all the consequences of a given action or series of actions; creative, think-stretching techniques.

7. *Awareness of Path Sequences.* Developing a perspective about strategic first steps and conceptions of the number of steps and the length of time required for a particular problem-solving sequence are crucial aspects of awareness which need to be explored in laboratory learning designs. Both the path of progress and PERT charting are ways to become aware of sequential step-designing, including time and commitment dynamics; a variety of diagnostic awareness tools are available including observation questionnaires, interviews, listening to audio tapes, seeing video tapes, etc.; what-follows-what can also be enacted nonverbally with verbal feedback.

8. *Awareness of Interdependence of Diverse Goals, Needs, and Means.* Often persons are aware of one or the other of these dimensions but often they build no interdependent connections between them. Such awareness can be built through: brainstorming all the possible connections; using films to illustrate interdependence of different variables; value dialogue to become aware of different ways to see and value interdependence; life planning exercises; using a collaboration simulation to increase awareness by participants of all the dynamics involved in collaboration of different agencies and organizations.

The Learning of Process-Centered Awareness

1. *Feelings About Self and Others.* It is important to know, sense, be aware of one's feelings about one's self and of feelings toward and about others. Awareness of feelings about self and others can be developed in a large variety of ways: non-verbal movement can be utilized to express feelings and to become aware of the variety of possibilities (for example, joy, caring, hostility, frustration, competition, fear, love, etc.); trust exercises to become aware of one's trust or lack of trust in others and vice-versa such as the blind-folded trust walk, being held horizontally in the air by a group of five or six persons being rocked; the brown bag technique is one in which the participant puts on the outside of a paper bag how he wishes to be known (using crayon, cutouts, crepe, and construction paper, glue, etc.) and on the inside of the bag all the things the client-participant wants to become more aware of and to learn; paired interviews, using file folders to record on so the folders can become a resource directory, taped on the wall, of how persons feel about self and others; group interview of client-participants by a peer and/or a trainer re awareness needs or/and feelings about self; being in the "hot seat" to talk about self and get feedback from peers and trainer(s).

2. *Awareness of Feelings About Things.* Most people have little awareness of their total surroundings especially if they are task-focused. To increase this awareness it is possible to have: guided observation trips of a city, neighborhood, a room, a building, a park; Braille trail is a technique in which participants are blindfolded and led by another person through a variety of smelling, tasting, sound, and touching experiences; multi-media experiences where sights, sounds, and kinaesthetic experiences involve the participant to increase simultaneous awareness; the trust walk increases awareness of one's trust and distrust feelings as one walks blindfolded led by a person who can see; nature walk led by someone who knows and can point out plants, animals, shapes, sounds; non-verbal touch techniques where participants touch and feel a variety of textures and shapes sometimes with music in the background.

3. *Awareness of Feelings From.* Feelings are received from a great variety of stimuli inside and outside the self. One can become aware that feelings from outside are there, and what they are, and one can learn how to cope in a variety of ways with the feelings from in the following ways: the internal dialogue can be utilized here to allow the voices of ambivalence to "speak" to each other; lying or sitting quietly becoming aware of one's breathing pattern and then varying this pattern; sending and receiving non-verbal movement messages in trios with an observer; projective techniques such as finger painting or clay modeling; mirroring with

or without music is a non-verbal way to become aware of feelings from self and other as two persons non-verbally mirror each other's movements and later discuss their discoveries; the T group offers many possibilities for increasing participants' awareness of feelings.

4. *Awareness of Feeling Into.* It is really hard to feel into unexperienced situations, or to feel into the challenges or problems of someone else. As one becomes more aware, it becomes possible to increase one's skill to feel into through: reversal of roles in role playing; movement to touch, feel, see; multi-media, audio-visual experiences; communication listening games; sounds — drums, screeching, music, bells.

5. *Awareness of Feeling Part Of.* This is important to a "we oriented" culture like ours. This can mean feeling part of a cause, a small group, a large group, a macro-system. To increase a person's awareness of the degree to which he feels or does not feel part of, it is possible to use the following: non-verbal ways to help a single person become part of a group; for example, one person joins another and this duo becomes part of a quartet — the quartet joins another foursome, etc., until all become one circle; problem-solving together such as doing a puzzle in a group; presentation of a series of societal trends (for example, increasing interdependence of social systems, changing world of work) and asking participants to discuss a variety of implications of each trend for them. There are new films that increase the feelings of being part of a bigger fate (for example, "Is it always Right to be Right?"). Slide-tape participatory presentations can be used.

6. *Awareness of Interdependence.* If one becomes aware of the interdependent part of self and the interdependence of self with others, it becomes possible to use the various parts to achieve a better product solution or decision through such learning activities as: team building games where without the team the task cannot be done; the trust exercises mentioned earlier; an erector set game where participants must build something together with the parts of an erector set they have been given; simulated tasks where a critical incident is simulated and must be solved by several people together; non-verbal techniques where persons describe their turf non-verbally and non-verbally decide to let people in or not or/and decide to leave their turf for that of others or not.

7. *Awareness of Causal Connections and Interrelations.* This can be increased through working on the circular process of cause and effect, thus, helping with learning of meaningful interventions: role-playing situations; it is possible to brainstorm all the things that will occur if ....; a self inquiry instrument can be used to help people become aware of connections within them; the published "Vicious Circle Package" is also available.

System Level Context (Column 3 on Charts)

Awareness at the task and process level of inter-group, organization, and community as well as at the micro-level of self, other, and group is essential to sensitive, effective, and productive diagnosis, decision making, planning, and problem-solving. Awareness training can result in client and practitioners becoming more aware at any level of a human system and, therefore, using such awareness, together with skills of various kinds, to increase the effectiveness of their performances. It is important also to integrate awarenesses across system levels and to be sensitive to and aware of the effects of one system on another. System level is identified in the third column of Charts 1A and 1B as an important dimension of awareness learning.

Awareness Level (Column 4 on Charts)

One can develop different degrees of awareness. There is probably an unconscious level. But, at the conscious and preconscious levels, the continuum might be as follows:

No Awareness	Peripheral Awareness	Some Awareness	Total Awareness

In awareness training, the effort is to help client-participators become more aware of themselves, others, and their surroundings, and to move along the continuum from no awareness toward total awareness. Variables affecting this movement include motivation, time and timing, and training design. Thus, it may be possible for people in a situation to be totally aware of self, but not at all aware of feedback or reactions from others. The training effort is to increase awareness of all the factors affecting a behavioral situation.

SKILL DEVELOPMENT

When Bobby Burns commented that "the best laid plans of mice and men gang aft agley" he was referring to the fact that there is often a discrepancy between our intentions to do something, and the actualization of these intentions in behavioral reality. The idea of *skill* as we are using it in this chapter, means *effective* behavioral implementation of goals, intentions, and plans, and *affectively* appropriate expression of feelings, values, ideas, opinions, and sensitivities.

For our goals, plans, feelings, and intentions to become a successful reality, we must have a repertoire of implementation competencies or behavioral skills to carry out the intentions. We believe that one of the most critical issues of human relations education is the general lack, or very low priority, of a curriculum focus on behavioral skill development. In other areas of learning — reading, writing, arithmetic, sports, cooking, music — there is a major emphasis on the importance of skill practice, of feedback, and of re-practice. This emphasis has been ignored and neglected in the crucial area of social relations and social problem-solving. One of the great strengths of laboratory education has been the emphasis on linking cognitive awareness and affective sensitivity to behavioral actualization in learning processes.

Why is Skill Development A Crucial Element of Laboratory Education Designs?

As we noted in Chapter 7, much educational effort has tended to encourage and support premature learning closures by focusing on and rewarding "getting the concepts right," or "developing sensitivity," or "expressing feelings," or "developing openness of communication." These are all important and necessary foci of laboratory learning activities but they need to be linked to a focus on developing the action skills to carry through on the implications of these cognitive and affective functions. Therefore, it is crucial that a focus on the quality of behavior be constantly present in laboratory learning activities.

Even when there is behavior carry-through of intentions, plans, and feelings, the behavior output often tends to represent very inadequately, inner intentions, plans, and feelings. The awkwardness or inflexibility or impulsiveness of the behavior often guarantees a high probability of failure and creates misunderstandings about motivations, feelings, and intentions. It is crucial, therefore, that learners develop a repertoire of behaviors which become as accurate and valid a representation of themselves as do their plans, intentions, values, and feelings.

Another important reason for emphasizing skill development is that the sense of behavioral competence, of knowing how to express and do, results in psychological security to be more innovative and risk-taking in expressing one's feelings and plans and intentions.

What are the Necessary Conditions for Skill Development Work as Part of Laboratory Education?

It is very hard to see ourselves as others see us and to experience the consequences of our behavior as others experience it. It is necessary that laboratory education designs create situations where we can discover and be confronted with the incongruities between our action-intentions and our action-effects. It is crucial that we receive the kind of feedback that gives us guidelines and motivation to re-practice, to try again and again to develop more communication clarity and behavioral competence.

This type of feedback often is hard to receive and utilize. Therefore, it is crucial that appropriate conditions for receptivity be created. This means, for example, that the learning situation must be one where the learners are "not playing for keeps" in trying out new behaviors and where peers provide an environment which supports the freedom to act and to provide feedback for re-practice.

What Kinds of Skills?

In the sections that follow, the reader will be helped by referring to Charts 2A and 2B, entitled "The Task-Centered Skill Development Matrix" and "The Process-Centered Skill Development Matrix." These two charts give, in schematic form, the material which is elaborated upon in the following sections.

The first question we have asked in attempting to summarize and articulate work on skill development and skill training is, what kinds of skills have been focused on and need to be focused on in laboratory education programs?

The left hand column of the two charts indicates our current version of such a taxonomy. It is relatively crude, but we believe it helps to clarify training objectives and relevant training activities for work on skill practice. We have classified skills as having a primary function of helping implement a problem-solving sequence of *task achievement* or as having a primary function of contributing to *human relations processes.* Productivity and personal satisfaction are simultaneously key aspects of the flow of goal-centered work.

Task-Centered Skills

We have identified eight clusters of task-centered skills, and in the second column of Chart 2A have noted illustrations of these particular skills. It is not feasible in this chapter to provide a "how to do it" manual of skill practice designs. An approach to the design of such activities is presented in Chapter 8.

At this point we would like merely to illustrate some of the type of skill practice activities mentioned in the right-hand column of the chart activities designed to help enhance skills in the various task-centered and process-centered clusters. These glimpses are intended to be illustrative rather than comprehensive.

1. *Goal Setting and Starting.* The setting of goals and the starting of a problem-solving sequence represent one of the most important areas for skill development both by trainers and by participants in laboratory learning programs. Here are a few of the skill development designs we have observed and used: problem census with rank ordering of priorities; taking an imaginary trip into the future and making observations of activities and states of

CHART 2A
TASK-CENTERED SKILL DEVELOPMENT

Type of Skill	*Examples of Skills*	*System Level*	*Skill Level*	*Illustrative Learning Activity Designs*
1. Goal setting Problem-solving Start-ups	Clarifying pain Projecting goal images Assessing the future	Intra-person Inter-person Group Inter-group Organization Community Macro-System	Macro Micro Behavior Ecological	—Image of potentiality exercise —Life planning program —Future trend implication
2. Diagnosis of readiness Alternatives Resources	Assessing readiness for change Discovering alternatives Finding resources for help	Intra-person Inter-person Group Inter-group Organization Community Macro-System	Macro Micro Behavior Ecological	—Group interviews —Internal dialogue —Resource directory
3. Designing for action-taking	Path and sequence projections Designing for collaboration Retrieving practice	Intra-person Inter-person Group Inter-group Organization Community Macro-System	Macro Micro Behavior Ecological	—Forcefield analysis —PERT diagraming —Design practice exercises —Exchange of practice designs
4. Anticipatory preparation for action	Anticipatory role-playing Simulation Retrieving experiences	Intra-person Inter-person Group Inter-group Organization Community Macro-System	Macro Micro Behavior Ecological	—Internal dialogue —Anticipatory tape episodes —Role-playing —Informant interviews —Team rehearsal

CHART 2A (continued)

Type of Skill	*Examples of Skills*	*System Level*	*Skill Level*	*Illustrative Learning Activity Designs*
5. Implementation activities	Leadership role Division of labor Coordination	Intra-person Inter-person Group Inter-group Organization Community Macro-System	Macro Micro Behavior Ecological	—Leader & member role practice —Human resource —Mobilization and utilization —Asking for help norms —Retrieval of technical knowledge
6. Support for action efforts	Involvement of sanctioners Peer commitments	Intra-person Inter-person Group Inter-group Organization Community Macro-System	Macro Micro Behavior Ecological	—Commitment review —Pair development —Decision-maker involvement —Personal feedback —Support, reward
7. Eliciting feedback, evaluation, documenting	Collecting data about progress Documenting work Assessing work satisfaction	Intra-person Inter-person Group Inter-group Organization Community Macro-System	Macro Micro Behavior Ecological	—Developing evaluation design —Documentation practice —Development of tools —Review of progress techniques
8. Processing feedback into implications for changes of goals and actions	Feedback Replanning Goal review	Intra-person Inter-person Group Inter-group Organization Community Macro-System	Macro Micro Behavior Ecological	—Reducing defensiveness —Implication statement session —Designing feedback sessions

affairs which have come to pass that please the goal setters with these images of potentiality; brainstorming discrepancies between behavior and operations as basis for deriving goals; deriving a set of predicted future trends from the futurists' literature and making implication statements about the derivations for goals from these trend statements; listing current confronting problems and selecting a confrontation as the basis for generating alternative ideas for action goals to cope with the problem; using life planning exercises to project own personal goals for development; writing a script for a documentary film or producing a documentary book describing life in the society at some time in the future; developing a plan for scanning the innovative practices of others to derive ideas for relevant goals.

This is just a sample of the many types of designs which help free up the imagination of would-be planners, provide support for the retrieval of information which has stimulus values for future-oriented thinking, and provide support for a discipline of action-oriented thinking about experiences and predictions which others have reported.

2. *Diagnoses of Readiness, Alternatives, and Resources.* The skills of diagnostic data collection are another of the critical clusters of task focused skills. The great variety of fact-gathering skills developed as research methodology are adaptable for educative use by laboratory educators. Usually, the tools need to be simplified to meet the needs of a particular laboratory population. Some of the most useful skills for development in this area, as we have observed them, are: the inner-personal dialogue technique to retrieve diagnostic data from within the self; developing a group interview schedule and skill practice in utilizing it with peers conducting group interviews with other peers; internalizing resistance and readiness to change by brainstorming liabilities and assets of a possible direction of change; techniques for identifying and recording the human and material resources needed for support of a course of action; a variety of pencil and paper data collection techniques such as questionnaires, sentence completion, forced choice, and critical episodes descriptions.

3. *Designing for Action Taking.* The skills in this area include the often-neglected skills of projecting a path and a sequence of activities, defining first steps, and designing of the collaborations needed to make action taking feasible. Particular skill development activities in this area of designing for action include: utilizing a forcefield analysis to make derivations of priorities for action; exercises in which the participants create alternative designs for presentation, critique by others, and redesigning; exercises in sequential step designing with indications of time and commitment; exchange of practice designs which identify and document a

variety of alternative possibilities from the successful action experiences of others.

4. *Anticipatory Preparation for Action.* The skills of designing for action-taking which we have just focused on are critical in making a linkage between goals and intentions and commitments. But the critical linkage often comes in bringing about effective connections between intentions and action commitments and the actual implementation of these in practice. Perhaps the most important linkage which laboratory education can provide for this aspect of successful problem-solving is to provide a variety of anticipatory practice designs where it is possible to try out alternative patterns of action and ways of behaving without the risk of "playing for keeps." There are a variety of skill practice designs for supporting the development of this linkage: creating anticipated confrontation situations on tape or through role playing and practicing alternative ways of coping, with observation and feedback by peers and consultants; conducting internal dialogue exercises between the internal voices supporting risk taking, and those supporting caution and resistance to new action; locating and interviewing informants who have had experience coping with the anticipated situations; the rehearsal of interpersonal support and division of labor in anticipated coping situations.

5. *Implementation Skills.* Many of the important skills of effective action which tend to be neglected in skill development programs focus on behavioral skills for influencing the development of norms about division of labor and resource use, and the skills of interdependent leader and member functions. Some typical exercises which support such skill development are: "round robin" exercises in which members practice leadership skills and membership skills in simulated group task situations; group problem-solving exercises in which the critical skill of how and when to ask for help is emphasized; exercises in retrieval and use of technical knowledge at times when it is needed in a problem-solving activity.

6. *Support for Action Efforts.* When the risk-taking of action commitment is under way, it becomes crucial to provide support for the action taker and the action-taking process. This may include the skills of appropriately involving power figures and sanctioners of the action being taken, of eliciting voluntary peer commitments for support and collaboration, and reinforcement when blocks and frustrations are encountered; developing and practicing "the buddy system" of pair responsibilities for tasks and for each other; design for "review of commitments" as stop sessions in the flow of work; techniques of involving decision makers and sanctioners as support mechanisms; practicing the

skills of giving supportive personal feedback and rewards.

7. *Feedback, Evaluation, and Documentation Skills.* Collecting data on progress toward a goal is one of the most important means of sustaining motivation and of revising direction to assure optimal success with minimum expenditure of energy. Therefore, the techniques of eliciting feedback and evaluation data about movement and direction are critical skills, as is the skill of designing and implementing a program of documentating the flow of activity. Some designs for skill development in this area are: practice in the development and critiquing of evaluation designs; practice in systematic documentation of activities; the development of feedback tools; practice in the skills of "selling evaluation" and briefing participants in the use of evaluation tools; designing personal projects to permit review of progress toward learning goals.

8. *Processing Feedback Into Implications for Change of Goals and Actions.* One of the clusters of skills which tend to be neglected are skills having to do with the utilization of feedback and evaluation in order to review the goals which are being pursued and the means which are being used to achieve them.

Often laboratory educators are quite effective in helping learners and client systems develop evaluation tools and procedures but tend to neglect the critical set of skills for processing and using such data in revising goals and courses of action. This cluster of skills may be developed by such designs as: role-playing sessions on coping with defensiveness and resistances in looking at feedback data; the designing of feedback sessions and the creation of the necessary software to communicate feedback effectively; skill practice in helping clients derive action implication statements from evaluation data.

PROCESS-CENTERED SKILL DEVELOPMENT (Chart 2B)

This is parallel to our task-centered taxonomy in Chart 2A. Although some of these process-centered skills may be quite comparable to task-centered ones, we believe it is important in designing training activities to recognize that some skill training has its major purpose to help with the development of skills for more effective and productive task achievement and that other skill training has as its purpose to help actualize interpersonal awareness and sensitivity, and to help learners cope with the issues of human relations and social process that underly and accompany effective work procedures and compatible living patterns between persons.

The two left-hand columns of Chart 2B indicate some of the

CHART 2B

PROCESS—CENTERED DEVELOPMENT MATRIX

Type of Skill	*Examples of Skills*	*System Level*	*Skill Level*	*Illustrative Learning Activities*
1. Communicating feelings	— Within self to other — About others	Intra-person Inter-person Group Inter-group Organization Community Macro-System	Macro Micro Behavioral Ecological	— Non-verbal exercises — "Mailbox feedback" — Fantasy attribution — T group
2. Diagnostic sensitivity Competence	— Listening to feelings and needs — Process problem identification	Intra-person Inter-person Group Inter-group Organization Community Macro-System	Macro Micro Behavioral Ecological	— Interview practice — Listening exercises — Problem census brainstorm — Internal dialogue — Self interview
3. Process Intervention Initiative	— Confrontations — Process feedback tools	Intra-person Inter-person Group Inter-group	Macro Micro Behavioral Ecological	— Stop sessions — Confrontation tapes — Critical episode role-play — Feedback tools
4. Affective support	— Legitimizing openness — Physical contact — Reassurance	Intra-person Inter-person Group Inter-group Organization Macro-System	Macro Micro Behavioral Ecological	— Strength bombardment — "Trust walk" techniques — Non-verbal support exercises — Group caring focus
5. Helping others express feelings	— Asking questions — Patience-timing — Testing	Intra-person Inter-person Group Inter-group Organization Macro-System	Macro Micro Behavioral	— Listening to encourage — Tape models — Expression media

Type of Skill	*Examples of Skills*	*System Level*	*Skill Level*	*Illustrative Learning Activities*
6. Dealing with positive and negative feedback	—Accepting compliments —Checking assumptions —Asking for help	Intra-person Inter-person Group Inter-group Organization Macro-System	Macro Micro Behavioral Ecological	—Role-play giving and receiving compliments —Asking for help exercises —Brainstorm inhibitions —Trio help exercises
7. Taking the role of the other	—Cross-cultural simulations —Empathy —Practice —Role-reversal	Intra-person Inter-person Group Organization Community Macro-System	Macro Micro Behavioral Ecological	—Role-reversal exercises —Cross-cultural simulations —"Mask" exercises —Film identification —Soliloquy practice
8. Making verbal and non-verbal behavior congruent	—Identifying double messages —Inner-dialogue	Intra-person Inter-person Group Organization Macro-System	Macro Micro Behavioral Ecological	—Videotape feedback —Verbal—non-verbal —Double message exercise —Value clarification re: ambivalence

typical clusters of skills that we believe belong in this area of skill development, and the right-hand column identifies illustrative skill learning activities.

1. *Skills of Communicating Feelings.* Some types of skill-development approaches we have observed are: non-verbal exercises in communicating feelings toward others; the "mailbox exercise" where envelopes with names of participants are mounted on a wall and everyone writes affective messages to others at any time; fantasy attribution exercises where each participant communicates feelings about self or others by selecting animals, plants, or objects which "you remind me of" or "that I think are like me"; the typical T group, of course, provides much skill practice in this area.

2. *Diagnostic Sensitivity Skills.* Much emphasis is put on this area of skill development — on skills of listening to the feelings and problems of others, as well as the skills of becoming sensitive to and able to articulate one's own ambivalences, that is, the internal forcefield which one is dealing with in understanding one's own feelings and motivations. Some approaches to skill

development are: skill practice in creating and using interview schedules; observation exercises, with chance to practice looking for different aspects of group process and checking observations against those of others; listening exercises in which different participants or sub-groups listen with different inquiry questions in mind; conducting problem census brainstorming; internal dialogue or self-interview exercises to develop skills of internal data collection and diagnosis.

3. *Skills of Process Intervention Initiative.* In laboratory education, the group may be a task-centered work group or a process-centered study group. In both cases, it is important for leaders or trainers to initiate skilled interventions to help the group or member look reflectively at the ongoing process in order to improve the quality of functioning and increase the sense of "awareness and control of what we are doing." Some of the techniques for helping develop such intervention skills are: designing and conducting "stop sessions" to look at "what's going on"; skill practice, by role-playing, of critical episodes in group life; use of confrontation tapes, or videotapes, to provide trigger episodes for skill practice; develop ways of asking participants for feedback in order to guide needed interventions.

4. *Skills of Giving Affective Support.* One of the most important areas of human relations learning is the area of skilled, sensitive support of the needs, intentions, and action of others. Some typical skill development activities are: non-verbal exercises in personal support through touch, gesture, affective expression; "strength bombardment technique" of giving positive supportive feedback to each other; various "trust walk" techniques of giving support and guidance to a blindfolded person; exercises where small groups focus on "expressing caring" for one member, then another.

5. *Helping Others Articulate Their Feelings.* To legitimize and support the expression of feeling by another is one of the core functions of a good trainer. A few illustrations of helping with this area of skill development are: listening exercises in encouraging another person to express feelings; creating tape "models" which legitimize overcoming barriers to expression by modeling "freed up" behavior; providing opportunities for "private sharing," such as putting feelings on tape while alone; providing media which encourage and support expressing feelings, such as clay, finger paints, and colored paper.

6. *Skills of Giving and Receiving Positive and Negative Feedback.* The manner of giving feedback makes all the difference in whether it can be listened to, and the skill of receiving and using feedback is a major support for the development of openness. Some illustrations of skill development in this area are: role-

playing exercises in giving and receiving compliments; skill practice in asking for feedback, including tool development; brainstorming all the reasons for inhibiting asking for or offering help and support; trio exercises in giving and receiving help, with one member acting as feedback observer.

7. *Skills of Taking the Role of the Others.* The skills of empathy and seeing things through the eyes of others are major foci for laboratory education. Some techniques for helping develop these skills are: role-reversal and alter-ego role-playing techniques; simulations of cross-cultural confrontation and negotiations with briefing sheets and "caucus" supporters; exercises using masks and other supports for experimenting with others' roles; films, with briefings to identify with different characters; soliloquy practice in "getting into the shoes of another" with a validity checker to test adequacy of the role portrayal.

8. *Skills of Exploring Congruence Between Verbal and Non-Verbal Behavior.* One frequently encountered dilemma in interpersonal transactions is the discovery that the actor judges his behavior by knowledge of his intentions and the receiver judges by the behavior he sees and by his inferences about intentions from the observed behavior. The two messages, that is, of intention and of behavior, are quite often discrepant. It is a challenge to help participants explore such discrepancies and develop skill in coping with them. Some approaches to skill development are: videotaping with playback to look for non-verbal and verbal incongruities; verbal — non-verbal exercises in projecting two messages, and identifying double messages from others; value-clarification exercises to identify ambivalence and polarization of personal or group values.

We hope that these illustrations have helped to clarify the great variety of training techniques available, and also to conceptualize a framework for thinking about skill development in its many aspects.

Some Basic Elements in Awareness Learning and Skill Development Activities

Although participative learning designs vary with the desired learning outcomes, the types of learners, size of learning group, and the personal style of the trainer, we believe any good learning design has several basic ingredients.

1. A learning objective of *personally or professionally relevant awareness or skill outcomes.*

2. An *inquiry question or confrontation* to be understood, or behaviorally coped with.

3. A learner role of *active participation* in inquiry and tryout of ideas, feelings, or behaviors.

4. A phase of *reflection, feedback, and review* following the active participation phase in order to integrate and to revise and re-direct learning efforts.

5. *Input from resource persons or materials* to provide data from the experiences and learnings of others.

6. *Integration of learning into larger* intellectual, affective, or action contexts.

7. *Work on and support of transfer of learning* from the learning situation to operating life situations.

8. Provision for *individualization of learning activities* throughout the design.

To ensure quality, flexibility, and relevance in this type of learning activity, it is crucial that the trainer-consultant-leader spend time retrieving diagnostic data about learning readiness and need, and developing a design of learning activities which will support learners in meeting their needs.

Perhaps the critical element underlying all participative learning has not been emphasized enough. This is the collaborative development, maintenance, and periodic review of a learning contract between trainer and participants.

The System Level Context (Third column of Charts 2A and 2B)

Although many basic skills are generic to all types of settings and situations, it is important in designing skill practice activities to recognize and be sensitive to the major context in which learners will be utilizing their skills in problem-solving activities and process work. There are indeed quite different skills involved in helping with goal setting at the personal individual level, at the level of interpersonal collaboration, at the level of group or organization goal development, or at the level of interagency relations in a community context, or at the macro-system levels of state or national or international bodies. Also, the skills needed in diagnosis of large system difficulties are quite different from those useful in small system diagnosis; different tools are needed, as well as different approaches to sampling decisions and data processing. This means that the contexts in which the clients are to utilize their skills is a critical input for trainers as they design skill development activities.

The Skill Level (Column 4 of Charts 2A and 2B)

In designing skill development activities for problem-solving work or process work it is important to provide opportunities for the development of several levels of skill. We have identified these as the (1) macro level, (2) micro level, (3) behavior level, (4) ecological context level. Let's look at these four levels in terms of one area of skill development—the development of diagnostic skills.

1. The *macro level* skill is that of designing a program of diagnostic work or diagnostic learning which will include a number of training objectives and a sequence of activities occupying a number of blocks of time, perhaps during several days or perhaps spaced out over a number of months.

2. The *micro level* of skill development is the designing of specific experiences relevant to one of the training objectives, such as sampling techniques or interviewing techniques. The micro skill level has to do with designing a learning component within a larger program design.

3. The *behavior skill level* has to do with guiding clients or learners in concrete behavioral skill practice. This might be behavioral practice of the techniques of asking questions or of probing in using an interview schedule.

4. The fourth level of skill development is often neglected. This is the skill of arranging the environment so that learning for problem-solving or process work may proceed effectively. It may focus on appropriate arrangement of the physical environment-seating, for example. Or it may focus on arranging for the resources, human and material, which will be needed during the course of an activity. We call this kind of level of skill — *ecological context* skills.

LINKAGE OF AWARENESS AND SKILL TRAINING IN LABORATORY TRAINING

We believe that there is a basic relationship between awareness and skill training in all aspects of laboratory training. How much of each or both is relevant in a particular design depends on the purposes of a particular laboratory session. If the laboratory is focused on process work, it will draw more heavily on awareness than on skill training, and much of the task work is transferred or deferred to other settings such as back home. If the laboratory is task-focused, skill training becomes more relevant, because the objective is doing better, being more productive, and being more satisfied with what one is doing. Here, awareness training is complementary but subordinate to task and skill training.

If laboratory training is thought of as a continuum from "pure" awareness training to a complete focus on task-centered learning, both awareness and skill training belong all along the continuum, though with different degrees of emphasis. Another variable is the trainer whose orientation, values, and competencies affect the design and choice of methods. Perhaps, if trainers continue their own "in-service" education, they can extend the range of their competencies all along the above-mentioned continuum.

CHAPTER 10

LIFE PLANNING

Herbert A. Shepard

Life planning is planning life-worth-living. The choices you make today create your future, as well as your here-and-now. And you have some freedom of choice, today, and tomorrow as well. We are only slowly emerging from an era of deterministic science, when it was assumed that today's choices are completely the product of yesterday's choices, and the very notion of choice a quaint illusion. The psychologists assured us that life after the age of five was merely an unfolding of a personality set in early childhood. And our culture demands of each of us so many promises and contracts that most of us seem to have signed away our future choices. We seal our fates.

Many people see their futures as fated in another way. They think of the future as something that happens to them. When they are asked to draw a line representing the way they think about their total lives — from the beginning in the past to the end in the future — they can portray certain aspects of their past, but are unable to map the future. The past can be re-interpreted, but it cannot be managed. Only the future is manageable, but these people have great difficulty in thinking about it that way.

Some people plan their careers and invest their energies in bringing about certain career achievements. Unfortunately, when people plan only their careers, the other aspects of their lives are unanticipated and sometimes unhappy consequences of their career choices. When these people draw their life lines, they draw only career lines.

Life planning is a self-confrontation. It is the induction of an identity crisis and a destination crisis for yourself. It requires the re-examination of basic values and assumptions. Many of us are enslaved to beliefs and fears that turn us into instruments used for some purpose outside ourselves. One therapist greets new patients with the question: "Why haven't you committed suicide?" The answers often lie outside the person and his joy in life, or lack of it: responsibilities to family, God and country, or even to the life insurance company. And if a married couple is asked: "Why haven't you divorced?" the answers are often outside their joy in each other, or lack of it: family responsibilities or social embarrassment.

Yet Fritz Perls' Gestalt Prayer[1] counsels:

I do my thing, and you do your thing.
I am not in this world to live up to your expectations
And you are not in this world to live up to mine.
You are you and I am I
And if by chance we find each other, it's beautiful.
If not, it can't be helped.

Who am I and who are you? The first answers that come to mind are usually "marketing" answers. They describe what makes you or me a respectable commodity: title, profession, memberships, loyalties, skills, hobbies, roles as parent, spouse, or manager. The answers that come later take us beyond the boundaries of such socially prescribed selves, and precipitate an identity crisis.

Who *should* you be? Our culture provides us with many reasons for being that lie outside ourselves, with many images of what we should be. The self-confrontations of life planning involve the unravelling of deeply, often automatically, held assumptions about shoulds and oughts, goods and bads. A dictator concerned only with the maintenance of his own power would value such qualities in the citizenry as loyalty, respect for authority, law and order, unselfishness, humility, and competitiveness. When you perform well, whom are you trying to please? When you are winning, is it ever at the cost of something more important? Is having a fine reputation at all like being trapped? Is being independent ever lonely? Is the greatest risk not risking?

On the subject of what one ought to be, Kahlil Gibran had this story to tell.

> It was in the garden of a madhouse that I met a youth with a face pale and lovely and full of wonder.
>
> And I sat beside him upon the bench, and I said, "Why are you here?"
>
> And he looked at me in astonishment, and he said, "It is an unseemly question, yet I will answer you. My father would make of me a reproduction of himself; so also would my uncle. My mother would have me the image of her illustrious father. My sister would hold up her seafaring husband as the

perfect example for me to follow. My brother thinks I should be like him, a fine athlete.

"And my teachers also, the doctor of philosophy, and the music-master, and the logician, they too were determined, and each would have me but a reflection of his own face in a mirror.

"Therefore, I came to this place. I find it more sane here. At least I can be myself."

Then of a sudden he turned to me and he said, "But tell me, were you also driven to this place by education and good counsel?"

And I answered, "No, I am a visitor."

And he said, "Oh, you are one of those who live in the madhouse on the other side of the wall."[1]

The location of the madhouse is less important than whether either the inmate or the visitor has learned to make his own life worth celebrating. What were those moments when you rejoiced in life, when you were fully alive, and living fully, and experiencing fulfillment? You're likely to find that many of them were quite "simple," and had little to do with the way you spend most of your time. If you can identify the conditions under which your life is fulfilling, you can set about creating those conditions.

Easier said than done. A basic fact of life — that it is to be lived fully — is difficult to grasp. Lyndon Johnson's widow, reflecting on their last years together, commented:

"To be close to death gives you a new awareness of the preciousness of life, and the extreme tenuousness of it. You must live every day to the fullest, as though you had a short supply — because you do. I said that glibly for years, but I didn't know how intensely one should live."[2]

Some people can apprehend the preciousness of life by writing their own obituaries, focusing on activities and feelings, and writing the obituary twice: once as an extrapolation of present life style, and again as one would wish it to be. But many others find this rather direct way of facing the question, "What shall I do with the time I have left?" too threatening to be taken seriously.

What are the conditions under which it is possible to rejoice in life? Perhaps one can learn from infants. An infant rejoices when it can affect its environment in ways that please it. It rejoices in loving and playful interaction with other beings. And it rejoices in the functioning of its own body. These three sources of fulfillment, translated into adult words, can be called autonomy, resonance, and tone.

As used here, autonomy refers to your ability to create a world worth living in for yourself. Typically, the autonomous person has many skills useful to himself and society, continually develops his physical, emotional, and intellectual capacities, can relate in many ways to others, is proactive and foresighted, imaginative and realistic, takes responsibility for his choices and their consequences, is open to new experience and learns from it. But the essence of autonomy is not in what one's resources are, but in how they are used, the purpose they serve: namely, the creation and maintenance of a world worth living in. Thus, autonomy differs from related terms like power, skill, achievement, independence, or wealth, which may become ends in themselves, or may be used to create a world for oneself that is not worth living in. The characteristics of such a world and of autonomy are not the same for every person. Robert Frost described the meaning of autonomy in the poet's world.

> The reason artists show so little interest
> In public freedom is because the freedom
> They've come to feel the need of is a kind
> No one can give them — they can scarce attain —
> The freedom of their own material:
> So, never at a loss in simile,
> They can command the exact affinity
> Of anything they are confronted with.
> This perfect moment of unbafflement,
> When no man's name and no noun's adjective
> But summons out of nowhere like a jinni.
> We know not what we owe this moment to.
> It may be wine, but much more likely love —
> Possibly just well-being in the body,
> Or respite from the thought of rivalry.
> It's what my father must mean by departure,
> Freedom to flash off into wild connections.
> Once having known it nothing else will do.
> Our days all pass awaiting its return.[3]

The second source of fulfillment is resonance, a relationship with other beings which is empathic, responsive, mutually stimulating, and expansive for all those involved. The term can describe a person's relationship with other environments as well. Resonance differs from the common meaning of love, which is usually understood to be an exchange relationship rather than a resonance relationship. Freya Stark describes the essence of resonance in the following passage.

> For it must be remembered that silence can be dead or living, and the two kinds must be distinguished. And perhaps the poles of Being are in the distinction — the one an end and a downfall and a destruction, and the other a part of that which has neither beginning nor end; and even in the humblest instance there is a difference in the silence

> of these two.
>
> There is, for instance, regrettably often a noticeable blank in the wedded silence, when a couple have been married a long time. One sees them in restaurants or on cruises — middle-aged, averted faces that turn toward each other with no light in their eyes and drop words of such astonishing triviality that one wonders how the air consents to carry them: surely the sort of conversation Sartre was thinking of when he described Hell as one prolonged domestic scene.
>
> Yet if a young creature were to ask for advice whether to say yes or no to the man or woman she or he thought of marrying, one might do worse than ask: 'Are you happy to be silent together?' That companionship is the living silence — a relaxation that finds speech superfluous, an atmosphere of well-being where nothing needs to be explained, a part of that current which can make not only men but most living things happy to be together. It is, I like to imagine, the stream that flows beneath all differences of language and carries each one of us from those cindery beginnings toward our undiscovered end.[4]

The third source of fulfillment, tone, is an alertness of all the senses and organs. The meaning we attach to the term "muscle tone" captures the quality referred to as the tone of the whole organism — sensory, mental, emotional, muscular, etc. The concept of tone differs from the concept of health. Health is usually defined as the absence of disease, and mental health is usually regarded as something different from physical health. Tone is a psycho-physiological concept: anxiety is as much its enemy as drugs. Lowen expresses this idea as follows:

> A person experiences the reality of the world only through his body.... If the body is relatively unalive, a person's impressions and responses are diminished. The more alive the body is, the more vividly does he perceive reality and the more actively does he respond to it. We have all experienced the fact that when we feel particularly good and alive, we perceive the world more sharply.... The aliveness of the body denotes its capacity for feeling. In the absence of feeling, the body goes 'dead' insofar as its ability to be impressed by or respond to situations is concerned. The emotionally dead person is turned inward: thoughts and fantasies replace feeling and action; images compensate for the loss of reality.... It is the body that melts with love, freezes with fear, trembles in anger, and reaches for warmth and contact. Apart from the body these words are poetic images. Experienced in the body,

they have a reality that gives meaning to existence.[5]

When autonomy, resonance, and tone are all high, we rejoice in life. This is a peak experience, and as Frost says, "Once having known it, nothing else will do." The three are closely intertwined: if autonomy is used in ways that reduce resonance, it will not produce a world worth living in; low tone will adversely affect resonance and autonomy. Treating them as separate aspects of life-worth-living may have some value in the life planning process for persons who have been spending all their energies on work and neglecting their relationships with others or their own bodies; or for persons who only feel strong when they are going against others and don't know that it is possible to be strong when going with others; or for persons who overeat at the expense of tone and resonance; or for persons with many resources, persons who possess the elements making for autonomy, but have experienced little fulfillment.

How does the infant's delighting in its experience of autonomy become transformed into the adult's striving for status or winning over others? How does the infant's joy in resonance become transformed into the adult's view of love as a commodity and commodities as substitutes for love? How does the infant's joy in its own body become transformed into emotional deadness? Perhaps it is because our socializing institutions demand that the child give up his search for autonomy in exchange for packages of pseudo-romance. Whatever the telling events in the process of socialization are, many people "grow up" having learned "truths" that blind them to life. Such distorting values are reflected in the following excerpt from a paper examining the relevance of Taoist and Buddhist philosophy to modern man in modern organization.

The second piece of advice is: Observe the cormorant in the fishing fleet. You know how cormorants are used for fishing. The technique involves a man in a rowboat with about half a dozen or so cormorants, each with a ring around the neck. As the bird spots a fish, it would dive into the water and unerringly come up with it. Because of the ring, the larger fish are not swallowed but held in the throat. The fisherman picks up the bird and squeezes out the fish through the mouth. The bird then dives for another and the cycle repeats itself.

To come back to the second piece of advice from the neo-Taoist to the American worker:

> Observe the cormorant, he would say. Why is it that of all the different animals, the cormorant has been chosen to slave away day and night for the fisherman? Were the bird not greedy for fish, or not efficient in catching it, or not readily trained, would society have created an industry to exploit the bird? Would the ingenious device of a ring

> around its neck, and the simple procedure of squeezing the bird's neck to force it to regurgitate the fish have been devised? Of course not.
>
> Greed, talent, and capacity for learning, then, are the basis of exploitation. The more you are able to moderate and/or hide them from society, the greater will be your chances of escaping the fate of the cormorant.
>
> . . . . It is necessary to remember that the institutions of society are geared to make society prosper, not necessarily to minimizing suffering on your part. It is for this reason, among others, that the schools tend to drum into your mind the high desirability of those characteristics that tend to make society prosper — namely, ambition, progress, and success. These in turn are to be valued in terms of society's objectives. All of them gradually but surely increase your greed and make a cormorant out of you.[6]

One need not view the fate of the cormorant as gloomily as does Siu to recognize that he provides a novel perspective on some attributes — ambition, talent, and capacity for learning — which are prized in our culture. Life planning is essentially an invitation to explore new perspectives from which to view past experience, one's current life, and future alternatives. As Siu implies, the value system we inherited is not necessarily designed to make life worth living.

The discovery and creation of perspectives that deepen our appreciation of ourselves in the universe is the fourth aspect of life-worth-living. It is akin to resonance, as suggested by the terminology William O. Douglas used to describe what is meant here by perspective:

"Man is whole when he is in tune with the winds, the stars, and the hills as well as with his neighbors. Being in tune with the apartment or the community is part of the secret. Being in tune with the universe is the whole secret."[7]

In everyday experience, being in tune with the universe, or having an adequate perspective, means seeing problems from above rather than from underneath, means not getting locked in to one end or the other of a presumed polarization, means being free in your situation rather than dependent on it, means owning your behavior rather than claiming someone else's behavior "caused" yours.

Life planning is a quest, and it is also a continuous part of life-worth-living. And while the life planning process and outlook described here may help you to live more fully, it will not protect you from pain. Developing towards higher levels of autonomy, resonance, tone, and perspective faces you with all the awkwardness, mistakes, and painful choices involved in any learning. Living more fully means investing yourself more fully in the creation of your experience: and anything you invest yourself in to the point that it can bring you great joy can also bring you great grief by its loss.

AN APPENDIX

If you ask a person why he is in his present job, he is quite likely to tell you how he got into it rather than how he is using it in the accomplishment of his purpose. Life planning is learning to see the environment through the eyes of your purpose, and the principal work of life planning is the creation of purpose. You become what you think. "A man defines himself by his project."[8]

Logically, career planning is a part of life planning. But psychologically and culturally, the two are often separated. For some, work or career or profession is the sole source of self esteem, the only justification for being permitted to exist. For others, it is not felt to be a part of life at all, and life planning refers to the time outside of work, when they can live a little.

Life planning is to make life more whole, to make living a good Gestalt, so that the parts of one's life are mutually enriching. Work belongs in life, along with love, laughter, prayer, and all the other elements of human experience.

Life planning has several aspects: arousal of motivation, freeing of imagination, generation of data about oneself, identification of themes in the data, formulation of purpose, and development of action plans. Many vehicles are available for taking this trip, and the ones noted below are examples.

Draw Your Life Line. Draw a line that represents ways you have of thinking about your life. Maybe it will be a straight sloping line drawn between the coordinates of chronological age and maturity. Maybe it will be a chart of your educational and work life. Maybe it will be two lines, one representing your career, the other the rest of your life. Maybe it will be jagged, with lots of peaks and valleys. Maybe it won't be a line at all, but a string of pictures, or something that looks like a tree, or a map. Maybe it will be several lines, each concerned with a different aspect of your life.

Make it a complete life line: beginning with your birth and ending with your death. Put a mark on it to show where you are right now. Let yourself play with the future part of the line. Be sure to bring the line to an end: the decision on how long to live is best made by yourself, and you can change your mind about it tomorrow.

When you have completed your drawing, its meaning is apparent only to yourself. If you explain to some others what you tried to portray, their questions and comments may lead you to discover additional meanings, and you can also gain perspective on your own life by learning how others represent theirs.

Identity Search. The next steps are explorations of the space between the "now" mark on your line and the future end of the line, beginning with the now mark: your current identity. Find as many answers as you can to the question "Who am I?" The first answers that occur to you probably will be the roles you take: your occupation, your family roles, your memberships, etc. Then explore the many other sides of yourself: adjectives that describe some aspect of you and your life: personality traits, beliefs, skills, attitudes, habits; impulses and inhibitions; dreams, wishes, fears and regrets; the kinds of relationships you form with other people; the things you like about yourself and the things you don't; the things you're not; the other people who are part of your life.

If you are in the company of someone who knows you, ask her or him to make a list of answers to the question "Who are you?" to provide you with additional data for your identity search. Now look over your list item by item, and spend some time assessing the importance of that item to your sense of yourself. Suppose it were suddenly removed, how would you feel? You may find that some are so important that if they were taken away you'd be lost and terrified; you may find some whose disappearance would be a relief.

Then review the list again, marking those aspects of your identity you want to maintain, and perhaps enhance, in the future, and those aspects of which you want to rid yourself. Add any new identities you want to become.

The identity search is enriched by being shared with others; for example, some of the items on their lists probably belong on yours, too.

Write Your Obituary. After exploring the now mark on your life line in this way, move to the future end of the line and look back over your whole life, especially the part you haven't lived yet. Write your obituary, covering as many aspects of your life as you can, and concentrating on the part between the now mark and the future end of the line. Write about the way your life will probably turn out if you continue in your current life patterns and trends. If you don't make any major shift in life-style, priorities, values, etc., what will your obituary say? After you've written it and shared it with the others, you can think about any changes you want to make in it.

Newspaper Clippings. The next steps are explorations of the space between now and the future end of the line. Take the Sunday edition of a large metropolitan newspaper and clip out items that intrigue you. They may be news items of a political, educational, scientific, sports, or cultural nature; or travel advertisements and descriptions of other countries; or cartoons and pictures; or business and real estate opportunities; or jobs and occupations; things offered for sale; perhaps a portion of someone's obituary.

Paste the clippings on a large sheet of paper and share them with others. See what patterns you can find in the things that interested you.

Fantasy Day. Somewhere in the space between now and the end of the line, create a special day for yourself. Give your fantasy free rein: don't ask whether you can afford to do what you want to do in that day; don't ask whether all those things could be fitted into one day. Just plan a day that you would love to have.

After you've lived that day in fantasy, and shared what you dare about it with others, look at it more critically. Did you build into that day any wishes or dreams that you want to take seriously and turn into plans? Many people suppress and altogether forget youthful dreams and wishes when they become "responsible adults." Dreams that were unattainable when you were younger may no longer be out of reach. See if you can recapture some of your wishes. Are they still attractive? Are they realizable?

A Way of Life. Take a larger segment of the line between now and the end, perhaps a year, and describe a life style you'd like to try. Again, don't be too "realistic." Take the segment from far enough in the future that you'd have time to do something about the obstacles that stand in the way of spending such a year. And after you've written and shared it, think about whether you mean any of it seriously enough to start planning.

A Review of Highs. What can you learn from your past that you can use in creating your future? If you can identify the conditions under which your life was fulfilling, you may be able to recreate those conditions.

Think back to the times when you felt best about yourself and your life. Some of them may have been brief moments; peak experiences. Some of them may have been projects that took years to accomplish. Some may have been work, some pure play. Some may have been solitary experiences, others full of people.

Write a paragraph about each one, describing it in as much detail as you can. Give yourself lots of time to recapture these highs: a whole evening, or a weekend. After you've described a number of them (try to find at least ten), go back over them in search of patterns. What strengths did you display or develop in each of the experiences? What did you contribute to the creation of the experience? What were the sources of your satisfaction in each experience? Ask others to help you with this analysis: they are likely to see strengths that were too obvious for you to see yourself.

Psychological Tests. Through the use of psychological tests, you can generate more data about your identity and your potentials. For example, the Thematic Apperception Test can give you a new perspective on your needs for achievement, influence and intimacy. FIRO-B reflects your needs in the areas of control, affection, and inclusion. The Strong Interest inventory tells you how your patterns of interests, likes, and dislikes match those of people who have been successful in various occupations.

Getting it all Together. By now you have amassed so much information about yourself that it will take some time and thought to assimilate it and comprehend it. As you look through it all, you will find the same set of messages, in different words and contexts, many times. You may also find some seeming contradictions and paradoxes. Some of these may be artifacts of the method used in generating the data: for example, the product of a particular mood you were in during one of the exercises. But often the paradoxes contain the possibility of discoveries about yourself that can be important to you in creating your future. A person with whom you have good rapport can be helpful to you in the process of sorting it all out and getting it all together.

Purpose and Themes. When you have identified some of the themes that you want to be central in your life, try to formulate a statement of mission or purpose that organizes the themes into a good Gestalt, a wholeness that is satisfying to you. Your purpose may evolve logically and obviously from your study of the data; it may have emerged clearly in the process of generating the data; or it may continue to elude you and then appear as a flash of insight. It may also be that you cannot formulate a purpose until you have made some further explorations.

Your Partners in Life. If you have a partner or partners in life, you should probably have been together throughout the process described above. But partners do not build identical life plans, nor plan to do everything together. The partners are separate beings who have created a third being, the couple, and the welfare of the couple is not served by imprisoning the partners within it. The couple should reserve itself those areas of mutuality which are fulfilling for both partners, and the partners need to discover what those are and can be. Beyond that, the value of the gift of being or having a partner is in serving as resources to each other in creating the life that the other is seeking.

FOOTNOTES AND REFERENCES

1. Frederick S. Perls, *Gestalt Therapy Verbatim,* Real People Press, Utah, 1969.

2. Kahlil Gibran, "The Madman" in *The Wanderer,* Heinemann, London, Knopf, New York, 1932.

3. Ladybird Johnson, *TIME,* May 21, 1973, p. 41.

4. Robert Frost, "How Hard It Is to Keep From Being King when It's in You and in the Situation," in *The Poetry of Robert Frost,* Holt and Rinehart, New York, 1969, p. 453.

5. Freya Stark, "On Silence," *Holiday Magazine.* Reprinted with permission © 1965, The Curtis Publishing Company, also John Murray, Ltd., London.

6. Alexander Lowen, *The Betrayal of the Body,* Macmillan, New York, 1967, pp. 5-6.

7. Ralph Gildi Siu, "Work and Serenity," *Journal of Occupational Mental Health, 1,* 1, 1971, p. 5.

8. Attributed to William O. Douglas, Associate Justice, U.S. Supreme Court.

9. R. D. Laing and G. O. Cooper, *Reason and Violence,* Tavistock, London, 1964, p. 61.

CHAPTER 11

INTERVENTION: THEORY, STRATEGY, AND STYLE

Kenneth D. Benne, Leland P. Bradford, Jack R. Gibb, and Ronald O. Lippitt

From the standpoint of the practitioner, trainer, teacher, consultant, or applied researcher, the most crucial problems in utilizing laboratory method are problems of intervention. As a practitioner stands over against a client, his vexing dilemmas are not alone the gross Hamletian dilemma of "to intervene or not to intervene," but all of the sticky in-between questions of when and how and in what style and with what content and how frequently to do so. Thoughtful responses to these dilemmas bring into juxtaposition his values, knowledges, skills and motivations, his imaginal audience of fellow practitioners with their expectations of him, his diagnosis of the needs and expectations of his client, and his sense of the quality of his relationship with that client. These components are not always consistent one with the other. In fact, they are often contradictory with respect to the character of the intervention required, if any. These components must be reconciled somehow in the intervention judgments which the practitioner makes and upon which he acts. There is always risk in any intervention a practitioner makes and a strong likelihood of surprise and unanticipated consequences. For this very reason, an adequate theory and general strategy of intervention is a centrally important part of the conceptual equipment of a professional practitioner of laboratory method.

Laboratory practitioners accept Argyris' definitions of intervention and of the intervention situation.[1]

> To intervene is to enter into an ongoing system of relationship, to come between or among persons, groups, or objects for the purpose of helping them ... Our view

acknowledges interdependencies between the intervener and the client system but focuses on how to maintain, or increase, the client system's autonomy; how to differentiate even more clearly the boundaries between the client system and the intervener; and how to conceptualize and define the client system's health independently of the intervener's. This view values the client system as an ongoing self-responsible unity that has the obligation to be in control of its own destiny. An intervener, in this view, assists a system to become more effective in problem solving, decision making, and decision implementation in such a way that the system can continue to be increasingly effective in these activities and have a decreasing need for the intervener.

The intervener-client relationship, as emphasized before, is thus not reducible to any of the several human relationships with which it may be compared and with which it is not seldom confused. It is by no means equivalent to the leader-follower relationship, nor to manager-subordinate, working-colleague to working-colleague, or friend to friend relationships. It may and does incorporate elements from any or all of these, but its peculiar genius lies in its goal of helping the client to grow in autonomy through experiences within the closeness and interdependence of the relationship. Its ultimate criterion of success is a severing, a termination of the relationship, with the client grown strong enough to function and to continue changing and learning on his own. It is a relationship which blends, often in a bewildering way, nurturance with weaning, rooting in relationship with a pulling-up of roots. An intervener needs a guiding theory of intervention, partly because of the distinctive relationship and purpose which actual interventions serve or fail to serve in the career and development of client systems.[2]

In planning this chapter, the editors were confronted with a choice. We might ask one thoughtful practitioner of laboratory method to formulate his or her theory and general strategy of intervention. Or we might gather considered statements about intervention practices and rationales from a population of laboratory practitioners and summarize the results with attention both to agreements and differences. The first plan would provide a more systematic and elegant theory of intervention. The second would give a better picture of the current status of thinking about intervention within the emerging profession of laboratory practice.

We finally decided upon the second plan. We prepared a questionnaire[3] and sent it to thirty outstanding laboratory practitioners with an eye on maximum heterogeneity. Replies came from thirteen practitioners in addition to those from the editors.[4]

The seventeen respondents represent a population quite heterogeneous in several dimensions. There are women and men in the sample. They come from several national cultures and subcultures. Their disciplinary backgrounds include social psychology, clinical psychology, psychiatry, philosophy, education, economics, sociology, and social work. Some typically specialize in laboratory activities whose objective is personal growth, others work typically in organizational development programs and still others work in community development projects. All, however, are also generalists, with successful experience in all or several of the current specialties of laboratory practice. Their religious commitments are diverse.

We will summarize their responses, noting agreements and differences. We will intersperse brief interpretive comments throughout our summary, with a summary interpretation at the end.

OBJECTIVES OF INTERVENTION

Objectives for all respondents were expressed in terms of augmented or enhanced capacities for the client or client system. The general capacity of the client which interventions by the helper aim to enhance seems to be a capacity to cope more effectively with conflicts and problems arising within the client's internal environment, his external environment, or in the connections between the two. There thus seemed to be an action-orientation in the stated aim of all respondents, whether they were discussing directly the action-taking abilities of the client or his perceptual, moral, cognitive, or diagnostic abilities.

It was not surprising to find a focus on individual capacities in the stated aims of interveners who work habitually in T Groups or other training activities oriented to personal growth. But this focus was present also in the statements of respondents who work habitually in organizational or community development programs. Objectives of intervention may be summarized in relation to three levels of human organization which furnish "targets" for learning and changing — person, group, and larger system.

Some respondents emphasized the action capacities of individuals as aims for intervention, others emphasized perceptual and cognitive capabilities, and still others stressed linkages within the person and linkages between individual and environment. Abilities of learners to learn and inquire were a principal concern of some respondents.

Action Capacities of Persons. Three aspects of persons were most often mentioned as providing objectives for intervention. The first of these was the *potency* of the person to cope with his environment. The aim of intervention is to help persons augment their actual and perceived potency to face and grapple with reality. A second aim was to support persons in *owning* their own desires and motivations and the effects of their actions on themselves and others. This involves exploration by individuals of their boundaries *vis-a-vis* other persons and affirming themselves in the self-identity thus clarified. Owning one's motivations and actions was seen as essential to the assumption of *responsibility* in personal choice and action. A third aspect of personal behavior was the person's perception of the range of action alternatives open to him. The aim of interventions was to enlarge a person's range of images of potentiality. Opening up of new alternatives was seen as closely related to *freedom* of response and to the enhancement of freedom in choice and action.

Less frequently mentioned objectives of intervention were to assist a person in mobilizing his instinctual energies and to decrease the power of his cultural imbeddedness in shaping his conduct.

Perceptual and Cognitive Capacities of Persons. There was less agreement among respondents concerning the cognitive capacities of persons which interventions should serve to enlarge than in the case of action capacities. Nearly all respondents emphasized greater self-awareness as an aim of intervention. A few stressed understanding and awareness of primary processes. More spoke of understanding of the effects of their own behavior on other people. And listening and observing skills were emphasized as important tools in attaining and maintaining self-awareness.

Other respondents emphasized the feeding in of appropriate concepts, models, and information to persons as tools for diagnosing their situations and their own place and part in these as a function of intervention.

Less often mentioned as desirable cognitive goals of learning were: achievement of a grasp of contradictory social processes within the person; the clarification of projections and assumptions; awareness of transferences; and an understanding of the way individual roles maintain the groups and organizations in which persons function.

Linkages Within Learners and Between Learner and Environment. Most respondents mentioned the importance of more adequate linkage within persons between intentions, values, and overt behavior. This was described qualitatively in terms of authenticity, congruence, and integration. An alternative way of describing the quality of response which interveners model, encourage, and support is a linkage or integration between the affective, cognitive, and motoric aspects of personal response.

Frequently mentioned as a goal of intervention was a working interdependence between the needs and resources of members within a group. From a personal standpoint, this interdependence requires a capacity of persons to act autonomously both in receiving help from and in giving help to others.

Closely related to autonomy in interdependence is the capacity of persons to link themselves to needed human and material resources both in the training or consultation environment and beyond it as well. Several emphasized the importance of encouraging linkage between laboratory learnings and the world and tasks outside the laboratory.

Abilities to Learn and Inquire. Another level of goals for laboratory learning which interventions should support and enhance was frequently stated as learning how to learn and/or how to inquire. More specific aspects of this general goal were emphasized by many respondents — internalization of problem-solving methods as a way of dealing with confusion and conflict; increased capacities for trust and, correlatively, for risk-taking, experimental responses; ability to collect and share relevant behavioral data; ability to clarify personal goals and to integrate these with the disparate personal goals of others; and understanding of the conditions of learning, and commitment to building such conditions into more of the relationships of life.

The stated aims for interventions which take the group as a target of intervention cluster around three aspects of group structure and function — goal setting and decision-making; group culture; and group climate.

Goal Setting and Decision Making. Two main emphases with respect to goal-setting and goal-clarification were present in the questionnaire returns. The first of these was to broaden the range of alternative paths of action taken into account by a group as it decides on its priorities and direction of movement. Some mentioned pointing out the neglect of goals suggested by some individuals, particularly by "minority" members, as "the group" rushes toward closure. Others suggested ways of getting beneath conventionally expected activities and helping group members to examine their feelings about what they *really* want to do and to accomplish. Others mentioned supporting groups in developing visions of the future which excite them, before reality testing alternative action steps for bringing the envisioned future into actuality. All respondents seemed to accept as a valid goal for a group a direction which integrates the goals and serves the needs of all group members.

The second emphasis was on interventions designed to help a group decide on *a valid goal*, when confronted with the complexity and conflict of diverse individual and sub-group preferences. Some respondents stressed the importance of a group's learning of win-win, as over against win-lose, strategies in decision making, and conflict management. Others emphasized the disclosure to the group of authority and power structures as these influence its making of decisions. Several respondents stressed the building of evaluation processes and periods into the group's life in order to revise goals and improve decision-making processes.

Group Culture. All respondents recognize that group members bring a normative "culture" with them from their significant associations as they enter a training or consultation situation. These normative orientations toward groups and persons, toward authority and leadership, toward work and play, may be explicit or implicit, conscious or non-conscious. Moreover, a group which meets through a period of time develops a normative culture of its own. All respondents saw many of their interventions aimed toward making implicit cultural patterns explicit, pre-conscious feelings conscious, and toward helping a group to function with expanded awareness of the influence of various external and internal cultural factors upon its functioning.

Specific factors mentioned by three or more respondents as needing to be made explicit in most groups, are interpersonal and interfactional tensions and conflicts, peer rivalries, authority relations, power relations within the group and assumptions about power, and group boundaries and their effects on group development and member behavior.

All interveners see the function of their interventions as helping a group they are training or consulting to expand its consciousness of the forces at work within its development and work and helping the group to collect relevant data as a basis for group decisions and actions. Some would see their function stopping at this point. Most others would see their interventions extending beyond this more or less neutral role into inducing a group to adopt and try out certain norms in the course of its life. Norms mentioned by many respondents are collaborative decision-making, an experimental and risk-taking approach to problem-solving with periodic evaluation of provisional try-outs of actions built in, open and trustful communication, and reciprocity and mutuality in relations between members and between members and trainers or consultants. The justification of such persuasive interventions is that certain norms are required as conditions of learning and growth. The commitment of interveners to optimize learning and growth in the human systems with which they work requires commitment to helping build the conditions which make integral learning and growth possible. This latter view is in line with the role of "methodological advocate" which we attributed to laboratory practitioners in Chapter 2.

Climate for Changing and Learning. Many respondents stated as an aim of their group level interventions the encouragement of a climate which supports continuing learning and change, through the responsible efforts of group members, after their relation with the group is terminated. In part, this is a repetition of the aim of building growth-supporting norms into the culture of the person, group, or organization. An additional element is the stress of several respondents on establishing effective feedback mechanisms in the ongoing life of the group. This means regularized data collection about the group's external and internal environments, the budgeting of time and effort for the analysis of data so collected, and the derivation of needed goals and programs of action and change from the analysis.

At the level of abstraction at which objectives of intervention were stated, no marked differences between the aims of intervention proposed for the group and for the larger system — organization, community, group interface — were noted. A similar emphasis on the importance of experiencing and learning participative methods of goal-setting and decision-making marked the responses of all respondents who differentiated the macro-system as an intervention target. A climate of open communication, the feedback of behavioral data concerning actual system functioning, the combination of support and challenge in consultant-client relations and in relations between the parts of the client system were all proposed as ways of lifting the implicit culture of the system into consciousness and of surfacing suppressed tensions and conflicts within and among parts of the system. The use of interventions to widen the range of alternatives in solving problems and to encourage win-win strategies for managing conflicts, thus brought into consciousness, was emphasized by nearly all respondents.

The intergroup character of behavioral events at the level of the larger system was noted by several respondents and understanding of intergroup dynamics suggested as a learning need. The importance of learning to use linking roles and linking mechanisms at the interfaces between interdependent but segregated groups was mentioned by some respondents.

The multi-centering of decision making in large organizations was suggested as an aim of intervention by a few respondents.

The responses to the question on successful trainer interventions and those to the question on the objectives of intervention tended to be the same. These have been summarized together.

The question concerning the effects of unsuccessful interventions brought out some additional ideas about the perils that hedge the life and career of the intervener. Again the responses clustered around the person, the group, and the larger system.

Effects of Unsuccessful Interventions on Persons. Most respondents called unsuccessful those interventions which mobilized and augmented persons' doubts about their own potency to cope with situations, which increased the dependence of persons upon the helper, or which over-exposed persons by pointing out aspects of their behavior with which they are not ready to deal responsibly. Similarly, respondents called unsuccessful interventions which discouraged ongoing voluntary participation by persons, which reinforced their defenses against open expression, and which augmented anxiety to the point where over-defensive and regressive behavior occurs and persists.

On the other hand, the same respondents deplored interventions which took persons in conflict off the hook before insight came, which smoothed over negative feedback before persons had heard and considered it, or which reinforced unrealistic aspirations in persons and colluded with persons in their confusion of "fantasies" with "facts."

It is clear that these concerns of laboratory practitioners about unsuccessful interventions constitute a dilemma. Conflicts, anxiety, and reorganization of unrealistic self-images are inescapable aspects of personal growth. Re-education does not occur without the experiencing of conflict, without anxiety, and without the reorganization of self-images by the persons involved. Yet conflicts which leave persons helpless, anxieties which prevent open and adaptive responses, and shattering challenges to self-image can lead to retrogression, to withdrawal of energy from attempts to change, rather than to achieve growth.

No theory of intervention can make judgments concerning these fundamental conditions of helping or hurting for an intervener. There is an art to intervention, in addition to a theory; an art which is always being learned and relearned by an intervener as he tries to use himself wisely in processes of helping other people. This is no argument against a working theory, but it is an argument against failing to recognize and remember the limitations of theory. Several respondents emphasized this wisdom.

Effects of Unsuccessful Interventions on Groups. Most

respondents pointed to augmented dependence or counter-dependence by the group *vis-a-vis* the trainer as marking an unsuccessful intervention. Some saw the group's ignoring of what the intervener said and going on with their interactions as if there had been no intervention as evidence of its ineffectiveness. But these respondents and others also pointed to a kind of "sleeper effect" of some interventions. The intervention may be ignored at first and later the group will bring it up again, discuss, and act on it. This means that interveners should not judge the effectiveness of interventions on the basis of a group's immediate response alone.

Other effects which respondents named as evidence of an ineffective or mal-effective intervention are: premature closure of an issue or conflict; increased scapegoating of individuals and sub-groups by the majority of the group; group flight from the event to which the intervener called attention (a move toward intellectualizing or to safer topics outside the life of the group); withdrawal of member energy from the work of the group; and increased polarization among factions in the group.

Effects of Unsuccessful Interventions on Larger Systems. The effects noted here tended to parallel those named for the group. Reinforcement of unrealistic goals and aspirations and augmented confusion in the organization between ideal images and behavioral actualities were named most often. A correlate of these — a reduced sense of the potency of the organization to solve its actual problems — was named by some respondents.

Premature decision-making on controverted issues was noted by several as evidence of an ineffective intervention.

Finally, augmented polarization between parts of the larger system and increased commitment to win-lose strategies for settling conflicts, following an intervention, were noted as evidence of its ineffectiveness.

EVIDENCES AND CLUES OF SUCCESSFUL INTERVENTIONS

The evidence which most respondents depend on in judging the effectiveness of their interventions is evidence gathered by their own skilled behavioral observations, including listening, checked against the observations of trainees in open discussion. Some respondents stressed the importance of checking such evidence against more systematically collected data, gathered by the trainer/consultant and group, or by independent investigators.

The evidence mentioned by respondents falls into four categories: changes in relationship between intervener and client;

changes in relationships within the client system; changes in functioning of the client system; and changes in task effectiveness. The responses will be summarized for each of these categories.

Changes in Relationship Between Intervener and Client. Most often mentioned as evidence of successful intervening were signs of more initiative, more voluntary action, more open critical questioning of the intervention by the client system, in the presence of the intervener. Closely related are movements toward more interdependence and reciprocity in exchanges between intervener and client. This is evidenced by more spontaneous feedback to the trainer/consultant's ideas and behavior from the client and vice versa. A few mentioned greater readiness of the client to ask for help from the intervener and from peers as evidence of a healthy relationship between intervener and client.

The converse evidence most frequently mentioned as indicating unsuccessful intervention included more dependence or counter-dependence in the client *vis-a-vis* the intervener. This may be masked by greater formality in relationship, or more lip-service agreement with the intervener's ideas or observations. Also stressed was evidence of greater passivity, less initiative, on the part of the client.

Changes in Relationships Within the Client System. Evidences most often mentioned as signs of growth are: more collaborative relations between parts of the client system (more building on each other's contributions, better listening); more open confrontation of conflicts within the system and more energy focused on resolving such conflicts; and more accepting attitudes toward deviants along with more effort to bring deviants into the circle of collaboration. Other evidences mentioned less often were: more giving, asking for and using feedback about one's membership and role behavior; and more comfort with silences.

The converse evidences of unsuccessful interventions reported were: more "game-playing" among parts of the client system and between client and intervener; preoccupation with idiosyncratic member behavior; maintaining a myth of mystical togetherness within the client system; and solidified polarizations between parts of the client system and between client and intervener.

Changes in Functioning of Client System. Most often mentioned as signs of growth in client functioning were: more open expression of thoughts and feelings, positive and negative; more risk-taking behavior (displays of courage and hope in behavior); more investment of energy in process inquiry; and more acknowledgment and sharing of insights gained.

The converse evidences noted were: inordinate emphasis on control of the group rather than on its productivity; increased attempts to get the group to adopt a single, official, language and/or value system; and a heightened level of verbally unexpressed anxiety.

Changes in Task Effectiveness. The evidences of growth in task effectiveness most frequently mentioned were: more clarity of goals; more exploration of alternative ideas and actions without polarization; more focusing of energies on goal attainment and more commitment to group decisions; and more readiness to evaluate the work of the group and to make changes, if indicated by the evaluation.

The converse evidences included: poor use of many resources in group; avoidance of process inquiry and evaluation of work; investment of inordinate time and energy in discussing unimportant issues; and passivity and lack of joy in work.

Similarities and Differences Among Respondents. The similarities in goals of intervention among respondents are striking and require no summary. The clues and evidences which interveners look for and use in evaluating their interventions, while revealing important convergences, also reveal differences which are worth noting. Respondents differ in the weight they give to evidences of healthy and unhealthy internal functioning of the client system and to evidences of the effectiveness or ineffectiveness of the client system in its impact on its external environment. In general, those who emphasize personal growth and learning as goals of intervention look for evidence of success or failure in the internal functioning of person and group. Those who stress more effective task work and problem-solving as goals of intervention focus on evidence of impact effectiveness.

A second difference in emphasis in gathering evaluation data is between a focus on intervener-client relations and a focus on relations between parts of the client system. The former focus seems correlated with learning about authority and power relations as a major or prior goal of interventions. The latter emphasis goes with a heavy weighting on improved peer relations, collaboration skills, and cooperation as goals of intervention. This may reflect a strategic, rather than a theoretical, difference among respondents. Some might say that until a group or organization clarifies its authority relations, it cannot focus energy on improving peer relations. Others might argue that until a group or organization builds strength through peer collaboration, it cannot effectively attack its problems with authority. These positions might lead helpers to different strategies and timing of interventions, although their ultimate criteria of client growth and health are the same.

A third difference is in the importance attached to information about changes in personal behavior and information about changes in group behavior as evidences of effective or ineffective interventions. A large minority among respondents impose a self-limitation upon themselves as laboratory educators, not necessarily as therapists. They analyze only group processes and interpersonal relations within the group setting as they work educationally with groups. They avoid public observations and analyses of personal behavior and intrapersonal processes. The majority of respondents do not place this limitation on their interventions. They may collect and use data about persons, groups, and larger systems as the system problem being clarified and solved requires such data.

A final difference is in the salience of client pain or distress as over against client aspirations and opportunities for growth as an occasion for intervention and as relevant evidence in evaluating the effects of an intervention. In bold contrast, this may demarcate preference for a "medical model" from preference for a "growth model" in conceptualizing the process of helping. Most respondents seem to find both "pain and distress" and "unactualized aspirations and images of opportunity" as legitimate foci of intervention and providing legitimate grounds for evaluating interventions.

CRITERIA FOR MAKING AN INTERVENTION

There are far more marked differences among the responses to this question than among the responses already summarized. Some respondents stated that they were led to intervene by their own gut feelings that an intervention is needed. A kind of preconscious, mind-body sense of readiness prompts an intervention or, conversely, prompts these helpers to abstain from intervention.

Other respondents are guided by their perception of the readiness of the client to receive and make use of an intervention or by their perception of client need which the client's own available internal resources are failing to meet. Examples of perceived readiness are: members of a group seem ready to listen, to learn, to receive help; or a group or larger system seems ready to work effectively on a critical process issue such as dependence or authority. Examples of perceived client need are: members or the whole group seem unable to do something that needs to be done — handle a dominant member, handle an immobilizing conflict, clarify a goal, make a decision.

Still other trainer/consultants are moved to intervene in order to serve some goal which the trainer/consultant believes is right for the client system. Examples are: to move from a "there and then" to a "here-and-now" focus of discussion; to establish a feedback system; to reduce subservience to status and ritual; to protect a "fragile" member; or to reduce confusion.

We are confronted here with differences which probably root in the differing personal styles of interveners. Some persons are more "intuitive," some more "inductive," others more "deductive" in making a decision to act. And it would be surprising if these personal differences did not extend to their actions in intervening as in other actions. If authentic response is valued in interveners' uses of themselves in helping others, authentic differences will show up in different styles of intervention. Interveners who agree on the goals and values of intervention, even on strategies, still will be differentiated in style. Again, we are reminded that "intervention" is an *art*, as well as a science.

FREQUENCY OF INTERVENTIONS

Here again, differences in responses indicate stylistic or strategic differences among our respondents.

Many trainers seem to favor a low frequency of interventions. Some accept this as a *general* policy — let the group or larger system do its own work, don't impose the helper's need to participate on the client, don't act if unsure, ignorant, or in doubt. Others counsel a policy of low frequency *at certain times* in the development of a training or consultation project — early in a group's life, near the end of a group, when the group is jelling as a group, when I, the intervener, feel secure.

Some trainers are oriented to a high frequency of interventions, especially at certain times in the helping process — in early stages of organizational development work; at the times when problems of authority and dependency are being worked on; when a learning group is beginning to define its goals and stragegies; when a group is terminating its relationship with a trainer or training team.

Still other trainers and consultants say that frequency is not a critical consideration in their interventions. They find other considerations more important. Frequency may vary "naturally" with these. Examples of this viewpoint are: I do what I feel; I do what I see is necessary; I do what I perceive is appropriate to my resources; I do what the developmental phase dictates; and I do what the client system is ready for.

KINDS OF INTERVENTIONS MOST FREQUENTLY USED

We have already discussed one classification of interventions. This is the level of human organization to which acts of intervention are addressed — person, group, or larger system. Three other bases of classification were used by respondents.

Classification by Trainer Functions. Several respondents stressed the functions of trainers in macro-level interventions. These have to do with providing scenic (or ecological) factors which fit the purposes and methods of particular training or changing events or dramas — the place of meeting, the duration of meetings, furniture arrangements, and appropriate equipment and supplies.

Another macro-level intervention is to help develop an overall plan for the effective use of time and resources in relation to the learning or change objectives. Such macro-level interventions might include attempts to influence the groupings of participants, the sequence of sessions or of learning events in a session, or the alternation of work and relaxation periods.

Most respondents stressed functions of interveners in their direct, face-to-face transactions with clients or with the client system. Five micro-intervener functions were mentioned approvingly by some or all respondents: 1) *Role model* — authentic expressive behavior, giving and receiving feedback, confessing limitations, and needs for help; 2) *Procedural, technical resource* — suggesting appropriate activities and methods, providing conceptual tools, linking learners to appropriate resource materials or persons outside the group; 3) *Methodological helper* — collecting and sharing behavioral data, training in methods of data collection and interpretation, training in participant observation; 4) *Confronter*, disconfirmer, agent of dissonance, Socratic questioner; and 5) *Supporter.*

Forms of Intervention. Two main forms of intervention were noted. The first has to do with the kinds of "language" employed in communicating the meaning of an intervention. All respondents report the use of the *language of behavior inquiry* at times in their interventions. Some respondents report using the *language of allegory and myth.* Incitive language is recommended by some — the *language of action.* And a few respondents emphasize the economy of the *language of gestures and movement* — modeling of movement in exploring and expressing affective states and processes. Language preferences no doubt are related to differences in personal style as well as to situational requirements and learning objectives.

The second classification of interventions had to do with

differences in grammatical and rhetorical form. Some respondents report extensive use of *questions* in intervening. The interrogative intervention seems to invite inquiry by the client. Other respondents report using *terse, open-ended statements.* Some respondents recommend *expressive communication* when the major content of the intervention is affective. Some respondents report the use of *explanatory and interpretive statements* while others deplore their use but would recommend *reports of behavioral observations.* Almost all respondents report the use of *summarizing statements* when these are not supplied by members of the client system.

Styles of Intervention. In general, respondents counsel the use of an open and direct style of intervention, a style which should be congruent with the personal style of the intervener.

All respondents seem to accept that a helper becomes a participant observer in the process of helping a client system. He must become, in some measure, a member in the time-bounded system of learning and changing which emerges out of his contracting with the client system. This is necessary in order that he may gather "inside" data about the state of the client system — its hopes and fears, its crippling and supporting history, its strengths and weaknesses. But he remains a "special" member — he cannot perform his function of consciousness and capacity-expander if he becomes "just one of the boys and girls." The principal differences among respondents with respect to style of intervention stem from different views of how far the intervener can and should become "member-like" in his interventions without losing his required capacity to challenge, to objectify and to open up novel images of functioning for the client system. These differences may reflect different theories of changing and of the change agent. But we suspect that they reflect differences in the personal styles of interveners — their most congenial and effective ways of meeting, greeting, and influencing their social worlds.

ADVICES TO AN APPRENTICE OR INTERN

We will list the advice which our respondents would give to apprentices, whose professional development they are assisting, without comment or interpretation. Actually, this advice also becomes advice both to readers who may be concerned with their own professional development, and to those who are seeking earmarks of professional wisdom in professionals whom they, as clients or consumers, might employ to assist them.

The stylistic and strategic differences which we have already noted among our respondents show up in their advice. The general agreement on the values which should guide interveners in a helping relationship also pervades these counsels of wisdom.

We have arranged their advice, beginning with those who see the person as the basic target of intervention, through those who favor the group as the target, to those whose orientation is toward changing larger human systems.

1. Know and understand yourself, your role, your motives, feelings, insecurities, and behavior patterns. Know also the effects these have upon recipients of your interventions.

2. Take care of yourself first; keep in touch with yourself; use your uniqueness; you can only be you, not someone else.

3. Be open with the group; share your motives, feelings, theories, and fears when the group needs to know these in order to deal openly with you and with other members.

4. Trust the group and the helping process. The client has many, if not all, of the key resources which need to be identified and used in the change process.

5. Focus on learning and growth, not member liking and comfort; interventions are in the service of client learning and growth.

6. Every intervention you make has an authority loading whether you want it to have such a loading or not. Actually, the trainer or consultant is an authority of a sort. You must deal with authority-responsibility-dependence issues at times in your relationship with clients. The trainer/consultant has a joint responsibility with participants/clients for initiative taking and for the effects of initiatives taken.

7. Focus on group phenomena, group processes, group norms, group conflicts, and group growth.

8. Focus on diagnosis of the client system. Diagnosis is a critical entry process in helping as well as a continuing responsibility of the client system.

9. Each intervention is time-bound and time-related, whether in individual, group, or larger system development. A "good" intervention at one phase of development may be a "bad" intervention at another.

10. A mutual scouting period between helper and client is necessary before valid contract development can take place.

11. Development of a support system for risk-taking behavior and experimentation is a key responsibility of the trainer/consultant.

12. It is crucial/helpful to develop an outside-inside temporary system to support integral personal and system change and growth.

13. Social change works from below upwards.

14. Social change requires mobilization of instinctual energies,

which "free" both persons and system from the hold of established constraints on behavior.

15. Social change requires working on exposed contradictions in persons and in the system.

16. Social systems are most effective when they generate public data, are collaborative among sub-systems, and when they generate public expressions of feelings and commitments.

We have not summarized the "intervention traps" against which our respondents would warn their apprentices or interns. In general, they are conditions which result from neglect of one or another of the counsels of wisdom.

SUMMARY COMMENT

We hope that we have revealed the present state of thinking about intervention within the emergent profession of laboratory practitioners. In spite of marked differences in culture, professional, and disciplinary background, and specialization in laboratory practice among our respondents, their responses reveal a considerable community of "theory." This community lies in a common conceptualization of helper-client relationships and of the values which should guide the helper-client transactions within those relationships.

Yet there are also marked differences in their views on the practice of intervention. Some of these arise realistically from the different levels of human systems with which various respondents habitually work. Other differences we have ascribed to differences in intervention strategy — the time sequencing of work on authority and power problems and on problems of peer relations, and the amount of pre-planning required for a fruitful learning encounter are examples. Still other differences we have attributed to differences in personal style. These are more evident in discussions of the "art" of intervention than in discussions of its "scientific basis" and "theory."

The evidences of community reassure us that teamwork among professionals is possible and that there are valid grounds to support the development of an emergent profession. The evidences of difference within that community reassure us that laboratory practice is not a dogmatic cult.

FOOTNOTES AND REFERENCES

1. Chris Argyris, *Intervention Theory and Method: A Behavioral Science View,* Addison-Wesley, Reading, Mass., 1970, pp. 15-16.

2. At first glance, Argyris' definition seems to limit "interventions" to

relationships between a client system and a helper from outside the system. This would seem to exclude from the scope of intervention theory and practice the helping actions of trainers and consultants internal to an organization in their relations with persons and groups which are parts of the same organization.

We do not accept this interpretation of the definition. An internal consultant, for example, one attached to the Personnel Department of a school system, can develop a helping contract with the principal, teachers, and students of a school building within the system. And the same theory and strategy should guide his interventions in this "internal relationship" as in an "external" consultant's relationship with a school system that does not regularly pay his salary. On the other hand, such an internal consultant would find it difficult or impossible to establish a helping relationship with the Personnel Department of which he is a working part or with the Superintendent of Schools in his system and the group of Associate Superintendents of the system. The practical difficulties arise from the clash between the expectations and requirements of the internal consultant's ongoing colleague relationships in his department and his subordinate relationship to the Superintendent and his group with the expectations of the helping relationship which intervention, as we are discussing it, requires. The difficulties are thus, we believe, "practical" rather than "theoretical."

3. Our questionnaire included the following eleven items — 1) The effects of successful trainer-consultant interventions are; 2) The effects of unsuccessful interventions are; 3) The clues (evidences) of successful intervention are; 4) The clues of unsuccessful interventions are; 5) The criteria I use most frequently for making an intervention are; 6) My orientation toward frequency of intervention is something like this; 7) What are some of the *major objectives* for intervention you use; 8) What kinds of intervention do you most frequently use; 9) If you were responsible for teaching a laboratory intern your theory of intervention, *what three or four propositions would you wish to emphasize*; 10) What types of traps about intervening (or not intervening) would you want to warn him about; and 11) What statements of rationale would you wish to defend as *your* orientation?

4. In addition to returns from the editors, the following distinguished practitioners of laboratory method completed and returned our questionnaire — Chris Argyris (Massachusetts); Boris Astrachan (Connecticut); Max Birnbaum (New York); William Dyer (Utah); Gunnar Hjelholt (Denmark); Gordon Lippitt (Washington, D.C.); Max Pages (France); Juan Rosello (Puerto Rico); Eva Schindler-Rainman (California); Richard Schmuck (Oregon); Marjan Schroder (The Netherlands); Robert Tannenbaum (California); and John Weir (California).

PART III

APPLICATIONS TO PERSONS AND GROUPS

PART III

INTRODUCTION

In this part of the book the focus is upon the application of the laboratory method to individual learning and changing, and to the development of the small group.

An earlier organizational title of NTL Institute, *National Training Laboratory in Group Development*, clearly and accurately focused on the centrality of the small group in early practices of laboratory method. Many disciplines, and a great variety of practitioners, received new and exciting nurturance from the then fresh developments in applied group dynamics.

The individual learner was viewed as a social and interpersonal being, with much of his behavior influenced by and to be understood in the light of group-member roles, responses to group norms and pressures, needs to solve common problems, and feelings and perceptions in the presence of others. Similarly, the small group became a focus of fresh insights into organizational and community dynamics. Organizations and communities can be conceptualized, in part, as social fields, in some way made up of continually changing and overlapping small-group systems that interact in powerful ways. Large systems can also be viewed as analogues of the small group, with dynamics that are similar in significant ways.

Gibb, in Chapter 12, defines the training group and shows how it has evolved over the years, as it has been adopted and adapted by a wide range of disciplines and professions.[1] Individual learning is the focus of therapy, counseling, and vocational rehabilitation groups. While therapy groups usually focus upon remedial processes designed to relieve distress in people who see themselves as sick and needing treatment; and training groups usually focus upon current interpersonal processes designed to improve competence and skills of people who see themselves as well and in need of further learning, there has come to be a mutual enrichment and great overlap in processes, technology, and aims between these two kinds of groups. Weir, in Chapter 13, describes one pattern of group learning in which therapy and training have blended into a focus upon personal growth. Personal growth groups vary in underlying theory, in method, in environmental content, and in style of leadership. The common interest is in accomplishing such aims as increasing personal potential, releasing creativity, and enriching personal life. The methodology is an innovative and fermentative meshing of such sources as yoga, Eastern religion, interpretive dance, psychodrama, cultural anthropology, and clinical psychology. New methodologies arise continually and include some creative, exploratory, or intuitive mixing of hypnotism, sensory awakening, bio-energetics, altered states of consciousness, dream analysis, calligraphy, or any other experience that might open the person to new energy sources or to an enriched life. Petzold, in Chapter 16, shows how psychodramatic role-playing can be used in a wide range of training, personal growth, and therapeutic experiences, and how training groups can be made more powerful by the use of this technology.

The design and structuring of the training laboratory can have powerful effects upon the focus and nature of the personal and group experiences within it. Astrachan, in Chapter 14, shows how an overall laboratory or conference strategy can be used to accomplish specific learning goals and to focus learnings. Methodology and design are highly interrelated with training objectives, as he clearly shows.

More traditional educative groups and processes have interacted with the training group over the years. While an instructional group usually focuses upon content, knowledge outcomes, and cognitive and ideational problems; and a training group usually focuses more upon process, behavioral change, and affective states, there is a large overlap and mutual enrichment in aims and foci between the two. The T group has been fused with or added to the instructional group in many settings. As shown by Gibb in Chapter 3, considerable research has focused upon the T group as a medium for accomplishing educational aims such as reduction of prejudice, increasing knowledge, improving skills, or changing attitudes. Birnbaum, in Chapter 15, describes such a directional effort in the "Clarification Group," a special educational invention to help persons understand and accept their social selves. This grew out of the accelerating depth and severity of interethnic and interracial conflicts in our pluralistic society. Birnbaum hopes that the clarification group process can be used to accomplish various educational outcomes in affectively powerful and more or less predictable ways.

The small group has been used in a variety of contexts for a number of different purposes. A group may train itself or be trained for such purposes as managing a system, planning a program, sharing ideas or perceptions, assessing the potentials of its members, carrying out a program, changing member attitudes, remedying member deficiencies, or creating a climate for member growth. The T group technology of here-and-now, process-oriented, minimal-structure activities can be used in custom-designed ways to enhance such aims and purposes. It is the purpose of the chapters in this section to show how this technology has been and can be adapted to the service of various objectives.

Training groups can be classified according to the theory used by the trainer. If one knows the theory base, one can predict something about the format, content, technique, or focus of the group. Although individual leaders differ greatly, and small groups differ widely, the experience is likely to be influenced considerably if, for instance, the theory base is psychoanalytic, bio-energetic, Lewinian, psychodramatic, TORI[2], Synanon, or that of Transactional Analysis.[3] Weir's tube theory helps to integrate, for both the trainer and the trainee, the experiences described in Chapter 13. The Tavistock theory adds meaning to the group relations training model described in Chapter 14 by Astrachan.

The training group has served as a medium for reducing the cognitive and affective dissonance among disciplines. The traditional barriers among fields such as social work, nursing, clinical psychology, rehabilitation, sociology, business administration, education, psychiatry, and recreation have been reduced somewhat through inter-disciplinary research, action, and training projects in which T group methodology has been used with effectiveness. The methodology is so diverse and so effective that many people with otherwise-conflicting models can work together with understanding, and learn ways in which each can contribute to the other.

FOOTNOTES AND REFERENCES

1. It may be of historical interest to readers to compare Gibb's synoptic treatment of the T group in this volume with the more lavish treatment of T Group Training in a book published ten years ago — L. P. Bradford, J. Gibb and K. Benne (Eds.), *T Group Theory and Laboratory Method*, Wiley, New York, 1964. The comparison reveals dramatically the rapid evolution of this form of training in the past decade.

2. The TORI theory and practice of training is the invention of Jack and Lorraine Gibb. It has been described, among other places, in Jack Gibb, "TORI Theory: Non-Verbal Behavior and the Experience of Community," *Comparative Group Studies, 3,* November, 1972, and Jack Gibb, "TORI Theory and Practice" in J. E. Pfeiffer and J. E. Jones (Eds.) *The 1972 Handbook For Group Facilitators,* University Associates, Iowa City, IA., 1972.

3. For a popular, readable and generally dependable account of the human potential movement, of which the approaches named here are parts, see Jane Howard, *Please Touch: A Guided Tour of the Human Potential Movement,* McGraw Hill, New York, 1970.

CHAPTER 12

THE TRAINING GROUP

Jack R. Gibb

The purpose of this chapter is to describe the laboratory training group (the T group), something of how it has changed and come of age in recent years, and how rapidly increasing research and more adequate theory has created new and enticing options for the training group leader. The training group has been seen by many participants and by some theorists as the dramatic core of the laboratory method.

In the beginnings of its development, the T group was relatively easy to describe and define — both in theory and in customary practice.

The focus was upon the *existential experiences* of the group in the here and the now, rather than upon the past experiences of the members or their future plans or expectations. The primary concern was upon the *processes* of the group, rather than upon content. Activities emerged in *low structure*, rather than being planned or designed in advance, and were minimally directed by the leader, except for procedural or process matters. The focus was, in a historically significant social-engineering invention, upon the *group qua group*, a social reality seen as transcending and enriching the intra-personal or dyadic (usually leader-member, occasionally member-member) focus of most action groups or remedial groups. Interaction was largely verbal, with a minimal emphasis upon the processes of non-verbal communication. The purpose was centered on *interpersonal and group competence*, rather than upon therapeutic, remedial, or personal-growth outcomes. Internal dynamics of the group were stressed rather than externally-oriented productivity or task outcomes. The group was purposefully composed of members who were in cultural and geographical isolation from their external environment — the everyday work, home, or play world.

During the last quarter century, the T group has somehow managed to maintain a relatively clear identity in the research literature, in theories of training and learning, and in popular parlance, in spite of gradual expansion of each of the above eight definitive criteria of T groupness.

EXPANSION AND DIVERSITY OF THE MODEL

The classic T group, as defined in the eight criteria described above, and as described in detail as it was in the theory and practice of the 50s in *T Group Theory and Laboratory Method*, has maintained a surprisingly classic integrity of form and style, especially as practiced by many leaders, and as practiced in some contexts, perhaps, by all. By now, almost everyone knows what a T group is. It is not unusual for a norm-breaking T leader to be called to task by a newcoming member: "You aren't doing what a T leader is supposed to do!" Everyone has, of course, projective expectations, which have wide across-person differences, but a common pattern is there. The model is demonstrably powerful. The early theory, grounded so little in research data, has held up surprisingly well.

Though the classic lines of the model are easily recognized (particularly existentiality, process orientation, and relatively low and emergent structuring), there are many modifications. The model is a very flexible one that has been adapted to a variety of purposes. There has been much cross-fertilization of theory and technique between the T group and other disciplines where groups have been a significant aspect of professional technology: psychotherapy, rehabilitation, counseling, group work, community development, and education. The T group model has created change and has been changed in the process. That is, while maintaining an existential base, the T group has been used as a medium for clarification of personal concerns about the past and about the future (see Shepard's Chapter 10). Many relatively puristic T group leaders are quite comfortable in prospecting residual feelings about past events, particularly if they are personal, represented in live current concerns and options, and related in some way to current behavior. All T group leaders would presumably aid the group to return frequently to here-and-now concerns, even in the most team- or task-oriented training groups.

Leaders of various theoretical persuasions have been willing to focus upon content-level interactions when the T group is an integral part of an action or learning group focused on such concerns as woman's awareness, racial confrontation (see Birnbaum's Chapter 15), executive development, acquisition of professional skills, or attitude change, to mention but a few of the programs reported in the literature. Research, reported in Chapter 3, indicates that the T group format is readily adaptable to successful programs in these program areas.

The T group format has, with some trainers, moved from its original low-structure state to various manners and degrees of structuring. The research studies reported in Chapter 3 describe a variety of T group research programs in which the groups have as a central focus some structured experiences such as role-playing (see Petzold's Chapter 16), non-verbal interaction, skill training, simulated organizational decision making, or other leader- or group-planned activity. Such structuring may follow principles of design discussed in the Lippitt and Schindler-Rainman Chapter 8. A related modification of the T group design is so to control the instructions or environment of the group as to accentuate the power dynamics, authority dynamics, or intimacy dynamics of the group, and thus hopefully to focus and accelerate selected learnings (see Astrachan's Chapter 14, and Pages' Chapter 17). Often these foci are used as a means of bridging the gap between training-group learnings and transfer to other life situations. The research suggests that this is accomplished to a significant degree in many cases, without unduly sacrificing the primary learnings of the original T group format.

The early group *qua* group focus has been preserved by many group leaders, but powerful forces have moved many leaders and group members (see the clear statement of this position in the Weir Chapter 13) toward a primary focus upon intra-personal and interpersonal dynamics. Particularly among humanistically oriented leaders, and among leaders who are likely to call the experience an encounter group (the basic dynamic is presumably an "encounter" between persons), a personal growth group, or an awareness group, the movement is toward "I statements," owning one's feelings, talking to another person rather than to "the group," and other earmarks of personal and dyadic interaction. In this milieu a remark oriented toward process or group-level reality is likely to be viewed as violating an unconscious, or often an explicit, norm of the leader and/or the group. This trend away from group-level focus is certainly evident in the protocols of T groups in a variety of settings. What seems to be occurring is some kind of synthesis of foci that will include legitimate interaction at any of several significant levels.

Protocols of current group literature indicate that there has been a dramatic increase in the use of non-verbal experiences and techniques designed to induce them. The non-verbal experience, once a hallmark of the growth-movement groups, now is a common happening in the T group, either as an unplanned aspect of the group experience, or triggered by leader structuring. Research evidence is conflicting, but there is some indication that non-verbal experiences add to the inductive power of the T group. The effects are likely to be influenced by the leader's freedom in communicating with the body and in allowing and joining emergent movement out of the boundaries of word communications. The frequent focus upon other-than-verbal activities need not change the definitive focus of the T group upon the here and the now, the process level, or the minimal structure, but is, indeed, likely to rapidly accelerate such focus. Members move, hug, frown, and fight in the moment. Nor need a non-verbal supplementation alter the preferred focus of the leader in directing, suggesting, allowing, or joining the activity of the group. Regression to the pre-verbal is congruent with other structure-reducing regressions of the group in the T group setting. Words are simply non-nonverbal or possibly less-organic ways of communicating.

T group leaders have the option of focusing upon the level of skill and competence or of behaving in such a way as to help move the group toward therapeutic, counseling, or personal-growth objectives. Interactions of T group practitioners with leaders who work in growth centers and with encounter groups has caused a mutual enrichment of these streams of activity. There are sharp differences of opinion among T group practitioners and theorists about the activities and outcomes of groups that move from the original interpersonal-competence level of analysis toward more personal-growth experiences. The literature contains lively and informative debates on this issue.

The T group model has expanded to include direct work on the task, problem-solving, social-action, and productivity level. Whether these task-and-process groups are composed of heterogeneous members, simulated teams, or organizational teams in the work, family, or school environment, they usually include similar techniques, purposes, trainer interventions, and group dynamics.

When the T group was first used in an organizational setting it was simply transplanted into the company or school system, for instance, and heterogeneous groups within the system were given training. It was later found that natural teams could be trained in this manner. A more recent and productive development (described in detail in the Gibb Chapter 3, the Beckhard Chapter 18, and the Schindler-Rainman Chapter 19), in the context of a long-range, integrated, and total-system-oriented approach to organizational and community development. Here the T group model can be effectively adapted to whatever is custom-designed by the system or by the consultant to meet organizational objectives. Both research and application experience show this approach to be very promising.

STATE OF THE ART

During the last quarter of a century a number of changes have occurred that deeply influence the diversity of the T group model — the art, science, and engineering technology of the training group. Each of the changes discussed below has a profound effect upon the trainer. The plan of the rest of the chapter is to discuss eight significant changes as they affect the options open to the trainer, and then to discuss, in detail, in the last section, the five classes of options open to the trainer who wishes to help create a T group that will lead to significant individual, group, and organizational learning and change: theory, primary focus, ecology, methodology, and leader style options.

Range of Options. The dramatic change for the trainer is the increase in the pool of viable and attractive options available, choices of design, style of intervention, model of structuring the environment, and other choices of engineering technology. In the earliest decade of T grouping, the road was uncharted. Leaders had few bases for choosing an intervening mode other than hunch and guess. Few leaders felt secure, knew what to do, or what would be the outcomes of their efforts. This made life exciting — and fearful. Some of the road now has been charted; a range of models has been tried; there are some meaningful data on what will happen when certain options are taken.

Societal Readiness. As described earlier, the laboratory has deep roots in widely diverse, often complex and antithetical historic forces. These changes that churn our society relate to the basic issues that people continue to face in the T group. The T group, partly because of its low directional structure, is a projective mirror of the culture. Where would the boundaries of freedom be? How do we create what kind of law and what kind of order? What part does authority play? How do we organize for work and play and worship? How much of our lives can we control? How much can I "do my own thing?" How can we handle conflict? How can we "make love, not war?" How honest and open can people be in a "real" world? Am I my brother's keeper? These issues continue to involve members of each T group. Each issue is a concern, at vocal or pre-verbal levels, of every group, organization, or nation in which a member has some involvement. The T group is life itself, and also is a surrogate simulation of the families, committees, boards — and all other groups that form the fabric of the culture.

The rising controversy around sensitivity training exists because T groups are so important. They reflect, exacerbate, or help solve all of the central value clashes in our culture.

The culture is more ready for the laboratory method than it has ever been. The forces creating rapid change in our institutions, that give us alternative schools, families, and churches, are forces that ready people for the gut involvement of people with other people around issues that matter.

Centrality of Values. Values — what matters — are of central concern to the increasing numbers of people who are seeking a new life or trying to preserve an old one. Freedom, authority, conformity, openness, love, conflict, duty — all are T group concepts that touch off deep value conflicts and re-examinations.

Cross-fertilization. The expansion of the T group model, discussed above, has helped create a broad base for potential support systems that now exist in many institutions and in many disciplines where support was once lacking and much needed. This is very convincingly seen in the results, presented in Chapter 3, which show the broad base in university departments which not only allow but encourage programs of research on T groups and application of these results to professional training programs.

Availability of Theory. Advancement of theory is highly interdisciplinary in this field. Conceptualization in T group theory shows clear sources in clinical psychiatry, cultural anthropology, sociology of power, political science, modern dance, calligraphy, physiotherapy, topological mathematics, astrology, energy-system physics, Chinese philosophy, economics, and game theory — to mention just a few of the explicit sources of recent writings in the T group field. In search of understanding, training models, and heuristic formulations, theorists are reading materials and talking with people that a decade ago they did not know existed. New journals, cross-disciplinary seminars, growth centers, and multidisciplinary graduate programs all contribute to this resource stockpile available to the leader.

New Research Data and Technology. Chapter 3 gives a brief survey of some developments in measurement and disciplined observation that make new data available for the trainer to use to test methods and designs. Effective laboratory group training is an integration of research and training processes. The effective group uses a data base for decision making, progress evaluation, directional steering, and continual re-evaluation. The organism is a scientific instrument and process. The new trainer can provide new technological resources to the group — from videotape to outcome instruments. The tools are improving.

Social Engineering. Expanding the resources available to the new professional is a wide range of technological interventions and training designs that have been tried, measured, described, and reported. Think of a new way of doing something in a group or an organization — and if you ask around it is likely that you will find that it has been tried. It is often possible to find out if it was seen as a success or a failure, what caused this, and what improves the technology. Groups have been tried with simultaneous translation, with deaf-mute members, with insane felons, in the nude or with varieties of clothing, with computer data feedback on current feelings and perceptions, on shipboard and on mountain hikes, with group sex or physical violence allowed, with white workers present with black bosses, with no leaders or rotating leaders, with bio-feedback, with meditation or total silence for prolonged periods — with a wide variety of technologies, populations, and purposes — with an articulated theory under test or seemingly simply to see what happens. The range of partially tested options is large.

Professional Trainer Pool. A greatly increased pool of professionally skilled trainer-consultants makes possible the broadening of the diversity and competence of a training team, consultation for new programs, reciprocal internships among co-professionals, peer learning, professional organizations, emotional support, creative conflict, and a general resource diversity which is deprovincializing the field.

Each of the developments has possible negative aspects: attraction of people with unprofessional values or motives to the training field, a dilution of quality; a cultural backlash produced by overenthusiastic cult members; a rush to do seemingly easy and popular research without adequate theory base; or a multitude of possible side effects which may have negative consequences.

The current state of the art is such that it appears that a new broadly based profession is emerging.

TRAINER OPTIONS

The options available to the trainer are greatly expanded. The options will be discussed in a contingency sequence. Each decision about a prior option will affect subsequent decisions and range of options available in the subsequent option categories. Neither the sequence nor these categories are viewed as other than an expository guide. They provide a convenient set of checkpoints for a professional to examine his self growth, training gaps, and restrictive areas of vision. The sequence is meant as a set of check points in looking at career growth as well as in preparing for a specific training program.

Theory Options. The leader has a wide range of articulated, published, and field-tested theory to use as a framework for approaching the task: Lewinian, self, role, non-directive, bio-energetic, Gestalt, TORI, Transactional Analysis, psychoanalytic, and Psychosynthesis, to mention a sample of many that are in current use. Propositions from each of these theories have been tested, directly or indirectly, in the studies listed in the research bibliography in Appendix A. Material on each is available in published form, with extensive protocol material making relatively explicit what a trainer might do who was attempting to make an application of such a theory.

A theory is a useful tool for the practicing trainer. Each trainer in reality creates his own theory, some integrated set of contingent assumptions, that helps in several important ways. A theory is a selecting instrument that gives criteria for all the subsequent choices the trainer makes — the design, choice of subjects, kind of intervention, and a whole range of other major and minor options described below. Selection and design are thus less opportunistic than they would otherwise be. Theory helps in diagnosis, in selective perception of the training group and the seemingly infinite range of variables to look at. It helps in guiding interventions — gives a basis for deciding when and how to act or not act. It helps in deciding what to evaluate or measure and what data might be selected for feedback. Because theory gives a rationale and justification for choices, it is a potential base of emotional support. So much that a trainer does is untested or untestable, intangible, and responsive to unforeseen ambiguity that it is important for the trainer to reduce unnecessary ambiguity and potential stress points.

The theory is likely to be optimally useful to the trainer if it (a) comes out of a level central to the person and is integral to the trainer's experience, values, and belief systems, if it (b) is suited to his level of skill, experience, and knowledge of the theory, if it (c) is internalized and specific enough to allow him to come into the T group with a feeling of confidence in knowing how he will cope with a wide range of events in the group.

In a sense most available theories are "true." There is an increasingly broad area of common empirical and experimental phenomena. Every useful theory has to take account of this growing body of empirical data. Theories differ in the hypothetical substrata that are inferentially assumed to account for the observations, upon which there is much greater common agreement. The test of worth of a theory for a trainer is not so much in its general validity (of which there is a rather narrow range in existing theory), but in its functional usefulness for the trainer.

Does it help in diagnosis, in communication of feedback, in understanding, and in telling the trainer and the trainee what to do next? Is it useful in everyday life to people who are likely to be in one's groups?

Primary Focus Options. Following the choice of an existent and organized model of learning and/or group life, or the creation of one's own framework, the leader has several viable options for primary focus, the choice of which is related to but may not necessarily be dictated by the theory chosen. The foci most often used in practice and most often tested in research studies are: the focus on cognitive-perceptual integration, process awareness, feedback flow, climate, group development and norms, personal growth, or structured technique. These foci are obviously not mutually exclusive, but do form the basis for a major concern for each trainer. The protocol and coding data suggest that leaders tend, when faced with recurrent intervention choices, to zero in on or return to preferred foci.

The evidence seems to indicate that most trainers (and therapists and teachers, as well) in developing an intervention focus, follow deep-seated habits and tendencies rather than the theory they describe to explain what they do. This is likely due to a number of factors which are presumably susceptible to T group training influence. As trainers build more specific theories that are integrated in the trainer they are more likely to be more congruent (do what they say they are doing, or change the theory, the intervention behavior, or both). The conditions of the T group (direct feedback in a trusting climate, opportunity to try out, get new feedback, and try again) are presumably designed to produce this congruence.

The trainer cannot focus on everything. The versatile and sensitive trainer may respond at appropriate times to any event, at any level. To have optimal effect, in terms of his theory, it is probably best to intervene at a level and in a manner that will focus client learnings.

If the theory predicts that cognitive organization, dissonance, or simplicity, say, is critical to learning, then, by and large, interventions tend to cluster at the cognitive-perceptual level.

Others may believe that the essential medium for learning diagnostic sensitivity, say, is process awareness. The theory may or may not specify the processes that are most critical. A bioenergetics theorist will focus on bodily processes and direct energy toward awareness and/or change specifically related to bodily energy systems. Some process people may ignore cognitive processes or their verbal counterparts completely, believing them irrelevant to change and growth.

If the focus is on feedback flow, then the theorist may be

much interested in the processes and procedural devices which facilitate bio-feedback, feeling expression, or idea-exchange, depending on his theory of feedback. See the discussion in the last section of this chapter, and Chin's presentation in Chapter 23.

If the focus is on climate, than ecological design, interventions, and other decisions will be related to trust building, empathy, or whatever focal element of the climate is seen by the theorist as the key leverage variable. Energy will be directed toward climate change. It may be worth noting that knowledge of the theory or the theorist may not be sufficiently differentiated to be able to predict with accuracy what interventions lead to climate change. At least the trainer/theorist is refining the theory to the point where it is more susceptible to experimental, empirical, or clinical test. Some theories are so stated that they cannot be tested. In an empirical system such as a laboratory T group, such untestable theories are of little use.

If the primary medium for change is the group stage or group norm, then the design calls for norm observation, focus on group stages, process observations at the group level, and a language appropriate to the sociology of the small group.

Weir describes in Chapter 13 how much a focus on personal growth and the choice of a relevant theory affects everything about his integrated training effort. His theory is useful to him in many ways. It enables him to ignore a whole range of data that others might pay attention to, and to *focus* his energy upon the data that his theory specifies as relevant to the changes he hopes will take place on very clearly defined variables. There are a wide variety of other theories which also steer the practitioner toward a personal growth focus, but which, in many cases, specify very different interventions, designs, and outcome variables toward which the trainer would focus energy.

Many trainers have specific theories which have a focus on a technique. The technique becomes the center of design focus, and the technique is the assumed medium of leverage. The technique, well used, is assumed to be associated with the desired level and quality of outcome. Petzold describes in Chapter 16 how a well-differentiated technique (role-playing) is used by a professional to attempt to get learning and change on specific outcome measures.

Ecological Options. The creation of a theoretical framework, and differentiation of this into a primary focus related to the theory, will predispose the trainer to create a format for the training.

Experience and research have increased the complexity of the format choice. For instance, much data from a variety of diverse fields indicate the powerful effect of macro-ecological factors. Whatever the theory, there is a necessity for the training team to plan or engineer the external environment in which the group experience occurs. The macro-environmental factors probably are more powerful than the internal environment of the group, granting a certain competence and expertise on the part of the trainers involved in providing a group experience. The total environment field affects all of the internal variables. The whole Watergate *Zeitgeist* impacts citizen reactions, trust in government, confidence in the courts, and all variables within the citizen. Institutional norms strongly influence dress, speech, trust, and attendance. Workers steal from open stock shelves in one company and are rewarded by the other workers; in another company stealing hardly ever occurs. One campus is rebellious, and another is conforming. The controversy over sensitivity training creates a bed of suspicion or an atmosphere of trust, depending upon the climate in the organization.

If a program of T groups is to accomplish widespread and enduring individual and institutional change, the trainer consultant must work with the total system on management policy, reward systems, information sharing, organizational decision-making, and other long-range climate-setting variables before spending energy on a program of group training, however massive it is or however saturated the system may become with "trained" members.

This means that trainer planners might take into account such factors as: integrating the administration of the laboratory with the group training philosophy; pre-planning with system participants to set expectations; co-planning with community or organization members for post-training actions and support systems; working with citizen groups or community members in attitude-forming sessions before engaging in group training; and paying attention to training system factors such as inter-group spatial relations, housing arrangements, ways of collecting data, community recreation, manner of payment of fees, and a whole variety of training-community norms.

In practice these factors are often ignored or relegated to "coordinators" or secretaries as less important factors than the training itself. There is increasing evidence that these factors are more powerful in determining change-maintenance than the within-training factors. It is likely that the wide variations in reported success of large T group programs and in measured outcomes of the research studies are due, in large part, to institutional and community variables that cause one massive study to show no significant outcomes of any kind and a similar program in another institution, in a widely different atmosphere, to show large, statistically significant gains.

Ecological factors include psychological, geographical, architectural, spatial, managerial, and many other aspects of the oft-ignored contributions to training effectiveness. Trainers have joked for years about the large tables, rural dynamics, and spatious lawns at Bethel — perhaps they were more important than trainers thought.

Internal Environment Options. The role expectations, norms, and demands of the external system (the institution or macro-system, and the training community itself) will have a powerful effect upon the internal environment of the training group, whether it be a company team, a growth-center weekend group, or a heterogeneous group of adults in an NTL laboratory. The group itself generates its own forces. One of the enduring contributions of early NTL sessions was that practitioners began to look seriously at the group *qua* group. Group therapy is not simply a matter of a therapist doing successive therapy sessions with individuals in a group setting. Management of a team is not a matter of a cluster or series of dyadic relationships between the manager and each team member. Family parenting is not merely a matter of a mother or father differentially rewarding or punishing individual family members according to perceived individual needs. Parenting, managing, therapy, and training may be carried on through effective, informed, and skilled leadership which involves the centering upon and building of powerful, free, cooperative, and effective groups. The group climate, created in such collaborative, laboratory-method ways, becomes the mediating mechanism for creating system outcomes (productivity, learning, family satisfactions, or whatever).

The trainer, then, to become effective, focuses upon the internal environment of the group. Research suggests that the following variables contribute appreciably to this environment: the leader style, particularly warmth and supportiveness and manner of controlling; the composition of the group; the amount and kind of feedback; the "therapeutic" quality of the group climate; the macro-environment; and possibly the method used and the length of training.

The role of the trainer in setting the climate for learning is described by Bradford in Chapter 5, and by Weir in Chapter 13. The specific influences of the trainer style and methodology are discussed below. Protocols of research reviewed in Chapter 3 suggest that the "flavor" of the internal environment differs widely and has differential effects. This flavor comes through even in the necessarily truncated written descriptions of the way the training is conducted. An examination of the intervention strategies in Chapter 11, representative of a variety of experienced trainers, shows the wide range of presenting selves shown by the trainers. One can only guess at the effect of these different strategies upon the internal environment of the groups they lead.

Research reports clearly indicate that the variance across groups and across trainers is large.

Awareness of the significance of the internal environment helps the leader to examine his own behavior as a norm-setter and what ecological impact may result from such factors as sitting on the floor or at tables, having flexible meeting times or prescribed time boundaries, rewarding initiators, or such things as how people dress, how laughter is regarded in the group, how decisions are made, what "contracts" are made, how physical touching is regarded, how conflict is handled, and how latecomers and absentees are perceived by the leader and by other members.

The available protocols of both training and research indicate that the length of session time and total training time is reducing appreciably. It is likely, as total training hours get shorter, that significant positive effects, already tenuous and of probable short duration, will get less, and that potential negative effects will be greater. It is not likely that twenty to thirty hours of training time is sufficient to accomplish in any effective way the hoped-for outcomes of conscientious trainers. It is realistic to expect that members who come with the expectation and implicit commitment to a longer period of time will be more apt to have enduring effects that will carry over to home and job behaviors.

The trainer who sees his role as that of internal-environment engineer will do a great deal of thinking about methodology and procedure. In recent years a wide variety of materials has been published on methodology. The professional has new and varied resources. The methodology focuses on everything from organizational and cognitive inquiry to personal growth in depth. Whatever its flavor, the method is likely to be focused on enrichment of the data collection and feedback systems. Methods, tests, and machines have been devised to help the group and the member get more reliable and valid data on an endless variety of states, "chosen" for examination by the dictates of the theory, the primary focus, or the ecological considerations of the trainer or the group. It is helpful to the trainer to be aware of and to examine the wide range of data selected for focus by current trainers, such as: peer perceptions, personality test scores, individual and group fantasies, muscle tone, posture, inner-role conversations, primal memories, body odors, alpha rhythms, facial and bodily states viewed on videotape, sensations from toe sucking, bodily states produced by yoga or prescribed group diet, reactions to music, group or individual finger painting, various altered states of consciousness from drugs or controlled sensory stimuli, reports from sensory-deprivation chamber experiences, sub-group or individual decision speed or quality, discussion content, values, talking rate, member roles, and on and on through a wide range.

The methodological aids to feedback and use of such data are comparably diverse. Trainers have used such devices as complex computer systems, videotapes, audiotapes, bio-feedback systems, newsprint, data panel boards, coded observation systems, process observers, role reversals, Gestalt trips, guided group fantasies, body painting, nature walks, silent meals, simulations, nude marathons, group screaming, community meetings, inter-group competition, inter-group observations, and a wide variety of diverse methods to intensify, simplify, focus, or otherwise improve the effectiveness of the data processing. The group is a medium that makes possible great enrichment of the awareness (data collection) and organic-integration (data processing) aspects of group training.

The same (and other) methods have been used to improve the motoric and action-taking aspects of group training. A major advantage of group training over most other forms of therapy, education, and social action is that members have frequent opportunities to try out new functional behaviors in an internal environment of relatively low threat, optimal current feedback relative to the new behavior, and norms conducive to experimentation and growth.

The professional trainer will have available a vast array of tested alternative methods and techniques that may never be used on individual occasions, but will increase the options that may be used to help structure the external or the internal environment. The availability increases trainer confidence, reduces anxiety about competence in unforeseen emergencies, improves effectiveness of role as procedural resource, and expands the vistas and options open to the group. Such diversity imposes clear demands on programs for training trainers. (see Chapter 20). A respectable body of professional technology now is available. The integration of this technology with data-based training theory is steadily improving the professional competence of the group-training field.

Leader-Style Options. Selection of a theory, choosing a primary focus, and building a range of competencies in methods must all be integrated into an individual training style that will achieve an organic quality in the training experience.

Leaders differ greatly in personality, style, theory preference, competence, experience, spontaneity, confidence, self-esteem, and other aspects related to presumed leader impact. It is likely that organic integrity-congruity is a more important variable than is method chosen, theoretical orientation, amount of experience, or choice of a leadership pattern. If the trainer comes across as a full person, genuine, authentic, and "having it together," he is likely to be more effective than if he tries to adopt a style, method, or theory that is not his own. Research corroborates this. Perceived genuineness is a significant leader and therapist variable.

Early research at Bethel disclosed a fairly narrow range of trainer styles within a prescribed process-centered and non-structuring model. The present T group model encompasses not only the highly divergent patterns described in the first paragraphs of this chapter, but also a greatly expanded range of personal leader styles.

There are very few positions one could take on leader-style issues that would not be congruent with one or another of the current theories and counter to others. Many behaviors and attitudes, within a rather wide range, are sanctioned by some theory, practice, or research evidence. One can confine interventions to process observing, or can take an active position in the interpersonal conflicts in the group. One can be personally close or intimate with group members in or out of the group meetings, or can maintain a professional role relationship at all times. One can be aggressive, confronting, demanding, and central to the action; or one can withdraw to less assertive positions in the group. One can exercise formal authority and role prerogatives or allow and encourage interdependence and peer relationships.

As has been stated clearly in other parts of the book, there is, however, a fairly clear range of role expectations and behaviors that constitute and define the "laboratory method" as herein treated. Application of the method implies a common set of value assumptions; a broad range of intervention strategies (see Chapter 11), and a general set of assumptions and perspectives defined by Benne in Chapter 2.

Within the particular theoretical orientation, and when centering on a primary focus, the leader puts his own person, style, and flavor into the interaction. The data suggest that how the leader learns to manage and express emotional support or behavioral control are the two most significant style options that influence differential learning outcomes. While much support and control behavior is partly out of the conscious control of the leader, the general assumption (controversial, but probably warranted) is that leaders do learn more and more effective and organically authentic styles of expressive behavior. The T group is an arena where the leader learns, along with others, to be more interpersonally competent. This includes the growing learning of a public presenting style that is centered in the core of the person, available to group analysis and interpretation, relatively congruent with the trainer's verbalized theoretical model, appropriate to the primary focus of interventions, and consonant with the methodology of preference.

The personal need system of the trainer will certainly predispose the selection of a theory and a focus that will mesh with the need system. This process of building an organic integrity of style and theory will allow the trainer to be most effective in working with the range of techniques, outcome aims, and situational contexts that are most appropriate.

Some of the apparent inconsistency of research outcomes is probably produced by the fact that belief and theory are self-fulfilling. A leader who deeply believes that expressive and genuine warmth is more apt to fulfill his prophetic system than is the confused and unintegrated trainer who has not as yet found an organic center, is not sure of his theory, or not sure that his behavior will influence outcomes in a powerful way. One cannot provide unconditional positive regard or even conditional warmth without a high degree of self-esteem in depth, or minimal needs to punish and control. One cannot provide an energizing and unblocking structure without developing a satisfactory and integrated way of coping with authority and power, and handling his own dependency needs.

Some trainers work best in participative modes, others in more directive modes. Even though the laboratory method presupposes some degree of participativeness for its success, the method must be applied in a manner suited to the trainer's current growth level, need system, and style of handling control systems.

Building an effective trainer style implies a personal confrontation of one's value and ethical system with one's expressive behavior. In effective training sessions a pre-professional or professional trainer has many opportunities to integrate values with expressive behavior. It may be that a trainer's value system may be unsuited to the effective and unambivalent application of the laboratory method itself. It would be wise for that trainer to adopt other methodologies. It may be that the trainer can arrive at a particular theory of training that will allow him to mesh successfully his deep values with his selected focal options and style, all within the broad definition of the laboratory method. One's trainer style must be congruent with one's deeper values.

One's trainer style develops as growth occurs, as needs change, as new research forces re-examination, and as new expressive behavior is learned. Presumably the trainer is a continually growing system, susceptible to great growth and modification as internal forces interact with wider bands of social reality. The trainer who does not experience himself or herself as continually changing in inner need systems and in outer presenting style is not learning and is likely not to be applying and living the laboratory method. As is continually evident in this book, all aspects of the laboratory method are undergoing constant appreciable change — including the individual trainers who are using the method.

The training group is a powerful medium for individual, group, and organizational change.

CHAPTER 13

THE PERSONAL GROWTH LABORATORY

John Weir

Personal growth is the dual process of maturation and development whereby an individual moves toward the fulfillment of his physical, emotional, intellectual, and spiritual potential. By this definition, personal growth training is older than recorded history and most of our established institutions are personal growth "centers." Schools, hospitals, factories, churches, prisons, bordellos, the military, the family, psychotherapy, and human relations training frequently subscribe to goals congruent with this definition. They are just a few of man's inventions in the effort to find growth.

They differ mainly in the theories and methods they use and in the results they obtain. The most commonly used methods involve pain, fear, punishment, isolation, rejection, threat, external control, confrontation, assault, exhortation, and evaluation. Less frequently love, caring, personal autonomy, acceptance, affiliation, self-determination, and freedom are used. Results vary from sustained personal growth, on the one hand, to developmental rigidity and fixation, violent resistance and delinquency, regressive dependency and passivity, and psychotic withdrawal, on the other. The critical question becomes: which theory, what goals, and what methods are to be used? Each institution has its answer, with its own dogma, myths, and rituals.

The practitioners within the human potential movement in the United States seem to be in general agreement on their major goals. Simply stated they are: to help the participant become more self-accepting, more self-directed, more responsible, more effective in his relations with others, more efficient in the use of his biological energy, more in contact with his physical and psychic processes, and better able to discover and actualize his potentialities. The emphasis is more on the process of Becoming than on the content of Being.

The methods to reach these objectives are not so widely agreed upon. For many years verbal exchange has been the principal method, extended somewhat with psychodrama and sociodrama. In recent years, however, there has been a rapid proliferation of new approaches. Among them are sensory awareness, body movement, non-verbal activities, dramatic improvisation, behavioral prescriptions, finger painting, clay modeling, drawing, dance, nudity, primal screaming, bio-energetic expression, consciousness-expanding drugs, Yoga, dreams, guided fantasy, pseudonyms, rituals, meditation, desensitization, and Gestalt experiments. Each has dedicated proponents and contemptuous critics.

A thorough examination of even part of this maze of purposes, practices, and results would require several books and a lifetime of laboratory participation. It would indeed be presumptuous of anyone to attempt to cover this subject in a single chapter. My solution to this problem is to describe in detail the personal growth workshop I am conducting at the present time. Thus I can give a detailed report of at least one way personal growth training can be conceptualized, designed, and conducted.

My justification is that I am very familiar with the origins of this design and with the reasons for its particular structure. My reservations are, first, that you, the reader, can never fully understand the process of personal growth simply by reading about the content, structure, and theory of a workshop in which it may occur. It must be experienced to be understood. And, second, this processs is an ever-changing interaction among the participant, those around him, and the working design. What happens is the consequence of where he is in his life at the moment of interaction. The circumstances of personal growth are always new, and always organic to the here and now of their emergence. So while my description can detail the fine structure of how I use the laboratory method for personal growth training, the experiential and the personal components of the subject matter will elude us. I am saddened by this realization.

PERSONAL BACKGROUND

I am convinced that the design and conduct of a particular laboratory represents a personal expression of the knowledge, experience, and values of its staff members. I can only "be" me and "do" me at all times, so to know me is to know my lab, and vice versa. Perhaps your understanding of my point of view will be increased if I recount a bit of personal history and note some of the experiences which, I now see, strongly influenced my thinking. At the time, I was not aware of the significance of these events nor did I anticipate how they would contribute to my differentiation.

I can now trace the professional me back to my studies in the late 1940s. At that time, I discovered my "Holy Trinity" of Gestalt psychology: Koffka, Kluver, and Koehler. Their principles of figure-ground relationships and the selective nature of perception provided the framework for my personal epistemology and led me eventually to the development of the percept language. Arnheim's theory of isomorphism gave me the basis for a theory relating stimulus input patterns, mental imagery, and motor output patterns. I use it to help a participant recover any of these elements of a past experience lost because of the pain or fear that originally accompanied them. Much of the laboratory work on body awareness, transference, and physical expression is based on this concept.

I have never forgotten my excitement at the insight into human behavior I gained from Prescott Lecky's *Self-Consistency* and Marguerite Sechehaye's *Symbolic Realization.* These were two small books that had a big impact on my thinking. Hans Reichenbach introduced me to scientific philosophy and demonstrated the tremendous power inherent in selecting a set of premises and pursuing them to their logical conclusion. This strategy enabled me to devise and then develop first, cross-group observation or fish-bowling, then microlabs, then pseudonyms and blind walks, then tube theory, and transference accommodation, and most recently the percept language. Reichenbach also made it possible for me to appreciate and admire the elegance of Skinner's *Behavior of Organisms.*

At this time I was having my first group experiences as a part of my internship in clinical psychology. I worked with groups of five to ten "patients" diagnosed as "sick" and given "psychotherapy" by the group "therapist" who was usually a psychiatrist, occasionally a psychologist. These were called "group therapy" groups and the goal was to "make the patient well." Here my immersion in Freud and Fenichel was intense, exciting, and illuminating. Transferences and counter-transferences were the coin of the realm, their elucidation the Holy Grail we all pursued. I am still on that Quest.

The early 1950s was my Wilhelm Reich period. His *Character Analysis* provided me the bridge between psychoanalysis and physiology. I read and reread *The Function of the Orgasm* and *Cancer Biopathy.* I searched for verification of his clinical observations, repeated his bion experiments, and built an orgone accumulator. I explored some of his notions of muscle-armoring, such as studying the relationships among body movements, the expression of hostility, and the frequency and timing of seizures of a group of epileptics. This work was in the direction of the contemporary theories of bio-energetics of Alexander Lowen and of Stanley Keleman. Reich's thesis of the mind-body identity was most convincing. I dismissed that dichotomy from my thinking and from then on conceptualized the human organism as a unitary, integrated system. I prize this orientation as a valuable professional asset.

My Rorschach instructor was Bruno Klopfer, the most wily of tricksters, perhaps even more sophisticated than Hermes. I went with him on long journeys of discovery deep into the underworld of Carl Jung where I learned about archetypes, symbolic processes, individual differentiation, and the racial unconscious. I haven't seen a Rorschach in many years; I see what I learned from Klopfer and Jung in every laboratory session.

It was at this time that I began to learn about "T groups" and laboratory education. These were groups of eight to fourteen "normal" adults experimenting with an exciting new way of learning about human relations and collaborating in the study of group processes with the aid of professional educators (teachers, professors, scientific researchers). The leader's (trainer's) task was to help the members learn about group structure and process and their effects on individual and group behavior. People met around a large table and discussed whatever they chose, pausing frequently to identify the emerging interpersonal and social processes. The educational goal was to increase the member's awareness of group processes, his skills in group membership, and his ability to give and receive personal feedback. Participants in these "Human Relations Laboratories" were mostly "newcomers" who had not been in a T group before.

In the late 1950s my earlier acquaintance with Carl Rogers developed into a deeper friendship. He had always astonished me with the ease and intensity with which he could give me his full attention, but now I experienced my autonomy, my personhood through him in a new way. His theory and application of Non-Directive Counseling took on a new meaning and importance for me. I see now that, for me, I began to develop a new concept of individual responsibility. Herrigel's *Zen in the Art of Archery* initiated my movement away from organizing and precipitating training events. I began creating conditions and opportunities and waiting for the Gestalt to emerge; for the target to attract the arrow. Rosen's *Direct Analysis* showed the way and gave me the courage to work directly with unconscious processes.

In the early 1960s I became dissatisfied with talking as the only mode of communication. It was too removed from behavior. It was easy to dilute or distort or obscure the meaning or the intention of the speaker. It became clear to me that verbal expression and exchanges were, in a sense, behavior substitutes. I wanted to work more directly with behavior. In my first experiment in this direction, when one group member said to another, "I'd like to know you better," I suggested he get out of his chair and say this to the other persons without words. They met in the middle of the group and expressed feelings with a glance, then a handclasp, then a hug, and finally a long, searching look into each other's eyes. It was evident to everyone that a thousand words had been spoken with clarity in the two minutes this exchange required. I excited myself with a fantasy of how productive a group could be if it devoted much of its energy to this kind of exchange. I began to experiment with very simple non-verbal interventions. I did away with the table, heightened the emphasis on personal feedback, and switched theory input from formal presentations in general sessions to timely and relevant "lecturettes" during the T group sessions. To the previous goals were added encouragement to try new behavior, and efforts to increase the long-term effects of the laboratory learnings. Participants were still mostly "first-timers" and the laboratory was still referred to as a Human Relations Laboratory.

About this time I also began conducting so-called "Advanced Human Relations" workshops. These were for people who had had previous laboratory experience. Many were T group trainers, ministers, counselors, educators, and other members of the helping professions. Working with these more experienced participants in an "advanced" setting I was free to experiment with new methods and new or expanded training goals.

In 1964, I started working with my wife, Joyce, on the design of a different approach to laboratory education. We came together as convergent streams from quite different origins. Mine, as sketched above, hers from expressive dance, Yoga, dance therapy, group psychotherapy, and the fine arts.

We replaced much of the conventional T group verbal exchange with non-verbal and physical encounters, and increased the attention given to physiological and symbolic processes. We removed all furniture and began to work in an empty room, using cushions for the sit-down periods. We introduced the use of lab pseudonyms, improvisations, finger painting, clay modeling, and behavioral prescriptions. We designed sessions in sensory awareness, body movement, and non-verbal activities. To the training goals we added increased sensory awareness, behavioral spontaneity, and self-control.

This began a process of design development and synthesis, and training strategy refinement that still continues. Joyce and I have learned to do our own individual and interpersonal growth work together and to apply the resulting personal learnings to our professional work. We have learned that there is a very close relationship among our individual personal growth, its effects upon each other, and the changes that emerge in the design and conduct of our labs. Furthermore, as we move toward greater self-differentiation, our lab design and the way we work together and separately becomes more precise, more congruent, more differentiated, and more effective.

The new methods worked well. After a while we stopped using the format of three or four T groups of ten to fifteen people with a trainer. Instead, we brought everyone together and did all our work in a "community-of-the-whole" consisting of the thirty-five to forty-five participants and three to five staff members.

The first time we tried this experiment we were apprehensive, but found almost immediately that we had much more data and more resources with which to do the work. The richness and variety of resources of the larger group soon excited everyone and we all quickly discovered that with a little self-discipline the large group could work more effectively and be more helpful to individual participants than a small group. From that time I have always preferred a large group and multiple staff.

It was becoming clear that personal growth, as we had come to know it, was a life process, present in everyone and occurring in an unconscious, fortuitous manner depending on chance events in an individual's life. In 1969-1970 we began to learn how this process could be identified, facilitated, and managed in a deliberate, conscious manner if a person had the necessary knowledge and motivation. Our laboratory goal then became the teaching of the principles and practices of managing one's personal growth processes. They were to be learned and practiced in the laboratory and applied to one's life thereafter. We called this a Laboratory in Self-Management.

Currently, we see that the ultimate biological function of personal growth is to enable one to develop the personal qualities, skills, and the life style for which he has the potential. Self-management enables one to do so in a conscious program of reaching for ever higher levels of maturity or individuation. This is accomplished through the resolution of parental transferences whereby the participant discovers his unique identity, frees himself from dependence and counter-dependence on parental images, embraces his existential aloneness, and accepts sole responsibility for the management of his life.

Our strategy to help the participants make this journey is to provide them with theories and with as many opportunities, techniques, and strategies as we can devise for them to experience and understand this differentiation process, both during and after the laboratory, and to acquaint them with the various resources, both internal and external, that are available for their continuing differentiation. Our basic objective is to help them learn how to grow themselves. A goal that seems identical with the nature of organismic development, that is to enable each person to travel toward his own personal distinction, to become more fully differentiated into his unique individuality. This is our Laboratory in Self-Differentiation.

This brings me to the present in the review of what I now see as some of the significant professional and intellectual experiences that brought me to where I am today. To these should be added the usual living experiences of sickness, operations, injuries, deaths, successes and failures, marriage and parenthood. Some of these experiences seemed tragic or unfortunate, but, congruent with the Law of Opposites, I find I have learned important things from and through each of them. I continue to do so. If I had missed any of them I believe I would be less differentiated today. Again, I am reminded that *all* experience can be, and usually is, growth-producing. Only sensory isolation, awareness-dulling, and inactivity are anti-life and lead to a living death.

I also recognize the influence of a large number of co-workers and participants on my professional and personal development and on the evolution of the kind of laboratories I conduct. Through and with them I have done much of my personal growth.

We are now ready to look at the Laboratory in Self-Differentiation in detail.

THE SELF-DIFFERENTIATION LABORATORY

Our preference is for a lab of thirty-five participants equally divided as to sex, and varied as possible for age, education, occupation, religion, and race. We prefer four staff members; ideally, two male and two female. A group of this size and composition contains large varieties of physical and personality types, of life styles, and potential transference images. Consequently, there will be a wide range of sensations, perceptions, and reactions to the experiential sessions. This offers the younger, the less experienced, or the naive participant an expanded view of life, and provides a rich background against which everyone can compare his personal experience. There's a friend, an enemy, and a stranger for everyone. The body movement and activity sessions are done with the total group. Some are done in pairs, some in trios, and some in quartets, and always in sessions-of-the whole, which we have come to call community sessions, where everyone is present and participates in the activities.

Duration

The amount and kind of work that can be done in a residential workshop vary significantly with the time available. Lasting personal growth of any magnitude can occur only within a time-span that permits the participant to orient himself to the design, develop a high degree of trust, confront himself at a deep level, reorganize his perceptions, then live with this reorganization long enough to become familiar with it, and to identify the process that produced it.

The pace of this sequence seems to be the same for most participants. For the kind of laboratory goals we wish to achieve, five continuous days seem to be the very minimum. And this is true only for some participants. It will not be sufficient for all. Eight continuous days, or two weeks, with open week-ends, seem to enable nearly everyone to do significant work. Week-end labs are too brief. They may generate intense feelings of exhilaration and social intimacy, but as vehicles for lasting growth, I have found them inadequate, so I no longer do them.

Staffing

The composition of the staff and the areas of their professional competence are extremely important in this kind of personal growth laboratory. As power figures, staff members are the most frequent objects of the participants' transferences. So they must know how to recognize, accommodate to, and work with such relationships.

A staff member whose style is to get into the group and "do his own thing" becomes oblivious to the transference processes of the participants. He needs to have enough separation and enough distance to respond to transferences sensitively and appropriately; not to initiate but to respond. He must be mature enough to observe himself as he would a participant, being what he needs to be, doing what he needs to do for his own growth, only if it does not disrupt the work of the participants. After the lab, on his own time, his observations of himself and his lab experiences will provide the data for his continued personal work.

Staff also must be able to facilitate and guide the transference relationships that develop between participants. If this is done properly, the person doing the transferring usually experiences some resolution, and the transferee isn't used beyond the limits of his willingness to cooperate or his ability to understand his role and respond.

They must be familiar with, and able to work with the wide

range of dramatic, highly emotionally charged episodes that occur when participants are confronting themselves and others at deep and meaningful levels. They must know when to encourage greater risk-taking, when to set limits, and when to be silent. It is essential that staff members do significant amounts of work on their own transferences. They must be familiar with their own symbolic processes. They must have a highly developed clinical insight. They must be willing and able to give themselves fully to the process. The more often a staff member has been where the participant needs to go, the more guidance and reassurance he can provide.

Staff members must have the physical stamina and adaptability to participate fully in the movement and activity sessions along with participants. They must be able to model ways of working in these sessions and of processing the personal data that are generated.

The staff team is composed so as to provide as many as possible of the needed transference and archetype images such as father, mother, brother, sister, child, trickster, warrior, witch, devil, clown, etc. Then the participant will have the opportunity to make the transferences necessary for his personal work. In addition, each person's culture and social class gives him success images to emulate, but does not permit or encourage the exploration of other dimensions; a process that is necessary for full differentiation.

I have been fortunate in having had the opportunity of working many labs with the same staff members. These long-term relationships, plus an intimate knowledge of my own personal growth experiences, have led me to a strongly held conclusion. This is that a staff member will design a lab and will make his training interventions in some relationship to where he is in his journey toward his own self-actualization. His growth urges, his fears, and his longings always assume central importance in his laboratory work. As he increases his self-awareness, his interventions become richer and deeper. As he resolves his specific transference residuals, that particular type of transference will no longer be prominent in his interactions. As he continues his differentiation, his lab work becomes wiser and has more impact. In his areas of blindness, he will continue to generate from certain participants stereotyped reactions in a repetitive manner. As he grows, so does his lab. As he gets stuck, so does his lab. Maturity of lab design and execution results from maturity of staff.

Introduction to the Laboratory

Our participant's laboratory experience begins when he reads the description of the laboratory theory, goals, methods, and expectations and makes application for admission. The description says in part:

> Personal growth is a continuing process of self-differentiation. From conception to death, one is always in transition, moving toward ever greater degrees of individual uniqueness. This process is an orderly one, with change occurring in sequential phases and with its facilitation and inhibition partly a matter of personal choice. The movement of a person through this developmental sequence can be facilitated through increased self-love, personal autonomy, self-understanding, and will. Self-management theory provides a set of guidelines whereby this process of self-differentiation can be enhanced and "managed" more consciously and more deliberately. It can supply a "design for living" with explicit directives for continued self-differentiation.
>
> The central objectives of the workshop will be to help the participant (1) assess his present state of differentiation, (2) experiment with the application of self-management theory to his personal growth processes, (3) focus his energy in the service of his continued self-differentiation, and (4) gain a keener appreciation of the inter-relationships among his present environment, his life style, and his growth needs.
>
> The necessary elements for successful differentiation through self-management include awareness and acceptance of physical and psychological functions, access to unconscious processes, sensitivity to interpersonal relations, acceptance of responsibility for one's existence, behavioral flexibility, and self-discipline.
>
> Exploration of these elements will be sought within the framework of general theories of self-development, self-management, and self-differentiation. It is intended that the workshop participant will continue thereafter to use these theories and his workshop experiences as guidelines for his continued psychic, somatic, and spiritual development.

Formal application affirms interest in and acceptance of these statements and implies that the applicant may already be working toward these same personal growth goals.

The second interaction occurs when he next receives a letter suggesting he adopt an assumed name. This letter says, in part:

> One of the objectives of this laboratory is to provide you with the opportunity to experience yourself in as many new ways as possible. Giving yourself a pseudonym, and a new back-home biography, if you wish, is one of the

more successful we have discovered. We invite you to try it in the lab we are going to do together.

Pick any name you'd like, classical, mythological, symbolic, a noun, verb, adjective, etc. Perhaps you've always wanted to be called by another name. Perhaps you've always disliked the name your parents gave you and would like to experience yourself freed of all the negative connotations accumulated over the years. Or perhaps you'd like to see if people would respond to you differently or if you would experience yourself differently if you had a different name. A name may emerge as you think about where you are now at this time in your life. It may represent a state of being, a current transition you'd like to experience more fully, or an exploration of an as yet unrealized potential. It may become a self-confrontation, a self-disclosure, or a self-liberation.

You may also choose to construct a new personal history made up in the way you think would be most helpful in your personal growth. It can be simple or elaborate, realistic, or fantastic and you can reveal as much or as little of it as you wish. Or, if you prefer, you may withhold all background facts about yourself and let people experience you as they encounter you in the here and now without the labels, relationships, status symbols, etc., that usually pre-condition their reactions to you.

You may change your name and biography as often as you like during the lab and whenever you decide, you may drop your assumed name and take on your back-home name. Let the laboratory registrar know as soon as possible what your new name is. She or he will arrange to have your mail, phone calls, and messages translated into your assumed name before delivery to you. Come to the lab using it wherever possible. There will be no disclosure of your back-home name and personal data until you make it, at the time and place of your own choosing.

Assuming a new name has many personal growth possibilities. Through it a person may experience a new self-image. He may live his "ideal" self. He may indicate his condition, aspiration, or illumination of the moment. He may explore the dark side of himself or the frightening side. He may live with aspects of himself that he does not like. He may intensify his transference. He may inflate, belittle, or laugh at himself. He may symbolize new growth urges. He may regress, express moods, feeling, and emotional changes. Almost any aspect of human experience can be interiorized through personal names and explored at explicit and symbolic levels. Assuming a new name always initiates a continuing self-confrontation.

Beginning of the Laboratory

We begin the workshop in the late afternoon with an opening "ceremony" of about an hour's duration. This ceremony has both verbal and non-verbal components. It is sometimes designed, rehearsed, and staged by the staff, sometimes allowed to develop spontaneously. Our intention is to provide a common initial experience, to convey important themes of the lab, to start participants on their personal journey, and to present a scenario from which we can build a separation ceremony at the end of the lab.

The first evening we share how we came to select our pseudonyms. This tells us something about where each of us is in our journey through life as we begin our work together. It also initiates the process of community building and provides each participant an opportunity for an initial public commitment to his or her personal work.

This is followed by a discussion of the dream process, its relevance for personal growth, how we will use dreams in the lab, and suggestions on how to remember what we dream. Participants are urged to keep a dream journal and to report their dreams to someone the morning after they have had them. Analytical interpretation or speculation as to their meaning is discouraged. Guided fantasies will be treated similarly with the reporting done during the community sessions. Dreams and fantasies are important aspects of this lab, especially in times of high stress when these processes become most significant.

The first morning session is devoted to reporting the previous night's dreams. At this time, we introduce a special point of view which we will emphasize throughout the lab. We start with the centuries-old philosophical theory of solipsism which states that only the self exists, or can be proven to exist. In our application, we take the position that, as far as I, the perceiver, am concerned, the external world "exists" only inside me as sensations and images. Objects, as experienced, are solely the consequence of my perceptual processes. If I close my eyes and drop the pen with which I am writing, it no longer exists for me, except as a memory. All my experience takes place solely within me, within the confines of my body. It occurs continuously, from moment to moment. I live only in the here and now.

This process of perception is selective. In the formation of an internal image, I "select" specific elements from my total memory field, my awareness at that moment, and omit others. So I may see the vase in Figure 1 while others may see the two faces or vice versa.

Our frame of reference for the lab, then, is that each of us is continually perceiving and organizing his world in his unique way, never precisely the same as anyone else. I am "doing" myself and

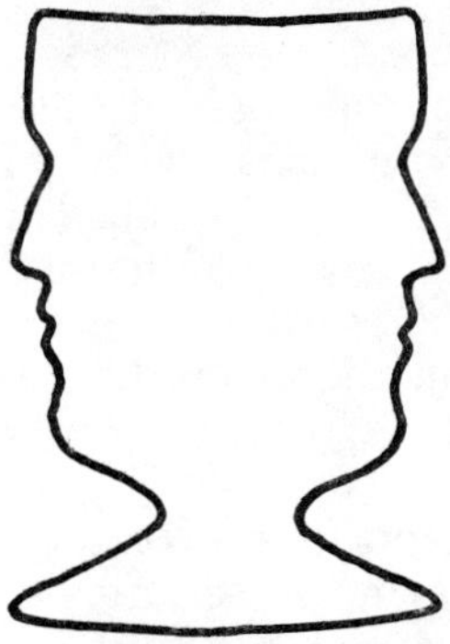

Figure 1

you are "doing" yourself. Your "existence" is for me always my perception of you, the "you-in-me," and I "exist" for you only as the "me-in-you." You are there, you act, you may even physically influence me. This has the consequence of changing the "you-in-me" and the "me-in-you." How I "do" the "you-in-me" is determined by my needs, my perceptions, and my past experiences. It is, I am, always my own responsibility. This is true both for how I do myself and how you do yourself. We conclude that the perceptual elements of our interpersonal interactions consist of a "you," a "me," a "you-in-me," and a "me-in-you."

We use this frame of reference as the basis for processing all of our lab experiences. For example:

My dreams take place entirely inside of me. The images, the feelings, and the actions are all of my own construction. They are therefore also my own responsibility. During dreaming, my sensory systems are turned down or off to the point where my dream imagery is stimulated, not from the outside, but from the inside. Even if I experience a sensation from some external stimulus that is impinging on me while I sleep, I incorporate it into my dream sequence in such a way as to make it congruent with the ongoing content and imagery of my dream work. My dreams are my own doing: I "do" me when I "dream me." I can deny them, or repress their content, but they still remain solely me "doing" me. Dreaming is *my* process.

My fantasies are my associations. I construct them from my memories, my images, my longings, and my fears. They may be influenced a little or a lot by stimulation from without, but I remain the sole agent of their construction. I "do" me when I "fantasy" me.

You are there. So I experience you. But I can never experience an absolute or "true" you, only the "you-I-know-at-this-moment," the "you-I-perceive," the "you-in-me." I experience you in my own selective way, imposing my perceptual organization on the elements of you I am able and permit myself to experience. I form an internal image of you, this "you-in-me," and react to this perception as "you." You are and always will be this product of my perceptual process, this "you-in-me." Our neurophysiology prohibits it, us, from being otherwise. In general, all my perceptions of others, my projections, my transferences, my blindnesses, and my illuminations take place within me. They are my doing and my responsibility.

The object in my hand exists for me only so long as I can see or feel it/me. If I close my eyes and drop it/me, I cease having awareness of its/my presence. Without sensory input I experience only my internal processes. I experience *me* through these processes, plus my sensory input. This is the active process of me "doing" me. Whatever I experience and whatever I make out of my experience is my doing and my responsibility. Change can occur only by me "doing" me in a new or different way.

One consequence of conceptualizing these four varieties of experiencing in this way is that I can now look at any one of them/me as if it/I were any other. For example, I illuminate me when I consider me awake as if I were dreaming and when dreaming me, as if I were awake. Making this reversal and living in it/me, for a while has led me to an expanded self-awareness and convinced me of their/my interchangeability. When I discover and fully take into myself the realization that all the "good" and "bad" aspects of myself, awake or asleep, are the consequence of me doing myself, I exhilarate myself at the promise of greater management of my existence, delight in the freedom of no longer being so controlled by the "others-in-me," and expand with the ownership of formerly rejected parts of myself. Honoring personal aspects of myself gives me the opportunity to integrate them into my conscious awareness.

One of the early goals is to live in this frame of reference until it becomes our mode of conceptualizing and reporting our experiences. We have found it helpful to employ a "language" that constantly reinforces the orientation and confronts the speaker with the consequence of his changed perspective. At various times we have referred to it as transference language, ownership language, and responsibility language. At the present time we have settled on percept language as being the most definitive.

A few rules and examples will illustrate how the language may be spoken.

I behave. I sense me. So I must own my experience. There are no impersonal pronouns such as "it," "one," "you," "that," etc., in the percept language. For them, substitute "I," "me," "mine," etc.

NOT	BUT
It's frightening	I am frightened
It makes me angry	I make me angry
It's a pleasure	I'm a pleasure
One gets scared	I get scared

I am the agent responsible for my sensations and my behavior, therefore only verbs in the active mode can report my experience:

NOT	BUT
I am frightened	I frighten me
I make me angry	I anger me
I'm a pleasure	I pleasure me
I get scared	I scare me

I "know" external objects only by my perception of them. That perception always takes place "in" me. Therefore the only objects I know are the "objects-in-me." Similarly with people — for me there is no "you" other than the "you-in-me."

NOT	BUT
You are beautiful	The you-in-me is beautiful
George is mistaken	The George-in-me is mistaken
I can't understand Ann	I can't understand the Ann-in-me
You are lying	The you-in-me is lying
I don't trust you	I don't trust the you-in-me
He suspects me	The him-in-me suspects the me-in-him
I know you will like him	I know the you-in-me will like the him-in-me
You are angry at him	The you-in-me angers himself at the him-in-you
They don't like each other	The them-in-me don't like the other-in-each-of-them

We continually urge participants to report all their laboratory experiences in this language and in the present tense. A simple example may illustrate how this is done. A participant made the following report:

"I climbed a mountain today. It was a hard climb. When I got to what I thought was the top I took my clothes off. I felt a little guilty. I walked around and discovered I wasn't at the top yet. I hiked through some undergrowth, became apprehensive, and put my jeans and boots on. Then I came to the main trail. I took my clothes off and climbed toward the top about a quarter of a mile away. I felt great. A ski structure came into view. It angered me to discover someone had built a building on this inaccessible peak. At the top I found people had left a horrible mess of garbage around. This disgusted me and I became more angry. Then I realized I could clean up the mess if I wanted and I felt relieved."

Translated into the percept language and into the present tense the participant would hear himself say:

"I go up the mountain part of me today. I am a hard climb. I get to what I think is the top part of me. I take the clothes part of me off. A part of me says I shouldn't do me this way. I tell this part of me to go to hell. I walk around me naked. I discover I haven't reached the top part of me yet. I go through an undergrowth part of me that I frighten myself with. I put on the jeans and boots part of me. I go through the undergrowth part of me and come to the main trail part of me. I take the clothes parts of me off again and continue my climb toward the top part of me about a quarter mile away. I am feeling me beautiful. Now I see a ski structure part of me. Some other people parts of me have structured me. I anger me when I discover other parts of me have structured me in this inaccessible part of me. I take me to the top part of me. I find the other people parts of me have left a horrible mess of garbage on the top part of me. I disgust me with these parts of me and anger myself. Then I realize I am alone on the top part of me and I can clean up this messy part of me and make me clean again. I feel me good with the knowledge of this power part of me."

This report can be heard as an account of a dream, a fantasy, or a physically experienced event. Telling it in this way helps the experience become a relevant part of the teller's existence and may provide him with some clues as to how and where he might grow himself.

At this time in the lab the teller was working on his parental transferences and experimenting with greater self-management. His report was a clear and concise statement of where he was on this journey at the time of telling.

TRANSFERENCE COMMUNITIES AND SMALL GROUPS

Much of the theory we use is derived from Freud's concept of transference. This is the notion that a person "projects" onto another the important qualities and aspects of significant others in his life such as parents, siblings, and teachers. We consider this process to be central in the work of differentiation in the years fifteen to fifty. We do everything we can to activate, identify, illuminate, and resolve these transferences as a major part of our laboratory work. We accomplish this partly by making explicit the relationships among the participants and staff as transferences emerge among them, and partly by showing the way the laboratory activities and theory can be used by the participants in the service of their individual work.

Talking in the percept language constantly focuses everyone on the transferences that underlie most of their perceptions and interactions. The usual small group structure and processes emerge as individual participant processes embedded in transference relationships. As a consequence, there are significant differences between the group processes that occur in the transference community and those that may occur in other types of training or encounter groups. The effect is to modify or eliminate some of the usually dominant training issues and conflicts. A brief description of several of them may further delineate important aspects of this type of differentiation laboratory and illustrate some of the essential values and attitudes that are offered for the participant's consideration.

Participants are joined in a common endeavor. Each is to make his own journey in his own way and in his own time. Dependency and counter-dependency are soon identified as transferences. They are usually parental; occasionally sibling. There are no staff "leaders" in a differentiation lab, only guides, protectors, and stimulators. The staff responsibility is to provide as many opportunities as possible for participant self-discovery and the enrichment of experiencing. Each participant has sole and total responsibility for his own "leadership" and for no one else's.

The participant's energy is invested in bio-energetic expression and in maintaining and resolving his transferences. A major laboratory goal is to help the participant discover and keep his own power, rather than to give it away or let it be taken from him. This is self-ownership. There is no possibility of, and no reward for, trying to accumulate group power or influence. That can be given only by the transferrer and always in the service of his transference and of his growth. Resolution of the transference dissolves this delegated influence as the participant reclaims his personal autonomy.

I discover my uniqueness by taking ownership of myself and my experience, and by assuming responsibility for my behavior. I cannot compete with you, or anyone else in this process. I, and only I can "do" me in my own way. Moving always at my own pace, there can be no win-lose. I am what I am, when I am. I Become when I am ready to Become. My transference needs are mine alone. They are unique to me. They can never be anyone else's. I can't "do" anyone else even if I want to, or am asked to. I can compete, and win and lose, but only with my own transferences.

I am the sole authority over me, the sole responsible agent for me, and the sole determiner of my behavior. I have no responsibility for anyone else's work. If I perceive another as an authority, I look to my transferences to see why I give him or her this power over me. The staff accepts no responsibility for my personal growth. That responsibility is mine alone. There is no staff leadership position in a transference laboratory, therefore there is no authority to resist or to lean on except as a transference image.

Transference is an unconscious process. Its resolution in a laboratory setting results from consciously recognizing and confronting it. No one can help another to do this except by agreeing to accommodate to the transference image projected upon him. If he can provide a good screen, he can perform a valuable collaboration and be very helpful.

The "friendly helper" always gets in the way as he tries to do the transferrer's work for him, or tries to change the other's feeling state in order to feel comfortable himself. So, too, the analytic helper who tries to demonstrate his omniscience by giving his psycho-analytic interpretation of everything that happens. He is almost always wrong with these projections of his own transferences. When occasionally he is close to being correct, he succeeds only in robbing the participant of the joy and rewards of self-discovery. None of these "helping" strategies lasts long under the spotlight of the percept language.

Resistance to personal growth is always determined by the transferrer in the service of his transference. When he decides to "do" himself, he melts his resistance. It is not functional for him to resist the staff, design, or schedule except as his transference dictates. They are not imposed, but are there for the taking. We avoid making demands on the participants as this only stiffens the resistance by reinforcing the transference. The participant is the sole responsible agent for his existence.

Likewise, the participant's motivation for working on his personal growth is not a staff responsibility. The staff member may explore the participant's resistance with him, but whether the participant will work or not is his own decision. Staff members will also accommodate to transferences made on them within mutually agreed upon limits but will not initiate such programs.

The reduction of these common training issues and conflicts frees participants to concentrate on their own self-actualization. It also releases large amounts of energy for the pursuit of personal growth through transference resolution. The concept of self-responsibility is basic to most of these process differences.

We encourage each participant to be on the lookout for emerging feelings and memories. When this begins to happen we encourage him to "go with" his experience, to experience himself fully and completely in all aspects of his sensations, emotions, perceptions, and movements. If he asks for help it is given. If he wants to be left undisturbed so he can experience himself without distraction we see to it that his desire is respected. We protect him from the friendly helpers, the amateur psychoanalysts, the aggressively dependent, and the envious who may try to steal part of his experience for themselves. When a formerly long-avoided memory and feeling is fully experienced with all its attendant agony and despair, the participant is able, for the first time, to reintegrate it into his conscious life. As he does so, he frees himself to let other aspects of his past, present, or future emerge into awareness to be confronted and managed with greater self-assurance. We do everything we can to minimize aborting this emergence through premature interpretation, evaluation, or closure.

The First Week

Our design emphasis for the first week is on building interpersonal relationships among staff and participants and on increasing the awareness of body structure and function. We accomplish this through the pseudonyms, dream and fantasy work, the percept language, and a sequence of verbal and non-verbal activities. For the body awareness part of the lab, I derive my design decisions and training interventions from a physiological model that organizes human behavior in terms of sensory-motor experiences.

In this model I think of the human organism as a simple tube, about three feet long on the outside and thirty feet long on the inside. It has appendages that aid in locomotion (arms and legs) and a concentration of communication centers at one end (the head). It is an energy exchange system designed to bring itself into contact with and ingest various natural compounds (food) at one end, chemically break them down and recombine them (metabolism) in the middle, extract energy in the process, and expel the residue (feces) at the other end. The energy profit from metabolism is expended mostly in building and maintaining the structure and function of the organism and powering its food-seeking behavior. It is always active, operating on a principle of least effort for maximum energy return.

The tube maintains contact with the world around it through more than a dozen sensory systems (vision, hearing, taste, smell, light pressure, heavy pressure, heat, cold, touch, pain, thirst, hunger, sex, suffocation, nausea, position, balance, weight, and vibration) by ingestion or rejection of a variety of chemical compounds other than "food," and as the recipient of externally applied forces. It functions optimally when it obtains biologically appropriate foods, has adequate use of its maintenance systems, is fully sensitive to sensory stimulation, and reactive within the full range of its response capabilities. It pulsates, expanding and contracting with varying rhythms. It contracts under stress, deprivation, or pain and expands under gratification, security, or pleasure. Under continued pain or stress it contracts chronically in such a way as to inhibit its motor reactions and to desensitize itself to the accompanying feelings. These actions are always to maintain the integrity of the system at some level of functioning.

The tube is always fully engaged in its existence. It is always experiencing sensory excitation, processing this input and emitting behavioral responses. It is most vital, most alive, when it is most response-able, when using all its capabilities or even extending them, in the service of its needs, its wishes, and its protection.

We use this model to design a program to sensitize and energize the tube and to activate repressed and undeveloped response capabilities. We employ a variety of activities intended to focus attention on body processes and to intiate interpersonal relationships among the participants at a non-verbal level.

We explore light and heavy touch, tension and relaxation, strong and gentle contact, balance and imbalance, controlled and random movement, posture, physical coordination, and body fantasies. We experiment with new ways of moving to music and help each participant find his natural movements, rhythms, and pace. Dancing is an important part of the lab design. We dance before, during, and after the scheduled sessions.

The model calls for a wide variety of non-verbal experiences that facilitate the expansion of sensory awareness. For example, silent meals to concentrate on tastes, smells, and oral textures, body movement exercises to explore balance, position, movement, and coordination, blindfold walks to renew and increase familiarity with subtle and often ignored smells, sounds, tastes, and textures, with orientation by body position, and to experience the extent to which the perceptual process is usually dominated by vision.

A "tube" lab calls for attention to diet, self-poisoning through smoking, alcohol, drugs, and plastic foods, to physical exercise and physical release, to the physical aspects of emotional states, and to sleep behavior. There is also practice in learning to read body feeling states and changes, to know which are needed, which are excessive, and which are unnecessary. The varieties of ways one can breathe and the effects of each are examined and the consequences compared.

We stress the importance of the feet in balance, contact, sensitivity, and body movement control. All activities are done barefooted to begin restoration of the sensitivity of the bottom of the feet. A large pan of water filled with ice cubes is provided. Standing in it, participants experience extremes of cold, pain, and sensory acuity. They frequently make important discoveries about their reactions and accompanying feelings of fear, tension, relaxation, and exhilaration that come from moving from one sensory extreme to another. At various times during this "foot work" participants may experience the recall of early childhood memories, sudden mood changes, behavior insights, increased physical sensitivity, increased physical contact with the ground, a heightened sense of balance, and a greater tolerance for physical and emotional pain.

An important staff responsibility is to provide as many and varied ways as possible for a participant to experience himself. This increases the likelihood that he will experience himself reacting or behaving in a particular way while participating in a variety of activities. For example, he may experience his fear, his anger, his aggression, his strength, or his weakness in his dreams and his guided fantasies, while clay modeling or finger painting, while improvising, while listening to a staff member, while being led on a blind walk, while dancing, etc. Uncovering such consistent ways of perceiving or reacting in a variety of situations can provide increased self-awareness and a rich source of personal insight.

As the lab progresses, the pace and vigor of the physical activities increase. This is accompanied by an increase in vitality from heightened body energy levels. With this revitalization, the participants experience a sense of greater strength and personal power. This, in turn, encourages them to take greater personal risks with deeper and more meaningful self-confrontations at all levels of consciousness. Self-images expand, dreams and fantasies become richer, self-acceptance increases, and enhanced physical capabilities emerge. New body awareness facilitates new social awareness. Increased body security is accompanied by increased personal security. The verbal work follows a parallel course of increasing vitality, openness, and directness. The concept, "I am my body" becomes more and more meaningful and more appropriate.

Almost any sensory, fantasy, or motor experience may reawaken long-forgotten visual or body images. As they emerge into consciousness, they may be experienced with almost their original intensity. Such "reliving" usually results in the confrontation of past trauma and the discharge of the accompanying feelings, frequently resolving them.

This kind of experience can be activated by beginning anywhere in the experiential loop of↔sensations↔images↔recollection↔feeling states↔body movement↔sensation↔etc. One of the strategies of "tube training" is to provide opportunities for this reactivation process to occur.

The basic learning formula for a tube lab is: I have an experience that reveals to me an inhibition or a facilitation of a sensory or motor capability. As a consequence, my awareness is increased. I know myself in a new way: I have new data. These data render incomplete my present self-perception, putting me into a state of confusion, anxiety, or excited expectation. Ultimately, a new organization emerges, I am reintegrated and I experience release, stillness, exhilaration, and a heightened sense of power, of well-being, and of personal worth. This process is a movement toward greater self-differentiation. If I pursue it deliberately and self-consciously, I am managing myself.

In percept language: I experience me inhibiting or facilitating my sensory or motor capabilities. As a consequence, I increase my awareness of me. I know me in a new way. I have new data. With these data I make me incomplete. I confuse me, "anxious" me, or excite me with expectations. Ultimately I organize me, I reintegrate me and release and quiet me. I make me feel better than before, more powerful and more valuable. This is how I grow myself. I move me toward greater differentiation. If I move me deliberately and consciously, I am managing myself.

Here it is the job of the staff to encourage sensory exploration, help promote greater acceptance and use of the body and body processes, help participants extend the limits of their physical movements, and model exploratory and experimental behavior. They will resist attempts to alleviate the confusion and anxiety of the amorphous state. They will help the participant recognize these feelings as a sign of movement and to value and embrace the state for what it is, a necessary precursor to personal growth.

We have scheduled sessions morning, afternoon, and evening. In each session we usually have an activity with part of the time spent in sharing and working this experience with the rest of the community. We also consider, and take advantage of, the remaining time as work time. This includes meal times, play time, and sleep time. We "work" twenty-four hours a day, living our relationships and our transferences, dreaming, fantasizing, and conducting our self-explorations. All our experiences provide data for personal growth.

The focus of tube theory is on neurophysiological processes. I find the theory adequate for the design of personal growth laboratories that are focused largely on physical experience. I find it satisfactory to concentrate, as tube theory does, on input and output and ignore the intervening or internal processes. With adequate understanding and acceptance by the participant of his sensory and motor processes, I am convinced that his symbols, fantasies, and dreams will undergo parallel differentiation without deliberate attention. However, there will be limited insight into, and verbal understanding of the processes of personal growth, self-management, and differentiation unless these inner processes are examined in detail. Therefore, we are careful to provide ample opportunity to conceptualize these processes as they emerge. My preference is to use a type of transference theory for this purpose.

The Second Week

One of the consequences of the first week's activities is that complex relationships have had opportunity to form, with the percept language constantly surfacing and illuminating their projective or transference basis. In the second week we maintain our emphasis of the first and increase our attention to these transference relationships as they come to assume a more central position in most everyone's experience. We need a cognitive map for understanding and working with them. We provide one through lecturettes by the staff on a transference theory of human development and socialization plus some of Jung's ideas on archetypes and the collective unconscious. Briefly, the transference theory we use is as follows:

My existence begins in the womb. I am sustained without effort. I am fed, breathed, warmed, shock-protected, and purified. I have no responsibility and no obligations. Life is peaceful, quiet, and secure. If this serene existence is seriously disturbed, the chances are that I will be damaged. The after-effects may linger on in me for years, perhaps even for life.

If I am fortunate, everything is comfortable and serene until the day of pressure, pain, and suffocation.

I am born into an existence that must always be at times cold, hot, noisy, rough, uncomfortable, painful, famishing, and abandoning. At other times, it can be pleasant, loving, gratifying, peaceful, and secure. From this day on I will never again have my every need filled completely and at once. Often I will live frustration, failure, pain, and loneliness. Furthermore, I am now responsible for my own survival and the unknowing recipient of obligations and expectations imposed upon me by those with the power to give and to withhold.

Four strivings will govern and guide me for life: self-love, self-identity, sexual identity, and self-differentiation.

What is my value? Am I prized, desirable, lovable? Am I another hungry mouth to feed? A nuisance, a burden? Am I wanted? Am I welcome? Or am I an intruder?

My thinking is magical. Before my birth the world was me. Gratification was immediate and complete. Now I must compete, adjust, submit, wait. My feeling of omnipotence rapidly diminishes. How others, especially my parents, treat me establishes my value to me. If they prize me, I prize me. If they belittle me, I belittle me. If they reject me, I reject me.

Regardless of how I am treated, my impotence and the frustration I experience over and over launch me on a lifelong search for my birthright. It is my quest for self-discovery, self-acceptance, and self-love, not because I have earned them, but because they are my right. Because I'm me.

I have now lived a few years. I am beginning to sense, in a vague way, that I am an entity, separate from others around me. I know nothing about me, but I am curious to learn.

Who am I? Where do my parents end and I begin? Where are the boundaries of me? What is within these boundaries? What are my strengths and my weaknesses, my abilities and my incapacities? What do I look like inside and out? What am I like in your eyes? How do I affect you? Do you like me? Tell me! Give me feedback!

I find my answers in the way I experience others treating me. I am conditioned by their power, their experience, their authority, and their need for control. They mold me in the images they desire, without my knowledge or my permission.

My self-differentiation begins within the constraints of conformity. I capitulate when I must, resist when I can, and struggle to find a "me" in my confusion. It is likely I will spend most of my life in this search.

I thank the ancients for the gift of the Oedipal myth! It is my thread through the labyrinth of man-woman relationships.

My parents instruct me in the qualities of maleness and what is proper behavior for a growing young boy. I learn to take them as models of proper behavior and to do as they do. I seek to "possess" my mother, the most important female in my life, and in the process to become manly like my father.

Likewise, my sister will learn to become a woman like her mother, and to be appealing and flirtatious with her father. Each of us explores, experiments, and discovers our sexuality through counterpoint with our opposite-sex parent. Given the nuclear family, how could we possibly do otherwise?

Then I marry someone I love, that is, someone who is the unconscious, and occasionally the conscious projection of my mother. By this transference I have my mother all to myself. My wife has, in her turn, picked me, the transference image of her father. Our reward is that, for the time being, we have satisfied our Oedipal longings. I have married my mother, she has married her father, and society has given its approval.

Now the marriage must live out its mission: to permit each of us to have our other-sex parent until we have fully experienced adulthood through our possession of them. Then we become ready and able to give them up and go on to rediscover our mates, this time without the transference loading. It is as if the institution of marriage as we know it were a social invention for the completion of this Oedipal journey.

I continue to define my sexuality within my marriage relationship. When I have lived through my Oedipal strivings and can experience my sexuality without transference, I am ready to work directly on my self-differentiation at the sexual level.

As an infant I waited. As a child I obeyed. As an adolescent I conformed. As an Oedipal marriage partner I cooperated. Even when I was rebelling, I was reacting against a common enemy in an accepted way, another variety of obedient conformity.

I was learning skills, values, and proper attitudes. I was liking myself occasionally. I was identifying aspects of me in a limited way. But my parental transferences set narrow limits within which to experience myself.

As I dissolve each transference image, I am able to identify and love a little more of myself, to own a little more of myself, know a little better who and what I am, and take in and accept more fully my experiences in the present. I come to see more clearly the processes and forces of my inner and outer existence. I increase my ability to manage my existence and to facilitate and prize my further self-differentiation. Time is limited, but the process of discovery is continuous and becomes more and more exhilarating. It will continue for the rest of my life.

This theory of developmental stages is wedded to the concept of transference. Almost from birth we project parental images onto those around us, reacting to these transference images as if they were the original parent. Only after we have resolved them are we able to perceive the significant people in our lives with objectivity. It suffices for me that most of the events that occur among young and middle-aged adults in a personal growth laboratory can be understood and adequately dealt with in terms of transference theory. It is clear to me that the transference process is a basic growth process. It permits us to continue to react to and deal with the significant figures in our youth long after they are gone from our presence.

There is a long transition to adulthood. It is not something suddenly achieved at a particular age. Even when we are generally adult there are parts of us that haven't "kept pace." There is still work to be done, crucial experiences we must have in order to bring those parts into congruence with the trends of the whole: love, hate, jealousy, guilt, grief, and depression are feelings that accompany this work. They may dissuade us from making the necessary effort unless we have learned there is a tolerable limit to pain. In terms of this theory, then, we can define personal growth as the process of transference resolution.

After the transferences are largely resolved, usually but not always by middle age, the growth process is concentrated more fully on continued differentiation and the transformation of life experiences into wisdom. This is accompanied by an increased inward turning of psychic forces and a confrontation and coming to terms with aging and death. As far as I can determine, transference mechanisms do not seem to be used in these later stages of personal growth.

As one lives through these four existential stages of growth — (self-love, self-identity, sexuality, and differentiation), the degree of success experienced in any specific stage sets the limit on the success that can be obtained in the succeeding stages. If I experience insufficient love in stage 1, I will have great difficulty finding my self-identity in stage 2, I will be confused concerning my sexual identity in stage 3, and my differentiation will be restricted. With adequate love in 1, I will be more likely to establish my identity in 2. If I fail here, then I will have difficulty establishing my sexual identification and differentiating, etc. These developmental "arrests" are similar to the psycho-analytic concept of fixation.

Participants work through this sequence in reverse order. So we design our sessions and work phases to be congruent with this order. We start with differentiation activities. Then we confront Oedipal transferences. Next we go on to personal feedback and self-confrontation to clarify the self-identity. Finally, we seek to develop self-acceptance and self-love through acceptance of one's body structure and processes, and ownership of the self "as is."

This reversal seems to be a function of the degree of confidence the participant has in the staff that he will not be deserted on his journey, plus the amount of personal risk he is willing to take at the moment. It takes more trust and requires more risk to work at the Oedipal level than on differentiation, still more when working on self-identity, and most when trying to rebuild self-love.

Not everyone works at all four levels during any one laboratory experience. Some will be working at each level, and some will work at more than one. It depends upon where they are on their journey toward resolution, how self-managing they are, and the strength of the resources at their disposal. Repeated laboratory attendance enables some participants to work on earlier and earlier stages in each succeeding laboratory.

This transference theory is the principal guideline for the design and conduct of the second half of the workshop. More and more attention and energy are devoted to exploring each participant's transference experience, partly to help him resolve it, and partly to educate everyone in the identification and exploration of transference in the lifelong service of personal growth.

In the selection of movement activities, the focus is gradually changed from sensory and body awareness to the re-enactment of family dynamics and of racial myths and symbolism, such as evolution, rebirth, rites of passage, and archetype identification.

For example, one member said to another, "I have had an exciting experience with my name. I called myself Fury, meaning the focusing of the energy of the unconscious, the daemonic energy, the energy of the beast which can be harnessed and used for power and growth and transformation. I felt the tremendous energy in me and could hardly contain it (me). I was different in my living style and in relations with people. Of course, some of the difference was due to people's reaction to the name, their fear and fascination of the connotations of the name Fury. As time went on, my image of the energy was that of riding a powerful horse, that I could feel it between my knees, that I had to grip with my knees and hang on tight or get thrown. I had to use incredible force to rein in and let out the energy in useful ways and not let the beast under me take over. I got tired. I longed to get off and rest. I couldn't until the end of the journey (lab). I looked forward to getting safely to my destination and putting the animal in the corral and resting. Now, at the end of the lab, I have the most lovely feeling of well-oiled coordination, well-being and restfulness, coupled with acute sensations."

When I translate what I've said into the concept of the animal in us, the devil part of us that is uncivilized, savage, undisciplined, and the struggle of the godlike part of us to train and use the energy that has to be put down, hidden away by society in its attempt to civilize us, I remember that you are doing this with your stallion. That on a real and physical level you are doing what must be done later on a metaphysical level, in order to come into your full power as a woman and as a human being. This latter task seems to be one of maturity, to be done after much living has been undertaken.

We continue to explore the extremes of sensory and behavioral polarities. We use guided fantasies to extend our access to unconscious processes. We design behavioral prescriptions for various participants in whatever form their personal work requires.

The journey into these deeper recesses of memory and experience culminates with the rising to consciousness of repressed memories and feelings and leads to the expression of long-hidden urges, fears, and angers in the appropriate activity or movement session.

When a participant is successful in surfacing and discharging a repressed experience there is a clear beginning, middle, and end to his encounter with this part of himself. Immediately after he is finished, he feels a strong sense of release, peacefulness, and satisfaction. It is as if long-inhibited muscle action patterns had finally been discharged and there was no longer any need to hold them out of consciousness. It is clear that the release and satisfaction are feelings resulting from the adult-as-child getting revenge for early childhood punishments and deprivations, experienced or imagined. Once the revenge is expressed, the participant is able to experience and accept his love and dependency. The ambivalence toward the parent is on the way to being resolved.

My own personal experience, after having "encountered" the revengeful parts of me many times over the years, is a reduction of hostile destructive impulses and actions and an increase in what I would call positive initiation or constructive aggression in my interpersonal relationships.

The Principle of Necessary Opposites

The principle of necessary opposites also influences many of our training decisions. It states that every functional image or social role requires a polar opposite for its delineation. The physician needs his patient, the slave his master, the officer his private, the con man his patsy, Christ his Judas, and God his Devil. And vice versa.

The principle also states that sensory, perceptual, and motor patterns have their opposites — their polarities. For example: hot-cold, up-down, open-closed, big-small, contract-expand, happy-sad, burdened-unburdened, suspicious-trusting, listen-ignore, accept-reject, initiate-follow, aggressive-passive, loving-apathetic, hating-apathetic, balanced-imbalanced, and controlled-spontaneous. If a person invests his energy and experiences himself in only one side of a polarity, he limits his adaptability, constricts his range of experiencing, and limits his breadth of differentiation. One needs to be able to live anywhere along a polarity's continuum, depending on his state of being and the circumstances of the moment.

We use this concept in the lab to encourage participants to explore the hidden sides of themselves. To discover childhood by being a parent, parenthood by being a child. To discover masculinity by exploring femininity, and femininity by exploring masculinity. To know pleasure through pain, and pain through pleasure. To differentiate thoughts from feelings and sensations from emotions.

We also use it in our insistence that self-discipline is a necessary aspect of spontaneity and freedom of expression. Contrary to what has sometimes been said, the kind of personal growth training being described here is not an orgy, or a training program for the expression of hostile impulses, or an excuse for licentiousness. We discourage hostile physical contact. We forbid participants to injure themselves or others. The aim of sensory exploration, physical contact, and expressive movement is to reacquaint the participant with his body and its processes. The conscious management of these processes demands a high degree of control and a type of self-discipline that approaches a form of asceticism. One will no longer permit the abuse, neglect, or denial of his newly understood, respected, and prized self. Participants frequently assess this acquisition of self-control as one of the most valuable achievements of their lab experience. It gives added reality and a sense of permanence to their experience of autonomy, ownership, personal responsibility, and self-management.

In principle, one becomes freer to be spontaneous and expressive over his entire range of possible behavior as he becomes more aware and capable of greater self-discipline. Only when one is completely aware and self-disciplined can one be completely spontaneous. Freedom derives from conscious, self-managed awareness, not from blind self-indulgence.

It is essential that participants share their experiences with others. Verbal sharing helps them discover and understand added implications and meanings of their experiences. The sharing also performs a kind of witnessing.

Witnessing seems to be extremely important in connection with many ritualistic and ceremonial activities. Participants frequently reactivate a memory or a body fantasy, act out a personal improvisation or a bio-energetic release, or experience another participant in a new way. We ask that whenever possible this be done in the group, or at least in the presence of group members, so the experience can be witnessed. Witnessing, and sharing, for that matter, seem to validate the event and to give it and the participant public sanction and acceptance. The sanction prevents the generation of guilt feelings. The acceptance enables the person to own the experience, making it a part of himself and contributing to his personal growth.

It is as if the participant returns to his childhood, recalls images or expresses behaviorally motor patterns (accompanied by the appropriate feelings) that were originally repressed, and then needs the accepting observation of the witnesses, especially his transference objects, to be assured that his behavior is approved, respected, and perhaps even genuinely admired. The more of his existence he can take into himself, the more secure he becomes. The ultimate may be a state of complete self-acceptance and internal security. He would then be free to let all parts of himself be seen, to disclose whatever aspect of himself he wished without fear or trepidation.

The last day or two of the lab is spent in consolidating the learnings made by some, and in continuing the uncovering and working through for those who still have unfinished business. During this time the group culture is one of acceptance of individual differences, mutual affection and respect, and strong feelings of community. Compared with the beginning of the lab, the level of energy and excitement is high. Sensations are intense, images are rich, behavior is spontaneous and open, and work is efficient and productive. At the same time there is an atmosphere of peace and quiet with the serenity that follows having made an arduous journey. The emphasis on self-responsibility has produced for some the exhilaration of greater acceptance of self, greater sense of ownership or autonomy, knowledge of how to grow one's self, the price and rewards of increased awareness, increased access to unconscious processes, greater zest for living, etc. For others, there is a new appreciation of how they deaden themselves to experience, how they immobilize themselves with fear or anger, how they enslave themselves to the needs of others, how they have degraded, abused, and rejected their bodies, how they deny their sexuality, and avoid the life decisions they can or must make, etc. These keener appreciations are not accompanied by depression and despair, but faced with anticipation and resolve.

We end the lab with a ceremony designed to be congruent with the one used for the opening. It focuses on feelings of separation and departure. In the opening, our ceremony brought us together, in the closing, it separates us and sends us on our way. We go with a sharper distinction between "me" and the "them-in-me." Many leave with a new appreciation of the strength and peace one can feel when one fully accepts his existential aloneness.

At the end of the lab, people often say they are ready to leave. They feel able to stand alone. They do not feel dependent on the lab community and they look forward to leaving to start dealing with the "world out there" in new ways. For them, the so-called re-entry problem is not a big issue. For others, the central concern is how they will be able to alter their living environment to make it more congruent with their new self-awareness.

Actually, the end of the lab is not the end of the experience, nor the end of the work. As a matter of fact, most of the work remains to be done. The laboratory focus is on *how* to identify and work with one's growth processes. Most participants return home and continue to "do" themselves. The laboratory learnings have only started or aided them on a journey that will continue for a long time to come.

OVERVIEW

There are many beliefs and assumptions underlying the theories I employ for laboratory design and the strategies of my training interventions. Among the more important that I recognize are the following:

1. As long as I live I am a functioning unitary organism. I am not composed of parts, such as body, mind, psyche, soul, feelings, thoughts, ego, id, etc.
2. I am my body; nothing more, nothing less.
3. I have an innate urge to grow, to realize my potential, to differentiate.
4. I learn, I grow by experiencing.
5. No one can give me knowledge, insight, or wisdom. I must gain them through my own efforts; from my own experiences.
6. I cannot and will not change, grow, or understand until I am ready.
7. I am the only one responsible for my existence.
8. I am the sole authority over my inner life and feelings.
9. I am frequently the unwitting captive of my childhood experiences. Only I can free me.
10. To experience and to grow is good.
11. Everyone has a right to personal autonomy.
12. Everyone has the right of self-determination.
13. Autonomy, self-determination, and differentiation follow transference resolution.
14. Whatever I feel at any point in time is an appropriate feeling to have at that time.
15. All of my behavior is functional for me. At all times, I always do the best I can with what I have.
16. My perceptions are never "wrong" though they always differ from those of everyone else.

I am keenly aware of these assumptions and the theories I use and how strongly they influence my laboratory designs and training strategies. I have already said they derive from my experience, my background, and my value system. I wish they had a more solid foundation of scientific verification than they do at present. They cannot, because the scientific data do not exist. I know of no adequate scientific research on the effects of personal growth training. We have no convincing scientific validation of the theories and procedures we use; no clear guidelines, scientifically based, for future developments, and only limited demonstrations that present methodologies are dependable, safe, and effective.

Like many other workers in this field, I have done questionnaire research and follow-up surveys, and have collected long-term autobiographical material from participants. These kinds of data provide a variety of exciting, dramatic, and inspiring testimonials that convince me that personal growth training can be influential in clarifying a person's attitudes, values, and life style as profoundly as other life experiences. But none of these reports or other research studies satisfy me. No one has yet devised the research design, the comprehensive measuring instruments, and the sophisticated analytical techniques commensurate with the extreme complexity, variety, and subtlety of the processes of personal growth. My conviction that the processes of human differentiation into ever-expanding uniqueness are becoming observable and definable gives me hope that this will not always be the case.

Let me make explicit what has so far been only implied. I am of the opinion that one must have a theory of some sort, either explicit or implicit, as to the nature of personal growth if one is going to do effective personal growth training. The adequacy and validity of that theory will strongly influence the quality and effectiveness of the laboratory design and the training procedures. Without a theoretical orientation that is clearly understood and consistently applied, personal growth training is apt to be experienced by the participant as incoherent, contradictory, and confusing. The learning will be limited and the impact will be slight.

The two theories I have described above represent a personal bias synthesized somewhat from my study of Freud, Reich, Jung, and Rogers, but mostly, from my personal growth struggles and a multitude of significant events shared with workshop participants in more than 350 laboratory experiences. These theories are my metaphors, my fantasies, my "as-if" formulations and conceptions. They work for me; they reduce my anxiety. I need them to design a laboratory. I need them to tell me when and where to go with a participant. I need them to tell me what is meaningful and what is irrelevant in both process and content. They structure my world.

I emphasize the "my," the personal origin of these theories, not out of arrogance or possessiveness, but from a conviction that I have no choice but to order my world the way I do. The theory that results therefrom is, and must inevitably be, solely my own. We each construct our own order out of what we experience, what we do, and what we think. My theory can never be another's and theirs can never be mine. Personal growth, self-differentiation, and theory building are always subjective and internal processes. They can be described and discussed, but never transferred. Our existential aloneness is the precondition for everything we feel, do, and think.

I have come to the end of my sharing with you my bit of order in the confusion of contemporary human relations training. I end with a quotation from T. S. Eliot that captures, for me, the essence of personal growth:

> We shall never cease to explore, and the end of all our

exploration will be to return to the place from which we started and know it for the first time.

Each time around is fuller, richer, and more enlightening. I excite me with this realization.

BIBLIOGRAPHY

Herrigel, E., *Zen in the Art of Archery*, Random House, Westminster, Maryland, 1971.

Lecky, Prescott, *Self Consistency: A Theory of Personality*, Island Press Cooperative, New York, 1945.

Reich, Wilhelm, *Character Analysis*, Farrar, Straus and Giroux, New York, 1949.

______, *Discovery of the Orgone*, Volume 2, *The Cancer Biopathy*, Orgone Press, New York, 1948.

______, *Discovery of the Orgone*, Volume 1, *The Function of the Orgasm*, Orgone Press, New York, 1949.

Rosen, J. N., *Direct Analysis*, Grune and Stratton, New York, 1953.

Sechehaye, M. A., *Symbolic Realization*, International Universities Press, New York, 1960.

Skinner, B. F., *Behavior of Organisms: An Experimental Analysis*, Appleton, New York, 1938.

CHAPTER 14

THE TAVISTOCK MODEL OF LABORATORY TRAINING

Boris M. Astrachan

"Crazy," "stupid," "confusing," "exhausting," "exhilarating," "demonstrating life in groups as it really is," "not personally helpful" are among the pungent descriptions of Tavistock Study Groups (laboratory training groups).

"Exciting," "overwhelming," "educative," "bringing out the worst in people" are some of the ways in which trainees have spoken about Group Relations Conferences (in-residence workshops). Dominant emotions of frustration and anger are associated with experiences of being less competent or even deskilled interpersonally. Out of confusion and charged emotionality, a somewhat unique learning environment is created: an environment in which one may learn about the covert forces operational in groups and organizations, the ways in which individuals may be moved to "irrational" behavior by the structures we create.

In this chapter, the focus will be on understanding the rationale behind the utilization of the various exercises in the typical Group Relations Conference, and of the Conference as a whole. Because these conferences arise from some of the same intellectual roots as the T group tradition, we begin with a brief summary of the history of Tavistock Conferences.

The history provides the intellectual underpinning of the work, its roots in analysis and social psychology, and its increasing reliance upon systems theoretical constructs. The development of a systems perspective allows one to view the conference as a small bounded social system, importing members (and staff), processing them through various discrete yet interrelated exercises (the small study group, the large group exercise and the intergroup exercise) and then exporting them back into their environments of origin (via application groups and learning about the individual in the organization).

HISTORICAL DEVELOPMENT

The Tavistock method of group training has its intellectual roots in the psychoanalytical work of Melanie Klein and W. W. Bion.* A psychoanalytical approach makes the assumption that certain *fundamental* human behaviors may be examined and understood by carefully observing individuals in settings in which physical comfort is assured, boundaries (that is, membership, time span, use of space, etc.) are clearly identified and the person in authority, clinician, analyst, consultant, or experimenter, behaves in a manner that is work relevant, but socially deviant. That is, expectations that the authority will provide direction or will satisfy individuals' wishes for emotional gratification are not met. The primary stress is placed on understanding behavior (and the influence of structure) rather than upon the development of change-oriented strategies.**

It seems clear that settings which are physically comfortable, carefully bounded and in which authority figures behave in a non-gratifying, task relevant manner facilitate the emergence of relatively primitive human emotions. The stimulation of diverse affiliative and sexual fantasies in the psychoanalytic situation is well known. In group settings with a psychoanalytic orientation phenomena concerning authority, leadership and projection (Bion 1961, Rice 1965, Astrachan and Redlich 1969) continually emerge.

Such carefully bounded structures can also be understood from social psychological, and social systems theoretical perspectives (Lewin 1951, Boulding 1968). Utilizing these frameworks the relationship of parts of a group to the whole, and the parts to one another may be explored. Issues of group development (Bennis and Shepard 1956, Mills 1965, 1967), group leader interaction (Slater 1966, Rioch 1971, Singer and others, mimeographed paper) and group revolt (Mann 1967) can be studied.

---

*An excellent overview of the early history of group dynamics can be found in Durkin (1964); the specific development of Tavistock conferences was described by Rioch (1970a).

**The stress on comprehensive understanding as a necessary precursor to change has been criticized as elitist and as leading to either reinforcement of established patterns of behavior or to limited change. It is as vigorously defended as basic learning which must precede attempts at developing change oriented strategies.

The Tavistock small group (study group) brings together psychoanalytic, social psychological, and social systems theories to study individual and mass behavior in well-bounded structures. By clearly establishing boundaries and carefully controlling transactions across them while minimizing emotional gratification, psychological projections about leadership and group are facilitated and the relationship of members to group, to each other, and to authority can be studied.

The first Tavistock group conference was held in 1957 at the University of Leicester (Rioch 1970a). Initially, the conference was primarily a setting in which small groups were studied and the application of small group theory to organizational life explored. Other group events were gradually introduced (Higgen and Bridger 1964, Rice 1965). In 1962, A. K. Rice assumed leadership of Tavistock-Leicester conferences and directed all such conferences until 1968.* Under his leadership there was a consistent change in the focus of these conferences from the study of the small group and issues of authority and leadership, to the study of the conference as an *organization.* Under his leadership there was also a consistent effort to attempt to understand conference behavior from interconnected theoretical perspectives rather than from any unitary position (e.g. psychoanalytic or social psychologic or social systems theory).

The late 1960s witnessed an explosion of interest in group experiences in this country. The small Tavistock study group prospered in this popularization of group experiencing, and various authors began to describe such experiences and to do research on them (Redlich and Astrachan, 1969; Alderfer, 1970; Rioch, 1970a; Musto and Astrachan, 1968; Harrow, et al., 1971; Kohler, et al. (mimeographed draft a). The development of Tavistock conferences was more modest since these require a more extensive time commitment, a more or less exclusive commitment to learning, a willingness to travel to a site distant from one's home and work location and a correspondingly substantial financial commitment.

THE TAVISTOCK GROUP RELATIONS CONFERENCE AS AN ORGANIZATION

In the remainder of this paper the focus will be on the Tavistock Conference in the American setting, its separate

*In the early sixties a number of American mental health professionals attended these conferences and Dr. Margaret Rioch became the leader in attempts to introduce such training into this country. Dr Rice was invited to conduct a group relations conference at Mt. Holyoke College in 1965 under the sponsorship of the Washington School of Psychiatry, Yale University Department of Psychiatry and the Centre for Appied Social Research of the Tavistock Institute of Human Relations.

components and its overall organization. The typical conference brings together staff and trainees from a variety of backgrounds, industry, government, the various mental health disciplines, clergy, academia. The Tavistock Conference currently combines experiences in small group, large group, and intergroup exercises as well as application sessions which attempt to understand the conference as an organization and to apply conference learnings to back-home situations. A continuing problem for members and staff of the conference is the omnipresent awareness that each exercise, although studied as though it were a free-standing experience, is always influenced by and in turn influences all of the other elements of the conference, and to an extent the communities in which the conference is being held. The examination of the interpenetration of exercises and of conference and community and the establishment of boundaries which facilitate task accomplishment of each conference exercise and the conference as a whole is a major task of conference management.

Rice (1963; Miller and Rice, 1965) has described organizations as open systems which import materials from the environment, modify the imports so that they are more highly valued by the environment, and then export the products to the environment. Although any segment of the organization can be studied as if it were a closed system, isolated from the environments in which it exists, this fiction is supportable only so long as management is able to adequately regulate exchanges between organization and environment. Thus, a major managerial task for organizations and their parts is the regulation of boundary exchanges.

Throughout Rice's work (Rice 1963, 1969, Miller and Rice 1967) and in the work of his followers (Levinson and Astrachan, in press) effective organizational boundary management is correlated with selective boundary permeability to those exchanges necessary to task-accomplishment and selective boundary impermeability to those exchanges which inhibit task performance.

The task of the Tavistock Conference as a temporary educational organization is to provide opportunities for members to learn about psychological processes which exist in group, intergroup and organizational life and which facilitate or inhibit organizational task accomplishment. To facilitate this task staff and members who have some commitment to this work are recruited. A variety of exercises analogous to organizational structures are utilized. These exercises are treated as though they are independent of one another in order that the interaction between exercises and issues of boundary permeability may be highlighted.

Import of Staff

Concomitant with the importation of the Tavistock Conference to the United States were extensive negotiations to establish an organizational home in this country. A firm organizational base was desired to sanction conference activities on the basis of demonstrated competence and to insure that trainers would be carefully selected and adequately trained. Under the leadership of Dr. Margaret Rioch, the Washington School of Psychiatry initially assumed this responsibility. Following several successful conferences a separate structure, the A. K. Rice Institute, was formed with headquarters in Washington and several regional sections. Conferences are sanctioned by these groups and conference directors approved. The conference director selects the staff. The staff agrees to work within the organizational framework of the conference and empowers the director to act for the total staff.

Staff members generally have a background in one of the social sciences, although they may work as managers, executives, clinicians, organizational consultants, etc. Staff will have participated as members in a number of conferences. They may have functioned as observers at conferences prior to being selected for staff roles. As staff members initially, they are carefully supervised in first one and then another conference exercise. In supervision they spend much time with more experienced staff members carefully reviewing the work and in particular studying their own behavior in the conference setting.

Import of Members

Members are recruited from a variety of organizations. They are advised through written brochures about the tasks of the conference and each of the exercises. Generally they are individuals who are in middle-managerial positions in academic, mental health, industrial, governmental, and religious organizations. Prospective members are advised that the purpose of the conference is learning, not individual psychological benefit, and that the focus will be on group, not individual behavior. Letters of support are required and in the request for such letters it is noted that the conference may be psychologically stressful. It is recommended that those individuals currently experiencing significant life stress or those individuals with limited coping resources not apply. Scholarships are generally available for some categories of members (that is, individuals who represent community organizations, individuals from organizations having limited resources, students, etc.).

Approximately fifty to seventy members are selected for each conference. The conference site is chosen for its relative isolation, comparative comfort and ability to house members and provide adequate work space. The members, on arriving, are notified about room assignments and all the amenities (location of bank, bookstores, phones, etc.). They receive small study group assignments, groups composed insofar as possible of individuals who do not know each other. Members also receive assignment to application groups structured on the basis of comparable work interests.

The first meeting is of the entire membership and staff. This *conference opening* is primarily devoted to restating the tasks of the conference and making appropriate announcements. During this meeting all staff are present. They are indentified as having as their primary task the facilitation of member-learning. They model certain behaviors, but insist on no specific member behavior. Staff arrive promptly, they attend carefully to their work, they speak only when they believe they can further the attempts of the members to work upon the specified tasks. Staff are identified as consultants to indicate that their role in the work is more of an educative than a leadership nature. At the conclusion of this meeting the import process as it relates to the members is completed. Insofar as is possible, the boundary between conference and community is established.

The Study Group — (Small Group)

The first group experience for the membership is in the small group. Conference members most often will have two small group sessions prior to the introduction of other exercises. The study group consists of nine to thirteen members and one consultant meeting together to explore group behavior in the "here and now." Prior to the group meeting the room is set up. A circle of chairs is formed, with exactly enough chairs to accommodate all members and the consultant. If staff observers are to be present, their chairs will be located outside the circle. At precisely the time noted for the beginning of the session, the consultant arrives. In this and other ways, the behavior of the consultant continually demonstrates his awareness of the boundaries of the exercise. The consultant accepts the boundaries because he has contracted to do so, and because he believes that his focus on the task of the group, the study of its internal life, will be highlighted by the group's constant exploration of his behavior and its exploration of group boundaries. The consultant's punctuality is the least intrusive "leadership" behavior. If he is early or late his real behavior can become a focus for the group, and he can too easily become more or less loving, more or less manipulable and far less available as a receptacle for the projections of the group and less available to concentrate on his work. By working to establish a clear boundary he allows for the exploration of phenomena within the boundary, and he can clearly note when the group attempts to do work beyond its boundaries. Other common boundary issues involve questions about the conditions for group membership, normative behavior and the control of deviance, and the legitimacy of discussing outside events from the larger conference within the study group. The consultant will identify such issues when they become problematic for the group, yet he will give no advice and will respond to no questions. He only comments when he believes that his comments further the work of the group.

His demeanor is extraordinarily attentive. He continually observes and struggles with the meaning of group behaviors. Yet he rarely speaks. The task of the group (to study its own processes) is ambiguous and members expect assistance or confirmation for their efforts from the consultant. This happens even when they are quite aware that the consultant cannot do the group's work for it. The potential helper, the consultant, begins to be viewed as distant, rigid, authoritarian and powerful (Harrow and others, 1971; Klein and Astrachan, 1972). Members experience a sense of isolation from one another, of disconnectedness, and in order to begin to establish some sense of self they endow the consultant with magical authority. The authority he possesses as expert is ignored as members attempt to have him accept authority and leadership in tasks of satisfying member emotional needs (Bion, 1961; Rioch, 1970b; Slater, 1966). The consultant's attention to his task, and to the work of the group is perceived as rejecting. Angry outbursts by members may be ignored or identified as attempts to coerce the consultant into a desertion of his work, a modification of his role. Instead of accepting member-dependency and utilizing that dependency to stimulate group action, the consultant will comment only on the dependency and his experience of the group's demands upon him. Within the group, members find themselves accepting roles as a way of preserving some measure of individuality within the context of the undifferentiated mass. The role serves to legitimize some individual behavior, while limiting other behaviors. Some members tend to assume those roles that have been successfully assumed in the past — regardless of the adequacy of those roles for task accomplishment in the study group. When the small study group is not held in the context of a conference, members often begin to test boundaries of the group. Children or dogs have been brought into meetings and some members regularly miss the third meeting and become the object of great group concern. However, when the small group is held in the context of the conference, other exercises begin which are perceived as even more threatening to individual identity and the small study group often begins to be viewed as an oasis of safety in a world gone mad (Turquet, in press; Astrachan and Flynn, in press; Kohler et al., in press b).

As members begin to view the small group as a sanctuary, the consultant more insistently keeps the task of the group in the forefront of awareness. As members make him into a friendlier, more helpful, caring individual, he avoids seduction and emphasizes the ways in which members seek to establish comfortable relationships with each other to have some relief from the chaos they experience elsewhere. He must identify the ways in which increased group identification facilitates task performance or inhibits that performance, whether it feels good or not.

The Large Group

The first large group session generally takes place after one or two small group meetings have occurred. A large room is set up for the total conference membership. Chairs set up in three or four concentric circles are available for exactly the total of all members, plus the two to four consultants. Chairs for staff observers, if present, are located outside of the circles. Because of its size, the large group is not a face-to-face situation. In the conference this group may meet intensively over a relatively short period of time (two or more meetings a day). The work of the consultants is to identify projections as the members seek to make them receptacles within which to place distressing group contents. The consultants assist the group to identify the large group as a bounded system in order to help the members in their attempts to encompass and understand the situation.

Each member is faced with his own lack of importance in this massive undifferentiated group. There are no rules save that the consultants will enter and also leave at the appointed time; there is no agenda. Personal agendas are not heard, the ability to follow conversational streams is interrupted continually by idiosyncratic member needs, and members continually experience the conviction that the only possible way for the group to unite would be for a religious convocation, an orgy, or a lynching. One member's comments on his emotional state may be followed by a second's observations on the group process and by a third's protest about the exercise. A response to the first member generally is lost in the competition for "air time."

Member attempts to encompass and simplify the exercise include attempts to form sub-groups (black-white; male-female; consultant-members) and sub-subgroups (members from study groups supporting each other; old friendships called upon). Other members may opt for a role on the periphery of the group, only marginally participating in its activities. Members may attempt to split the consultants, to see one or another as more or less helpful or to insist that the problems in understanding interaction in the exercise are problems of the consultants. Frequently in this exercise one or perhaps a few members are projectively identified with a variety of uncomfortable group emotions: confusion, madness or rage, and as scapegoats for the group they carry these emotions while the group behaves as if their experience was unique.

Individuals are not understood, their comments are attributed to others, motivation is assumed and little reality testing and feedback are possible. Dyadic alliances are short-lived and subgroups are rarely stable, shifting almost constantly. Task accomplishment, the study of the large group in the here and now, is confounded by the dilemma of maintaining individuality in the large group and by the continual emergence of intergroup issues. Indeed, often the individual with the clearest identity is the one whose chair is unoccupied, or the scapegoat. In all of this, the consultants attempt to maintain their focus on behavior in the large group, commenting upon attempts to disrupt the external boundaries of the group or to form new internal boundaries, elucidating the problems encountered in attempting to work in the group, and the members' demands for structure, simplification, and authority while continually deprecating the authority of the work task.

The Intergroup Exercise

The intergroup exercise usually begins after a meeting or two of the large group. Two different exercises have been utilized (Rice, 1965; Astrachan and Flynn, in press). In one, the consultants are placed in each member group attempt to assist the members in understanding the interaction of groups one with another. Here, all intergroup staff are assigned to member group sections and they do not form a staff group. In the second exercise, the consultants form as a group in the exercise and are available to consult only at the request of member groups. This second exercise is particularly important in understanding the conference as an organization, and will be the exercise discussed below.

The intergroup exercise opens in a large meeting including all staff and members. The task of the exercise is described, "to study behavior in and between groups as it occurs." The staff is identified as a separate group in the exercise. Staff announces its willingness to consult with those groups which may form in the allocated sectors (rooms). During this exercise one less room than the total number of study groups is set aside for the formation of member groups in order to forestall a too-easy splitting of the membership into pre-existing study groups. At the conclusion of his remarks, the conference director asks for questions, and then leads the entire staff to its sector. Members may begin to try to identify some rational way of splitting into groups to accomplish the task, but are unable to do so. Members often consider remaining in study groups to at least preserve the ties to one another that have developed, but to do so they would all not only have to agree to this split but also to manage the difficulties that would result from one group's having no defined territory. (For example, there is one less room available than the total number of study groups.) The members must begin to confront the difficulties involved in group formation. Generally small groups develop without any planning as some members burst out of the large meeting in order to "occupy" small group rooms. At times some territories are staked out and members may even struggle for possession of a room. The exercise has become a reality.

The small groups that form in this exercise do so more for reasons of coping with the anxiety of the members not knowing where they belong than because of any attempt to split into groups to accomplish the task. The groups that form then painfully begin to attempt to establish some sense of group identity while also attending to the behavior of other groups. When requested, consultants attempt to help groups understand their reasons for forming and to understand how those reasons influence further group development. Some groups form as sanctuaries, others to focus the aggression of the membership, others to reconstitute old groups, etc. Groups make initial attempts to organize, to develop some kind of structure, but experience great difficulty in doing so. Overtime members routinely develop positive in-group attitudes and negative attitudes towards other groups (Howenstine and Miller, mimeo; Kohler and others, in press b). The staff group, reasonably well organized and reasonably clear about its boundaries, is perceived as controlling and manipulative. The staff's ability to control itself may be interpreted as a staff wish to control others. Members and groups tend to hear consultant interventions as either calls to action or as interpretations designed to prevent it. Member hostility to and frustration with staff often reaches a peak in this exercise with calls to aggressive action (that is, to revolt, capture the consultant's space, capture a consultant and hold him prisoner, etc.).

The consultants in their meetings, which are open to all for observation, and in their consultation to sectors, attempt to help the membership understand the problems involved in group formation, group development, and intergroup activity. They identify the ways in which boundaries are formed about groups without reference to task, how barriers arise inhibiting information flow in intergroup interaction, how some groups fail to develop any boundaries and are continually overwhelmed by the environment. An important member-learning (although difficult membership accomplishment) is that member group collaboration is necessary for members to have any sense of effectiveness in their interaction with staff.

Application Groups

As the conference is moving to its conclusion, the final exercise begins.* In the application group, there is an opportunity to see the way in which all of the exercises are interrelated. In the application group members may trace the manner in which behavior in one exercise influences behavior in others. For example, a small study group may have experienced the consultant's behavior as excessively depriving. Members of that group could have been incensed at their inability to be supportive of one another in the large group, and might have decided to stay together in the intergroup exercise. Their behavior in that exercise might be directed to establishing a warm friendly group isolated from the environment thus inhibiting the efforts of other groups to effectively engage in intergroup interaction with them.

It is possible to explore how malfunctioning or dissension in one part of a system may be spread throughout the system, to study the ways in which problems in one sector tend to be re-identified as problems in other sectors or as failures of those in authority; to observe the ways in which one's own group is identified as being equated with goodness and truth while other groups are disparaged.

In the application group the small study group may be viewed as a small section of a larger organization. The relationship of task accomplishment and emotional interaction can be examined as can the consequences of carrying over boundaries that work well in one area into another area (that is, attempts to reproduce the study group in the intergroup exercise). Group needs to endow the consultant with authority may be explored with staff now actively participating in describing the dilemmas of the consultant. In this exercise, he is free to answer questions concerning when to intervene or how to comment when the group is insisting that each comment is an order. The large group may be examined for its parallels to a meeting of most of the members of the organization. In the organization when boundaries are ambiguous, members may belong to multiple small groups simultaneously (that is, section, union, racial, ethnic, sex-based groups, etc.), and affiliations may shift dependent on individual need rather than organizational goals. Cohesion of a large section or department may be facilitated by projection of uncomfortable feelings into management just as may have occurred in the large group with the consultants.

*Application groups were first utilized as attempts to understand the conference as an organization by Turquet in the 1966 Mt. Holyoke conference.

Organizational scapegoats may be identified in the real, back home situation, and the mechanisms producing such scapegoating related to the scapegoating of members in the large group.

The intergroup exercise may be viewed with special relevance to the organization. In the exercise described, staff has a role similar to that of management, but in spite of their reasonably adequate organization, their regulation of their own boundaries in the service of task accomplishment, they cannot impose task accomplishment on the members. Although the individual may at times feel as though the complexity of each group and of the relationship of group to group is more than he can fathom, he is nonetheless always aware of the connectedness of the individual and the whole, and of their great interdependence. In the exercise, the learning remains each individual member's responsibility. Member groups may form that to some extent gratify member emotional needs, but unless the groups evolve ways of regulating their boundaries to effect interaction with others, the members will perceive themselves as having only poorly accomplished their work.

In the application, group issues from the larger community that have impact on the conference may be explored. In recent conferences major social issues that were reflected in the conferences included issues of female authority and male-female relationships; issues of black authority and black-white relationships and issues of campus militancy, and the establishment of a counterculture within the conference. These issues are in society at large and are reflected in issues of membership selection, in member-member interaction, and in the ways in which members interact with consultants. These issues can be discussed in relationship to back home situations where pressing societal problems may alter boundary permeability of organizations, even to changing internal structures (Butkovich and others, in press).

As the discussion of the conference as an organization progresses, it becomes possible to ask individual members to contribute specific work experiences or dilemmas to the discussion in order to explore the utility of the learnings in understanding back home situations.

THE INDIVIDUAL IN THE ORGANIZATION

The Tavistock laboratory method is oriented to learning about the significance of group and social structure and the ways in which individuals are called upon to fill roles for groups in the absence of clear, task-relevant division of labor. Members are helped to explore the ways in which groups relate to one another and the manner in which diverse tasks are managed in groups and among groups. This learning takes place in groups, but as the conference is a residential one, the learning and the utilization of knowledge are individual matters.

Rice (1969) has written that "the effectiveness of every intergroup relationship is determined, so far as its overt purposes are concerned, by the extent to which the groups involved have to defend themselves against uncertainty about the integrity of the boundaries." He identifies as a major task for individuals, groups, and organizations the regulation and control of boundaries. Throughout the conference, the individual is confronted by a plethora of ambiguous boundaries.

His own personal boundaries in the small group are initially unclear, his attempts to identify with others move in a variety of directions. He may seek clarity by identifying with a group, thus giving up a piece of self with the hope that his group or some leader will know how to most effectively set priorities and deal with conflict. His group may gratify some of his needs, but will deny others. Faced with greater uncertainty (the large group; the intergroup exercise), he may seek to recreate one or another small group, or to project his chaos and confusion into others. In intergroup relationships he discovers that collaboration among groups is difficult to accomplish without some sense of one's own group's integrity, but that a sense of one's own group is insufficient to guarantee collaboration. Indeed it may even lead to disparaging other groups, prejudice, and efforts at manipulation. He discovers that group work tasks are easily discarded for security, power, or "good-feeling" goals. The individual discovers that his actions and his group's actions have significant consequences to the total organization, even when they are discounted! In the organization, for example, individuals may consider staying home from work individual acts, yet such choices may contribute to a high rate of absenteeism that steadily undermines the achievement of widely valued organizational goals.

The member experiences the remarkable complexity of organizations, the loneliness of the mass, even when one "knows" many in the mass and the peculiar interconnectedness of the one with the whole. Hopefully, he learns that in confusion, even if others are insisting that all must be equally confused, it remains possible to reflect, to question, to work, and to try to behave responsibly to self and others. Regardless of his degree of success, he may at least learn that the task is worthwhile.

REFERENCES

1. Alderfer, C. P. Understanding Laboratory Education: An Overview. Monthly Labor Review, December 1970, pp. 18, 27.

2. Astrachan, B. M. and Redlich, F. C. Leadership Ambiguity and its Effect on Residents' Study Groups. Int. J. Grp. Psychother. 19, 1969, pp. 487-494.

3. Astrachan, B. M. and Flynn. H. R. The Intergroup Exercise: A Paradigm for Learning about the Development of Organizational Structure. In Task and Organization, edited by E. Miller. Tavistock Publications: London (in press).

4. Bennis, W. G. and Shepard, H. A. A Theory of Group Development. Human Relations 9, 1956, pp. 415-437.

5. Bion, W. W. Experiences in Groups. Tavistock Publications: London, 1961.

6. Boulding, K. E. General Systems Theory — The Skeleton of Science. In: Modern Systems Research for the Behavioral Scientist. Ed. W. Buckley, Aldine Press, Chicago, 1968.

7. Butkovich, P., Sullivan, M. and Astrachan, B. M. Boundary Structures and Responses of Community Mental Health Centers to Pressures for Change. Proceedings of the 33rd Annual Meeting of the Academy of Management, 1973 (in press).

8. Durkin, H. The Group in Depth. Int. Univ. Press: New York, 1964.

9. Harrow, M., Astrachan, B. M., Tucker, G. J., Klein, E. B, and Miller, J. C. The T group and Study Group Laboratory Experiences. J. Soc. Psychol. 85, 1971, pp. 225-237.

10. Higgen, G. and Bridger, H. The Psychodynamics of an Intergroup Experience. Human Relations 17, 1964, pp. 391-446.

11. Howenstine, R. A. and Miller, J. C. Group Development in Intergroup Relations (mimeographed draft).

12. Klein, E. B. and Astrachan, B. M. Learning in Groups: A Comparison of Study and T groups. JABS 7, 1971, pp. 659-683.

13. Kohler, A. T., Klein, E. B., and Miller, J. C. Relationships between Sex of Members and Consultants in Study Groups. (mimeographed draft)

14. Kohler, A. T., Miller, J. C., and Klein, E. B. Some Effects of Intergroup Experience on Study Group Phenonmena. Human Relations. (in press)

15. Levinson, D., and Astrachan, B. M. Entry into the Mental Health Center: A Problem in Organizational Boundary-Regulation. In Task and Organization, Ed. by E. Miller, Tavistock Publications: London (in press).

16. Lewin, K. Field Theory in Social Science. Harper: New York, 1951.

17. Mann, R. Interpersonal Styles and Group Development. John Wiley & Sons: New York, 1967.

18. Miller, E. J., and Rice, A. K. Systems of Organization: The Control of Task and Sentient Boundaries. Tavistock Publications: London, 1967.

19. Mills, T. M. Group Transformation. Prentice-Hall: Englewood Cliffs, New Jersey, 1965.

20. Mills, T. M. The Sociology of Small Groups. Prentice-Hall: Englewood Cliffs, New Jersey, 1967.

21. Musto, D., and Astrachan, B. M. Strange Encounter: The Use of Study Groups with Graduate Students in History. Psychiatry 31, 1968, pp. 264-276.

22. Redlich, R. C., and Astrachan, B. M. Group Dynamics Training. Am. J. Psychiat. 125, 1969, pp. 1501-1507.

23. Rice, A. K. The Enterprise and its Environment. Tavistock Publications: London, 1963.

24. Rice, A. K. Individual, Group, and Intergroup Processes. Human Relations 22, 1969, pp. 565-584.

25. Rice, A. K. Learning for Leadership. Tavistock Publications: London, 1965.

26. Rioch, M. D. Group Relations: Rationale and Technique. Int. J. Grp. Psychother. 20, 1970a, pp. 340-355.

27. Rioch, M. J. The Work of Wilfred Bion on Groups. Psychiatry 33, 1970b, pp. 56-66.

28. Rioch, M. J. All We Like Sheep (Isaiah 53:6) Followers and Leaders. Psychiatry 34, 1971, pp. 258-273.

29. Singer, D. L., Astrachan, B. M., Gould, L. J., and Klein, E. B. A Group is not a Group is not A Group: Psychological Work in Groups from an Organizational and Systems Perspective. (mimeographed draft)

30. Slater, P. E. Microcosm: Structural, Psychological and Religious Evolution in Groups. John Wiley & Sons: New York, 1966.

31. Turquet, P. M. Threats to Identity in the Large Group: A Study in the Phenomenology of the Individual's Experience in Groups. In Task and Organization, edited by E. Miller. Tavistock Publications: London (in press).

CHAPTER 15

THE CLARIFICATION GROUP

Max Birnbaum

The Clarification Group (C Group) is a small group process which typically focuses on the exploration of group identifications: racial, religious, ethnic, etc.[1] The C Group utilizes life history and other experiential data together with appropriate sociological and social psychological knowledge to create a systematic teaching methodology. The method is potentially applicable to other disciplines in addition to intergroup relations.

The C Group was devised to deal with an urgent social need — the amelioration of inter-group tensions. In the course of its development, the exploration of the influences of primary group origins became a necessary first step in the process of coming to terms with one's own ethnocentrism. This coming to terms seemed essential to the surfacing and examination of the hostile and aggressive feelings which sought their targets in persons of different origins. C Group methodology presumes the significant and enduring impact on individuals of their early group identifications.

All this, however, was a prelude to enabling individuals of different ethnic and racial stocks to carry on the business of life in a democracy with minimal pathological conflict. We are today, however, witnessing a massive change in traditional group relationships. The explicit assertion of group rights as opposed to that of the individual in all areas, economic, social, and political, is a new phenomenon in America. The traditional definition of self, in individual-idiosyncratic terms, now is giving way in many quarters, because of social pressures and constraints, to the need to define and be defined in group terms — black, white, WASP, Catholic, Jew, Chicano, Spanish-speaking, woman, youth, etc. The poignant cry of Dennis in the film "Where is Prejudice?"[2] "I don't want to be known only as Dennis the Jew, I want to be looked at as Me!" is perhaps fated by the present climate to be denied in many quarters. Inter-group relations for the foreseeable future will emphasize more the conflict of group interests and the demand for swift rectification of past wrongs. There is need for a methodology which makes these issues and forces explicit and cultivates the personal capacity to deal realistically with the massive changes these social forces will invoke. Facing us now is the demand from many to turn a heterogeneous society into a pluralistic community.

On the level of interpersonal relations there is a need for frank and open interaction where possession of culturally created prejudice is not denied; a premium is placed on candor and an injunction upheld against polite denial and evasion. All this, while maintaining the freedom to fashion one's own relationship with culture and subculture without the need to conform to a single model. The seemingly conflicting demands to assimilate, to integrate, to maintain cultural independence are bewildering challenges. The C Group is an attempt to contribute to the resolution of the implicit dilemmas.

Current interest in the C Group has been heightened by the growing realization that T Group methodologies have not been so successful in changing prejudiced attitudes toward members of other groups as originally had been hoped. It now appears fallacious to assume that a change process involving interpersonal experiences based on contact and emphasis on human similarities will significantly influence the complex feelings and prejudices which are rooted in group identifications.[3]

The development of a norm of focusing primarily on individual and interpersonal dynamics often encourages participants in their quest for interpersonal and group intimacy to avoid discussion of group differences among members. Valuable and genuine as this experience may be on one level, the growth of this feeling of group intimacy is inimical to the realistic recognition of the intergroup factor and its sobering, divisive implications.

The need for an alternative model was commented on in 1968 by Donald Klein, then Program Director of NTL's Center for Community Affairs, in a letter to a fellow practitioner:

> The difficulties and successes you report appear to reflect many of the dynamics which have been noted elsewhere, but not, as far as I know, reported in the literature. The application of sensitivity training without modification to the field of intergroup training does not appear to work. In fact, as the blacks suggested in your project, sensitivity training may have the effect of by-

> passing the intergroup hostilities and tensions just because the individuality of people is emphasized. In usual sensitivity training efforts it rarely becomes necessary to open up and deal with group stereotypes. In fact, such material takes on the quality of "there and then" and, therefore, prohibited material.
>
> Your experience underscores, I feel, the necessity for making major changes in sensitivity training and of bringing to it much of the earlier intergroup relations training approaches when dealing with black-white or other intergroup problems.[4]

Currently, there are three basic uses of the C Group employed by the Boston University Human Relations Laboratory where current experimentation with the method is a high priority: 1) as the central small group experience of a residential laboratory; 2) a shortened form employed as part of a larger organizational improvement project; and 3) as a seminar in the graduate school setting. The first, the residential laboratory C Group, will be discussed in detail below, the other two uses, subsequently.

C GROUP AND THE LABORATORY

The most dramatic and effective use of the C Group is within the context of a total laboratory experience where it approximates the centrality of the T Group in its sister Basic Human Relations Laboratory. The C Group in a Summer Lab setting is the methodology in its purest form. At Osgood Hill the usual process begins with Phase I, where life history material is elicited via the structured group interview,[5] usually conducted by the trainer with increasing participant assistance. Methods other than the structured group interview may be used to begin the C Group, but a directed focus on life history data by the trainer has proved to be most practical. The life history data are controlled by the trainer to *avoid highly personal idiosyncratic material and restricted to those data which easily can be related to one's ethnic, religious, racial, social class and regional, primary and secondary group influences.* Greater emphasis is given to societal influences which have genetically or historically anchored racial or religious roots, in contrast to the temporary or transitory regional or occupational identifications. This opening phase of the C Group is designed to emphasize the continuing influence of the social self, even though often overlooked and denied. The process leads to the recovery of much that has been heretofore submerged and neglected by C Group members. In rare cases, life history data below the preconscious level have been recovered in these sessions, but these instances have been rare, and are deliberately discouraged by the trainer.

Phase II of the process now begins to encourage the participant to examine his view of the world, especially his view of other people with different social selves, as well as to become aware of their views of him. This phase also leads to the surfacing and recognition of prejudices, fears, and stereotypes regarding persons from groups other than one's own. The first phase might be dubbed the recovery of the social self, the second as the recognition of ethnocentrism, which leads to the third and last phase of the C Group process, the exploration and confrontation of the participant's present feelings. The trainer raises and helps the participants to begin to raise a variety of questions in order to facilitate movement through these stages. These questions may be roughly classified in three categories (not necessarily parallel to the three stages, but rather to be raised repeatedly throughout the fabric of the C Group process).

(1) *Who am I in terms of my group identifications?* How do I feel about my race, religion, etc.? How aware am I of the influences these group identifications have had upon me? In what ways have my awareness and feelings changed over time? How have I responded to the group memberships with which I was born and why? Have I strongly affirmed, strongly rejected, accepted, denied, ignored, etc., my ethnic identity, religion, geographic background, etc.? Do I have mixed feelings about any of these memberships? Are there areas in which I have not come to terms with who I am?

(2) *How do others respond to me in terms of my group identifications?* What generalizations do others tend to make about me because of my Catholicism, Protestantism, Jewishness, blackness, femininity, etc.? Which of these generalizations are valid and which are stereotypes? How do I compare with others from my own group, that is, in what ways are my opinions, attitudes, feelings, behaviors, etc., typical of members of my group and in what ways are they atypical? In what ways am I influenced by my consciousness of the valid generalizations and stereotypes about my group? Do I, for example, resent the stereotypes and (consciously or unconsciously) try to act differently, or do I sometimes find myself playing a role that is expected of me, instead of being myself?

(3) *How do I respond to others in terms of their group identifications?* What stereotypes and what generalizations do I make? What prejudices do I have? For example, do I as a white, tend to clump all blacks together in my mind, without realizing the significant differences which social class, regional background, etc., make? Do I, as a black, tend to clump all

whites together without realizing the significant differences that ethnicity, religion, etc., make? Do I misinterpret others' behavior as being based on one aspect of social self when it is actually based on another aspect, or do I confuse social self with individual, idiosyncratic self? Can I, for example, distinguish when a person is angry at me, whether it is because I am a male, because I am a Catholic, or simply because I am me and there is something about me, completely unrelated to my social self, which makes that person angry? Do I use my group identification as a shield, assuming that people of another race who dislike me are prejudiced in order not to have to look at whether there is really something about me personally that some people dislike? On the other hand, do I tend to personalize things, assuming that people are responding to my personal self when they are really reacting to my social self? Am I able to distinguish when I am acting out of prejudice and when I am acting out of conflict of group interests?[6]

The final phase of the C Group (exploration and confrontation of participants' present feelings) is the most delicate and divisive of the entire experience. C Groups come to their close with an unsettling awareness of the impossibility of resolving historical group differences through "love" or "trust" or normal strategies suitable to individual relationships, even in a temporary society like the Lab. Facing reality with all its complexity, shades of gray instead of clean and easy black and white, induces fear and anxiety in many, and a sobriety in the reality-oriented. They know more than ever before the nature of the problem of intergroup relations and the limits as to what can be done to minimize possible pathology. This ending of the Community Lab experience raises significant methodological questions, answers to which do not come readily. A few of these questions follow. Roughly parallel to the substantive phases of the C Group described above, there is a progression of group feeling from non-cohesion to substantial cohesion to post- or anti-cohesion. In Phase I where each person is sending his or her message in response to the task — dredging up the influences which created the social self — the common task and the basic similarities of familial influences create a confraternity which encourages group cohesion. In Phase II, all men and women are equal since all enjoy the common boon of consciousness of kind and suffer the curse of ethnocentrism. Phase III, however, sets each subgroup in opposition to the others, with society's unresolved intergroup problems underlying group differences and creating the final state of the C Group atmosphere, post-cohesion. Post-cohesion should not be construed in this context as a term of negative connotation. It should be understood rather as a state of group development where simplistic conceptions of the disappearance of group differences, conflict of group interests, and the elimination of prejudice through the achievement of personal trust are seen as improbable. It involves a realistic recognition that the effects of group differences can be understood, lived with and controlled, but never dismissed or eradicated.

The training field has assumed that group cohesion is an essential causative factor in individual change.[7] The baffling question is just how does the C Group which never develops the cohesive quality of the T Group and ends in an anti-cohesive mood, produce individual change? There are at this point sufficient personal testimonials which cumulatively attest to the effectiveness of the C Group as a change methodology. Many of these testimonials refer to new awareness and acceptance of one's previously disregarded social self and prejudices against persons of other groups. Others testify to a new-found courage to stand up to excessive pressure from overly demanding minorities. Still others who are members of minorities, blacks and others, affirm a new-found appreciation of the differences between the culturally prejudiced and those who discriminate. One conjectures that the meaningful support group for change consists of fellow ethnics in the Lab across C Group lines. This deserves further investigation. Another possibility, directly contradictory, suggests that group cohesion is not necessary for individual change, but what is sufficient is the availability of a group undertaking a common task of introspection and re-education. This may be enough to encourage individuals to tackle cultural influences and come to personal terms with them. In any case, the field is wide open for investigation.

The C Group in a laboratory setting cannot be comprehended fully unless the other inputs stemming from that setting are evaluated. These influences arise from two sources: the cognitive input consisting of theory, concepts, information, and issues, and consultation on back home problems. The latter has by far the greater impact and without exception almost equals the C Group in perceived value to the participants. Starting on the very first afternoon with a focus on institutional and community problems, groups are carefully chosen from those with common interests and problems and are staffed to deal with these within an organizational or community focus. If the system problems are not intergroup in a classical historical sense, then they are interface problems. In any case, the phenomena seen clearly in intergroup encounters are also frequently seen in interface encounters. Thus, those interested in either macro- or micro-settings see common relevance in analysis of either intergroup or interface encounters.

Cognitive input consists primarily of exercises and experiences highlighting ethnicity, social class, racial and religious confrontations, nature of stereotypes, with a bow to more contemporary intergroup issues — male-female, age-youth. All of these influence interaction within the C Group whose membership reflects this heterogeneity of the Lab population and provide further stimulus to and reinforcement of C Group learnings.

With the seventh annual Community Relations and Community Dynamics Laboratory at Boston University recently concluded, a considerable body of experience with C Group processes has been accumulated. My chosen way of dealing with these findings is to discuss them under the following five headings: (a) Trainer Behavior; (b) Process Problems; (c) Personal Growth Outcomes; (d) Short Term C Group; (e) C Group Process as Teaching Methodology. The latter will include C Groups in other than laboratory settings and some thoughts on the C Group as a teaching methodology, useful for areas of study, in addition to that of intergroup relations.

Trainer Role

The ideal Clarification Group trainer is a person with equal mastery of small group leadership skills and a broad knowledge of those social and behavioral sciences which contribute to an understanding of intergroup relations, past and present. A firm grasp on racial and ethnic politics of the present era would round out the armament of the C Group leader. The need for substance is essential and constitutes a major difference between effective C Group leaders and those who use small-group methodologies for other change purposes. The C Group has didactic components based, if possible, on leads suggested by the trainer or by knowledgeable participants. Misinformation or outright stereotyping tends to influence considerably the individual change process in the C Group and thus the need for appropriate and judicious input. Moreover, the C Group tends to be closer to the classroom learning model than are the other small group methodologies, which are closer to the therapeutic end of the continuum from education to therapy. The following is an example of the deliberate introduction of substantive material designed to inform but also to influence the process.

The C Group discussion centered on the situation in some city universities currently besieged by black and Puerto Rican demands for admission requirements to be based on a quota system rather than on academic achievement. The trainer pointed out that Jews have traditionally been opposed to quotas because quotas have been restrictive to them. Blacks want quotas because these would be in their favor. Jews are not opposed to entrance examinations whereas blacks are. He suggested this might be a conflict of group interests rather than a racial issue.

There was much disagreement in the group as to whether college admission policies are discriminatory to blacks. The Sister thought they were. "One of the problems of the black man is his inability to participate in decision-making within institutions. Unless more and more blacks are in a position to make decisions relative to their destiny, they won't be able to get out of their bag."

Challenging the Sister's comments, the trainer pointed out that neither have white students traditionally participated in the decision-making of educational institutions and suggested that the problem might be broader than this. Certain of the universities under fire have achieved distinction for the top quality of the graduates due in part to their entrance requirements. It is being said that if blacks' and Puerto Ricans' demands are met, these institutions will change and will instead inherit a "mess of pottage." The Jewish psychologist agreed and offered an example from his own experience. Out of forty black students admitted for a special program at his college, eight survived and the rest flunked out. He suggested that the students were selected poorly and that it was a tragedy to admit students who were unequal for college work under the false assumption that it might be less unfair to admit them on the basis of their blackness than on the basis of their credentials. A black man in the group disagreed. "Why must I be kept out of college because I attended your inadequate high school?"

The Lutheran minister said he could only conclude that there was no answer other than separate schools for whites and blacks. He indicated displeasure with his conclusion. The black woman in the group suggested this would indeed be acceptable as long as the schools were of equal quality.

Commenting on research being done in education, the trainer commented that studies such as the Coleman Report have indicated that part of the problem might be due to the possibility that teachers have not really learned how to teach nor to create the climate within a classroom necessary for learning. Instead, they have built upon the motivations brought to them by students from certain socio-economic levels of our society and have reinforced them. Students coming without this built-in motivation, lower class whites as well as lower class blacks, confound their teachers by their inability to profit from educational experiences designed for their more affluent peers. There was some agreement in the group with the black woman reiterating an earlier comment about the importance of early family experiences as a preparation for learning.

Leadership styles of successful C Group trainers differ as much as those employed by T Group trainers. These vary from comparatively non-directive to directive or confrontationist models. The qualification attached to the first label is significant because it is doubtful that a C Group which always demands didactic input can be designated a non-directive experience. Indeed there are some indications that the Rogerian behavioral model is counterproductive in C Groups, where intergroup tensions frequently reach a high emotional pitch. Silence on the part of the trainer at those moments has often added to group suspicion and resistance. The C Group appears to demand, on the contrary, an open self-disclosure leadership model.

C Group experience has demonstrated repeatedly the necessity for the trainer to lead off, establishing a model of openness and definiteness about his own biases. This is an odd but very crucial distinction between C Group trainer behavior and that of, for example, the T Group where self-disclosure by the trainer at the beginning of the group experience may seriously impair the trainer's subsequent usefulness. This is especially true for those T Groups where the transference phenomenon is important to trainer strategy. Transference is too difficult to manage where the initial act of disclosure tends to make the trainer appear to be "a member of the group" with only the disadvantage of that ambiguous role. Additional complications regarding transference and the C Group will be discussed shortly.

To use self-disclosure as part of the training process and still maintain the objective stance of the non-member or special member of the group is a role fraught with difficulties. To negotiate the contradiction successfully requires one to be in far better command of one's own biases than is the usual case. In addition to the two criteria already mentioned: the need for skill in small group leadership and substantial knowledge of substance, the C Group leader must also be thoroughly aware of and in control of his own intergroup prejudices, which almost by necessity include a clear understanding of the influence of his own group identifications. Denial or rejection of the latter will interfere considerably with an effective C Group leadership posture. Undoubtedly, the last requisite may be the most onerous and difficult of all.

Mention has been made of the transference pheonomenon. This is commonly encountered in small group change models, especially therapy groups and almost always in the T Group. There appears to be a minimum manifestation of certain types of transference in the C Group. Trainer behavior, more "normal" than that of the T Group trainer, tends to discourage the growth and maintenance of initial transference feelings. Trainers may often actually discourage discussion of process problems deriving from transference phenomena. Psychological manifestations: projection, displacement, denial, etc., are common but the nature of the phenomenon investigated in the C Group, the social self, appears to change the quality of projectivity usually involved in traditional transference. A typical manifestation of the interaction of transference with the classic psychological defense mechanisms in a C Group setting may help to illustrate the way in which familiar interpersonal and intrapersonal dynamics take on a somewhat different light in a C Group. Often in the initial stage of a C Group when the trainer is actively probing for acknowledgment of cultural prejudice, a participant will deny he has ever had such attitudes. When the trainer continues to probe, a second participant (often of a group background that is racially, religiously, or ethnically polar to that of the first) may then accuse the trainer of being too hard on the first participant. He thus ascribes a motive to the trainer which is in fact a projection of his own unconscious or pre-conscious angry reaction to the first participant. He displaces his anger on the trainer because this serves the dual purpose of aiding his denial of anger, stemming from prejudice toward the first participant, and providing a group legitimate outlet for whatever negative transference toward the trainer he may have developed.

At first, the absence of more explicit transference phenomena was assumed to be a consequence of role-modeling, but closer scrutiny including comparison of somewhat different styles of leadership does not bear out the first hypothesis. The C Group essentially does not become a "family." It should be noted that overt transference manifestations in the psychoanalytic sense, derived from infantile familial relationships, are minimal in the C Group; however substantial "cultural transference," that is, latent attitudes stimulated by the trainer's ethnic and racial identity, does occur and furnishes valuable data for learning. Participants respond to the trainer (as they do to one another, although probably the response is usually heightened by the authority status of the trainer) in terms of their past experiences with persons of group identification similar to those of the trainer.

Process Problems

The surfacing of group process issues in C groups, aside from their side-tracking of C Group major themes, has often complicated the relationship of trainer and group members to the point of derailing the entire enterprise. The significant progression from non-cohesion through cohesion to post-cohesion, which must be based on participant reactions to C Group relevant themes and material, becomes instead a conflict between the trainer and a segment of the group over the legitimacy of excluding idiosyncratic personal data or including legitimate life history material.

As a general rule, three distinct types of resistance develop in C Groups. The first will arise out of the usual process problems familiar to T Group leaders — issue of authority, dependence, and counter-dependence; the second from the need for interpersonal closeness which the process does not encourage; and finally, a set of phenomena directly related to C Group issues and therefore theoretically functional and appropriate to the C Group process. Each of the first two types of resistance provide problems of a different order of difficulty to the C Group trainer and the group, but neither can be said to offer much opportunity for C Group related learning. The working through of the phenomena reflected in the third category is essential to C Group learning. A functional way of dealing with the first two types of resistance will be discussed subsequently. The following are some examples of the third category:

(a) Undoubtedly the unique resistance is that of members of a black subgroup refusing to confront or give feedback to each other; in many cases, caucusing outside the group and deciding to cut to the barest minimum their presentation of family background. This "political" resistance arises from the conviction that whites should begin to examine and study themselves and not use blacks for their education or edification. In one recent experience, the rest of the C Group was constantly being told, "Tell us how you feel to be white. We are tired of telling you what blackness means to us." The fact that very few whites ever have done anything but take their Caucasian state for granted created an impasse for much of the first week.

(b) Members of the dominant group, usually WASPS, have never seen themselves, on some levels at least, as different. This psychological acceptance of being the norm of the society is quite similar to the inability of the whites to see themselves as blacks do. Complicating this resistance is the widespread acceptance of this WASP assessment by many minority group members: Jews, Catholics, and various ethnics. How then can the WASP see himself as a different subgroup, one ethnic among a group of ethnics, if the latter shields the WASP by behaving as if the non-WASPS alone were different?[8] Some WASPS sit in C Groups, smug or bewildered, but genuinely unable to lend themselves to the process.

(c) With other WASPS, however, it is not a naive inability to acknowledge difference, but an intense awareness of threat which poses as ignorance of difference. They are aware of differences, being conversant with their own prejudices or those of their significant reference groups. This subgroup becomes defensive, sometimes resists the process by asking for more "gut level" issues, meaning T Group issues (if this were to really come to pass, they would likely be just as frightened). This subgroup is very much aware of being different, but this awareness is of the common variety associated with simple rejection of the strange and unfamiliar. This difference makes them feel superior, not inferior. There are many Catholics of Anglo-Saxon or West European origins who join with the WASPS in this genuine feeling of superiority, which also spells difference for them. Members of this class of resisters will frequently complain that the trainer or the process creates tensions and conflicts where none really exists.

(d) A poignant type of resistance to the C Group process is presented by those minority group members (often middle-class Jews in the learned professions, as well as comparable middle-class ethnics, Italians, Greeks, Chinese, blacks, etc.) who have papered over the isolating feelings stemming from prior unpleasant experiences and who do not wish to have these uncovered. The resistance of this group presents a complicated problem, for their unwillingness to lend themselves to the process creates an opportunity for Group *C*, which now has an ally from an unexpected source. This resistance alliance usually does not persist for too long, for the frequent revelation of the motivations of Group *C* makes members of Group *D* uncomfortable and even the need for joint defense as whites confronting blacks cannot re-cement the alliance.

(e) Finally, the Clarification Group often has at least one member of either in-group or out-group who has achieved a state of cosmopolitanism where preliminary C Group issues are no longer significant. These persons are ready to move on to Phase II and their impatience to explore what remains of their ethnocentrism is reflected in their behavior. This group, however, reacts to the two preceding phases with good humor, aware that most of the other resisters are marching to other tunes.

As has already been stated, it is only when the resistances are clearly in the realm of challenge to the authority of the trainer or the rationale of the C Group that matters become sticky, for these are not functional to C Group processes. In order to deal effectively with this type of resistance, one would have to create a T Group transaction within the C Group. At least one C Group trainer, Kenneth Benne, is persuaded that a fusion of the two methodologies is essential. It is difficult to accept Benne's position for several reasons. First, legitimizing the discussion of group process issues takes too much time and build-up, thus reducing time more appropriately spent on C Group issues. Second, the focus on interpersonal and intragroup issues very often is an escape from the demands of the C Group, a strategem already mentioned.[9]

The oft-repeated phenomenon of non-functional resistance

within the C Group to the twofold task of learning about one's social self and then about how one regards strangers as a consequence, has at least two causes. The first is the need to develop an integrative connection with a group of strangers. Thus the task of the C Group is perceived as antithetical — it asks for things which will divide people rather than unite them. The second cause comes at a later time in the life of the C Group and is often a manifestation of resistance to the confrontation phase of C Group life. It frequently masquerades as an attempt to get at "deeper" more "gut level" issues than those characterized as less crucial to the group development. An example here may help illustrate the complex interaction between resistance to the intergroup focus and the transference phenomenon. A young white Protestant woman consistently challenged the trainer (the trainer was a WASP), indicating her feeling that he was not helping the group to get at the "real" issues. A young black man in the group was also challenging the trainer's authority, explicitly indicating his unwillingness to talk about his background. As group pressure mounted on the black man not to withhold his participation, the white Protestant woman became highly vocal in challenging the black man. However, when he challenged her in turn, and began to ask whether her reaction to him stemmed from her background, she rapidly backed down and dropped the subject, indicating that this might well be true and was a very helpful question. Counterdependent behavior was also elicited from her by other males in the group. Sometimes her attacks were couched in the context of her identification with women's liberation. She had special difficulty in challenging the black man, more so than in challenging white men in the group.

In a T Group, the trainer would have explored her reaction to authority. In a C Group, the behavior was used as a vehicle for exploring the male-female and black-white dimensions, raising questions as to the meaning of her behavior toward men and her difficulty in confronting the black man as an instance of the dilemma of whites unable to get angry at blacks due to racially associated fear and guilt. Her inconsistent behavior toward the black man had the effect of making her appear to be anxious to move the group forward, while in actuality, her behavior was an avoidance of opening up her racial feelings to exploration, and in effect consisted of an unconscious pairing with the black man in resisting the process. This paradoxical juxtaposition of interpersonal versus intergroup concerns does serve the need to avoid facing the potential intensity of intergroup encounters. Persons can, despite many interpersonal differences, get along in a temporary system such as a laboratory, but persons brought into touch with their latent tribal feelings will have great difficulty in bridging the chasms which frequently appear.

Here one must respect the voices of those who insist on the value of having a group experience which first deals with the interpersonal and then, after a group cohesion has been affected, with the social self. There is the possibility, however, that being subsequently asked to confront tribal differences may cause many to feel that the initial T Group methodological emphasis was a shell game. They may feel that they had been euchered into acceptance of each other without being confronted with the need to accept with the other person the full meaning of their differences.[10]

Human beings in our society or others generally do not band together to exterminate each other on the basis of presumed personal psychological traits, but history and the present era is replete with the instances of ferocious hatred or violence stimulated by religious, tribal, or national differences. In fact, the potentialities for these conflicts are in all likelihood more deeply rooted in the unconscious than is social class conflict, which has been heretofore the most highly publicized universal confrontation.

Personal Growth

The C Group does not achieve or attempt to achieve the degree of personal insight as do small group processes such as group therapy and its variants, or even the T Group in its less classical and more psychological forms. Some personal changes do occur, however, and these vary from the acceptance of one's primary group origins, to the diminution of non-rational hostile feelings toward members of groups other than one's own. Although the returns are not in by any means, it has become quite clear to those involved in the direction of C Groups that one can anticipate a coming to terms with one's own background and a reduction of denials about negative feelings toward other persons with different backgrounds. Parenthetically, this acceptance of the influence of one's social self can be devoid of ethnocentrism as far as one can tell with the naked eye. Protocol material for four cases involving a Lutheran, a WASP, a Catholic Nun, and a black male are offered as examples of what has been achieved through a C Group experience. A fifth case, involving a young Jew, is summarized; comparable protocol material is not available at this time.

The Lutheran was born in the Middle West of Scandinavian parents. Their circumstances were mean, and the often unlovely strategems of the poor became identified in his mind with his subgroup, causing him to reject both parents and their background. This rejection took classical forms including the development of behavioral norms, values, speech, etc., which were polar to those of his parents. Marriage to a WASP with a native American background and thoroughly middle class completed the 180-degree reaction. During the C Group experience, after personal resistance from the Lutheran consisting of insistent demands for T Group interaction, the breakthrough finally took the following turn:

The Lutheran Minister commented that for the first time in his life, someone at the laboratory had referred to him as a WASP. "I don't understand why, I really haven't put myself in that role." Another participant suggested that perhaps he had. The minister went on to say that he felt in a minority for the first time, suggesting that what happened to him was occurring in three stages. He described these as (1) not wanting to look at differences, (2) conceding intellectually that perhaps the trainer was right in stressing their importance, and (3) suddenly "bombing" the night he felt the negative response of the group toward him. He suggested he felt in a minority because of "personality factors," explaining that he had grown up in a Norwegian-German community, had gone to a Lutheran College and a Lutheran Seminary, had moved to the Dakotas to an almost all Norwegian, all American-Lutheran community, and had served, ". . . in the biggest church in town which was attended by all the important people." He spoke of his father as being all Norwegian but said he had found it difficult to identify with him because of his accent which many people found amusing.

There was some discussion about the reputation Norwegians have for hard drinking to the point of frenzy and how this detracts from their work orientation, which is the antithesis of Calvinism. The Lutheran minister suggested his father was a WASP in this respect, although his grandfather had been a drunk and had behaved "in the way Norwegians fear." He suggested that in rejecting the grandfather's behavior, the father had taken on the WASP mentality regarding work. The minister added that he, too, valued the importance of work.

Another participant remarked that the Lutheran had taken such apparent glee earlier in the Laboratory when he described himself as different from the other participants in that he did not need to acknowledge differences. She pointed out to him that he had a background of his own, he found it easier to deny that of others. She added that though the minister has said that his father has assumed the WASP mentality, she had gathered from what he had said earlier that his father had not achieved WASP respect.

The trainer asked the Lutheran if his parents had rejected their Norwegian heritage. He replied that his mother had but his father ". . . is not bright enough to reject it . . . too stupid to reflect on it." The trainer remarked on the minister's use of the word "stupid," suggesting that if one were to ask the participants here to distinguish among Norwegians, Swedes, Germans, and WASPs, the majority might make no distinction between Norwegians and WASPs. The minister reflected that he probably felt resentful about his being designated a WASP. The trainer asked him if this were because he had not enjoyed the WASP advantages. The minister, voice rising in volume and hand pounding on the table in emphasis, referred again to the experiences of his youth, of his family all having accents, all being farm people and poor people.

The Jew was a somewhat similar case, but here the complication was that, because of appearance and social class upbringing, he had passed as a WASP during college and afterwards. Passing is an American phenomenon not restricted to Jews by any means. Blacks have frequently passed as a means of self-protection and a desire to evade societal restrictions. The need to pass illustrates in a dark way the stratagems which out-group members use to cope with our endemic group exclusiveness! What happens psychologically to those who have to live in constant denial of who they are is not pleasant to contemplate. No great insight into good mental health is necessary to encourage an end to this practice. For a Jew (as well as some minority groups) passing is seen as a rejection of themselves and brings a hostile response from them as well as guilt feelings to the passer. The blacks until recently have been in a different position because their own group saw this as the ultimate retaliation against an oppressive majority.

To return to the Jew: his C Group experience required a disclosure first of his true origin, and secondly, a description of his personal accommodation. Fellow Jews in the group reacted typically, not with sympathy and understanding, but with hostility. The non-Jews reacted with a mixture of shame for their "responsibility" for the exclusionary state of affairs as well as some feelings about being tricked. Caught in such a bind, the Jew could only make peace with both groups by a genuine acceptance of his own roots. This has continued until now, more than a year after the redemption experience.

The WASP (Methodist), a counselor in a Jewish setting, was unable and unwilling to consider that his own background and subgroup influences (like those of an ethnic) were responsible for his likes and dislikes, his values, norms of behavior, etc. WASPS encountered in C Groups typically cannot see themselves in ethnic terms unless they have been resident for a period of time in a predominantly Catholic or Jewish or other explicitly ethnic setting. Everyone else but the WASP is different; an outsider, a foreigner. To a significant degree, this is an accurate assessment of the historic realities of our society. The C Group as a microcosm emphasizes again and again that, for the WASP and the non-WASP to come to terms, all subgroups must see themselves in ethnic group terms; thus equalizing their experiences and creating a new and more equal level of discourse. Pertinent excerpts from the protocol material follow:

The trainer asked the WASP what anti-black or anti-Semitic feelings he had. He replied that he was not sure but that when he had gone home that weekend, he had wondered to what extent he had been trying to make Jews over into Gentiles by trying to institute athletic programs at the university with which he was affiliated.

He added that he had told himself that to be athletic was healthful but was now questioning his motivations. He felt he had worked through much of his Negro prejudices but could not be sure about the Jews or the Catholics.

The WASP continued by saying that "this sickness" was directed toward other minority groups and that ". . . Jews were considered okay as long as they were Christians." He added that he had always had funny feelings about Jews and that he was not sure about Catholics. When Kennedy was President, he remembered joining his family in saying that the Pope was now running the country. When Kennedy died, he had not felt anything, and was angry with his wife because she had cried. He added that, subsequent to Kennedy's death, he had written numerous papers on the assassination as a cultural phenomenon, further adding, "I don't know how much of this I've really dealt with. My wife has helped me a great deal this way."

The next day, the WASP started the group session by announcing, "There's a new ethnic group on the scene: the WASP." The night before he had been struck by the realization that this was not a WASP group. He had realized also that his experience at the predominantly Jewish university had tended to segregate him as a WASP. He recalled being asked at the university about his group affiliation and reported that he had replied that he had none. He acknowledged that, at that time, he was unaware of any group affiliation, but now he was aware and also recognized what this meant. He added that he had been struck by two things here: his difficulty in getting into the group and not knowing how and also the "weakness of the WASP" in terms of his never having had the kinds of experiences mentioned by some of the blacks and the Jews in the group. "I can't feel strong in terms of these kinds of things." He recalled walking around as a kid with his fists doubled up and a chip on his shoulder; angry at the world. He suggested, however, that the fences he had to climb ". . . were never so high nor so hostile" as those referred to by other members of the group.

One of the black participants suggested that not only were the fences he had to climb less high and less hostile, but survival was not an issue as it is with minority groups. The WASP admitted that he had never experienced feelings associated with survival but had experienced the difficulty of gaining acceptance in situations where he felt he was an outsider.

The Catholic was a nun, active in race relations and vigilantly insistent that she harbored no prejudices. Hers appeared to be a classical reaction formation, managing unconscious hostilities by opposite behavior. Her relationship with blacks in a group was thus poisoned by the double messages emanating from her. Most of the blacks, sensitive to surface sweetness and underlying hostility, treated her in a gingerly fashion at first, and then more roughly. Not too surprisingly, those blacks who had spent their lives denying their own blackness were most eager and ready to accept the counterfeit coin she offered. Some excerpts from these encounters will illustrate points already made.

The sister introduced herself to the group during the first session as a religious woman of Irish origin currently in community work and no stranger to prejudice, either religious, racial, or ethnic. She added that she knew she could take off her habit (she wore secular dress during the laboratory), but that the blacks could not take off their skins.

During the next session, a black woman remarked on the inability of some whites who take the time of a group such as this to inquire as to its purpose while the blacks feel an urgency to get things done. She indicated that perhaps blacks were attempting to go faster than they needed, but she felt at the same time that whites should be aware of their tendency to dawdle. The sister, apparently accepting this indictment as applicable to herself, commented that perhaps part of her own problem stemmed from the fact that she came from "structure." She marveled at how a black friend of hers could more fully experience new situations in which he found himself than she could, suggesting that perhaps he could enter them without any preconceived notions of what would occur.

During the next session, the religious were once more targeted for holding themselves aloof from the group, this time by another of the black participants, who added that only the sister had participated to any great extent. Under her breath and outside of the sister's range of hearing, a black woman muttered, "Just because she's talking doesn't mean she's in touch."

The black woman said she felt the sister held stereotyped notions about the behavior of black women in general and sensed that the sister had been disappointed to find that she, as a black woman, did not fit the stereotype.

The discussion then turned to some of the ways in which

minority group members are discriminated against and also how sometimes minority group members are capable of hurting each other. Joining in this discussion, the black woman contributed an example from her own experiences, but managed in an oblique way to score a direct and somewhat unexpected hit on the sister during the process. The black woman said she was prepared for the kind of hurt she got from the sister, ". . . that kind of patronizing, over-complimentary manner of approach. The kind of approach that suggests I'm black, but I'm okay. I expect that. But I'm less prepared for the kind of attack I get from the Negro male when I least expect it."

It was not until the second week of the laboratory that the sister asked for some time to explore the reasons why she came across in a way that had led to the black woman's ". . . pounding me about my strong prejudices against blacks." She suggested that what she might feel was not prejudice so much as guilt, mentioning that she had reacted very strongly at the time of Martin Luther King's death.

Reflecting on the black woman's response to her, the sister said she had experienced similar problems with other Negro women. She suggested that she has too strong a tendency to want to say something nice to people in order to please. She wondered if this might have been one of her problems, as it was easy for her to give to people in this way, but she became uncomfortable when they began to reciprocate. She wondered further if she might really not trust people and thus unconsciously act in the way she does in order to keep them at a distance. Perhaps her choice of religious life as a vocation was to some extent influenced by this.

The black was a professional in the community relations field with personal experience and convictions reinforced by the current Black Power mood. His interventions were confrontationist in style. Any questioning of black motives was immediately challenged; no concession to the whites was allowed. He also attempted to coerce other blacks in the group to maintain a solid front against the trainer and the other participants. In this case, he was not successful. A massive confrontation by the trainer became necessary to pierce his shield of denial. The protocol material follows:

The black participant introduced himself to the group by announcing, "I'm Black and Beautiful!" In an aside to the recorder, he added, "Be sure to write that down." He went on to identify himself as a psychiatric social worker who found he could not be promoted because he would then be supervising whites. (There were sympathetic "hmmmms" from some of the white participants accompanied by affirmative head nodding.) He added that he had then discovered ". . . politics in the black community" (more "hmmms") and spoke of his work with the government and his interest in making the black community more viable, so that its people might be on a more "... equal footing with their white brothers." He expressed concern about "... the white racism in our institutions," adding that he had come to the laboratory on one of many forays in search of answers for his concerns, but doubted that he would find them here.

Later in the session, the black remarked on the inequities which exist in a white society and which need to be taken care of. He recalled a recent personal experience when he had been denied service in a restaurant and another when an airline stewardess had ignored his request for a glass of water, "... because I'm black, and besides, I was sporting a beard and a wild shirt at the time." The trainer questioned this last assumption, suggesting that he himself might have been ignored had he boarded an airliner in such a get-up. The black chuckled and commented, "Maybe so, but at least let me have my own paranoid feelings." Into the laughter which broke out, the trainer commented that it was just such fantasies which he would challenge in this group. The black remarked that he had had so much experience with prejudice, that he had internalized it to the point that he assessed situations in which he found himself and frequently made the judgment that he was about to become the victim of a discriminatory practice.

The trainer suggested that blacks were sometimes criticized because they expect to be discriminated against and often create the conditions wherein their expectations are fulfilled. He asked the black if he could differentiate between those situations in which he was actually being discriminated against and those in which he was not, explaining that this was what was meant when he said he would not let this participant indulge in his "paranoia." The black admitted that this was one of the safeguards he had and agreed that it might be considered a form of defensive behavior. The trainer asked if this type of crutch was necessary for all blacks at this particular time. Another black participant replied by suggesting that it probably was not, but that the need for such a crutch on the part of some blacks might be another manifestation of black insecurity.

During a subsequent session in response to a comment about anger, the black said he had been struck by the glaring absence within this group, and also within others in which he had participated, of white anger. He suggested whites had been willing to view black anger, "... to put the blacks on the operating table," but were not willing to confront what he viewed as the real problem: "black anger is the product of white society. I want to hear what the whites expect to do to make restitution for this."

The trainer remarked that the black might need to recognize

that whites have certain imperatives that he as a black person does not have and that more and more, whites will have to do their own thing. He added that whites who think they can do only what the blacks tell them to do will become separated from their own community. The black commented appreciatively that when the trainer said things such as this, he could see him as being helpful. It is not often that blacks are helpful to each other because they tend to be overly concerned. He felt it to be important for people to question each other with the intent of helping each other to see things more clearly. He suggested that so many whites are so concerned with how they express themselves to blacks that they end up not being helpful at all.

The case of the Lutheran and the Jew belong in the category of escapist behavior. To help the two to stop escaping; face reality and accept themselves for what they had been and are, were two clear examples of helpful personal growth which probably had a good chance to endure long beyond the lab experience. The WASP's conversion to a recognition of equal ethnicity may or may not prevail. One must continue to doubt the psychic and social rewards for a member of the majority to continue looking at himself as another minority. One would have to continue to work at it, to make the insights stick. The changing nature of intergroup relations, however, may produce social forces to maintain this new equilibrium.

A better chance for continuation of the change does exist for the Catholic. The elimination of reactive behavior brings some reduction of intra-psychic conflict, and greater acceptance by the very group whom one has been trying to reach by previously learned dysfunctional behavior. Parenthetically, an "automatic liberal" behavior syndrome appears to be quite common among clerics of all faiths who enter C Groups. This phenomenon deserves a separate discussion beyond the limits of this chapter.

The experience of the black emphasizes an issue which has already been alluded to. C Groups are very difficult to manage and learning is reduced if any subgroup decides to act as a non-participative caucus. A typical black strategy is to agree outside the group never to give negative feedback to each other and to deny that they are there to afford a learning experience to the whites. Whenever this common front appears, it must be dealt with openly because it reduces the learning potential for all members. This aspect of resistance, a unique phenomenon, has yet to be successfully confronted. As previously stated, this deserves further investigation and experimentation. For the black, in this instance, his strategy failed, and paradoxically, his learning may have been benefited.

Short Term C Group

The C Group process in an attenuated or truncated form has been used on numerous occasions with selected personnel from institutions involved in an organizational improvement or development process. A description of this use is given in Thomas Cottle's "Strategy for Change."[11] It is based on several days of observation and study of a Bristol Township School System training session. Later, similar two-day events were incorporated into organizational improvement designs for a very large urban school system and a 20,000 population suburban system. In both systems, a diminution of teacher tensions and a significant increase in willingness to deal openly with intergroup issues followed.

The C Group is particularly applicable where improvement in an organization or in community relations wherever a direct focus of the C Group on those group identifications which are central to organizational and community problems is needed, thus providing a clearly job-related rationale for its use. A modified C Group consistently related to on-the-job problems avoids some of the pitfalls accompanying the use of other small group processes in organization development. The C Group deals primarily with subject matter which is public knowledge or with personal material related to matters shared by members of groups. It does not deal with idiosyncratic, personal material and therefore does not tend to be as subject to controversies over the right of an organization to ask its personnel to undergo such personal revealing experience. In addition, it avoids opening wounds among people who must work together on a day-to-day basis.

The C Group, outside the lab setting, has been offered three times as part of the Practicum in Human Relations at the Center for Applied Social Science, Boston University. The three seminars resulted first in a moderate success; the second was a near failure, and the third, a highly successful experience. The first two were six-week offerings with three hours per session. Evaluative comments on the twelve-week Practicum are available. It appears possible to conduct a reasonably good short course in intergroup relations by combining interaction-intensifying exercises developed at the Community Lab, and a judicious input of theory and research data.

All C Groups benefit enormously from heterogeneous group composition. If the group composition is lacking in significant ethnic, racial, and religious membership, it may make the task of the instructor so difficult as to raise questions concerning the desirability of this format for teaching intergroup relations. An experimental form of C Group, meeting two hours a week for fourteen weeks, is currently being offered to seniors in Boston University's School of Nursing. If the experiment proves successful, it will open up other possibilities for use in other professional schools within the helping professions.

C Group Process as Teaching Methodology

A combination of selected personal history data, didactic input, and student readings has been utilized in teaching seminars in social class and social stratification. These have been uniformly successful. The group composition of the seminars was a significant factor, both groups had a range of social classes from upper-lower to upper-middle. Lecture input and selected reading were used to fill in the social class lacunae — upper class and lower-lower. The process was an extremely meaningful one for the students. The investigation of social self — in this case, one's own social class — incorporated the students into the teaching-learning transaction, and made the cognitive input more personally relevant. A similar procedure can be utilized whenever the life experience of the student makes him simultaneously both student and informant; learner and teacher. It should not be too difficult to experiment in this fashion with classes in adolescent psychology and child psychology, values and ethics, illness and death (for nurses), patient care (for doctors), etc. The absence of the affective component in the teaching of disciplines where affect is otherwise all-present may be the most persuasive argument for this method of teaching. A useful technique and process to create the ambience necessary for success in this type of instruction is the *Structured Group Interview* which has been described elsewhere.[12]

Conclusion

The search for effective small group change processes has been stimulated from its inception by the existence of various societal as well as individual problems. Our endemic problem of intergroup relations has always been high on the agenda of social need. It is not surprising, therefore, that the search for solutions to racial and religious impasses indirectly led to the establishment in 1947 of Bethel and the T Group via its precursor — the New Britain Workshop in 1946.[13] The same impetus created the Rutgers Workshop in Human Relations and the early beginnings of the C Group, the year Bethel began. Unlike the T Group, however, the long-range impact of the C Group experience on individuals and on institutions has as yet not been surveyed systematically. The development of effective evaluation instruments and procedures to assess this impact is now high on the agenda of the Boston University Human Relations Laboratory.

FOOTNOTES AND REFERENCES

1. All citations from C Group case material have been especially prepared for this chapter by Professor Irene Allard of Boston University. These have been drawn from extensive original protocol material prepared by her in the course of the Third Annual Laboratory in Community Relations and Community Development (now Community Dynamics) in 1969. A volume on the Clarification Group based on this and other C Group protocols is being prepared for publication by the writer and Professor Allard as co-authors.

Other protocol material has been supplied by Dr. James Small and Professor Kenneth Benne. Dr. Small's editorial contributions to this chapter merit special mention.

2. National Education Television; released December, 1967.

3. See Irwin Rubin, "The Reduction of Prejudice Through Laboratory Training," in *Journal of Applied Behavioral Science*, Vol. 3, No. 1, pp. 28-50, for an inconclusive single study asserting the contrary. Rubin's study, oddly enough, was based on data gathered at Osgood Hill. Two of the T Group trainers whose groups were part of the study were Kenneth Benne's and mine.

4. Letter from Dr. Donald Klein to Dr. Richard Wagner of Bucknell University, October 29, 1968.

5. James Small and Max Birnbaum, "Structured Group Interview" in *Training and Development Journal*, September, 1971, pp. 26-32.

6. Questions taken from a short description of the C Group prepared by Dr. James Small, Associate Director of the Boston University Laboratory in Human Relations.

7. For documentation of the significance of group cohesion in small group change process, see Dorwin Cartwright and Alvin Zander, *Group Dynamics, Research and Theory*, pp. 73-121, 263-264. Row, Peterson and Co.; Evanston, Illinois, 1953.

8. Compare this with Gerald Suttle's experience in Chicago, where in an Italian stronghold, situated adjacent to three other ethnic turfs, he was considered an object of pity because he could not be located in any of the known categories of difference. Gerald D. Suttles, "Anatomy of a Chicago Slum," in *Transaction, 4*, 1969, pp. 16-25.

9. Experience at the Boston University Laboratory in Community Relations and Community Dynamics during the Summer of 1972, suggests a possible solution to the dilemma. This involves scheduling an all-lab-community group process in which trainers would deal with classic encounters in T Group development, especially issues of authority, dependent and counterdependent behavior, and other traditional T Group member resistance behaviors. These all-lab-community sessions might profitably include theoretical input on C Group methodology emphasizing the rationale for isolating and concentrating on one facet of human development, the influence of the social self.

10. See page 342, Dr. Donald Klein's letter.

11. *Saturday Review*, September 20, 1969.

12. See footnote No. 5.

13. Lippitt, Ronald, *Training in Community Relations*, New York; Harper and Row, 1948.

CHAPTER 16

PSYCHODRAMA AND ROLE-PLAYING IN GROUP WORK

*Hilarion Petzold**

HISTORICAL DEVELOPMENT

Since ancient times, dramatic performance has been used as an instrument for education (Coggin, 1956; Hausmann, 1959) and therapy (Barrucand, 1971). Springing from the cultic celebrations of Dionysus, the theater in Greek and Roman antiquity and in the Byzantine and Western middle ages acquired, along with its cultic character, an educative function which found its clearest expression in the didactic-instructive religious play and the Latin school drama of the sixteenth century (Kindermann, Vol. II). The drama was not always the finished work of an author presented by professional actors for the spectators, but rather, in its medieval forms, drew in the audience and made them fellow actors on the common stage of the market place or church nave (Duvignaud, 1965).

The sociodramatic character of the educative drama was lost with the institutionalization of the theater and with the separation of actors and audience by the Renaissance Terentian stage. The educational character of the theater was reduced to an instructional process; its one-way communication turned the spectator into a passive receiver of the presentation. The creative interaction among all involved in the performance continued only in the improvisational plays of the touring companies, the offshoots of the *Commedia del arte*, and in the shrovetide plays. We repeatedly

---

*We acknowledge with gratitude the services of Dr. Daniel Papero, Vanderbilt University, in translating the first draft of this chapter from German to English.

encounter the dramatic performance as a therapeutic instrument in the histories of the theater and of medicine. The psychiatric textbooks of the eighteenth and nineteenth centuries record attempts to cure the mentally ill with the help of theatrical performances, apparently based on medieval practices (Petzold, Schmidt, 1972). Reil (1803, 209 ff.) states in his outline of a "psychic cure method" that the patient must repeatedly be confronted in the various phases of treatment with dramatic procedures which he takes in at first passively but with growing attention and in which he should finally participate himself as an active performer with the progressive improvement of his condition.

The theater presentations of the Marquis de Sade at the beginning of the nineteenth century, which he staged with patients during his internment in the psychiatric clinic at Charenton, took a similar direction (Schutzenberger, 1966). Systematic attempts to use the theater's potential for pedagogical and therapeutic purposes were first made, however, in the late nineteenth and early twentieth centuries. Three sources should be mentioned above all.

Russian Theater Experiments. The theater experiments in Russia by Stanislavski and his students Sulershitzski and Vachtangov, who are said to have taken their point of departure from the great sociodramatic actions of the revolutionary theater (Ruhle, 1963). Yevreinov and Meyerhold should be named here, too. Vachtangov wrote in 1918: "We must portray the rebellious spirit of the people . . . it would be good if someone would write a piece with no individual roles. Only the masses would appear in all acts." These ideas were realized in largely improvised mass presentations in which up to 10,000 soldiers of the Red Army participated (Ruhle, 1963).

Iljine's Therapeutic Theater. A second source is the experiments of the Russian professors, Vladimir Iljine and Basilius Zenkovski, who in Kiev in the years 1909-1917 used improvised theater and drama within a pre-arranged frame for the treatment of the mentally ill (Iljine, 1909, 1910, 1942) and for the instruction of students (Zenkovski, 1935); they thus developed the "therapeutic" and "didactic" theater. They were doubtlessly influenced by contemporary theater experiments, for example, Gorki's plays (Petzold/Schmidt, 1972, 27).

Ferenczi's Analytic Role Play. A third source is the psychoanalytical role play of Sandor Ferenczi. S. Freud had already dealt with "psychopathological characters on the stage" in a study written in 1904 — it remained a private possession for more than thirty years and was only finally published in 1948. Although Freud clearly points out the therapeutic possibilities of the drama, he never returned to this approach. Ferenczi, on the other hand, did not stop with fragmentary notes on the theater (for example,

Bausteine III, 55) but used role plays in his "active technique" in the early nineteen twenties, as clearly described in the case of the Croatian singer (Bausteine, II, 67-74).

These attempts remained on the fringe or were forgotten, like the analytic role play of Ferenczi. Stanislavski's impulses have found continuance in recent years with Grotovski (1968) and in many off-off-Broadway experimental theaters. Iljine and Zenkovski finally were able to continue their work in Paris with a small circle in the Russian immigre colony (Zenkovski, 1935; Petzold, Iljine, Zenkovski, 1972).

The Psychodrama of Moreno

The attempt to win overall recognition of the scenic drama as an instrument of therapy and pedagogy is found in the early theater experiments of J. L. Moreno in the early nineteen twenties. Moreno, who was born in 1892 in Rumania and studied philosophy and medicine in Vienna, reports from his childhood that as a four-year-old he had led theater performances of neighborhood children (Leutz, 1967). The actual origin of the psychodrama is to be found in the plays which as a young medical student Jakob Levy Moreno put on with children in the gardens of Vienna. By observing the childish plays, Moreno found the elements of his later psychodramatic therapy: spontaneous improvisation, scenic portrayal, and creative solutions to conflicts, role taking, role reversal, and role play (Moreno, 1968).

Moreno's later theater experiments are clearly marked by these spontaneous plays with children; one of his early theater manifestos, "Die Gottheit als Komodiant," bears the sub-title "Children's Stage 1911" ("Kinderbuhne," 1911). The "Rede vor dem Richter," 1925, also makes this connection clear. "In the year 1923 in the hall of the *Stegreiftheater* I was endeavoring to try out a sort of social play with adults — a recollection of hundreds of children who knew how to amuse themselves in this splendid fashion before the war in the public gardens. Talks and conversations took place, which, at the least, revealed the idea of the theater."

In the *Stegreiftheater*, which Moreno founded in 1921 in the Maysedergasse of Vienna, the psychodramatic techniques, like the "living newspaper" as an improvised processing of the day's events, and the sociodrama were born. The Viennese *Stegreiftheater* must therefore be considered one of the most important roots of modern group work and group psychotherapy.

Moreno's experiments, which continued after his emigration to the U.S.A. in 1925 in New York performances of the "living newspaper," had, to be sure, a clear psychotherapeutic orientation but also a strong pedagogical and socio-therapeutic accent. The latter is revealed in Moreno's suggestion for sociometrically organizing a refugee camp at Mittendorf near Vienna where he served as a doctor. In 1934, he used socio-therapeutic oriented psychodrama in his classical sociometric work with a reform school at Hudson, N.Y., which he transformed into a "therapeutic community" with the help of sociometry and psychodrama. The founding of the first psychodrama theater in Beacon, N.Y., in 1936, and of the Psychodrama Institute in New York in 1942, has turned out to be extraordinarily fruitful for the development of psychodrama, sociodrama, role play, group dynamics — in short, for psychological group work in general.

Moreno's creative *elan* and the multiplicity of his ideas have inspired and stimulated numerous theoreticians and practitioners to develop further his approaches or to go their own ways. Thus, for example, psychological group work and human relations education were advanced by three men who incorporated insights and techniques of Moreno into their basic orientation to the concepts of Kurt Lewin, the philosophy of John Dewey, and the profession of adult education. Ronald Lippitt, Kenneth D. Benne, and Leland P. Bradford experimented with psychodrama, sociodrama, role play, and sociometry in the nineteen forties (Lippitt, 1943, 1947; Bradford, Benne, Lippitt, 1947) as they applied Lewin's concepts in the development of laboratory education.

Alvin Zander (1947), Alex Bavelas (1947), and numerous other social scientists who were trained in social psychology and group work incorporated some insights and techniques of Moreno into their professional work. Moreno also exerted a fruitful influence on men like F. S. Perls. Most schools and forms of psychodrama, sociodrama, and role playing have been inspired and influenced by J. L. Moreno. Nonetheless, there are numerous types which reveal an independent approach.

The "therapeutic theater," as employed by V. N. Iljine in 1909 in his work with psychic patients and from which he developed the "didactic theater" in collaboration with B. Zenkovski at approximately the same time, proceeds from a frame which determines the structure of the event and provides room for free improvisation. In the therapeutic theater the frame is written by the therapist focusing on conflict identified through anamnesis for the particular situation of the patient. In the didactic theater the group itself writes the frame play. They work out a theme together which is relevant to all members. This theme is formed into a frame play which is realized in the following performance. The performance is then analyzed, and, from the insight gained, a new play is written. For pedagogical tasks, the "didactic theater" offers not only an instrumentarium for developing creativity and for joining cognitive and affective learning, but also the opportunity jointly to acquire and transmit information in a fascinating manner (Petzold, Iljine, Zenkovski, 1972).

Fritz Perls, within the framework of the Gestalt therapy developed by him, used elements of psychodrama to clarify Gestalt—therapeutic processes. Perls rejects the use of auxiliary egos and the double technique in order to exclude possible projections of other group participants in the therapeutic process (Perls, 1969). The protagonist assumes all roles in the performance himself. An empty chair is his interaction partner. Alongside the role play, Gestalt therapy uses a sort of "internal psychodrama." In dialogues between feelings and scenes from dreams, conflict (open psychic Gestalt) is identified, acted out, and the emotional Gestalt closed.

George Kelly's *Psychology of Personal Constructs* (1956) is one of the few works which presents an original anthropology and theory of the personality along with a diagnostic and therapeutic instrumentarium as well (Rillaer, 1969/70). Kelly assigns decisive significance to the personal constructs as they are expressed in the behavior of the individual. The therapeutic activity begins with an assessment of the constructs, with a sort of role inventory, from which a "fixed role" is developed for the patient which he consequently has to act out over several weeks (Bonarius, 1967). For this period of time he assumes the role of another personality with the goal of breaking through rigid role cliches, experiencing behavioral alternatives, and drilling new ways of behaving. Kelly's "Fixed Role Therapy," which he has been developing with his colleagues since 1939, is inspired by Moreno but has developed both in theory and practice into an independent form of therapy.

Sociodrama was developed by J. L. Moreno as a socio-pedagogical and socio-therapeutic instrument (Moreno, 1943, 1947) to deal with problems going beyond the individual situation. The sociodrama is divided into a warm-up and planning phase, in which the goal of the performance and its realization are planned, a performance phase and a socio-analysis, as a result of which strategies for social change can be developed and tried out in the performance (Petzold, 1973). In the socio-analysis, the social conditionings of the situations, the connections between social groups and the social roles within a group are investigated (Lippitt, Bradford, Benne, 1947).

Hypnodrama was developed by Moreno and Jim Enneis (1950). A protagonist is hypnotized and in this state acts out his conflicts. The technique is suited to the working through of dream content (Wollman, 1967), for reducing resistance and for the treatment of highly inhibited patients. The hypnodramatic technique is cultivated particularly in Japan (Naruse, 1967). Petzold (1971, 1974) and Greenberg (1974) have further developed the hypnodramatic procedure so that the entire group is hypnotized and acts under hypnosis, a procedure which has proved particularly useful in the treatment of drug addicts.

Ferenczi's analytic role play has not remained the only form associating dramatic performance and psychoanalysis. In France various schools of analytic psychodrama have been formed. Lebovici and colleagues (1958, 1972) represent the position that in the psychodrama, the most important therapeutic factor is transference, which is clarified by the performance. But only the analytic "interpretations of the psychodramatic happening turn this form of therapy into more than an acting out or a symbolic wish realization" (Lebovici, 1972). Anzieu (1956; 1969/70) and his school incorporate more strongly the concept of role theory into the analytic work. They see interpretations indeed important but not as indispensable. Special variations of the analytic psychodrama are practiced by Paul and Genie Lemoine (1973), Petzold (1969), Friedemann (1972), and Widlocher (1961).

This is based on Moreno's triadic concept of group psychotherapy, sociometry, and psychodrama and attempts to connect these three elements. In the French model of the triadic psychodrama (Schutzenberger, 1968; 1969/70; Petzold, 1971; 1973) this occurs by combining with each other the scenic performance, group dynamic setting, and group analytical method in order that the potential of the methods named are integrated. In practice, the sessions take place in such a way that either the group dynamic, analytic, or psychodramatic activity is being emphasized at any one time.

The tetradic psychodrama was formulated by Petzold (1971). It is divided into four phases: 1. the diagnostic-anamnestic phase in which the conflict of the patient is psychodramatically remembered and diagnosed; 2. the psychocathartic phase in which conflictive situations are acted out with the goal of facilitating an emotional experience (repeating); 3. the analytic-communicative phase provides for sharing, that is, the emotional communication of group members among themselves as well as feedback about the preceding performance (the latter is given verbally or by performance [psychodynamic aspect]) and, furthermore, is investigated from the perspective of learning theory. The goal is rational insight (working through); 4. drawing from the emotional experience and rational insight a direct consequence which is expressed in the formulation and drill of new behavior (change) (Petzold, Schulwitz, 1972).

Behavior drama was developed by Petzold (1969, 1971) through the consequent application of learning theory principles as a form of behavior-therapeutic role play. Systematic desensitization occurs in situational performances arranged hierarchically

(Petzold, Osterhues, 1972) or assertive training is practiced. Through demonstration performances of situations the possibility for imitation learning is given (Bandura, 1968). By repeat performances of situations, desired behavior is rewarded, undesired behavior ignored (in order to extinguish it) or punished.

The various forms of role play were developed chiefly in the United States during the nineteen forties and fifties primarily for three areas: therapy, pedagogy, and organizational training programs. Lippitt (1943), Bradford and Benne (1946, 1947), Bavelas (1947), and Maier (1952) developed role play techniques to train leaders and instruct personnel in industry, finance, and government. Such role play techniques stimulated further development by Francks (1959), Corsini, Shaw, Blake (1961), and by Peters and Phelan (1959) among others. Essentially, all have a didactic and behavior-modifying character. They are intended on the one hand to make patterns of social behavior clear and on the other to drill behavior alternatives.

The pedagogically oriented role play has similar goals. For "reality practice" (Zander, Lippitt, 1944) and for the clarification of interpersonal relations, role plays have great value in the teaching situtions. As a rule they are conducted on the basis of pre-established themes (Chesler, Fox, 1966). In this way the therapeutic variables of role play are reduced to a minimum and are in all cases easily controlled. In addition, subject matter can be directly conveyed. Due to the pre-established themes, role plays need less intensive warm-up since they produce no resistance as is often the case in the therapeutic process. Alongside Chesler and Fox, George and Fannie Shaftel (1967) particularly have worked with pedagogical role play. The Shaftels' approach consists of reading stories which present a particular social situation for which a solution must be found. The group must then complete the "problem stories" by continuing them in a performance.

The theorems of learning and social psychology essentially form the theoretical foundation of the pedagogical-didactic role play as employed in industry and teaching. Learning-, role- and communication theory have served to explain the processes occurring in role play (Learning theory: Scott, 1957, 1959; Sturm, 1965; Petzold, 1971, 1972. Role theory: Sarbin, Allen, 1964; Biddle, Thomas, 1966). Theories which have been strongly influenced by the scientific study of the role play itself also have been influential: the theory of cognitive dissonance (Festinger, Carlsmith, 1957); and incentive theory (Janis, Gilmore, 1965). Indeed, the conflict between these two social psychological schools lay largely in their varying explanations of role play (Elms, 1969). At the root of the therapeutic role play lie various psychotherapeutic theories. Corsini (1966), in his handbook, *Role Playing in Psycho-*

therapy, refers to Moreno's theory of creativity and concepts of role theory — he speaks of "role therapy." Sarbin (1945) also bases his explanation of therapeutic process on role theory. Solomon and Fentress (1947), Bromberg (1958), and Derblovsky (1969), among others, have used role play in analytic psychotherapy, O'Connell (1963), Shoobs (1956, 1964) in Adlerian psychotherapy. Even Rogers' school (Goodman, 1962) and behavior therapy (Wolpe, Lazarus, 1966) have included role play in their arsenal of treatment techniques.

APPLICATION AREAS OF PSYCHODRAMA, SOCIODRAMA, AND ROLE PLAY

There are probably no procedures in psychological group work which have been applied in such various areas as have psychodrama, sociodrama, and role play. The number and variability of the techniques are as much responsible for this as their reality-related procedures. There are hardly any limits set to dealing with real situations *in situ* and to working through fantasies on the psychodrama stage. It is not possible to give even a brief review of the rich literature on the individual application areas in this context. Therefore, only some have been selected and other extensive literatures referred to.

Psychodrama as a psychotherapeutic instrument in the therapy of neuroses and psychoses has been described in numerous studies. Straub (1969) successfully treated compulsive neurotics, depressives, and phobics with psychodrama; Dedne and Hanks (1967), Chase (1962), and Parrish (1958), among others, have treated psychotics in the framework of psychiatric clinics with good results. Psychodrama has proven itself also within the framework of therapeutic communities since Moreno used it for the first time to construct such a community (Stroka, 1967; Seabourne, 1972; Ploeger, 1972).

Since Tierney (1945) employed psychodrama in the treatment of alcoholics, psychodramatic therapy with the addicted has increasingly spread (Weiner, 1965, 1966; Bonabesse, 1970; Petzold, 1970). Psychodrama has proven itself in work with drug addicts as well (Eliasoph, 1955; Friedman, 1967; Petzold, 1974; see the latter for further literature).

Psychodrama has found a place as a sociotherapeutic instrument in work with prisoners (Haskell, 1957, 1960; Lassner, 1950) and with juvenile delinquents (Head, 1962; Eliasoph, 1963). It is not only a question of the treatment of sociopathy but also of the drill of new, socially more adequate behaviors, of conflict intervention within the repressive prison situation, and of preparation for situations after being released.

Psychodrama has been employed with success not only in child psychotherapy with behaviorally disturbed children (Straub, 1972; Anzieu, 1956; Widlocher, 1962) or retarded children (Fontaine, 1972) but has also been used in preschool pedagogy and in kindergarten work (Lippitt, 1954; Petzold, Geibel, 1972). Improvised performance greatly attracts the preschool child (Gording, 1971) and stimulates his creative capabilities. The combination with dolls (Kors, 1964) and with creativity techniques (Krantz, 1971) has proved particularly effective.

Psychodrama has established itself alongside the role play as a technique of modern instruction (Haas, 1949; Carpenter, 1968). For the clarification of social interactions, for the transmission of subject matter, and for communication and perception training it is a superb didactic instrument in the hands of the teacher and a procedure for the improvement of class structure and of the school climate. (See Petzold, Schulwitz, 1972 for further literature.)

Psychodrama has been used in technical institutes and universities for the training of students of pedagogy (Schonke, 1971), those studying social work and the helping professions (Cuvelier, 1972), students of medicine, psychology, and theology among others. The aim was, on the one hand, to provide a personal therapeutic experience and to give, on the other hand, an introduction to psychological group work along with communication training. (See Petzold, 1973 for further literature.)

With similar goals as in work with students, psychodrama has been employed in adult education (Andragogik) (Sturm, 1967; Petzold, Sieper, 1973) and in the education of the aged (Geriagogik) or geriatrics (Leveen, Priver, 1963). The flexible procedures can be advantageously brought to bear for optimal cognitive and affective learning, particularly in adult education. (See Petzold, 1973, 1974, for further literature.)

Psychodrama offers numerous possibilities for work with ambulant parent groups (Webster, 1968; Wolpe, 1957). The graphic clarity of the event facilitates in the shortest possible time understanding of problem situations. Counseling as an accompanying measure to therapeutic and pedagogic work with children is much simplified in this manner. Psychodrama offers similar advantages for marital and family therapy (Moreno, 1940, 1952). Techniques like role play make insight into the situation of the other possible and also promotes problem-solving behavior.

Both in pastoral therapy (Sturm, 1963; Zacher, 1961) and in ministerial responsibility (Green, 1961; Bobroff, 1966) psychodrama has found application. The goals were to further the process of communication between the pastor and congregation members and among congregation members themselves; in the pastoral therapeutic situation, the goal was to provide the possibility for self-discovery and self-realization. (See Petzold, 1972, for further literature.)

THE CLASSICAL PSYCHODRAMA BY MORENO

Psychodrama, group psychotherapy, and action learning have their origin, already noted, in the Moreno's Viennese *Stegreif-theater.* As the Viennese psychiatrist Freud concerned himself essentially with the individual dimension of the human being, so the attention of the Viennese psychiatrist J. L. Moreno was directed primarily to the social dimension. If one assumes that the therapy of pathological conditions requires the therapy of the pathogenic environment, then one can view the group psychotherapeutic and sociometric research of Moreno not as the antithesis of psychoanalysis, but as an important complement to every form of individual psychotherapy. In its therapeutic and pedagogical efforts psychodrama is oriented toward reality, the individual reality of the individual person with his specific dynamics and toward the social reality of the group to which the individual belongs and to the group dynamic processes active therein. Dealing with reality is as complex; as multi-faceted as reality itself, in which the dimensions of the present, the past, and the future (time factor) come into play as well as that of the spatial environment.

The classical psychodrama is composed of three progressive phases: the initial or warm-up phase, the action or performance phase, and the conclusion or discussion phase (Leutz, 1970, 1974). In each of these phases specific techniques are used.

The initial phase is directed toward collecting diagnostic material, reducing resistance, and establishing a field of communication in which group participants can deal with each other openly and without anxiety. During the warm-up phase the group themes crystallize or a protagonist for a psychodramatic performance is found. Setting the scene, that is, the reconstruction of the place (for example, the parents' living room) and the assignment or selection of roles follow.

The action or performance phase begins as soon as the scene has been set. Situations are acted out, the past becomes the present, and the future is brought to the here-and-now. On the stage of the psychodrama reality of life (*Lebenswirklichkeit*) takes shape. The protagonist and the group experience the performance with an intensity which hardly differs from the real situation. The goal is the catharsis of the protagonist and the group.

In the concluding phase, when the performance is finished, the protagonist awakes as if from a dream. He steps out of the reality of his performance into the reality of the group which supportingly and protectively gathers around him. In the *sharing* which follows, each of the participants relates his feelings and experiences during the performance. Expression is not limited to the verbal. A friendly gesture or an embrace are not rare as expressions of spontaneous emotionality. A taboo with respect to physical touching, as we find it in the classical forms of psychotherapy (Forer, 1969), does not exist.

Whether the psychodrama is applied as *individual* or *group treatment* or as *long* or *short term therapy* depends in the last analysis solely on the question of the symptomatic indications, the details of which we cannot go into this context. It is a common but nonetheless inaccurate assumption that psychodrama is exclusively a form of group psychotherapy. From his first therapeutic experiments Moreno used psychodrama in three ways: as individual treatment, as individual treatment in group, and as group therapy. Furthermore, the psychodrama was used as an instrument of group pedagogy.

Types of Psychodrama

The classical psychodrama is applied in two forms: as protagonist-centered and as group-centered performance (Leutz, 1970; Moreno, 1959). We have ourselves differentiated two further procedures: the group-oriented and the theme-centered approach.

When the protagonist has stepped onto the stage of the psychodrama, he is alone with the therapist. The group steps back, which is particularly evident where there is a lighted stage in a darkened room. By various techniques, for example, the *dialogue interview*, a situation fully comparable to individual therapy is created.

The psychodrama is person- or protagonist-centered. We have already pointed out that by involvement in the performance and processes of identification the group is affected to a certain degree by the therapeutic activities in a protagonist-centered psychodrama. In homogeneous groups it can go so far that the problem area of one protagonist at the same time opens up paradigmatically an area relevant to the entire group. The psychodrama is *group oriented.*

The *group-centered psychodrama* deals with the situation of the group in the here-and-now. The interaction between the individual group members and the behavior of the participants in the group become the subject of analysis and process. By taking up and acting out general themes, for example, the question of authority, the line between psychodrama and sociodrama becomes fluid.

The *theme-centered procedure* allows the psychodramatic activity to move around a theme which either the leader has presented or which the group itself has worked out and is prepared to follow. The theme-centered approach can be problem-oriented, but may also serve didactic ends. For example, such themes as "authority," "prejudice," and "sexuality," can be explored in psychodramatic role playing formulated on an *ad hoc* basis.

No matter which of the described procedural forms one chooses, certain diagnostic and therapeutic components are inherent in the psychodramatic process; to be sure these can be emphasized in one way or another according to the orientation and technique of the psychodramatic therapist, but they are found in every psychodrama.

ELEMENTS OF THE PSYCHODRAMA

The classical psychodramatic performance, according to Moreno (1959), requires six elements: the stage or performance area; the protagonists; the leader or director of the psychodrama; the psychodramatic techniques; the assisting therapists (auxiliary egos); and the group participants.

The stage or performance area clearly differentiated from the group circle (Leutz, 1970), offers a space in which the reality of the group, the here-and-now of the interaction between the individual participants can be extended and expanded, in which the individual past and future of the protagonist, the excerpts from his life situation, but also his fantasies and dreams can take shape. The reality is increased; it becomes *surplus reality*, to use Moreno's expression (1971). The stage of the psychodrama provides possibilities for the exploration of reality, revealing the constellations of interactional conflicts, the role behaviors of those involved, and the structure of behavioral patterns. An analysis of behavior on the basis of learning theory principles (Kanfer/Phillips, 1970) gives the psychodrama a high diagnostic value for the unraveling and understanding of individual and social behavior.

The protagonist in the psychodrama can portray his conflict. He does not remain limited to a verbal description but can experience on the psychodramatic stage the place, the surroundings, and the time of his conflict, that is, he can give it a certain quality of reality. As a result of this close approximation of reality, which includes all non-verbal expression, movement, gesture, and mimicry, affective participation is so mobilized that the emotional experience in the "semi-reality" of the psychodrama does not fall short of the real emotional event. Not only can the protagonist become better acquainted with his personal reality, in that he explores it together with the leader/therapist and the group, he can also experiment with himself, investigate his potential, and expand and develop his capabilities.

The director of the psychodrama has the task of stimulating a climate in the group in which the psychodramatic processes can develop. With the warm-up exercises he structures the initial situation of the group and thereby accelerates the group processes so that in a short time vital personal problem areas can be approached.

The psychodramatic techniques serve as tools for the leader to start, steer, and keep track of the therapeutic processes. According to function we differentiate among warm-up, action, and summing up techniques (Petzold, 1972). In addition there are the "frame techniques."

The auxiliary egos or assisting therapists aid the protagonist and the leader in carrying out the psychodrama. They assume the function and roles of persons from the protagonists's *social atom* (Moreno, 1967) or *conflict field* (Petzold, 1972). By portraying those persons with whom the protagonist is or has been involved, the auxiliary egos make possible the repetition and the bringing to the present of past traumatic or conflictive events or the acting out of the protagonist's imaginary images and fantasies. The auxiliary egos have to work their way into the roles assigned them by the leader or protagonist (role-taking). The role of auxiliary ego can be carried out by trained therapists or by group members, from whom role-flexibility, empathy, spontaneous acting, and reactions appropriate to the situation and role are required. As a result, intensive training in these capabilities is accomplished.

The participants of the group, in addition to the function of auxiliary egos mentioned already, have the job of providing a communications system in which the therapeutic processes can be effective. Only in a climate of mutual trust and acceptance is it possible to reveal and act out personal conflicts. A. Schutzenberger, (1970), has called psychodrama "*thérapie en profondeur du groupe; une thérapie par l'action de groupe, dans le groupe, par le groupe, avec le groupe, et du groupe,*" and thus has pointed out the significance of the group and its participants in the psychodramatic process. The group offers the setting for the psychodrama and the participants carry out the following functions: sharing, feedback, and analysis of events performed.

THE TETRADIC SYSTEM OF PSYCHODRAMA AND ROLE PLAYING

The classical psychodrama with its three-phase structure includes in each of these phases various diagnostic and therapeutic possibilities. In order to make those components which surface during the course of treatment more readily available for specific application, we have attempted to restructure the psychodramatic process by expanding the triadic concept of Moreno and the French School to a four-stage structure and, taking up a suggestion of Moreno (1963), have added to the psychodrama a behavior therapy-oriented section.

We differentiate the following phases: the diagnostic-anamnestic; the psychocathartic; the analytical-communicative; the behavior modification phase.

We have briefly described the "tetradic system" above. In other studies (Petzold, 1971, 1973) we have dealt in detail with the underlying theory. We intend here to convey the theoretical approach by interpreted examples based on classroom teaching experience.

The tetradic psychodrama was first developed as a therapeutic method (Petzold, 1971), but has in the meantime found more and more application in the pedagogical field (Sieper, 1972; Petzold/Schulwitz, 1972). To illustrate our preceding discussion we intend to show by examples how the tetradic system of psychodrama and role playing can be used in work with school children. We have conducted continuous courses, workshops, and laboratories in a similar fashion with older students and within the framework of adult education.

Protagonist-centered procedure is seldom applied in work with the entire class and, when applied, only to peripheral problem areas. It makes the appropriate therapeutic and psychodramatic training of the leader absolutely essential. In small groups of eight to twelve pupils it can be used successfully, however. In every class there is the "problem child," whose academic production and behavior present the teacher with a difficult task which cannot be dealt with in the concrete pedagogical situation since the causes of the difficulties lie outside the class. Social-psychological research has shown repeatedly the interdependence of environment (family, household, local, and religious community), psycho-physical development and productive/unproductive performance in school. These "stress factors" (*Belastungsfaktoren*) resulting from environmental circumstances must be dealt with, for they hamper a healthy intellectual and mental development as well as an adequate social and school behavior by crippling, inhibiting, frus-

DIAGRAM 1

Structure of a Tetradic Psychodrama

(Application possibilities: person-centered, group-oriented, group-centered)

diagnostic–anamnestic phase

remember

exploration of learning history | exploration of biography

I. behavior analysis | projective material

conflict–centered procedure

psychocathartic phase

repeat

II. action catharsis | spectator catharsis

emotional experience
experiential learning

analytic–communicative phase

working through

verbal and psychodramatic interpretations | sharing, feedback

analysis of behavior patterns

III. clarification of psychodynamic connections | clarification of behavior

rational insight
insight learning

behavior modification phase
(behaviordrama)
change

IV. desensitization, assertive training, aversion training, imitation learning, shaping, flooding, etc.

reward | punishment

social, instrumental and self-reinforcement

trating, burdening, causing painful environmental pressure, constricting living space and thereby disturbing development. The range of symptoms that indicated the use of the protagonist-centered tetradic psychodrama is thereby outlined: disturbances in learning and in social behavior.

We cite the case of pupil K. for the protagonist-centered tetradic psychodrama: fifteen years old, in his ninth year of school, toward the middle of his class, capable of relating well, nonetheless often absent, and when present, aggressive toward his fellow pupils and although somewhat more reservedly, toward the teacher.

The group, consisting of nine pupils — five boys and four girls — had not been working together long; nonetheless good group cohesiveness was present, although the initial scenes had been marked by great reticence because the pupils all knew each other. At the beginning of the first meeting the teacher had given a short introduction about the point of the psychodrama and in so doing had emphasized that openness, not histrionic production, would be expected. After an initial silence, superficial themes from every day school life were introduced.

Phase I. Hans K. reported in a meeting about his difficulties with a teacher whom he "can't stand." This teacher was too authoritarian for him. Upon probing by the group leader he reported: "I told him why I hadn't done any homework for today. But he wouldn't even accept my apology and we had a fight." — Silence — "It's okay. They all pick on me, anyway." — Agreeing exclamations from the others (identification). The scene is set and the real incident repeated. Hans K. expressed his apology in a somewhat irritated tone to the teacher who stood there in a provokingly superior and distant manner. In a role-reversal, Hans K. in the role of the teacher gave the pupil a cold brush-off: "I don't care about your reasons. I know your type." Another role exchange. Playback of the scene in which Hans K. (now in his own role) retorted to the teacher: "You never listen, I know that. To you we're only slaves!" With this scene the leader interrupted the performance. "Do you see yourself as a slave only with Mr. F. (the teacher)?" — "Mostly with him, he's unbearable. Exactly like my old man." A psychodrama with a first scene between Hans K. and his father then began. The performance of the initial scene had been interrupted by the leader at a key point, which was revealed by Hans K.'s inappropriately vehement reaction to the teacher, Mr. F. A breakthrough to the underlying problem with the father became possible in this way.

Phase II. In the scene with the father we found the same pattern of communication as with the teacher. The father was rejecting and has an authoritarian attitude. In this essentially insignificant scene, Hans K. was slightly aggressive and thus reinforced the rejecting attitude of the father, who expressed criticism, releasing in turn an open outbreak of aggression in Hans K., which the father then answered with a slap (Hans in the role of the father). Hans swallowed his rage and obeys the bellowed command of his father. "And now beat it before I beat you black and blue, you snot!"

Role exchange. Playback of the scene (Hans in his own role). At the slap a group member spontaneously jumped up and doubled. "I'll kill him, the old man, I'll get him!" With that, Hans threw himself at his antagonist, then broke off his aggressive action and burst into tears.

Phase III. Two group members took Hans in the middle. The girls and the boy who had been the double cried also. Others comforted Hans and shared similar experiences with him (*sharing*). The group calmed down again. People began to speak about the scene and told Hans how they have experienced him in the scene with the teacher and the father (*feedback*). The leader had certain sections reenacted by other pupils. In this way Hans K. can observe his behavior. The attention of the group was directed to the behavior pattern evident in both scenes (with the teacher and the father), and Hans together with the group recognized the mechanism of the "escalation of emotions." To the *emotional experience* of the cathartic aggressive explosion and the support of a group of young people in similar situations was added the *rational insight* into a rigid relationship mechanism which made any communication impossible from the start. All came jointly to the conclusion that Hans and his father must get beyond this frozen behavior pattern if they are ever to converse and reach understanding, and that it is unreasonable to transfer a cliché arising from a very particular situation to relationships with other people, for example, the teacher. The group also recognized the difficulty in approaching the father. The situation must be clarified, not only to improve Hans' relationship with his father but, above all, so that Hans can adjust and become more controlled in his reaction.

Phase IV. The emotional experiences and the rational insights gained in phases II and III have clarified the situation to the point that a behavior modification effort now is possible. Hans K.: "There are other things with my father, that's not all, but I see that more clearly now." We returned in later sessions to this comment and worked through other situations.

At the leader's suggestion other scenes were performed which offered Hans the opportunity of practicing adequate behavior. Situations were worked out with the teacher he disliked. Hans learned to react flexibly to the critical, cold manner of the teacher by reenacting the difficult situations again and again with the group rewarding desirable behavior and disapproving of undesirable behavior. At certain points Hans did not progress and fell back into his aggressive behavior. The situations were interrupted there with the behavior drama technique, developed by Petzold, of "action stopping" (Petzold/Osterhues, 1971), but the new attempt did not lead any further. Another pupil spontaneously interjected: "My God, don't you understand? Let me do it!" The scene was recast; Hans watched and repeated. His reaction was clearly changed (*imitation learning*). The group applauded (social reinforcement), and the leader allowed a refreshment break. Hans did not have to pay for his soft drink (instrumental reinforcement). (A group fund exists for such things.)

The behavior therapeutic effect consists of the systematic approach to the desired behavior (successive approximation), in that positive responses are reinforced and negative responses criticized. This process of *shaping* is furthered by the possibility for imitation learning offered by the pupil's intervention demonstrating the desired behavior to the protagonist. At the same time, however, the spontaneous reaction of the intervening pupil revealed another problem area, which is taken up in the expanded feedback following the behavior drama of phase IV.

Hans received a spectrometric self-reinforcement schedule (Petzold, 1972, 1973); a card with a table on which he can record successful behavior in those situations of everyday life difficult for him. Such possibilities of self-reinforcement and regulation have proved decidedly helpful and effective (Kanfer/Phillips, 1970) after the entire situation has been worked through first in the tetradic psychodrama.

The tetradic sequence of the protagonist-centered psychodrama not only led quickly to the core of the conflict (phase I, *diagnostic-anamnestic*), but also has facilitated emotional experiences (phase III, *psychocathartic*) leading to rational insights (phase III, *analytic-communicative*) on which a specific behavioral change could be based (phase IV, *behavior modification*).

Group-oriented psychodrama can be applied in the class unit as well as in the small group. Homogeneity of the class is helpful but not absolutely necessary to the process, since we can reckon with similar difficulties and questions. A school class with a number of heterogeneous factors offers a potential for generally relevant and specific school problems, providing good conditions for a group-oriented psychodrama. The case of a school girl who, as a result of changing schools, was faced with the difficult task of learning new material in a relatively short time, will be taken up as an example. Due to the special structure of the school (a German school abroad) a large part of the class was either in a similar situation or had at least been in the same situation at one time. The excessive achievement standard in various subjects, the environmental change and the nostalgic reactions associated with it, the difficulties fitting in, the pressure for achievement from the parents, all were factors placing the child in a permanent situation of overwhelming demands (Petzold, 1968). The result was a serious decline in achievement in subjects in which the child otherwise did well. Sleep disturbances, perspiration attacks when called upon by the teacher, and continual aggressive irritability were the consequences.

Phase I. In an oral vocabulary test the girl burst into tears; she had had enough of school. When asked what was bothering her, she answered: "My old school was totally different, but here you can only cram and there's nobody to play with." In reply to the question "Whom did you most like to play with at home?" the girl told about two girl friends. An *ad hoc* psychodrama with these two friends took place in the class. The strong connection among the girls is evident. In the course of the scene, the grandparents, with whom the girl had often stayed and on whom she had greatly relied, entered the play. The performance showed what close relationships the girl had left behind in her homeland. At her new home no new areas could open up; in part due to language difficulties. Even though the scene made a diagnostic view of the child's situation possible, it already had a decisively therapeutic character. The reliving of happy memories (minerva experiences, Otto, 1969) calmed and comforted the girl.

Phase II. In contrast to scenes from the native land, scenes from the new environment were performed. In a sequence of scenes it became clear that the child did not feel herself accepted and understood in her surroundings by her parents, fellow pupils, and children in the street. At home, school achievement was all important. It was the only topic of conversation. The relationship between parents and child was reduced totally to this theme. The afternoon was spent with the mother. The atmosphere was nervous and tense. There were tears and scoldings.

Phase III. A few children in the class began to cry during the last scene. The leader asked if things happened similarly at their houses. Two other psychodramas with other children were performed in which similar situations became recognizable. Just as in our example above, phases I and II blended; so also III and IV. By performing scenes which coincided with the problem areas of the main protagonist, a cathartic experience was facilitated for the second and third protagonists which simultaneously represented a *sharing* for the first protagonist. During the feedback about the psychodramatic scenes most of the children in the class expressed that they had been or still were in similar situations. They thus brought their own difficulties into the class community and in the process of verbalization found release for their emotions stirred up by identification. Performance and sharing brought about not only the action catharsis of the active performers but a group catharsis for spectators as well. The protagonists saw that they were not unique and above all not alone with their problems. The class recognized how isolated many classmates were, particularly the new arrivals, and they decided to go visiting more often and to do schoolwork with the newcomers so that the situation at home would become less tense. During the discussion of the scene with the mother, the leader had the protagonist repeat the situation in a playback and then had it mirrored by another pupil, so that the protagonist could observe "from outside" the interaction with her mother at the same time. It became clear to her in the process that she reacted insecurely and haltingly to a nervous comment by her mother and was not in a position to express her thoughts, and that, on the other hand, her mother became more nervous and irritable as a result of her hesitant speech; they became increasingly rigid in their behavior. The result: the daughter said nothing and began to cry, the mother shouted.

Phase IV. With their decision to develop a closer relationship to the newcomers, the class introduced a modification in group behavior. The group-oriented psychodrama cannot only stimulate and effect changes in the individual, but also in the social environment (*social change*). Even for the protagonists, the entire situation and its influencing behavior patterns became reviewable. The situation was dealt with in the behavior therapeutic role play. The mother was played by a very decisive schoolgirl who, as the star of the class, occupied a dominant and, for the protagonist, anxiety-producing role, anyway.

The performance achieved a very intensive realism. The behavior drama was designed as assertive training. When hesitation in speech occurred, a supporting double — a role assumed by the second protagonist — intervened and verbalized the anxieties of the protagonist. As long as the mother's irritability did not exceed a certain level, the double could bridge the situation. The girl began to speak more freely. If the mother became more vehement, the old reactions appear. Here the leader calls for a role-reversal. By intervening he interrupted the undesirable behavior in accordance with *action stopping* and transferred the protagonist to the role of the mother, where she experienced the latter's reactions and at the same time saw her antagonist, now in the role of the girl, behaving adequately. The exchange of roles took the pupil out of the anxiety-filled situation, interrupted undesirable behavior, and made imitation learning possible. Returned to her own role, the protagonist's behavior was less anxious and she answered even impatiently asked questions calmly. The class applauded and reinforced the behavior. Then the other two protagonists with their similar situations were brought into the performance. Through the behavior drama of the first protagonist, both had the opportunity for imitation learning. The second protagonist, by functioning as a double, was already somewhat desensitized to the situation. She adapted an adequate behavior more quickly.

The *group-oriented* tetradic psychodrama reached the class as a whole and a few pupils in particular with the psychodramatic performance of the second phase and involved them in the *sharing* of the third phase by working through the problem area of *one* pupil which was relevant to the majority of the class. The result was a change in individual and social behavior. Similarly in the fourth phase, the entire class and a few particularly affected pupils were drawn in along with the protagonist. As a consequence, a few parents, whose children had reported about the psychodrama project in the class, approached the leader with the request to organize parent-counseling. A small parent group (ten persons) formed, coming together every two weeks and beginning to work psychodramatically as well. This parallel parental endeavor had a decidedly favorable impact on the children. We see here possibilities for pedagogical activities which cannot be valued highly enough.

Tetradic System — Group-Centered Procedure

Composition of the class: twenty-four pupils, twelve boys (average age 15.1), twelve girls (average age 14.8). The class had experience in didactic theater, which essentially had been used for illustration and practical application of subject matter. On the basis of a sociometric investigation, the class structure was seen as not well integrated. (Cf. zone profile by Ruppert, *Die seelischen Grundlagen der sozialen Erziehung*, Weinheim, 1969.) Diagram 2 shows zone profile of the class at the beginning of the psychodramatic activity (diagram 2a) and after six months of psychodrama (diagram 2b).

Particular tensions emerged repeatedly in the relationship between the boys and girls of the class. While the boys were divided into several subgroups with leaders of approximately the same strength, the girls gathered around one star who had succeeded in driving both her rivals completely into the position of outsiders. The girls had without exception boy friends from upper level classes. The academic work of the girls, for the most part, was considerably better than that of the boys in verbal subjects. There was no significant difference in the natural sciences. The attitude of the girls was superior and arrogant. The boys did not feel they were taken seriously, for their part reacted with crude, sometimes

Diagram 2

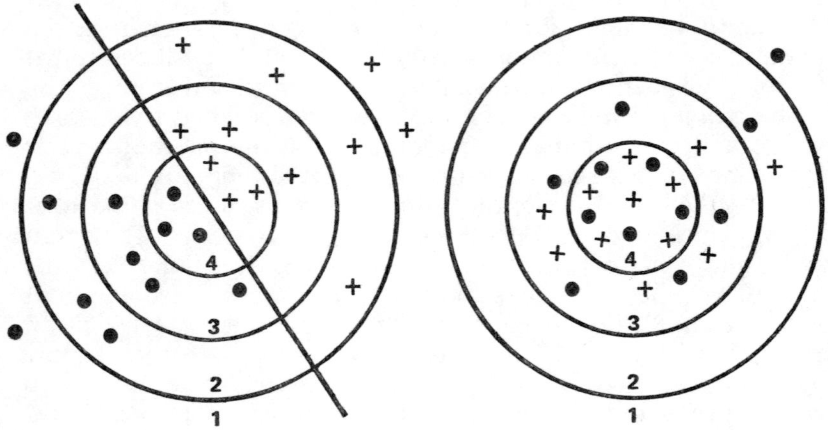

2a 2b

Legend:

1 — Outer zone
2 — Border zone
3 — Middle zone
4 — Core zone

+ = Girl ● = Boy

Diagram 2a
Negligible integration
Division into cliques

4 Children outside
7 Children on the border
7 Children in the middle
6 Children at the core

Diagram 2b
Good integration

1 Child outside
2 Children on the border
10 Children in the middle
11 Children at the core

even rough behavior. The division into two camps led frequently to teaching disruptions and often placed the teachers in unpleasant situations, since they were called upon as the "judge" by both parties ("The boys just ... the girls just ..."). The general situation was repeated in numerous personal animosities between individual boys and girls of the class.

As the result of a confrontation where the class appealed to the teacher demanding a decision, he parried the demand with the comment that he did not see himself as the judge of affairs internal to the class. In general, he thought the class was completely capable of solving its own difficulties. As a consequence, discussion took place among the various participants in which some at first denied that there were far-reaching differences in the class. A few pupils made a strong protest. The teacher intervened here with the question as to whether they agreed where the difficulties lay. The question triggered some perplexity. They decided to look into the matter. The diagnostic phase was thereby introduced.

Phase I. At the suggestion of the teacher, the class divided itself into four subgroups in which they began to collect material about the class feuds. The specific confrontations, experiences, and feelings of individual pupils were brought together and thoughts about the general situation were set down. The subgroups came together again with this material and began to report jointly. Since the subgroups had been formed by free choice, the respective leaders and their followers were collected in them. So we find a block A (girls) standing in sharp opposition to block B (boys). Block C (girls) coalesces with block A. Block D remains relatively indifferent. Those outer and border zone pupils, who are minimally involved in the event, are represented in it.

The situation soon slipped from factual discussion into a very intensely conducted confrontation between group A + (C) and group B, with whom group D then also sided. The psychocathartic action phase began.

Phase II. The instruction that no one may present unsubstantiated assertions caused the discussants to go all out to bring in documentation for their arguments. Single situations were introduced where the girls by their behavior were accused of having contaminated the class climate. The situation was described differently by both sides. People became tangled in contradictions. The leader suggested that the entire scene be repeated one more time with an observer from each group remaining outside the performance in order to get an objective overview. The scene — dealing with the allocation of seats in a bus during a class trip — got underway quickly. A pupil from group D played the bus driver, another the teacher presented at that time who apparently was not equal to the situation. In the quarrel over the seats some of the girls ended up in tears. The scene was played and experienced so genuinely that even in the psychodrama the tears flowed again. The result was that the teacher in the performance gave the window seats to the girls for the trip. The boys argued that the girls had only bawled in order to get the window seats. The entire trip was tense. The girls were content with their victory but not happy, because the boys gave vent to their displeasure by teasing, delays, shouts, etc.

Phase III. After the performance, the scene was talked through (*analytic-communicative* phase). The participants gave each other feedback about how they experienced each other in the performance. The "observers" added to the picture. A discussion evolved. The girls defended themselves against the boys' charge that "the howling was only a show to get the good places," and conceded that they could really have exchanged places during the two days. While discussing the situation, the class observed that the irritated tone, otherwise the usual form of communication, had disappeared. "Usually we insult and tease each other, but we never speak with each other." "Each assumes the worst about the other." "We don't take the boys seriously at all." (One boy's reply: "We don't want you to take us seriously," was rejected by others.) The class began to consider what other factors had made the climate worse. They hit upon the tense relationship between the star of the girls' group and a star from the boys' group. A psychodrama with both of them got underway. During the course of it, the old follower groups formed and took sides. The leader interrupted at this point and confronted the group with what happened. The process of taking sides became obvious. The class saw that many other difficulties must be openly laid on the table in order to improve the class climate. The result: "We don't want to be cross immediately, but to try to speak with each other."

Phase IV. At the teacher's suggestion the bus scene and the class trip were performed again with instructions to get together somehow and change their behavior toward each other (behavior modification phase). The scene went along without friction. The boys behaved gallantly; the girls considerately. In the feedback to this scene the pupils saw that gallant behavior and "magnanimity" neither are necessary nor desirable, but only that they mutually accept one another. The predominantly *group-centered* and *group-oriented* psychodrama was performed during the next half of the school year once a week during a class period. In this time period the cohesion of the class has undergone a fundamental improvement, as was evident from the zone profiles of the class set up before and after the psychodrama sequence. (See Diagram 2.)

CONCLUSION

Psychodramatic role playing has proved itself, in its classical and tetradic form, to be a highly effective instrument in the field of education. The principles of the therapeutic procedure have been easily modified to meet pedagogical tasks. The theoretical and, beyond that, the philosophical-anthropological bases of psychodrama have remained unchanged; they are equally valid for pedagogic and therapeutic tasks.

BIBLIOGRAPHY

Anzieu, D., *Le Psychodrame chez l'enfant*, P.U.F., Paris, 1956.

Barrucand, D., *La catharsis*, Epi, Paris, 1972.

Bavelas, A., Role playing and management training, *Sociatry* 1/2, 138 (1947).

Blatner, H., *Psychodrama, Role Playing and Action Methods*, Thetford, 1970.

____, *Acting In*, Springer, New York, 1973.

Bonabesse, M., L'utilisation du psychodrame dans le traitement des alcooliques, *Bulletin de Psychologie*, 13/16, 834 (1969/70).

Bonarius, J. C., De fixed role therapy van George A. Kelly, *Neederlands Tijschrift foor de Psychologie*, 8, 482 (1967).

Bradford, L. P., R. Lippitt, Role playing in supervisory training, *J. Personnel*, 1, 258 (1946).

____, R. Lippitt, K. D. Benne, Sociodramatic clarification of leader and group roles *Sociatry*, 1, 82 (1947).

Bromberg, W., Acting and acting out, *Am. J. Psychotherapy*, 12, 264 (1958).

Carpenter, J. R., Role reversal in the classroom, *Group Psychotherapy*, 3/4, 155 (1968).

Chesler, M., R. Fox, *Role-playing in the classroom*, Science Research Associates, Chicago, 1966.

Coggin, P. A., *Drama and Education*, London, 1956.

Corsini, R., *Role playing in Psychotherapy*, Aldine, Chicago, 1966.

____, M. E. Shaw, R. R. Blake, *Role playing in business and industry*, The Free Press of Glencoe, New York, 1961.

Cuvelier, F., Gruppengerichtetes Psychodrama in der Ausbildung von psychiatrischem Pflegepersonal, in: *Petzold* (1972a).

Dedne, W., V. Hanks, Psychodrama in a mental hospital, *Group Psychotherapy*, 1/2, 43 (1967).

Derbolowsky, U., Die Drei-Satz-Technik beim Rollenspiel in der gruppenzentrierten analytischen Psychotherapie, *Zeitschr. Psychotherapie und medizinische Psychologie*, 19, 202 (1969).

Duvignaud, J., *Sociologie du theatre*, P.U.F., Paris, 1965.

Elms, A. C., *Role playing, reward and attitude change*, Van Nostrand Reinhold, New York, 1969.

Eliasoph, E. A., A group therapy and psychodrama approach with adolescent drug addicts, *Group Psychotherapy*, 8, 161 (1955).

____, A group therapy and psychodrama program for delinquent boys, *Berkshire Farme Monographs*, 1963.

Festinger, L., J. M. Carlsmith, Cognitive consequences of forced compliance, *J. Abnormal and Social Psychology*, 58, 203 (1959).

Ferenczi, S., Bausteine zur Psychoanalyse, 4 vol., Huber, Bern, 1964.

Fontaine, P., Psychodrama mit geistig und korperlich Behinderten, in: *Petzold* (1972a).

Forer, B. R., The taboo against touching in psychotherapy, *Psychotherapy, Theory, Research and Practice*, 6, 229 (1969).

Franks, T., *Role playing in industry*, Sociometry Monographs, Beacon, 1959.

Friedman, A., Psychodrama of addictness, *Group Psychotherapy*, 3/4, 158 (1967).

Goodman, J. M., Nondirective psychodramatic play therapy, *Amer. J. Orthopsychiatry*, 32, 532 (1962).

Gording, E., Dramtisches Spiel. Von kindlicher Improvisation zum Jugendtheater, Friedrich, Velber, 1971.

Greenberg, I. A., *Psychodrama and Audience attitude change,* Thyrsus, Beverly Hills, 1968.
____, Group Hypnotherapy, inedit. Manuscr. 1974.
Grotowski, J., *Das arme Theater,* Friedrich, Velber, 1970.
Haas, R. B., *Psychodrama and sociodrama in American education,* Beacon House, New York, 1949.
Haskel, M. R., Psychodramatic role training in preparation for release on parole, *Group Psychotherapy,* 10, 51 (1957).
____, Group psychotherapy and psychodrama in prison, *Group Psychotherapy,* 13, 22 (1960).
Hausmann, G., *Didaktik als Dramaturgie des Unterrichts,* Quelle & Meyer, Heidelberg, 1959.
Head, W. A., Sociodrama and group discussions with institutionalized delinquent adolescents, *Mental Hygiene,* 1, 127 (1962).
Iljine, V. N., Improvisiertes Theaterspiel zur Behandlung von Gemutsleiden, *Theatralny Kurier,* 2 (Kiew 1909) suppl. (Russian).
____, Kranke spielen Theater — ein Weg zur Heilung des Leibes und der Seele, *Theatralny Kurier,* 4 (Kiew 1910) suppl.
____, *Therapeutisches Theaterspiel,* Paris, 1942 (Russian).
____, Therapeutisches Theater, in: *Petzold* (1972a).
Janis, I. L., J. B. Gilmore, The influence of incentive conditions on the success of role playing in modifying attitudes, *J. Personality and Social Psychology,* 1, 17 (1965).
Kanfer, F. H., J. S. Phillips, *Learning foundations of behavior therapy,* Wiley, New York, 1970.
Kelly, G. A., *The psychology of personal constructs,* W. W. Norton, New York, 1955.
Kindermann, H., *Theatergeschichte Europas,* 10 vol., Wien, 1957 — 1970.
Kors, C., The use of puppets in psychotherapy, *Am. J. Psychotherapy,* 17, 54 (1963).
Lassner, R., Psychodrama in prison, *Group Psychotherapy,* 1, 77 (1950).
Lebovici, S., Analytisches Psychodrama, in: *Petzold* (1972a).
Lebovici, S., R. Diatkine, E. Kestemberg, Bilan de dix ans de therapeutique par le psychodrame chez l'enfant et l'adolescent, *Psychiatrie de l'enfant,* 1, 63 (1958); repr. *Bull. Psychol.* 13/16, 839 (1969/70).
Lemoine, P., G. Lemoine, *Le psychodrame,* Laffont, Paris, 1972.
Leutz, G. A., Vom kindlichen Spiel zum Psychodrama, *Schweizer Theater — Jahrbuch,* XXXIII (1967).
____, Ubertragung, Einfuhlung und Tele im Psychodrama, in: *Petzold* (1972a).
____, Psychodrama — *Theorie und Praxis,* Springer, Heidelberg, 1974.
Lippitt, Ronald, The psychodrama in leadership training, *Sociometry,* 6, 286 (1943).
Lippitt, Rosemary, Psychodrama in the home, *Sociatry,* 2, 148 (1947).
____, Psychodrama in the Kindergarten and nursery school, *Group Psychotherapy,* 4, 262 (1954).
Maier, N. R., *Principles of human relations,* Wiley, New York, 1952.
Moreno, J. L., *Kinderbuhne 1911,* Wien, Privatdruck, 1911.
____, *Einladung zu einer Begegnung,* Anzengruber, Wien, 1914.
____, *Die Rede uber den Augenblick,* Kiepenheuer, Potsdam, 1923.
____, *Das Stegreiftheater,* Kiepenheuer, Potsdam, 1923. Second edition, Beacon House, Beacon, 1970.
____, Psychodramatic treatment of marriage problems, *Sociometry,* 3, 1 (1940).
____, Sociodrama of a family conflict, *Group Psychotherapy,* 1, 20 (1952).

____, *Psychodrama*, vol. I, Beacon, 1946; vol. II, Beacon, 1959; vol. III, Beacon House, Beacon, 1969.
Moreno, J. L., J. Enneis, *Hypnodrama and psychodrama*, Psychodrama Monographs 27, Beacon House, Beacon, 1950.
Moreno, Z., *Psychodrame chez l'enfant*, Epi, Paris, 1973.
____, Psychodrama in the crib, *Group Psychotherapy*, 3/4, 296 (1954).
O'Connel, W. E., Adlerian psychodrama with schizophrenics, *J. Individual Psychology*, 19, 69 (1963).
Otto, H., *Group Methods to actualize human potential*, Beverly Hills, 1970.
Parrish, M., The effect of short term psychodrama on chronic schizophrenic patients, *Group Psychotherapy*, 12, 15 (1959).
Perls, F. S., *Gestalt Therapy Verbatim*, Real People Press, Lafayette, 1969.
Petzold, H., Psychodramatische Techniken in der Therapie mit Alkoholikern, *Zeitschr. f. praktische Psychologie*, 8, 387 (1970).
____ (Ed.), *Angewandtes Psychodrama in Therapie, Padagogik, Theater und Wirtschaft*, Junfermann, Paderborn, 1972a.
____, Psychodrama als Instrument der Pastoraltherapie, der religiosen Selbsterfahrung und der Seelsorge, *Wege zum Menschen*, 2/3, 41 (1972b).
____, *Methoden in der Behandlung Drogenabhangiger.. Vierstufentherapie*, Nicol, Kassel, 1972c.
____, *Gestalttherapie und Psychodrama*, Nicol, Kassel, 1973a.
____ (Ed.), *Kreativitat und Konflikte. Psychologische Gruppenarbeit mit Erwachsenen*, Junfermann, Paderborn, 1973b.
____, Triadisches Psychodrama in der Ausbildung von Studenten, in: *Petzold*, (1973b).
____, *Drogentherapie. Modelle, Methoden, Erfahrungen, Junfermann*, Paderborn, 1974a.
____ (Ed.), *Gruppenhypnose*, Urban & Schwarzenberg, Munchen, 1974b.
____, *Psychodrama — Theorie und Praxis*, Anwendung, Springer, Heidelberg, 1974c.
____ (Ed.), *Psychotherapie und Korperdynamik*, Junfermann, Paderborn, 1974d.
Petzold, H., I. Schmidt, Psychodrama und Theater, in: *Petzold* (1972a).
Petzold, H., Ch. Geibel, Komplexes Kreativitatstraining in der Vorschulerziehung durch Psychodrama, Puppenspiel und Kreativitatstechniken, in: *Petzold* (1972a).
Petzold, H., I. Schulwitz, Tetradisches Psychodrama mit Schulkindern, in: *Petzold* (1972a).
Petzold, H., U. J. Osterhues, Zur verhaltenstherapeutischen Verwendung von gelenkter katathymer Imagination und Behaviourdrama in einem Lebenshilfezentrum, in: *Petzold* (1972a).
Petzold, H., V. N. Iljine, B. Zenkovskij, Didaktisches Theater in der schulischen Erziehung, in: *Petzold* (1972a).
Petzold, H., J. Sieper, Zur Verwendung des Psychodramas in der Erwachsenenbildung, in: *Petzold* (1973b).
Reil, J. Ch., *Rhapsodien, Uber die Anwendung der psychischen Curmethode auf Geisteszerruttungen*, Halle, 1803.
Rillaer, J. van, Une therapie des roles figes: l'apport de G. Kelly, *Bulletin de psychologie*, 13/16, 793 (1969/70).
Ruhle, J., *Theater und Revolution*, dtv, Munchen, 1963.
Sarbin, Th. R., Spontaneity training of the feebleminded, *Sociatry*, 7, 389.
____, V. L. Allen, Role enactment, audience feedback and attitute change, *Sociometry*, 27, 183 (1964).
Schutzenberger, A., Marquis de Sade, a French precursor of psychodrama, *Group Psychotherapy*, 1/2, 46 (1966).

____, Triadisch Psychodrama, *Folia Psychodramatica*, Louvain, 1, 301 (1968).

____, Presentation du psychodrame, *Bulletin de psychologie*, 13/16, 969 (1969/70).

____, *Precis de Psychodrame*, Editions Universitaires, Paris, 1970.

Scott, W. A., Attitude change by response reinforcement: Replication and extension, *Sociometry*, 22, 328 (1959).

Seabourne, B., Psychodrama und therapeutische Gemeinschaft, in: *Petzold* (1972a).

Shaftel, G., F. Shaftel, *Role playing for social values*, Englewood Cliffs, 1967.

Shoobs, N. E., Individual psychology and psychodrama, *Am. J. Individual Psychology*, 12, 46 (1956).

____, Role-playing in the individual psychotherapy interview, *J. Individual Psychology*, 20, 84 (1964).

Siroka, R., Psychodrama in the therapeutic community, *Group Psychotherapy*, 3/4, 123 (1967).

Straub, H., Erfahrungen mit psychodramatischer Behandlung von Zwangsneurosen, *Zeitschr. f. Psychotherapie und medizinische Psychologie*, 19, 192 (1969).

____, Theoretische Anmerkungen zur psychodramatischen Behandlung von Phobien, Zwangsneurosen und anderen psychischen Storungen, in: *Petzold* (1972a).

Sturm, E. I., The behavioristic aspect of psychodrama, *Group Psychotherapy*, 1/2, 50 (1965).

____, Psychodrama in an adult education program, *Group Psychotherapy*, 3/4, 181 (1967).

Tierney, M., Psychodramatic therapy for the alcoholic, *Sociometry*, 8, 76 (1945).

Webster, H., Procedures for group-parent counseling, *J. Speech and Hearing Disorders*, 2, 128 (1968).

Weiner, H., Treating the alcoholic with psychodrama, *Group Psychotherapy*, 1/2, 27 (1965).

Widlocher, *Le psychodrame chez l'enfant*, P.U.F., Paris, 1962.

Wollman, L., Hypnodrama, *Group Psychotherapy*, 3/4, 207 (1967).

Wolpe, J., A. A. Lazarus, *Behavior Therapy Techniques*, Oxford, 1966.

Zacher, A. N., The use of psychodrama in pastoral therapy, *Group Psychotherapy*, 3/4, 1164 (1961).

Zander, A., Role-playing: a technique for training the necessarily dominating leader, *Sociatry*, 2, 225 (1947).

Zander, A., R. Lippitt, Reality-practice as educational method, *Sociometry*, 7, 129 (1947).

Zenkovskij, B., Dramatization and theater performance as methods of religious education, *Byulletin Religiozno-Pedagogischeskago Byuro*, Paris, 1935 (Russian).

PART IV

APPLICATIONS TO LARGER SOCIAL SYSTEMS

ORGANIZATIONS AND COMMUNITIES

PART IV

INTRODUCTION

In Part III, a range of applications of laboratory method in support of integral personal and small group growth and development was described. Rationales for various forms of personal and group training also were presented.

In Part IV, the focus of application shifts to processes and problems of changing and development in larger social systems — organizations and communities. The programs described and noted illustratively still are applications of laboratory method. The model employed is the cooperative action research model. The central spiral process of changing, decision-action-feedback-learning-new decision-new action, is "the same" for larger system clients as for personal and group clients. The change agent, now often functioning as consultant, plays his familiar linking-bridging roles — helping to bridge between segregated parts of the client system, between the client and its environment(s), and between the disclosed needs of the client and the resources of the applied social and behavioral sciences. Clearly we have not left the world of laboratory method as we shift to its applications in larger units of human organization.

But there are differences, too — differences in the process of contracting between change agent and client, differences in the mix between task and process focus, more massive problems of power relations, more complicated interface and intergroup relationships to diagnose and deal with, and new variables and variable relationships to help clients recognize and manage. It is these differences that lend fascination to Chapters 18 and 19. We shall return to these chapters shortly.

Chapter 17, written by Max Pages, is not of a piece with the two other chapters in this part of the volume. The program he describes takes place in a residential laboratory, in many respects not unlike those described in Part III. It differs from these in his attempt to focus attention for purposes of learning upon the laboratory in its development as a miniature "capitalist" society, not upon intrapsychic, interpersonal, or group processes occurring within it. In lifting up the "political" and "economic" dimensions of laboratory development for conscious experiencing and learning, struggles over the composition of authority and power in the organization and management of laboratory life are brought to the center of the stage. And the training staff, because of its position of initial ownership and authority in the laboratory, are involved in the struggles toward more communal ownership and authority that ensue.

Power and authority are almost always part of the major focal issues in human and social relationships. Oftentimes, the larger the system, the more pervasive and important questions about the maldistribution of power become, and the more difficult they are for individuals and small groups within the system to deal with, except by open rebellion, sabotage, surrender, or passivity. Some seek power overtly, some covertly, and pay great prices — psychologically, physically, politically, and economically — for its acquisition. To paraphrase Shakespeare — "Some are born with power, some achieve power, and some have power thrust upon them."

Others in a social system may avoid struggles for power, or even deny their existence, for a number of reasons. They may accept dependence on those possessed of power, while both fearing and hating them. Sometimes the hostility of the dependent ones is latent and unrecognized; sometimes it is acted out in subtle ways. Others feel powerless in situations where the power of a ruling group is stabilized and legitimized, and see no way to break out of the situation. And some persons, fortunately, are free both from the personal need to exercise power over others and the need to be subject to external authority.

Some trainers feel that power and authority issues provide the major focal point in human relations training. Most believe that, while these issues are important, other issues are of equal importance — personal security, self-understanding, intimacy, collaborative peer relationships among others. In fact, none of these issues stands alone. They are intertwined with each other and not least with factors of power and authority.

So universally accepted in society is the factor of established authority that many people see it as "natural" and unchangeable, when, in fact, it may and should not be so considered. People tend to regress to childlike ways of behaving when stable authority and power structures become confused or disappear. Such regressive behavior, which is reported from Pages' "Flexible Structures Laboratory," becomes the occasion for fundamental learnings about authority and power in social structures and in personal lives.

In effect, Pages is trying to bring the historical development of societies into the ambit of laboratory experience, analysis, and learning, as Southgate and Benne suggest in Chapter 4. His work is of a pioneering nature. In a less historically oriented way, Gunnar Hjelholt in Denmark, has attempted to bring societal problems into the laboratory for direct experiencing, experimentation, and illumination. Annually, he composes a residential laboratory society with a composition isomorphic with that of contemporary Danish society. The laboratory population includes blue collar and white collar workers, managers, young people, old people, men and women. Each group has the opportunity to work out relations with other groups as they choose from day to day, and to observe, experience, and study the processes and outcomes. The work of Pages and Hjelholt extends laboratory method into learnings about societal level problems, about "society" as a macro-system. It is because of this that we have placed Chapter 17 in this part of the book.

In Chapter 18, Richard Beckhard discusses organization development (OD) as a species of laboratory practice. He discusses the theory, strategy, and tactics which guide the interventions of change agents who try to help organizations to diagnose their needs for development and renewal and to mobilize energy and effort to meet these needs. His discussion of the consultant role *vis a vis* the organization client is rich and insightful.

While Beckhard draws his case illustrations from OD programs in business and industrial settings, he and other OD specialists have worked in similar fashion with hospitals, voluntary organizations, government agencies, and educational systems. If space had permitted, we would have included chapters which described OD programs in some of these other settings. The principles are the same, but the details of application differ widely. We have appended a short bibliography to this Introduction to indicate some of the current variations in OD work, including differences in institutional settings.

In Chapter 19, Eva Schindler-Rainman, out of wide consultant and training experiences with the volunteer and the professional segments of local community life and with the two in combination, discusses the application of laboratory methods in programs of community development. She recognizes the overlap between OD and community development work but stresses the problems which interagency and intergroup conflicts bring to those who would cultivate more collaborative approaches in the diagnosis and solution of community-wide problems. Her ideas are illustrated with the description and analysis of two concrete programs in community development. Her approach stresses the importance and the problems of teamwork between outside and indigenous training and consultation resources.

BIBLIOGRAPHY

1. Argyris, Chris. *Interpersonal Competence and Organizational Effectiveness,* The Dorsey Press, Homewood, Illinois; 1962.

2. Argyris, Chris. *Intervention Theory and Method: A Behavioral Science View,* Addison-Wesley Publishing Company, Reading, Mass.; 1970.

3. Argyris, Chris. *Management and Organizational Development,* McGraw-Hill, New York; 1971.

4. Bidwell, C. D. "The School as a Formal Organization" in March, J. G. (Ed.) *Handbook of Organizations,* Rand-McNally, Chicago, Ill.; 1965, pp. 972-1022.

5. Burke, Warner W. and Hornstein, Harvey (Eds.). *The Social Technology of Organization Development,* NTL Learning Resources Corporation, Fairfax, Virginia; 1972.

6. Gordon, C. W. *The Social System of the High School,* Free Press, Glencoe, Illinois; 1957.

7. Margulies, Newton and Raia, Anthony P. (Eds.). *Organizational Development: Values, Process, and Technology,* McGraw-Hill, New York; 1972.

8. Schein, Edgar H. and Bennis, Warren G. *Personal and Organizational Change Through Group Methods,* Wiley, N.Y.; 1965.

9. Schmuck, R. A. and Miles, M. B. (Eds.). *Organizational Development in Schools,* National Press Books, Palo Alto, Calif.; 1971.

CHAPTER 17

THE FLEXIBLE STRUCTURES LABORATORY

Max Pages

THE CONCEPT OF FLEXIBLE STRUCTURES

This experiment is based on the recognition of the central importance of structural phenomen in social life. By structural phenomena I mean not only the task structure (the arrangement of activities in time and space), the frontiers of groups and subgroups, the communication network, the set of norms, etc. — what I would call functional structures, but also more fundamental structures of power and authority. Power and authority structures, hidden behind the functional structures, influence and distort them in many ways, so that no problem, in a group or in an organization, is solved on purely a functional basis for rational reasons pertaining to the task requirements.

The fundamental structures, authority and power, have four main characteristics.

1. They introduce a basic and stable dichotomy between a privileged subgroup or privileged group and the rest of the group. The word privileged is taken here with two meanings: a psychological meaning, which connotes a focal psychological relationship, the archetype of which is the parent-child relationship; a political-economic meaning which indicates that interests of all kinds of the privileged groups are given precedence over the interests of other groups. By authority I mean a relationship of absolute (independent from time and circumstance) superiority between the privileged and the non-privileged, at the psychological and economic levels. By power I mean the possibility for the privileged to procure "absolute" protection and destruction, psychologically,

politically, and economically.

2. Psychological attitudes and images, most of which are unconscious, are present in the relationship between the privileged groups and the others. The privileged figures are unconsciously felt as protective and destructive. They hold absolute powers to protect from all evils as well as the power to destroy. The psychological relationship with them is dependent and counterdependent, in an ambivalent way. It performs, following Jacques' hypothesis, a collective function of defense against anxiety for the group, protecting the group against the anxiety of taking initiative, of assuming one's own individuality, of facing concrete differences with other groups or individuals, including the privileged figures. Identification with external figures, which represent a benevolent and/or destructive power, localizes and limits the fears of destruction inherent in active social interaction. This means also that the privileged figures are internalized and projected onto other individuals or groups, so that they influence all aspects of social interaction. They are the basis of psychological security for every member of the group.

3. The power and authority of the privileged group are not only of a psychological nature, they are embodied in means of social control of the social structures of production, in the Marxist sense (property in a capitalistic society), concentrating economic and technical resources, unilateral or manipulative decision-making, instituting norms which consolidate the status of the privileged groups, producing ideologies which assure conformity, and ultimately the use of violence to enforce decisions.

4. The authority and power structures at all levels of social life are linked with broader social institutions. The latter give legitimacy to the former and support them in many other ways, while in turn the former sustain the latter.

At this point, I shall draw only two consequences from this rationale. The first one is the pervasiveness of the structures of authority and power. Psychologically, they are the focus of the defenses of the individual, the refuge where are hidden the deepest and most unconscious defenses against autonomy, risk-taking, creativeness, and relationship with others. Through an overall network of identifications and projections, they influence, at least partially, the whole field of social interaction. They are the foundation of a world of unrecognized fear, false brotherhood, and latent destruction; a world where the other does not exist as such but only unconditional allies or irreconcilable foes, both projections of self. At the political-economic level even minute decisions are at least partially influenced by the structures of authority and power. Initiative from below, cooperation between individuals and between groups, however "rationally" based on task requirements and concrete needs of individuals, are threatening to interests of the privileged, fundamentally irrational in nature. All sorts of mechanisms operate, which tend to limit them; for instance, group segregation, encouraging competition between groups.

The second consequence concerns the correspondence between the poltical-economic and the psychological aspects of authority and power structures. One can conceive of the relationship between the two as a circular one. On the one hand, economic structures have psychological meanings: the defense of economic privileges of subgroups performs functions of psychological defense for the total group. It is one way for the group to protect itself against anxiety. Economic structures have in turn psychological consequences; economically privileged groups have support for identifications, projections, and ambivalent attitudes of submission and aggression. The economic structures of a given group have, of course, links with structures in the larger society; these pre-exist in the group, so that they influence the psychological life of the group, exogenously, while they are in turn reinforced by it, or, possibly changed.

The results of all this for a strategy of change are central to our purpose. It means that: 1) No significant change can be expected without some change occurring in the structures of authority and power. 2) No significant change in the areas of authority and power can occur if it does not happen simultaneously on the political-economic and psychological levels. Political-economic change without its psychological counterpart will tend to be superficial and formal, and archaic patterns of power and decision-making will form themselves again informally, as can be observed in many cases of "social reforms" introduced bureaucratically. Psychological changes which do not have political-economic repercussions also are very limited, and probably tend to die out. For example, an increased capacity of expressing personal opinions and feelings, of "expressing one's own personality" will not subsist if individuals see no possibility of taking action on them because of unchanged social controls. How many internal training programs within organizations started with enthusiasm and stopped, because of the resistances of the hierarchy to listen to what trainers had expressed? Thus, rather than to speak of "personality development," "expressing one's self," as psychologists tend to do, we will speak of individual *initiative*, as one goal of training, recognizing that the word initiative has not only a psychological, but also a political-economic meaning. The individual who tries to change tends both to change the political-economic structure which surrounds him and to sort out better his aspirations, wishes, and feelings. The processes involved are complex and confused; the action toward social transformation can be an indirect expression of psychological conflicts, an acting out, in technical terms. In reverse, psychological growth may very well cover enabling the field of social action. But the assumption I make is that it is in helping both processes to develop that each one can become clearer. It is by helping individuals to change their surroundings that they can progress in "expressing their personality," in "psychological growth." Clarification of feelings, goals, and values lead in turn to social reorganization. Psychological and social changes are to be treated as parts of one single process, rather than separate, and then necessarily conflictual elements.

This assumption is the basis of a methodology of flexible structures training laboratories. It has long been recognized that training cannot be limited to psychological goals. Ever since Kurt Lewin, modern training has been linked with training "social change agents." Over the years this tendency probably has increased, as is shown, for instance, by the development of a methodology of intraorganizational change, by an increased recognition of economic and political variables, by the emphasis on "designing" at the level of laboratory as a whole, by schools of thought like "institutional analysis" in France which insists on the importance of economic and political variables, and by similar developments in psychiatry (Laing, Basaglio). All these efforts, however diverse and sometimes opposite, have one common feature: *the structures of authority and power within training itself, between trainer and trainees, become an operational part of the training strategy*. They are recognized as symbols of external structures of authority and power and they are used to initiate restructuring authority and power in the training institution, as well as in the outside world.

But in this area, which I believe probably is the most difficult and the most central of training methodology, it is necessary to clarify hypotheses and methods as much as possible. Roughly speaking, it seems to me that we can identify three different orientations.

The first is the *classical psychoanalytical orientation*, which has almost disappeared among trainers in the U.S.A., but remains dominant or very influential in other parts of the world. Its features are well-known: the functional structures of training (time-periods, fees, activities, group composition) are fixed by the trainers unilaterally; deviations from them, when they occur, are permitted but in no way do the trainers cooperate with the trainees in elaborating new structures; deviations are analyzed in psychological terms, as expressing various aspects of dependency, counterdependency, and the like, toward the trainers. Social action within training is systematically interpreted as acting out, and even sometimes coercive rules are enforced to limit it (Freudian principle of abstinence). The rationale behind the trainer's conduct is: 1) that the analysis of fantasms is the motor of individual change; 2) that the analysis of fantasmatic conflicts can develop more fruitfully against the background of a stable social structure. The hypothesis here is completely opposite to the one I made above: that psychological conflicts, including unconscious ones, depend upon and influence the social structure itself.

The second orientation follows what I shall call the *induced democracy model.* It is implemented in the practice of many laboratories organized by NTL Institute in Bethel, Maine, in the U.S.A., and also, I believe, in some experiments in France, inspired by the revolutionary ideology of "auto-gestion" (self-government). Here, contrary to the previous orientation, the functional structures of training are, at least in part and for some periods of time, made flexible. For instance, the training staff proposes that the trainees plan the second week of a laboratory, either offering or not offering guidelines as to the procedures of planning. The characteristic feature in this orientation is that initiative is *granted* to the participants by the trainers, not taken by the former. Most often it is canalized along procedural lines which the trainers provide (negotiation between groups, for example, in a joint trainers-trainees committee, or, as in auto-gestion, by the total group acting as a formal governing body). These democratic institutions are part of a masterplan designed by the trainers and controlled by them. The trainers act as institutions of democracy; they teach democracy to the group; they introduce and induce in the group a definite social structure. This enables them at the same time to preserve their own status and power. Politically-economically they preserve their ultimate control at the level of the overall design, at the cost of minor "sacrifices" concerning the task structure. Psychologically, they present the image of benevolent rulers, protecting the group against the risk of chaos, diffused aggression, destruction. This means that, in spite of the appearances and rationalization, the structures of authority and power are not changed in this orientation. They remain fixed and stable throughout the laboratory experiment, and basically authoritarian.

While the classical psychoanalytical laboratory resembles the organization of a traditional firm, where a paternalistic boss controls all details of the work authoritatively, the induced democracy laboratory resembles more a modern firm where competent and well-intentioned managers anticipate the needs of "their" people, and provide various ways of self-expression and realization, and a considerable amount of freedom at the level of task arrangements, thus augmenting the efficiency of production, while preserving their overall control of the process. The control is facilitated by the anticipatory approach which "kills in the egg" changes initiated from below.

These thoughts led me to the necessity of conceiving of a third orientation. In a flexible structures laboratory the attempt is to render flexible not only the functional structures of the laboratory, but the more fundamental structures of authority and power, as they develop in the trainers-trainees relationship. The assumption here is that trainees will tend to produce various structures of authority and power as the laboratory develops. For instance, they may start with an archaic structure of childish dependency upon the trainers, requesting decisions to be made by them and building them into a God or parent-image, all protective and potentially destructive. Occasionally, they can revolt against the trainers impotently, and try to force decisions upon them or upon other members of the group. At some time it may happen that they build an internal power within the trainees, replacing the archaic power of the trainers, at the same time displacing some of the problems they had with the former power-group onto the new power-group. They could enter a state of utter chaos and disorganization, where every member is felt as a power figure, threatening, and threatened by all the others. Eventually, they could also build radically new structures where authority and power, in the sense we have defined them, tend to dissolve, where threat is reduced and concrete cooperation made possible. Each of these developments has both psychological and economic components, involving a psychological reorganization (change of authority figures and attitudes toward them) as well as political-economic organization: who takes decisions and how. The trainers' part in this process is to offer as little resistance as they can to these changes at both psychological and political-economic levels. They accept being treated as all-protective gods who make decisions for the group, or at other times, being ignored and rejected and seeing decisions for the group taken out of their hands, or negotiating with the internal power (the "union"), or to cooperating with individuals and subgroups, according to the dominant trend. This role can be defined as helping latent structures of authority and power to emerge from within the group in a process which involves a reorganization of their own status. At the same time they aim at understanding the process along with the members of the group, in particular discovering the meaning of the structures which are built and their relationship to underlying anxieties. It is a circular process of action and analysis in the large sense of the word; structure-building and expression of emotions, feelings, ideas. Trainers participate jointly with trainees in both aspects of the process, focusing on defining and redefining their own roles, as well as on their psychological relations with others.

The practical aim of this type of training is to develop initiative among participants, which involves not only clarifying one's motivation, working through unconscious conflicts, "psychological growth," but also a capacity to change alienating social structures, so that one and others have more adequate conditions of psychological growth. Participants are expected to understand various social structures out of the laboratory situation better, as well as their economic and psychological dynamics, and to be more able to insert their own action in those structures, so that potentialities of change are maximized.

A scientific aim of these experiments is to make social structures and the conditions of their change an object of scientific study, to better understand in particular the complex interconnection between social structures and psychological conflicts. This could possibly project some light on similar phenomena on the larger social scene, such as union formation, various forms of political revolution, and the like. One could hope thus to be able to build progressively general theories of social change on an experimental basis, under conditions of thorough investigation.

The logic of the flexible structure methodology is to study social change as it occurs spontaneously, rather than in forms planned by the formal leaders. The variables of the authority and power structures which in my opinion are frozen in other training methodologies, are here permitted to vary, so that new avenues for change and for scientific study are opened. In that sense, the flexible structures laboratory can be described as a *generalized T group*. If the T group invention consisted of opening a free space of movement for intragroup phenomena as well as an opportunity to study them in the making, the flexible structures laboratory is a T group at the level of the laboratory organization as a whole. Small group formation and intergroup relationships are studied in the same way intragroup phenomena are in the T group, that is, without being planned by the trainers. The condition for this is to include in the variables the authority and power within the organization, which usually rest with the trainers, solidly anchored in their role of organizational leaders.

The laboratory thus turns into an organization which develops spontaneously and simultaneously studies itself while doing so. We touch here on a limit of the experiment. While the "internal institution" of the laboratory is made flexible, "external institutions" remain rigid, which have some influence on the laboratory life, that is, trainers' and participants' permanent organizations, and the overall social structures which support them. If the laboratory is not to be Utopian, part of its task should be to analyze those constraints.

One can also present this methodology as an attempt at

generalized dialogue. From a certain angle, the processes in training and therapy can be viewed as opening new channels of dialogue, discovering new languages; for example, play, symbolic language, bodily movements, graphic and plastic expression. In each of these cases, human activities which had been considered as insignificant, literally as non-language, or at least as closed realms of communication, restricted to specialists or fans, have been discovered as conveying individual and social meanings of universal significance. They tend now to be incorporated into a strategy of change. Trainers and therapists have learned to use them and to convert them into one another. But the areas of power and decision-making have not yet in general been incorporated. They are the locus of violence, and one resorts to them in order to cut or limit dialogue, probably because there hide the deepest anxieties of destruction. In the methodology I am trying to describe, power and decision-making phenomena are treated as a language among others, connected with the language of emotions, feelings, ideas, not as solid and isolated *facts*, but as messages, as human products, owned by man and changeable by him, rather than as parts of nature. The attitude of the trainer toward power, his own and of others, is neither to revere it and treat it as a sort of fatal god, loved and/or hated, nor to be afraid of it, but rather to use it as a necessary means to express himself, to answer others and to understand them, while at the same time trying to understand some of the covert meanings hidden in the use of power. He wants to permit the experience and the analysis of power, for himself and for others, in its varied forms, with the expectation that in the process the more defensive and violent forms of power will be reduced, while some of the underlying threats are identified, so that individuals, including himself, will tend to act more on the basis of autonomous, truly individual aspirations, less under a compulsion to protect themselves against potential destruction.

THE EXPERIMENTAL LABORATORY: OVERALL DESIGN

This experiment derived partly from theoretical conceptions such as those I have just outlined. It was also in line with my evolution as a trainer over the past years, where I tried more and more to open avenues for a generalized dialogue with participants. In the summer preceding this laboratory, I was able to engage in an experiment at Bethel, somewhat similar to this one, although more restricted, in a Human Relations Laboratory of the NTL Institute, thanks to the interest of the Dean, Matthew Miles, and other trainers. This encouraged me to go one step further.

The laboratory was held in France under the sponsorship of

Arip, and one important dynamic of the experiment was that a member of this group, Jean Dubost, showed interest in my project and volunteered to share the responsibility with me, in spite of the fact that my views were heavily criticized among this group, and that he himself had reservations about them. Thus, at the outset, the laboratory was placed under the sign of mutual interest and a spirit of research among the two senior trainers. Two co-trainers, who were following a training of trainers program with Arip, eventually joined the team.

The laboratory was announced in a brochure as focusing not only on individual and group relations, but on collective decision-making as well, and the concept of flexible structures was introduced.

Twenty-four participants joined; males and females coming from social work, industry, church, training, and teaching.

The laboratory was planned to consist of five three-day sessions, with a space of five to six weeks between sessions, from October, 1969, until May, 1970. The participants had contracted for five individual interviews with the trainers, the co-trainers, or a consultant (psychoanalyst) if they so wished.

It had been decided in preparatory meetings that neither the place of the meetings (two mansions outside of Paris), nor the periods of the sessions, nor the fees, were to be changed. These structures were fixed, either for practical reasons (previous arrangements), or because the trainers were not prepared to see them amenable to change, or because the parent institutions would not accept changes. The trainers realized that this factor should be accounted for as perhaps an important limit of the experiment. All other aspects of the work, allocation of activities in time and space during the sessions, type of activities, number and composition of groups, presence or absence of trainers, were subject to possible changes and to be treated as I tried to describe above.

In the account I am now going to give of the laboratory, I shall focus on events which directly or indirectly seem to me to affect the structures of the laboratory as a whole. I shall thus leave aside many important aspects of the laboratory, in particular, the evolution of the individuals and the dynamics of small groups, partly for lack of systematic data and partly for the sake of clarity and brevity of this report. The account is based on the notes and memories of the trainers and of some participants, who volunteered to join in a three-day session after the laboratory to help draw a picture of the event.

First Session — November, 1969

The trainers had decided to present a program and a schedule for the first session, under the assumption that this would meet participants' expectations. The program was a standard one for Arip, including T groups in two groups (previously arranged), plenary meetings and intergroup meetings (small trainerless groups with participants from both T groups). The trainers started the session by stating their objectives and hypotheses, presenting the program and the reason they had for presenting a program at this stage, adding that it could be changed at any point and that in this case one task of the laboratory would be to understand the meaning of those changes. They introduced the distinction between the fixed structures of the laboratory (place, periods of the three-day meetings, starting and leaving time for the meetings, meal periods, fees) and the flexible ones (all other elements). This presentation was received rather passively by the participants; two or three of them expressed some criticism of the amount of structuring proposed by the trainers, but they did not try to push their point very much and they were not supported by the others. Two or three participants demanded to change their T group membership and this was arranged on the spot. Two participants stated that they had known me beforehand and did not appreciate my style very much and they preferred to work with someone else, while another said the contrary — that he wanted to work with me. One can interpret this reaction as meaning that the demand for change, the contestation, was held very much under cover, with people expressing themselves mainly through minor changes affecting only the individual.

Contrary to our expectations, the first attempts to change the overall structure of the laboratory happened in the very first day, after the first period of the afternoon, which was a T group. At the end of the period, the members of my T group "decided" to stay as a T group during the second session of the afternoon (which was scheduled to be a plenary session). The decision process was not clear. The person who had initiated the proposal had left the room before a clear decision had been reached; nevertheless, when I asked if a decision had been taken, I was told yes, and that the decision was to stay as a T group for the next period and for me to inform the other group about this decision. I then replied that I had personally no objections to continuing as a T group, but that I refused to inform the other group because I did not like to be ordered about and that I should consult the other trainers before deciding to join the T group; that I was going to meet them over tea and that they could contact me there if they so wished. Nobody did.

After the pause the trainers went to the room scheduled for

sessions, which was located between the two rooms for the T groups, with movable walls right and left. This ecology proved very convenient, because it gave the opportunity for everyone to visualize materially the confused structure of the group at that time and they could work from there. Walls were half open; members of Jean's T group were seated in the middle room (the plenary room), in an open half-circle, obviously following the program's suggestion; members of my T group were seated in "their" room, with one or two exceptions who were in the middle room, while one member of the other group was seated among them. The trainers at the beginning were standing near the outside door of the middle room, because we did not want to fix the situation by sitting here or there.

Communications started to flow from one group to another. Members of Jean's group expressed their frustrations and anger toward the other group. They analyzed the other group's behavior as violence over them and violence over the trainers (my being instructed). My group responded with expressions of guilt and justification. Toward the end of the meeting, this conflict seemed to resolve itself, and a new decision was reached concerning the rest of the three-day period, three members belonging to both groups pressing and cooperating in this. The decision seemed rather symbolic and involved very superficial changes over the old program, a mere permuting of periods for some proposed activities. I intervened at some point to facilitate decision-making by putting down suggestions over a paperboard, and this intervention was received with anxiety first and then with relief when participants realized I was not against their making a decision.

During the rest of the session, the participants expressed no concern whatsoever for programming, decision-making, and the like, neither for this session, nor for the one to come, which surprised the trainers. During the second night, a spatial change occurred: the plenary was held in the lounge instead of the usual room. A "delegation" of participants negotiated this with three trainers, but it was not clear whether they were truly delegated and by whom. At that time I was making a telephone call and I arrived late at the meeting. After the meeting, a conflict arose between Jean and the other trainers on one side and myself. They reproached me for showing carelessness in arriving late at the meeting and also they said they had had the feeling I had "sent" a participant, a member of the "delegation," to them in order to "inform" them of the change in place.

The Tam-Tam. The last afternoon was very interesting. The participants talked about an event which had occurred in the morning, in one of the intergroups. In this group (seven or eight people belonging to two T groups, without trainers), participants had engaged in a tam-tam, as they described it, alluding to the African custom, making a great deal of noise with furniture of various kinds. The tam-tam was felt by its participants as bearing the meanings of "beginning," "invitation" (to the other intergroups) to feast, incantation, play, protection and denial against the trainers. They also said it was a noise designed to stop the "noise" felt in the laboratory, by which they meant two things: 1) superficial ways of communicating (interpreting, explaining oneself complacently) and 2) confused aggressions. All this was expressed somewhat reluctantly with long intervals of silence, but was extracted by the trainers. Finally, one participant said they felt some guilt at bringing out a behavior felt as childish before the trainers felt as parents.

Tentative Interpretive Remarks Concerning First Session. At this stage I shall attempt only prudent interpretations, leaving broader generalization for later.

1. I am struck by the fact that the first attempts at change were made without any explicit decision, with the exception of the first plenary the first afternoon, where help was provided by a trainer to carry through the process (the promoter of the first decision left before conclusion, the "delegation" without mandate the second night). This suggests that participants at this stage avoided responsibility for the decisions they made.

2. In content, the decisions altered the program proposed by the trainers very little. The decision-making process involved very little discussion of alternatives and no imagination. The horizon, the space of alternatives, the creativeness of participants were very restricted. In fact, the decisions were governed by the pattern set by the trainers at the outset. The decisions seem to have been symbolic ones, and to have functioned as a way for the participants to reassure themselves as to their power to make any decisions at all.

3. Consulting with other group members, or even informing them previously, was minimal or absent. The pattern of decision-making was coercive and authoritarian. It expressed violence done to others but the need for violence was unrecognized, and it expressed itself indirectly, through deciding for others, through acting over the institution (schedule, activities) presented as separated from the people. This means that the institution was felt as unowned by the people.

4. At the feeling level, the dominant feelings were of being violated, placed before *a fait accompli*, manipulated, not respected (reactions of Jean's group to mine, conflict between trainers) with the associated feeling that one had to violate others to see one's wishes taken into account. I believe these feelings were dominant, but remained unconscious most of the time, and were expressed

more openly when a group first attempted to change the situation. They also conflicted with the feelings that the trainers and the institution they had set up offered adequate help, and also a protection against the unknown.

5. The fact that my group played the aggressive role reflects the status situation between the two senior trainers (Jean and myself; the co-trainers were ignored at that time), and the felt relationship between them, partly fantasmatic, partly real, as a relationship of domination-submission. During one meeting, Jean's group had described him as fragile, almost feminine, and needing to be protected, and myself and my group as extroverts, the big muscle type, aggressive, and masculine. Apparently both groups had identified with their trainers projecting on one a need to aggress and to be aggressed, and on the other a need to protect and to be protected. The aggression of my group was as much directed against me, the felt aggressor, as it was against other people.

6. I believe the tam-tam to be very important. To me it is the first sign of initiative taken by participants. The other moves, as I have shown, were still very much influenced by the pattern set by the trainers. Remember that the tam-tam was described as both a beginning and an invitation to others to join. To me, it was as a formation of a new group, the initiative of which rests with the participants, not with the trainers. But interestingly enough this group formed:

a) out of the presence of the trainers and of the threat they represent;

b) as a protest and a denial of them;

c) as a denigration of *speech* which was felt as the instrument of lies and aggression. Speech also was the official language of social interaction, and the language of the officials (the trainers). Breaking with it and expressing oneself non-verbally was a way out of the trap in which one felt oneself in the relationship between power and powerless groups. It was a reaction against both external and internal censorship.

d) The tam-tam also was a way of getting contact with instinctual impulses, censored internally and externally.

e) It was also a protection against a possible punishment of initiative. After all, one could say if this "turns wrong" (evokes aggression), this was only childish play. Remember how reluctantly the participants talked about it in front of the whole group and of the trainers.

I was very impressed with the dimness of these first signs of initiative in a group, how cautious are individuals and groups to show and how unable they are to express initiative in rational ways, translatable and acceptable by the leaders of the institution, who usually feel that "these people do not know what they want!" To me this means how profoundly they are alienated by the social structures, how alert one has to be to perceive these signs and not ignore them, or discard them as childish play.

7. As an overall interpretation of this session, I propose that it was dominated by unrecognized feelings of aggression by the trainers, particularly by the one with the higher status, conflicting with the image of trainers as good and offering a protection. The trainers partly collude with these feelings. Their political-economic behavior was consistent with this psychological structure. They offered a program, in order not to frustrate the participants' expected dependency, thus protecting and aggressing against the participants, and offering themselves as a target for feelings of dependency and aggression. This is typical of what one would call, after Weber, a charismatic or parental structure of power, although it added complexities to Weber's analysis.

Another trait of this structure is that aggression was unrecognized mainly on the part of the trainers and toward them. It was mostly displaced onto other individuals or other groups. Identification with the trainers formed rapidly and tended to be high, either on the aggressive or on the protective side. Conflicts between participants developed partly as a result of conflicting identifications with the trainers.

The *institution* was used by trainers and participants as a way of expressing aggression and protection. They were expressed through manipulating schedules, activities, group composition, in an impersonal and indirect way. Manipulating the functional structures of the group was used as rational pretext for expressing needs for aggression and/or protection.

The institution was disowned by the people; was felt as a substance separate from the people; as alien to them. For the trainees, it was felt as owned by the trainers and some of them tried to appropriate it, with violence, guilt, and fear; some tried to adjust and use it as a protective house. The trainers probably felt more that they owned the institution, but they also felt guilt and uncertainty as to their power. The institution was used by both groups to express these unrecognized feelings of guilt, aggression, and need for protection. Its functioning, in spite of the overt speeches, was very little guided by rational considerations, much more by the necessity of treating those emotional conflicts.

Creativity and imagination were very low. Changes were proposed in an aggressive way, with little consultation and information. Failure was experienced when one first tried to change something. Even in their attempt at changing, individuals were alienated in the model set by the authorities. Nevertheless through these attempts, which were not stopped by the authority, some confused understanding of the underlying forces began.

More profound initiative had to come from very far, nonverbally, in a sort of childish regressive play, outside the official world of trainers, outside of the official language and admitted means of social communication, as a radical contestation of the ordinary world and of the participants themselves and at the same time as a sort of confused appeal for something unknown and desired.

Second Session — January, 1970

At the beginning the trainers again proposed a program for the session. The trainees began to express some dissatisfaction about this, saying that the trainers were too paternalistic, but no action was taken at first. During a night plenary on the second day, for the first time, the trainees became conscious of the risks of destruction (by others) and aggression (by themselves) experienced in the laboratory. They expressed how helpless they felt in the plenaries, particularly in front of the trainers, who held competence, and also how tempted they were to react to the unstructured situation in a fascist way, aggressing and destroying others. This reduced some of the unconscious threat and probably enabled the group to take action at the political level. The last day a sort of spontaneous union formed at lunch time. Some people democratically consulted every participant and negotiated a change of program for the last day with the trainers. But the union "leaders" were in turn attacked by some others, in a far-left style, for reintroducing discipline and authority, illegitimately restricting freedom. It appeared that some of the conflicts with the traditional authorities (the trainers) were lived again in relation to the new leaders. Eventually this conflict was resolved, the group became very creative, and it decided unanimously to ask the trainers not to plan the next session and from now on to let them take full responsibility for their lives. The trainers accepted.

This session is interesting on several accounts. First, one sees in it the reproduction within the laboratory of large scale social structures (union, far-left radical contest) and it sheds some light on their meanings as socio-emotional states, reorganizing both external power-structures and psychological components. The threat of destruction being diminished, it became possible for the group to form new authorities from within (the union). But the union incorporated some of the old fears and needs for protection-aggression. The far-left structure was an attempt to eliminate radically the external threat, but the threat of destruction remained active internally and was now projected onto all others, not only authorities, old or new. Secondly, one can see that the conflict resolves when the group takes full responsibility for its life. One sees also that the conflict decision of self-management had been announced, at a much earlier date, by the tam-tam. This shows that *non-verbal expression not only has individual or interpersonal meanings, but that it expresses political unconscious wishes on the part of the group, and that it can be used in that way as a process of social change.*

Third Session — March, 1970

Opening of the session. The group used the first part of the morning to decide on a program. Monique suggested setting a short limit (one hour) to make a decision and it also was agreed to plan only the first day. The decision was reached within the set time; three people acting as leaders, with little discussion. The program was rather conventional T groups in the afternoon and a plenary at night. All this points to a certain anxiety in the group over potential conflicts, and a desire to make a decision without raising them.

The Emergence of Chaos. During the night plenary the situation changed progressively into a completely different climate. Participants started to wonder how they had in the morning accepted the decision so easily, particularly being led by three of them. They began intervening very actively, raising questions, stating individual goals of their own. At times almost everybody was speaking at the same time, without listening to the others. The climate was one of excitement, participation, and commitment.

Gerard, for example, was sitting in the middle of the room solid as a rock, repeating that he wanted a plenary in order to answer three questions: *where* do we take decisions? *who* takes them? *what* is the role of the *trainers?* When somebody asked him, "But, Gerard, in order to have a plenary must you have other people's consensus?" he started all over again "I want a plenary, I want us to answer three questions," and so on.

Such was the climate: insistence upon and commitment to one's own wishes, neglect of the others' wishes and even hostility toward them. Some, like Gerard, wanted to solve practical issues, others wanted to have T groups, others wanted to explore differences among various dimensions, men-women, talking-non-talking, political-emotional. A bottle of whiskey was circulating in a sort of bacchic atmosphere. The feeling of buoyant and joyful war was lacking. We left the room exhausted, around 1:30 a.m., without having taken any decision.

Next morning it started all over again. It became increasingly clear that we were not to reach a decision. Attempts at integrating the various ideas failed. Toward the end of the morning I made a sort of desperate move: I proposed that we meet after lunch, standing and not sitting, that we try to locate ourselves where we would like "and then we would move or not move, we would interact or not with some other people, verbally or non-verbally, and perhaps the situation will develop from there." The suggestion was accepted with enthusiasm very quickly.

In the afternoon the situation changed rapidly. At one time there was a group sitting on the floor, playing a game of collective free association, while others, more peripheral, were listening to them. Then a split occurred, a larger group remained in the group centered around Gerard, in a minor group, and the minor group went to the adjacent room. Each group contained participants of both formal T groups. The trainer teams were split, the co-trainer who had worked with Jean came with me and *vice-versa*. Interestingly enough, we had discussed this possibility months before, when we had composed the trainer teams, and we had wished that at some point changing the teams would occur. But now it had occurred with no consulting among ourselves, nor, I believe, was there any conscious decision about it. The same was true with the participants.

After tea, in the group I was with, one participant came from the other group and informed us they had taken two decisions: 1) to remain as a group for the time being; 2) that anyone was free to leave the group or to join it.

Interpretive remarks over the chaos and the change. To me, the chaos was a state of overt paranoia. All individuals were for the first time conscious of their desires and really committed to them and, on the other hand, felt all others as potential enemies, apt to destroy them and what they wanted. I believe the possibility of experiencing real chaos in this sense was a *condition* for further change. This is what individuals had feared from the beginning but they had always been protected against experiencing it by formal structures, by authorities from without or from within, and by their own defenses.

I believe a chaos of this kind is a foundation of social life, but society protects its members against it, and never fully allows it to happen. Class segregation, political and economic controls, ideology, and psychological defenses are a converging means to protect against chaos. One of the limits of social change on a broader scale in present society probably lies in the inability of people to understand and accept chaos as a constructive step toward change.

I have reflected several times over the opportunity of my suggestion of the second morning. I have wondered if I had not acted as the Savior of the group, thus defending myself and the group against a fuller experience of chaos. On the other hand, it seems to me that the meaning of this intervention was to open a new channel for expression of wants and fears. Participants were wrapped in traditional patterns of expression: verbal behavior, plenary sessions, T groups, decision-making patterns, and other traditional *organization forms.* What I did was to introduce the possibility of a new *language* for the building an organization — the language of desire, which meant the possibility of reconciling these two apparently antagonistic terms, organization and desire.

Ultimate Phase of the Laboratory. I shall not discuss in detail the following sessions of the laboratory, which is unnecessary for the purpose of this chapter. I prefer to describe some general characteristics of this period.

1. *Entering a new world.* Participants used this expression to describe this phase. They felt they had trespassed already-known behavior and forms of organization in an irreversible way.

2. *Decisions were made in a particular fashion.* Usually decisions were not made at meetings, and there was no formal and complicated discussion over them. People did not sit and say "let us now decide something," as if decision-making was something solemn and special, separate from ordinary life. Usually decisions were made by one individual proposing to other specific individuals to do something, and then those agreeing doing it without asking permission from anyone. Three characteristics of such a process of decision-making strike me as:

a) informality — no reference to "the group" as an entity, no reference to set procedures, no attempt to reach "the best solution" in the abstract;

b) self-commitment;

c) commitment to work with others on an interpersonal basis. Decisions were treated as personal matters involving self and specific others.

3. *Groups were open.* The standard set by one group in the second afternoon after the chaos, came to operate throughout. Individuals were at any time free to leave or join. Sometimes conflicts arose over that issue; some people resenting people leaving or entering. These conflicts were treated as interpersonal issues for those concerned, not as matters of principles or rules. At times we had one group, at times two, three, or four, while some individuals remained out of any group for most of the time.

4. *Groups were set on operational criteria.* They were formed to perform a certain task, and lasted no longer than the task itself. In a sense one could say that groups dissolved in the usual sense of the word. They existed no more as entities separate from the individual members. Groups tended to become what they are supposed to be — *free associations of people temporarily linked by a common purpose.* This led me to reflect on the traditional, so-called task-centered groups, as in industry, for example. These groups are prearranged and individuals do not choose to be members. Tasks or purpose are superimposed by people above, and are felt as superimposed. The result is that these groups are far from

being as task-centered as they claim to be. Much of their energy is overtly or covertly used in fighting over power.

5. *Mobility* was very great. Tasks, groupings, and methods changed rapidly, with little inertia.

6. *Differentiation* also increased. Some groups engaged in non-verbal interaction, some in political analysis, some in emotional exploration.

7. *Power* became decentralized or, better, *multi-centered.* Initiative was not localized with the trainers, nor with any other individuals or subgroups. Neither was there a pyramidal chain of decentralization, with the scales above *granting* a limited amount of their power to the scales below. On the contrary, initiative would come from any part of the organization, including a single individual, and the responsibility would rest with every individual or temporary subgroup to react to it.

8. *Trainer-participant* relationships changed in a drastic way. Trainers had no established status, or role, or clientele any more. They were expected to participate in what was going on, according to their resources, if any.

This involved a large amount of threat for the trainers, and probably constituted the part of the experience from which they learned most. For instance, we would go out at breakfast time, looking where participants were, not knowing what was to happen, where to go, and if we were at all needed somewhere. We realized how much we depended for our security upon our professional role, upon a fixed clientele of participants, and how difficult it was to find our identity within a community without these securities.

A very intense conflict arose one day when I had stayed alone most of the time. I felt my presence was not desired by any group, while I personally did wish to join. Eventually, some participants came to me asking me to join and I did, but others resented it tremendously to the extent that one person left the laboratory until the next session. They said I was acting out of "coquetterie," waiting to be asked, and thus trying to reinforce my status as a trainer. The assumption was that it was my responsibility (not theirs) to join if I so desired, and to face possible rejection. Of course, one could interpret the very intensity of the reaction as unresolved dependency upon the trainer, but I believe the symmetrical interpretation made by some participants is equally correct, as an unresolved dependency of the trainer upon participants, and the desire of the trainer to stick to his privileged position.

9. All these characteristics point to the idea that we had to a large extent become a *productive organization.* Using Marx's terms, our organization was based largely on *productive forces*, on

the infrastructure, while the influence of structures and superstructures (economic, political, and ideological controls) was reduced to a minimum. If we use this framework, we also must realize that we have to expand Marx's concepts, in order to include some psychological elements. By productive forces we mean not only technical resources of participants, such as ideas and methods, but also emotional resources, motivations, and more deeply the possibility of erotic investment. By cooperation among workers, which also was underlined by Marx as a fundamental condition of social change, we mean not only the technical conditions of cooperation, set by necessity of collective work, but emotional conditions as well, such as the desire to work together. On the repressive side, not only economic-political-ideological elements are present (power in the usual sense of the word), but psychological factors as well, mainly psychological structures acting as defenses against unconsciously felt aggression.

10. An important element of the last phase of the laboratory was the emphasis on *analysis and action toward outside institutions*, primarily those to which the participants belonged. The contradiction was felt as acute between the laboratory life and the institutional life experienced by participants. The tendency was to recognize that it was not the purpose of that laboratory to change institutions, but to recognize contradictions experienced by the participants, so that they could themselves better take action concerning these contradictions.

A particular emphasis was given to the analysis of the contradictions of the sponsoring institution, Arip, as revealed by this laboratory: contradiction between its legal status as an open association and its real functioning as a small closed group; contradiction between its status as a non-profit organization and its similarity to a commercial firm selling services; contradiction between a laboratory like this one, having initiative and autonomy as ultimate goals, and the very setting by the organization of such laboratories, decided for participants by the organization, sold to them, and maintaining them in a dependent status at least over matters of policy. Trainers were accused by more political participants of being hypocritical, ambiguous, and contradictory. As a result of this, participants used the opportunity of a meeting with some staff of Arip; others used the trainers to question these points. The meeting ended with little mutual understanding. Some participants also asked to join evaluation meetings within Arip about the laboratory, but their demand was rejected by Arip.

Incidentally, this laboratory had one non-negligible institutional consequence — my leaving Arip, of which I had been General Secretary since its foundation twelve years before. When I stated my intention again to organize a laboratory of this kind for the year to come, my colleagues violently opposed me, and eventually forbade me to do so under Arip sponsorship. I did not accept their decision. I left the organization and invested in a new one. This conflict had, of course, many other indirect causes, linked with the history of my relationship with Arip as a founding member. Its direct cause, however, lies with this laboratory, and with the political, theoretical, practical issues it had raised.

CONCLUDING REMARKS

I should like in conclusion to make a few schematic theoretical remarks about social change, which this experiment and other similar ones inspired in me.

1. Social change is a *collective process*. The forces toward and against social change apply simultaneously to groups and individuals, according to their situation.

2. Social change is a *multi-dimensional process*. It implies political-economic-biological-psychological-ideological dimensions, to say the least, which combine at any stage of the process, in *socio-emotional systems*. Effective action on the system is a simultaneous action on all these dimensions, and not on one single dimension taken out of the complex. Action on one single dimension may result in maintaining or reinforcing alienation, because it does not give people control over essential parts of their lives.

3. As a corollary for training, training should concern itself as much with decision-making, altering political and economic structures, as with psychological insight and change, which have been traditionally its primary concerns. Training should open avenues for people, the power structures they live in, both within laboratories and without, as well as avenues for expressing their desires and fears in the situation.

4. Social change works *from below upward*, upon the initiative of people politically, economically, ideologically, psychologically oppressed and repressed. The task of the social scientist is to liberate group potential for expression and action of the oppressed as much as he can in his situation. He has nothing to teach to anyone.

5. As a corollary for training, the objective of the trainer is not to introduce new social models of functioning from above (new norms, values, decision-making practices, a new concept of social hierarchy), however refined or ethically appealing these may be, but to give way to latent models emerging from within. This implies that the trainer be in a constant state of reappraisal and change of his values and practices, along the dimensions stated above, psychological-economic-political.

6. The *energy for change* in the political-economic sphere and in the personal-sexual-emotional area is basically the same. *Mobilizing impulses* (sexual and aggressive) and facilitating their expression, verbally or non-verbally, is part of the task of the social change agent. This means working not only with the individual but with the group. Since impulses are organized in groups, they are a response to the group's situation as much as to the individual's and they have group meanings.

7. In a similar way, collective emotional systems of defenses combine with political-economic systems of control to maintain a given social state. These defenses consist mainly of defenses against unconscious felt-desired aggression. Polarization of affect on privileged persons or groups, identification with them, need for protection by them coupled in an ambivalent way with unconscious fear, are the mechanisms. It is crucial for the study of any socio-emotional state to describe and understand in detail the psychological systems of defenses which are an essential part of its functioning. The task of the social change agent is to increase awareness of these systems among the people he works with.

8. Chaos is a fundamental but usually repressed experience of social life. In chaos, political-economic-ideological controls are loosened, creative energy and impulses are mobilized, as well as formerly repressed fears-desires of aggression. It is a state of creativity and overt generalized paranoia. Conflicts are maximal, internal psychological conflicts between the desire to create, unite, cooperate, and the desire to destroy as well as the fear of destruction; so are conflicts between each individual and all the others, felt as potential enemies. Chaos is thus a state where chances for change are maximal, the possibility for a group really to experience chaos maximizes future changes for this group. It maximizes chances for future cooperation, creativity, productive work, and social responsibility. Society ordinarily represses and limits chaos in many ways — so does social science by non-committed study, manipulation from above, segmenting its work and focusing exclusively on psychological, political, or economic dimensions in isolation.

9. A particular aspect of segmentation is segmentation of training from social action, as one usually does in training laboratories. Training then offers a methodology, as if in the abstract, which is not related to concrete social groups and concrete social problems. Thus, it performs in part a mystifying, limiting, and conservative function, because it disconnects people from the social groups they belong to and where lies energy for change. While people are busy being trained, and trainers busy training them, existing social powers are busy doing their ordinary business. Training thus colludes in limiting social change (this criticism

applies to the experiment described in this chapter). Probably a reorientation of training on this line is desirable, by which training would offer distance and protection to participants, as it does now, but would address itself clearly to specific social problems (for example, self-government in industry, urban life, family life), to specific parts of the population motivated for change, and would prepare action in specific social loci of every day life.

10. Social change is a *contradictory process*. People involved in change experience a fundamental psychological contradiction between a desire to change, to create, to unite with others in new ways, and a need to protect themselves against the fears of destruction evoked by the desire to change. At the social level the desire to fight existing social powers, and their alienating function, is balanced by the fear of missing the security they provide. Another type of contradiction concerns micro-*versus* macro-social change, individual *versus* small group change, small group or organizational change *versus* societal change. While macro-change can be seen as a condition for macro-change, it can also inhibit or limit it, and *vice-versa*. A similar contradiction applies to long term *versus* short term changes. Another type of contradiction exists between changes along the various dimensions of the social process. Psychological and political changes, for example, may foster each other, but also one can obliterate the other. Any aspect of change can thus be seen as both a facilitator and an inhibitor of a global change process. The social change agent and the people he works with are constantly caught in all these contradictions. His main task may be to recognize them for himself and take a stand in the midst of them, and help his clients do the same, that is, recognize the contradictions they are caught in, and take their stands in relation to them.

BIBLIOGRAPHY

Basaglia, P., *L'institution en negation*, seuil, Paris; 1970. Original Italian edition, Giulio, Torino; 1968.

Hjelholt, G., "Mini-Society: Results of the 12th, 13th, and 14th of June." Unpublished document written by Mico Kriger, Copenhagen; 1968.

Laing, R., and Esterson, A., *Sanity, Madness and the Family, Families of Schizophrenics*, Tavistock, London; 1964.

La Passade, G., *Groupes, Organizations et Institutions*, Gauthier-Villars, Paris; 1967.

_____,*L'autosuggestion Pedagogique*, Gauthier-Villars, Paris; 1971.

_____,*L'analyseur et L'analyste*, Gauthier-Villars; 1971.

Lourau, R., *L'analyse Institutionelle*, Ed. de Minuit, Paris; 1970.

Meigiez, R., *Pathologie Sociale de L'enterprise*, Gauthier-Villars; 1965.

Pages, M., *La Vie Affective des Groupes*, Dunod, Paris; 1968.

Southgate, J., "Report on the Conference on Power and Group Work Held at the Polytechnic of North London." Unpublished document, London; 1971.

CHAPTER 18

ORGANIZATION DEVELOPMENT IN LARGE SYSTEMS

Richard Beckhard

The focus of this paper is on assisting complex organizations through consultative or training interventions.

To sharpen this focus, I would first like to share with the reader my assumptions about *laboratory methods; organization change; intervention practice;* the *relationship* between *change managers* (organizational leaders) and *change agents* (consultants, trainers).

I will focus the major part of this chapter on the *intervenor* (change agent, facilitator, consultant). I will examine what the intervenor brings to the relationship — issues he faces in deciding on his intervention strategy — choices in initial interventions — values and ethical issues he faces.

I will describe a model of diagnosis and strategy planning. Finally, I will look at some change strategies in organizations. *Laboratory method* — the laboratory method as applied to organization interventions for me means the use of an *action research mode.* By "action research," I mean collecting information about the state of events primarily for the purpose of *actively planning* to improve them. The process of action research includes collecting information (for the purpose of planning), giving the information back to those who produced it (for the purpose of ordering the planning), and doing the planning, preferably by those people who will have to implement whatever is planned. The laboratory method is often associated exclusively with small group training, sensitivity training, and team building. In fact, those are applications of action research methodology. Data is produced behaviorally; it is analyzed, looked at, and fed back and generalized. The option is then open to those in the group to plan some change in either individual, group, or total system functioning. Action research guiding organizational interventions also is a use of the laboratory method.

A Definition of Organizational Effectiveness and Health

An effective organization is one in which:

1. The total organization, the significant subparts, and individuals manage their work against *goals* and *plans* for achievement of these goals.
2. Form follows function (the problem, or task, or project determines how the human resources are organized).
3. Decisions are made by and near the sources of information regardless of where these sources are located on the organization chart.
4. The reward system is such that managers and supervisors are rewarded (and punished) comparably for: short term profits or results, growth and development of their subordinates, creating a viable working group.
5. Communication laterally and vertically is relatively undistorted. People are generally open and confronting. They share all the relevant facts, including feelings.
6. There is a minimum amount of inappropriate win/lose competition between individuals and groups. Constant effort exists at all levels to treat conflicts as *problems*, subject to problem-solving methods.
7. There is a high "conflict" (clash of ideas) about tasks and projects, and relatively little energy spent in clashing over interpersonal difficulties.
8. The parts of organization see themselves as interacting with each other and with a larger environment. The organization is an "open system."
9. There is a shared value, and management strategy to support it, of trying to help each person (or unit) in the organization maintain his (or its) worth, integrity, and uniqueness.
10. The organization and its members operate in an "action research" mode. There are built-in *feedback mechanisms* so that individuals and groups can learn from their own experience. The organization is consciously self-renewing.

Some Assumptions About Organization Change

1. It must be "owned" by the key people in the organization — usually at several levels.
2. It must be *managed* from the top.
3. It must be system oriented — relating to the total organization or significant parts.

4. It must have an extended time frame.

5. It must be related to the organization's mission and goals.

6. Change efforts must be responsive to organization-environmental interfaces. It is no longer practical to improve internal effectiveness, without explicit prior attention to the relationship of the organization to its environment.

7. It must be implemented through leadership behavior from the organization's leaders. Facilitators can help in the planning. The implementation must be *managed* by the organization's leadership.

8. Real *organization change* will not take place and stay maintained unless three conditions obtain:

a. There must be real dissatisfaction with the status quo; a high enough level of dissatisfaction to mobilize energy toward some change.

b. There must be in the organization leaders' "heads" some picture of a desired state which would be worth mobilizing appropriate energy.

c. There must be in the organization leaders' "heads" a knowledge and picture of some *practical* first steps toward this desired state, if energy is to be mobilized to start.

If any one of these three conditions does not exist in strength, the "cost" (economic and emotional) of changing is likely to be too high.

I want to look now at the "going-in" condition relationship between the organization leader(s), whom I will call "clients," and the intervenor(s), or change facilitator(s), whom I will call "consultants."

Assumptions About Initial Relationship Between Leaders (Clients) and Change Facilitators (Consultants)

1. There is likely to be some dependency by the client on the consultant.

The client probably will feel the need for expert help with whatever problem he is bringing to the consultant. A characteristic of a dependency condition, with particular implications for consultant-client relationships, is that dependency is okay and comfortable when the thing or person on which you are dependent does not have skills or competence that you want. For example, I wallow in my dependency on TV repair men. Even if they tell me that I could "do it myself" for half the price, I would much prefer to have them make the repair and fix the set! I have no need, desire, or interest in becoming expert at repairing television sets. On the other hand, most managers and organization leaders see themselves as *needing* to be *competent* in managing human affairs in organizations. Therefore, the "dependency" on the "expert" is a two-sided coin — on the one hand, they want some help and guidance; on the other hand, they *resent* that they need it. With outside consultants, this "ambivalence" is likely to take the form of over-dependence; getting the consultant to make the decisions, so that if something goes wrong, the client knows whom to blame. With inside consultants, it is likely to take the form of "prove that you're more competent than I am about this problem or situation."

2. There is likely to be some suspicion of the consultant's motives and/or competence.

This produces a real dilemma for the "consultant:" either to *prove* that he does have skill and competence; or to induce some client anxiety, by not immediately behaving in ways that show his "competence."

3. There could be some threat to existing traditions, ways of work, relationships, and rewards.

The very need for change probably means that some kinds of well-established forms, norms, ways of doing things must be replaced. It may mean that some people may have to be replaced. It probably means that work will be reorganized and/or structures will be changed and/or reporting relationships will be changed and/or the "pecking order" will be changed. The "client" probably knows this, but also probably finds it somewhat threatening. If the threat is great, there is a likelihood that he will transfer the "threat" to the consultant.

This produces another dilemma: how much to behave as the champion or advocate of new ways, *vs* how much to help the client face up to his (the client's) concerns or feelings of threat (to be a process diagnostician).

4. There is likely to be pressure for early results. This dynamic can subvert any change effort, particularly if there are budget consequences. There may be strong needs on the part of the entry client (first client in a system), to prove either to his bosses or to his colleagues the worth of investing in the change effort. Many complex change programs require pilot projects or experiments. Many "clients" have needs to make a big impact on the organization quickly, and therefore want to see some massive change effort introduced during their "time in office."

5. There could be some confusion around the amount of perceived power a "consultant" has and/or should have.

Depending upon the consultant's outside reputation, track record, access to other parts of the organization — the entry client may see him as all-powerful, down the scale to low power. At the beginning of the relationship, the power is "perceptual," that is, it is the amount of power to influence the client that the client *gives* the consultant that governs the client's behavior. I believe that there is a need for clarifying at a very early stage the *client's perceptions*, the *consultant's perceptions*, and the likely perceptions of *other key people* in the organizational system about the consultant's roles and influence.

6. There are likely to be unrealistically low expectations by the organization leaders of the requirements for their own *personal investment* of time and energy in the change effort.

Entry clients — particularly those at the top of an organization — frequently assume that by bringing in a consultant, they can *delegate* the "management" of the change effort to him; that their role is to be permissive and supportive of the activities. This assumption is valid insofar as it is their job to make sure that the support conditions are there for changes. It is incorrect, however, to assume that the top of the organization can avoid significant commitments of their personal energy toward *managing* the change effort.

7. There is likely to be an unrealistically low connection in the organization leader's mind between the organization's needs to *act* differently and the organization's need to *learn* how to act differently.

This may produce resistance to "educational" activities or training programs, or development programs as being irrelevant to the desired change.

Implications for Consultant's Behavior

1. Find ways of reducing the dependency. Somehow deal realistically with the client, meeting enough of the dependency needs not to lose the connection, but resisting some of them and moving the client toward independence and ownership. One must repeatedly resolve the dilemma: when to be "consonant," and when to be "dissonant" to the client.

2. Find ways of exposing both his motives and his competence. One must find some way of communicating to the client "where he's at" and what he wants. The consultant is faced with a very major value or ethical choice or dilemma. To what degree does the consultant wish to be an advocate (of a position or value system or goal)? And to what degree does he wish to be a methodologist (assisting the client to find ways of working and solving the problems)?

For example, if a client wants some help in how to prepare his organization for the hiring of more racial minority members and females into management positions, the consultant has a choice of how to use his influence position and his own values. He can urge the client to take an aggressive, socially responsive position; to take a strong stand for the change. He can communicate the "rightness" of the change. Or he can work as a methodologist

— helping the client assess the forces in the situation, looking at options, assessing resistance to the change; looking at options for "postures" toward the change by the client.

The choices for the consultant are very difficult. What values should he share? What should he suppress?

There is another dilemma around exposing competence. Often a client needs to have evidence that the consultant can be *helpful* in working the problem. There's also the consultant's need to prove, both to himself and to the client, that he is competent. Over-reaction to the client's needs can produce too much of the "expert syndrome" or premature solutions. On the other hand, paying no attention to these needs may terminate the relationship at a very early stage. The consultant needs to find ways, experiments or pilot projects, or initial diagnosis, that prove to the client that the consultant understands the total problem; can deal with the development of a desired state of change, and has some suggestions of practical first steps for getting there.

3. Find some ways of dealing with threat. As mentioned, he must somehow find a way of communicating to the client that he understands and empathizes with the fact of threat, and that change will involve costs and upsets; and that there is a great need for both of them to keep this explicitly in mind throughout the relationship.

4. Find ways of helping the client develop a realistic, practical time frame.

The consultant needs to help the client look at the consequences of immediate superficial success and over-expenditure of energy too soon.

5. Find ways of getting the organization leaders to make personal commitments of time and energy to manage the change effort.

This means confronting the entry client and/or the leaders of the organization with their role as "culture managers," as people with whom the rest of the organization identifies, as policy makers, and as "role models." One needs to help them look at the consequences of their behavioral commitment or lack of it, and help them make appropriate managerial choices about time investment and cost.

6. Find ways of identifying and defining *educational* and *learning* needs, and outcomes necessary to get behavioral or procedural change in the organization. He must help the client system look at what kinds of "unfreezing" from old attitudes, behaviors, norms, traditions, etc., are necessary; what kinds of new learnings around new knowledge, new technology, new skills, and new insights into both self, organization, etc., are necessary, in order for real behavioral and organizational change to take place. If, for

example, a computer is to be introduced to replace a hand bookkeeping system, what kinds of education and learning, what kinds of changes in knowledge, understanding, and attitudes are necessary prerequisites for effective behavioral change on the part of those who will either have to learn to use the computer or will find their work being taken over by the computer?

Another illustration: An organization has large numbers of managers whose style is heavily autocratic or paternalistic and the organization management wishes to change toward a more participative style. It may well be necessary to provide some educational interventions, such as a Phase One Managerial Grid seminar or a "styles of management" program for all middle managers. It may also be necessary to send certain key people to outside management courses, in order to provide some unfreezing of traditional attitudes, so that the conditions for trying new ways can get established.

THE INTERVENOR

So far, I have looked at some assumptions about organization change; some assumptions about the relationship between the change managers or organization leaders, and the change agents or consultants. I'd like now to focus further on the consultant or intervenor or change agent, taking a look at what he brings to the relationship, what specific issues he faces around his personal behavior, how he determines his intervention strategies, and his organization diagnosis.

A Definition of Intervention

Interventions are behaviors that inject into the ongoing social processes of a system. They may intervene or stop interaction between individuals; interaction between groups; the procedures used for: transmitting information, making decisions, planning action or setting goals; the strategies and policies guiding the system, norms or unwritten ground rules or values of the system; the attitudes of people toward: work, the organization, authority, social values; and the distribution of effort within the system.

What the Intervenor Brings to the Engagement

He has a set of values and assumptions about excellence, or an ideal state, which affect his behavior.

He has a set of attitudes toward the client systems' goals and values, which affect his behavior.

He has some degree of need to influence the client system to change.

He has some amount of need for success and approval by the client system and by the entry client.

He has a mixture of needs to control the situation and to *help* the situation.

He has a set of attitudes about the potential for growth and actualization of people in general, and people in the client system, in particular.

He has some motivation to stay with the client system during the change.

He has some "mix" of skills as: organization diagnostician, theory interpreter, consultant, designer of training activities, trainer, structural analyst, and change planner.

He has some amount of knowledge about: the nature of human nature, motivation theory and principles, the nature and dynamics of organizations, the styles of managing and their consequences, the process of change and resistance to change, organization development — planned organization change, and systems analysis.

As he intervenes in the system to help with organizational change, he must "manage" all of the above.

Entry and Contract Issues

Operationally, the consultant-intervenor is faced with establishing a working contract with the client as a way of managing the above issues.

He needs to decide, in his initial relationship establishment, how he will handle: sharing of expectations between consultant and client about ways of work, outcomes, power arrangements, etc.; sharing of values — between the consultant and the first client, other clients, and the whole system; definitions of the organization problems and change problems; accepting the client's initial diagnosis, or other data from the system; sharing of feelings and attitudes of the entry client toward the task and the client and toward the organization; what kind of a role relationship should be developed; what early roles?

One other part of the contract setting is the establishment of boundaries of the consultant's access to the system. Does he have complete freedom to enter the total system anywhere he wishes? Can he work only through the entry client? Can he work within certain levels, or certain departments, or certain areas? If the boundaries as defined by the client are unacceptable to the consultant, it is quite possible that the relationship should terminate at that time. Similarly, if the consultant's requirements are not acceptable to the client, the relationship should terminate.

Another operational issue is a choice of when to function as a *consultant* (helping the client to work the problem) and when to be an *expert* (providing solutions or action recommendations). This is a continuing choice throughout the life of the relationship but is crucial during the early stages. It defines *behaviorally* the consultant's ways of work. It also meets or does not meet client expectations and desires for consultant behavior. Open discussion of the conditions under which the consultant will behave (as expert, procedural technician, process consultant, *or* counselor) will help the initial relationship considerably.

Another issue is the determination of those areas where the consultant can and/or should contribute *substantively*. Some OD consultants see themselves as *purely* process consultants and therefore only intervene around interpersonal, intergroup, or group processes. Often, from the client's point of view, this, although helpful, is not of priority relevance. The client's *needs* frequently are for some assistance in actually comparing his actions with some other experience, or looking at what a proposed action might mean in terms of organizational consequences. The consultant may have considerable background from working with other clients or organizations. To ignore this is for the client to lose a resource. On the other hand, if the consultant's contributions are seen as prescriptions, this will increase dependency and perhaps establish an unhealthy relationship. The fine line between these is a continuing problem. It can be handled if the client and consultant establish some ground rules and a feedback system early in the relationship.

The outside consultant is more likely to have early credibility with a client based on the client's perception of the consultant's knowledge and/or experience. Clients tend to project more competence and credibility onto those who can command high professional fees, which is a symbol of a good track record or a lot of experience, or being with the "right" university.

Internal consultants have a more difficult task. Their track record in their specialty probably is known to the client. They probably have some past, present, or future *authority relationship* with the client.

One way to help the credibility issue is for internal consultants to have more contact with the outside seminars and events.

A MODEL FOR CHANGE PLANNING

I would like to propose a model of diagnosis and change planning that has had high usefulness to me in virtually every large system intervention I've made. Like any other model, it is no panacea, but it does seem to ask the right questions, the answers to which give a basis for a relatively trustworthy judgment on early interventions.

Assessing A Need for Change

When a change effort is initiated, either the client and/or the consultant, or some other part of the system, has in fact determined that there is some need for changing something. An initial diagnostic step is to analyze what those needs are; whether they are shared perceptions, or are very differentiated among parts of the system. For example, let us suppose top management in an organization sees as a major need the improvement of the supervisory behavior of middle management. The personnel staff in the organization sees as a *prior* need, the change in managerial behavior of the top management and a change in the reward system. There are two very different perceptions of the priority of need for initial change, but there is a common perception that there is a need for changing things.

As a part of determining the need for change, it is useful to collect information from various parts of the system.

Defining the Change Problem

Definition of the change problem should be thought of in two distinct ways. One way is the organization change needed or desired. For example, is the issue to change the state of morale, the way work is done, the communication system, the reporting system, the structure or the location of the decision making, the effectiveness of the top team, the relationships between levels, or the way goals are set, or what?

The other aspect of defining the change problem is what *type* of change is desired and what is the *hierarchy* or *rank-ordering* of these types? One should ask if the *primary* initial change requires a change:

Of attitudes? Of whose?
Of behavior? By whom and to what?
Of knowledge and understanding? Where?
Of organization procedures? Where?
Of practices and ways of work?

Rank-ordering the various types of change processes helps to determine which early interventions are most appropriate.

Defining the Appropriate "Client" Systems

Once having defined the change problem or problems from the point of view of both *organizational change* problems and change *process* problems, one can then look at the organization to determine which specific subsystems are primarily related to this particular problem. The appropriate systems may be the organizational hierarchy, may be pieces of it, may be systems both inside and outside the formal structure, may be parts of the formal structure, and not other parts. An identification of those parts of the total system which primarily affect or are affected by this particular change helps to cut down the number of subsystems to be considered, and also helps to clarify directions for early intervention.

Determining Each (Sub)System's Readiness and Capability for Change

Readiness, as used here, means either attitudinal or motivational energy directed toward the change. Capability means the physical, financial, organizational capacity to make the change.

For change to be possible and for the commitment to occur, there has to be enough dissatisfaction with the current state of affairs to mobilize energy toward a change. There also has to be some fairly clear answer about what the state of affairs would be if and when the changes are successful, in order for energy to be mobilized toward it. A desired state needs to be consistent with the values and priorities of the client system. There also needs to be some client awareness of practical first steps, or starting points toward the desired state.

An early diagnosis by the consultant of which of these conditions does not exist, or does not exist in high strength, may provide direct clues as to where to put early intervention energy. For example, if most of the system is not really dissatisfied with the present state of things, then early interventions may well need to aim toward increasing the level of dissatisfaction. On the other hand, there may be plenty of dissatisfaction with the present state, but no clear picture of what a desired state may be. In this case, early interventions might be aimed to get strategic parts of the organization defining the ideal or desired state. If both of these conditions exist, but practical first steps are missing, then early interventions may well be to pick some subsystem; for example, the top unit or a couple of experimental groups, and to begin improvement activities.

A case illustration: A general manager was concerned that the line managers weren't making good use of the resources of the staff specialists. He felt the specialists weren't aggressive enough in offering their help. He had a "desired state" picture of what "good" use of staff by line would be. He also had a *practical first step* in mind: send the staff out to visit the units on a systematic basis; as a control they would report back to him after their visits. He sent a memo to all staff and line heads announcing "the plan." Staff went to the field; they had a variety of experiences, mostly frustrating. The general manager got very busy on other priorities and did not hold his planned follow-up meetings. After one round of visits, the staff stopped its visits except in rare cases. Things returned to "normal." An analysis showed that the general manager's *real* level of dissatisfaction with the previous state of affairs wasn't big enough to cause him to invest personal energy — follow-up reporting — so the change didn't stay changed.

Capability is sometimes within one's control but frequently is outside personal control. For example, a personnel or training manager may be very ready to initiate a management development program, but have low *capability* for doing it because he has no funds or support. Two subordinates in an organization may be equally ready and motivated toward some change in their own functioning or leadership skills. One may have reached the ceiling of his capabilities and the other may not. This variable is an important guideline in determining interventions.

Identifying Consultant's Own Resources and Motivations for the Change

In addition to defining where the system is, and where the client is, and determining with the client the rank-ordering of change priorities, it is necessary for the consultant to be fairly clear with himself and preferably also with the client about what knowledge and skills he brings to the problems and what knowledge and skills he does *not* have. One of the results of the early dependency on a consultant, particularly if the first interventions are seen as helpful, is to transfer the expertise of the consultant in a particular field to being expert in anything. I have had clients ask my advice on investments, family life, which kind of car they should drive, and all sorts of items on which my competence to help just isn't there.

Consultant's Own Motivations

In assessing one's own motivations, one of the fundamental choices that the consultant must make is when to be a substantive advocate, and when to be a methodologist.

The values of the consultant and the values of the system and their congruence or incongruence come together around this point. The choice of whether to work with the client, whether to try to influence the client toward the consultant's value system, whether to take an active or passive role, are a function of the decision that is made around the choice of substantive advocacy *vs* methodological advocacy.

This is not an absolute decision that, once made at the beginning of a relationship, holds firm throughout a change effort. Rather, it is a choice that is made daily around the multitude of interventions throughout a change effort.

Determining an Intermediate Change Strategy and Goals

Once change problems and change goals are defined (particularly the kinds of goals that are concerned with moving toward "health" or "effectiveness"), it is important to look at intermediate objectives, if enough positive tension and energy toward change is to be maintained. For example, let us suppose a change goal is to have all of the work teams in an organization looking at their own functioning and systematically setting work priorities and improvement priorities on a regular basis. An intermediate goal might be to have seeded the various diversions or sections of the organization with at least one team per unit having achieved this condition by a certain time.

Determining First Steps

One other set of diagnostic questions that I find relevant is to look at the subsystems again in terms of:

Vulnerability or *readiness* of each system to influence by the consultant and/or entry client.

Accessibility of each of the subsystems to the consultant or entry client.

Linkage of each of the subsystems to the total system or organization.

In the earlier illustration of starting a management development program, if the personnel director were highly vulnerable to influence by the consultant and highly accessible to the consultant, but had low linkage to the organization; and if the president were much less vulnerable to influence by the consultant and entry client, who might be the training manager, which of them should sign the announcement of the program to the line management? The correct answer is not necessarily the president, with his higher linkage, nor the personnel man, with his accessibility and commitment. The point is that weighing these three variables helps the consultant and client to make an operational decision based on data.

The concepts of systematic system analysis and system change help develop a realistic, practical, and more attainable strategy and goals.

INTERVENTION STRATEGIES IN LARGE SYSTEMS

To this point we have been looking at the process of intervention — its dynamics and characteristics; at some issues around the relationship between the intervenor and the entry client; at the processes involved in problem identification, and early diagnosis. I'd like now to examine briefly what kinds of conditions in organizations tend to need large system interventions. I want to discuss a few of these that I consider most relevant:

Change in relationship of the organization to its environment;
Change in managerial strategy;
Change in organization structure;
Change in ways work is done; and
Change in the reward system.

Change in Relationship of Organizations to Their Environments

The number and complexity of outside demands on organization leaders is increasing at a rapid pace. Pressures from special interest organizations, minorities, youth, governments, consumers — each with strong demands for priorities of organization effort, have *required* organization leaders to focus on creative adaptation to these pressures. The autonomy of organizations is fast becoming a myth. More and more organization leaders are recognizing that the institutions they manage are truly *open* systems. Improvement strategy based on looking at the internal structure, decision making, intergroup relationships, *exclusively* both is incomplete and not realistic. A more relevant method is to start with looking at how the organization and its key subsystems relate to the different environments with which the organization interfaces. One can then determine what kinds of organization structures, procedures, and practices are necessary for *each of the units* in the organization, to optimize the interface with its different environment. Once having identified these, management then can turn its energy toward the problems of integration (of standards, rewards, communications systems) which are consequences of the multiple interfaces.[1]

Clark, Krone, and McWhinney have developed a technology called "Open Systems Planning." It helps the management of an organization to systematically sharpen its mission statement; to look objectively at its present environmental relationships.

Such a planning method serves several purposes: it forces systematic thinking; it forces people to think from outside-in (environment to organization); it forces empathy with other parts of the environment; it forces facing the realities of today; and it forces a systematic plan for priorities in the medium term future.

There is an increasing demand for assistance in helping organization leaders with these macro-organization issues. Much current change agent training almost ignores this market need. Major changes in specialist training are called for, if OD specialists are to

*This concept is further developed by: Paul Lawrence and Jay Lorsch, *Organization and Environment: Managing Differentiation and Integration*, Harvard University Press, Cambridge, 1967.

stay organizationally relevant.

Change of Managerial Strategy

A change in the *style* of managing the human resources of the organization can come about when top management is changing its assumptions and/or values about people and their motivations. It can come about as a result of new inputs from the environment; for example, loss of a number of key executives, or difficulty in recruiting young people or females into the organization, or government requiring new employment practices.

Whatever the causes, once such a change is planned, help is likely to be needed in: working with the top leaders; assessing middle management attitudes; unfreezing old attitudes; developing credibility down the line; and dealing with interfacing organizations, unions, and regulatory agencies.

Help can be provided in organization diagnosis, job design, goal setting, team building, and planning. Style changes need considerable time and patience; perspective is essential and is often lost by the client. Both internal and outside consultants can provide significant leadership in providing perspectives. Some of the questions about key managers needing answers in planning a change in managerial strategy are:

To what degree does top management encourage influence from other parts of the organization? How do they manage conflict?

To what degree do they locate decision making based on where information is located, rather than by hierarchical roles? How do they handle rewards that they control? What kind of feedback systems do they have for getting information about the state of things?

Change of Organization Structures

One key aspect of healthy or effective organizations is that the structures, the formal ways work is organized, *follow* and relate to the work to be done; in many organizations the structure relates to the *authority* system: who reports to whom. Most organizations are designed to simplify the structure in order to get clear reporting lines which clearly define the power relationships.

As work becomes more complex, it becomes impossible, in any large system, to have *one* organization structure that is relevant to all of the kinds of work to be done. The basic organization chart rarely describes the way even the basic work gets done. However, more and more organization leaders recognize and endorse the reality that organizations actually operate through a variety of structures which are in addition to the "permanent" organization chart, project organizations, task forces, and other temporary systems.

Let me give an illustration of a firmly fixed organizational structure which was a major resistance to getting required work done.

In this particular consumer organization there was a marketing department that was primarily concerned with competing in the marketplace, and a technical subsystem that was primarily concerned with getting packages designed with high quality. Market demands required that the organization get some sample packages of new products in supermarkets as sales promotions. The "rules of the game" were that for a package to be produced, it must go through a very, very thorough preparation, including design and considerable field testing. These standards were developed for products which were marked extensively, in a market where the company had a very high share. The problem in this division was that the company had a very low share of the market, and was competing desperately with a number of other strong companies. Because of the overall company rules about packages, the division marketing people were unable to get the promotion packages into the stores on time. The result was they were losing an even greater share of the market. The frustration was tremendous, and it was felt right up to the president.

Within the marketing organization there was a very bright, technically oriented, skilled, abrasive entrepreneurial type. He kept very heavy pressure on the technical package people. He was convinced that he could produce the packages himself within a matter of weeks as opposed to months that the technical people required. Because of his abrasiveness, he produced a great deal of tension in the technical department — to the point where the managers wouldn't even speak to him. The tensions between the two departments increased. At one point, the heads of the two departments were on a very "cool" basis. The president of the company was "climbing the walls" at the loss of markets. He had earlier attempted to do something about the situation by giving the marketing "entrepreneur" a little back shop in which he could "prove" his assertions of being able to produce a package in a short time. The man did produce them, but when he took them to the technical people for reproduction, they called up all the traditional ground rules and policies to "prove" his package wouldn't work and couldn't be used.

The client — in this case the president — had diagnosed the problem as one of non-cooperation between the departments and particularly between individuals. Based on this diagnosis, he asked for some consultative help on working the interpersonal problem between the marketing entrepreneur and the people in the technical department. He also thought perhaps an intergroup intervention might be appropriate to increase collaboration between the groups.

My diagnosis was that although either of these interventions was possible and might, in fact, produce some temporary change, through lowering the "heat" in the situation, I could not see the possibility of either event producing more packages. The change problem, as I saw it, was one of an inappropriate structure for managing work.

I suggested that the leaders of the marketing and technical developments get together to develop a flow chart of the steps involved in moving from an idea to a finished promotion piece on packages. Then I suggested they isolate those items which clearly fitted within the organization structure, such as the last few steps in the process which were handled by the buying and production department. The remaining steps, I suggested, needed to be managed by a *temporary* organization created for just that purpose. I proposed that for each new promotion, a temporary management organization be set up consisting of one person from packaging, one from marketing, one from purchasing, and one from manufacturing. This organization would have, as its charter, the management of the flow of that product from idea to manufacturing. They would analyze the problem, set a timetable, set the resource requirements, and control the flow of work. The resources they needed were back in the permanent structures of which they were also members. This task force would report weekly and *jointly* to the heads of both departments — technical and marketing. The president would withdraw from the problem.

The intervention produced the hoped-for result: promotion packages available in one-fifth of the time previously required. The interpersonal difficulties remained for some time, but gradually decreased as people were required to collaborate in getting the job done.

Change in Ways Work is Done

This condition is one where there is a special effort to improve the meaningfulness as well as the efficiency of work. Job enrichment programs, work analysis programs, development of criteria for effectiveness — all of these can be listed as interventions. To give an example, an intervention might be to work with a management group helping them take a look at their recent tasks.

Based on this analysis, a replan of work can emerge. It can have significant effects on both attitudes and behavior. The output of such an activity, by a group at the top, means that work gets re-allocated to the next level and thus a domino effect is set in motion, which can result in significant change.

Another illustration describes an organization-wide change

effort to improve both the way work is done and the management of the work.

The total white collar staff of this organization consisted of about forty thousand people. During a six-month period, the total organization met in their family groups or work teams, to develop criteria, against which that team wanted the performance of their work unit to be measured. They then located their current performance against those critieria and projected their performance at a date about six months in the future against the same criteria.

These criteria and projections were checked with senior management committees in each subsystem. If okayed, they became the work plan and basis for performance appraisal for that group.

With this one intervention, the top management distributed throughout the whole organization the responsibility for managing the work to the people who were doing the work.

The results of this program were a significant increase in productivity, significant cost reductions, and a significant change in attitudes and feelings of ownership among large numbers of employees, many of whom were previously quite dissatisfied with the state of things. A great deal of latent energy has been released and continues to be used by people all over the organization who feel responsible and appreciated for *their* management of *their* work.

Changing the Reward System

One significant organization problem is getting the reward system consistent with the work. How often we see organizations in which someone in a staff department spends 90% of his time in assisting some line department; yet at his annual review, his performance is evaluated solely by the head of his staff department probably on 10% of his work. One result of this is that any "smart" person behaves in ways that please the man who most influences his career and other rewards, rather than those with whom he is working. Inappropriate reward systems do much to sabotage effective work as well as organization health. An example of an intervention in this area: the group vice president of one of the major groups of businesses in a very large company was concerned about the lack of motivation of his division general managers in working with him on planning for the future of the business as a whole. He was also equally concerned that they were giving lip service to the development of their own subordinates. In his opinion, this was standing in the way of their own promotions. He had spoken of these concerns many times. His staff had agreed that it was important to change, but their behavior was heavily directed toward maintaining the old priorities: meeting short-term profit goals. This group existed in an organization where the reward system was very clear. The chief executives in any sub-enterprise were accountable for their short-term profits. This was their *most* important assignment. Given that company's reward system, whatever the group vice president wished, it was predictable that his managers would work to the organization's real reward system, even if only because of the fear of negative consequences if they didn't. Division managers knew that if they did not participate actively in future business planning, or if they did not invest energy in the development of subordinates, they would incur the group vice president's displeasure and perhaps be spanked. They also knew, however, that if they did not meet their short-term profit objectives, they probably would not be around. The company had an executive incentive bonus plan (considerable amounts of bonus money were available to people in the upper ranks for good performance). In trying to find a method for changing his division managers' priorities, the group vice president looked, with consultant help, at the reward system. As a result of this, he called his colleagues together and told them, "I thought you'd like to know that in determining your bonus at the next review, I will be using this formula. You are still 100% accountable for your short-term profit goals — but that represents 60% of the bonus. Another 25% will be my evaluation of your performance as members of this top management planning team. The other 15% will be your discernible efforts toward the development of your subordinates."

Executive behavior changed dramatically all over the place. The reality — the reward system — and the desired state now were consistent.

I have looked very briefly at several types of organization phenomena which need large system oriented interventions. I would like now to move back to look at initial interventions, and to examine in another way the choices facing the intervener.

EARLY INTERVENTIONS

There are a number of choices about where to intervene, of which the following are several. My intention is to lay out a map of possibilities.

1. The top team or the top of a system.

2. A pilot project which can have a linkage to the larger system.

3. Ready subsystems — those whose leaders and members are known to be ready for a change.

4. Hurting systems. This is one class of ready system where the environment has caused some acute discomfort in a generally

unready system.

5. The rewards system.

6. Experiments. A series of experiments on new ways of organizing or new ways of handling communications.

7. Educational interventions — training programs, outside courses, etc.

8. An organization-wide confrontation meeting, bringing together a variety of parts of the organization, to examine the state of affairs and to make first step plans for improvement.

9. The creation of a critical mass.

I want to elaborate a little on this last concept. It is most difficult for a stable organization to change itself; that is, for the regular structures of the organization to be used for change. Temporary systems are frequently created to accomplish this. As an example, in one *very* large system — a country — there were a number of agencies involved in training and developing organization leaders. The government provided grants to them for training activities. These grants provided funds to support the agency staffs for other purposes. Because of this condition each agency was busily mounting programs for the same small clientele. Each agency kept innovations secret from its competitors.

As an attempt to move this competitive state toward a more collaborative one, a small group of people developed a "*non-organization*" called the Association for Commercial and Industrial Education. It was a luncheon club. Its rules were the opposite of an ordinary organization. It could make no group decisions; it distributed no minutes; no one was allowed to take any one else to lunch; there were no dues; there were no officers or hierarchy in the organization.

In this context it was possible for *individuals* from the various competing agencies to sit down and talk together about matters of mutual interest. After a couple of years it even became possible to mount a national organization development training project — a four week course which was attended by top line managers and personnel people from all the major economic and social institutions in the country. Only this non-organization could sponsor such a program. From this program a great many other linkages were developed.

MAINTAINING CHANGE

To *maintain* change in a large system it is necessary to have conscious procedures and commitment. Organization change will not be maintained because there has been early success. Many organizations are living with the effects of successful short-term change results which have not been maintained.

Perhaps the most important single requirement for continued change is a continuing *feedback* and information system that lets people in the organization know where they are in relation to a desired state. Some feedback systems that are used fairly frequently are:

1. Periodic team meetings to review where a team is and what its next goal priorities should be.

2. Organization sensing meetings — the top of an organization meets, on a systematic planned basis, with a sample of employees from a variety of different organizational centers, in order to keep apprised of the state of the system.

3. Periodic intergroup meetings between interdependent units of an organization.

4. Renewal conferences. One company I know has an annual planning meeting with its top management. Three weeks prior to that meeting the same management group and their wives go to a retreat for two or three days to take a look at where they are, where their personal and company priorities are, what are the new forces in the environment, what do they need to keep in mind in their upcoming planning, what has happened in the way they work and in their relationships that need review before the planning meeting.

5. Performance review on a systematic goal directed basis.

6. Periodic visits from outside consultants to keep the organization leaders thinking about the organization's renewal.

There are many other possible techniques but these are probably the most commonly used methods.

SUMMARY

Toward *helping* organizations improve their operational effectiveness and system health, I have examined:

1. Some conditions for organization change;
2. Some assumptions about relationships between the system and the facilitator or consultant;
3. Some implications of these dynamics for the behavior of the consultant;
4. An analysis of what the consultant brings to the relationship;
5. His operational choices in establishing a contract;
6. A model for determining his early organization interventions;
7. Some choices of change strategies;
8. Some choices of early interventions; and

9. Some choices of strategies for maintaining change.

As I said at the beginning, the focus of this chapter has been on what the third party or facilitator can do as either a consultant, expert, trainer, or coach, in helping organization leaders diagnose their own system and to plan strategies for development toward a better state. This focus includes process intervention but is not exclusively that. It also includes skills of system diagnosis, of determining change strategies, of understanding the relationship of organizations to external environments, of understanding such organizational processes as power, reward systems, organizational decision-making, information systems, structural designs, and planning processes.

A final comment — it is this writer's experience that the demand for assistance in organizational interventions and large system organization change is increasing at a very fast rate. It is my personal opinion that it is increasing faster than there are qualified resources to meet the demands. As the world shrinks, as we have more multi-national organizations, as the interfaces between government and the private sector and the social sector become more blurred and more overlapping, large system interventions and the technology and skill available to facilitate these will be in continuing greater need and demand.

BIBLIOGRAPHY

Books

Beckhard, R. *Organization Development — Strategies and Models*, Addison-Wesley; Reading, Mass.; 1969.

Blake, R., and Mouton, J. *Building a Dynamic Corporation Through Grid Organization Development*, Addison-Wesley; Reading, Mass.; 1969.

Dyer, William G. *The Sensitive Manipulator*, Brigham Young University Press; Provo, Utah; 1973.

French, Wendell L., and Bell, Cecil H., Jr. *Organization Development*, Prentice-Hall; Englewood Cliffs, New Jersey; 1973.

Galbraith, Jay R. *Designing Complex Organizations*, Addison-Wesley; Reading, Mass.; 1973.

Hornstein, Harvey A., et al. *Social Intervention*, The Free Press; New York; 1971.

Lawrence, Paul R., and Lorsch, Jay W. *Developing Organizations: Diagnosis and Action*, Addison-Wesley; Reading, Mass.; 1969.

Likert, Rensis. *The Human Organization*, McGraw-Hill Book Company; New York; 1967.

McGregor, Douglas. *The Human Side of Enterprise*, McGraw-Hill; New York; 1960.

Myers, M. Scott. *Every Employee a Manager*, McGraw-Hill; New York; 1970.

Schein, Edgar H. *Organization Psychology*, Second Edition, Pretice-Hall; Englewood Cliffs, New Jersey; 1970.

_____ *Process Consultation*, Addison-Wesley; Reading, Mass.; 1969.
1969.

ORGANIZATIONS AND COMMUNITIES

Articles

Beckhard, R. "The Confrontation Meeting," *Harvard Business Review, 45,* 2; March—April, 1967.

French, Wendell, and Bell, Cecil. "Organization Development: An Overview," *Journal of Contemporary Business, 31,* University of Washington; Summer, 1972.

CHAPTER 19

COMMUNITY DEVELOPMENT THROUGH LABORATORY METHODS

Eva Schindler-Rainman

Interest in community development and participation of citizens in shaping their own environment, social relations, and way of life is at an all time high in our country and in the world. Therefore, the art and applied science of community development have been increasingly refined over the years, and we now know a variety of ways to help people learn community development technology, particularly through participative laboratory methods. It is the aim of community development to plan and implement plans for improving the quality of human life in geographic and functional communities. Usually community development happens in one of the many functional communities that may be found in any geographic community. These include the religious, educational, recreational, welfare, health (both physical and mental), political, economic, mass media, public safety, and cultural communities. It is the aim of community developers to improve existing situations, or to initiate new developments, using the data and experience of previous efforts and future trend predictions to improve the patterns and conditions of living. For instance, there are great efforts in many communities to develop child care centers, so that working mothers can have their children taken care of. There are many efforts in the educational community to change the nature of education. All of this is part of total community development.

ESSENTIAL INGREDIENTS OF COMMUNITY DEVELOPMENT

The essential ingredients of this process include the following:

1. Citizens who will be affected by such planning and development be included in the planning and development.

2. Agencies, organizations, and institutions who have appropriate and relevant connections to any given community development effort be involved collaboratively in the planning and action phases.

3. The professional, paraprofessional and the volunteer, the public as well as the private sectors of the community, be involved.

4. The groups to be involved include a vertical slice of community, from policy-makers and power figures to volunteers and citizens; people with or without particular status or title, elected and selected leadership persons, men and women, from all sectors of the community.

5. The planners and implementers of community development be inter-racial, intergenerational, and come from various social and economic groups in the community. For development means development of particular processes or projects by a variety of people representing themselves and/or a variety of organizations, agencies and institutions. Therefore, community development must always be an interorganizational, inter-group process.

THE COMMUNITY ORGANIZATION PROCESS

Community organization, on the other hand, here is defined as the process of organizing the community to work on various developmental projects. Community organization is the organizing of the sectors of community mentioned above in order to produce developmental processes. The community organizer may be the change agent, giving leadership or providing consultation, enabling the sectors of community to work together on community development projects and processes.

Organizational development, on the other hand, is the organization and coordination of the internal units and processes of the functional community agencies and organizations within the geographic community. Richard Beckhard gives this definition of organization development: "Organization is an effort, (1) planned, (2) organizationwide, and (3) managed from the top to (4) increase organization effectiveness and health through (5) planned interventions in the organization processes, using behavioral science knowledge."[1] Within community development are both community organization and organizational development existing so that the community, as well as its organizations, can function at maximum effectiveness to implement the community developmental processes.

SOME SIMILARITIES AND DIFFERENCES

There are some interesting differences as well as similarities between community development and organization development. The *differences* include the following:

1. In the community, the process is always *intergroup*, that is, between groups and organizations who must collaborate on given projects, while in the organization the process is within one organization. It may be interdepartmental, or within one unit of the organization.

2. The second difference has to do with *loyalty*. Within the geographic community there are many loyalties to be dealt with, loyalties to several different organizations; often loyalty to the geographic community itself; loyalty to sub-communities; and loyalty to a variety of causes. In the organizational context there may be loyalty to the organization, and perhaps to one's department or superior, but it is a different kind of thing than the many different "loyalty hats" people wear within a community.

3. A third factor is the *commitment* factor. In an organization, part of the commitment, if an employee has it, is due to the fact that he is paid in money for his services. Commitment to community causes is often of a different variety. There may be strong religious, ethical, or philosophical commitments to particular causes or particular projects.

4. Another difference is that in the community one almost always works with both *professionals and volunteers*, while that is not true in most organizations.

5. Also, the *multiple agenda* of communities need to be considered. While there might be the question of child care centers and improved education within the community, there are many other agenda. There will be many other kinds of things equally important to various people, all the way from urban-suburban planning to passing the bonds for the water district, to electing new board of education members, to rapid transit plans. Within the organization, though there may be multiple agenda, their extent is not nearly so vast or complicated as those of the total geographic community.

6. Another difference is that often in community development projects the *efforts* of people, both professional and volunteer, *are voluntary;* that is, people can be asked, requested, but not

required, to come to meetings, and participate in a planning or action process. But in an organization it is possible for management to require participation of employees. The participation may or may not be willing, but it can be required. This is much harder to do in a community setting.

7. Another possible difference is that in community development there is a maximum effort to include *different sectors* of community population, and this is probably a neater group to draw from than would be found in any organization, even if all the different sectors of an organization were included in the development and the planning processes.

What are some of the *similarities* of community and organization development? There are many:

1. In organization development the *change effort may be or may not be organizationwide.* In community development the change effort may or may not be *communitywide.* The change effort may be initiated by only one functional part of the community, and may not involve the other functional sectors of community. For example, the planning of day care centers may not involve all ten functional sectors of community, although perhaps the election of municipal officials would.

2. In both cases, the *change effort* is a *planned* one, including diagnosis of the situation, development of strategies for changing the situation, and mobilizing human and material resources to do so.

3. *Resistance to change* certainly will be found in both the functional and geographic communities, as well as in the organization, and may be due to some of the same causes in both contexts.

4. Another similarity is the *necessity for involvement of those to be affected by the change.* In both cases this would include the planners as well as the consumers of change.

5. Another similarity is that change or development in both cases is surely *designed to increase effectiveness*, the quality of life, and the ability of people to do their jobs.

6. In both cases, *vertical and horizontal participation* is necessary in the community and in the organization.

7. Also in both cases, *ongoing evaluation* should be part of the developmental process.

8. *Planned interventions*, using behavioral science knowledge, would be another similarity in both community and organization change processes.

9. The need for an *inside-outside change agent team* usually is evident in both settings. This means that, in order to have effective community and/or organization development, it is necessary to combine resources and talents of outside consultants. They, to-

gether with a larger group of representative persons, plan the change process, and lead participants through it.

10. Another similarity is that in both cases these developmental processes are *long term efforts*, not "one-shot" affairs. They must be carefully planned, carefully implemented, carefully replanned and evaluated, and the goals and implementation steps are such that they usually take a long period of time to carry out.

11. The programs and projects are *action oriented.* This is particularly true in this day and age, when studies alone often are not what is desired by either communities or organizations. Studies are required to be of the kind that can be translated into actions of specific kinds.

12. The developmental efforts in both community and organization largely are done *through groups* rather than through individuals, so that groups and teams are the basic units through which developmental efforts toward effectiveness, improvement, and greater health are made.

Some of the *conditions for success* of community development and organization development projects are also quite similar. These include:

1. A felt need for change;
2. Skilled leadership to bring about this change; both inside and outside leadership;
3. Openness to a variety of alternative solutions, rather than looking for one pretested recipe;
4. Willingness to commit to long-term change goals;
5. The necessary budget available, or the expertise and willingness to get the needed funds;
6. A pain great enough to warrant change; or a strong image of potential improvement;
7. The willingness to take risks in trying new patterns in collaborative work or new relationships;
8. Stepwise successes that can be seen, felt and known along the way to support and maintain motivation;
9. The commitment to action is based on careful diagnosis and analysis, as well as tentative alternative strategies that are creative and exciting to the participants;
10. There are positive support and recognition as changes happen that are successful, so that new practices get some acceptance;
11. Appropriate and relevant people from different sides of issues with differing opinions and a great variety of resources are participating in the process;
12. Failure experiences are shared and used as a basis for evaluation and change.

PRESENT AND FUTURE SOCIETAL TRENDS AFFECTING COMMUNITY DEVELOPMENT TRAINING

As one looks at the community development picture, it becomes evident that it is very much affected by the kinds of present and future societal trends that both define and forecast some of the major community development confrontations and challenges. "Trend," as used here, means a dynamic process that is already happening somewhere in the society, but will probably spread and intensify as time goes by. We do not see a societal trend as something which will begin at some magic date in the future, when a particular curtain is raised.

Collaboration and Interdependence

Thus, for example, the *collaboration and interdependence of community agencies and organizations will increase* in the future. We are seeing beginnings in the 70s of this trend or phenomenon. John Platt, in an article entitled "What's ahead for 1990?" says: "We are in the midst of a great world transformation to new levels of energy, communication, human interaction and planetary organization. The necessary limits and outline of the new system — if we are to survive — are already fairly clear." He said later: "If we can design new institutions to control our crisis in time, what will life be like in the world ahead? I think there will be new patterns of politics, new patterns of rights, and new patterns of human relations."[2] This indicates that the central focus for change will be in our communities where the old institutions will have to change to meet new demands, confrontations, and needs, and will succeed only as people now separated learn to collaborate and work with each other. The need and requirement to become increasingly interdependent and collaborative is caused by a variety of factors, including the demands by private and public funding bodies, requiring that projects to be funded be carried out collaboratively by all relevant systems in the community. For example, if a new drug education program for teenagers is to be innovated, the funding agency, whether it be the United Way of America, a private foundation, or a federal funding source, will require that all the people and all the organizations that can help with this project are involved, referred to, and called together to make a sustained collaborative effort to build such a program, instead of either a new organization doing it, or one of the old agencies "going it alone." The latter has been the trend for a long time, and is not an easy one to divert, since going it alone is somehow inextricably bound up with private initiative, individual enterprise, and "doing your own thing." Another pressure for interdependence is the need for far better planning in both the public and private sectors. This means involving not only more units, but more persons of a variety of backgrounds in the planning process.

Changing Power Bases

A second trend is the trend toward *changing bases of power.* We are seeing the trend of shared power; shared between the provider and the consumer, between the employer and the employee, between the young and the older, between the decision-makers and the decision "carry-outers."

Polarization

A third trend is the trend towards *polarization,* which is certainly a counter trend to interdependence. As groups gain identity and power in our society, there is increasing polarization. For example, the polarizations between black and white, between oriental and white, between young and old, between establishment and non-establishment. One of the confrontations for a community is how to help polarized groups bridge, if not close, the gap or gaps. New patters of human relations will have to be found, including ways for groups with polarized ideas, ideals, and commitments to find creative compromises, to find ways to maximize their differences in a way that helps them come out with new and creative solutions, new ideas, that would not have happened if the differences had not been openly aired. Methodological advocacy is a necessary tool here.

Rights of the Individual

A fourth trend is the move toward looking for individual identity and *new rights for the individual.* As ethnic and minority groups gain more power and more identity, so individuals, men, women, and the young also are seeking new rights. Perhaps the phrase "doing your own thing" characterizes the search as well as any. Also the movement toward demands for humaneness in treatment by the consumers, whether in individual psychiatric treatment, legal treatment, or treatment by public agencies, be they welfare, health, or probation, is another focus on the individual that is developing. We also are seeing increasing demands by individuals for rights to share in decision making that affects their destiny. Other forms of the search for individuality are new patterns of living, including a variety of communal forms. The challenge to community developers is to be sure to include people whose lifestyles and values are different from those of the majority in the community development and social change ventures that affect them.

Changing Work Life

The *changing world of work and voluntarism* is another dynamic affecting community development. Not only are the places changing where work for pay can be done, but many people either are working fewer hours or fewer years in their lifetime, and are, therefore, available for volunteering or for other kinds of service roles and new careers in the community. More people are not working, whether by design, or because they cannot get jobs, and are, therfore, recruitable for community development efforts. This connects with another related trend, which is the changing world of the volunteer. More and more people are available to give of their time, ideas, ideals, skills, and resources in voluntary capacities of their own choice. It seems we are moving into an age of commitment in which many people, young, middle and older, from all ethnic, racial, social and economic and religious backgrounds are available to volunteer as long as they can do so in an area in which they have interest, or in a cause to which they are committed.

Complexities of Society

The *complexity of the society* and of living has been increasing at an extremely rapid rate. It is difficult to keep up with all of the changes, plus the very complexity of change increases resistance to change on the part of many people. One of the areas in which the complexity can be of great help to the community is in the area of media technology. Information is much easier to spread around and may be had almost instantaneously, rather than being deferred through a time lag. Television is making it possible to involve people in new ways, in planning, in information giving and getting, and a variety of other ways. Through video- and audio-tape, people can be involved in new ways. The world of news media offers confrontations to the community developers to learn to utilize these media to involve more people in more exciting, creative ways than ever before.

Federal Funds and Programs

The vastness and pervasiveness of federal, state, and local government interventions of funds and program resources are affecting community development as much as any of the other trends. There are few areas of community life in which the government does not intervene in one way or another. It may be by making funds, or human, or material resources available, or it may be because it provides a monitoring function. This trend has both positive resource characteristics, as well as the negative invasion of privacy and restrictions of local autonomy.

WHY LAB EDUCATION IS A GOOD APPROACH TO COMMUNITY DEVELOPMENT TRAINING

1. *Persons learn about what is going on within a group and between people, as well as how to do a particular task.*

2. *Participants in the community development process are involved from the very beginning.*

3. *There is an emphasis on feedback.*

4. *The work is done in small face-to-face groups.*

5. *Conflict is legitimized.*

6. *Difference and diversity are utilized as a resource.*

7. There is a concept of *learning to learn* new ways of learning.

8. There is *support for the linkage of values and intentions to action taking.*

9. This is done through *skill development learning.*

10. *Retrieval, use, and adaptation of research-tested social and behavioral knowledge* is another aspect of laboratory learning.

11. *Learning to live with multiple loyalties* might be considered another value and outcome.

12. *Commitment to helping produce healthy community and organizational environments* is an important value.

SOME ASSUMPTIONS AND HOPED-FOR OUTCOMES

Among the assumptions that can be made of laboratory education as an approach to community development are the following:

1. That planned social change in communities can be brought about by teams of interested and trained social scientists with community collaborators.

2. That persons, in order to feel skilled and able to cause change to happen, must participate in the planning and carrying out of these changes.

3. That a series of supports is needed by the change agents. These include inside as well as outside team members. These supports can be developed in the laboratory learning environment through interaction with peers, bosses, trainers, team-mates, and consultants.

4. That laboratory settings can offer a simulated situation of real life community settings for experiencing, in an anticipatory way, the kinds of experiences one will have in a real way in the community change process.

5. The laboratory method is adaptive to community popula-

tions with different needs, resources and skills.

6. That the diverse resources of trainers and participants can be utilized and maximized in collaborative work on community problem solving.

With these assumptions as our orientation, what are some of the kinds of outcomes that various laboratory designs for community development would have in common? What would we hope participants in this kind of experiential training would learn, or increase their learning about, during and as a result of the process? Among these would be:

1. An increased understanding of the dynamics of change, including such things as (a) how to handle resistance to change to community change efforts, (b) how to diagnose the readiness for change, and (c) how to plan for change and cause change to happen.

2. Learning alternative strategies to help change to happen.

3. Increasing the feeling of ability and power to cause change, on the part of the participants. This is a particularly important outcome in an age in which so many people feel powerless. The objective is both to help individuals feel powerful as individuals, and also as teams and groups in the community.

4. Participants will have learned the skills of planning, designing and carrying out change projects with consultative support of a variety of kinds.

5. Participants will have learned how to discover and utilize diverse talent, skills and resources, including their own.

6. Participants will have developed a large variety of basic skills, both human relation skills and action skills, in order to translate plans and intentions into skilled behaviors and strategies.

7. There will be an ability to assess and appreciate stepwise movement (often small steps) toward goals.

8. There will be an ability to transfer what has been learned in one community development learning experience to other community settings.

9. Participants will have increased ability to relate to people different from themselves.

10. Participants will have increased faith in themselves, and in others, and in the democratic system as a method that can facilitate change through collaborative planning and action, in concert with other human beings.

IMPORTANT INGREDIENTS FOR COMMUNITY DEVELOPMENT LABORATORY EXPERIENCES

Laboratory learning of community development processes now is being accomplished in a variety of settings.

1. *In a Laboratory Community.* This is a setting where, over a period of time from three days to two weeks or more in a workshop setting, community volunteers, professionals and paraprofessionals learn together planned strategies for change. They utilize all of the resources of each other and the trainers to do so, and may use a variety of designs, including simulation, emergent designs, and participant-planned designs. Often these kinds of laboratory communities are set up away from the real geographic community, as a kind of cultural island for the teaching-learning transactions. Such a laboratory may be variously sponsored, for example, by the NTL Institute for Applied Behavioral Science, alone or in cooperation with a university, by a network of community agencies and organizations, by university extension or continuing education division, or by others.

2. *In the Geographic Community.* The laboratory training may take place within the geographic community, where the actual development project is underway. Participants from a given community, therefore, or from a cluster of communities, come as individuals or in teams, and the training often includes action research, action planning, inter-agency or organization collaboration, specific problem solving, evaluation techniques, and others.

The interesting thing about this approach is that the training can become a part of an on-going community development project, since people may meet intermittently (for example five times a year, or twelve times a year, or twice a month) utilizing their own projects as the learning material in the laboratory. Often in such a case the team may be an outside-inside team of trainers, and it may include some experienced community people as part of the teaching team.[3]

3. *Within one Agency or Community Segment.* Sometimes the laboratory takes in one of the functional communities, for example, the health services community. The training may be mainly for interdisciplinary health teams, and may, therefore, take place in the large meeting room of a hospital, or in one of the voluntary health agencies. This, too, may be ongoing, or a three-day to two-weeks workshop, usually with follow-up at later intermittent times.

It is becoming evident that community development laboratory training should be of an ongoing nature, and cannot be successful if it is a one-time, one-shot kind of training. Therefore, no matter where it takes place, or for what length of time, some kind of ongoing training meetings need to be provided to help people look at both the process and the task in which they are involved, and to give them some "booster shots" as they go, both in terms of theoretical knowledge and skill development. This kind of ongoing training gives the participants the support they need in order to stay motivated and committed.

DESIGN INGREDIENTS

Anyone who participates in community development experiences, regardless of the setting or the timing, needs to be exposed to the following kinds of content ingredients.

1. *Strategy of Entry and Start-up.* How does one begin a community development change process? Included in the entry and start-up, learning experiences would be: how to develop a contract between the change agent and the community or communities; inside-outside team development; clarification of roles of different team members; discussion and planning of who should be involved, by whom and when, in the start-up process.

2. *Support mechanisms.* Included here would be the kinds of supports needed in order for the change process to take place, at the beginning and during the change project. The development of peer support, other agencies' support, and power figure support are important content and practice dynamics here. Also included here would be the development of the inside-outside change agent team, and how they will work together to support each other.

3. *Renewal mechanisms.* Important items to include are a variety of feedback techniques, different meeting designs, and the planning of meetings to get ideas and critique from consumers and participants. Also practice in designing and redesigning can be offered through role playing, case presentations, audio and/or video taped live situations techniques.

4. *Documentation.* As part of any laboratory training method participants learn how to document each step of the way, and how to utilize this documentation in order not only to have a history of what they have been doing, but also in order to improve their processes as they go, as well as to provide the basis for handing out and disseminating information to others during and after the change process.

5. *Dissemination.* This includes learning how to disseminate information, to whom, and when to do so. Actual practice in designing the dissemination items should be part of the laboratory learning process. This includes reports, questionnaires, reaction sheets, rating scales, and feedback instruments and their results.

Woven through these ingredients are the following

kinds of learnable methods and skills: (a) consultation skills within and between systems; (b) skills in inter-agency collaboration either to improve ongoing collaboration or to initiate a collaborative network; (c) alternative designs for problem-solving tasks; (d) methodological advocacy skills, sometimes known as third party mediation; (e) confrontation skills; (f) action research skills; (g) training skills; (h) diagnostic skills, including understanding the power and influence structures within the community, within organizations, and between systems; (i) learning how to motivate and utilize idigenous human resources of a great variety of kinds; (j) understanding of different values through value dialogue, discussions and confrontation.

Thus the design ingredients and the threads running through them are aimed to implement some, if not all, of the already mentioned outcomes. It is very important that participants in community development laboratory experiences receive help and support as they move through the process, as will be illustrated in the next section.

TWO CASE ILLUSTRATIONS

1. Collaboration for Future Planning

Background Information. This series of events took place in a middle-sized midwestern community. The Junior League decided that it had funds and was willing to sponsor a community wide planning conference. It was the hope of the League to help the community look at some of the current problems that needed present and future planning. A private foundation was contacted for purposes of financial co-sponsorship. A community organization consultant was contacted to help plan. The nationally-known consultant was not a member of the community, but was known to the organization. Through correspondence and telephone conferences between League planners and the consultant it was determined that a planning meeting involving the kinds of people they hoped to involve in the events should take place at least six months prior to the event. The meeting was held with professional and volunteer citizens from both the black and white communities and from all the functional communities in the geographic community participating, as well as a representative from the private funding organization. As a result of this one-day planning meeting a conference, "Perspective 70," was clearly outlined, designed and planned for six months hence. Co-sponsoring groups were the Junior League, the local War on Poverty agency, and the private foundation. Because of the mixed planning committee all kinds of cross organization fertilizations began and have continued since then.

The outside consultant teamed with the chairman of the conference, in order to form an inside-outside planning team. Also several subcommittees were developed to help with the implementation of the two-day conference to be held early the following year.

The conference was designed to awaken participants to the problems of the community, and to stimulate positive action development of a variety of kinds. Another purpose was to help develop new and better understanding among all the participants, and to work for collaboration among community organizations. People were invited from all walks of life and from all parts of the community. There were scholarships available for people unable to pay the registration fee. A free baby-sitting service was developed, as were personal ways to select and recruit participants. Since this meeting was to be a bringing together, among others, of the black and white groups for the first time in this community, it was decided that the outside team should represent a man/woman, black/white combination. Another consultant was, therefore, recruited to become part of the oustide consulting team.

Design of Activities. The two days were carefully designed to give maximum participation to the registrants. Persons preregistered, and were assigned to mixed table groups of eight the first morning. The first activity was to fill out a sheet that was on the table where they could initial where they fitted into the community in terms of which of the sectors they participated in, either professionally or as a volunteer. The next activity was a short input by the two trainers of some of the societal trends that are affecting communities and community change. After each trend there were table discussions about "how does that trend effect our community, and what are the implications for us?"

Each table group was then asked to look forward a year, and to brainstorm all the things they saw happening a year hence that pleased them because of the improvements that had taken place in their community since a year ago. After the brainstorm of these "images of potentiality," each table group selected two goal image priorities for their community. During lunch they summarized their priorities on newsprint sheets, and put them on the wall for others to see. There was much consensus on priorities among the 250 participants. The consultants then presented the steps of diagnosis and planning, and an input on forcefield analysis, to prepare the participants for the next day.

The trainers grouped the goal image priorities into ten goal areas. Each of these was put on a sheet of newsprint, and as people came in the second day they signed up for the task force group of their first choice. Some blank sheets were also put up for anyone who had a priority that had not been caught in summarizing the priority goals. It was the purpose of the second day to organize and begin work as task forces. The task forces chosen were:

a. Development of a voluntary Action Center;

b. Home retention and repair;

c. The development of a welfare rights office;

d. A youth cultural center;

e. Information and referral service;

f. Development of a citizens' advisory group to the city council;

g. Health services for the poor;

h. Coordination of youth services in four counties;

i. Development of a collaborative drug committee;

j. Development of community-coordinated child care services.

There was an opportunity for task forces to report out and get reactions, help, and consultation from other people in the room. Also a senator from the state was there to hear and react from his viewpoint to ideas and plans reported.

Outcomes of this Community Laboratory Training Event. There were a number of major outcomes.

a. Many of the recorders and facilitators who were trained the evening before the meeting became skillful leaders in their own groups. The recorder-facilitator pair at each table represented the sponsoring groups. In many cases, it was a black-white pair.

b. Ten groups still are active.

c. A continuing committee made up of some participants and some members of the sponsoring groups have kept track of the ongoing activities and meetings.

d. A meeting was held a year later at which each of the task forces presented their projects. This helped reinforce their goals and gave them support to continue.

e. As the oustide consultant change agents moved out, the leadership was taken over totally by community people.

f. New channels of communication were opened up between people from different segments of the community and continue to be open.

2. Action Research and Feedback to Mobilize the Socialization Community

Research on the education and socialization of children and youth has revealed that each day of his life the young person receives a variety of often competing and conflicting inputs from a variety of adult agents who have some type of socialization responsibility, for example, the teacher, the parent, the religious educator, the employer, the recreation leader, and the police officer. In coping with this "medley of voices," the young person frequently adopts styles of reacting which are both harmful to himself and which cut off the influence of the adult community. These findings led into the decision to combine action research and laboratory education techniques in trying to establish communication and collaboration between the various sectors of the socialization community. This approach was tried in a community of about 100,000.

Design of Flow of Activities. First, five key informants were located and interviewed. Because of their position and seniority of experience they had wide knowledge of influential leadership persons across all sectors of the community. Each of them was asked to nominate the key policy making influencers in each of the sectors of the community. They were asked to rank order the high influencers in each area of community activity. There was very high agreement among informants. From their nominations thirty to forty influential people from different community sectors were invited to meet in group interview sessions, seven or eight at a time. In these group interviews, which were conducted by one of the change agent team and one of the internal community collaborators, the group was asked among other things what they regarded as a "good product" of the socialization efforts of the community (that is, to describe behavior values, attitudes, of approved young people). The interviews typically were evening sessions of two to three hours, with the group becoming highly involved, usually requesting a second session. The final question for each interviewed group was a request to nominate the most effective and successful administrators and program leaders in the various sectors. Again, there was high agreement among the nominators, and a second round of interviews was held with groups of operating program leaders in all sectors of the community. These program leaders were requested to nominate the most creative, innovative direct workers with youth in all areas of the community.

Group interviews were conducted with these creative workers in groups of seven or eight, with members from different sectors. They in turn nominated influential older children and youth, with the requirement that their nominations include half "pro-establishment" and half "anti-establishment" young people of both sexes and from all sectors of the youth culture. Group interviews were conducted with these nominated young people.

The findings from these interviews were analyzed and converted into generalizations, and into critical issue summaries for feedback sessions with horizontal groups at the policy and administrative leadership level, and vertical groups going from leadership to youth within the various sectors. In each of these feedback sessions the stimulus materials from the findings were used as a trigger for small groups to brainstorm derivations and implications for improvement of collaboration, and improvement of the quality of the efforts to help youth grow and develop. The following cross-community, cross-agency task forces emerged with such tasks as:

a. Developing an approach to value education;

b. Developing a community-wide training program for youth leaders;

c. Developing collaboration on outreach efforts to neglected young people;

d. Development of a program for work with parents of young people in trouble;

e. Developing of a co-ordinating committee for the total socialization community;

f. Development of a youth-initiated program of intergenerational value discussions with parents and teachers.

The change agent team of external helpers from the university and internal helpers from within the community helped with consultation to task forces, the linking of the task forces to each other, the development of training opportunities which were needed to help maintain and develop the quality of the planning and action growing out of the priorities developed by the task forces.

This case illustration provides an example of a typical lack of a community mechanism to carry out a core function for a community, that is, the educating, socializing, integrating of the young into the life of the community. The development of needed community competence requires collaboration of community groups and agencies which cut across conventional turfdoms, such as school systems, families, churches, agencies, and other socialization activities. Laboratory education methods are particularly critical in helping develop the process of the group interview situation, the participative designs of effective feedback and action-derivation sessions, and for facilitating the organization and operation of task forces, and the training for new styles of leadership which are required.

The above cases are only samples of community development processes that utilize laboratory method. They do, however, illustrate the connection between community development and a variety of laboratory, participative learning experiences mentioned earlier in the chapter.

CONCLUSIONS

Consultants, trainers, organizational specialists, community organization consultants, in order to work with total community systems, obviously need a variety of competencies. Here are some of the kinds of core competencies that need to be included in the tool bag of the community development practitioner.

Knowledge and Understanding of:

1. Community networks;
2. Power bases;
3. Influentials and informants;
4. Community resources, including the agencies, organizations, and people operative in the community;
5. The regional and national bodies connected with the local agencies;
6. The purpose, mission and programs of the agencies, organizations, governmental structures, labor, business, industry;
7. Different life styles of cultural, ethnic, racial, religious groups;
8. The history of the community;
9. The status of relations between community organizations;
10. Evaluation and feedback strategies and instruments.

Needed Skills:

1. Diagnostic skills;
2. Intervention strategies, including entry, start-up, contract development, support development, and the use of both inside and outside resources;
3. The ability to work with a wide variety of people;
4. Skill in designing different kinds and sizes of conferences and meetings;
5. Communication skills;
6. Skills in mobilizing support for action strategies;
7. Problem solving and decision making skills;
8. Skills in handling conflicts and confrontations;
9. Skills in the methodological advocate role;
10. Short and long term planning skills;
11. Skills in dealing with resistance to change;
12. Skills in follow-up designing;
13. Feedback and evaluation skills.

From the above it can be seen that the laboratory method has much to offer to the field and the practice of community development. In summary, the laboratory method can help to:

1. Decrease polarization between peoples;

2. Increase public-private collaboration;
3. Develop networks of vertical decision making groups;
4. Develop a variety of mechanisms for inter-agency collaboration;
5. Develop experimental models of merger designs;
6. Develop meaningful evaluative and feedback mechanisms.

FOOTNOTES AND REFERENCES

1. Richard Beckhard, *Organization Development: Strategies and Models*. Addison-Wesley Publishing Company, Reading, Massachusetts; 1969, p. 9.

2. John Platt, from *The Center Magazine, V*, 4; July—August 1972, p. 21. Publication of The Center for the Study of Democratic Institutions.

3. Eva Schindler-Rainman and Ronald Lippitt, *Team Building for Community Change*, University of California, Riverside, California; 1972.

BIBLIOGRAPHY

Connor, Desmond M. *Understanding Your Community*, Development Press, Ottawa, Canada; 1968.

____, *Diagnosing Community Problems*, Development Press, Ottawa, Canada; 1968.

Fox, R., Lippitt, R., Schindler-Rainman, E. *Towards a Human Society: Images of Potentiality*, Learning Resources Corporation, Fairfax, Virginia; 1973.

Ross Murray G. *Community Organization: Theory and Principles*, Harper & Bros., New York; 1955.

Schindler-Rainman, E., and Lippitt, R. *The Volunteer Community: Creative Use of Human Resources*, Center for a Voluntary Society, Washington, D.C.; 1971.

PART V

ISSUES OF PROFESSIONALIZATION AND QUALITY CONTROL

PART V

INTRODUCTION

In Chapter 4, it was noted that the development of laboratory practice during the past quarter of a century presents a double face to the world. In one aspect, it is a popular social movement. In another aspect, it is an emerging field of professional practice.

In a recent critical survey of the human potential movement, which has developed around the use of the technologies of laboratory practice and related technologies, Kenneth D. Benne has identified the movement as one of the liberation movements that have burgeoned in the recent history of industrialized societies.* Two of his comments about the human potential movement are worth quoting here.

> Like other social movements toward liberation, the [human potential] movement . . . incorporates many variations in style, technology, and rationale. What seems to unite practitioners in the movement is a conviction that interactions and transactions among people can, under specially designed conditions, help these people get a clearer vision of who they are as persons, in actuality and in potentiality, can help them surface and face conflicts in themselves and choose among alternative ways of seeing and managing themselves, ways which are "right" for them, can support participants in achieving fuller integrity

*Kenneth D. Benne, "The Tearing Down of Walls," *Literary Currents,* Boston University, Boston, Mass.; December 3, 1970. This article has been included in the publication series, *Training Reports and Items,* #206, Center For Applied Social Science, Boston University, Boston, Mass.

> among the divided and compartmentalized parts of their persons as now functionally organized, including their bodies and their affective, cognitive, and conative powers, and can help participants become more fully autonomous centers of expression, communication, and evaluation in continuing processes of growth and learning.

But, as in most popular social movements, people, eager to gain promptly the liberation which group and interpersonal experiences of the sort described seem to offer, and distrustful of all elites, professionals among others, discount the need for especially educated expertise in designing and guiding such experiences toward desirable outcomes.

> Men and women, individually and in groups and organizations, become diagnosticians of their own human malaise, prescribers for the alleviation of their own unsatisfactory human condition. Of course, such resolution by men and women to take responsibility for freeing themselves, for replacing false consciousness in themselves with more reality-oriented views of themselves, in actuality and potentiality, is indeed a healthy step toward personal, social, and cultural rebuilding. Free and responsible persons in a free and responsible society cannot come to be without such a resolution and commitment on the part of many, ideally of all, people.
>
> The danger is that they will cripple themselves, limit themselves, delude themselves in seeking to benefit and improve themselves and their situations without the benefit of the knowledges of man, the images of human potentiality, the technologies for facilitating human growth and learning which now exist, under-utilized, fragmented and compartmentalized, in various non-communicating [disciplines and] professions of social practice. Responsibility for the spread of anti-intellectualism lies as much in the thought ways, attitudes, and social organization of the learned as in the thought ways, attitudes, and social organization of the unlearned, who take the diagnosis and treatment of their alienated condition into their often untutored hands.

While the popular social movement was raging about them, responsible laboratory practitioners have, for more than twenty years, been trying to develop themselves into a new profession of social practice. This effort has several dimensions — defining core competences and competences for specialties within the emerging profession, developing programs for assisting persons in becoming professionally competent, clarifying the ethical dilemmas confronted in trying to help others and creating ways of managing these, educating the public concerning the virtues and limitations of their craft, and building self-correcting and self-improving processes of feedback and evaluation research into their ongoing work.

It is these bootstrap efforts to professionalize laboratory practice which the first four chapters in this part of the book attempt to describe, analyze, criticize, and project into the future. For the most part, these efforts have been undertaken with a view to preserving the valid strengths of the popular social movement, which their inventions have helped to trigger and release, while mitigating its excesses and invalidities.

In Chapter 20, the editors describe and criticize past and current efforts to develop programs for educating professionals, paraprofessionals, and volunteers to meet the accelerating demands for the services of laboratory practitioners. They also describe various efforts to achieve appropriate organizations for accrediting professional laboratory practitioners, with special attention to the recently formed International Association of Applied Social Scientists.

In Chapter 21, Robert A. Luke, Jr. and Kenneth D. Benne discuss the ethical issues and dilemmas which laboratory practitioners have encountered and are encountering in their work. They are concerned to illuminate the conditions for developing an ethical code which is useful in guiding the choices of laboratory practitioners and which is not designed primarily to ground and justify disciplining of practitioners accused of unethical practices.

Gordon L. Lippitt, in Chapter 22, explores the processes and problems of educating the general public and the public of potential and actual clients and consumers concerning the virtues and limitations of laboratory practice and concerning the earmarks of professional practice. He considers this a necessary complement to the professionalizing efforts dealt with in the two preceding chapters.

In Chapter 23, Robert Chin sketches the outlines of evaluation research of educational and action programs as it has developed outside the province of laboratory practice. He notes the dissonance between some of the emphases of this main line of evaluation and the commitment of laboratory practice to a cooperative action research model of data collection and utilization. And he projects ideas about models of evaluation research and documentation congruent with the value orientation of laboratory practitioners. It is not necessary to emphasize the important place which effective evaluation plays in attaining and maintaining quality control in programs of laboratory practice — the central theme of this part of the book.

The editors, in Chapter 24, undertake a prophetic role in projecting "A Look Into The Future." They are concerned to identify areas of unsolved problems in the career of laboratory practice from the vantage point which the preparation of this book has provided to them. They also venture recommendations concerning desirable directions to be pursued in seeking solutions for some of these problems.

CHAPTER 20

THE PROFESSIONALIZATION OF LABORATORY PRACTICE

Ronald O. Lippitt, Kenneth D. Benne, Leland P. Bradford, and Jack R. Gibb

Today, most of the human service professions are, and should be, in a flux of self-examination and redevelopment. The needs for human services today far outweigh the quantity and expanded competences of trained professionals to meet these needs. In many cases, the professionals have not been trained for, nor have they otherwise developed, the basic empathy required to serve well the various populations now most in need of services. The professions have tended to be too narrow and too exclusive. For example, in medicine, the general practitioner, the family physician, has been accorded a low status compared with various specialists. In several of the professions, training for and respect for generalists slowly are re-emerging. In general, the professions have not yet recognized and responded to the widespread human problems resulting from increased population, mobility, runaway technology, and the perspectives and aspirations of "new" consumers of services. Some who up to now have been content with, or who have had to settle for, untrained or even primitive levels of service are now expecting and demanding more. Some of the critical issues for professions may be highlighted by an illustration or two.

In a large hospital, the MDs were so few in numbers that each doctor's caseload approximated 150 patients, an impossible burden. So, with some winking at tradition, nurses carried on many of the medical services "normally" limited to doctors. But each nurse had a caseload of over 100 patients, and with their increased "medical" responsibilities, they found their nursing duties overwhelming. So, aides and volunteers, still short in number, took on nursing duties. Housekeepers took on the duties of aides. What was wrong with this essentially necessary team development and functioning was that 100 years of traditional separation and "segregation" of roles made it almost impossible for this fact of required teamwork to be recognized, legitimized, and developed at a conscious level. Thus, there was no planned team formation, team training, or planned supervision. No reciprocal peer relations and flexible patterns of collaboration could be built, except by happy accident.

In a large school system, the failure of the bond issues for increasing the ratio of professionals to students resulted in a class size of nearly forty. But the increasingly active concern of parents in the community for better education resulted in greater and greater pressures for individualization of instruction. As a result of this, in several of the school buildings, two innovations were adopted. One was the use of older students as "Cross-Age Helpers" to help in classroom teaching and the other was the development of squads of adults as school volunteers including parents and older citizens. Again, the resistance of the professionals to the utilization of these resources resulted in a poor level of training for student and volunteer helpers, uncreative supervision, and a lack of responsibility taken by professional teachers for team development and team leadership in the educational process.

In medicine and in education, as well as other areas of professional practice, the "images of potential" for the development of a high quality of human service by new ways of deploying scarce professional resources are clearly emerging, but professionals are showing great reluctance to initiate and assume creative leadership in these processes of change.

In the United States, in contrast to many countries, there has always been a commitment to voluntarism and volunteers, but it has often been limited to a concept of the affluent periodically moving in to help the poor and unfortunate. Now what is beginning to take place is the formation of organizational and community teams in which volunteers, with the help of a few professionals to give consultation, training, and supervision, are taking on themselves responsibility for working as teams in the creative solution of service needs and social problems. In some underserviced situations, residents look on professions with distrust and even hostility. Frequently, volunteers and paraprofessionals from such neighborhoods are more effective in providing service than the professionals can be. With some surprise and anxiety, professionals are observing neighbors getting more help from neighbors living in the same local environment, in the rearing of their children, for example, than they are getting from the "experts."

But there is another side to the coin. To widen the concept of service in this way does not mean that the professionals can or should abdicate their responsibility to keep up with and contribute to the development of new levels of service and new developments in theory and research. The challenge to professionals is to devise ways of training others to share in the new knowledge and to learn some of the skills and values needed to function on service teams under the leadership of professionals increasingly competent to lead democratically.

THE SOCIAL-HUMAN CONFRONTATION FOR LABORATORY EDUCATION

The professionalization of practice in laboratory education faces most of these same problems. There are too few professional generalists. The field covers a multiplicity of disciplines and fields of professional practice. It is too new to have differentiated adequately the types of needed team responsibilities; too new to be very certain about what training experiences should go into the development of the professional trainer-consultant. The fields of application extend across practically all sectors of society. The values, ethics, and theories of practitioners differ to a considerable extent.

And as we scan the challenges to be met by this new field of professional practice, we become aware of some of the critical social and human confrontations which are in need of the services of laboratory educators. Here are just a few of them.

1. More and more people, individuals and groups, are expressing concerns about their identity, who they are, and where they belong in this complex society.

2. Individuals everywhere are attempting to find meaningful collaboration with others as an outgrowth of loneliness and lack of self-identity.

3. Discouragement with the possibility of exerting meaningful influence has brought not only disillusionment with government and politicians, but is also resulting in poor government and an increasing danger of loss of democracy. Some believe that one way to handle the self-identity crisis is to seek and to be satisfied with extreme dependence on a "Fuehrer" and to accept a nonparticipative existence.

4. Great confusion over relevant basic values leads to the passive condoning of crime and to depersonalization of relationships at all levels.

5. The continuing acceleration of the industrial revolution makes more and more jobs psychologically meaningless for workers.

6. The increased affluence and leisure of some, and the relative and actual poverty of many, along with the increased volume of TV and other mass media inputs, accentuates awareness of discrepancies of life opportunities and life styles, often making their own work and pattern of living seem even more meaningless and unsatisfying to many.

7. And the physical mobility caused by technological and occupational changes is pulling up the geographic and neighborhood roots which traditionally have lent security to the lives of many people.

This context of social, human problems, individual and group, generates many of the challenges for the needed creative growth and application of the theory and technology of laboratory practice.

PROFESSIONAL DEVELOPMENT CONFRONTATIONS

Those of us who are concerned about the development of adequate and high quality laboratory practice must cope creatively with a variety of questions about the continuing development of this area of professional work. Here are a few of the questions which are crucial and which are explored in later sections of this part of the book.

1. How can good public education about the availability and potentialities of laboratory education be accomplished? By whom?
2. How frequently do poorly trained and unethical practitioners use technical knowledge of this field for destructive human and social consequences? How can this be prevented?
3. Might there be a rejection of this whole field of professional practice by the public because of inappropriate practices, and misleading presentations in the media, thus drying up support for research, for the development of the profession, and for the recruiting of high quality young professionals?
4. Will legislation force the field to be prematurely narrowed and rigidified?
5. Is it possible to develop some type of valid accreditation of competence?
6. How can key decision makers and leaders be helped to recognize the significance of this resource and use it intelligently?
7. To what extent should every child and adult be given an opportunity for laboratory education training?
8. How can significant new laboratory education practices be widely distributed to support the continuing professional development of competent workers in the field?

9. How can the basic research and conceptual resources of the behavioral sciences and humanities be more adequately linked to professional laboratory education and more adequately integrated as an interdisciplinary base for professional practice?

In the remaining sections of this chapter we will explore some of these questions, beginning with analysis of some areas of competence which we believe should be part of the repertoire of practitioners of laboratory method.

AREAS OF COMPETENCE FOR PRACTITIONERS OF LABORATORY EDUCATION

Before examining some emerging areas of specialization within the field of laboratory practice, we will identify some of the dimensions of competence which have emerged as core areas in the performance of all professionals. It is our belief that generalists in laboratory practice must be competent in seven areas of professional functioning and should be able to apply these competences in working with individual, group, and organizational client systems. The curriculum for professional development in these areas of competence should include the following kinds of items.

Diagnostic Competences consist of the: ability to take a system view, to see the person or institution, or group, or nation as a system in interrelation with other systems; ability to get out of his "ego-centric" predicament without losing his sense of self; have a wide range of experiences with various types of systems and people; know instruments and methods for data-collection and feedback; see feelings and perceptions as "facts;" have a broad view of multiple levels and kinds of data; and the ability to help a system diagnose itself, to collaborate in action research rather than to make the diagnosis alone.

Competences in Entry and Contract Development consist of the: ability to live and function rationally in the grey areas of inclusion, to be "of the world but not in it," to be both in and out of the system, and to be a creative marginal member; ability to assess his own strength and to help others assess theirs, to have role flexibility, and to know what contracts are possible and feasible for him; ability to reject non-viable contracts or to withdraw appropriately from a relationship; ability to be flexible in coping with contract violations and to be creative in creating new contracts; and the courage and skill in bringing into the open the hidden and "unmentionable" aspects of formal or informal contract.

Design Competences consist of: a wide range of experiences in various settings; a wide range of experiences with varied designs;

knowledge of the limitations of various types of designs; ability to settle for less than perfection in design and to allow and help the system to produce, in collaboration, its own designs; ability to start a design "where the client now is;" ability to allow for and encourage emergent or serendipitous designs; and the imagination and creativity in individualizing designs to meet the unique needs and readinesses of particular clients.

Intervention Competences consist of the: ability to be proactive and to risk when the path is unclear; to cope with ambiguity; ability to accept "errors" and "failures" and to convert these into learning opportunities; ability to expose his intervention style to public view, analysis, and feedback; role flexibility in utilizing various styles, tools, paths, and forms of intervening to help produce movement and growth in the client; ability and willingness to hold back, wait it out, listen, let the client do the major work; ability and willingness to let others take credit for intervention success, giving credit quickly and facilitating the risk-taking of others; ability to be the target of hostility, transference, counter-transference, and to handle personal feelings about these processes; insight into his own tendencies to manipulate and control and to understand the responses he gets in interaction cycles when he does so; ability to accept the role of central figure, and skill in utilizing the role creatively rather than coercively; and the sensitivity to hidden dependencies and ability to handle his feeling of having others depend on him in various phases of the helping relationship.

Ethical Decision Making Competences consist of the: ability to handle his own values, guilt, and ethical dilemmas; insight into the handling of his judgments of others, how to share these, how to get them into the data system in constructive and manageable ways; insight into how his values affect his behavior, his choices, his decisions; and recognizing and acknowledging his own needs for power and how these affect his behaviors and have consequences for others.

Competences in Continuity, Follow-Up Support and Termination consist of the: ability to terminate relationships appropriately and handle dependencies, guilts, and griefs involved; a wide range of experiences and skills in helping with transfer of learning; ability to build flow, flexibility, and continuity into relationships with clients; and the ability and readiness to make appropriate commitment for follow-up support.

Peer Team Building Competences consist of: skills in being autonomous in interdependence, in teaming with peers; sensitivity to role needs in team functioning and readiness to supply missing roles in a team where needed; a broad conceptual schema which handles interdependent systems and allows a wide variety of paraprofessionals, volunteers, professionals, and technicians to function as team members on a peer basis; and the readiness and ability to function as a peer with a wide range of people in problem solving quests.

SPECIALISTS WITHIN LABORATORY METHOD

There are various ways of classifying professional specialists in application of laboratory method. We recognize the fact and economy of specialization, but we hope that most specialists will work to become generalists, cultivating the competences already outlined for generalists, in the course of their pre-service and in-service education.

1. *Organizational Development.* Specialists in this area have a rapidly growing store of practice designs, special literature, and theoretical frameworks to internalize as they work in consultant and training relationships with macrosystems of various sorts. Some of these are described in Chapter 18.

2. *Community Development.* Laboratory practitioners in community development have a very wide and diverse set of theories and practices, a very scattered literature, and a complex interdisciplinary base to make their own in their practice in projects and programs of community improvement. Some of these practices are described in Chapter 19.

3. *Group Development.* Part III of this volume describes some of the developing theory and practice in this area of specialization. This field of specialization is more highly differentiated, and encompasses a greater number of practitioners than do the other three. Work on professional accreditation of practitioners probably has proceeded furthest in this area of specialization.

4. *Personal Growth Facilitation.* These specialists are greatly varied in background and technical skill and often fuse many areas of practice in their work; for example, dance, music, art, psychotherapy, psychiatry, religion, and psychodrama. The pathways to professional competence in this area are highly diverse. There is little standardization of practice, and certification is especially difficult. Chapter 13 gives an extended description and rationale for one mode of personal growth facilitation within laboratory practice. Chapters 10 and 16 are also relevant.

Another approach to classifaction of specialists is in terms of educational level and status-acquired competence. Although it is clear that there is much overlap at the present time, professionals have a fuller range of the competences described above in the discussion of general professional training; paraprofessionals have a narrower range of experiences in training and more specialized responsibilites; and volunteers play a wide variety of roles, and their status and functions tend to be less clearly defined, as is also true of *interns* and *co-trainers* or *co-consultants.*

Still another approach to the classification of specialists in laboratory education is in terms of their functioning as "insiders" or "outsiders" in relation to client systems. Outside consultants may specialize in one or more kinds of systems (for example, religious, educational, governmental, public health, therapeutic, military, industrial, or others). Such consultants may have acquired the specialized language appropriate to more than one kind of systems and have developed a "feel for the turf" of several different kinds of systems. Inside practitioners specialize in particular institutions and institutional roles. It often helps if they have had line managerial experience in the organization in which they work, but typically they influence the system from such staff roles as personnel directors, training officers, organizational development specialists, and research and development practitioners.

We believe that all seven dimensions of competence are important for all the types of specialists mentioned above, although the range of experience and the level of skill may vary from the most widely trained and experienced generalists to the more narrowly trained and experienced specialists. In the continuing development of the field of laboratory education we must be concerned with the training and development of the total range of practitioners indicated above.

THE EDUCATION (DEVELOPMENT AND MAINTENANCE) OF HIGH QUALITY PERFORMANCE BY LABORATORY EDUCATORS

Springboards

Laboratory educators emerge from many different settings and backgrounds. They may be trained in a discipline such as psychology or sociology or anthropology and want to extend their role beyond the department and the campus. Or they may be trained in a profession — social work, education, medicine, public health — and want to extend their professional competence in pre-service education as well as to function more effectively in in-service activities off campus. Or they may be graduate students involved in inter-departmental interdisciplinary training and have a strong motivation to function as applied behavioral scientists in a variety of social problem-solving contexts. Or they may be highly trained in fields such as the humanities, or engineering, or philosophy, and be highly motivated to develop the skills and the roles of laboratory educators. Or they may be laymen who, in functioning as volunteers, have developed the perspective and the skill and the motivation to extend their citizen role into the area of laboratory education activities.

In other words, the practitioners of laboratory education are a very heterogeneous population, some of them from academic departments, some from professional schools, some from organizations and agencies in the community, others from consulting firms, others from private practice, and still others from activist citizen roles and organizations. This heterogeneity indeed presents problems, represents a challenge, and suggests a great breadth of resources in the continuing development of the field. Clearly, they have a wide variety of personal resources and developmental needs and are seeking different types of professional growth programs and are hoping to achieve preparation and "certification" for a wide variety of roles and responsibilities. If they come from academic departments, they may be seeking new skills as teachers, or hoping to develop an off-campus practice as a trainer-consultant. If they are based in professional schools, they may be seeking new competences in pre-service and in-service education, or new roles and income as consultants. If they are located in graduate programs, they may be wanting to explore occupational alternatives. If they are based in the staffs of organizations and agencies, they are often wanting to increase their potency as "internal change agents." Those from independent consulting firms are wanting to increase their competitive advantage among other professional helpers.

Almost all such seekers for further learning of the concepts and skills of laboratory education recognize that there is a great surge in the need for service in individuals, groups, organizations, and communities, and that a new profession of laboratory practice is emerging. The need and readiness of participants in all sectors of community life to seek out and respond to such opportunities for learning and renewal generate a demand far greater than the resource pool of well-trained practitioners can easily supply. Several patterns of training for the role of laboratory educator have emerged. Several approaches to quality control and certification are currently developing and are reviewed later in this chapter. Certainly no systematic and comprehensive curriculum for the training of laboratory educators has developed up to this time. But several emerging designs can be identified.

There are several interdisciplinary doctoral programs in universities which provide graduate students with an opportunity to develop themselves as applied behavioral scientists and laboratory educators with a base of disciplinary training in several departments and with professional training in one or more departments such as education, social work, public health, business administration, and public administration. Most of these programs include supervised field work in laboratory training and consulting activities and also provide experience as a member of a sensitivity training group. An important supplement to such campus-based graduate programs is the special program in laboratory training (education) developed by the NTL Institute for Applied Behavioral Science. This program provides an effective sequence of laboratory learning experiences which is designed to supplement basic disciplinary and professional training in behavioral science departments and professional schools.

An important contribution to post-graduate professional education is being provided by the learning community program of the NTL Institute. This is a program especially for consultants and trainers who have had considerable experience in inside or outside organizational consultation and training. A sequence of modules is available, equivalent to about eight weeks of professional development activities, starting with a core program of two weeks followed by a variety of optional modules depending on the development needs and specialized interests of the participant. Other similar "trainer-of-trainer" programs are being developed at other training centers in this country and abroad.

A third pattern of development for laboratory educators is a less formal sequence, followed by many, in which the learner functions as a co-trainer or intern in a variety of laboratory education designs, selecting several senior trainers to work with and getting both feedback assessment from his or her supervisor and help in securing connections with other senior practitioners with whom to work in a co-training or colleague capacity.

A fourth pattern can be observed in the on-the-job development of young professionals by consulting firms and companies who employ promising young behavioral scientists and support them in securing a series of growth experiences on-the-job and off-the-job as part of their occupational development.

Probably a fifth pattern should be noted. This is a pattern where a "practitioner" or "scientist," who may or may not have completed a graduate program in social science or behavioral science or in a helping profession, makes a personal decision that he or she has just as much to offer as some of those already practicing in the field. He or she, therefore, "hangs out a shingle" and develops his or her own base of experience at the expense of uninformed and uncritical clients who enter into a contract to get training or consultative help from an inadequately prepared practitioner.

With this brief review of some of the current patterns of development of laboratory practitioners, we are ready to turn to a more analytic assessment of some of the issues and problems current in this emerging field of social practice.

UNSOLVED PROBLEMS IN THE PROFESSIONALIZATION OF LABORATORY PRACTICE

We have already described how members of the emerging profession of laboratory practice have tried over the past several years to meet two of the essential requirements of a developed profession: (1) an agreed-upon definition of the competences needed by professional practitioners, and (2) the launching of processes and programs of education and training to support candidates for professional membership in acquiring these competences. It is clear from this description that both of these aspects of professional development still are in transition, marked by improvisation, and very far from being settled or routinized.

Other aspects of professionalization are in a similar transitional state. One of these is a code of ethics commonly accepted by professional practitioners, and enforceable, in some part, through self-policing by the organized profession. The ethical problems in laboratory practice are dealt with in Chapter 21.

Another aspect of professionalization is the understanding and acceptance by the public of the importance of professionalized competence in meeting the personal and social needs which practitioners claim to be competent to meet. Potential consumers and clients as well as the "general public" now have very spotty knowledge and acceptance of laboratory practice as a way of meeting needs for re-education and changing of people in their living and working relationships. Problems raised by this uneven public awareness and acceptance of the strengths and limitations of laboratory practice are dealt with in Chapter 22.

Before reviewing the present state of organization of laboratory practitioners, another earmark of a developed profession, two distinctive difficulties in professionalizing laboratory practice require further discussion. We began this chapter by noting difficulties which all service professions are currently experiencing. The emerging profession of laboratory practice, of course, shares these difficulties. But two inherent characteristics of laboratory method confront its practitioners with distinctive dilemmas in achieving adequate professionalization.

The first of these is the cross-disciplinary and cross-professional view which laboratory practitioners have taken of their craft from its beginnings. Its ablest practitioners have brought backgrounds in psychology, sociology, anthropology, economics, psychiatry, philosophy, history, and the humanities to their development as practitioners. And others have been recruited from various service professions — clinical psychology, nursing, education, medicine, religious work, social work, and professional management among others. Many retain primary identification with one or another discipline or profession. Cultivation of an exclusive profession of laboratory practice would sever important linkages of laboratory practice with various disciplines and helping professions. This would prejudice the very much needed function which laboratory practice has served as a meeting ground for teamwork among various fields of specialized expertise in achieving more adequate diagnoses of and more holistic approaches to contemporary human problems. Some sort of non-exclusive inter-profession which encourages its members to sustain memberships in other disciplinary and professional associations will be necessary if this potential strength of laboratory practice is to be maintained and extended.

The trend toward greater and greater specialization in research fields, including research in the human sciences, is generally recognized. And a similar trend toward specialization has marked the recent development of professional practice in health, welfare, education, and management. This specialization has brought economy of effort in the unprecedented amassing of refined knowledge and technology which is sometimes named the "knowledge explosion."

But specialization has brought also the dangers of non-communication and fragmentation — fragmented diagnoses of human problems and fragmented and competing proposals for their solution. We mentioned earlier that teamwork among specialists is much needed as a way out of fragmentation and toward more rounded and "human" diagnoses and solutions of human problems. Because of their competences in group formation and development and in methods of organizing collaborative effort, practitioners of laboratory method have been called upon increasingly to coach and train team-building efforts among specialists in various practice settings. And such assistance should be a continuing part of the services which laboratory practitioners can provide to our society.

It would be ironic indeed if, in their efforts to professionalize their own field of practice, laboratory practitioners would lose the capacity for teamwork among their own emerging specialists and specializations. We have reviewed already some of the specializations which have taken shape in the evolution of laboratory practice. And we will note later how these specializations are reflected in the current organization of the profession. One part of the answer to this difficulty is to maintain esteem and recognition for generalists as well as specialists in developing the profession. Another part of the answer is to maintain continuing efforts to define a generic core of knowledge, skill, and value for the education of all laboratory practitioners — generalists and specialists alike. And still another part of the answer is to cultivate and honor teamwork and community among various specialists of laboratory practice in programs of research, education, and action.

The second difficulty arises from a value commitment which has been emphasized again and again in this book as central to the practice of laboratory methods. *This is the value attached to collaborative relations, not alone between practitioners in helping teams, but between practitioners and clients as well.* This is a derivation from the democratic orientation of laboratory practice. It also represents a rebellion against the fixed hierarchical status which characterizes helper-client relationships in many areas of professional practice, not least in educational settings and programs of "engineered" change.

There is a strong "populist" strain in the leaders of this rebellion, some of whom are also practitioners of laboratory method. In the rhetoric of extreme "populism," any attempt to identify some persons or groups of persons as more able than other persons or groups of persons and to counsel that the less able follow the leadership of the more able is seen as "elitist" in spirit. And, virtually by definition, to be "elitist" is to endorse existing inequities and fixed hierarchical relations among people, to be anti-democratic, to abet the mad status-striving which characterizes established society. It is clear from this point of view that moves to professionalize, and to exclude from professional membership persons who are judged by persons now included not to meet established standards, are "elitist" in intention and consequence and so to be opposed and avoided on ideological grounds. In its extreme form such a "populist" view is opposed to all professionalization of practice, not only of laboratory practice.

It is easy to denounce this view as anti-intellectual, as making no distinction between knowledge-based, ethical practice, and practice by self-appointed helpers who ground their claims to be able to help others on superstition, charisma, or other irrational grounds, including the ideological "correctness" of their value systems. And it is easy to point to the ultimate logic of this view as leading to no protection of clients or the public from the ministrations of charlatans, quacks, and enthusiasts of various sorts — a protection which the development of professions allegedly provides.

We recognize and accept the dangers in such a totalistic rebellion against professionalization of practice. But we see also that the rebellion is in part a reaction against pathologies in professionalism as it has developed historically. It is true that professions have sometimes confused credentials with competence in admitting some persons to professional membership and in excluding others. And credentials have more and more been defined in terms of external badges of schooling, degrees, and other evidences of completion of some rigidly defined single track of required "professional" development. It is further true that organized professions have operated at times solely as protective agents of the economic interests of their members. They have resisted expansion of their numbers against a clear demonstration of a social need for augmented services of the type which they purport to provide. And they have at times resisted the development and use of paraprofessionals in the field of social need which they are expected to meet. They have been tardy in recruiting and training volunteers for a responsible part in their delivery of professional services. They have tended at times to cultivate a mystique in the public concerning their professional lore and skill rather than to educate the public concerning the strengths and limitations of their craft. Finally, established professions have tended to tie themselves into the complex of established institutions and to respond more willingly and effectively to the wishes of those in control of these institutions than to those not in a position of power and control. This is evident in the differential responsiveness of the health, welfare and education professions to the needs of the poor, the blacks, the Indians, as these needs have been uncovered and articulated, as over against their response to needs of those with adequate economic means to pay for professional services.

There are thus pathologies in "professionalism" as it has developed in industrialized societies. And the "populism" of the counter culture, as it resists "professionalism" is an over-reaction against these pathologies. The wise course to follow in professionalizing laboratory practice is, it seems to us, to avoid these pathologies. Put positively, ways of educating professionals, of organizing the profession and of cultivating relations between profession and public which avoid these pathologies should be developed and institutionalized.

Some counsels of wisdom for our emerging profession may be summarized out of the preceding discussion.

1. Standards for professional membership should be defined in terms of demonstrated competence, *not* in terms of credentials. And evidence of competence should be gathered from relevant experiences of consumers and clients as well as from the observations of professional leaders.

2. Multiple experiential tracks for the development of professional competences should be recognized and honored. Competences are learned from various experiences, not from prescribed programs of schooling alone.

3. The knowledge-base for professional practice should be multi-disciplinary and should be acquired in close connection with ethical awareness of the uses to which knowledge can and should be put.

4. Qualifications for professional membership should be subject to periodic review and re-examination. The expectation should be one of continuing growth and re-education for all professionals.

5. Professional laboratory practitioners should encourage the recruitment and development of paraprofessionals in their field of practice. They should commit themselves to working in equal status collaboration with paraprofessionals without denying the reality of differences in competence and experience in the allocation of responsibilities.

6. Professional laboratory practitioners should welcome collaboration with volunteers in their work. They should assume responsibility for helping to recruit and train volunteers and for learning from them.

7. Professional laboratory practitioners should try to inform the public — both the "general" public and potential and actual clients and consumers of laboratory practice — concerning the virtues and limitations of laboratory practice. They should seek to demythologize the nature of their practice and to substitute accurate information for myths, positive and negative, in their relations with their public.

8. The profession of laboratory practice should welcome responsible evaluation of their practices and programs both by "laymen" and by "academics." It should try to learn from the feedback coming to it from such evaluations.

The Organization of the Profession of Laboratory Practice

The earliest professional association of practitioners of laboratory method developed under the auspices of the National Training Laboratories (NTL), later to be expanded under the names of NTL Institute of Applied Behavioral Science and NTL Institute. The NTL network, as it was called, was comprised of persons who collaborated in planning, conducting, and evaluating programs of laboratory education, sponsored by NTL. The original group was small and in face-to-face contact with each other as they planned and worked together. In addition to their work on specific programs, network members met periodically in seminar fashion to work on generic problems of rationale and value orientation and independently to invent designs and technologies and review research results.

As applications of laboratory method expanded to new populations and geographic locations, under NTL and other auspices, the network grew in numbers and altered in function. It was no longer a close association of working colleagues. New practitioners sought membership in the network as an insignia of professional competence, since no other accrediting agency was available. The first code of ethics for laboratory practice was developed by a Committee on Professional Development, staffed and sponsored by NTL. Standards of competence were developed for each of the three classes of membership which evolved in the NTL network — Fellow, Associate, and Professional Member. And these standards were applied through a rather elaborate system of committees with supportive staff work. At its largest, the NTL network expanded to about 700 members with membership not alone in the U.S. but in Canada, Europe, Latin America, India, and the Philippines as well.

This expansion produced tensions in the organization of NTL with respect to the assignment of its limited staff and other resources. NTL Institute was primarily an agency for experimentation and programming in laboratory education, organizational development, community development, and the professional development of laboratory practitioners. The maintenance of an expanded network added the functions of a professional accrediting agency to its already over-taxed resources. In 1970, the Board of NTL Institute decided to disband the network. This decision was made in the prospect of a new professional organization with accrediting functions which was then in the planning stage. The International Association of Applied Social Scientists (IAASS) will be described later as the most massive current effort to deal organizationally with the problems of professionalizing laboratory practice.

Before discussing IAASS, other kinds of organizational efforts to define and apply professional standards to laboratory practice will be illustrated and discussed briefly. The rapid spread of laboratory practices — a spread more rapid than the expansion of the supply of adequately trained practitioners to supervise and conduct the programs — has become an object of concern to professional practitioners, to related professions and disciplines, and the general public as well. The concern has been with the personal casualties which use of group methods under inept and unethical leadership can produce. Concern has been felt also with the debasing of the repute of responsible use of laboratory methods which results from inept and sensational misuse of the methods and the lurid reporting of such misuse through various media of publicity. Both concerns focus on the need for developing standards of professional competence and ethics in the use of laboratory methods and to find ways of applying these in accrediting practitioners and in disciplining misusers of the methods.

Four sorts of organized efforts to meet these needs, in addition to the over-all approach of IAASS, have emerged in the past two decades. We cannot describe all of these but will illustrate each kind of effort before describing IAASS in greater detail.

1. The basis of the first kind of effort to organize and accredit practitioners of laboratory method is geographic. The geographical basis may be a state or province as in the case of laboratory trainers in the Canadian Province of Manitoba. The geographical base may alternatively be a nation. Such an organization is the Australian Institute of Human Relations with its headquarters in Melbourne and chapters in the state capitals of Brisbane, Sydney, and Perth. The geographical basis may be multinational as in the case of E.I.T. in Europe. The current name for this association of laboratory practitioners is European Institute for Trans-national Studies in Group and Organization Development.

All such geographical associations seek to serve a standard-setting and/or accrediting function for laboratory practice in their areas. In some cases, they have also sponsored programs and experiences for the professional development of practitioners.

2. A second basis for professional organization is an institutional setting in which a sizable number of laboratory practitioners are working. This is well illustrated by the Association for Religion and Applied Behavioral Science in the U.S.A. This was an organization which invited applied behavioral scientists whose principal work setting was in churches and church-allied programs into professional membership. The organization worked out standards of professional competence and procedures for applying these to applicants for membership in the association.

3. A third basis for organization is around some particular technology within the broader repertoire of laboratory methodologies. This is well represented by the A. K. Rice Institute which has grown around the professionalizing of group training methods pioneered by the Tavistock Institute of Human Relations in England and applied and extended through its use in America. (Chapter 14 provides a discussion of this variant of laboratory practice.) The A. K. Rice Institute is a federation of regional chapters throughout America. It has worked out standards of professional competence and procedures for applying these in the accrediting of professional members. Since 1972, the A. K. Rice Institute has formed an affiliation with IAASS. About thirty members of the Institute are also members of IAASS. Institute members are represented on the IAASS Board and Committees.

4. The fourth basis for professional standard-setting for labo-

ratory practice is through activities sponsored by "older" disciplinary or professional associations whose memberships include sizable numbers of qualified laboratory practitioners. This type of activity is represented by work in the American Psychological Association, The American Psychiatric Association, and the Association for Humanistic Psychology. The work of these related associations includes sponsorship of studies of the effects of laboratory method in group settings, efforts to define standards of professional competence and to adapt existing ethical codes to the conditions of laboratory practice.

IAASS. The International Association of Applied Social Scientists was incorporated in 1971 as a professional association to bring into membership qualified practitioners who work scientifically and collaboratively in programs designed to effect changes in persons, groups, and larger social systems. As its work has developed, so far, four specializations have been recognized — organizational development specialists, community development specialists, laboratory educators, and personal growth group consultants. Members are accredited in one or more of these four divisions.

IAASS has so far concentrated on developing standards and procedures of accreditation which seek to avoid the pathologies of "professionalism" already discussed. The accreditation process places primary importance upon an applicant's demonstrated competence as a practitioner, not on academic or other credentials. An applicant for membership must be sponsored by an IAASS member who has first-hand working knowledge of the applicant's competence as a practitioner. The applicant must submit a record of his experiences as a practitioner, along with a statement of his philosophy and theory of professional practice and peer evaluations of his work by practitioners with whom he has worked over at least two years. The applicant must also provide client evaluations of his competence.

Applicants for membership meet with a peer review panel in one of the eight regions into which the American membership of the Association is currently divided. Operating as a total group in the review process, the panel assesses: (1) the adequacy and extent of training of the applicant in his specialty or specialties; (2) the extent and adequacy of the applicant's professional experience; (3) competence as a practitioner as reflected in the clarity and coherence of his stated theory and ethical viewpoint; and (4) competence as a practitioner as reflected in evaluations of his work by peers and clients. Whether or not the applicant is admitted to membership in the Association, he is provided with a summary of the findings and recommendations of the peer review panel to serve as a basis for planning his continuing development as a practitioner.

Qualified but newly trained or relatively inexperienced practitioners may receive accreditation for two years in contrast to a five-year review process for other accredited members. IAASS hopes to have avoided the pathologies of "professionalism" in the unique accreditation process which it has developed.

A board of trustees sets policy for the association. The nucleus of the board consists of an elected representative from each of the eight regions now recognized in the U.S.A., the paid president of IAASS and a representative from the A. K. Rice Institute. The nucleus of the board must complete its membership by appointing additional members to make it adequately representative of the four recognized specialties and of "minority" members of the Association — blacks, women, and others.

The Association works through four standing committees: a committee on standards and admissions which revises policies and procedures for accreditation as required; a committee on ethics which establishes and revises criteria for the ethical conduct of members; a committee on discipline which investigates allegations of ethical misconduct and/or failure to meet professional standards of competence on the part of any member; and a committee on the education of its publics. A Foundation for Applied Social Science has been formed within the Association to collect and disburse funds particularly in the discharge of the Association's educational functions — informing various publics, including potential consumers and clients, concerning proper and needed uses of applied social science knowledge and technology.

While the membership of IAASS is now mainly from the U.S.A., negotiations are underway with groups of qualified practitioners in various nations or in multinational areas outside the U.S.A. to form chapters of the Association in their areas. Such chapters will, of course, share fully in the accrediting, educational, and governance functions of the Association.

Concluding Observations

The scope and diversity of laboratory practice illustrated throughout this volume should, we hope, help a diverse population of "people helpers" or applied behavioral or social scientists, to find bases for common cause in laboratory practice. Hopefully, this will help in the development of motivations, and techniques, and occasions for the sharing and pooling of high quality practice and sharing and acting on common concerns about the development and maintenance of high standards of professional ethics and competence.

Another common concern, we hope, will be the attracting of competent and motivated young people into this area of professional service, and providing them with "turned on" personal and professional development experiences. The interpersonal patterns of sharing knowledge and skill between senior practitioners and the younger or less experienced must be at the core of all designs for professional development.

Another base for the successful development of laboratory education as a major contributor to personal growth and social problem-solving must be the readiness of professionals to share the challenge and opportunity with associates who have had less conceptual and technical training. We believe the involvement of volunteers and paraprofessionals in the development of laboratory education service teams is one of the most important images of the future in our work. New role functions for the professional laboratory educator are implied — as a trainer of trainers, a team leader and consultant, and a linker to conceptual and research resources for colleagues who have less academic training.

The challenge to the universities is to overcome their curriculum fragmentation by creatively blending the knowledge resources of the several behavioral science departments, the knowledge resources of the professional schools, and the practical experience resources of related community agencies and institutions. Under pressure from enlightened graduate students and an increasing number of truly cross-disciplinary faculty members, such training sequences are emerging, but slowly. We must accelerate this trend.

And, finally, we must both educate and protect our present and potential clients — from the elementary school learner to corporations, communities, and nations. We must educate them about what they can and cannot gain and what they have a right to expect in using the resources of laboratory practice. And we must exercise control over ourselves — developing guidelines of competence, of ethical practice, appropriate definitions of general and special areas of practice, and appropriate differentiations of roles and patterns of teamwork to meet the critical needs of personal and social development which now confront and challenge all of us.

CHAPTER 21

ETHICAL ISSUES AND DILEMMAS IN LABORATORY PRACTICE

Robert Luke, Jr., and Kenneth D. Benne

One of the earmarks of most developed professions is a code of ethics to which persons entering the profession subscribe and agree not to violate in their professional work. "Entering a profession" usually means, operationally, being accepted for membership in an organization of professionals — an organization which purports to "represent" the profession in its relations with its public(s). Subscribing to a code of ethics is part of the ritual of initiation of a neophyte into professional membership. Just as "subscribing to the code of ethics" is a condition of inclusion in the professional association, demonstrated violations of the code by a member provide grounds for exclusion of that member from continuing collegial association with other professionals.

The usual justification of such professional codes of ethics is that they are useful in protecting clients and consumers of the services which the profession offers to the public from unscrupulous acts by members of the profession which violate the "rights" of clients and consumers or harm them in some way. An ancillary function of such codes is self-protective — to provide a basis for actions by an organized profession to protect its public reputation and the public reputation of its brand of service by disciplining members whose actions violate the code. Organized professions usually are jealous of their autonomy in advancing and protecting the interests of their members and their mode of social practice. And self-policing of members' conduct is an important ingredient of professional autonomy. Codes of ethics serve a quasi-legal and quasi-judicial function in the self-policing activities of organized professions.

When one thinks of the "ethics" of laboratory practice with this meaning of "ethics" in mind, he thinks of ways of developing a code of conduct to which members of our emerging profession will voluntarily subscribe and which they will be willing to apply in disciplining colleagues. He thinks of the kinds of conduct on the part of laboratory practitioners which now endanger and dupe clients, which respected members of the profession see as undermining the good reputation of laboratory practice among potential clients and among members of related professions, and which, if continued, will invite governmental legislation to control the conduct of laboratory practitioners. In brief, he thinks legally, judicially, and defensively.

Of course, "ethics" has another well-established meaning quite distinct from the meaning we have been discussing, which concerns an area of inquiry into the moral choices which persons make in taking actions. Actions require a moral dimension as they have consequences both for the actor and for others who live and work in relationship with him. In its general form, ethics is inquiry into the meaning of "right" and "wrong," of "good and bad" as applied to types of classes of choice situations or perhaps to *all* choices. Of course, choices always are made in particular, concrete situations. Situations are unique. Choice situations confront actors with normative conflicts, with competing "shoulds." Ethical principles and policies, while they may guide actors in processes of choice, can never make judgments for them. So ethical inquiry must include an examination of the processes and methods of judgment which actors use in making concrete choices, where questions of "good" or "bad" or, more likely, "better" or "worse" are at stake in the judgment.

When one thinks of the "ethics" of laboratory practice in this sense of "ethics," he is concerned with ways in which laboratory practitioners can become more sensitive to normative conflicts as these present themselves in relationships with clients, with colleagues, and with the "public;" how they can become more resolute in facing up to normative conflicts, how they can learn better ways of diagnosing and settling normative conflicts, and what helps they need from other people in thinking through the ethical judgments they unavoidably must make. And, since laboratory practitioners are educators, in whatever format they work, the ethics of laboratory practice should extend to ways of stimulating and supporting clients in learning better methods of ethical inquiry and judgment as they encounter normative conflicts in their life and work, including their work with trainers and consultants. In brief, one thinks like an educator, and, more particularly, like a laboratory educator.

WHICH EMPHASIS ON ETHICS DOES LABORATORY PRACTICE NOW NEED?

The authors are members of the Committee on Ethics of the International Association of Applied Social Scientists (IAASS). IAASS already has been described in this volume as the organization most centrally devoted to the professionalization of laboratory practice at this time. We have volunteered to conduct a study for the Ethics Committee with a view toward improving the ethics of our profession. Since our study is in its early stages, this chapter should be seen not as a final report, but as a report of work in progress. We will raise more questions than we will answer.

As we have communicated with members of IAASS and thought about the problem, the first issue we have encountered is an issue concerning how IAASS should now be investing its energies in improving the ethics of laboratory practice. The distinction we have already made between different meanings of "ethics" becomes important at this point. Should we concentrate on developing an acceptable and enforceable code of ethics for laboratory practitioners? Or should we initiate an educational and re-educational program among our membership and beyond, designed to increase awareness of ethical dilemmas involved in the practice of our profession and to encourage responsibility in dealing with these dilemmas in ways congruent with the moral orientation of laboratory practice?

This is itself an ethical issue. And our way of dealing with it will help to clarify both what we mean by an ethical issue and what we see as a defensible way of inquiring into such issues. Those who favor concentrating on developing an enforceable code of ethics for our profession are impressed with the current volume of shoddy and unprofessional offerings of service that are now being foisted on an unknowing public, in the name of laboratory practice. They are particularly concerned with offerings which take the names of "encounter groups and marathons," "sensitivity training," and "personal growth experiences." They point to the evidence of psychic damage which a sizable percentage of participants suffer from unprofessionally led encounter group sessions and marathons.[1] In addition to the lack of professional competence on the part of many leaders or trainers, those who favor work on a code of ethics are mainly concerned with four sorts of "unethical" practices — fraudulent advertising of offerings, promising miraculous healing and educational outcomes; lack of screening of participants to exclude highly vulnerable people; lack of responsibility on the part of trainers for what happens to participants during training sessions; and lack of follow-up of participants and referral to special help for those who need it. A code of ethics should label such acts of commission and omission as unethical. Even though IAASS has no control over incompetent trainers, who would not qualify for membership in any event, by adopting a code of ethical practice, it can disengage itself from those who practice unethically and help the public to distinguish between ethical and unethical practice.

Those who favor an educational approach to the problem point to a discrepancy between formulating codes which proscribe certain acts and enjoin other acts and the inherent morality of laboratory practice. When in a training situation, for example, a trainer encounters an act by a participant which disturbs or shocks or hurts others, including himself, he does not proscribe the act. Rather, he encourages a joint inquiry into the action, into the intentions of the actor, into the situational factors related to the act, into alternative ways in which a better fit between intention and situation might be attained. Moralistic or legalistic judgment of the act is suspended in the interest of understanding and learning. And when moral judgment is undertaken it has more to do with the methodology a person (or group) uses in making his (or its) choices and decisions, than with the wrongness or rightness of particular behavior. The "same" behavior may be "right" for an actor in one situation and "wrong" in another. And the "same" behavior may be "right" for one actor and "wrong" for another in the "same" situation. Laboratory practitioners practice a morality in their work which honors the "uniqueness" of persons and the "uniqueness" of situations and finds its guiding normative principles in a methodology designed to utilize these differences for common benefit. Stereotyping of people and behaviors as wrong or right without taking into respectful account the differences among people and situations is immoral. And doesn't a legalistic code of ethics tend to do just that? Why shouldn't we treat our colleagues who annoy or offend us or hurt us by their actions as we would treat participants who offend us in a training situation, or, indeed, as we would choose to be treated, when we're at our best, when our own behaviors annoy or hurt others?

The argument against reliance upon codes to enhance ethical behavior goes on to point out that overt compliance with prescribed norms of conduct by laboratory practitioners, as by anyone else, does not ordinarily lead to internalization of self-shaped and self-accepted normative principles to guide continuing ethical choices and inquiries. In fact, codes may work in the opposite direction. Laboratory practitioners who comply with a *legal* code of ethics prescribed by their professional organization may feel that they have solved their "ethical" problems and fail to confront the ethical issues internal to their work and to continue growing, ethically as well as technically.

A third kind of voice speaks to those embattled on both sides of the issue. This voice reminds the detractors of professional codes that they are "idealizing" laboratory practice with respect to its alleged failure to proscribe and enjoin certain behaviors in training situations. The usual training group, in effect, operates within certain prescribed norms laid down in the laboratory design — to meet in certain groups at certain hours of the day, for example. John Weir's Personal Growth Laboratory (Chapter 13) proscribes physical attacks by a participant upon other participants. Max Birnbaum's Clarification Group (Chapter 15) proscribes the group from probing into intrapersonal and interpersonal issues. Even Max Pages' Flexible Structures Laboratory (Chapter 17) has some limiting normative structures — it is "flexibly" structured, not unstructured. Detractors of offical codes are quite right about the inherent morality of laboratory practice with respect to deviant behavior. This morality counsels an educative and re-educative approach to deviance. But this deviant behavior occurs within the limits of a narrower or wider normative structure, enjoined or prescribed by authority.

Would it not, therefore, be possible and wise for IAASS to work toward consensus on a code of conduct for its members? It should not be externally imposed but, rather, self-imposed. It should not be borrowed wholesale from another practice profession. The codes of other professions can be used as raw materials but a code for IAASS should be tailored to the particular conditions of laboratory practice and be tuned to the distinctive ethical sense and sensibilities of laboratory practitioners. And it should be subject to continuous revision as the consensus changes.

To those who stress the central importance of a professional code of ethics, the third voice also speaks confrontingly. You are, no doubt, concerned with the danger of psychic damage to which unethical laboratory practices subject participants. But doesn't your primary animus against "unethical" practice stem from its threat to the good reputation of the mode of social practice to which you are committed and, by extension, to your reputation and your way of making a living? There is nothing wrong in protecting ourselves and our reputations from threat. Survival in good repute and economic well-being is a value and one not to be derogated. But, as laboratory practitioners, we like to be clear and honest about our motivations. I'm sure you accept this value as an ethical value, too.

Don't you think you may be putting too much emphasis on adoption of a code of ethics as a way of promoting a continuing search by our profession for defensible ethical foundations for its practice, foundations congruent with the inherent morality of laboratory practice? Don't your opponents have an excellent point in their insistence that this search be essentially an educational search, based upon the experiences by members of ethical issues which confront them in their practice, an inductive search which builds on an analysis of relevant cases, rather than on derivations from an *a priori* set of ethical principles? Why shouldn't IAASS pioneer in initiating a new kind of continuing search by a profession for ethical guidelines?

We, the authors, have decided to heed the counsels of the third voice. We are planning to institute a process of working toward a consensus statement of a code of ethics for laboratory practitioners. And we plan to invest more of our energies in an inductive and educational process of identifying concrete ethical issues and dilemmas inherent in our professional work and of submitting these to analysis and "resolution" by as many IAASS members as we can recruit into the process.

Process Comment

We hope that the issue presented and discussed above illustrates more concretely what we mean by an ethical issue. With finite energy and resources at our command, we are confronted with a choice concerning how to expend our energy and resources. Two courses of action, each with values supporting it — it wouldn't be an ethical issue if all positive values were on the side of one alternative — are conflicting in the arena of judgment. If the values were equally balanced, the situation would present an *ethical dilemma.*

The process of choice involves a clarification of the values at stake in the choice. In ethical conflicts, polarization of positions is a part of the process. Only in this way can value clarification take place. If listening can be maintained between all sides to the conflict, opposing value orientations get clearer all around. And usually, some of the conflict is internalized by opponents. This makes creative compromise possible.

The third voice is a bridging, confronting, third party voice, seeking a synthesis in the conflict, creating a workable basis for joint action, if not conflict resolution. We believe that the values inherent in laboratory practice are consistent with such a methodology of value clarification and of value-conflict management. We believe, further, that professionals of laboratory practice can and should use such a methodology in working through its issues with respect to professional ethics.

We don't know how well we have used the methodology in reaching our decision in this case. We welcome critical feedback. But we hope the primary thrust of the criticism will be to reveal inadequacies in our methodology and the way we have applied it in this case. We can learn from such feedback. We will learn little from claims that our "answer" is ethically less adequate than an "answer" favored by our critic, without an indication of where and how we went astray in our processes of thinking and deciding. We believe this point is worth underlining. There is an analogy between what we are saying and the commitment of a "new" mathematics teacher to evaluate a student's work in mathematics not by the correctness of his answer but by the adequacy of the process by which he sought to solve the problem. Traditional teachers who know the correct answer in advance of inquiry have difficulty in understanding this commitment. Traditional ethicists who know the right answer to ethical issues and dilemmas independent of inquiry will have similar trouble in understanding our emphasis upon method and process. If ethical quandaries are to be brought into the range of responsible inquiry, along with technical and factual puzzles, and we believe they should be, we cannot be too attentive to the adequacy of our methods of ethical judgment.

HISTORICAL BACKGROUND OF ETHICAL CONCERNS IN LABORATORY PRACTICE

We, of course, realize that work on the ethical problems inherent in laboratory practice did not begin with our work in and for IAASS. Such work began early in the history of laboratory education. And it has taken both the forms identified in our discussion above. We will first review attempts to incorporate ethical concern and inquiry into processes of laboratory education.

Education for Ethical Sensitivity and Responsibility

In the Introduction to Part I, it was noted that one of the three papers prepared for the first summer laboratory at Bethel, Maine, in 1947, was a paper written by Kenneth Benne dealing with democratic ethics, scientific method, and social engineering. This paper was studied by staff, distributed to participants, and used as one of the major strands of the laboratory curriculum, along with the more cognitive analyses of group development and the change agent role and skills.

This analysis of ethics in terms of methodological norms to guide processes of laboratory learning and changing was not intended or taken as an ethical Bible. It was discussed and criticized in many laboratory staff seminars and meetings and operationalized in terms of its meanings for trainer diagnoses and interventions. It was published in 1949 in revised, if not definitive, form and has since that time been reprinted in various publications dealing with planned change and laboratory education.[2] Its substance, in revised form, is included in the final section of Chapter 2 of this volume and need not be repeated here.

For many years, presentations and discussions of ethical problems of the change agent were standard parts of laboratory programs at Bethel and elsewhere. Explicit attention to the ethical dimensions of laboratory practice tended to be relaxed as the numbers and influence of clinically oriented psychologists and positivistic behavioral scientists increased among laboratory practitioners. The professional problem became one of educating practitioners to attend to ethical issues in training and consultation along with issues of technique and instrumentation. Many practitioners were unable to distinguish between the two kinds of issues and to use methodologies differentiated appropriately to the two. Another paper by Kenneth Benne may be used to locate this shift in ethical emphasis in laboratory practice. This paper was part of a symposium on group and organizational consultation, edited by Ronald Lippitt and Jack Gibb for the *Journal of Social Issues* in 1959.[3] Benne's effort here was to help practitioners distinguish between "ethical" and "technical" issues arising in the practice of consultation. In brief, "ethical" issues were defined as issues which precipitated value conflicts within the practitioner along with conflicts among the expectations of various of his significant associations upon him. The resolution of such issues requires a reconstruction of the self in its value orientation and significant associations. Technical issues are externalized and are reducible to processes of determining alternative means-end and cost-benefit relations. Benne tried to identify examples of both kinds of issues as they confront group and organizational consultants.

With the recent emergence of humanistic psychology and phenomenological sociology and their increasing influence among laboratory practitioners, ethical problems are again very much on the agenda of professional laboratory practitioners. And so we are back to the Luke-Benne ethics project for IAASS in the 1970s.

Developing a Code of Ethics for Laboratory Practitioners

The stimulation and support of ethical inquiry as an integral part of laboratory education has thus been an early and continuing concern of many laboratory practitioners. Interest in a professional *code of ethics* developed only during the 1960s. This interest was stimulated by the rapid expansion of the human potential movement. Unconventional and sometimes bizarre approaches and technologies for stimulating and supporting processes of personal growth, which began to be practiced and publicized during the early and middle sixties, caused concern among many members of the NTL network, which, as noted in Chapter 20, was at that time the principal accrediting agency for laboratory practitioners. The NTL Board instructed the NTL Committee on Professional Development to develop a code of ethics for NTL practitioners and to publicize this code along with the standards of competence which were currently being applied to candidates for admission into the NTL network.

The concern of the NTL Board and network which prompted this move was mainly to protect the reputation of laboratory practice by disengaging NTL's version of professional practice from what they regarded as the unprofessional excesses of parts of the human potential movement. It was in the 1960s that anti-establishment protests became prevalent, that proponents of the counter-culture became articulate and assertive, that Hippie culture thrived, and that various liberation movements became clamorous on the American and world scene. There was some overlap between proponents of the counter-culture and those of the human potential movement. And frightened members of "establishment" culture saw much more overlap than actually existed. NTL by no means wished to oppose the counter-culture or liberation movements. Its network members worked in programs which were so self-labeled. It did want to maintain an image which did not prejudice its access also to established culture. OD work was beginning to thrive in business, industry, and government agencies. The move to develop and publicize standards for laboratory practice grew out of this context.

The results of this work appeared in printed form in 1969.[4] The pamphlet which outlined NTL's official definition of laboratory method, program standards, and standards of competence for professional practitioners has been widely circulated in various interested "publics." In this pamphlet, NTL endorsed the Ethical Standards of Psychologists, developed and published by the American Psychological Association, and urged its members to guide their conduct according to this code.

OUR PROJECT IN IAASS TO IMPROVE THE ETHICS OF LABORATORY PRACTICE

We mentioned earlier that our project has two aspects. The first of these is to initiate a process within IAASS designed to develop consensus on a code of ethics for that organization. Since this process has just begun, we can only illustrate here the kinds of deliberations which it will require of laboratory practitioners.

Developing a Code of Ethics for Laboratory Practitioners

It seems appropriate to use the Ethical Standards of Psychologists as a point of departure, since NTL's endorsement of it has made it the nearest thing to a code of ethics for laboratory practice now available. Our examination and criticism of parts of this code are our own and have no official status in IAASS or any other organization. We are not questioning its adequacy as a code for professional psychologists. Our criticisms have to do rather with its adequacy as a code for laboratory practitioners. We have offered criticisms. We have not ventured formulations of principles which meet our criticisms.

We have found some difficulties with the first standard.

> The psychologist recognizes the boundaries of his competence and the limitations of his techniques and does not offer services or use techniques that fail to meet professional standards established by recognized specialists in particular fields. The psychologist who engages in practice assists his client in obtaining professional help for all important aspects of his problem that fall outside the boundaries of his own competence. This principle requires that provision be made for the diagnosis and treatment of medical problems.

We have no difficulty with the notion that the laboratory practitioner should recognize the boundaries of his competence and the limitations of his techniques. And we would willingly endorse the notion that the laboratory practitioner should assist his client in obtaining professional help for important aspects of the client's problem that fall outside the boundaries of his own competence.

Our difficulty arises in the prohibition upon a professional's offering services and using techniques that fail to meet "standards established by recognized specialists in particular fields." This seems to us to be using a code of ethics to underwrite and maintain the present system of specialization and sub-specialization and sub-sub-specialization which characterizes the established organization of both basic and applied social science today. Specialized expertise has its limitations in the diagnosis of human problems. Specialist diagnoses are often partial and fragmentary diagnoses. Laboratory practitioners are very much aware of the fact of what Thorstein Veblen once called trained incapacity both in themselves and in other "experts." They are aware of the dangers of trained incapacity in helping human systems to change. Laboratory practice is committed to cross-disciplinary and cross-professional work both in helping clients to diagnose their difficulties and in helping them to plan ways of dealing with problems as diagnosed. Laboratory practice has maintained respect for generalists among its practitioners partly because of its affinity with cross-disciplinary approaches to human problems and partly because of its recognition of the need for teamwork among specialists in programs of changing. Generalists are needed to make teamwork work. We would seek a statement of an ethical principle which supported rather than contravened these justifiable values of laboratory practice.

Let us turn now to the third ethical standard for psychological practitioners.

> A psychologist who advertises or makes public announcements of his services, describes them with accuracy and dignity, adhering to professional rather than commercial standards.

We would endorse the principle of accuracy and honesty in advertising or publicly announcing the availability of services by a laboratory practitioner. We gag a bit over the contrast between "professional" and "commercial" standards of honesty. Much of the hypocrisy in the helping professions stems from a concealment or denial that helping professionals make a living out of selling their services to clients. And this is true whether we work for a salary or for fees. We are part of a commercial society and not members of a priesthood which has taken the vow of poverty. This is not to say that laboratory practitioners are motivated only by economic rewards. But this is a part of their motivation. We would seek a way of stating the ethical principle of truth and honesty in advertising services with less hypocrisy.

Now for a look at Ethical Standard 5.

> The psychologist in the practice of his profession shows sensible regard for the social code and moral expectation of the community in which he works, recognizing that violations of accepted moral and legal standards on his part may involve his clients, students, or colleagues in damaging personal conflicts.

This seems to us a counsel of prudence rather than a counsel of ethical integrity. Perhaps the underlying assumption here is that practice is carried on in dyadic relationships between a psychologist and an individual client which operate in semi-isolation from the culture of the client. But when the client is an organization or a community, as it is in important varieties of laboratory practice, part of the target of change likely will be "the social code and moral expectation of the community in which he works." If joint diagnosis by a laboratory practitioner and client shows that part of the client's difficulty lies in the prevailing social code and moral expectation, then that moral code and social expectation must be called into question and ways of helping the client to change them invented and tested. Even when the client is a person, the same logic should prevail. This ethical standard as stated seems mainly to require the practitioner to stay out of trouble. We would seek an ethical principle which counseled laboratory practitioners to stay out of unnecessary trouble but to handle unavoidable trouble creatively — like an effective change agent.

We hope that we have communicated the flavor of the deliberations in which the first part of our project will involve laboratory practitioners as they seek consensus on a code of conduct that is self-imposed and that is congruent with the values inherent in laboratory practice.

Collecting, Analyzing and Studying Cases Involving Ethical Issues

The major part of the study we are starting in IAASS began with the collection of incidents, first from members of the Committee on Ethics and later from a larger sampling of IAASS members. We asked for brief descriptions of incidents which the respondent had encountered in his work as a laboratory practitioner which had presented an issue or dilemma in personal or professional ethics to him. We also asked how he had handled the issue and for any generalization with respect to the handling of such issues which grew out of his reflections on the experience. We have appended one reported case incident to give readers the flavor of our protocol materials.

Our first responses showed a healthy variety in several respects. They came both from practitioners who work typically as consultants with larger systems and from some who customarily work with training groups. They referred to incidents which occurred in various stages of practitioner-client relationships. The value conflict involved in the issue may occur in various "regions" of practitioner-client relations and transactions. They may arise within the person of the practitioner, for example, between personal commitments and norms associated with the role of helper. They may be connected with the practitioner's relationship with his client. They may stem from dealings of the practitioner with the sponsor and/or funder of a laboratory program.

We are now engaged in a more systematic approach to the collection of incidents incorporating ethical issues for practitioners. We are, in effect, trying to fill out a matrix of incidents. One dimension of the matrix is the stage of the helper-client relationship in which the incident occurred — contacting, contracting, working, and terminating. The second dimension is the relationship in which the issue or dilemma was precipitated — self-self, practitioner-client, practitioner-colleague, practitioner-sponsor/funder, and practitioner-public. We also are seeking incidents that occur both in training and in consultation relationships.

We are asking our respondents to be more explicit about the processes they used in "settling" the issue, including the kinds of help, if any, they received from others in the process of deciding. After all, we are not looking for answers which will be "right" for all practitioners and for all specific situations. We are concerned with better processes and methods for managing ethical quandaries, appropriately to the self of the practitioner and to the situation.

Before too long, we hope to develop a casebook of ethical issues for laboratory practitioners. This casebook will be primarily an educational instrument. We will invite its use by members of IAASS, preferably in group discussions. We hope that it will also be discussed by members of other helping professions. And we would encourage its use in "pre-service" seminars for laboratory practitioners in training.

In all situations where the casebook is studied and discussed, we hope that criticisms and refinements, along with new cases, will be reported to and pooled by the Ethics Committee of IAASS. The casebook will be revised from time to time, reflecting the results of feedback. If this process can be made to work, and we know the "if" is a large one, it should represent a novel approach by a professional association to the problem of enhancing the sensitivity of member-practitioners to ethical issues and dilemmas inherent in their work and of developing better processes and methods for handling such ethical issues ethically. And, we hope, it is an approach congruent with the inherent morality of laboratory practice.

FOOTNOTES

1. See Morton A. Lieberman, Matthew B. Miles, and Irvin D. Yalom, *Encounter Groups: First Facts*, Basic Books; New York, 1973.

2. Kenneth D. Benne, "Democratic Ethics in Social Engineering," *Progressive Education*, *26*, 1, May, 1949.

3. Kenneth D. Benne, "Some Ethical Problems in Group and Organizational Consultation," *Journal of Social Issues*, *15*, 20, 1959, pp. 60-67.

4. *Standards for the Use of Laboratory Method*, NTL Institute, Washington, D.C., October, 1969.

APPENDIX

A PROTOCOL REPORT OF AN ETHICAL ISSUE

Through a referral by a colleague, my name was mentioned to an organization development firm that had received a large contract to work with one of the federal government's largest agencies. After I had been interviewed and accepted by the firm's representative, I was interviewed by the firm's chief executive officer. He noticed that my hair is rather long (down to my neck), and asked me, "How attached are you to your long hair?" The discussion centered around the ethical dilemma of whether or not an organization development consultant should seek to conform to certain standards of dress when in such an atmosphere.

After a day's time, I called the chief executive of the firm and told him I felt that if I cut my hair, it would say something about me and the way I see myself as a consultant, something that violates my ethics. The hair had long been a decision that I had made, representing the way I felt about myself and my appearance. To comply with an external standard, and to have cut my hair, would have meant that I rejected my own value.

In summary, my value is that a consultant is not distinguished by his ideas, work, or skills apart from himself. He and his abilities are integral components. The freedom of an individual to express himself, or herself, in a visual manner, is a very real part of the consultant's style of intervention. Thus, to try to make one's consultative intervention in terms only of designs, interventions, programs and the like, is to curiously separate the consultant from the process of his consultation. He is now, nor should he be, an interchangeable part of an organization. That, unfortunately, is the model which characterizes most of those who have surrendered to institutional invisibility, and represents much of what is wrong within organizations. Consequently, for an organization development consultant to reflect that same behavior in his work, is to feed the very kind of behavioral condition that requires more inventive approaches in O.D.

CHAPTER 22

ORIENTATION OF CLIENTS TO THE USES OF LABORATORY METHOD

Gordon L. Lippitt

In the two preceding chapters the authors have examined some of the ways in which quality can be attained and maintained in programs of learning and changing which employ laboratory method. These ways all emphasize the responsibilities of laboratory practitioners for the professionalization of their chosen mode of practice — through clearer definition of standards of professional competence, through more adequate programs of professional development, through continuing work on the ethical issues and dilemmas inherent in their efforts to help various human systems, and through the achievement of appropriate organizations of professionals.

It does not detract from the importance of these professionalizing efforts to say that they will not, by themselves, be sufficient to attain and maintain quality in laboratory practice. Clients and consumers of laboratory practice, potential and actual, must be educated to an understanding of the virtues and limitations of laboratory practice, of the differences between shoddy and adequate laboratory offerings, and of ways of determining the fit, if any, between their own needs for learning and changing and the resources of laboratory practitioners, before quality control can be firmly established. The orientation of potential consumers and clients to the nature and use of professional resources is, of course, important for all professions. But it is perhaps peculiarly important for the profession of laboratory practice. This is because of the central importance which laboratory method ascribes to active collaboration between practitioner and client in all stages and phases of a learning and changing effort. Collaboration requires knowledge of the other on both sides of a relationship.

ORIENTATION OF THE GENERAL PUBLIC

In our age of mass media communication and mass education, we tend, when confronted with a problem of public interpretation, to think first of ways of informing a general public about a service or an activity by messages beamed to the public through various media. And there is certainly a problem, in the case of laboratory practice, of getting more reliable and valid information about this relatively new mode of social and educational practice to the general public. For confusion and misinformation characterize the current thinking of most people about the various and diverse modes of learning and changing which are presented in this book as differentiations of laboratory method.

In part, this very diversity of clients and of helping technologies and the different names given to its various modes of practice and to its various practitioners accounts for current confusions in the general public about the nature and uses of laboratory method. Laboratory method does present a complexity of approaches to its public of potential consumers and clients. This entire book is an effort to show the unifying concepts and value orientations which underlie and pervade the evident diversities which have emerged in the evolution of laboratory method.

But the preceding chapters of this book have, for the most part, been beamed to professional students of laboratory practice and to professionals in closely related professions and disciplines. They have not been written with a view to answering the questions which plague a prospective client as he decides whether or not laboratory practice promises to help him better to meet his needs for learning and changing and, if yes, as he chooses laboratory practitioners or programs which are appropriate to his needs and which meet standards of professional quality.[1] This chapter, on the other hand, is written from the viewpoint, not of the professional, but rather from the viewpoint of clients, actual and potential, of laboratory practice.

Before presenting a classification of potential consumers and clients and trying to formulate and respond to questions they differentially do and should ask about the resources of laboratory practitioners and about themselves, a few more words are needed about the confusion, misinformation, and suspicion which prevail in the "general public" with respect to laboratory practice. Some of this misinformation and suspicion no doubt are due to widespread, unprofessional offerings of training experiences in the name of laboratory practice and to the unrealistic claims about the miraculous results of participation which have been used in overselling such offerings to the public. Other authors have already noted the proliferation of unprofessional offerings as part of the social movement which has accompanied the development of laboratory practice (See Chapter 4). And they have attributed the promotion of such offerings to two major motivations — the zeal of converts who have found in laboratory practice a cult of salvation, and the desire of some to make a quick profit through exploitation of the alienated and lonely in our mass society.

If one combines the fact of such offerings with the typical way they have been reported through the mass media with an eye for the lurid and sensational — encounter groups in the nude, uninhibited orgiastic sex-expression, etc. — it is small wonder that the general public is misinformed and often suspicious about what they believe laboratory practice to be and what their participation in laboratory programs would require of them.

Another result of such publicity has been to focus public attention on only one small part of the spectrum of laboratory practice: intensive, highly affective, and personally oriented experiences in small groups. As a result, many in the "public" identify laboratory methods of education with "sensitivity training" or "encounter groups" or "therapy for normals" — names which have been used to designate learning activities in this part of the spectrum.

What the "general public" needs to recognize is the range of formats in which laboratory method is applied and the differential demands which various formats make upon self-disclosure and self-examination by participants. Warren Schmidt[2] has represented this range graphically in the accompanying diagram.

What this diagram makes clear is that all processes of laboratory learning and changing incorporate re-learning of dysfunctional patterns of behavior deposited in past experiences and new learnings of concepts, theories, and value orientations drawn from various sources outside the learners' narrowly personal experience. The mix of re-learning and new learning varies in different programs and program formats — all of which are *bona fide* forms of laboratory practice. If this fact of variety in laboratory practice is known to a prospective client, his decision as to whether to employ the services of a laboratory practitioner is no longer narrowed, as it now tends to be, to "Shall I participate in a group counseling or sensitivity training program?"

When the question is raised concerning ways to clear up confusion and misinformation in the "general public" concerning the uses of laboratory practice, two approaches seem to have

Continuum of Learning Processes

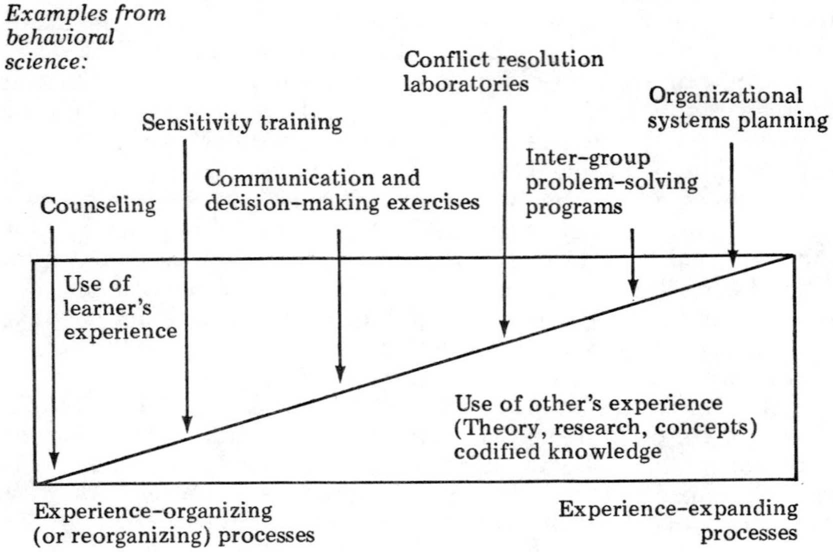

worked best in the past. The first is to recruit writers and publicists into participation in various laboratory programs with the understanding that they will use their skills in communicating to the general audience the purposes, methods, and varieties of laboratory practice.[3] The second approach is to support professional laboratory practitioners who have a flair for communication to non-professional audiences in using some of their energies and time in preparing and delivering intelligible messages to the "public" of potential clients and consumers.[4]

TYPES OF PROSPECTIVE CLIENTS

While there are values in sending messages to a "general public" about the purposes, methods, and varieties of laboratory practice, the most effective setting in which to orient prospective clients is a decision setting. The prospective client feels "distress" or has images of potential improvement which cannot be actualized through the mobilization of internal resources alone. The client needs help and is deciding whether the resources of laboratory practitioners might supply this help. Such a decision requires two kinds of knowledge. The first, already emphasized, is knowledge of the kinds and formats of helping which fall within the range of laboratory method. The second is knowledge of his own client system, particularly of his readiness to enter into the processes of self-study and self-experimentation which participation in laboratory programs will require. There are general questions which any prospective client may address himself in assessing its readiness for laboratory participation. But specific questions vary with different kinds of clients. I will discuss both appropriate self-directed questions and appropriate questions to be put to laboratory practitioners by five types of prospective clients in turn: individuals, couples, groups, organizations, and communities.

Questions Which All Clients Should Ask Themselves Before Seeking the Help of Laboratory Practitioners

Laboratory practice is not a panacea, good for all client ills and all types of clients. Warren Bennis has recommended a process of self-examination which any client should undertake before entering a laboratory program or engaging the services of a laboratory practitioner as a consultant.[5]

FIVE-STEP MODEL FOR DIAGNOSING STATE OF TARGET SYSTEM

1. Are Lab Training change goals appropriate to target system? If *yes*, then:	If *not*, *stop* and reconsider appropriateness of Lab Training.
2. Is the "cultural state" of target system prepared for: Lab Training? Degree and type of value conflict? Legitimacy of interpersonal phenomena? Degree, range, intensity, and resolution of conflict? Concepts of control and authority used? Interdependence of target system? Relationship of trust and confidence between change-agent and target system? If *yes*, then:	If *not*, *stop* and examine areas where more preparation is needed or where value conflicts should be reduced.
3. Are key people involved and committed? If *yes*, then:	If *not*, *stop* and examine ways to develop more commitment to program.

4. Are members of the target system adequately prepared for, and oriented to Lab Training? If *yes*, then:	If *not, stop* and examine ways to develop more commitment to program.
5. Is voluntarism (regarding participation) ensured?	If *not, stop* and examine attitudes toward Lab Training or *why* people do or do not want to go to labs. After diagnosis, attempt to indicate the place of Lab Training in career development accurately.

Bennis stresses a state of readiness in the client system and "voluntarism" on the part of participants entering a laboratory program as key factors in program effectiveness. These conditions will not guarantee the success of a program. But they will help insure that participants are not entering a training or consultation experience under conditions that make success very doubtful indeed.

Individuals. A person may choose to enter a laboratory experience as an individual. He might be a professional, seeking to improve his interpersonal skills; a student wanting to learn more about himself; an administrator searching for new approaches to leadership; or a volunteer worker wanting to relate more effectively in and to groups. Such persons will ordinarily seek admission to a residential laboratory program.

Each individual who participates actively and thoughtfully can expect to gain a clearer picture of the impact he makes on other members of a group. He can assess the degree to which that impact corresponds with or deviates from his own conscious intentions. He can get a clearer picture of the range of perceptions people form toward his actions. It is as important to understand how and why different people see "the same" behavior differently — as supportive or aggressive, relevant or irrelevant, clear or ambiguous — as it is to understand one's impact upon one other individual.

Perhaps the individual will choose to try out behaviors in a laboratory setting he has never tried before — but wanted to. Such experimentation can enlarge his view of his behavioral potential and provide a basis for continuing experimentation and skill development.

There are some people whose paid positions or volunteer assignment involve them in responsibility for encouraging changes in other persons or in the system with which they are connected. Such persons may gain more comprehension of the theories and skills for creative change.

Some individuals, perhaps those who have already participated in a basic human relations laboratory, may wish to achieve more sensory awareness of their own mind-bodies, increased intimacy with others, greater self-discipline. For them, a Personal Growth Laboratory, such as those described in Chapter 13, may be helpful.

Couples. Sometimes couples choose to enter into a laboratory experience. They may attend a general residential laboratory or a program formed specifically for couples. The client might be a married couple searching for insight into marital difficulties; or two lovers testing the depth of their love; or a boss and subordinate seeking better communication with each other; or two peers from any small organization where their effective collaboration is essential to the work of the organization.

A laboratory experience may help them to see their relationship more realistically. As a pair, they may test their pre-lab perceptions of each other against the perceptions of others in the laboratory community. They can be helped to see better how to relate, give and receive feedback, and express anger and love. They can practice skills of conflict resolution and management.

Groups. The prospective client may be a group. A group may seek help in a laboratory which is heterogeneously composed. Or they may enter a laboratory program organized for members of their organization. In some cases, a group may employ a consultant to work with them over a period of time.

Whatever the format, the group may learn more about group behavior generally and apply it to themselves in achieving greater satisfaction and productivity from their group life and work. They can learn how groups form through the desires and acceptance of all members, rather than by authoritative fiat. They can learn of the roles and actions by members required to keep a group functioning effectively, in doing its tasks and in surfacing and dealing with interpersonal conflicts and rivalries which may be impeding group development. They can learn how to develop and change group norms or standards toward those that support productive group functioning and member satisfaction.

Groups face relations with other groups, whether in an organization or in a community. In competitive situations in a laboratory, they can experience and review the consequences on themselves of winning over or losing to another group. They can see and assess the consequences of winning or losing on other groups. And they can learn the skills and values of intergroup cooperation on a larger task.

Qualifications for Effective Individual, Couple, and Group Clients

Before continuing with a look at organizations, institutions, and communities as clients in laboratory practice, what are some of the questions which individual, couple, and group clients should put to themselves in testing their qualifications as clients?

Are they serious about investing energy in learning and possibly changing their behavior and beliefs? Do they expect to be taught entertainingly and painlessly by an expert? Are they willing to involve themselves in participative learning? Are they willing and able to discover and acknowledge, in the presence of others, that their behavior, beliefs, attitudes, and stereotypings of others may have been incorrect? Are their defenses low enough and/or their inner strengths sufficiently great to face the possible need for changes in their self-image? Will they work to use learning gained in training in their situations back home? How much dare they risk of themselves? How open can they be to help from others? How much of themselves will they extend in trying to be helpful to others?

Such questions should be considered carefully as an individual, couple, or group client chooses whether or not to enter a laboratory experience. Such questions are applicable either when the learnings sought are personal learnings or when the hoped for learnings are about group behavior. The requirements of effective laboratory learning are much the same for both kinds of learnings.

Qualifications Rightly to be Expected of a Laboratory Trainer

A client may rightly expect certain competences in a trainer whose help he seeks. These competences can be classified in three areas. While all of these are not easily predetermined by a prospective client, they do provide cues to help clients to know whether to continue with a particular laboratory program they may undertake.

1. *Personal Qualifications.* The trainer must have sufficient self-understanding to be in touch with his own motives. He must have sufficient discipline to act in a professional manner, which means not using client, individual, or group, to meet his personal needs, whether these be for love, affection, acceptance, or dislike. His behavior should not be punitive. He should be able to give empathy and emotional support to clients when these are needed. He needs personal security so that he doesn't panic at an unexpected event, or create anxiety and needless tension in the group. He should have genuine respect for other people. Coming out of his personal security will be a willingness to share leadership roles with others and appropriately to relinquish authority in the learning process as training proceeds. Such personal security will also allow the trainer to participate in the rather wide range of interpersonal situations that are inherent in a laboratory program, and to be able to deal with the many ambiguous and hostile situations which may arise. He needs sufficient internal strength so

that he is himself as open to feedback from others for his learning and changing as he hopes others will learn to be.

2. *Training and Experience.* The trainer should have background knowledge about individual and group behavior. Although a professional degree in aspects of human and social behavior does not guarantee training competence, the concepts and constructs that come from a thorough academic background are valuable aspects of his qualifications. He should be experienced in at least most of the techniques derived from general laboratory method. This means that he should have experienced a laboratory group as a member, should have engaged in a program for training trainers, should have served as a co-trainer under the supervision of an experienced trainer, and should have had training experience on his own.

3. *Training Abilities.* He should, first, be able to help create a participative, trusting, and non-defensive learning environment (see Chapter 5). He should have the diagnostic ability to recognize when an intervention on his part is needed by an individual or group for support, for group data collection, for report of his own observations or feelings, for encouraging review of what has occurred. He needs the flexibility of knowing a variety of possible learning activities or the ability to create them on the spot, rather than having only a few pre-set activities which he must run through, whether or not they are relevant. He should be able to sense both individual needs for help, and meet them as far as he can, and to sense individual resources among participants and encourage these to come forth. He should model, through the openness of his own behavior and his receptivity to feedback, ways in which individuals and the group can learn. He needs to be competent in his knowledge so that he can give cognitive explanations and descriptions to clarify incidents that have occurred. He should know how to collect data from the group and make these available for group analysis and use.

Organizations and Institutions as Clients

Organizations and institutions ordinarily use the resources of laboratory practitioners in a format of continuing consultation rather than for all members of an organization to participate in residential laboratory programs. Some members may attend such programs as part of a design for changing. Consultation may be performed by consultants coming in from outside or by qualified internal consultants employed regularly by the organization or institution. Frequently, a team of external and internal consultants is developed in continuing change and renewal programs.

A prospective organizational client has questions to ask of itself similar to those already outlined for individuals, couples, and groups. But the head of an organization or a group representing an institution, will have further questions to ask before seeking consultation from an organizational development specialist. Are others who work for or with us willing to undergo change in the culture of their organization? What would be the consequence if we proceeded to contract with a consultant who uses laboratory method? Can change in our philosophy, managerial style, and our structures be brought about without too much disruption of our ongoing work? Will laboratory methods lend themselves to helping our organization to look at itself and plan steps for change? What should be the first steps to minimize polarized conflict in the organization? Should a team from our organization attend this kind of program before we really get started? If so, which persons should be encouraged to attend? We have been thinking of acquiring another organization. What preliminary steps should be taken to minimize bad human consequences of a merger?

I wonder if a consultant we might employ is familiar with organizational problems? Will he be honest with us about his abilities and limitations? Can we trust him to recommend effective methods and procedures? Certainly we should talk to him and indicate that we will be whole-heartedly behind any reasonable move. Or will we be?

Qualifications to be Expected of a Trainer-Consultant to an Organization

Besides the qualifications described above for a laboratory educator, the trainer-consultant for an organization, institution, or larger social system should have had experience with organizational life, not necessarily as an inside employee, but certainly through other consultant experiences. First, he should have interview and other data-collection abilities so that he can see the human and structural problems, the resistances that might occur, the readiness to have something happen, and the hierarchical perceptions and misperceptions that clog the system. He needs to be competent in feeding data back to those who have contributed the data for a number of reasons. First, it is important that those who gave the information recognize in its synthesized form, that it is still their information. Second, they need to discuss the meanings of the data and what should be done, with full knowledge that their ideas have been heard and considered. Thus, the consultant should be both highly competent in leading groups in discussing sensitive data, and trustworthy as an honest linker between levels of the organization.

If one indicated action step is a series of team-building meetings with the head and immediate subordinates, he must be able to recognize both human and method problems and be capable of bringing both to the surface for analysis and action planning. He should not become fixated on intrapersonal and interpersonal problems only or primarily. Equally, he, or a competent partner, should be capable of team-building activities in levels below the top of the hierarchy. He should have competence in serving as a third-party between two conflicted groups, or two persons failing in communication.

In summary, he needs to be able to see the intertwining of human and structural forces, of group interfaces and group loyalties, and of authority and subordination factors and of helping the client system to see and deal with this kind of issue (see Chapter 18).

Communities as Clients. A prospective community agency client needs to ask itself most of the questions other clients have asked to test its readiness for self-study and self-improvement. In addition, it has the following questions to ask about itself. What are our personal motives in seeking change in the community? How are we viewed by other individuals and organizations? What long-held prejudices or points of view are held by certain groups or organizations? Which ones? Can they be changed? How? Are there other agencies or organizations, or even an individual, that can better serve as an initiator of change than we can? How can others be reached in a collaborative effort? What specific plans for collecting data and using it wisely can we develop or discover? What kinds of outside third-party services will we need in order to get community development started?

Qualifications to be Expected of the Community Trainer-Consultant

In addition to qualifications already mentioned, the community consultant-trainer needs to know the historical intricacies of the composition of most communities, how to gather data from all parts of the community, what the racial and ethnic groupings are and what their attitudes generally are toward each other, and toward community changes. The community trainer, if he brings the leaders of various groupings together, will need to be able to put at their disposal a variety of methods for getting started. He will need to to be master of third-party techniques to use in enlisting the collaboration of traditionally embattled agencies and community segments in identification and diagnosis of community problems. He should be versed in dealing with problems of volunteer-professional cooperation (see Chapter 19).

GENERAL QUESTIONS WHICH ANY PROSPECTIVE CLIENT MIGHT ASK

There are other modal, less specific, questions which the development of laboratory practice as a social movement have made salient. Some of these, along with hopefully non-defensive answers to them, follow.

1. *What is the Optimum Length for Laboratory Programs?* Programs vary greatly in length, dependent mainly on client needs and convenience. For those who seek professional training, whether as a behavioral scientist working occasionally as a consultant, a consultant without an adequate academic background, a trainer or consultant within an organization, programs conducted by NTL usually run from four to eight weeks, and are usually followed by shorter sessions spaced over time.

For individuals, whatever their purposes, who wish to attend a Basic Human Relations Laboratory, they will find programs running from two weeks to a long weekend. Some organizations run short programs repeated at intervals over a period of several months. There is as yet no conclusive research concerning optimum length (see Chapter 3). Nevertheless the individual who wishes more than superficial learning should choose a longer program.

In working within organizations on team-building projects, the usual length of the initial session is from two to three days, followed at intervals of three to six months with other sessions. Such sessions continue as long as all parties feel they are profitable. In most cases, the role of the trainer-consultant will vary from one meeting to another. Toward the end of the series of sessions, the trainer-consultant merely observes for progress made and points out occasional errors.

2. *Heterogeneous or Homogeneous Groups?* Again, programs vary as to whether they are stranger programs, drawing individuals from different organizations, or whether they are "in-house" programs. In the latter case, after various trials in organizations, opinion favors bringing together individuals who work together. The purpose of these programs is to solve situational problems. They deal with intrateam behavior and some interpersonal behavior as relevant. Problems of the work setting are inevitably a part of such in-house training and the improvement of team work is often the central reason for the meetings.

3. *Instrumented or Trainer-led Programs?* Some experimentation has been done with instrumented laboratory groups.[6] The instruments consist of both individually and group-administered questionnaires in which reactions can be coded,

analyzed, and fed back to the participants. A trainer does not sit with the group, but does assist in designing the questionnaires. The group spends much of its time examining the feedback provided by the questionnaires. The trainer may lead general data-summarizing sessions or presentations as well as assist the groups with skill practice exercises.

While the results of such programs indicate that learning does take place, most specialists in the laboratory practice field believe that instruments cannot take the place of a competent trainer in helping with interpersonal feedback and group analysis. In any event, most trainers feel that instrumented training should utilize a professional at all times during training events. Otherwise, it is felt, the questionnaires may not hit the essential point for any given individual, or that groups may fail to make effective use of the data collected. Frequently, trainers in trainer-led groups use instruments to provide data for analysis and self-steering.

4. *Outside vs. Inside Organization Trainers and Consultants?* Some organization leaders ask the question: "Can't my training director do this kind of training?" Perhaps he can if he has had extensive training.[7] Certainly, such a person can work with groups in the organization, if he is properly trained, where inhibiting status and hierarchical forces are not present. He might find it difficult to give honest, but painful, feedback to a superior, and, if given, his interventions might be ignored.

One of the best answers to this problem, and one usually made as part of the contract between an outside consultant-trainer and the organization when he starts work is that one of his tasks will be to discover and help to train special inside resources. Or, if inside employees are already well-trained, to collaborate with them in defining areas in which each will work and arrange time for the inside-outside team to analyze difficulties discovered in their work or in their relationship. Perhaps the outside consultant-trainer will arrange further training at a laboratory program for inside trainers so that their joint efforts will gear better together and the training capability of the organization will be enhanced.

It may well be that the inside training director's job is so demanding that he has little time for doing training himself and, if the organization is a large one, he may find himself organizing and coordinating the work of teams of outside and inside trainers.

5. *Cultism Versus Research and Theory?* A charge by some critics is that the laboratory method is no more than a cult. Often persons coming back from a program are so enthusiastic they leave their friends with a similar impression. Dr. George Odiorne[8] indicates that he feels that many human relations laboratories have

become "... perverted into psychological nudist camps which end up mainly as self-flagellation societies." On the other hand, Dr. Douglas McGregor[9] says this kind of training can "... bring about significant improvements in the skills of social interaction." And Dr. Rensis Likert[10] believes there is a body of knowledge about the dynamic factors that emerge when people work in groups, and the more a person understands these factors, the more effectively he can work with people in work groups. Research on morale and productivity indicates that people potentially meet their needs and accomplish work in the face-to-face work unit of the organization.

Dr. Kurt Back did a study a few years ago.[11] He started with the premise that laboratory method is a cult, and he finished with this conclusion, as researchers often do. He said that very little research had been done in the area. This hardly squares with the evidence offered in Chapters 3 and 6 of this book.

To say that there is not enough research is true, because there is never enough research in any field. But after reading Chapters 3 and 6, as well as the rest of this book, and examining the length and depth and range of the bibliographies, the reader can judge whether laboratory method is a cult or an educational method peculiarly suited to linking behavioral science knowledge drawn from a number of disciplines to vexing and difficult individual and social problems.

6. *How Does Laboratory Education Differ from Therapy?* Laboratory training of all kinds is designed to help "normal" adults improve their understanding of themselves, their interpersonal skills, and their group, intergroup, and organizational understandings and skills as leader and member. While the line between education and therapy may sometimes be hard to draw, one difference is that a laboratory training activity generally focuses on "here-and-now" data. In therapy, pathology in members is usually assumed and the leader sees himself as a healer rather than an educator. As stated by the American Group Psychotherapy Associations:[12]

> Therapeutic groups are established for the purpose of treatment. The therapist is responsible for the effects of his practice and maintains responsibility for his patients. It is expected that he will: 1) have some way of screening prospective members, 2) have the group's goals clearly stated, 3) make a commitment to and contract with the group members, 4) indicate he has in mind the possibility that there may be a need to make provisions for helping group members who might find the group situation too upsetting, and 5) maintain interest in evaluation and follow-up of his group members and his group practice.

Jerome Frank[13] has discussed the major differences between therapy and training, pointing to a de-emphasis in laboratory training upon learning about internal dynamics of self. Others disagree and point to a steady trend toward de-emphasizing group knowledge and increasing emphasis upon knowledge of self.[14]

HOW CAN PROSPECTIVE CLIENTS GET INFORMATION TO ANSWER THEIR QUESTIONS ABOUT LABORATORY PRACTICE AND PROGRAMS?

There is, unfortunately, no simple or unequivocal answer to this question at the present time. I have already discussed the problems of producing published, popular yet accurate accounts of laboratory practice and laboratory programs. A few such publications are listed in Footnote 3 of this chapter. And the bibliographies of various other chapters in this book include many more of these. Reading is one way for clients to get needed information.

One does not discount the values of reading even as he recognizes its limitations. Reading cannot answer questions about the quality of specific laboratory offerings or the qualifications of particular laboratory practitioners. Nor can it answer questions about the fit between client purposes and needs and various laboratory services and various formats through which these services are made available to clients.

Counseling with *dependable persons who know* is needed to supplement what prospective clients may learn through reading. One counseling resource is clients experienced in laboratory programs — individuals or couples who have participated in extended laboratory programs or persons in organizations or community agencies which have employed laboratory practitioners as consultants over a period of time. If you have a good relationship with such persons you will be able to get past what is likely to be their first response to your questions, "You will have to experience it to know what it's like." They are, of course, right in saying that "telling about" is not the same as "experiencing." But they will be able to tell the prospective client about their experiences and he will have to apply such reports to his own person and situation.

Some client questions may require professional answers. The International Association of Applied Social Scientists in Washington, D.C., now accredits laboratory practitioners. You can find from their office the names of accredited practitioners geographically near to you. Take your questions about laboratory method to one of these accredited professional practitioners.

There is, of course, no substitute for one's own experience in making up one's mind. Attend a weekend laboratory program before you decide to attend one which lasts for two weeks. Most professional practitioners insist on a short trial period with a client before deciding to contract for an extended consultation relationship. Clients also should insist on such a trial period, wherever possible.

SUMMARY

There is no one set of questions or answers that can express completely the interests and concerns of potential clients of laboratory practice. In this chapter, I have posed questions that "typical" consumers might ask of themselves and of those knowledgeable about various forms of laboratory practice.

In his dissertation, Daniel Hogan has described the current situation in laboratory training very well.

> The potential value of human relations laboratory training for our society cannot be underscored enough. Technological change, alienation, social mobility, bureaucratization, and the rigidity of traditional social institutions have brought about a situation where people in society have lost their sense of belongingness, their sense of stability, and their sense of intimacy. The small laboratory group represents a place where these needs can not only be met, but where new methods can be learned to deal constructively with the problems in our society today.
>
> Human relations training provides us with a tool to learn to adapt to change, and it has provided many techniques that have proven useful in psychotherapy. The research evidence indicates that human relations training can be useful for personal, group, and organizational development.
>
> But, as is true with any powerful phenomenon, human relations training has the capacity for bringing about harm as well as benefit. It is this dual potentiality that makes the question of regulation so vital.[15]

His recommendations for regulation, like those of this book, are for more effective professional standards and associations, not laws. But the consumer still needs guidelines in deciding for himself what kinds of laboratory training, if any, are appropriate for him, his organization, or his community. I hope that this chapter will serve that need.

FOOTNOTES AND REFERENCES

1. I started to write "he or she" each time I referred to practitioners or clients in the third person singular. This proved awkward, so I adopted the practice of using "he" to include both male and females. I recognize that many of our ablest laboratory practitioners are women and that at least half of the clients of laboratory education are women. I plead the poverty of the English language in my defense, if defense is needed.

2. Warren Schmidt, *Transferring Knowledge into Impact — The Teacher and Learner Process*, a paper delivered to the National Conference of the American Society of Training Directors, 1969.

3. Examples of the products of such collaboration between writers and laboratory practitioners are Stuart Chase, *Roads to Agreement*, Greenwood Press; Westport, Conn., 1951: and Jane Howard, *Please Touch: Guided Tour of the Human Potential Movement;* McGraw-Hill; New York, 1970.

4. Excellent popular accounts of laboratory method have been published by professional laboratory practitioners like Warren Bennis, Max Birnbaum, Malcolm Knowles, Gordon Lippitt, and Warren Schmidt.

5. Warren G. Bennis, *Beyond Bureaucracy;* McGraw-Hill; New York, 1972.

6. Robert Blake and Jane Mouton, "The Instrumented Training Laboratory" in *Issues in Human Relations Training*, NTL, National Education Association; Washington, D.C., 1962.

7. Gordon L. Lippitt, "Leaders for Laboratory Training," *ASTD Journal*, March, 1967.

8. G. S. Odiorne, "Managerial Narcissism — The Great Self-Development Binge," *Management of Personnel Quarterly, 1*, s, Spring, 1962.

9. Douglas McGregor, *The Human Side of Enterprise*, McGraw-Hill; New York, 1960.

10. Rensis Likert, *New Patterns of Management*, McGraw-Hill; New York, 1962.

11. Kurt Back, *Beyond Words*, Penguin Books; Baltimore, 1972.

12. American Group Psychotherapy Association, Inc., *Position Statement on Non-Therapy and Therapy Groups*, January, 1971.

13. Jerome Frank, "Human Relations Training Groups and Therapy Groups," a chapter in L. P. Bradford, Jack Gibb, and K. D. Benne (Eds.), *T Group Theory and Laboratory Method*, John Wiley; New York, 1964.

14. I. Weschler, F. Massarik and R. Tannenbaum, "The Self in Process: A Sensitivity Training Emphasis" in *Issues in Training*, Learning Resources Corporation; Fairfax, Va., 1962.

15. Daniel Hogan, *The Regulation of Human Relations Training: An Examination of Some Assumptions and Some Recommendations*, Unpublished Thesis, Harvard U. Law School; April, 1972.

CHAPTER 23

EVALUATION RESEARCH AND DOCUMENTATION IN PROGRAMS USING LABORATORY METHOD

Robert Chin

How can evaluation research be done on programs of learning and changing using Laboratory Method? What unique issues need to be faced in conducting useful and relevant studies? How can evaluation research efforts be strengthened through modifications of conventional approaches to evaluation research?

A hurried scanning of the development and current state of affairs in evaluation research generally and in specific fields will reveal the surrounding and the forces impinging upon evaluation research as it is applied in laboratory education. Following this survey, the ideas of usable feedback, currently employed in face to face interactions, will be presented and then extrapolated to the conducting of evaluation research, its audiences, and its elements. Finally, I will make some recommendations for facilitating evaluation research of laboratory education programs and for optimizing objective evaluation research.

The point of view of this chapter is simple: evaluation research is a sub-process of a more inclusive process of changing. Awkward as this phrase may sound, I am deadly serious about the necessity of conceptualizing evaluation research on laboratory education to include a much wider range of feedback of information than is ordinarily included. Evaluation research, applied to laboratory education, is necessarily a sub-process of the action-feedback-action dynamic which is central to laboratory practice.

GENERAL DEVELOPMENTS IN EVALUATION RESEARCH

The pace of evaluation and evaluation research in many practice fields has quickened recently. Indeed we are now being flooded with demands for and attempts to do better program evaluation. The flood has over-run the usual banks and channels, burying familiar features of the landscape. The flood, fostered by Federal governmental requirements mandating evaluation of funded programs, consists of (1) tens of thousands of substantive evaluations of projects and programs in educational and social action, (2) methodological studies by aroused researchers, and (3) occasional essays on evaluation theory.

Chart I shows the several major strands of work in evaluation research since 1945. Early in 1953, Henry Riecken prepared a memorandum on evaluation pointing to the more than twenty fields then undergoing empirical evaluation of different sorts, including agency programs and projects as well as innovative social practices. His memorandum warned of the issues and difficulties in goal definition, program specification, and measurement. Unfortunately, his warning was little heeded. It was written to guide foundations and did not reach a general audience until much later.[1]

The profession of education has a long tradition of seeking to evaluate new programs and curricula. Formulations about the influence of group factors and processes in education have emerged in the last two decades as worthy of direct study. But the major focus has been on developing a set of instructional "packages" of subject matter intended to revise and improve the learning of students. These new curricula have been force-fed by large sums of federal money to modernize the teaching of subject matters in the schools. New institutions were created to innovate and to spread these innovations widely. In the research and development of innovations and change techniques, evaluation research was brought to a frenzied peak of empirical activity. New achievement scores were developed, based methodologically on the more typically used achievement tests in reading and in quantitative skills. The Sputnik-triggered spurt of interest in bringing the science curriculum up to date also generated large-scale studies of the claimed superiority of the content and objectives of various new curricula. The federal government's role in this, and in accompanying developments of experimentation in education to remedy inequities in the achievements of children from minorities and the poor, was to insist on an evaluation component in all funded programs. As a result, the last decade and a half have produced vast quantities of empirical evaluation research studies, a

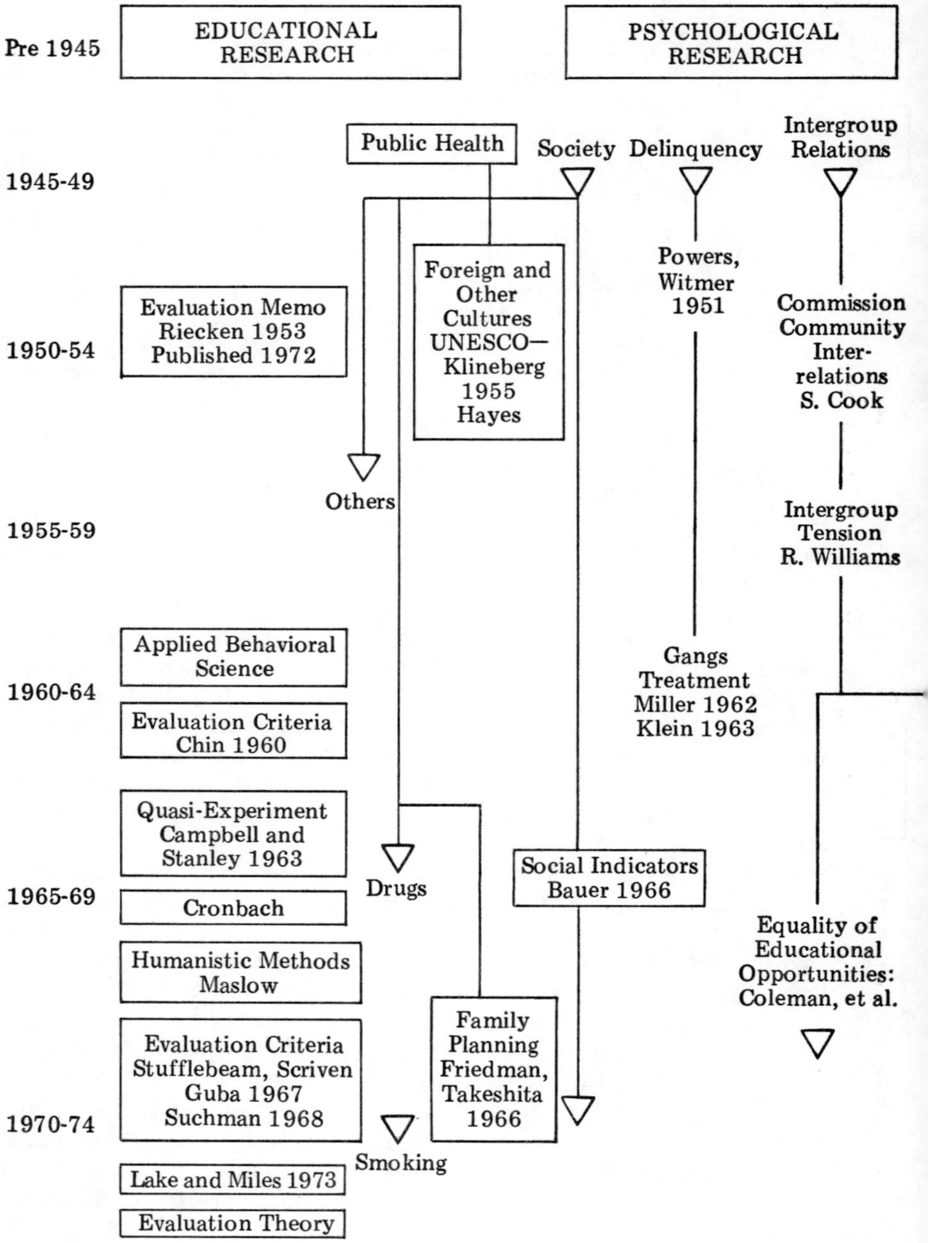
Pre 1945
EDUCATIONAL RESEARCH
PSYCHOLOGICAL RESEARCH
1945-49
Public Health
Society
Delinquency
Intergroup Relations
1950-54
Evaluation Memo Riecken 1953 Published 1972
Foreign and Other Cultures UNESCO—Klineberg 1955 Hayes
Powers, Witmer 1951
Commission Community Inter-relations S. Cook
Others
1955-59
Intergroup Tension R. Williams
1960-64
Applied Behavioral Science
Evaluation Criteria Chin 1960
Gangs Treatment Miller 1962 Klein 1963
Quasi-Experiment Campbell and Stanley 1963
Drugs
Social Indicators Bauer 1966
1965-69
Cronbach
Equality of Educational Opportunities: Coleman, et al.
Humanistic Methods Maslow
Family Planning Friedman, Takeshita 1966
Evaluation Criteria Stufflebeam, Scriven Guba 1967 Suchman 1968
1970-74
Smoking
Lake and Miles 1973
Evaluation Theory

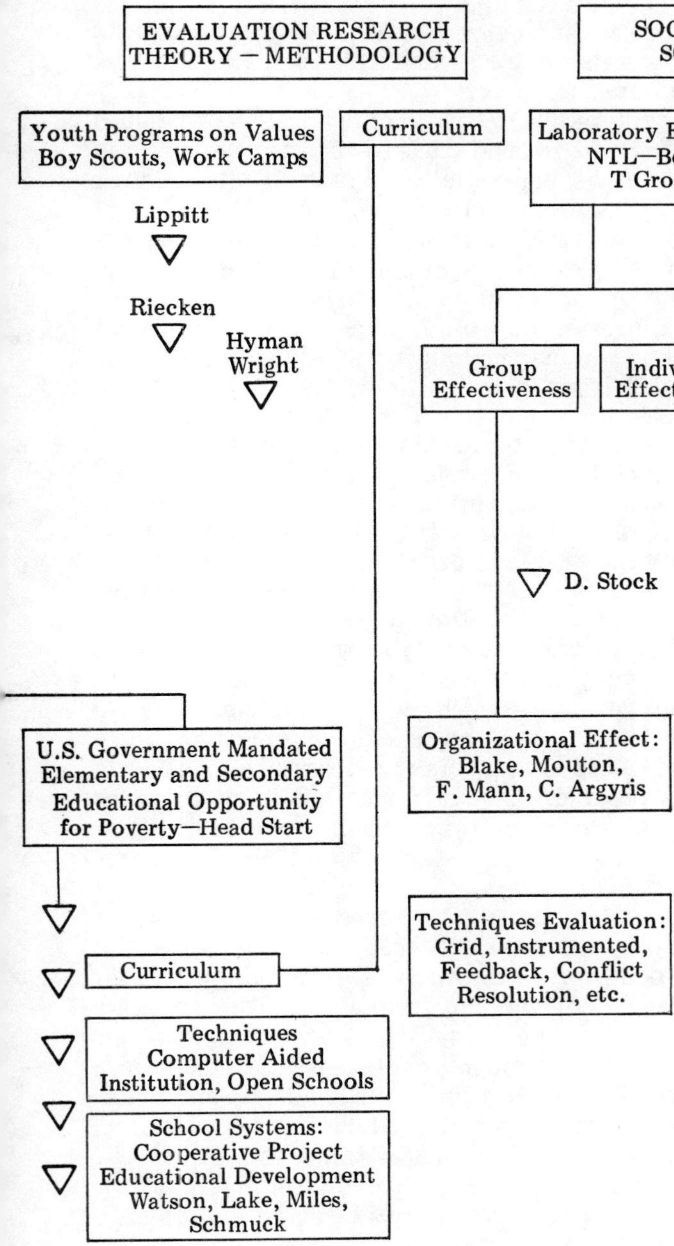
EVALUATION RESEARCH THEORY — METHODOLOGY
SOCIAL PROBLEMS SOCIAL ISSUES
Youth Programs on Values Boy Scouts, Work Camps
Curriculum
Laboratory Education NTL—Bethel T Group
Testing
Attitude Change Measures
Lippitt
Psychotherapy Methods - Measures
Riecken
Hyman Wright
Group Effectiveness
Individual Effectiveness
D. Stock
U.S. Government Mandated Elementary and Secondary Educational Opportunity for Poverty—Head Start
Organizational Effect: Blake, Mouton, F. Mann, C. Argyris
Techniques Evaluation: Grid, Instrumented, Feedback, Conflict Resolution, etc.
Curriculum
Techniques Computer Aided Institution, Open Schools
School Systems: Cooperative Project Educational Development Watson, Lake, Miles, Schmuck

floodtide of overwhelming magnitude with discouraging outcomes both in demonstrating the accomplishment of desired outcomes and in assessing various technologies of teaching and learning. At best, the evaluation results on the actual attainments by learners are controversial and non-conclusive.[2]

The objectives of the individual programs, and the techniques for remedying the problems seemed clear to many — namely, the rapid increase in accomplishing equality of attainments through new curricula, open classrooms, alternative schools, pre-school programs, and a host of other innovations. The advocates, the innovators, the program developers of remedial action both resisted and embraced the opportunity of having their programs subjected to evaluation research. Most frequently, in order to get the funding, they had no choice but to accept some sort of "evaluation." Yet, aside from their emotional attachments to the innovations themselves, the evaluation results were largely unattended by the advocates. It is interesting to note that research and development of instructional materials, such as programmed instruction, made evaluation of step attainments an integral part of the development process. Stepwise evaluation was similarly built into instructional techniques in computer-aided instruction. Units of small size were identified in cognitive learning, with cumulative stages lacing together these units to form larger units.

Learning theorists, instructional theorists, and psychometricians from psychology and education set to work to develop tools for evaluation research which would implement these studies. Out of these developed several salient outcomes. First, the emphasis became that of specifying concrete observable behavioral objectives. That is, a program that had broad goals and purposes must be able to state the intended outcomes in terms of concrete observable behaviors. The concept of behavioral objectives was only an extension of the long-accepted position of operationalism in research and testing. Therefore, there was no break with research tradition. There was generally ready acceptance of the necessity of stating behavioral objectives. Further, there was an unhooking of the dependent variable from its network of independent and intermediate variables, the focus now being placed on criterion variables borrowed from psychometrics. Second, there was general neglect of the specification of intermediate and mediating technologies which were used to produce the intended outcomes. A composite program in broad outlines was the result. Staffs tended to be eclectic in orientation, multi-disciplinary in skills and procedures, and under pressure to be active and quickly productive. The network of independent and mediating variables represented in the technologies was scantily specified. Third, a beginning was made on delineating the equally important requirement of specifying the conditions under which the technologies were to be applied and the outcomes achieved. The techniques and procedures were applied with a broad brush, hoping that later statistical analysis, *if* positive outcomes were found in the evaluation, could sort out all of the other interactions of the techniques with the nature of the persons and groups to whom it was applied, the settings and other conditional factors which mitigate or define the situation, the nature of the user of the technique and procedure and of his interventions, his relationship to other participants in the program and all such other factors and sub-factors. The dazzling availability of the powerful ingestive and digestive capacity of computers fed this hope.

A major outcome was the development of more sophisticated designs and multi-variate statistical techniques such as the landmark statements by Campbell and Stanley on modifications of research designs,[3] by Harris on measurement issues,[4] and by Cronbach on change scores.[5] Paradigms[6] and lists such as those of Lake, Miles, and Earle abounded.

Another major strand of development in empirical evaluation research stems from attempts to meliorate the social problems of race, crime, and health beginning in the mid-forties. The problems of inter-group relations and racial justice forced attention to techniques for reducing inter-group tension, to conflict and conflict resolution, and to removing barriers to justice and equality. Evaluation of on-going social action programs as compared to "experiments and demonstration programs," and isolated techniques for changing attitudes and values were stressed. By the mid-fifties, these gave way to situational variables; attitudes and values yielded priority to situational determinants such as housing, jobs, and income. The very nature of the problem of racial inequalities and relations among groups forced attention to nature-of-the-people variables. Overlooked were value issues, since, for most of those concerned, there was seeming agreement on program purposes, conceptual frameworks, and techniques of action. For example, it was not until the last five years that controversy over environment *versus* heredity brought to the fore issues of values implied by the conceptual and procedural frameworks for conduct and analysis of action programs in inter-group settings.

The early studies in delinquency, of youth gangs and their treatment, emphasized "hard" variables as compared to "soft" variables. "Hard" variables meant such behaviors as arrests and court appearances, as contrasted with "soft" variables — attitudes, values, personality changes, and group affiliations. Similarly, public health evaluation studies which did recognize people's attitudes, values, and sub-cultural values as mediating processes in health practice also forced attention to outcomes in terms of behavioral health practices or non-practices. Did they or did they not brush their teeth more regularly after the treatment than they did before? Drug treatment evaluations, family planning programs have glaringly obvious concrete, objectively required variables that must be attended to, in contrast with the verbal and phenomonological variables of self-supported insights and changes in attitudes and values. This panorama of developments in evaluation research has unavoidably impacted on evaluation studies of laboratory education in ways not necessarily congruent with the values of laboratory practice. The proliferation of evaluation research in general has brought judgment standards from these fields to bear on evaluation research efforts in laboratory education.

LABORATORY EDUCATION

How can present evaluation research efforts be transformed and embedded in the unique approach of laboratory method to the stimulation and support of human change and growth? We will deal with two countervailing inputs.

One facet of the work in this field is of special interest, namely the early and continuing interest of laboratory practitioners in "action research." In the specific and unique use of the term "applied behavioral science" by laboratory educators, there is an additional unique meaning. Action research is not merely research on action, but in the specific meaning of Lewin, Lippitt, and others, "action research" requires the involvement of the people who are undergoing change in gathering and interpreting data and in deriving action-implications from the data. This meaning of action research is also present in the writings of some early educational theorists and indeed was the chosen position of some social reformers.[8] Though "action research" was one of the wellsprings from which the T group and laboratory method generally was created, its conceptual and methodological impact on evaluation research has been buried and blurred by more traditional models of research wherein the researcher is not only a resource on methodology and on technical measurement questions, as well as process skills, as in action research and laboratory education, but also assumes responsibility for deriving the meanings and implications of the data gathered. The sources of the data are only "subjects" in the traditional research use, instead of "self-experimenting subjects" and "co-investigators," as in the specific usage of laboratory educators.

FEEDBACK

If evaluation research is part of the process of changing, it is but one phase of the decision-action-feedback-decision-action paradigm. Evaluation research is the sum of the more or less formalized activities which provide a valid and reliable data base for decision and action. Let us try to build upon the smaller size paradigm of interpersonal and group feedback processes. The reason for taking this approach is to examine the ways in which evaluation research can be transformed to become consistent with laboratory method — its concepts, values, working approaches, and technologies. In doing so, we should give fair warning that the questions about the one set of usual purposes of evaluation research namely, does "it" (laboratory education) produce valuable results, may be finessed and ducked. At best, it may be embedded in the context of information serving the purpose of providing valid information for decisions and actions, and perhaps in some non-rational factors as well. The alternative view of researchers standing outside the framework of laboratory education and making judgments about "it" is more typical and will be examined in a later section.

Feedback is the central process of laboratory practice. The process is one where the actor collects information about the consequences of his action in a problematic situation. In his inquiry, information about the behavioral consequences of his actions is collected from the significant others in the setting, who thus take on a unique and special responsibility. The feedback is information in a form which, when made available to the actor, increases optimal utilization by the actor. The conditions of *usable feedback* in processes of laboratory education are derived from a value system and ideology as well as from pragmatic experiences of practitioners and clients. Feedback is deemed to be useful and growth-oriented for the actor when it is *descriptive* of the words, actions, and behaviors of the actor, with minimal attention to the inferred intentions of the actor. It is concerned with the *effects* of these descriptions. The ones providing feedback are coached to provide feedback in *concrete* terms *specific* in time, space, and setting. It is usable and growth oriented when the reported-upon behaviors and their consequences are *alterable*, especially within the value assumptions and intentions of the actor, although not solely so since the value system itself may be at stake in the transaction. In implementing usable and growth-oriented feedback, the feedback opens up responsible *choices* and *decisions* for the actor and encourages further *mutual inquiries* by the actor and the one(s) providing feedback. The mutual inquiry recognizes and values the individual differences of both the actor's interests and those of the one(s) providing feedback. The consequences of such two-way, reciprocal exchanges are twofold: increased desire to *engage further* in these activities as well as an eagerness to *learn* about the processes at work in the relationship which make the feedback mutually useful.

Feedback from this perspective avoids the ritualization of "objective truth," however defined and by whatever means validated. Extending the feedback approach of laboratory education to evaluation research and documentation poses questions, which require a new orientation to evaluation research in laboratory practice.

AUDIENCE, ELEMENTS, LEVELS

We need to think of the actor as having a role as the interested audience of evaluation research reporting with an expectation of using the feedback for improved action. We need to think of documentation as describing what happens in these activities. There are many participants and potential participant-observers in a change program. The actor as actor and also as audience, most frequently focused upon, is the first order or first level practitioner, directly "on the firing line." His concern is with a concrete problem presented by a particular concrete client system (whether a person, a group, an organization, or a larger system). He uses a specific technology, here, the laboratory method of re-education, a *genus* of technologies as well as *species specific* techniques. Second-level applied behavioral science does not purport to deal directly with individual concrete clients, but works on a class of applied problems.[9] The first order applied behavioral scientist is distinguished from the second order behavioral scientist by primary motivation, intention, and consequent behavior. The second order applied behavioral scientist may create a new technology or a new theory formulation in laboratory practice. A reliable and valid data base drawn from a number of concrete cases, which gives a set of frequencies and probabilities for forecasting other cases, can be the same for practitioners working at both levels. There are specific information and data needs additionally and separately characteristic of each. Basic behavioral science is still another level of abstraction (Chart II).

The information needed and the usable feedback must be examined by various types of actors as decision makers and as audiences for feedback. The classes of these are varied. First are the sponsors-funders. Each sponsor may have different decisions to make and thus have different information needs, again with

CHART II

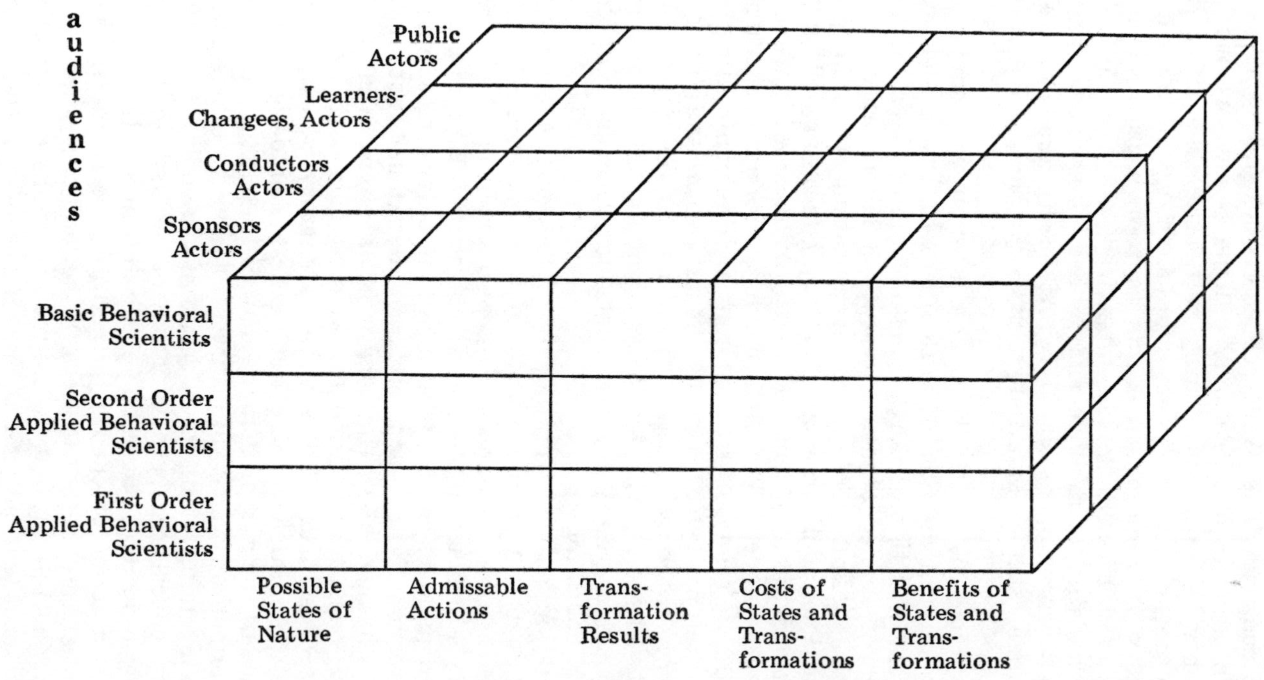

Elements of a Theory of Action

some overlap. Each set of confronting decisions-actions has different conditions of usable feedback and admissible alternatives which it can undertake. And each enters into both unique and general interactions and relations with the conductors of a program. (Chart II does not convey sufficiently the interactions among actors and audiences.) Also, for laboratory education evaluation, there is a more active role as co-investigators for the changees and learners as already emphasized.

A formulation of the "elements" of action programs, whether in formal instruction as stated by Atkinson from whom these elements are taken,[10] or in laboratory education, is the crux of evaluation. Outcome evaluation or summative evaluation has been primarily concerned with the middle column, the outcomes of transformation of the state of nature that results from each action or program of action. The preceding column has been the major definition of applied behavioral science as laboratory education. Within this definition there are specifications of training and change actions admissible in laboratory education — T groups, organizational development and consultation — within learning and inquiry models. The first column, the possible states of nature, the description of the persons and the confronting problems, is often neglected by both. The last two are the cost-benefit dimensions, not only in terms of dollars and cents, but also in terms of social and psychological costs and benefits in the growth of persons and groups in society constitute a major purpose of laboratory education.

Evaluation research for the use of the sponsor as an actor-audience is usually in the context of the first order level of the concrete case and requires the step of assisting the actor to examine his own action alternatives and the kinds of information needed to guide his choices rationally, both before and subsequent to the program. Systematic interviews to determine what he wants as data, why and how data might be used, and what are the necessary steps to determine the kind of data to be sought in processes of evaluation. Indeed, the laboratory educator should integrate these problems as part and parcel of his design. (It is the experience of the author that the sponsor frequently is concerned with information which will justify his actions to others and not for the informing of his own decisions, an indication that the laboratory educator and evaluator may not be in direct touch with the strategic decision points.) Typically, his needs are stated pragmatically in terms of changes in performance of the system or some system part. Berkowitz goes further and urges the evaluator to accept the responsibility to select among these pragmatically stated areas, situations and their variables which will be most "persuasive, confirmatory, and powerful" in three classes of situations: "tough nuts to crack"; "typical" situations currently existing and representing barometric situations; or high readiness and favorable situations.[11] Such a delineation made beforehand by the sponsor-actor-audience along with the laboratory educator and evaluator maximizes the probability of producing usable feedback for the use of the sponsor. Control groups and designs with statistical tests are not needed under these circumstances. If behavioral measures are agreed upon as evidence, there is face validity in the achievement of successful outcomes.

However, if the decision options are to engage or not engage in further activities in laboratory education, by extending the training, or through applying the same kind of program to a wider number of units, the decision-maker needs to have data bearing on the degree of transferability or generalizibility of the approach and program to new or to different situations, persons, units in the organization, or to a wider set of social problems. It is at this point that the decision-maker frequently wants to have the program conductors "do exactly the same thing," elsewhere; develop a canned program. And it is at this point that the laboratory educator insists on going through a complete cycle of individualized diagnosis and program design with the people in the new units and situations.

If the sponsor has a very large number of units under his purview and responsibility, he must have data that illuminate his policy decisions as to whether or not to proceed to wider application with the hope of some lowering of "costs." To respond adequately to this need, the evaluator must shift to the skills and methodological requirements of the second order practitioner. As such, he must be able to assert the degree to which the just-evaluated instance represented a class of situations within the population of all possible problematic situations of concern to the decision-maker. But since the laboratory educator and evaluator did not and probably could not have exercised control over the selection of the original instance and cannot know the valid boundaries of the total class or classes of instances, he cannot use the logic of scientific proof; he cannot assert that his instance represented some approximation of a total class of instances, a condition of external validity.[12]

The principle for laboratory education may now be stated. Evaluation research for the use of the sponsor depends upon clarifying *with* the sponsor the decisions he faces, the conditions under which he must make the decisions, the scope of responsibility for which he needs information. *In short, the laboratory educator and the evaluation researcher must engage the sponsor in action research on his own situation, as well as contributing criterion outcome variables for a more formally established pro-*

gram of laboratory education. Data and information should fit the conditions of usable and growth-oriented feedback consistent with the laboratory educator's approach. Sponsors and decision-makers have growth needs, too.

Evaluation research for the use of the conductors of programs — the first order laboratory educators — takes the form of assessing specific techniques, the participants' reactions to the educator's personal characteristics that may present obstacles to his desired effectiveness, and, in general, informing the choices he makes and illuminating the choice points in his own continuing learning. As actor and audience for information about the nature of people, procedures, outcomes, about the costs and benefits of existing states and of their transformation, both due to his actions and to the effects of other people and forces, he adopts an observer role for himself or uses others as evaluation observers and researchers to assist him. Frequently, in actual practice, this role of external observer and provider of data and information is most often performed by his interns and associate trainers. It should be noted that this evaluation and feedback role will not work well if the laboratory educator sees the trainee-intern as one who is ignorant and who has nothing to teach him. Where the data being provided are seen as problems solely of the intern to be "corrected" out of the wisdom of the laboratory educator, the educator is not considering these situations as in turn new problematic situations where he is a receptive audience for the evaluation of his responses and interventions.

Laboratory educators are important audiences for one another. To be useful to this imaginary audience, the evaluator would need to assess the information needs of this audience, its needs for usable feedback. The assumptions, logic, the entry, the social contracting, the tactics of the laboratory practitioner would need to be scanned, documented, and reported. The mode of documentation and communication would take the form of a case history, rich enough in detail to allow other laboratory educators to "be there" vicariously. While the present communication filters between laboratory educators tend to feature and reward reports of innovations and new techniques, responsibility for reporting and evaluation of "well-established" approaches and procedures must be undertaken as well. The documentation of the old and the new technologies and actions must be extensive enough for laboratory educators to learn from each other as they deal with comparable problematic situations. Laboratory practice may well need to establish its own files of case histories written with this purpose in mind.

Documentation must be about several aspects of the program of the laboratory educator. The customary mode of documentation is that of reporting formal program events. However, in trying to go beyond the formal program, the paucity of theory and concepts of laboratory education design has deterred the expansion of reportable and usable documentation. A simple and usable paradigm of "design" would report the elements indicated in Chart II, using a smaller unit within the program and furnishing information about several elements simultaneously. One metaphor for design reporting is that of a river's flow, with the formal events of the program representing the surface appearance. Underneath are several levels of currents: the organizational aspects of the group as a group, the interpersonal, the personal and the intrapersonal processes, and the influence of the ecological surround or environment of the laboratory program. Central to a meaningful report on the processes of laboratory education are the feedback mechanisms at work and the data they provide to guide and steer each of these process levels, their interactions and their relations to the whole process of the "unit." The size, duration, and sequence of the unit and movements at each of these levels or currents are dictated by the surface program events on the one hand and the diagnostic concepts of the laboratory educator on the other. Documentation must provide information directly gathered from the learners and participants or from the observations of the laboratory educator and/or evaluator or from both. While each laboratory educator has his own intuitive sense of the flow of a design and of the data usable to guide and steer the flow, reporting intended to increase comprehension by other laboratory educators and to accumulate a bank of usable information and data requires some agreed-upon formats. Units and episodes of the processes at each level are probably best reported in terms of the time units and events marked out by the surface program design.

Documentation of the several currents — the diagnosis of what is the state, the admissible actions, the transformation results, and the costs and benefits — makes explicit the decisions entering the laboratory educator's designing and intervention processes, his assumptions, and his data. Only through this kind of documentation will the seemingly mechanical packaging of familiar and innovative procedures strung together in a design be made useful to others.

CHOICES

Polarizing the differences between the position recommended for conducting evaluation research on laboratory education and the position taken in traditional evaluation research may dramatize my belief about how the orientation toward research in laboratory education needs to change. Chart III lists the more salient contrasts.

CHART III
SOME DIMENSIONS OF CHOICES

Evaluation Research as Generally Conducted	Evaluation Research in Laboratory Education
1. Concrete and objective goals specifiable *a priori*.	Emergent goals and objectives
2. Rigorous expert research design	Collaborative action research
3. Controlled pure variables	"Contaminated" variables
4. Technology–techniques–actions as causal variables	Equifinality of styled Gestalt of program as causal variables
5. Reliability and validity dependent upon knowledge building methods independent of investigator's values	Reliability and validity dependent on personal qualities and competence of investigator
6. Paradigm fact model	Metaphoric theory
7. Evidential critical proof	Experiences of problematic acts
8. Evaluation as autonomous, objective	Evaluation as feedback for action decisions in a system of change

Central to the approach and activities of laboratory practice in bringing about change in human systems is the disavowal of specific and concrete goals established *before* the program. In Chapter 2, Benne says that one of distinctive characteristics which set off laboratory education from other methodologies of re-education and of planned change in human systems is that the experiences are "problematic," and that the outcomes cannot be *fully* known in advance. It is not that the laboratory practitioner has no *a priori* goals or intentions. Rather he is alert to the emergence of collaboratively envisioned new goals as the process of laboratory education uncovers hitherto unforeseen directions and goals. But does this also mean that evaluation of laboratory education is hopeless? One answer is to state the real goals in terms of the facilitation and mastery of methodological and problem-solving processes. Bennis and Benne have suggested that such "meta-goals" be used as the criterion outcomes. Yet even with these universal goals, there are difficulties in specifying which ones are to be used or emphasized in advance in any concrete program. The counter-pressure from the orientation of general evaluation research is stated by Campbell and Dunnette in their comprehensive review of evaluation research on the effects of using T groups in organizational development. They conclude that there is a real need for specifying the concrete objectives and goals of a T group, in order to improve research on T groups.

The working resolution for the first order practitioner who wishes to do evaluation research for the audience of sponsors is to have the formal goals and direction stated, with an honest acknowledgment of the possibility of specifically emerging goals. The second-order practitioner must be more responsible for assessing achievement of the meta and process goals of learning and changing.

Collaborative action research fits the ideology and the working spirit of laboratory practice. The participants are both sources of data and co-investigators. Co-investigation requires that they derive the purposes and share the hypotheses of the investigation and influence the methods used in collecting and interpreting data. By so doing, they produce "contaminated" research. For it has been shown that researchers tend to produce data favorable to the hypothesis they assume or know is the purpose of their activity. Observations become biased, it has been found. Yet, as Argyris[12] has pointed out, the unintended consequences of rigorous research procedures also produce other serious contaminations often unrecognized by "value-free" researchers. Not the least of these are the reported feelings of participant-subjects of being controlled and dependent. This leads to various adaptive mechanisms in the subjects to protect their threatened interests. They give less than "authentic" answers to the questions put by their "oppressors." Argyris sees similarities between the reactions of research subjects in a rigorous research design to those of lower-level employees in hierarchical business organizations, namely, the consequences arising from top management's (or researcher's) assumptions of full-spirited cooperation by subjects in purposes and conditions which are not influenceable by those who are asked or ordered to "cooperate." The degree of rigorousness and precision which is compatible with the educing of valid data must be re-examined. For laboratory education's evaluation research, the swing must be toward the "action research" mode. This is research designed to produce valid data, with known and acknowledged determinants of contamination, to be used as usable feedback to one or another actor-audience of the research.

Laboratory practice emphasizes a system of variables no one of which by itself is a simple and sovereign "cause." Instead, there is an equifinality of outcomes; many roads can lead to the same place. Thus the causal mode of thought about technologies, techniques, or interventions used by the laboratory educator emphasizes the non-constancy and non-invariant determinants of the outcomes. Evaluation of laboratory education thus needs conceptualizations of some higher order of system-processes, with multiple patternings of these system-processes. Specific technologies and interventions function in the role of triggers, releasers, rather than as direct "causes." The evaluator of the first order practitioner's outcomes must, therefore, keep in mind that if the program outcomes turn out positive, the results could be achieved in other ways as well. The second order practitioner must meet different requirements, since the nature of the comparison group, and the proof of the wider usefulness of a particular program require additional ways of describing patterns and differences among patterns.

Overall, the purposes of evaluation research on and for laboratory educators' and related audiences' actions, must maintain consistency with the values and approaches of laboratory education. If evaluation research is a sub-process of the process of changing, its values and approaches must be congruent with the values and approaches of the more inclusive process. Evaluation research intended to provide usable information in and for programs of laboratory education must, therefore, use methods congruent with those of laboratory practice.

Can evaluation research be done on programs of changing which employ laboratory method? This question can be answered positively only when researchers decide to function as collaborative parts of the program — with special responsibilities for providing a usable and valid data base for the decisions which must be made by various persons and groups connected with the programs — first and second level practitioners, clients, sponsors, and funders.

Changing the orientation of evaluation specialists from the traditional research orientation to an orientation more congruent with processes of laboratory changing and learning sets a re-educative problem for evaluators and researchers. This means that they need to unlearn some familiar patterns of thinking and functioning and learn some new ones. Laboratory practitioners are skilled in stimulating and supporting processes of re-education. They must make themselves available in helping researchers with their own problems of re-education. In the future, evaluation researchers in laboratory programs should come to serve the learning needs of practitioners, clients, sponsors, funders, and of researchers, too.

FOOTNOTES AND REFERENCES

1. Henry Riecken, "Memorandum on Program Evaluation, 1953," in Carol H. Weiss, *Evaluating Action Programs: Readings in Social Action and Education*, Allyn and Bacon; Boston, 1972.

2. James S. Coleman, et al., *Equality of Educational Opportunity*, National Center for Educational Statistics, U.S. Govt. Printing Office, 1966.

3. Donald Campbell and Julian Stanley, *Experimental and Quasi-Experimental Design for Research*, Rand McNally; Chicago, 1963.

4. Chester W. Harris (ed.), *Problems in Measuring Change*, University of Wisconsin Press; Madison, Wis., 1963.

5. Lee J. Cronbach and Lita Furba, "How Should We Measure 'Change' Or Should We?" *Psychological Bulletin*, *74*, 1, pp. 68-80 (1970).

6. Robert Chin, "Problems and Prospects of Applied Research," in W. G. Bennis, K. D. Benne, and Robert Chin (eds.), *The Planning of Change*, 1st ed., Holt, Rinehart and Winston; New York, 1961. See also Robert L. Hammond, "A Systematic Approach to Planning and Managing Evaluation in Education," Mimeographed Paper, Center for the Advanced Study of Educational Administration, University of Oregon, Eugene, Oregon, N.D.; and Egan Guba, "Factors Influencing Evaluation Research," Unpublished Paper delivered to Division of Instructional Technologies Conference, University of Indiana, Bloomington, Ind.; July, 1973.

7. Dale G. Lake, Matthew B. Miles, and Ralph Earle, *Measuring Human Behavior*, Teachers College Press; New York, 1973.

8. Stephen M. Corey, *Action Research to Improve School Practices*, Teachers College Bureau of Publications; New York, 1953. See also Ronald Lippitt, "Value Judgments of Social Scientists in Action Research," in Bennis, Benne, and Chin, *Op Cit.*

9. Paul Meehl, "Second Order Relevance," *American Psychologist*, *27*, 10, pp. 932-940, 1972.

10. Richard C. Atkinson, "Ingredients For A Theory of Instruction," *American Psychologist*, *27*, 10, pp. 921-931, 1972.

11. Norman H. Berkowitz, "Audiences and Their Implications for Evaluation Research," *Journal of Applied Behavioral Science*, *5*, 3, pp. 411-430, 1969.

12. Chris Argyris, "Some Unintended Consequences of Rigorous Research," *Psychological Bulletin*, *70*, 3, pp. 185-197, 1968.

CHAPTER 24

A LOOK INTO THE FUTURE

Leland P. Bradford, Kenneth D. Benne, Jack R. Gibb, and Ronald O. Lippitt

In this book's predecessor volume, *T Group Theory and Laboratory Method*, the editors, at the end, ventured some prophecies about the then future of laboratory method. They spoke as prophets, not as predicters of future states of affairs. The prophet speaks to unsatisfactory conditions in the present which need the devoted attention, thought, and effort of people affected by and responsible for these conditions. He may point out trends toward the solution of unsolved problems which seem promising and desirable to him. But he believes too much in human freedom to think of a future which will predictably come to pass, no matter what people decide and do today and tomorrow. His effort is to call men and women to decision and action in shaping undesirable conditions in the present toward humanly desirable outcomes.

The editors of our predecessor volume prophesied about four unsatisfactory conditions; areas of unsolved problems, as they called them, with respect to laboratory method — inadequate professionalization of laboratory training; a need for expansion of research and theory development; the need for maintaining an experimental temper and posture in laboratory practice; and the need for extending laboratory practice from the residential laboratory into "non-laboratory" settings. They wrote their prophecies in 1964 — ten years ago at this writing.

We propose to venture our prophecies in 1974 by examining each of the aspects of laboratory practice which were identifiied as areas of unsolved problems in 1964. We will assess, in the light of this book's survey of the present state of laboratory practice, how far the problems in the areas which they saw as requiring thought and action have been solved and what problems, perhaps old ones, perhaps new ones, remain to be solved. And we will add two new *areas* of unsolved problems which seem important to us in the perspective of 1974.

THE PROFESSIONALIZATION OF LABORATORY PRACTICE

We were concerned ten years ago with the inadequate supply of qualified persons to meet the accelerating demand for the services of laboratory trainers. So we spoke of the need for more and better programs of professional training and development than existed at that time. We were also aware that the expanding inequation between demand and supply was encouraging unqualified persons to enter the training field and degrade the quality of laboratory practice and maximize the dangers to clients from inept and unscrupulous use of the technologies developed and developing within the field of laboratory training. We called for the development of more effective professional associations to define standards of competence and ethics and to apply these in accrediting professional practitioners and in disciplining members who fail to meet professional standards.

It may be discouraging to some to discover that the professionalization of laboratory practice still bristles with unsolved problems. It is true that some of today's problems grow out of what we have called the populist rebellion against all professional elites which crested during the past decade and is still highly active in 1974. What is encouraging, in a generally discouraging situation, is the wide awareness among laboratory practitioners in 1974 of the need for professionalizing their craft and the efforts now underway to grapple with the difficulties and complexities involved in meeting that need.

It is, we believe, encouraging that in this volume we have devoted four chapters (20, 21, 22, and 23) to problems of professionalization and quality control in laboratory practice while our predecessor volume had none. While the authors of the four chapters are somewhat futuristic in their approach, pointing to problems still to be solved and to images of potential solution, all authors build their statements around actualities now in being — inadequate, but still in being. This is true for all the problem areas with which professionalization and quality control confront laboratory practitioners — professional training, definition of standards of competence, development of ethical codes, professional organization, the education of the public concerning laboratory practice, and the development of modes of evaluation research congruent with the values of laboratory practice.

PROFESSIONALIZATION AND QUALITY CONTROL

There is no need to restate the findings and recommendations of these four chapters. But we have picked out for comment here two aspects of professionalization which we fear may be neglected in the welter of activities which the authors of the four chapters describe and recommend. We fear, with the strong need for developing and upgrading more professionals in laboratory practice and with the large outlay of expense and effort that this will involve, that the preservice and continuing training of various kinds of paraprofessionals and volunteers will be neglected. The services of paraprofessionals and volunteers will be needed, along with the services of fully qualified professionals, in the staff teams required to assist massive programs of action and education addressed to renovations in institutional and community life which we see as part of the future of laboratory practice. Much of the effort of professionals will be needed for organization, team-building, evaluation, and supervision of staff teams made up principally of paraprofessionals and volunteers, rather than in direct services to clients. We see this trend in the deployment of the resources of other professions and believe that it is indicated in the best future use of the resources of professionals in laboratory practice.

Paraprofessionals will not only need training, they will also need to be appropriately organized. We do not know whether they should be organized separately from professionals or whether one umbrella organization should find a place for both. Whatever answer to this question future history holds, we hope that status differentials will be reduced to a minimum as between professionals, paraprofessionals, and volunteer workers in laboratory programs. Status struggles now militate against badly needed teamwork in other fields of social practice. Laboratory practice should role-model a genuine team approach in its own internal working relationships.

Our second fear is that professional practitioners will neglect the building and strengthening of transnational bonds within their professional associations and within working relationships on transnational projects. We are favorably impressed with the spread of laboratory practice into various nations through the past twenty years. We feel certain this will continue. But we realize how easy it is to invest energy in national programs and to neglect the development of effective transnational programs and projects which a multi-national population of laboratory practitioners now makes possible. We hope this neglect will be avoided.

EXPANSION OF RESEARCH AND THEORY DEVELOPMENT

Ten years ago, we were concerned that the creative energies of laboratory practitioners would flow too heavily into the invention and tryout of new technologies and designs for training and too lightly into empirical research and theory development. It was an imbalance among three kinds of activities, all of them important, that we then feared. We also looked to two kinds of collaboration which laboratory practitioners needed to cultivate in order to insure adequate opportunities for empirical researches relevant to laboratory practice. We needed the collaboration of universities and university centers on the one hand. And we needed the collaboration of a variety of organizations and communities, on the other, to provide sites for longitudinal research studies which short-term residential laboratories fail to provide.

How have research and theory development fared in the past decade? We were certainly right ten years ago in seeing that much of the ingenuity of laboratory practitioners would flow into the invention of new technologies and new designs and formats for the linking of laboratory resources to clients with various needs. Parts II, III, and IV of this book furnish abundant evidence that such inventions have continued and are continuing.

Jack Gibb, in his investigation of trends in empirical researches into laboratory practice, showed that the volume of such researches has been increasing. He also showed that one of the kinds of collaboration which we thought important in 1964 has been forthcoming. An accelerating number of doctoral dissertations on laboratory practice are coming from various universities and from various university departments, schools, and centers. We will comment on the relations between universities and laboratory practice in a later section of this chapter.

Whether organizations and communities are providing more sites for longitudinal studies of the application of laboratory method in practice and action settings is less clear. Gibb did find a number of research reports on organization development programs.

Chin illuminates another aspect of the interrelations between laboratory practice and evaluation research. He found that the volume of evaluation researches had been greatly stimulated by recent requirements set by funders in the Federal government to the effect that funded action, education and demonstration programs be systematically evaluated. No doubt other fund sources have made similar requirements, as the slogan of "accountability" has gained power among funders of socially oriented programs. Chin observed that the main line of evaluation research has developed in ways which are incongruent with laboratory practice in its commitment to a cooperative action research model of changing and learning. This condition sets an important challenge to laboratory practitioners, particularly to those with a strong commitment to empirical research. How can we invent and try out formats of cooperative action research which can furnish valid data and information which clients, first and second level practitioners, sponsors and funders severally require in evaluating laboratory practice and programs. As Benne recalled in Chapter 2, Kurt Lewin once argued that properly designed action researches could serve the purposes of basic social and psychological research as well. Perhaps basic researchers should be added to the mix of audiences of action research already named. We seriously believe that the inventive bent and genius of laboratory practitioners need to be focused on ways of making the action research model more amenable to the research as well as the practice needs of laboratory practitioners. Perhaps we need to make a place for applied researchers as first class citizens in the professional associations of laboratory practitioners.

We feel that theory development in laboratory practice is still running a poor third behind technological invention and empirical research in the activities in which laboratory practitioners invest their talents and energies. With all the variety of options now showing up in laboratory practice — a variety which Gibb expresses so tellingly in Chapter 12 — there is a danger of laboratory practice falling into a kind of flabby eclecticism in its conceptual underpinnings. This eclecticism can lead to a kind of uncreative tolerance among and between practitioners — "You do your thing and I'll do mine." Part of the corrective to this condition is better evaluation researches focused comparatively on different varieties of laboratory practice. But part of the corrective surely lies also in inducing votaries of various modes of laboratory practice to join in dialogic efforts to build a more comprehensive theory, or, failing that, to clarify the theoretical issues and conflicts which at once divide and unite us. We hope that such theory-building seminars and conferences will be put prominently on the agenda of laboratory practitioners in the near future.

EXTENSIONS AND MODIFICATIONS OF LABORATORY METHODOLOGY

The prophets of 1964 were concerned whether laboratory practice — and they were concerned then primarily with the T Group and its other educational modes — would maintain its experimental temper as it came of age; whether the risk-taking innovation of its early years would continue. They were concerned with the standardizing influences that were beginning to operate in laboratory practice, particularly in its NTL varieties.

One standardizing influence — one which as we have already seen they favored — was the professionalization of laboratory practice. They saw professionalization as needed in the interest of better quality control in laboratory programs. But they recognized that an additional effect of professionalization "unless it is planned otherwise, may be to narrow the interdisciplinary range of influence by narrowing the variety of people admitted to the regular associations and colleague relationships of laboratory trainers."

While they recognized that the long-range hope for continuing innovation lay in stronger programs of empirical research and theory development, they were anxious lest such developments would also exercise a standardizing influence on laboratory practice. They saw such effects coming from the subordination of training interests to research interests, to the concern of the latter for pre-determined behavioral outcomes and for replications of designs. They also feared that a yen for respectability among laboratory practitioners might lead them to appease research orientations that were conservative in effect if not in intent and which were committed to values at variance with those of laboratory practice.

I think that we may say with confidence in 1974 that these fears of 1964 were unjustified. Innovations, particularly in training technologies and formats, have blossomed profusely in the past decade. We refer to the wide range of exciting training innovations described in this book — Shepard's Life Planning (Chapter 10), Weir's Personal Growth Laboratory (Chapter 13), Birnbaum's Clarification Group (Chapter 15) and Pages' Flexible Structures Laboratory (Chapter 17) among others. And again we emphasize Gibb's telling account of the wide range of options now open to the T Group trainer (Chapter 12). Innovation and experimentation have continued in laboratory practice, even as the production of empirical research has accelerated and as significant moves toward professionalization have taken place.

We do not reject the wisdom of the prophets of 1964 with respect to maintaining an inclusive rather than a narrowly exclusive stance in the continuing significant associations of professional laboratory practitioners. We have repeated this same wisdom in urging the maintenance and extension of collegial relationships between professionals, paraprofessionals, and volunteers in laboratory practice.

But we see now that we were not fully aware in 1964 of one major dynamic for continuing innovation which has been operating upon laboratory practice during the past decade. This is the fact of changing demands, interests, and needs on the part of consumers and clients of laboratory services. We have responded to innovative forces in the society, to novel problems that confront groups and persons and organizations in our changing society, to new visions of future potential which people are working to actualize. It is out of such responses of ours to changing client demand, interest, and need that innovations in technology, design, and format have been generated. We commend such openness to client and consumer influence as a continuing impetus to innovation with one caution. We, the group of laboratory practitioners, not any one or subgroup of us, should be responsive both to culture and counter-culture, to alternative school and to established educational systems, and to the old as well as to the young. Such catholicity of response is no deterrent to innovation, if we maintain collegial relations with each other. And it is a way of maintaining for laboratory practitioners the stance of methodological advocacy, and the role of supplying bridges between factions and segments of a complex society, so much needed in our conflict-ridden and divided world.

EXTENSIONS OF LABORATORY METHOD INTO "NON-LABORATORY" SETTINGS

Our predecessor volume was focused almost completely upon the operations of laboratory method in laboratory environments specially designed to facilitate and support those operations. The editors were quite aware of efforts to apply laboratory methods within or near to the "real life" situations of participants and clients. While they saw an important place for residential laboratories and "cultural island" training in the future of laboratory method, they believed that much of its future would consist in applications in "non-laboratory" settings.

They classified the settings into which laboratory method had penetrated in 1964 as academic and non-academic settings. With respect to the former, they noted deepest penetrations in college and university settings, particularly in professional school programs in business administration, in nursing, education, and in theological seminaries. They opined that applications in elementary and secondary levels would be slow in coming.

What has the decade shown with respect to the extension of laboratory method into academic settings? Laboratory method probably has been most used in parts of education least tied into the sequences of established schooling. Continuing and adult education, "alternative" schools, "free schools" within, yet outside, colleges and universities, "Head Start," and new community colleges can be named in this connection.

But penetrations into established elementary, intermediate, and secondary schools also have occurred. These penetrations have been of two sorts. The initiatives may have come from within the teaching force — particularly from social studies teachers and counselors — in moves to introduce more peer-directed participative and experiential modes of learning and growth into processes of instruction. Or the initiatives may have come from school administrators in introducing system-wide renewal and OD efforts into school systems.

Perhaps the principal impetus to changes which incorporate laboratory methods into school programs and systems has come from demands and pressures from the clientele of the school — from students, particularly at high school and college levels, sometimes from parents, and from embattled minority segments of community populations. The student "revolution" at the University of California in Berkeley came in 1965, one year after our predecessor volume was published. The entire train of student and minority protests against established schooling which followed took place during the past decade. Whatever undesirable effects student and minority protests may have had, some highly fortunate effects, from the viewpoint of laboratory practitioners, have flowed from the vigorous critique of the educational establishment which most protests embodied. They asked for more participation by students in determining the goals and methods of instruction and in setting priorities for whole educational systems, for more experiential and "relevant" modes of learning, and for deneutralizing education through a sustained focus on those value-laden issues, upon the wise resolution of which human survival now depends. All of these critiques might have been made and have been made by laboratory practitioners.

We believe and hope that educational programs now are ripe for renewal and reconstruction. And we hope that laboratory practitioners will involve themselves in helping along the inventions and widespread experimentations which such renewal and reconstuction will require.

The 1964 prophets saw OD efforts as the main extension of laboratory method into non-academic settings at that time. This volume shows the important gains made in OD work in the last decade. We see no reason why it will not continue, barring decisive victories by Fascism in our larger political life.

Community development work has also made gains in the past decade, as Chapters 15 and 19 attest. But this work has been hampered by the "politicization" of all aspects of community life. This "politicization" which protest and liberation movements have accomplished is all to the good in its dramatization of the pervasiveness of mal-distributed power in various relationships which most of us had tended to take for granted as "natural" and "inevitable" — woman-man, younger-older, black (or red or yellow) and white. Consciousness of mal-distributed power and of its often "antihuman" effects on people on both sides of these relationships is a necessary precursor to change in these relationships. But, at this point, falling back on traditional political methods to effect required changes can perpetuate destructive conflicts and prejudice human survival. We will have more to say about this difficult problem in the final section of this chapter.

THE UNIVERSITY AND THE FUTURE OF LABORATORY METHOD

We have chosen the interrelations between laboratory practice and universities as one of the "new" areas of unsolved problems which deserve comment in 1974. Universities are still the principal repositories of the technical and knowledge resources on which wise solutions of contemporary human problems depend. But they have not typically organized themselves in ways to facilitate the utilization of these resources in solving the human problems, often novel ones, which beset processes of social action and social practice. This is particularly true, so laboratory practitioners believe, in the area of applied social and behavioral science.

No doubt universities do need some degree of autonomy within society, of non-involvement in politicalized issues, to make possible their functions of supporting the production, garnering and refinement of basic, disinterested knowledge about a great number of things. But this valid claim has often become a defense of isolation, neutrality, and irrelevance in university life, as the universities have been battered by demands from all quarters for investment of their resources in socially and humanly significant programs and projects.

Universities also are feeling the pinch of inadequate funding. One kind of response to threatened bankruptcy is to cut off experimental extensions of university resources into collaboration with off-campus agencies, projects, and programs and to cultivate "excellence" in slimmed-down traditional, on-campus university activities in teaching, scholarship, and research. Another kind of response is to cultivate new sorts of collaboration with off-campus agencies and populations, incorporating off-campus experiences more fully into processes of both general and professional education, testing new mergers of applied and basic researches, honoring and rewarding cross-disciplinary teaching and research, etc.

We favor for the university the latter kind of "proactive" response to attack and indigence rather than the "reactive" former kind of response. Proaction promises greater "dividends" in revivified teaching, in knowledge building and utilization, and in more adequately knowledge-based programs of social action and social practice. It also promises readier relief from funding strictures.

For universities which take the proactive route of adaptation in their present plight, the resources of laboratory practitioners will be indispensable in helping them to face and solve the difficult human change problems which will be encountered — problems of flexible and functional organization, including the use of various temporary systems; problems of unaccustomed collaboration between university and non-university people; problems of teamwork between hitherto segregated disciplines and departments; problems of developing collaborative relations between teachers, students, and non-students, etc. The working home of many, if not most, laboratory practitioners is the university. Their services are typically employed with organizations and populations outside the university. We hope that their resources will be more fully employed in the near future in the renovation and renewal of university life and organization.

LABORATORY METHOD AND POLITICS

We mentioned earlier that attempts to extend laboratory practice into community development work had been hampered by the growing "politicization" of community life. We commended the contribution which "politicization" has made to a new consciousness of the fact of mal-distributed power in various relationships of life and of the anti-human effects of such mal-distribution on people on both sides of these relationships. What we deplored was the tendency of the politically conscious, confronted with inequitable distributions of power, to fall back on traditional political methods of win-lose power struggles, of substantive advocacy with its tendencies toward melodramatic exaggeration of the wickedness of the opposition, and of deliberate polarization of conflicting parties as a way to correct the condition. The "politically conscious" are often rich in the envisioning of ideal future states of affairs and highly impoverished in inventing means for the management of existential conflicts toward improved states of affairs which are accepted as improvements by all parties to the conflicts.

The work reported by Birnbaum in Chapter 15 and by Pages in Chapter 17 suggests that laboratory practice has important contributions to make in developing new more collaborative and experimental methods in political activity. We believe that such contributions are important for laboratory practitioners to develop in the years ahead. We cannot know the forms which such contributions will take. We believe that we do know some of their general requirements. They will require laboratory practitioners to be available for helping roles to *all* parties to conflicts and to play trusted third-party roles between contending parties within conflicts. They will require continuous interpretation of the virtues of "methodological advocacy" to conflicting parties. They will require cultivation of collegial relations between a variety of ideological perspectives within the professional associations of laboratory practitioners. We hope that these requirements can be met in the years ahead and that political processes can become tinctured if not imbued with the values of central importance to laboratory practitioners.

What is the future of laboratory practice? The answers are not now available. Answers will be found only in responsible efforts to solve the problems which now constrict its continuing development.

APPENDIX A

BIBLIOGRAPHY FOR CHAPTER 3

Ackerman, P. H. A staff group in a women's prison. *International Journal of Group Psychotherapy*, 1972, 22, 364-373.

Alderfer, C. P.; and Lodahl, T. M. A quasi experiment on the use of experimental methods in the classroom. *Journal of Applied Behavioral Science*, 1971, 7, 43-69.

Allan, T. K.; and Allan, K. H. Sensitivity training for community leaders. *Proceedings of the Annual Convention of the American Psychological Association*, 1971, 6, 577-578.

Anzalone, A. P. Personality characteristics relevant to research in human relations training. Unpublished doctoral dissertation, University of Nevada, 1972.

Argyris, C. Explorations in interpersonal competence — II. *Journal of Applied Behavioral Science*, 1965, 1, 255-269.

Armor, T. H. Peak-experiences and sensitivity training groups. Unpublished doctoral dissertation, University of California, Los Angeles, 1969.

Aronson, S. R. A comparison of cognitive vs. focused-activities techniques in sensitivity group training. Unpublished doctoral dissertation, University of Connecticut, 1971.

Bagdassarroff, B. J.; and Chambers, N. E. An evaluation of the encounter group process through assessment of value shifts and patterns of black and white educators. Unpublished doctoral dissertation, United States International University, 1970.

Baker, F. S. A comparison between two methods of teaching prospective counselors to provide high therapeutic conditions. Unpublished doctoral dissertation, Case Western Reserve University, 1970.

Baldwin, B. A. Change in interpersonal cognitive complexity as a function of a training group experience. *Psychological Reports*, 1972, 30, 935-940.

Bare, C. E.; and Mitchell, R. R. Experimental evaluation of sensitivity training. *Journal of Applied Behavioral Science*, 1972, 8, 263-276.

Bass, B. M. Reactions to "12 Angry Men" as a measure of sensitivity training. *Journal of Applied Psychology*, 1962, 46, 120-124. (a)

_____; Mood changes during a management training laboratory. *Journal of Applied Psychology*, 1962, 46, 361-364. (b)

APPENDIX A

Baumgartel, H.; and Goldstein, J. W. Need and value shifts in college training groups. *Journal of Applied Behavioral Science*, 1967, 3, 87-101.

Bebout, J.; and Gordon, B. The value of encounter. L. N. Solomon and B. Berzon (eds.). *New Perspectives on Encounter Groups.* San Francisco: Jossey-Bass, 1972, 83-118.

Bellanti, J. The effects of an encounter group experience on empathy, respect, congruence, and self-actualization. Unpublished doctoral dissertation, Pennsylvania State University, 1971.

Benedict, B. A.; Calder, P. H.; Callahan, D. M.; Hornstein, H. A.; and Miles, M. B. The clinical-experimental approach to assessing organizational change efforts. *Journal of Applied Behavioral Science*, 1967, 3, 347-380.

Ben-Zeev, S. Comparison of diagnosed behavioral tendencies with actual behavior. In D. Stock and H. A. Thelen (eds.) *Emotional dynamics and group culture.* Washington, D.C.: National Training Laboratories, 1958. Pp. 26-34. (a)

_____. Sociometric choice and patterns of member participation. In D. Stock and H. A. Thelen (eds.), *Emotional dynamics and group culture.* Washington, D.C.: National Training Laboratories, 1958. Pp. 84-91. (b)

Berlin, J. I. Program learning for personal and interpersonal improvement. *Acta Psychologica*, 1964, 13, 321-335.

Berzon, B.; Pious, C.; and Farson, R. E. The therapeutic event in group psychotherapy: A study of subjective reports by group members. *Journal of Individual Psychology*, 1963, 19, 204-212.

_____; Reisel, J.; and Davis, D. P. Peer: An audio tape program for self-directed small groups. *Journal of Humanistic Psychology*, 1969, 9, 71-86.

Berzon, B.; Solomon, L. N. Research frontier: The self-directed therapeutic group — three studies. *Journal of Counseling Psychology*, 1966, 13, 491-497.

Bidwell, W. W. A study of openness as a factor in the human relations training of preservice teachers. Unpublished doctoral dissertation, Ohio State University, 1966.

Bitner, J. A. Diabetes, self-concept, and an encounter group: A pilot study using phenomenological analysis and the Tennessee Self Concept Scale. Unpublished doctoral dissertation, United States International University, 1972.

Blake, R. R.; and Mouton, J. S. Some effects of managerial grid seminar training on union and management attitudes toward supervision. *Journal of Applied Behavioral Science*, 1966, 2, 387-400.

Bobele, H. K. An exploratory study of the use of body-movement as a personal growth adjunct in sensitivity training. Unpublished doctoral dissertation, University of California, Los Angeles, 1970.

Bolman, L. Laboratory versus lecture in training executives. *Journal of Applied Behavioral Science*, 1970, 6, 323-336.

_____. Some effects of trainers on their T groups. *Journal of Applied Behavioral Science*, 1971, 7, 309-326.

Bowers, D. G. OD techniques and their results in 23 organizations: The Michigan ICL study. *Journal of Applied Behavioral Science*, 1973, 9, 21-43.

Bramson, R. M. Changes in social senstivity in group training. Unpublished doctoral dissertation, University of California, Berkeley, 1969.

Brenner, A. M. Self-directed T groups for elementary teachers; impetus for innovation. *Journal of Applied Behavioral Science*, 1971, 7, 327-341.

Brook, R. C. Self concept changes as a function of participation in sensitivity training as measured by the Tennessee Self Concept Scale. Unpublished doctoral dissertation, Michigan State University, 1968.

Brown, L. D. "Research action: organizational feedback, understanding, and change." *Journal of Applied Behavioral Science*, 1972, 8, 697-712.

Bunker, D. R.; and Knowles, E. S. Comparison of behavioral changes resulting from human relations training laboratories of different lengths. *Journal of Applied Behavioral Science*, 1967, 3, 505-523.

Bunker, G. L. The effect of group perceived esteem on self and ideal concepts in an emergent group. Unpublished master's thesis, Brigham Young University, 1961.

Burke, R. L; and Bennis, W. G. Changes in perception of self and others during human relations training. *Human Relations*, 1961, 14, 165-182.

Burns, C. W. Effectiveness of the basic encounter group in marriage counseling. Unpublished doctoral dissertation, University of Oklahoma, 1972.

Byrd, R. E. Self-actualization through creative risk taking. Unpublished doctoral dissertation, New York University, 1970.

Calliotte, J. A. The effect of basic encounter groups on student teachers' personality traits and subsequent teaching behaviors. Unpublished doctoral dissertation, St. Louis University, 1971.

Campbell, J. P.; and Dunnette, M. D. Effectiveness of T group experiences in managerial training and development. *Psychological Bulletin*, 1968, 70, 73-104.

Carney, E. A. A measurement study of passively defensive persons in communication work-shops. *Dissertation Abstracts International*, 1971, 31, 12.

Carron, T. J. Human relations training and attitude change: A vector analysis. *Personnel Psychology*, 1964, 17, 403-424.

Cecere, G. J. Change in certain personality variables of counselor education candidates as a function of T-groups. Unpublished doctoral dissertation, Rutgers State University, 1969.

Cerra, P. F. The effects of T-groups training and group video recall procedures on affective sensitivity, openmindedness, and self-perception change in counselors. Unpublished doctoral dissertation, Indiana University, 1969.

Cherlin, D. L. Anxiety and consultant differences in self-study groups. Unpublished doctoral dissertation, Yale University, 1967.

Cimbolic, P. The effects of sensitivity training upon black clients' perceptions of counselors. Unpublished doctoral dissertation, University of Missouri, 1970.

Cirigliano, R. J. Group encounter effects upon the self-concepts of high school students. Unpublished doctoral dissertation, St. John's University, New York, 1972.

Clark, J. V.; and Culbert, S. A. Mutually therapeutic perception and self-awareness in a T-group. *Journal of Applied Behavioral Science*, 1965, 1, 180-194.

____; Culbert, S. A.; and Bobele, H. K. Mutually therapeutic perception and self-awareness under variable conditions. *Journal of Applied Behavioral Science*, 1969, 5, 65-72.

Clarke, J. F. Some effects of nonverbal activities and group discussion on interpersonal trust development in small groups. Unpublished doctoral dissertation, Arizona State University, 1971.

Cleveland, S. E.; and Morton, R. B. Group behavior and body image: A follow-up study. *Human Relations*, 1962, 15, 77-85.

Connolly, W. J. Participation in a communication training laboratory and actualizing changes in church leaders. Unpublished doctoral dissertation, United States International University, 1970.

Conyne, R. K. Facilitator-directed and self-directed sensitivity models: their effect on self-perceptual change. Unpublished doctoral dissertation, Purdue University, 1970.

Cooper, C. L. T-group training and self-actualization. *Psychological Reports*, 1971, 28, 391-394.
_____. An attempt to assess the psychologically disturbing effects of T-group training. *British Journal of Social and Clinical Psychology*, 1972, 11, 342-345.
_____. Coping with life stress after sensitivity training. *Psychological Reports*, 1972, 31, 602.
_____. The influence of the trainer on participant change in T-groups. *Human Relations*, 1969, 22, 515-530.
_____; and Oddie, H. Group training in a service industry: improving social skills in motorway service area restaurants. *Interpersonal Development*, 1972, 3, 13-39.
Costinew, A. E. The basic encounter group as an innovation in counselor education. Unpublished doctoral dissertation, Wayne State University, 1970.
Counseling Center Staff. Effects of three types of sensitivity groups on changes in measures of self-actualization. *Journal of Counseling Psychology*, 1972, 19, 253-254.
Croft, J C. Organizational development for Thornlea: a communication package and some results. *Journal of Applied Behavioral Science*, 1970, 6, 93-106.
Culbert, S. A. Trainer self-disclosure and member growth in two T-groups. *Journal of Applied Behavioral Science*, 1968, 4, 47-73.
_____; Clark, J. V.; and Bobele, H. K. Measures of change toward self-actualization in two sensitivity training groups. *Journal of Counseling Psychology*, 1968, 15, 53-57.
Danish, S. J. Factors influencing changes in empathy following a group experience. *Journal of Counseling Psychology*, 1971, 18, 262-267.
Davies, M. M. A comparison of the effects of sensitivity training and programmed instruction on the development of human relations skills of beginning nursing students in an associate degree program. Unpublished doctoral dissertation, St. Louis University, 1970.
Delaney, D. J.; and Heimann, R. A. Effectiveness of sensitivity training on the perception of non-verbal communications. *Journal of Counseling Psychology*, 1966, 13, 436-440.
Delaney, E. T. The effects of a group experience on the self-awareness of supervisor trainees and teacher trainees in supervision. Unpublished doctoral dissertation, University of Illinois, 1970.
DeMichele, J. H. The measurement of rated training changes resulting from a sensitivity training laboratory of an overall program in organization development. Unpublished doctoral dissertation, New York University, 1966.
Dietterich, P. M. An evaluation of a group development laboratory approach to training church leaders. Unpublished doctoral dissertation, Boston University, 1961.
Diller, J. V. The encounter group as a means of reducing prejudice. Unpublished doctoral dissertation, University of Colorado, 1971.
Dodson, J. P. Participation in a bi-racial encounter group: its relation to acceptance of self and others, racial attitudes, and interpersonal orientations. Unpublished doctoral dissertation, Purdue University, 1970.
Draeger, C. Level of trust in intensive small groups. Unpublished doctoral dissertation, University of Texas, Austin, 1968.
Dunnette, M. D. People feeling: joy, more joy, and the "slough of despond." *Journal of Applied Behavioral Science*, 1969, 5, 25-44.
Dunphy, D. C. Phases, roles, and myths in self-analytic groups. *Journal of Applied Behavioral Science*, 1968, 4, 195-226.

Durham, L. E.; and Gibb, J. R. *An Annotated bibliography of research, National Training Laboratories, 1947-1960.* Washington: National Training Laboratories, 1960.

Dyer, R. D. The effects of human relations training on the interpersonal behavior of college students. Unpublished doctoral dissertation, University of Oregon, 1967.

Dyer, W. G.; Maddocks, R. F.; Moffitt, J. W.; and Underwood, W. J. A laboratory-consultation model for organization change. *Journal of Applied Behavioral Science,* 1970, 6, 211-227.

Easton, C. W. The effect of the structure and emphasis of group training methods on communication skills, attitude change, and problem-solving ability. Unpublished doctoral dissertation, Rutgers State University, 1971.

Edwards, D. D. Effects of an extended encounter group experience upon counselor facilitation of client self-exploration. Unpublished doctoral dissertation, North Illinois University, 1971.

Egelhoff, E. A. Encounter group feedback and self-perception change. Unpublished doctoral dissertation, University of Texas, 1970.

Eisenbeiss, M. J. The effect of a sensitivity group experience on counselors-in-training and their understanding of counselee communication. Unpublished doctoral dissertation, University of Wyoming, 1972.

Eisenstadt, J. W. An investigation of factors which influence response to laboratory training. *Journal of Applied Behavioral Science,* 1967, 3, 575-578.

Elbert, W. E. Changes in self-concept, self-actualization, and interpersonal relations as a result of video feedback in sensitivity training. Unpublished doctoral dissertation, East Texas State University, 1969.

Elliott, A. L. Fostering self actualization of high school students through general semantics training in encounter groups. Unpublished doctoral dissertation, United States International University, 1969.

Elliott, G. R. The effects of the T-group method upon the communication and discrimination skills of counselor trainees. Unpublished doctoral dissertation, Kent State University, 1971.

Fadale, V. E. An experimental study of the effects of videotape feedback in a basic encounter group. Unpublished doctoral dissertation, East Texas State University, 1969.

Fennell, N. W.; and Kenton, R. W. Some effects on personality of a basic encounter group in a community college class. Unpublished doctoral dissertation, United States International University, 1970.

Fenwick, D. D. An evaluation of a planned program of human relations development for college students. Unpublished doctoral dissertation, University of Nebraska Teachers College, 1967.

Fisher, I. S. The relationship between selected personality characteristics and the effects of training to develop small group productivity skills and interpersonal competence. Unpublished doctoral dissertation, University of Miami, 1970.

Force, E. J. Personal changes attributed to human relations training by participants, intimates, and job colleagues. Unpublished doctoral dissertation, Michigan State University, 1969.

Foster, B. W. An investigation of changes in levels of dogmatism, self-concept, needs for inclusion, affection, and control, as a result of encounter group experiences with selected graduate students. Unpublished doctoral dissertation, University of South Dakota, 1972.

Foulds, M. L. Effects of a personal growth group on a measure of self-actualization. *Journal of Humanistic Psychology,* 1970, 10, 33-38.

____. Changes in locus of internal-external control; a growth group

experience. *Comparative Group Studies*, 1971, 2, 293-300.
_____; Girona, R.; and Guinan, J. F. Changes in ratings of self and others as a result of a marathon group. *Comparative Group Studies*, 1970, 1, 349-355.
Freid, J. B. The effects of input and feedback on accuracy of self descriptions in short-term sensitivity training. Unpublished doctoral dissertation, University of South Carolina, 1970.
Freidlander, F. The impact of organizational training laboratories upon the effectiveness and interaction of ongoing work groups. *Personnel Psychology*, 1967, 20, 289-308.
_____. A comparative study of consulting processes and group development. *The Journal of Applied Behavioral Science*, 1968, 4, 377-400.
_____. The primacy of trust as a facilitator of further group accomplishment. *Journal of Applied Behavioral Science*, 1970, 6, 387-400.
French, J. R. P., Jr.; Sherwood, J. J.; and Bradford, D. L. Change in self-identity in a management training conference. *Journal of Applied Behavioral Science*, 1966, 2, 210-218.
Friedman, V. S. The effects of sensitivity training on students at a major metropolitan university. Unpublished doctoral dissertation, St. Louis University, 1969.
Gage, N. L.; and Exline, R. V. Social Perception and effectiveness in discussion groups. *Human Relations*, 1953, 6, 381-396.
Gamez, G. L. T-groups as a tool for developing trust and cooperation between Mexican-American and Anglo-American college students. Unpublished doctoral dissertation, University of Texas, 1970.
Gamez, K. B. Transfer of learning from T-groups to other groups. Unpublished doctoral dissertation, University of Texas, 1970.
Garner, H. G. Effects of human relations training on the personal, social, and classroom adjustment of elementary school children with behavior problems. Unpublished doctoral dissertation, University of Florida, 1970.
Gassner, S. M.; Gold, J.; and Snadowsky, A. M. Changes in the phenomenal field as a result of human relations training. *Journal of Psychology*, 1964, 58, 33-41.
Geisler, J.; and Gillingham, W. The effects of a personal growth group experience. *National Catholic Guidance Conferences Journal*, 1971, 15, 183-186.
Geitgey, D. A. A study of some effects of sensitivity training on the performance of students in associate degree programs of nursing education. Unpublished doctoral dissertation, University of California, Los Angeles, 1966.
Gibb, J. R. Effects of role playing upon (a) role flexibility and upon (b) ability to conceptualize a new role. Paper presented at the meeting of the American Psychological Association, Cleveland, Ohio, 1953.
_____. The effects of human relations training. In Bergin, A. E.,; Garfield, S. L. (eds.) *Handbook of psychotherapy and behavior change*. New York: Wiley, 1971, 839-862.
_____. The message from research. In Pfeiffer, J. W.; and J. E. Jones (eds.), *The 1974 Annual Handbook for Group Facilitators*. Iowa City, Iowa: University Associates, 1974. In press.
_____; Smith, E. E.; and Roberts, A. H. Effects of positive and negative feedback upon defensive behavior in small problem-solving groups. Paper presented at the meeting of the American Psychological Association, San Francisco, September, 1955.
Gibb, L. M.; and Gibb, J. R. Effects of the use of "participative action" groups in a course in general psychology. Paper presented at the meeting of the American Psychological Association, Washington, D.C.,

September, 1952.
Gilligan, J. F. Personality characteristics of selectors and non-selectors of sensitivity training and the relationship between selector characteristics and training outcomes. Unpublished doctoral dissertation, University of Idaho, 1972.
Gilliland, S. F. Some effects of a human relations laboratory on moral orientation. Unpublished doctoral dissertation, Boston University, 1972.
Gold, J. S. An evaluation of a laboratory human relations training program for college undergraduates. Unpublished doctoral dissertation, Columbia University, 1967.
Goldberg, R. M. Changes in self-ideal discrepancies in sensitizers and repressors as a function of a sensitivity training experience. Unpublished doctoral dissertation, University of Cincinnati, 1970.
Goldstein, S. R. Differential effects of physical and non-physical encounter group techniques on dimensions of self-esteem, interpersonal relations, and defense. Unpublished doctoral dissertation, Temple University, 1970.
Golembiewski, R. T.; and Blumberg, A. Confrontation in complex organizations: attitudinal changes in a diversified population of managers. *Journal of Applied Behavioral Science*, 1967, 3, 525-547.
____; Carrigan, S. B.; Mead, W. R.; Munzenrider, R.; and Blumberg, A. Toward building new work relationships; an action design for critical intervention. *Journal of Applied Behavioral Science*, 1972, 8, 135-148.
Gordon, R. D. A quantitative investigation of selected dynamics and outcomes of the basic encounter group. Unpublished doctoral dissertation, University of Kansas, 1971.
Grant, S. J. The effects of a basic encounter group experience on supervision by supervisor trainees. Unpublished doctoral dissertation, University of Illinois, 1970.
Grater, H. Changes in self and other attitudes in a leadership training group. *Personnel and Guidance Journal*, 1958, 37, 493-496.
Green, F. The effects of a task-encounter workshop on the administrative staff of a public school system. Unpublished doctoral dissertation, United States International University, 1970.
Green, J. G. A study of expressed behavior changes occurring as a result of exposure to filmed classroom situations and T-group sensitivity training. Unpublished doctoral dissertation, Washington State University, 1969.
Greiner, L. E. Organizational change and development. Unpublished doctoral dissertation, Harvard University, 1965.
Haiman, F. S. Effects of training in group processes on openmindedness. *Journal of Communication*, 1963, 13, 236-245.
Hall, J.; and Williams, M. S. Group dynamics training and improved decision making. *Journal of Applied Behavioral Science*, 1970, 6, 39-68.
Hammann, K. A. Trainer orientation, member experience, and empathy; a true experiment exploring the source and kinds of impact of sensitivity training. Unpublished doctoral dissertation, University of Michigan, 1970.
Harpel, R. L. The effect of encounter group composition upon social and political attitudes. Unpublished doctoral dissertation, University of Colorado, 1970.
Harrison, R. Impact of the laboratory on perceptions of others by the experimental group. In G. Argyris, *Interpersonal competence and organizational effectiveness.* Homewood, Ill.: Irwin, 1962, 261-271.
____. Cognitive change and participation in a sensitivity training laboratory. *Journal of Consulting Psychology*, 1966, 30, 517-520.
____. Research on human relations training: design and interpretation.

Journal of Applied Behavioral Science, 1971, 7, 71-86.
_____; and Lubin, B. Personal style, group composition, and learning. *Journal of Applied Behavioral Science*, 1965, 1, 286-301.
Harrow, M.; et al. The T-group and study group laboratory experiences. *Journal of Social Psychology*, 1971, 85, 225-237.
Heck, E. J. A training and research model for investigating the effects of sensitivity training for teachers. *Journal of Teacher Education*, 1971, 22, 501-507.
Heiner, H. G. An application of T-group method to the teaching of family relationships. Unpublished doctoral dissertation, University of Washington, 1970.
Hellebrandt, E. T.; and Stinson, J. E. The effects of T-group training on business game results. *Journal of Psychology*, 1971, 77, 271-272.
Hill, W. F. The influence of sub-groups on participation in human relations training groups. Unpublished doctoral dissertation, University of Chicago, 1955.
_____. Hill interaction matrix (HIM). In Pfeiffer, J. W.; and J. E. Jones (eds.), *The 1973 Annual Handbook for Group Facilitators.* Iowa City, Iowa: University Associates, 1973, 159-176.
Himber, C. Evaluating sensitivity training for teenagers. *Journal of Applied Behavioral Science*, 1970, 6, 307-322.
Hipple, J. L. Effects of differential human relations laboratory training designs on the interpersonal behavior of college students. Unpublished doctoral dissertation, University of Iowa, 1970.
Holloman, C. R.; and Hendrick, H. W. Effect of sensitivity training on tolerance for dissonance. *Journal of Applied Behavioral Science*, 1972, 8, 174-187.
Holmes, C. B. The effect of sensitivity training on counseling behavior. Unpublished doctoral dissertation, University of Toledo, 1971.
Howard, R. D. The effects of structured laboratory learning on the interpersonal behavior of college students. Unpublished doctoral dissertation, University of Oregon, 1969.
Hull, D. The effect of laboratory training on self-concept and self-actualization. Unpublished doctoral dissertation, University of Missouri, 1971.
Hull, W. F. Changes in world-mindedness after a cross-cultural sensitivity group experience. *Journal of Applied Behavioral Science*, 1972, 8, 115-121.
Innis, M. N. An analysis of sensitivity training and laboratory method in effecting changes in attitudes and concepts. Unpublished doctoral dissertation, University of Houston, 1970.
Jacobson, E. A.; and Smith, S. J. Effect of weekend encounter group experiences upon interpersonal orientations. *Journal of Consulting & Clinical Psychology*, 1972, 38, 403-410.
Jeffers, N. E. An examination of new techniques for enhancing human growth experiences. Unpublished doctoral dissertation, Claremont Graduate School, California, 1971.
Jenks, R. S. An action-research approach to organizational change. *Journal of Applied Behavioral Science*, 1970, 6, 131-150.
Jepson, P. Some effects of self-actualizing growth on teenagers. Unpublished doctoral dissertation, United States International University, 1969.
Johnson, D. L. The relationships between human relations training for educational administrators and changes in their leader behavior. Unpublished doctoral dissertation, University of Maryland, 1969.
_____; Hanson, P. G.; Rothaus, P.; Morton, R. B.; Lyle, F. A.; and Moyer, R. Follow-up evaluation of human relations training for psychiatric

patients. In E. H. Schein, and W. B. Bennis (eds.), *Personal and organizational change through group methods.* New York: Wiley, 1965. Pp. 152-168.

____; Rothaus, P.; and Hanson, P. G. A human relations training program for hospital personnel. *Journal of Health and Human Behavior,* 1966, 7, 215-223.

Johnson, D. W.; Kavanagh, J. A.; and Lubin, B. T-groups, tests, and tension. *Small Group Behavior,* February, 1973, 81-88.

Johnson, J. J. Some effects of three kinds of groups in the human relations area. Unpublished doctoral dissertation, University of California, Los Angeles, 1967.

Johnson, L. K. The effect of trainer interventions on change in personal functioning through T group training. Unpublished doctoral dissertation, University of Minnesota, 1966.

Johnson, R. F. The effects of encounter groups on selected age-related variables in a volunteer geriatric population. Unpublished doctoral dissertation, University of Miami, 1970.

Joure, S. A.; Frye, R. L.; Green, P. C.; and Cassens, F. P. Examples of overuse of sensitivity training. *Training & Development Journal,* 1971, 25, 24-26.

Kassarjian, H. H. Social character and sensitivity training. *Journal of Applied Behavioral Science,* 1965, 1, 433-440.

Kegan, D. L. Trust, openness, and organizational development: Short-term relationships in research and development laboratories and a design for investigating long-term effects. Unpublished doctoral dissertation, Northwestern University, 1971.

Kelley, H. H. First impressions in interpersonal relations. Unpublished doctoral dissertation, Massachusetts Institute of Technology, 1948.

Kelley, H.; and Pepitone, A. An evaluation of a college course in human relations. *Journal of Educational Psychology,* 1952, 43, 193-209.

Kennedy, T. F. An exploration of the effects of sensitivity training upon selected personality traits. Unpublished doctoral dissertation, St. John's University, New York, 1972.

Kepes, S. Y. Experimental evaluation of sensitivity training. Unpublished doctoral dissertation, Michigan State University, 1965.

Kernan, J. P. Laboratory human relations training: Its effect on the "personality" of supervisory engineers. Unpublished doctoral dissertation, New York University, 1963.

Keutzer, C. S.; Fosmire, F. R.; Diller, R.; and Smith, M. D. Laboratory training in a new social system: evaluation of a consulting relationship with a high school faculty. *Journal of Applied Behavioral Science,* 1971, 7, 493-501.

Khanna, J. L. A discovery learning approach to in-service training. Paper presented at the meeting of the American Psychological Association, San Francisco, September, 1968.

King, W. R. The effects of a T-group experience on teacher self-perception and classroom behavior. Unpublished doctoral dissertation, Stanford University, 1970.

Klingberg, H. E. An evaluation of sensitivity training effects on self-actualization, purpose in life, and religious attitudes of theological students. Unpublished doctoral dissertation, Fuller Theological Seminary, California, 1971.

Knowles, E. S. *A bibliography of research on human relations training since 1960.* Washington: NTL Institute for Applied Behavioral Science, 1967.

Koile, E. A.; and Draeger, C. T-group member ratings of leader and self in human relations laboratory. *Journal of Psychology,* 1969, 72, 11-20.

Kolb, D. A.; Winter, S. K.; and Berlew, D. E. Self-directed change: two studies. *Journal of Applied Behavioral Science*, 1968, 4, 453-471.

Komins, A. S. An analysis of trainer influence in T-group learning. Unpublished doctoral dissertation, Boston University, 1972.

Koziey, P. W.; Loken, J. O.; and Field, J. A. T-group influence on feelings of alienation. *Journal of Applied Behavioral Science*, 1971, 7, 724-732.

Kraus, W. A. Laboratory groups: effect on the tolerance scale of the California Psychological Inventory. Unpublished doctoral dissertation, Ohio University, 1970.

Krear, M. L. The influence of sensitivity training on the social attitudes of educational leaders of racially imbalanced schools. Unpublished doctoral dissertation, United States International University, 1968.

La Boon, S. TORI: a theory of community growth. Unpublished master's thesis, United States International University, 1971.

Lakin, M.; and Carson, R. C. Participant perception of group process in group sensitivity training. *International Journal of Group Psychotherapy*, 1964, 14, 116-122.

Lasalle, A. J. The effects of encounter and programmed group treatments on self-concept. Unpublished doctoral dissertation, State University of New York, Albany, 1970.

Lee, R. E. Relationship between basic encounter group and change in self-concepts and interpersonal relationships of college low achievers. Unpublished doctoral dissertation, United States International University, 1969.

Lee, W. G. Differences in self-concept changes among three educative treatments. Unpublished doctoral dissertation, Florida State University, 1971.

Lee, W. S. Human relations training for teachers: the effectiveness of sensitivity training. *California Journal of Educational Research*, 1970, 21, 28-34.

Leiterman, P. H. Attitudinal and behavioral changes in self-directed and leader-directed personal growth groups. Unpublished doctoral dissertation, University of Kentucky, 1970.

Leon, J. E. Attitude change, as a result of a T-group session, in a pre-teaching population. Unpublished doctoral dissertation, Case Western Reserve University, 1972.

Levy, S. J. An empirical study of disclosing behavior in a verbal encounter group. Unpublished doctoral dissertation, Yeshiva University, 1971.

____; and Atkins, A. L. An empirical investigation of disclosing behavior in a verbal encounter group. *Proceedings of the Annual Convention of the American Psychological Association*, 1971, 6, 297-298.

Lieberman, M. A. The relation of diagnosed behavioral tendencies to member-perceptions of self and of the group. In D. Stock and H. A. Thelen (eds.), *Emotional dynamics and group culture.* Washington, D.C.: National Training Laboratories, 1958. Pp. 35-49. (a)

____. The relationship between the emotional cultures of groups and individual change. Unpublished doctoral dissertation, The University of Chicago, 1958. (b)

____. Sociometric choice related to affective approach. In D. Stock and H. A. Thelen, (eds.), *Emotional dynamics and group culture.* Washington, D.C.: National Training Laboratories, 1958. Pp. 71-89. (c)

____. The influence of group composition on change in affective approach. In D. Stock and H. A. Thelen (eds.), *Emotional dynamics and group culture.* Washington, D.C.: National Training Laboratories, 1958. Pp. 131-139. (d)

____; Yalom, I. D.; and Miles, M. B. *Encounter groups: first facts.* New York:

Basic Books, 1972.
Liebowitz, B. A method for the analysis of the thematic structure of T-groups. *Journal of Applied Behavioral Science,* 1972, 149-173.
Link, S. L. A study of degree of change in self-concept as a result of participation in a marathon T-group. Unpublished doctoral dissertation, University of Oregon, 1971.
Lippitt, G. L. Effects of information about group desire for change on members of a group. Unpublished doctoral dissertation, American University, 1959.
Lippitt, L. L. Participant learnings resulting from a human relations training experience for teacher trainees. Unpublished doctoral dissertation, University of Michigan, 1971.
Little, F. W. The effect of a personal growth group experience upon measured self-concept of a selected group of black college freshmen. Unpublished doctoral dissertation, Purdue University, 1971.
Livingston, D. G. The effects of varying group organization upon perception of power and benefit. Unpublished doctoral dissertation, University of Kansas, 1951.
Livingston, L. B. Self-concept change of black college males as a result of a weekend black experience encounter workshop. Unpublished doctoral dissertation, Arizona State University, 1971.
Lohman, K.; Zenger, J. H.; and Weschler, I. R. Some perceptual changes during sensitivity training. *Journal of Educational Research,* 1959, 53, 28-31.
Loper, M. D. Videotaped feedback and changes in self-concept during and after sensitivity training. Unpublished doctoral dissertation, University of California, Los Angeles, 1970.
Lubin, B.; and Zuckerman, M. Affective and perceptual-cognitive patterns in sensitivity training groups. *Psychological Reports,* 1967, 21, 365-376.
_____; and Zuckerman, M. Level of emotional arousal in laboratory training. *Journal of Applied Behavioral Science,* 1969, 5, 483-490.
Lumpkin, M. A. The effect of an encounter group experience on the role anxiety and therapeutic competence of student therapists. Unpublished doctoral dissertation, Texas Technological University, 1971.
Lundgren, D. C. Interaction process and identity change in T-groups. Unpublished doctoral dissertation, University of Michigan, 1968.
_____. Trainer style and patterns of group development. *Journal of Applied Behavioral Science,* 1971, 7, 689-709.
Lynch, A. Q. The effects of basic encounter and task training group experiences on undergraduate advisors to freshmen women. Unpublished doctoral dissertation, University of Florida, 1968.
Lynn, A. W. Measures of self-actualization changes and their relationship to interaction preferences among encounter group participants. Unpublished doctoral dissertation, University of Southern California, 1972.
Mann, R. D. The development of the member-trainer relationship in self-analytic groups. *Human Relations,* 1966, 19, 84-117.
Marchand, R. H. A comparison of T group and practicum approaches to the training of undergraduate resident assistants. Unpublished doctoral dissertation, Florida State University, 1972.
Maroun, T. J. Differential effects of two methods of encounter group training on the personal growth of counselor candidates. Unpublished doctoral dissertation, Indiana University, 1970.
Mase, B. F. Changes in self-actualization as a result of two types of residential group experience. Unpublished doctoral dissertation, Northwestern University, 1971.
Massarik, F.; and Carlson, G. The California Psychological Inventory as an

indicator of personality change in sensitivity training. Unpublished master's thesis, University of California, Los Angeles, 1960.

Mates, M. E. The effects of trainer personality on trainer behavior and on participant personality change in a sensitivity training experience. Unpublished doctoral dissertation, George Peabody College for Teachers, 1972.

Mathis, A. G. Development and validation of a trainability index for laboratory training groups. Unpublished doctoral dissertation, University of Chicago, 1955.

Maxey, J. H. The effects of interaction analysis training and sensitivity training on the verbal teaching behavior of pre-service teachers. Unpublished doctoral dissertation, University of Michigan, 1970.

McFarland, G. N. Effects of sensitivity training utilized as in-service education. Unpublished doctoral dissertation, George Peabody College for Teachers, 1970.

McGee, R. D. A study of sensitivity training as a method of changing self-concept. Unpublished doctoral dissertation, University of Tennessee, 1969.

Meador, B. D. Individual Process in a basic encounter group. *Journal of Counseling Psychology*, 1971, 18, 70-76.

Merriam, M. L. The effects of two group methodologies on interpersonal behavior. Unpublished doctoral dissertation, Pennsylvania State University, 1970.

Michael, E. M. The effect of human relations training upon the academic achievement of pre- and early adolescent children. Unpublished doctoral dissertation, Wayne State University, 1968.

Miles, M. B. Changes during and following laboratory training: a clinical-experimental study. *Journal of Applied Behavioral Science*, 1965, 1, 215-242.

Miller, G. M. The effects of sensitivity training design and personality factors upon the attitudes of group participants. Unpublished doctoral dissertation, Case Western Reserve University, 1969.

Miller, J. H. Sensitivity training with incarcerated criminals: personality correlates of participant duration and an assessment of therapeutic value. Unpublished doctoral dissertation, Auburn University, 1971.

Mindes, S. The differential effect of a modified encounter group experience on the achievement test performance of high and low-defensive pupils. Unpublished doctoral dissertation, New York University, 1970.

Minter, J. R. The effects of sensitivity training on self concept and attitudes of student teachers. Unpublished doctoral dissertation, East Texas State University, 1969.

Mitchell, M. D. Machiavellianism, control, and social desirability: their relation to certain outcomes of human relations training. Unpublished doctoral dissertation, Purdue University, 1967.

Mitchell, R. R. An evaluation of the relative effectiveness of spaced, massed, and combined sensitivity training groups in promoting positive behavior change. Unpublished doctoral dissertation, University of California, Los Angeles, 1969.

Morton, R. B. The organizational training laboratory — some individual and organization effects. *Advanced Management Journal*, 1965, 58-67.

Moscow, D. T-group training in the Netherlands: an evaluation and cross-cultural comparison. *Men en Onderneming*, 1969, 23, 345-362.

Myers, G. E.; Myers, M. T.; Goldberg, A.; and Welch, C. E. Effect of feedback on interpersonal sensitivity in laboratory training groups. *Journal of Applied Behavioral Science*, 1969, 5, 175-186.

Myrick, R. D.; and Pare, D. D. A study of the effects of group sensitivity training with student counselor-consultants. *Counselor Education & Supervision*, 1971, 11, 90-96.

Nadler, E. B.; and Fink, S. L. Impact of laboratory training on sociopolitical ideology. *Journal of Applied Behavioral Science*, 1970, 6, 79-92.

Nance, E. E. The effects of human relations training on selected personality variables. Unpublished doctoral dissertation, Western Michigan University, 1971.

Nath, R. Dynamics of organizational change: some determinants of managerial problem solving and decision making competences. Unpublished doctoral dissertation, Massachusetts Institute of Technology, 1964.

Nye, L. S. K. The development and implementation of two pre-practicum training approaches and an evaluation of their effects upon counseling performance. Unpublished doctoral dissertation, Purdue University, 1971.

Orsburn, J. D. Sensitivity training versus group lectures with high school problem students. Unpublished doctoral dissertation, Kent State University, 1966.

Osborne, G. E. The relationships between sensitivity training, self-perception, and student teaching behavior in a program for elementary education student teachers. Unpublished doctoral dissertation, Purdue University, 1970.

Oshry, B. I.; and Harrison, R. Transfer from here-and-now to there-and-then: Changes in organizational problem diagnosis stemming from T-group training. *Journal of Applied Behavioral Science*, 1966, 2, 185-198.

Parker, C. C. The effects of the group process experience on rigidity as a personality variable. Unpublished doctoral dissertation, Ball State University, 1971.

Parry, K. A. The effect of two training approaches on counselor effectiveness. Unpublished doctoral dissertation, University of Missouri, 1969.

Peters, D. R. Self-ideal congruence as a function of human relations training. *Journal of Psychology*, 1970, 76, 199-207.

Pfister, G. C. An investigation of the effectiveness of laboratory training in increasing interpersonal communication skills with police officers. Unpublished doctoral dissertation, University of Washington, 1970.

Pickhardt, C. E. Perceptions by self and others of female black and white teachers from segregated and desegregated schools before and after a six-week training institute. Unpublished doctoral dissertation, University of Texas, 1970.

Pilder, R. J. Some effects of laboratory training on married couples. Unpublished doctoral dissertation, United States International University, 1972.

Pino, C. J. Illinois Institute of Technology interaction in sensitivity training groups. Unpublished doctoral dissertation, Illinois Institute of Technology, 1969.

Piper, W. E. Evaluation of the effects of sensitivity training and the effects of varying group composition according to interpersonal trust. Unpublished doctoral dissertation, University of Connecticut, 1972.

Poe, B. J. The effect of sensitivity training on the relationship between risk taking and other selected behavioral factors. Unpublished doctoral dissertation, East Texas State University, 1971.

Pollack, D.; and Stanley, G. Coping and marathon sensitivity training. *Psychological Reports*, 1971, 29, 379-385.

Pollack, H. B. Change in homogeneous and heterogeneous sensitivity training groups. *Journal of Consulting and Clinical Psychology*, 1971, 60-66.

Powers, J. R. Trainer orientation and group composition in laboratory training. Unpublished doctoral dissertation, Case Institute of Tech-

nology, 1965
Pratt, W. M. The effectiveness of the use of the T-group laboratory method as an adjunct to a developmental approach to teaching. Unpublished doctoral dissertation, East Texas State University, 1969.
Pressman, M. L. A study of an intensive TORI weekend group experience and its effects on interpersonal skills. Unpublished master's thesis, University of Utah, 1970.
Psathas, G.; Hardert, R. Trainer interventions and normative patterns in the T-group. *Journal of Applied Behavioral Science*, 1966, 2, 149-169.
Pyke, S. W.; and Neely, C. A. Evaluation of a group communication training program. *Journal of Communication*, 1970, 20, 291-304.
Rand, L. P.; and Carew, D. K. Comparison of T-group didactic approaches to training undergraduate resident assistants. *Journal of College Student Personnel*, 1970, 11, 432-438.
Rankin, R. C. Attitudinal perceptions of black students and white students as influenced by an instrumented laboratory experience. Unpublished doctoral dissertation, Arizona State University, 1971.
Reddy, W. B. Sensitivity training as an integral phase of counselor education. *Counselor Education & Supervision*, 1970, 9, 110-115.
_____. Sensitivity training or group psychotherapy: the need for adequate screening. *International Journal of Group Psychotherapy*, 1970, 20, 366-371.
_____. Interpersonal compatibility and self-actualization in sensitivity training. *Journal of Applied Behavioral Science*, 1972, 8, 237-240.
_____. On affection, group composition, and self-actualization in sensitivity training. *Journal of Consulting & Clinical Psychology*, 1972, 38, 211-214.
_____. The impact of sensitivity training on self-actualization: a one-year follow-up. *Comparative Group Studies*, in press.
_____; and Byrnes, A. The effects of interpersonal group composition on the problem-solving behavior of middle managers. *Journal of Applied Psychology*, 1972, 56, 516-517.
Reisel, J. A search for behavior patterns in sensitivity training groups. Unpublished doctoral dissertation, University of California, Los Angeles, 1959.
Riley, R. An investigation of the influence of group compatibility on group cohesiveness and change in self-concept in a T-group setting. Unpublished doctoral dissertation, University of Rochester, 1970.
Ring, B. Recognized similarity: an investigation of significant events reported by encounter group participants. Unpublished doctoral dissertation, Boston University, 1972.
Rios, R. M. The comparative effects of tape-led, led, and leaderless groups. Unpublished doctoral dissertation, University of Southern California, 1972.
Rosenthal, D. Perception of some personality characteristics in members of a small group. Unpublished doctoral dissertation, University of Chicago, 1952.
Rothaus, P. Instrumented role playing in a psychiatric training laboratory. *Archives of General Psychiatry*, 1964, 11, 400-410.
_____; Johnson, D. L.; Hanson, P. G.; Lyle, F. A.; and Mayer, R. Participation and sociometry in autonomous and trainer-led patient groups. *Journal of Counseling Psychology*, 1966, 13, 68-76.
_____; Johnson, D. L.; and Blank, G. Changing the connotations of mental illness in psychiatric patients. *Journal of Counseling Psychology*, 1967, 14, 258-263.
_____; Johnson, D. L.; Hanson, P. G.; Brown, J. B.; and Lyle, F. A. Sentence-

completion test prediction of autonomous and therapist-led group behavior. *Journal of Counseling Psychology*, 1967, 14, 28-34.

____; Morton, R. B.; Johnson, D. L.; Cleveland, S. E.; and Lyle, F. A. Human relations training for psychiatric patients. *Archives of General Psychiatry*, 1963, 8, 572-581.

Rubin, I. The reduction of prejudice through laboratory training. *Journal of Applied Behavioral Science*, 1967, 3, 29-50. (a)

____. Increased self-acceptance: a means of reducing prejudice. *Journal of Personality and Social Psychology*, 1967, 5, 233-238. (b)

Rudman, S. Positive changes in self-concept as a function of participation in encounter groups and encountertape groups. Unpublished doctoral dissertation, Memphis State University, 1970.

Runkel, P. J.; Lawrence, M.; Oldfield, S.; Rider, M.; and Clark, C. Stages of group development: an empirical test of Tuckman's hypothesis. *Journal of Applied Behavioral Science*, 1971, 7, 180-193.

Russell, W. J. A study of changes in measures of inner-direction, open-mindedness, and intraception during laboratory training designs of the Methodist church. Unpublished doctoral dissertation, Syracuse University, 1968.

Rutan, J. C. Self-acceptance change as a function of a short-term small group experience. Unpublished doctoral dissertation, Boston University, 1971.

Sales, A. P. Rehabilitation counselor candidate change resulting from sensitivity group experiences. Unpublished doctoral dissertation, University of Florida, 1971.

Santucci, A. A. The effects of T-group process and study skill training on self-confidence levels of economic opportunity fund college freshmen. Unpublished doctoral dissertation, Lehigh University, 1972.

Scherz, M. E. Changes in self-esteem following experimental manipulation of self-disclosure and feedback conditions in a sensitivity laboratory. Unpublished doctoral dissertation, George Peabody College for Teachers, 1972.

Schmuck, R. A.; Runkel, P. J.; and Langmeyer, D. Improving organizational problem solving in a school faculty. *Journal of Applied Behavioral Science*, 1969, 5, 455-482.

Schubert, P. W. Personality type and self-perceived change resulting from sensitivity group experience. Unpublished doctoral dissertation, Purdue University, 1971.

Schutz, W. C.; and Allen, V. L. The effects of a T-group laboratory on interpersonal behavior. *Journal of Applied Behavioral Science*, 1966, 2, 265-286.

Schwartz, R. I. An experimental study of massed and spaced encounter. Unpublished doctoral dissertation, State University of New York, 1971.

Seashore, C. N. Attitude and skill changes in participative action training groups. Unpublished master's thesis, University of Colorado, 1955.

Sebring, R. H. The effects of human relations training on selected student teacher personality variables, attitudes, and behaviors. Unpublished doctoral dissertation, Pennsylvania State University, 1970.

Seldman, M. L. An investigation of aspects of marathon-encounter group phenomena: types of participants and differential perceptions of leaders. Unpublished doctoral dissertation, Temple University, 1971.

Shaevitz, M. H.; and Barr, D. J. Encounter groups in a small college. In L. N. Solomon and B. Berzon (eds.), *New Perspectives on Encounter Groups.* San Francisco: Jossey-Bass, 1972.

Shapiro, J. L. An investigation into the effects of sensitivity training procedures. Unpublished doctoral dissertation, University of Waterloo, Ontario, 1970.

_____; and Diamond, M. J. Increases in hypnotizability as a function of encounter group training: some confirming evidence. *Journal of Abnormal Psychology*, 1972, 79, 112-115.

_____; and Ross, R. R. Sensitivity training for staff in an institution for adolescent offenders. *Journal of Applied Behavioral Science*, 1971, 7, 710-723.

Sherwood, J. J. Self-identity and referent others. *Sociometry*, 1965, 28, 66-81.

Shilling, L. E. The differential effect of two small group training procedures upon the acquisition of interpersonal communication skills and the extinction of interpersonal anxiety. Unpublished doctoral dissertation, University of Georgia, 1970.

Shinn, R. The effects of sensitivity training on oral communication competence among secondary school social studies student teachers. Unpublished doctoral dissertation, University of California, Los Angeles, 1969.

Sikes, W. W. A study of some effects of a human relations training laboratory. Unpublished doctoral dissertation, Purdue University, 1964.

Simon, A.; and Agazarian, Y. *Sequential analysis of verbal interaction.* Philadelphia: Research for Better Schools, Inc., 1967.

Skinner, W. W. Effects of systematic human relations training on the organizational and performance characteristics of a medical unit. Unpublished doctoral dissertation, University of Georgia, 1971.

Slager, J. B. Leader personality type as a factory of change in T-groups. Unpublished doctoral dissertation, Purdue University, 1972.

Smith, D. J. A comparison of the effects of short-term individual counseling, group counseling, and sensitivity training on the self-concepts of male college students. Unpublished doctoral dissertation, Boston College, 1971.

Smith, O. P. Changes in self-actualization and self-concept as a result of the use of visual feedback in marathon sensitivity training. Unpublished doctoral dissertation, East Texas State University, 1970.

Smith, P. B. Attitude changes associated with training in human relations. *British Journal of Social and Clinical Psychology*, 1964, 3, 104-112.

_____; and Honour, T. F. The impact of Phase I managerial grid training. *Journal of Management Studies*, 1969, 6, 318-330.

Smith, W. D. A study of the effects of sensitivity training on the self-concept of student teachers. Unpublished doctoral dissertation, University of New Mexico, 1970.

Snortum, J. R.; and Myers, H. F. Intensity of T-group relationships as a function of interaction. *International Journal of Group Psychotherapy*, 1971, 21, 190-201.

Solomon, L. N.; Berzon, B.; and Davis, D. P. A personal growth program for self-directed groups. *Journal of Applied Behavioral Science*, 1970, 6, 427-452.

Spehn, M. R. Relationship between an intensive group experience and change in church leaders' religious attitudes. *Dissertation Abstracts International*, 1971, 31, 12.

Steele, F. I. Personality and the "laboratory style." *Journal of Applied Behavioral Science*, 1968, 4, 25-45.

_____. The relationship of personality to changes in interpersonal values effected by laboratory training. Unpublished doctoral dissertation, Massachusetts Institute of Technology, 1965.

_____; Zand, D. E.; and Zalkind, S. S. Managerial behavior and participation in a laboratory training process. *Personnel Psychology*, 1970, 23, 77-90.

Stinson, J. E. The differential impact of participation in laboratory training in collaborative task effort on intact groups and fragmented groups. Unpublished doctoral dissertation, Ohio State University, 1970.

Stock, Dorothy. The relation between the sociometric structure of the group and certain personality characteristics of the individual. Unpublished doctoral dissertation, University of Chicago, 1952.

____, A survey of research on T-groups. In L. P. Bradford, J. R. Gibb, and K. D. Benne (eds.) *T-group theory & laboratory method.* New York: Wiley, 1964, pp. 395-441.

____; and Ben-Zeev, S. Changes in work and emotionality during group growth. In D. Stock and H. A. Thelen (eds.), *Emotional dynamics and group culture,* Washington, D.C.: National Training Laboratories, 1958. Pp. 192-206.

Stockton, R. A. An investigation of the effect of sensitivity training on the attitudes of teacher education students. Unpublished doctoral dissertation, Ball State University, 1969.

Stone, P. A. Comparative effects of group encounter, group counseling, and study skills instruction on academic performance of under-achieving college students. Unpublished doctoral dissertation, University of South Dakota, 1972.

Stone, W. O. A study of pre-recorded relaxation training, rational-emotive and personal growth group counseling intervention techniques in the reduction of state anxiety in black multi-occupational trainees. Unpublished doctoral dissertation, Florida State University, 1971.

Stoudt, C. L. The comparative effects of sensitivity training, didactic training, and no training on the rating of responses to the Wisconsin counselor education selection. Unpublished doctoral dissertation, University of Wisconsin, 1970.

Sutfin, A. B. An evaluation of activities in a human relations training experience. Unpublished doctoral dissertation, Purdue University, 1971.

Tallant, W. J. Changes in pre-service teachers involved in a multi-cultural training program utilizing formal presentations, sensitivity training, planned social activities, and a cooperative living arrangement. Unpublished doctoral dissertation, East Texas State University, 1970.

Taylor, F. C. Effects of laboratory training upon persons and their work groups. Paper presented at the meeting of the American Psychological Association, Washington, D.C., September, 1967.

Tchack, E. Self-actualization and clarity of perception of self and others during sensitivity training. Unpublished doctoral dissertation, Columbia University, 1972.

Terleski, D. R. The relationship between unstructured and structured sensitivity group experiences and self-perceived changes of group members. Unpublished doctoral dissertation, Purdue University, 1970.

Thomas, M. D. Developing human potential through group interaction: a study of changes in personality factors, personal attitudes, and group functioning in university students participating in human relations training. Unpublished doctoral dissertation, University of Kansas, 1970.

Tilly, G. T. An evaluation of personality factors associated with changes following laboratory training. Unpublished doctoral dissertation, Louisiana State University, 1971.

Toelela, M. Effects of T-group training and cognitive learning on small group effectiveness. Unpublished doctoral dissertation, University of Denver, 1971.

Tompkins, D. S. Group effectiveness as a function of leadership style moderated by stage of group development. Unpublished doctoral dissertation, Ohio State University, 1972.

Treppa, J. A.; and Fricke, L. Effects of a marathon group experience. *Journal of Counseling Psychology,* 1972, 19, 466-467.

Trotzer, J. P. Process comparison of encounter groups and discussion groups using videotape excerpts. *Journal of Counseling Psychology,* 1971, 18, 358-361.

Tucker, M. F. An experimental investigation of human relations laboratory training among disadvantaged Job Corpsmen. Unpublished doctoral dissertation, University of Utah, 1969.

Uhes, M. J. Expression of hostility as a function of an encounter group experience. *Psychological Reports,* 1971, 28, 733-734.

Underwood, W. J. Evaluation of laboratory-method training. *Training Directors Journal,* 1965, 19, 34-40.

Vail, J. P. The effects of encountertapes for personal growth on certain specific aspects of the intellectual, behavioral, and self-concept development of culturally disadvantaged Negro girls. Unpublished doctoral dissertation, University of Georgia, 1970.

Valiquet, M. I. Individual change in a management development program. *Journal of Applied Behavioral Science,* 1968, 4, 313-326.

Varner, E. B. Impact of basic group encounter on self-actualization of junior college students. Unpublished doctoral dissertation, University of Florida, 1969.

Vogt, J. F. A cross-cultural study (Lebanon and United States) of perceptual, attitudinal, and behavioral effects of the laboratory method in a teacher education course. Unpublished doctoral dissertation, University of Michigan, 1970.

Wagner, A. B. The use of process analysis in business decision games. *Journal of Applied Behavioral Science,* 1965, 1, 387-408.

Walker, R. E.; Shack, J. R.; Egan, G.; Sheridan, K.; and Sheridan, E. P. Change in self-judgments of self-disclosure after group experience. *Journal of Applied Behavioral Science,* 1972, 248-253.

Washburn, R. W. Human relations training for confined delinquents. Unpublished doctoral dissertation, Colorado State University, 1968.

Wedel, C. C. A study of measurement in group dynamics laboratories. Unpublished doctoral dissertation, George Washington University, 1957.

Weigel, R. G. Outcomes of marathon group therapy and marathon group topical discussion. Unpublished doctoral dissertation, University of Missouri, 1968.

Weissman, H. N.; Seldman, M.; and Ritter, K. Changes in awareness of impact upon others as a function of encounter and marathon group experiences. *Psychological Reports,* 28, 651-661.

Weldon, F. A. The effects of a value seminar group experience in relation to selected student teacher needs, level of self-esteem, and attitudes. Unpublished doctoral dissertation, University of Montana, 1971.

Wheeler, W. F. Effects of encounter group methods upon selected measures of the body image. Unpublished doctoral dissertation, University of Southern California, 1971.

Wilker, P. B. The effect of sensitivity training on specific counseling skills. Unpublished doctoral dissertation, Rutgers State University, 1971.

Willis, R. J. A search for predictors of growth through interpersonal interaction. Unpublished doctoral dissertation, United States International University, 1972.

Wolfe, W. W. A study of a laboratory appraoch to in-service development programs for school administrators and supervisors. Unpublished doctoral dissertation, University of Texas, 1965.

Wyse, M. Sensitivity training versus group lectures with elementary school problem students. Unpublished doctoral dissertation, Case Western Reserve University, 1969.

Young, J. R. The effects of laboratory training on self-concept, philosophies of human nature, and perceptions of group behavior. Unpublished doctoral dissertation, George Peabody College for Teachers, 1970.

Zacker, J. W. The effects of experimental training upon empathy, interpersonal sensitivity, cynicism, and alienation in police recruits. Unpublished doctoral dissertation, City University of New York, 1971.

Zand, D. E.; Steele, F. I.; and Zalkind, S. S. The impact of an organizational development program on perceptions of interpersonal, group, and organization functioning. *Journal of Applied Behavioral Science*, 1969, 5, 393-410.

Zener, A. E. Human relations training and job corps adjustment. Unpublished doctoral dissertation, University of Utah, 1971.

Zener, J. H. The effect of a team human relations training laboratory on the productivity and perceptions of a selling group. Unpublished doctoral dissertation, University of Southern California, 1967.

Zimet, C. N.; and Fine, H. J. Personality changes with a group therapeutic experience in a human relations seminar. *Journal of Abnormal and Social Psychology*, 1955, 51, 68-73.

Zullo, J. R. T-group laboratory learning and adolescent ego development. Unpublished doctoral dissertation, Northwestern University, 1972.

APPENDIX B

BIBLIOGRAPHY FOR CHAPTER 6

1. Argyris, C. *Interpersonal Competence and Organizational Effectiveness.* Dorsey: Homewood, Illinois, 1962.

2. Aronoff, J.; and Messe, L. A. Motivational Determinants of Small Group Structure. *Journal of Personality and Social Psychology,* 1971, *3,* 319-324.

3. Asch, S. E. Studies of Independence and Conformity. A Minority of One Against a Unanimous Majority. *Psychological Monographs,* 1956, *70,* No. 9 (Whole No. 416).

4. Bales, R. F. The Equilibrium Problem in Small Groups. In Parsons, T.; Bales, R. F.; and Shils, E. A. (eds.), *Working Papers in the Theory of Action.* Free Press: Glencoe, Illinois, 1953.

5. _____. *Personality and Interpersonal Behavior.* Holt, Rinehart, & Winston: New York, 1969.

6. _____; and Strodtbeck, F. L. Phases in Group Problem Solving. *Journal of Abnormal and Social Psychology,* 1951, *46,* 485-495.

7. Bateson, N. Familiarization, Group Discussion, and Risk Taking. *Journal of Experimental Social Psychology,* 1966, *2,* 119-129.

8. Benne, K. D. From Polarization to Paradox. In Bradford, L. P.; Gibb, J. R.; and Benne, K. D. (eds.), *T-Group Theory and Laboratory Method.* Wiley: New York, 1964.

9. Bennis, W. G. Patterns and Vicissitudes in T-Group Development. In Bradford, L. P.; Gibb, J. R.; and Benne, K. D. (eds.), *T-Group Theory and Laboratory Method.* Wiley: New York, 1964.

10. _____; and Shepard, H. A. A Theory of Group Development. *Human Relations,* 1956, *9,* 415-537.

11. von Bertalanffy, L. The Theory of Open Systems in Physics and Biology. *Science,* 1950, *111,* 23-29.

12. Bidwell, C. E. The School as a Formal Organization. In March, J. G. (ed.), *Handbook of Organization.* Rand McNally: Chicago, 1965. Pp. 972-1022.

13. Bion, W. R. *Experiences in Groups.* Free Press: New York, 1961.

14. Bitterman, M. E.; and Kniffin, C. W. Manifest Anxiety and "Perceptual Defense." *Journal of Abnormal and Social Psychology,* 1953, *48,*

248-252.

15. Blau, P. M. *Exchange and Power in Social Life*. Wiley: New York, 1967.

16. ____. *The Dynamics of Bureaucracy*. University of Chicago Press: Chicago, 1963.

17. Bonacich, P. Norms and Cohesion as Adaptive Responses to Potential Conflict: An Experimental Study. *Sociometry*, 1972, *3*, 357-375.

18. Bradford, L. P. Membership and the Learning Process. In Bradford, L. P.; Gibb, J. R.; and Benne, K. D. (eds.), *T-Group Theory and Laboratory Method*. Wiley: New York, 1964.

19. ____; and Mallinson, T-Group Formation and Development. Unpublished manuscript, National Training Laboratories, Washington, D.C., 1958.

20. Brehm, J. W. Post-Decision Changes in the Desirability of Alternatives. *Journal of Abnormal and Social Psychology*, 1956, *52*, 384-389.

21. ____. A Dissonance Analysis of Attitude-Discrepant Behavior. In Hovland, C. I.; and Rosenberg, M. J. (eds.), *Attitude Organization and Change*. Yale University Press: New Haven, 1960.

22. Brown, R. *Social Psychology*. Free Press: New York, 1965.

23. Brozek, J.; Guetzkow, H.; and Baldwin, M. A. A Quantitative Study of Perception and Association in Experimental Semistarvation. *Journal of Personality*, 1951, *19*, 245-264.

24. Bunker, D. R. Individual Applications of Laboratory Training. *Journal of Applied Behavioral Science*, 1965, *1*, 131-148.

25. ____; and Knowles, E. S. Comparison of Behavioral Changes Resulting from Human Relations Training Laboratories of Different Lengths. *Journal of Applied Behavioral Science*, 1967, *3*, 505-523.

26. Burke, R. L.; and Bennis, W. G. Changes in Perception of Self and Others During Human Relations Training. *Human Relations*, 1961, *14*, 165-182.

27. Callahan, R. E. *Education and the Cult of Efficiency*. University of Chicago Press: Chicago, 1962.

28. Campbell, J. P.; and Dunnette, M. D. Effectiveness of T-Group Experience in Managerial Training and Development. *Psychological Bulletin*, 1968, *70*, 73-104.

29. Chandler, S.; and Rabow, J. Ethnicity and Acquaintance as Variables in Risk Taking. *Journal of Social Psychology*, 1969, *77*, 221-229.

30. Charters, W. W., Jr., Social Class Analysis and the Control of Public Education. *Harvard Educational Review*, 1953, *23*, 268-283.

31. Clark, R. D. Group-Induced Shift Toward Risk: A Critical Appraisal. *Psychological Bulletin*, 1971, *76*, 251-270.

32. Cohen, A. R. Attitudinal Consequences of Induced Discrepancies Between Cognitions and Behavior. *Public Opinion Quarterly*, 1960, *24*, 297-318.

33. Coleman, J. S. *The Adolescent Society*. Free Press: New York, 1961.

34. Cooper, C. L.; and Mangham, I. L. (eds.), *T-Groups: A Survey of Research*. Wiley-Interscience: London, 1971.

35. Coser, L. *The Functions of Social Conflict*. Free Press: New York, 1956.

36. Daniels, V. Communication, Incentive, and Structural Variables in Interpersonal Exchange and Negotiation. *Journal of Experimental Social Psychology*, 1967, *3*, 47-74.

37. Deutsch, M. An Experimental Study of the Effects of Cooperation and Competition Upon Group Process. *Human Relations*, 1949, *2*, 199-321.

38. ____. A Theory of Cooperation and Competition. *Human Rela-*

tions, 1949, *2*, 129-152.

39. ____. Socially Relevant Science: Reflections on Some Studies of Interpersonal Conflict. *American Psychologist*, 1969, *24*, 1076-1092.

40. ____; and Krauss, R. M. The Effect of Threat on Interpersonal Bargaining. *Journal of Abnormal and Social Psychology*, 1960, *61*, 181-189.

41. ____; and Krauss, R. M. Studies of Interpersonal Bargaining. *Journal of Conflict Resolution*, 1962, *6*, 52-76.

42. Dion, K. L.; Baron, R. S.; and Miller, N. Why do Groups Make Riskier Decisions than Individuals? In Berkowitz, L. (ed.), *Advances in Experimental Social Psychology*. Academic Press: New York, 1970, 305-377.

43. Dulaney, D. E. Avoidance Learning of Perceptual Defense and Vigilance. *Journal of Abnormal and Social Psychology*, 1957, *55*, 33-338.

44. Duncan, S., Jr. Some Signals and Rules for Taking Speaking Turns in Conversations. *Journal of Personality and Social Psychology*, 1972, *23*, 283-292.

45. Durkheim, E. *The Division of Labor in Society* (1st Ed., 1893). Translated by George Simpson. Free Press: New York, 1949.

46. Eriksen, C. W.; and Browne, C. T. An Experiment and Theoretical Analysis of Perceptual Defense. *Journal of Abnormal and Social Psychology*, 1956, *52*, 224-230.

47. Faucheux, C.; and Thibaut, J. W. L'Approche Clinique et Experimentale de la Genese des Norms Contractualles Dans Differentes Conditions de Conflit et de Menace. *Bulletin Centre d'Etudes Rech. Psychotech.*, 1964, *13*, 225-243.

48. Feffer, M. Developmental Analysis of Interpersonal Behavior. *Psychological Review*, 1970, *77*, 197-214.

49. Festinger, L.; and Carlsmith, J. M. Cognitive Consequences of Forced Compliance. *Journal of Abnormal and Social Psychology*, 1959, *58*, 203-210.

50. ____; Schachter, S.; and Back, K. *Social Pressures in Informal Groups*. Harper: New York, 1950.

51. Fraser, C.; Gourge, C.; and Billig, M. Risky Shifts, Cautious Shifts, and Group Polarization. *European Journal of Social Psychology*, 1971, *1*, 7-30.

52. Freeman, J. J. Set or Perceptual Defense? *Journal of Experimental Psychology*, 1954, *48*, 283-288.

53. French, J. R. P., Jr.; and Raven, B. H. The Bases of Social Power. In Cartwright, D. (ed.), *Studies in Social Power*, University of Michigan Press: Ann Arbor, Michigan, 1959.

54. Freud, S. *Group Psychology and the Analysis of the Ego*. (Translated by J. Strachey.) Liveright Publishing Corp.: New York, 1949.

55. Friedlander, F. The Primacy of Trust as a Facilitator of Further Group Accomplishment. In Cooper, C. L.; and Mangham, I. L. (eds.), *T-Groups: A Survey of Research*. Wiley-Interscience: London, 1971.

56. Gibb, J. R. Climate for Trust Formation. In Bradford, L. P.; Gibb, J. R.; and Benne, K. D. (eds.), *T-Group Theory and Laboratory Method*. Wiley: New York, 1964.

57. ____. Fear and Facade: Defensive Management. In Parson, R. E. (ed.), *Science and Human Affairs*. Science and Behavior Books: Palo Alto, 1965.

58. Glidewell, J. C. *Group Emotionality and Productivity*. Unpublished Ph.D. Dissertation, University of Chicago, 1953.

59. ____. New Psychosocial Competence, Social Change, and Tension Management. In Carter, J. W. (ed.), *Research Contributions from Psychology to Community Mental Health*. Behavioral Publications: New York, 1968.

60. ____. *Choice Points*. MIT Press: Cambridge, Mass., 1970.

61. ____. System Linkage and Distress at School. In Feldman, M. J. (ed.), *Studies in Psychotherapy and Behavioral Change, No. 2: Theory and Research in Community Mental Health.* State University of New York at Buffalo: Buffalo, New York, 1971.

62. ____. A Social Psychology of Mental Health. In Golann, S. E.; and Eisdorfer, C. (eds.), *Handbook of Community Mental Health.* Appleton, Century, Crofta: New York, 1972.

63. Gordon, C. W. The Social System of the High School. Free Press: Glencoe, Illinois, 1957.

64. Gouldner, A. W. The Norm of Reciprocity: A Preliminary Statement. *American Sociological Review*, 1960, *25*, 161-179.

65. Gullahorn, J. T. Distance and Friendship as Factors in the Gross Interaction Matrix. *Sociometry*, 1952, *15*, 123-134.

66. Harrison, R. Cognitive Change and Participation in a Sensitivity Training Laboratory. *Journal of Consulting Psychology*, 1966, *30*, 517-520.

67. Hearn, G. The Process of Group Development. *Autonomous Groups Bulletin*, 1957, *13*, 1-7.

68. Heider, F. *The Psychology of Interpersonal Relations.* Wiley: New York, 1958.

69. Herbert, E. L.; and Trist, E. L. The Institution of an Absent Leader by a Student's Discussion Group. *Human Relations*, 1953, *6*, 215-248.

70. Hinds, W. C. Individual and Group Decisions in Gambling Situations. Unpublished Master's Thesis, School of Industrial Management, M. I. T., 1962.

71. Homans, G. C. *Social Behavior: Its Elementary Forms.* Harcourt, Brace, & World: New York, 1961.

72. Horwitz, M. Training in Conflict Resolution. In Bradford, L. P.; Gibb, J. R.; and Benne, K. D. (eds.), *T-Group Theory and Laboratory Method.* Wiley: New York, 1964, 365-378.

73. Hovland, C. I.; Janis, I. L.; and Kelley, H. H. *Communication and Persuasion.* Yale University Press: New Haven, 1953.

74. Katz, D.; and Kahn, R. L. *The Social Psychology of Organizations.* Wiley: New York, 1966.

75. Kelley, H. H.; and Thibaut, J. W. Group Problem Solving. In Lindsey, G.; and Aronson, E. (eds.), *Handbook of Social Psychology.* (Revised Edition.) Vol. 4. Addison-Wesley: Cambridge, Mass., 1969, 1-104.

76. Kendall, P. Medical Education as a Social Process. Paper presented at the annual meeting of the American Sociological Association, New York, 1960.

77. Kleiner, R. Perceptual Defense or Perceptual Set. *Journal of Social Psychology*, 1959, *49*, 95-103.

78. Kogan, N.; and Wallach, M. A. Risk-Taking as a Function of the Situation, the Person, and the Group. In Mandler, G.; Mussen, P.; Kogan, N.; and Wallach, M. A. (eds.), *New Directions in Psychology.* Vol. III. Holt, Rinehart, & Winston: New York, 1967, 224-266.

79. ____; and Carlson, J. Group Risk-Taking Under Competitive and Noncompetitive Conditions in Adults and Children. *Journal of Educational Psychology*, 1969, *29*, 228-243.

80. ____; and Doise, W. Effects of Anticipated Delegated Status on Level of Risk-Taking in Small Decision-Making Groups. *Acta Psychologica*, 1969, *29*, 228-243.

81. Lacey, O. W.; Lewinger, N.; and Adamson, J. F. Foreknowledge as a Factor Affecting Perceptual Defense and Alertness. *Journal of Experimental Psychology*, 1953, *45*, 169-174.

82. Lake, D. G.; and Callahan, D. M. Entering and Intervening in Schools. In Schmuck, R. A.; and Miles, M. G. (eds.), *Organizational Develop-*

ment in Schools. National Press Books: Palo Alto, Calif., 1971, pp. 139-154.

83. Lakin, M. *Interpersonal Encounter.* McGraw Hill: New York, 1972.

84. Lamm, H.; and Kogan, N. Risk-Taking in the Context of Intergroup Negotiation. *Journal of Experimental Social Psychology,* 1970, *6,* 351-363.

85. Lazarus, R. S.; Yousem, H.; and Arenberg, D. Hunger and Perception. *Journal of Personality,* 1953, *21,* 312-328.

86. Levine, R.; Chein, I.; and Murphy, G. The Relation of the Intensity of a Need to the Amount of Perceptual Distortion: A Preliminary Report. *Journal of Psychology,* 1942, *13,* 283-293.

87. Levinger, G.; and Schneider, D. J. Test of the "Risk is a Value" Hypothesis. *Journal of Personality and Social Psychology,* 1969, *11,* 165-170.

88. Lewin, K. *Resolving Social Conflict.* Harper: New York, 1948.

89. Lieberman, M. A. The Relationship Between the Emotional Cultures of Groups and Individual Change. Unpublished Ph.D. Dissertation, The University of Chicago, 1958.

90. ____. The Relation of Diagnosed Behavioral Tendencies to Member-Perceptions of Self and of the Group. In Stock, D.; and Thelen, H. A. (eds.), *Emotional Dynamics and Group Culture.* New York University Press: New York, 1958.

91. Lieberman, M. S.; Yalom, I. D.; and Miles, M. B. *Encounter Groups: First Facts.* Basic Books: New York, 1973.

92. Likert, R. *The Human Organization.* McGraw Hill: New York, 1966.

93. Loomis, J. L. Communication, the Development of Trust and Cooperative Behavior. *Human Relations,* 1959, *12,* 305-315.

94. Lortie, D. C. *Structure and Sentiment in Classroom Teaching: A Sociological Analysis.* Unpublished manuscript, 1973. (Available from the author at the University of Chicago.)

95. Lundberg, G. A.; and Beazley, V. "Consciousness of Kind" in a College Population. *Sociometry,* 1948, *11,* 59-74.

96. Madaras, G. R.; and Bem, D. J. Risk and Conservatism in Group Decision Making. *Journal of Experimental Social Psychology,* 1968, *4,* 350-366.

97. Marquis, D. G. Individual Responsibility and Group Decisions Involving Risk. *Industrial Management Review,* 1962, *3,* 8-23.

98. McGinnies, E. Emotionality and Perceptual Defense. *Psychological Review,* 1949, *56,* 244-251.

99. Miles, M. B. Human Relations Training: How a Group Grows. *Teachers College Record,* 1953, *55,* 90-96.

100. ____. Human Relations Training: Processes and Outcomes. *Journal of Consulting Psychology,* 1960, *7,* 301-306.

101. ____ (ed.). *Innovation in Education.* Teachers College Press: New York, 1964.

102. ____.Changes During and Following Laboratory Training: A Clinical-Experimental Study. *Journal of Applied Behavioral Science,* 1965, *1,* 90-96.

103. ____. Some Properties of Schools as Social Systems. In Watson, G. (ed.), *Change in School Systems.* National Training Laboratories: Washington, 1967, 1-29.

104. Newcomb, T. M. *Personality and Social Change: Attitude Formation in a Student Community.* Holt, Rinehart, & Winston: New York, 1943.

105. ____. *The Acquaintance Process.* Holt, Rinehart, & Winston: New York, 1961.

106. Nordhy, F. *Group Interaction in Decision-Making Under Risk.* Unpublished Master's Thesis, School of Industrial Management, M. I. T., 1962.

107. Piaget, J. *Judgment and Reasoning in the Child.* Harcourt, Brace: New York, 1928.

108. ____. *The Psychology of Intelligence.* Harcourt, Brace: New York, 1928.

109. ____. *The Originis of Intelligence in Children.* Norton: New York, 1952.

110. Postman, L.; Bronson, W. C.; and Gropper, G. L. "Is There a Mechanism of Perceptual Defense?" *Journal of Abnormal and Social Psychology,* 1953, *48,* 215-224.

111. Pruit, D. G. (ed.), Special Issue on the Risky Shift. *Journal of Personality of Social Psychology,* 1971, *20,* 339-510.

112. ____; and Teger, A. I. Is There a Shift Toward Risk in Group Discussion? If So, Is It a Group Phenomenon? If So, What Causes It? Paper presented at the annual meetings of the American Psychological Association, Washington, D.C., 1967.

113. Rabow, J.; Fowler, F. J.; Bradford, D. L.; Hofeller, M. A.; and Shibuya, Y. The Role of Social Norms and Leadership in Risk-Taking. *Sociometry,* 1966, *29,* 16-27.

114. Rim, Y. Risk-Taking and Need for Achievement. *Acta Psychologica,* 1963, *21,* 108-115.

115. ____. Leadership Attitudes and Decisions Involving Risk. *Personal Psychology,* 1965, *18,* 423-430.

116. Secord, P. F.; and Backman, C. W. Personality Theory and the Problem of Stability and Change in Individual Behavior: An Interpersonal Approach. *Psychological Review,* 1961, *68,* 21-32.

117. Schachter, S. Deviation, Rejection, and Communication. *Journal of Abnormal and Social Psychology,* 1951, *46,* 190-207.

118. Schanck, R. L. A Study of a Community and its Groups and Institutions Conceived of as Behavior of Individuals. *Psychological Monograph,* 1932, *43,* No. 2 (Whole No. 195).

119. Schmuck, R. A.; and Miles, M. B. (eds.), *Organizational Development in Schools.* National Press Books: Palo Alto, Calif., 1971.

120. Schutz, W. C. *FIRO: A Three-Dimensional Theory of Interpersonal Behavior.* Holt, Rinehart, & Winston: New York, 1958.

121. Sherif, M. Group Influences Upon the Formation of Norms and Attitudes. In Newcomb, T. M.; and Hartley, E. L. (eds.), *Readings in Social Psychology,* (1st Ed.) Holt: New York, 1947.

122. Siegel, S.; and Zajonc, R. B. Group Risk-Taking in Professional Decisions. *Sociometry,* 1967, *30,* 339-350.

123. Simmel, G. *Conflict and the Web of Group Affiliations.* Free Press: New York, 1955.

124. Stock, D.; and Thelen, H. A. *Emotional Dynamics and Group Culture.* New York University Press: New York, 1958.

125. Stoner, J. A. F. A Comparison of Individual and Group Decisions Involving Risk. Unpublished master's thesis, School of Industrial Management, M. I. T., 1961.

126. Thibaut, J. W. The Development of Contractual Norms in Bargaining: Replication and Variation. *Journal of Conflict Resolution,* 1968, *12,* 102-112.

127. ____; and Faucheux, C. The Development of Contractual Norms in a Bargaining Situation Under Two Types of Stress. *Journal of Experimental Social Psychology,* 1965, *1,* 89-102.

128. ____; and Kelley, H. H. *The Social Psychology of Groups.* Wiley: New York, 1959.

129. Thelen, H. A.; and Dickerman, W. Stereotypes and the Growth of Groups. *Educational Leadership,* 1949, *6,* 309-316.

130. Tuckman, B. W. Developmental Sequence in Small Groups. *Psychological Bulletin*, 1965, *63*, 384-399.

131. Valiquet, M. I. Individual Changes in a Management Development Program. *Journal of Applied Behavioral Science*, 1968, *4*, 313-325.

132. Vidmar, N. Group Composition and the Risky Shift. *Journal of Experimental Social Psychology*, 1970, *6*, 153-166.

133. Vinacke, W. E. Variables in Experimental Games: Toward a Field Theory. *Psychological Bulletin*, 1969, *71*, 293-318.

134. Vinokur, A. Review and Theoretical Analysis of the Effects of Group Process Upon Individual and Group Decisions Involving Risk. *Psychological Bulletin*, 1971, *76*, 231-250.

135. Wallach, M. A.; and Kogan, N. The Roles of Information, Discussion, and Consensus in Group Risk-Taking. *Journal of Experimental Social Psychology*, 1965, *1*, 1-19.

136. _____; Kogan, N.; and Bem, D. J. Group Influence on Individual Risk Taking. *Journal of Abnormal and Social Psychology*, 1962, *65*, 75-86.

137. _____; and Wing, C. W. Is Risk a Value? *Journal of Personality and Social Psychology*, 1968, *9*, 101-107.

138. Waller, W. *The Sociology of Teaching*. Wiley: New York, 1932.

139. White, R. W. Motivation Reconsidered: The Concept of Competence. *Psychological Review*, 1959, *66*, 297-333.

140. Whitman, R. M. Psychodynamic Principles Underlying T-Group Processes. In Bradford, L. P.; Gibb, J. R.; and Benne, K. D. (eds.), *T-Group Theory and Laboratory Method*. Wiley: New York, 1964, 310-335.

141. Whittaker, E. M.; Gilchrist, J. C.; and Fischer, J. W. Perceptual Defense of Response Suppression. *Journal of Abnormal and Social Psychology*, 1952, *47*, 732-733.

142. Willard, D.; and Strodtbeck, F. L. Latency of Verbal Responses and Participation in Small Groups. *Sociometry*, 1972, *35*, 161-175.

143. Zajonc, R. B.; Wolosin, R. J.; Wolosin, M. A.; and Loh, W. D. Social Facilitation and Imitation in Group Risk Taking. *Journal of Experimental Social Psychology*, 1970, *6*, 26-46.

144. Zigler, E.; and Yospe, L. Perceptual Defense and the Problem of Response Suppression. *Journal of Personality*, 1960, *28*, 220-239.

CONTRIBUTING AUTHORS

Boris Astrachan, M.D., is Professor of Clinical Psychiatry at Yale University School of Medicine and Director of the Connecticut Mental Health Center. His most important memberships are in family (wife and four children), friendship groups, and a variety of work groups.

Richard Beckhard is Senior Lecturer in the Organizational Studies Group, Graduate Faculty, Alfred P. Sloan School of Management, Massachusetts Institute of Technology, and Director, Richard Beckhard Associates in New York City. His work with programs of the National Training Laboratories, particularly its programs in Organizational Development, dates back to the early 1950s. He has been consultant to industrial organizations in various parts of the world, including numerous multinational companies. He is also consultant to various health organizations in both the private and public sectors, including the American Association of Medical Colleges.

Max Birnbaum is Professor of Human Relations and Sociology, Boston University, and Director of that University's Human Relations Laboratory. He has pioneered in intergroup and community relations training. He is an educator who has been active for many years in both secondary and higher education, teacher training, and adult education. He has been administrator and staff member of numerous workshops and laboratories in applied social science and consultant to a variety of social systems.

Robert Chin is Professor of Social Psychology at Boston University. He has been connected with that University's Human

Relations Center, as co-founder, as staff member of its Pro-Seminar and Practicum Seminar, as its Director of Research, and as staff member and administrator of its Basic Human Relations and Organization Development Laboratories.

John C. Glidewell is Professor of Educational Psychology at the University of Chicago. He has done basic and applied research on health systems in public and in mental health, and on educational systems and processes. His experiences with laboratory method, both as researcher and trainer, extend from the early nineteen fifties to the present time.

Gordon L. Lippitt is Professor of Behavioral Science in the School of Government and Business Administration of the George Washington University. He was Associate Director of the National Training Laboratories from 1950 to 1960, and served as President of the American Society for Training and Development in 1969. His extensive writings have been in the fields of human behavior, leadership, and organizational effectiveness.

Robert Luke earned his doctorate in Sociology. His interest in laboratory training is of long standing, since he was in and around the NTL summer laboratories at Bethel, Maine, for several years as a small boy, while his parents served on the laboratory staff. He has served as head of organization development work in a large business, has worked on the staffs of numerous NTL programs, and has taught at the Boston University Human Relations Center. He now works in Washington, D.C., on the staff of the National Training and Development Service to state and local governments.

Max Pages, 47, lives in France and was educated there. Among his crucial professional experiences were his work with Carl Rogers in 1951, and with the National Training Laboratories at Bethel, Maine, in 1955. He is now Professor at the University of Paris IX — Dauphine, and President of the Laboratoire de Changement Social. He has published two books and now is preparing a third on "Contradictions et Changement."

Hilarion G. Petzold was born in 1944. He studied Theology, Philosophy, and Psychology at the *Institut St. Denis*, Paris, *Ecole Pratique des Hautes Etudes*, *Sorbonne*, and Medicine and Educational Sciences at the University of Dusseldorf. In 1968, in Paris, he obtained his Doctor of Theology degree and in 1971, his Ph.D. His training analysis was with V. Iljine, pupil of Ferenczi and originator of the therapeutic theater. He has studied with Fritz Perls and J. L. Moreno, and at the National Training Laboratories Institute. Currently, he is Professor of Pastoral Theology at the *Institut St. Denis*, Paris, and lecturer on group psychotherapy at the School of Social Work,

Dusseldorf. He introduced Gestalt Therapy into Germany and founded the Fritz Perls Institute for Gestalt Therapy and Creativity Training, Dusseldorf/Wurzburg. He has written and edited six books and has written more than fifty articles on group psychotherapy and psychological group work.

Eva Schindler-Rainman earned her doctorate in social work and is a member of the Academy of Certified Social Workers and charter member of the International Association of Applied Social Scientists. She is a consultant on community organization, organizational development, and the development of voluntarism with a national and international clientele. She is the author of many articles and co-author of three books: *The Volunteer Community*, *Team Training*, and *The Humane Society*.

Herbert A. Shepard is a pioneer in the application of behavioral science to organization and community development. He conducted the first large-scale organization development experiments in industry and founded the first doctoral program in organization development at Case-Western Reserve University. Currently, he has a varied teaching and consulting practice.

John R. Weir earned his doctorate in clinical psychology at the University of California. For seventeen years, he was a faculty member, director of student counseling and of institutional research, at the California Institute of Technology. His professional career has been in teaching, psychotherapy, laboratory training, and management and organization development. He is at present in private practice.

AUTHOR INDEX

SUBJECT INDEX